19

Human Resource Management

BUSINESS SERIES

Series Editor: Andrew Lock
Manchester Metropolitan University

The Contemporary Business Series is designed with the needs of business studies undergraduates and MBA students in mind, and each title is written in a straightforward, student friendly style. Though all of the books in the series reflect the individuality of their authors, you will find that you can count on certain key features in each text which maintain high standards of structure and approach:

- excellent coverage of core and option subject
- UK/international examples or case studies throughout
- full references and further reading suggestions
- written in direct, easily accessible style, for ease of use by full, part-time and self-study students

Books in The Contemporary Business Series

Accounting for Business (Second Edition)
Peter Atrill, David Harvey and Edward McLaney

Cases in International Business Strategy
Werner Ketlehohn and Jan Kubes

Human Resource Management: A Strategic Approach to Employment
Chris Hendry

Information Resources Management
John R. Beaumont and Ewan Sutherland

International Business Strategy
Werner Ketelhohn

Management Accounting for Financial Decisions
Keith Ward, Sri Srikanthan and Richard Neal

The Management and Marketing of Services
Peter Mudie and Angela Cottam

Organizational Behaviour in International Management
Terence Jackson

Total Quality Management: Text with Cases
John S. Oakland with Les Porter

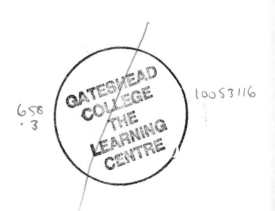

Human Resource Management
A strategic approach to employment

Chris Hendry

BUTTERWORTH
HEINEMANN

To Enid for her patience

Butterworth-Heinemann
Linacre House, Jordan Hill, Oxford OX2 8DP
225 Wildwood Avenue, Woburn, MA 01801-2041
A division of Reed Educational and Professional Publishing Ltd

A member of the Reed Elsevier plc group

OXFORD   AUCKLAND   BOSTON
JOHANNESBURG   MELBOURNE   NEW DELHI

First published 1995
Reprinted 1995, 1998, 1999

British Library Cataloguing in Publication Data
Hendry, Christopher
   Human Resource Management: Strategic
   Approach to Employment. -(Contemporary
   Business Series)
   I. Title II. Series
   658.3

ISBN 0 7506 0994 X

Printed and bound in Great Britain by The Bath Press, Bath

Contents

Figures

Tables

NOTE

It should be noted that research for the case study on pages 262–276 was carried out in 1989. Observations about the concept of 'key jobs', the competitiveness of pay for higher graded jobs, middle management briefings and updating of skills are now no longer issues of concern. Some competitor process reliability is now at least equal to the case study company. It should also be noted that comments about the role of the Union are those of the author and not supported by the company.

Preface

Since the mid-1980s, human resource management (HRM) has gained rapid acceptance in the UK – in job titles, in conference programmes, in business courses in universities and colleges, and in the titles of lecturer posts. This acceptance is far from universal and uncontroversial, though. The field of HRM is still in the process of forming. People dispute whether there is such a thing as HRM and whether it is significantly different from personnel management. Many dislike certain of its overtones, seeing it as a front for an anti-union strategy. Above all, it means different things to different people.

The result has been a rush of books with HRM in the title. Some are little more than traditional 'personnel admin.' dressed up. Others leaven this with a stronger element of 'organization behaviour', adopting in the process a partial reading of HRM to do with culture and leadership. The founding American texts have so far proved much stronger in terms of defining a new area, but tend to have a normative and prescriptive flavour. Clearly, HRM stands at the intersection of personnel management and business strategy. Yet most texts lack an effective grip on business strategy.

This book combines a number of features which it is hoped, will overcome these deficiencies:

1   It provides a critical perspective on the reality and practice of HRM and personnel management, while offering instances of what is possible. It goes beyond simple description of administrative techniques in the hope of providing some normative direction to students and practitioners alike in an area that is still seeking theoretical and practical definition.
2   In so doing, it aims to keep in view the various connotations that HRM has acquired, and provides some test of their validity.
3   It actively links personnel management to business strategy through appropriate models and examples, to establish a coherent rationale for personnel practice. This is, nevertheless, grounded in realistic accounts of organization strategy, largely based on research.
4   It is problem- and issue-focused, addressing issues in strategy and contemporary employment management. In doing so, it treats processes of change and the skills in managing change. Since the personnel function is far from having exclusive influence in these areas, it addresses the roles and responsibilities of personnel specialists, line managers, and the chief executive in HRM, and does not take only a personnel manager perspective.
5   The treatment of standard personnel themes, such as recruitment, pay, training, and IR, is anchored in organizational histories. These cover different types of employment systems and reflect the economic, social, and technological circumstances that gave rise to them. The cases

presented similarly emphasize the situational and context-specific nature of HRM/personnel management.

6   The practical nature of the text is informed by an 'agency' *and* 'systems' view – that is, it treats employment systems, trade union organization, and companies' business strategies in relation to wider circumstances, but also shows how these are capable of being proactively formed by managers and employees to change the circumstances an organization finds itself in. This is, after all, the special claim of HRM. Above all, it is hoped the reader will find in the juxtaposition of business challenges, opposite employment systems managed according to distinct groups, a perspective that is original and persuasive. An employment systems perspective on personnel management is itself, I believe, relatively unique and opens up a number of key concepts around which personnel management, regardless of any adherence to HRM as a concept, can profitably be ordered. These, needless to say, are central to the particular conception of HRM which is developed in this book.

In conclusion, this book is intended for a wide readership. It is not for the exclusive use of those who will specialize in personnel management and HRM. The attention to the strategic side of the business should ensure that. Decisions about the direction of an organization have human resource implications and all decision makers should be responsible for thinking these through. By the same token, HRM specialists should be able to relate human resource practices to business needs. All students of business should therefore find something in this book for them.

Equally, it is hoped students at all levels will find it relevant and accessible. It is certainly demanding in parts. However, more can be gained in the end from confronting serious ideas than accepting watered-down versions of reality. Ultimately, nothing helps to simplify understanding more or to guide practice better than rigorously thought-through ideas. The use of case examples should, nevertheless, make difficult ideas clear. It is hoped that the result will be read with equal profit by students at all levels, from undergraduates to MBAs, as well as by practitioners who are part of the changing scene in HRM.

Acknowledgements

For granting copyright clearance the author is grateful to the following:

- The Free Press, a division of Simon & Schuster, for Figure 1.2 from M. Beer, B. Spector, P. R. Lawrence, Q. N. Mills and R. E. Walton, *Managing Human Assets*, © 1984 by The Free Press.
- Gower for Table 3.1 adapted from N. Millward, M. Stevens, D. Smart and W. R. Hawes, *Workplace Industrial Relations in Transition: The ED/ESRC/PSI/ACAS Surveys*, 1992.
- Institute of Manpower Studies for Figure 9.4 from W. Hirsh, *Career Management in the Organization: a guide for developing policy and practice*, IMS Report No. 96, 1984; and Figure 18.1 from J. Atkinson, *Flexibility, Uncertainty and Manpower Management*, IMS Report No. 89, 1985.
- Prentice Hall International for Figure 4.1 from G. Johnson and K. Scholes, *Exploring Corporate Strategy*, 1988.
- Dr John Purcell for Table 5.1 from J. Purcell, 'How to manage decentralised bargaining', *Personnel Management*, May 1989.
- John Wiley and Sons, Inc for Figure 1.1 from C. J. Fombrun, N. M. Tichy and M. A. Devanna (eds), *Strategic Human Resource Management*, 1984; and Figure 4.4 from D. Ulrich and D. Lake, *Organizational Capability: Competing from the Inside Out*, 1990.
- John Wiley and Sons Ltd for Figure 6.1 from G. Johnson, 'Managing strategic change: the role of symbolic action', *British Journal of Management*, vol. 1, 1990.

Abbreviations

ACAS Advisory, Conciliation and Arbitration Service
BIFU Banking, Insurance and Finance Union
BIM   British Institute of Management (see also IM)
CBI   Confederation of British Industry.
IM   Institute of Management (formerly the BIM)
IPD   Institute of Personnel and Development
NGA   National Graphical Association
NUJ   National Union of Journalists
NVQ   National Vocational Qualifications
SNVQ Scottish National Vocational Qualifications

Part One
The Making of Human Resource
Management

1
Human resource management: an overview

Introduction

Human resource management (HRM) has gained rapid and widespread acceptance as a new term for managing employment. It remains, however, an ambiguous concept. People question whether it is any different from traditional personnel management, nor is it altogether clear what it consists of in practice.

This chapter sets out the background of ideas on which HRM is based. Three common interpretations are identified. HRM is then compared with personnel management, identifying the special shortcomings of personnel management and those it shares with HRM.

The chapter concludes by setting out the approach adopted in this book. This combines a view of organizations as employment systems set against the requirement to manage organizations in accordance with current business strategy.

What do we mean by HRM?

Our starting point is that HRM has different connotations for different people and does not yet constitute a unified theory. We are all familiar with such statements as 'our human resources are our most important asset'. In some cases, acceptance of the principles of HRM goes no further than this. Others emphasize that it is about matching employment practices to an organization's strategy. A corollary of this is that, taken as a whole, employment practices should combine together to reinforce one another. Part of this is that employment decisions should not be conceived in isolation, but ideally should be integrated through mechanisms such as personnel planning. At the same time, reward systems, the way promotions are made, who gets trained and why, all have effects on motivation and say something about what kind of organization it is and what behaviours it wants to promote. HRM is about making sure such personnel practices convey a consistent message.

A third connotation is to present HRM as having a distinctive philosophy underpinning it, not just any set of values. This philosophy emphasizes se-curing employee commitment and motivation in organizations characterized by high-trust relations, with scope for employees to exercise influence. Management style and organizational culture then become an important focus for action in their own right. It is not enough that employment practices cohere, nor even that they should express the values of the organization. These values are of a particular kind.

These are the three common expressions of HRM. However, they cannot simply be added together to produce a complete theory or prescription. While the first proposition sits comfortably with the last, it is very easy, for example, to conceive of employment practices conditioned by a business strategy that depends on producing at lowest cost in an unstable product environment. Such a business might rely on low pay, part-time working, and hire-and-fire arrangements which enable it to respond rapidly to fluctuations in orders – in other words, to use casualization as an employment strategy. Dock work once used to be like this, as the movement of cargo vessels changed by the day. If, on the other hand, employees have craft skills and/or high levels of effort are required in a concentrated period, casualization may be accompanied by high levels of pay – as in the construction industry. By this yardstick construction firms could be said to practise a kind of 'HRM'.

When someone talks therefore about 'creating excellence through a culture of commitment' and 'managing cultures to create excellence', while arguing also for personnel policies being linked with corporate objectives and strategic plans, we should beware. Such rhetoric obscures potentially incompatible definitions and ignores the reality of employment systems. Let us look a little more closely, therefore, at what is contained in these definitions and begin to sketch some of the potential weaknesses in the principles themselves.

Human resources are our most important asset

The idea of people as a valuable organizational asset has a sound pedigree in the economists' theory of human capital. It means something specific that is, in principle, measurable. So, for example, human capital can be enhanced by the further investment of education and training, just as the physical capital of a factory can be by modernization. Equally, both can deteriorate through ageing, obsolescence, and neglect.

In its more general use in the management literature, where it has been more or less explicit since Peter Drucker (1954), this idea tends to get watered down into 'motherhood statements' about people being important to the functioning of an organization. A number of academic writers have nevertheless been influenced by 'human capital' theory and have developed principles for action around it. Douglas McGregor (1960) (an educationalist-turned-management consultant), in his 'Theory X–Theory Y', argued that the way managers treat employees will affect how much of their talent, effort, and motivation can be harnessed for the organization. In other words, how much of the human capital can be tapped.

This opened the way for the behavioural science school (represented by people such as Herzberg) to incorporate psychological theories of personal

growth, particularly that of Maslow (1943), into their theories of organization. The underlying belief, which 'organization development' (OD) consultants turned into a programme of action in the 1960s/1970s, was made
explicit in Argyris's (1964) book, *Integrating the Individual and the Organization*, where personal growth was represented as entirely compatible with an
organization's objectives. In due course, human resource management has
picked up this convenient assumption.

Over the years this has attracted much criticism, since it plays down, for
example, the imbalance in power between the mass of individuals and that
exercised by the few in the name of the organization. The problem comes
back to the idea of people as 'assets' and 'resources' which John Morris
(1974) tellingly exposed in his pointed distinction between 'human resources'
and 'resourceful humans'. Human resources are the readily manipulated
footsoldiers of organizations; resourceful humans are the managers and
others, but particularly managers, who initiate. The best test of resourceful-
ness, then, is to go out and start one's own business.

We need not accept this conflict in quite such a stark way. It is clear
organizations, by definition, 'organize' people and that the majority of
people work within organizations. The recently popularized idea of 'intrapreneurship' (Kanter, 1984) suggests the importance of giving space to resourceful, entrepreneurial individuals *within* the organization, and ways of doing
this. 'Intrapreneurship' depends precisely on opening up a gap between the
pressures of organization and the individual, not on 'integration'.

Thus, writers like Kanter are concerned with how to mobilize people's
talents to advantage the organization, but do not take on board an overt
set of values about personal growth, nor other explicit elements of a theory
of HRM. The issue of integration has resurfaced in criticisms of HRM,
nevertheless, and we will consider these later.

Looked at historically, then, the early adoption of the title, 'human
resource(s) manager/director', in a handful of American companies during
the 1970s, before any theory of HRM had been elaborated, was probably
nothing more than a statement about the importance of people to an
organization (Janger, 1977). By the mid-1980s in the USA, and in the UK
by the late 1980s, the more widespread use of such titles harboured larger
ambitions.

Matching employment practices to business strategy

The first major theoretical advance came in the classic statement of HRM
by Fombrun, Tichy and Devanna (1984). Building on Alfred Chandler's
(1962) argument that structure should follow strategy or an organization
will be otherwise less efficient, two theorists of business strategy, Galbraith
and Nathanson (1978), extended this to argue that HRM systems should
similarly be adapted to match the requirements of strategy. Fombrun,
Tichy and Devanna (1984) then fleshed this out, adding various elements of
personnel policy:

Just as firms will be faced with inefficiencies when they try to implement new

strategies with outmoded structures, so they will also face problems of implementation when they attempt to effect new strategies with inappropriate HR systems.
The critical managerial task is to align the formal structure and the HR systems
so that they drive the strategic objectives of the organization (p. 37).

The key human resource (HR) systems for them were selection, appraisal,
development (including training), and rewards. These had the potential to
channel behaviour towards specific performance goals, if they were properly
aligned with one another – as their model of the human resource cycle
suggests (Figure 1.1).

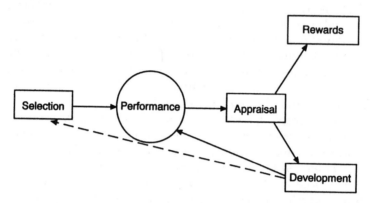

Figure 1.1   *The human resource cycle. (Source: Fombrun, Tichy and
Devanna, 1984)*

In a further elaboration, they introduced the idea of organizational
culture, or what they termed the 'dominant value'. HR practices implicitly
or explicitly create characteristic organizational cultures, and reinforce one
another insofar as they support a particular culture. As a result, 'culture'
becomes the crucial intervening variable.

There is one significant omission from their model, however, which will
be all the more evident when we look at the contribution of the Harvard
school to the theory of HRM. They omit industrial relations, or employee
relations, as a major focus of managerial activity. Fombrun, Tichy and
Devanna (1984) are principally concerned with the 'new labour force' (p. 8)
of managers, professionals, and white-collar workers – the changing occupational balance in favour of whom is one of the important contextual factors
that makes HRM desirable. The focus is on selection, appraisal, development, and rewards almost exclusively in relation to staff.

This omission is symptomatic and can be linked to other elements of
their thinking. Compared with the Harvard school, there is little sense that
choices might be contested or need to be negotiated. Although they imply
culture involves a choice, it is implicitly determined by whatever direction
business strategy is taking. Managers are not challenged to reassess their
personal values and those the organization embodies – either by other
employees or by the authors themselves. Indeed, sometimes there is a
feeling that choices are made and decisions taken without human
intervention.

For Fombrun, Tichy and Devanna business strategy precedes any other considerations, and HR systems are contingent upon strategic need. Although other contributors to their edited volume develop particular aspects of HR systems with varying degrees of attention to the nature of managerial choice and employee influences on this, they are generally all wedded to this contingency model. They and their imitators are thus active in devising frameworks that link different strategic circumstances to sets of HR practices. We shall look at these in more detail in Chapter 4.

Before turning to the Harvard school, it is worth keeping in mind that although managers *de facto* make choices daily to do with people, they may not consciously reflect on these. The needs of the business may well be uppermost in their minds, and implicitly they may reaffirm a set of values moulded around 'strategic imperatives'. Rarely do people review their fundamental assumptions about behaviour. There is a realism here, therefore, unintended though it is, about the extent to which managers can and do make conscious HR choices.

In a way, however, this backfires also on the idea that managers make deliberate choices about business strategy. As we shall argue in Chapter 4, making strategy and therefore determining the direction of an organization is rather more complex than these writers credit. HR theorists have in common a belief in managers being able to make deliberate choices, yet the whole question of managerial choice, in business strategy and employment systems, is far from straightforward.

HRM as a philosophy of management

If Fombrun and his colleagues represent one of the two schools of contemporary HRM in North America, Michael Beer and his colleagues at Harvard are the foremost proponents of the other. Their ideas are contained in two key books (Beer *et al.*, 1984; Walton and Lawrence, 1985), which were written to provide the conceptual underpinning for the new Harvard core course in HRM launched in 1981 – the first such innovation to the core programme, as they point out, in twenty years.

Where others draw on the strategy literature, the source of inspiration for the Harvard group lay within the human relations/human resources movement. A number, such as Paul Lawrence and Richard Walton, for example, had been prominent as consultants and writers in OD – although the fault lines running through OD meant that Michael Beer (1976) had been a notable critic, and Lawrence (1969) had co-authored a seminal text from a structural contingency perspective. These complications of history and intellectual development aside, in their representation of HRM they put more stress on *people* as 'human resources', with their needs and potential for personal development, whereas Fombrun, Tichy and Devanna appear to give greater emphasis to HR *systems*.

Thus, people are at the centre of the Harvard model, with management taking decisions affecting people day in, day out:

Human resource management involves all management decisions that affect the nature of the relationship between the organization and its employees – its human resources. General management make important decisions daily that affect this relationship (Beer *et al.*, 1984, p. 1).

They explicitly reject the idea that employment systems should be simply responsive to technical, social and economic factors, although they acknowledge that 'most firms' employment policies are less reflective of a coherent set of management attitudes and values than . . . of the economic environment in which that organization operates' (Beer *et al.*, 1984, p. 101).

Instead, managers can and should make choices about the organizations they want to create; these choices respond to a wide range of factors; and certain choices are preferable from a moral (and, in their eyes, a practical) point of view. Thus, their model (shown in Figure 1.2) is much more inclusive, business strategy, for example, being but one among a number of situational factors (or contingencies). Employee influence is a key area of decision (or 'choice'), and is affected by a number of other stakeholder interests than just management. By the same token, HRM practices have consequences not just for company performance but for the individual and society.

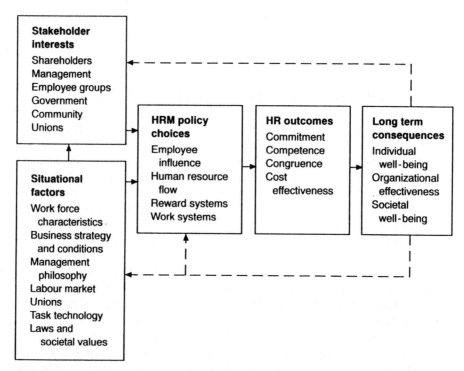

Figure 1.2 *Map of the HRM territory. (Source: Beer et al., 1984)*

The touchstone for HRM practices is not therefore simply whether they provide an efficient fit with the present, short-run business strategy. While this goal is reflected in the immediate outcomes specified by 'commitment', 'competence', and 'cost effectiveness', such a fit is qualified by the need to reconcile organizational with individual goals ('congruence'). 'Competence', moreover, implies an enhancement of the individual and his or her skills, and not simply what this can deliver to the organization. Above all, the key outcome which HRM policy needs to deliver is 'commitment'.

The Harvard group frequently argue for a distinctive philosophy in managing work relations around this value. It requires the creation of high-trust relations, which in turn (to bring us back to the point of departure) mean employees being able to exercise influence. The keystone to creating commitment is 'mutuality':

> The new HRM model is composed of policies that promote mutuality – mutual goals, mutual respect, mutual rewards, mutual responsibility. The theory is that policies of mutuality will elicit commitment which in turn will yield both better economic performance and greater human development (Walton, 1985, p. 64)

One other feature which marks their perspective off from the 'strategy' theorists is that the precise design of any one HRM policy is less important than the *gestalt* in which it fits. Thus: 'Pay typically needs to be less tightly tied to specific results or behaviour' (Beer *et al.* 1984, p. 147).

The 'strategy' theorists, by contrast, have tended to go to great lengths to relate specific policies to particular strategic ends through the behaviours they assume will be created. Their image is of organizations as control mechanisms, with employment policies creating strict means–ends chains between organizational goals and individual behaviours. Pay is typically at the centre of this kind of perspective – both in HRM and in personnel management generally.

In challenging such assumptions, the Harvard group are therefore saying that personnel management and managers in general should stop treating people as simple tools who can be 'motivated' (i.e. their behaviours can be manipulated) by tightly drawn employment systems. Creating broad commitment is more important since it means that people then become more self-directing, ready and willing to adapt to changing situations. This is better, as they see it, than having to rely on someone or something else to pull their strings. Often this doesn't work in any case; when it does it produces people who lack initiative or behave rigidly in other ways; and in contemporary organizations adaptiveness is the key to organizational survival.

'High-commitment work systems' therefore are entirely functional. They represent not only a moral imperative but also a practical one. The values which McGregor and Argyris expressed in the 1960s, and Harvard authors such as Walton sought to implement under the 'Quality of Work Life' umbrella, would appear, according to this prognosis, to be ideas whose time has come. In Chapters 2 and 3 we will put this claim to the test through evidence of the changing workscape. Meanwhile, it is instructive to compare the ideals of HRM with the professional model of personnel management in the UK, and to establish some of the limitations of personnel management in practice.

The professional model of personnel management

HRM has had little more than ten years to make an impact so far, and rather less in the UK. What evidence is there that it has made any sort of impact in this short time?

To answer this, we must first have a picture of what has gone before. How have firms managed their employment in the past; what does conventional personnel management look like; and what are its shortcomings? In other words, 'how does HRM differ from personnel management, both as an activity in practice and in terms of the professional model?' Is it 'old wine in new bottles' (Armstrong, 1987), substantively no different from the values that personnel management has long espoused (Fowler, 1987)? We can then move from a critique of personnel management at the point where HRM came in, back to the critique of HRM itself.

The evolution of personnel management in the UK is well known. From its welfare origins before the First World War, it shifted its focus to labour management and staffing (1920s/1930s); to the maintenance of consensus and the balance of interests through joint consultation (1940s); and on to industrial relations bargaining and manpower planning in the 1960s/1970s (Niven, 1967; Torrington, 1989). In the process, the range of tasks expanded, the fields of knowledge to support the necessary personnel skills were embellished, and the role shifted.

Two aspects of this evolution are of particular relevance to present purposes. How far does personnel management share with HRM a concern for 'mutuality' and 'high commitment' as a doctrine to get the best out of people? Second, what priority has it given to managing the human resource strategically in accordance with business objectives?

Personnel management as the satisfaction of mutual interests

The definition of personnel management, which the Institute of Personnel Management (IPM)* adopted in 1963, retained much of the image of the personnel manager as the arbitrator, or 'man or woman in the middle':

> Personnel management aims to achieve both efficiency and justice, neither of which can be pursued successfully without the other. It seeks to bring together and develop into an effective organization the men and women who make up an enterprise, enabling each to make his own best contribution to its success both as an individual and as a member of a working group. It seeks to provide fair terms and conditions of employment, and satisfying work for those employed.

---

*In 1994, the IPM merged with the Institute of Training and Development to become the Institute of Personnel and Development (IPD). All references throughout the text up until 1994 will therefore continue to refer to the IPM, and thereafter to the IPD.

In a sense, by emphasizing the 'balancing' role, this statement was more reflective of the 1940s when the IPM was formed and the emphasis was on managing consensus. The reality, however, was that personnel managers were being forced into giving up pretensions of professional neutrality in the 1960s/1970s by industrial relations strife and the need increasingly to be on the front line in defending the organization against disruption.

The balancing image is perpetuated in two of the key textbooks. Thomason (1976, 1978), for example, saw the personnel manager assuming a third-party role between management and employees, at a time when legislation sought to create a better balance between their respective rights and obligations. In doing so, the personnel manager harked back to the dual origins of his or her function and sought to reconcile these – 'the one paternalistically oriented towards the welfare of employees and the other rationally derived from corporate needs to control' (Thomason, 1976, p. 27). The IPM's twin ideals of 'efficiency and justice' are clearly visible here.

Torrington and Chapman (1983, p. 4) elaborated this 'balancing' philosophy by proposing that what binds employees to the organization is a series of implicit and explicit contracts:

> Our philosophy is based on the assertion that personnel work has three elements:
> (1) Determining the expectations that employees have of their organization and the expectations organizations have of their employees.
> (2) Setting up a series of contracts or agreements between organizations and employee(s) that describe the mutual expectation.
> (3) Servicing the contracts to ensure that the expectations are fulfilled.

Although this overplays the 'ethical' role (as the profession has often tended to), these images of personnel work do faithfully capture the 'juridical' element, to do with policing agreements, which dominated through the 1970s. As Torrington (1989, p. 60) has since put it: 'Legal wrangling became dominant in the 1970s, when a plethora of legislation protecting the rights of workers and trade unions gave managers a fright . . .'

The work of personnel management in the 1970s was thus often dominated by negotiating formal collective employment contracts; ensuring adherence to these; dealing with unofficial action outside procedural agreements; and ensuring that the organization did not infringe individual rights in such areas as dismissal, equal opportunities, and health and safety.

The main difference between reality and the model proposed by the IPM, Thomason, and Torrington and Chapman, was that, rather than standing as a neutral go-between, the role shifted unequivocally towards representing the organization on these contractual matters, thereby counterbalancing the power of trade unions and individual rights enshrined in legislation. In turn, this helped to secure the personnel profession unprecedented status and the first personnel directors were appointed to many company boards.

In saying this, we have to be careful, of course, not to see all personnel work as to do with industrial relations (IR). The more technique-oriented tasks, such as the administration of recruitment and selection, and the management of training, went on largely governed by technique, and in large organizations these were often specialized functions within personnel departments. The IR manager, however, became the most important figure in the department, and IR the aspect of his or her role to which the personnel manager/director gave most attention.

In the idealization of personnel management at this time, there is considerable similarity with Harvard's philosophy of HRM and its emphasis on 'mutuality'. This ideal of personnel management, however, was being swallowed up by the pressures of industrial relations to become more partisan. By the same token, HRM is also vulnerable to real-world pressures. 'Mutuality' and 'high commitment' are liable to be subordinated or distorted by other priorities. For both HRM now as for personnel management then, there is a big question-mark over whether the professional model accurately portrays practice and is sustainable.

Is personnel management strategic?

The second issue for personnel management in the UK is the priority it has given to managing human resources strategically. HRM's claim to take a strategic approach to employment touches a particularly raw nerve among personnel managers. *'Of course'* personnel management has *'always'* advocated a strategic approach. The preoccupation with industrial relations problems in the 1970s tended, however, to undermine personnel management as a strategic activity. This had a number of facets.

Industrial relations has often been characterized as a firefighting activity. There are many reasons for this. It is partly the nature of industrial relations problems that they involve crisis. In Britain, the element of crisis was exacerbated, in the eyes of many, by defects in the system itself. Workplace bargaining and the growth in shop steward power under conditions of full employment, along with fragmented union structures, were constantly seen, through the 1960s and 1970s, as a source of disorder. Thus, in the famous words of Alan Flanders, pay bargaining was 'largely informal, largely autonomous, and largely fragmented' (1970, p. 70). The effort to instill greater order by statute, through the Industrial Relations Act 1971, did little to arrest this tendency. It was deeply unpopular, and was repealed.

Accompanying this, managers were often themselves at fault in not having a strategy for industrial relations. Again in the words of Flanders, there was, in the 1960s, 'a growing abnegation by management of its responsibility to manage' (1970, p. 70). Long-term considerations disappeared in short-term responses to meet production targets or to buy off temporary industrial peace – resulting in institutionalized overtime, disputes over differentials, overmanning, and resistance to flexibility (Gowler, 1969).

These criticisms continued to be repeated into the 1980s. Thus, Thurley and Wood (1983) and Gospel and Littler (1983) criticized the failure of top managers to devote as much time to developing an industrial relations strategy as they gave to planning their financial and commercial strategies. Foreshadowing HRM, these critics also broadened the scope of industrial relations strategy to cover general employment policy. In a sense, it was precisely because firms did not see industrial relations in the light of wider employment issues that they tended to respond to it in terms of crisis.

A further issue is the suspicion that industrial relations management tended to be 'non-strategic' because that was the way IR managers preferred it to be. Managing problems is how personnel officers have typically established their importance to an organization (Drucker, 1954), and IR gave plenty of scope to running about, damping fires, acting as a go-between. Moreover, the 'informal' aspects of this – knowing the personalities and power networks on the union side better than others in the organization could find time for, resolving problems behind closed doors – contributed to the mystique of the role. This informality combined with the formal source of the specialist's power, namely the knowledge of employment legislation and industrial relations procedures.

The final point is that IR problems simply tended to dominate. It is not just the way industrial relations was conducted, but that it tended to pre-empt other concerns. A measure of this preoccupation, and with IR as firefighting, can be seen in a comment by the Group industrial relations manager at GKN:

> In the 1970s I used to get a daily report on disputes within GKN. Towards the end of that period, not a week went by when there was not some industrial action somewhere within GKN. It was a dreadful time. It ground managers down.

This refrain is repeated many times by IR managers who lived through that period. As a result, as the personnel director of Peugeot–Talbot has commented, reflecting on the time when the company was owned by Chrysler:

> It wasn't that we didn't want to behave strategically. We did. But there were so many problems bearing down on us and there wasn't the support from top management to take a position and see it through.

Turning from industrial relations to personnel management more generally, the lack of a strategic approach towards employment has been often commented on. For example, the ramifications of introducing new technology have invariably not been thought through (Rothwell, 1984; Burnes and Weekes, 1988); forms of flexible working have been introduced in piecemeal fashion (Atkinson, 1984); and training and management development have been bedevilled by short-termism (Hayes, Anderson, and Fonda, 1984; Coopers and Lybrand Associates, 1985). Tyson (1983) regarded it as a general failing of firms that they lacked an employment strategy, or, as Atkinson (1984) put it, they relied on 'manpower tactics', instead of having 'manpower strategies'.

This appears in flat contrast to the emphasis to be found in most personnel texts on having personnel policies. Policies are not, however, the same as strategies. 'Policies' belong with 'contracts' as a way of ensuring consistency and equity, often to avoid infringing employment legislation. They can be written on any subject as the need arises, and may not cohere together (unlike strategy, which is about thinking things through in relation to one another and to some overarching aim). The personnel department in any case may write policies but lack power to give them effect.

The emphasis on policies in traditional personnel texts betrays, therefore, a fundamental difference in outlook (and on occasion a basic misunderstanding of the nature of employment strategy). Thomason's (1978) standard text for the IPM, for instance, contains not one reference to strategy but thirty-five references to personnel policy (and, equally significant, sixty-three references to the static image of the organization as a system).

In any case, many organizations lacked even systematically formulated policies. In a study of ten organizations in the 1970s, Karen Legge (1978) found that while the larger, more sophisticated companies did have a broad range of personnel policies,

> the medium sized and smaller companies, however, tended either to have well-defined policies on certain issues (for example, on recruitment, conditions of employment, and collective bargaining arrangements) and none on areas less immediately pressing (for example, on management development), or to rely on rudimentary policy on basic terms and conditions of employment backed by observance of legal obligations.
>
> In fact, for large and small companies alike . . ., what was clear . . . was the basically reactive nature of their policy formulation. Thus, areas that had not caused specific problems to date tended to be ignored, while the strongest stimulus to action was legislative (p. 38).

When it came to decision making itself, there was a problem, on the one hand, of line managers' lack of a human resource perspective; and, on the other, the personnel specialists' lack of access to the highest levels of decision making:

> many issues that potentially have a direct bearing on human resource utilization are not considered from this perspective by the specialists concerned, while personnel specialists are not regarded as being legitimately involved (Legge, 1978, p. 42).

These two factors which Legge identifies together help to account for the lack of a strategic approach towards employment. Consequently, it has been a perennial complaint that the personnel function is excluded from business decisions.

One good reason for this is that until recently the professional training of personnel managers has omitted formal training in other business disciplines. In the 1960s, the decision was made to take personnel management down the route of professionalization, with an exclusive curriculum, modelled on the social sciences, rather than to associate it with general business training. While this secured the role as the specialist in the provision of personnel services, it largely disqualified professionally trained practitioners from an influence over the business decisions from which their specialist contribution flowed.

As a result, they were rarely party to decisions affecting the numbers and skills of people – the 'human resources'. This is one reason why manpower planning, which most thoroughly embodies personnel management's strategic pretensions, has largely remained a textbook discipline.

Therefore, when it is said that there is nothing new about the idea that 'the business of personnel is the business' (Fowler, 1987), the evidence is that personnel managers were in general ill-equipped for this role and were infrequently allowed to exercise it. Recent confirmation of this comes from Daniel's (1987) review of technical change in Britain, where speaking of the introduction of such changes and the decisions relating to it, he says: 'A very modest picture emerged of the part played by personnel managers' (p. 108).

The Harvard presentation of HRM has taken on board the issue of the personnel manager's status and role in organizations, and tackles it head-on. Since personnel managers could not be expected to display a strategic approach if they were shut out from business decision making, the obvious conclusion was that general managers, who do make strategy, should take direct responsibility for people-related decisions. The Harvard writers therefore explicitly direct their arguments at 'general management', and as a core module in the Harvard MBA, HRM is taken by future *general managers*.

Personnel management and HRM: towards an employment systems approach

It is evident that personnel management has been stronger in providing an integrative framework for employment decisions and management actions by means of employment policies than in structuring employment systems to implement particular business strategies. These two ideas have tended to be kept apart, with some writers stressing more the philosophical and ethical roots of personnel management (Kenny, 1975; Cuming, 1985), and others the resourcing aspects (Armstrong, 1979).

In practice, the ethical ideal has tended to be overwhelmed by external reality, encapsulated in industrial relations problems, while the systemic ideal, that personnel systems should support one another, has been effectively confined to saying that decisions should be focused through man-power planning – and the adoption of manpower planning, as we noted, has been limited. Moreover, manpower planning falls short of delivering what HRM aspires to – distinctive cultures geared to long-term business strategies.

The theory of HRM thus has the potential to sharpen up the discipline of personnel management. HRM is more explicit in both areas – in the exposition of a philosophy underlying employment strategy, and in its analysis of business strategy and associated employment strategies.

Personnel management and HRM, nevertheless, share the same ambivalence about the relationship between these, with the fault lines strongly reflected in the differences of approach taken by Fombrun *et al.* and the Harvard school. This ambivalence is not surprising, of course. It reflects a tension between corporate needs for control and individual needs for freedom and fulfilment which to some degree are always likely to be with us. At another level, it reflects also the economic, social, and political struggle for control of organizations between shareholders, top managers, employees, and community. The resolution of this struggle is open to considerable flux and ingenuity, from generation to generation, and country to country.

Europeans like to believe that the greater prevalence of trade unionism in Western Europe has ensured that personnel management here has a much more developed sense of the potential conflict of interests between the employer and employee, as well as more developed institutional arrangements for striking a balance between them. Consequently, many European critics see in HRM a managerial approach that skates over potential differences of interest. Either inadvertently, or as a deliberate instrument of policy, they see HRM making doubtful assumptions about the common interests of the individual and organization, and undermining trade union representation of employee interests against the employer. Thus, Guest (1989, p. 43) states:

> Its underlying values . . . would appear to be essentially unitarist and individualis-
> tic in contrast to the more pluralistic and collective values of traditional industrial
> relations . . .
> HRM values are unitarist to the extent that they assume no underlying and
> inevitable differences of interest between management and workers . . .
> HRM values are essentially individualistic in that they emphasize the
> individual–organization linkage in preference to operating through group and
> representative systems . . . These values leave little scope for collective arrange-
> ments and assume little need for collective bargaining.

These contrasts were, of course, thoroughly drawn some years ago by Alan Fox (1974).

As a result, certain practices identified with HRM are treated with suspicion. We will describe these in Chapter 3 in reviewing innovations that have taken place in personnel management during the 1980s. In broad terms, Guest (1987, 1989) identifies practices that have the aim of increasing 'flexibility' and 'commitment' as a threat to the British and European style of industrial relations. Note, however, that the threat is conceived in relation to 'traditional industrial relations and to the trade unions' (Guest, 1989, p. 44) – that is, to the status quo.

The other problem, which we will address in Chapter 3, is interpreting on the one hand the motivations of a company in initiating a particular practice and on the other the actual effects. Most of the time, observers have limited information about either of these.

Thus, 'flexibility' is interpreted as employees giving away control in some sense, and 'commitment' as giving away personal identity and competing affiliations (such as the union, family, community). It is ironic that much of the fire on this account has been levelled at the Harvard writers. The fact that they have framed their advocacy of HRM in terms of 'high commit-ment' makes them obvious targets. Yet they make a point of addressing stakeholder interests and the moral choices of management, and they frame their solutions in terms of arrangements for reconciling competing claims ('mutuality'). The strategy- and system-oriented advocates, on the other hand, entirely pass over these issues, although 'flexibility' and 'commitment' are implicit throughout in arguing for 'fit' between business strategy and employment policy.

The way forward

The theory of HRM can sharpen up the discipline of personnel management, yet is itself apparently flawed. How, then, should we proceed? Certainly, personnel management lacks adequate concepts of business strategy. One task in this book will be to explore competitive situations, under the variety of organizational forms in which these are encountered, with the employment strategies to match.

How do we preserve, though, the sense of intractableness that also characterizes employment – which preserves the human element and keeps alive issues of commitment, motivation, and segmented interests – without necessarily buying into the particular set of values with which HRM has become identified?

The values of HRM are defined by the Harvard writers in terms of four criteria which employment policies should satisfy – congruence, competence, cost effectiveness, and commitment. Guest (1987), similarly, has argued that HRM can only be considered as something distinctive if it can be shown to satisfy a set of clear criteria. He identifies these as strategic integration, high quality, high commitment, and flexibility. When policies meet these criteria, it is assumed there is a beneficial payoff for the organization.

Paul Lawrence (1985), one of the Harvard group, meanwhile, described employment systems generally in relation to 'specific technical, social, and economic preconditions' (p. 16). The 'high commitment work system' is just one of five types of employment system. It is the latest to emerge, but other forms still survive in particular sectors, or are practised by particular organizations. This, of course, accords with experience: employment systems differ between organizations.

The 'high commitment work system' should therefore be measured against a particular set of technical, economic, and social pressures. It may, indeed, be the case that modern conditions make it widely appropriate. Because economic circumstances demand high quality and innovativeness in products, firms need also to be innovative in their work practices. Modern technology demands high skills, adaptive behaviour, and the exercise of discretion. Independent of such factors, people also demand and expect to be given responsibility and discretion, as a result of higher levels of education. Finally, governments support such expectations through laws and infrastructure investment in education and training.

On the other hand, these conditions may apply only to certain kinds of business or to certain groups of employees. It is a matter of common observation, after all, that employees in the same organization get treated in different ways. Indeed, it has been suggested that there is a trend for firms to develop employment structures which differentiate between 'core' employees and those who are 'peripheral' (that is, less permanent or less critical to operations) (Atkinson, 1984). The 'high commitment' HRM strategy is likely to be especially applicable to the 'core' group, to bind them to the organization, but less so to 'peripheral' employees (Hendry and Pettigrew, 1986). As Karen Legge (1989) has argued: 'Clearly, we need to know more about the organizational and market circumstances that facilitate the adoption of the mutuality model, and how widely within an organization it can be applied' (p. 39). The particular values of HRM can, therefore, be regarded as a special case in an employment systems perspective on HRM.

However, the value-specific version may be of general relevance in the light of two trends that affect modern organizations. One is the changing character of markets in which firms operate and the rate of change that needs to be managed; the other is the degree of complexity and the need to manage this complexity in an integrated way (Hendry and Pettigrew, 1990, 1992).

When organizations operated in mass-markets and were dominated by large production/service functions, the primary task of personnel management and industrial relations was the maintenance of organizational stability. Job evaluation, gradings, contracts, disputes and grievance procedures, apprenticeship schemes, routine training programmes – these were the stuff of personnel management. As technological change has reduced the size of the production function, and as firms have had to adjust to rapid and continuing change in their markets, a different style of personnel management is required. This is more concerned with managing change, adjusting personnel systems to organizational needs, and adapting the structures and cultures of work systems and of the organization as a whole to strategic shifts.

Piore and Sabel (1984) have called this conjunction of technological possibilities and market imperatives 'flexible specialization'. This provides a broad justification for the systems model of HRM. But it also implies more individualized organizations, operating with higher levels of trust and commitment to allow such flexibility to be practised. Similar requirements apply to the growing market-oriented service sector. The limiting factor is, of course, how prevalent 'flexible specialization' has actually become, something which is disputed.

Managing change and maintaining flexibility is one imperative, therefore. A second imperative is coping with increased complexity in the external environment and the structural elaboration of the organization in the face of this. Influenced by Japanese models, this leads to the realization that organizational effectiveness depends on being able to integrate a variety of activities, and getting people to think 'whole organization' rather than just focusing on their own corner. This demands new approaches to training, career moves across traditional boundaries, perhaps forms of job rotation, information flowing more freely, team working, and attention to culture and management style. Personnel management cannot then also remain compartmentalized in its thinking, managing selection, training, and so forth in isolation. Again, while this provides a justification for the systems model of HRM, it also raises the importance of trust and commitment.

Complexity and change are therefore two particular circumstances to be considered in defining the 'technical, social, and economic preconditions' of employment systems. They give particular meaning to the values of 'flexibility' and 'commitment' identifed by Guest as central to HRM.

While this book will explore the varieties of employment system which firms practise, in the light of their particular needs and circumstances, we will therefore also keep a continuing eye on the relevance of the 'special version' of HRM. In doing so, we shall try to keep in mind the tension between the ways organizations manage different groups of employees, the pressure of external social and political influences, and the requirements of strategy. This also ensures that we think about the past, present, and future. Employment systems are inevitably anchored in the past, responding to earlier antecedents. The issue is often therefore to create more appropriate forms. This is precisely the challenge of HRM.

The most useful approach to HRM is that of the sceptic. It matters less, in the first instance, what the theorists of HRM say, than how organizations operate in practice. Personnel management has itself been bedevilled in the past by normative models of how it should work, instead of accounts that reflect the actual operating circumstances of organizations. An employment systems perspective aims to achieve the context-specific view of personnel management which Legge (1978) and others have long advocated. An employment systems perspective on personnel management, in addition, opens up a number of key concepts around which personnel management can profitably be ordered, regardless of any adherence to HRM as a concept.

Summary

Two principal schools of thought in HRM have been distinguished. One has roots which lie in the business strategy literature and addresses the implications of strategy for HR systems. The other traces a stronger line of descent from human relations and personal growth theory. The latter sees improved work relations and opportunities as a necessary condition for present-day organizations to be effective.

Although there are certain similarities between HRM and personnel management, HRM is more explicit in both areas – in its analysis of business strategy and associated employment strategies, and exposition of an underlying philosophy. However, the 'high commitment' version of HRM may be relevant only in certain circumstances. A more open approach is required which takes account of the variety of employment systems among organizations and within organizations, and the factors which sustain these.

The view of organizations as employment systems can then be set against the requirement to manage organizations to implement current business strategy.

2
The context for HRM

Introduction

Human resource management emerged in the 1980s as a response to specific challenges faced by firms. Its American protagonists prefaced their arguments for HRM with an analysis of these challenges and the ways in which their organizations were deficient in face of them. Firms in Britain experienced equally severe disruptions in their external environment and to their management of employment. This chapter briefly reviews the ways in which HRM was a response to identified defects in American organizations. It then traces the impact of economic change, labour law, government labour market policy, demographic change, and the political climate on UK organizations during the 1980s under the Thatcher government. In this way, it sets the context for the theory and practice of HRM.

The treatment of this background is more detailed than one might normally find in a book on personnel management. However, personnel practioners, as much as anyone in a firm, need a clear appreciation of business issues and economic factors – more perhaps than they have customarily had. The maxim applies in business as it does elsewhere, that 'he who forgets the past is compelled to repeat it'.

The failure of American industry

Whereas Organization Development (OD) and the Quality of Work Life (QWL) movement in the United States, with their ideas on job enrichment and more humane organizations, can be seen as an outgrowth of prosperity and social liberation in the 1960s, HRM was born of quite different circumstances. The most vivid aspect of this around 1980 was the perceived failure of American management and industry in the face of Japanese competition in international and domestic markets.

The ideals around which HRM is built, identified in Chapter 1, reflect deficiencies in American organizations. American firms (it was believed) failed to inspire the same kind of commitment that characterized Japanese firms. Ouchi (1981) compared 'Type A' ('American' or 'achievement') values unfavourably with 'Type J' (Japanese) values. 'Type A' stood for short-termism and lack of teamwork. American firms, he argued, were characterized by employment insecurity, quick promotion, specialized careers, bureaucratic control, an emphasis on individual decision making and responsibility, and a narrow focus on departmental interests, to the detriment of the organization as a whole.

George Lodge (1985), a Harvard professor of business administration, summed up the problem in terms of American business being caught between an old individualist ideology, which was losing legitimacy, and an emerging 'communitarian' ideology, more like that in Japan and some European countries. Incidentally, he saw Britain caught in a struggle between *three* conflicting ideologies:

1 An older, medieval communitarianism which continued to nourish hierarchy and classes
2 An individualist philosophy which derived, as did the American, from the principles established by John Locke (namely, individualism, property rights, marketplace competition, the limited State, and scientific specialization); and
3 The modern form of communitarianism represented in Germany and Japan.

This modern communitarianism consisted of revised notions of equality backed by consensus, personal rights and duties deriving from membership of organizations, the legitimate claims of the community over individual and corporate interests, an active, planning State, and a sense of interdependence. Clearly, though, this lost out to individualism in the Britain of the 1980s.

The short-term, or non-strategic, orientation of American firms was closely associated with the ideals of individualism. Fombrun (1983, p. 200), for instance, echoing Pascale and Athos's (1981) analysis of Japanese firms, underpinned his argument for a strategic approach in HRM as follows:

> Human resource systems in American organizations have tended to drive a short-run orientation in business strategy through a philosophy that largely stresses bottom-line performance. Japanese organizations emphasize loyalty as the dominant value in the human resource cycle and encourage it through a set of sub-systems that are tied to long-run concerns.

Beer *et al.* (1984) similarly wrote that most firms' employment policies were 'less reflective of a coherent set of management attitudes and values than . . . of the economic environment in which that organization operates' (p. 101) – that is, dictated by short-term financial considerations.

As an instance of short-termism, American firms in the 1980–1982 recession were alleged to have made larger redundancies than necessary (Perry, 1985). Japanese companies, in contrast, first seek to reduce pay, starting at the top, rather than resort to firing loyal workers (Inohara, 1990). One of the reasons for this short-run outlook is the requirement in the USA for publicly quoted firms to produce quarterly accounts. Coupled with this is the concentration of ownership in the hands of institutional investors – the pension and insurance funds – and their focus on short-term 'return on equity' to maintain their own rates of return on policies. This means that to preserve their stock values firms are likely to be more sensitive to employment costs and therefore to hire and fire labour more frequently. Japanese firms are relatively insulated from these pressures by a different structure of stock ownership and bank lending:

> The US corporate pursuit of relatively short term profit goals ... tended to emphasize cost reduction as a mechanism for profit growth rather perhaps than growth itself. Thus, in times of economic decline the natural reaction of US firms and those European companies influenced by this pattern of organization, was to cut short term discretionary expenditures such as training, marketing and research, to reduce capital investment and, in particular, to reduce corporate headcounts (Channon, 1991, p. 9).

The same criticisms have been made of British firms, especially in relation to their negative performance on training (Keep, 1989a).

Many critics, from different quarters, saw a solution in giving more attention to the 'people side of organization'. In an influential paper, Abernathy, Clark, and Kantrow (1981) argued that the failure could be explained in terms of two sets of factors:

- 'Hard' factors to do with the adoption of new technology, new working methods, and new forms of manufacturing organization to improve efficiency
- 'Soft' factors to do with attitudes.

The latter were especially important in improving product and service quality. In parallel, Pascale and Athos (1981) extolled Japanese management practice in terms of their attention to both 'hard' and 'soft' elements. Peters and Waterman's *In Search of Excellence* (1982) was an extended plea for the importance of organizational values and for taking seriously the 'soft' side of organizing in the creation of organizational culture.

The argument for treating organizational culture as a central issue in managing organizations thus preceded the more specific elements of a theory of HRM, and became entwined with it. In most treatments of HRM culture becomes a key linking concept.

Industrial failure was thus a dominating theme in the early 1980s, while there was also a sense of national failure in the political sphere, with President Nixon's near-impeachment and President Carter's failure over the Iran hostages. As Guest (1990) has noted, the optimistic and humanistic message in Peters and Waterman and in HRM promised renewal for the American Dream.

In addition, there were other practical challenges in the economy and society to be addressed:

1 The pace of technological change, specifically the effect of microelectronics in stimulating automation
2 The effect of higher education on people's work expectations, accompanied by the increase in white-collar 'knowledge workers', as the structure of the economy shifted from manufacture to services
3 The impact of increasing globalization on political decision making (Fombrun, Tichy and Devanna, 1984; Beer *et al.*, 1984).

The changing context for personnel management in the UK

Organizations in the UK also faced their share of difficulties and opportunities in the 1980s. These are now reviewed, with their broad implications for personnel management.

The economic context

The 1980s can be viewed in terms of three eras – the severe recession (or 'slump') of 1980–1981, the so-called 'economic miracle' claimed by the government between 1985 and 1988, and renewed recession from the second quarter of 1990 when economic growth ceased.

Recession 1980–1982

In describing the policies pursued by the government of Margaret Thatcher to deal with the immediate crisis of the early 1980s, it is worth bearing in mind that these were intended at the same time to tackle longstanding and underlying structural problems. As one economist put it:

> Britain's relative economic decline has a longer history than is often assumed by contemporary observers. . .
> It is clear . . . that many of the factors that inhibited modernization in the late nineteenth century survived after 1945: the low status of industrial employment; managerial shortcomings; an inadequate educational system, especially in relation to technical training; conservatism and suspicion of change in the labour movement; adherence to craft techniques; a capital market that is too little concerned with long-term industrial development; a State lacking the apparatus or the political authority to promote industrial modernization effectively.
> The absence of any traumatic shocks to the British economic system explains why so little effort was made to achieve transformations (Singh, 1977).

Supporters of the government's economic policies, which fell so heavily on manufacturing industry, consequently saw these as a necessary shock for British firms to modernize their plant and work practices, and to bring about a change in attitudes (Maynard, 1988). Much was therefore heard about the importance of establishing a climate for change. Sir Keith Joseph, Secretary of State at the Department of Industry from 1979, believed with Schumpeter (1939) that economic advance is characterized by periods of 'creative destruction', when old technologies and social organization are swept away. He therefore saw the traumas of industry as a necessary process.

It is also worth remembering that the loss of manufacturing capacity which so alarmed people during the recession of 1980–1982 had been gradually occurring for some time. In 1975, for example, the Labour Chancellor of the Exchequer, Denis Healey, had warned in his budget against the remorseless process of 'de-industrialization', and this theme was repeated through the 1960s and 1970s (for example, Bacon and Eltis, 1976; Caulkin, 1983). The difference during the 1980s was that the Conservative government appeared to welcome the decline of manufacturing *vis-à-vis* services, as an inevitable process in a modern economy.

The fortunes of the British economy in the first two phases of the 1980s, and before that back to the recession of 1974–1975, can be directly related to sudden movements in the international price of oil. The graph in Figure 2.1 shows the two sharp increases in 1973–1974 and 1979, each of which triggered severe recessionary phases, and the equally sharp drop in price in 1985–1986 which preceded the 'economic miracle'. The effect in each case was not only to disrupt the level and pattern of demand in the world economy. The price of oil also, of course, fed through into industrial costs and the price of goods, and generated inflationary (or, after 1985, disinflationary) pressures in the UK. The drop in the price of oil in the mid-1980s, when in real terms it was nearly back at its 1973 level, thus coincided with the low point in UK inflation in the 1980s. Similar shifts in the international price of other commodities (non-food and food) also contributed to the high and low peaks of inflation since 1979.

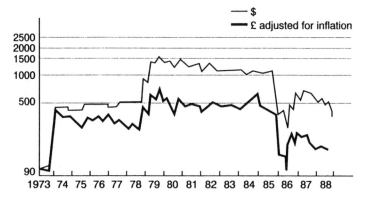

Figure 2.1   *Changes in the price of oil, 1973–1988*

In addition to externally induced inflation which affected raw material costs, the competitiveness of British-based firms also suffered from persistent wage-cost inflation. Tackling wage inflation consequently became one of the main priorities of the Conservative government after the explosion in wage demands in 1979 had helped to bring down the Labour government.

One instrument for tackling wage inflation was trade union and employment legislation designed to weaken employees' bargaining power. The other was the recession. As the Prime Minister constantly warned, people priced themselves out of jobs if they demanded, and were conceded, pay rises that were not justified by productivity increases.

Despite the downward pressures on wage inflation, however, increases in average earnings have continued to run ahead of inflation, testifying to the intractableness of the problem.

While dealing with wage inflation, the government sought to squeeze general price inflation from the economy through strict monetarist policies.

This meant restricting the money supply by means of high interest rates, cutting government expenditure and borrowing, and applying a severe deflation to consumer spending, principally by increasing indirect taxation (VAT) to 15 per cent in the 1981 budget.

While deflation directly affected sales, the reliance on a high interest rate policy bore on firms in two ways. By raising borrowing costs, it added to overall costs, increased the pressure to shed jobs, and helped to precipitate the high rate of insolvencies during the recession. Second, by attracting foreign funds into the UK and thereby maintaining the pound at a high valuation, the terms of trade for UK firms deteriorated. This meant that imports became cheaper as foreign firms were drawn to the UK market, and manufactured exports became dearer and harder to achieve.

Aggravating this were the perverse effects of North Sea oil. Throughout the 1980s Britain was self-sufficient in oil. Firms in the UK, however, did not directly benefit through cheaper energy costs, since the price of oil was internationally determined. Instead, they suffered from the fact that it helped to sustain a high exchange rate (1) from the direct effect on the balance of payments and (2) by strengthening the Exchequer as a result of the £65 billion tax revenues it generated in the course of the decade.

The causes of the recession in 1980–1982 were thus complex, with government policy arguably aggravating the situation for British firms. The effects of the recession, on the other hand, are well known and less in dispute.

There was a collapse in manufacturing generally, which hit older industries particularly, such as steel, textiles, engineering, and shipbuilding. Although other European countries such as France and Belgium also had to make severe adjustments in mature industries like steel and coal, Britain arguably had many more such sectors, and the overall impact was therefore greater. The positive gloss put on this by the government was that this was the overdue rationalization of industry which featherbedding by successive governments had put off, with distorting effects on the whole economy. Large areas of industry were thus forced to confront competition and tackle problems they had put off, or die. Many died; many emerged leaner and fitter.

The collapse had a number of effects:

1 It produced large-scale unemployment at well over 3 million for almost five years, with large regional imbalances.
2 In making forced redundancies and closing marginal units of production, firms greatly improved their productivity and unit-cost situation in the medium term.
3 It stimulated many firms to seek greater flexibility in working practices in order to be able to operate with fewer employees, and many traditional demarcations were ended or weakened.
4 It encouraged investment in labour-saving technology, including the widespread adoption of technology based on microelectronics – although initially there was a fall in manufacturing investment by 11 per cent in 1980 and 25 per cent in 1981, and net fixed investment declined each year from 1979 to 1983.

5 Coupled with changes in organization and technology, it led firms to seek more efficient ways of managing materials, including the adoption of 'just-in-time' principles and systems.

6 It led many firms fundamentally to reassess their products and markets, turning away from areas of low added value to where they could earn higher profits. This itself represented not just a shift towards more productive use of economic resources: it also reflected a more pervasive concern with profit.

The economic miracle (1985–1988)?

The result for those companies that survived was a dramatic recovery in profitability, liquidity, and their capitalization values, to levels not seen since the 1960s (Figure 2.2). While this reflected the elimination of marginal plant and the shedding of labour to a greater extent than at any other time since 1945, it also reflected firms' desire to restore liquidity before committing themselves to reinvestment (Henry, 1984).

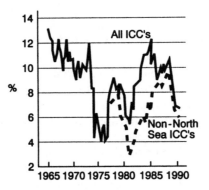

Figure 2.2 *The profitability of industrial and commercial companies (return on capital). (Source: Bank of England)*

For the economy at large, however, wiping out large chunks of manufacturing capacity severely depressed aggregate output. In 1980, manufacturing output dropped by nearly 9 per cent and by a further 6 per cent in 1981; GDP declined by around 3½ per cent; and it was 1986 before output recovered again to 1979 levels. In the longer term, this loss of overall capacity can be seen to have contributed to the adverse balance of payments from 1987 and to the 'overheating' of the economy when too much money once again chased too few home-produced goods.

The other outstanding feature of the recovery was the productivity improvement, particularly in manufacturing. While economic growth from 1979 to 1989 averaged 2.2 per cent per annum, productivity in manufacturing grew at an unprecedented 5 per cent per annum. More significantly, as a measure of the 'economic miracle' claimed, Britain went from the bottom to the top of the productivity growth league table among OECD countries.

Views differ as to what accounted for this – whether it was fewer people simply doing more work, as workforces were cut and reorganized, and the same amount of work was spread round; or whether it was due to additional and improved technology.

What seems to have happened is that in the first phase, between 1979 and 1983, the improvement came from eliminating marginal plant and employees ('rationalization') and from better use of existing capital, by removing restrictive practices and increasing work intensity. Thereafter, with manufacturing investment leaping by 33 per cent in 1984–1985 from its depressed levels of the previous few years, the improvement came from the use of more and better technology, more efficiently used. One study which has attempted to separate out these two sets of factors suggests that the latter has been far and away the more important (Smith-Gavine and Bennett, 1990).

Recession 1990–1993

In contrast to 1980–1982, which occurred against a background of world recession, the recession that took hold in 1990 was much less the result of global recessionary trends and more the result of government policies themselves, including the tacit abandonment of monetarist philosophy. The effective cause was an increase in money supply from two sources.

First, there was the boost in personal, commercial property, and industrial debt. This can be traced to three sources:

- The ending, in 1980, of direct controls on what banks could lend and to whom
- The 'Big Bang' in the City in October 1986 which boosted share dealings and company values, and encouraged borrowing against these inflated values
- The deregulation which officially allowed building societies greater scope to lend from 1 January 1987.

The result was a doubling of consumer debt from 1980 to 1988 (particularly from wider house ownership, as people bought their council houses following the Housing Act 1980); and a decline in personal savings as a percentage of GNP to historically low levels. Company interest repayments relative to income, meanwhile, hit a 25-year high in 1990.

Second, accompanying this increase in debt, cuts in direct personal taxation in the 1988 budget gave an immediate and large fillip to the money supply. The inflation that resulted was an old-fashioned demand-led inflation. When oil prices started to rise temporarily in autumn 1990, inflation was already well established.

The means used to control it – namely, the raising of interest rates to reduce money in the economy – created once again the familiar pincer effect on firms, depressing demand in the economy and increasing borrowing costs. Compounding the pressures on firms, and completing the recipe of inflation and recession (or 'stagflation'), trade unions once more began to push large wage claims to offset factors such as higher mortgage repayments. The immediate consequence was a sharp fall in liquidity levels and high levels of company insolvencies. The second consequence, with interest repayments on debts to be met, was attempts to cut costs which could readily be cut – as so often, investment in research and training, and labour costs through redundancies.

The present recession has been more prolonged, but not as deep as that of 1980–1982. While affecting manufacturing, it has also hit services sectors previously immune. It also seems that manufacturing firms have reacted more quickly this time than they did in 1980; that they have become more resilient; and that they are behaving differently. This must be one of the litmus tests for HRM.

Economic change and personnel management

What are the implication for personnel management and HRM of these economic changes during the 1980s? At one level, it is simply to recognize the importance of the business cycle in managing firms. As the director of one large company, which was severely hit, put it rather ruefully: 'We seem to need to rediscover the business cycle every few years.' This argues for realism in proposing HRM as some kind of humanist philosophy for managing employment.

Setting aside the aggravated circumstances of trying to bring about a once-and-for-all catching up, some aspects of personnel management have perennial relevance in the context of the business cycle and an economy subject to global demand factors and government macro-economic management. These involve managing pay costs, handling redundancies, controlling industrial relations, and managing the effects of technical change.

Managing pay costs

Managing pay levels is a constant requirement for keeping costs in check. In the early 1980s, rising unemployment made it relatively easy to resist wage and salary claims. Improved profitability and low general inflation in the mid-to-late 1980s, coupled with the re-emergence of skill shortages, then made companies willing to concede a higher rate of increases. Only lately, has wage-cost inflation become an issue once again.

One factor may have changed in all this, however, and that is the reduction in wage and salary costs as a proportion of firms' total costs because of capital substitution from investments in new plant. Since the marginal effect of pay increases on total costs reduces, it becomes less important to concentrate on holding down pay, and attention may be better devoted to developing other aspects of the employment relationship. This is more true for manufacturing, however, where there has been heavy investment in technology. Newer service industries remain less capital intensive, which is one reason why the recent recession has fallen more heavily on services.

Handling redundancies

In the early 1980s, the major preoccupation for many personnel managers was making people redundant. As one manager put it, having had to handle eighteen separate redundancies in an engineering firm of no more than 500 people, 'I had almost forgotten how to recruit'. Managing redundancy is likely to be a second perennial task, which general recession or the particular circumstances of company decline brings on.

Managing industrial relations

Controlling pay and making redundancies could in turn be a recipe for industrial relations strife. Managing or preventing this remains another key task for the personnel manager. In fact, industrial relations disputes have tended to be associated with periods of relative prosperity, just as trade union density has suffered during high unemployment (Bain and Price, 1983; Hyman, 1989; Kelly, 1990). There are a number of reasons for this, to do with raised expectations. Trade unions are encouraged to push pay demands, knowing that companies can afford to concede them and will eventually do so rather than face disruption when they have a strong order book. A membership whose employment is relatively secure will also be more emboldened to seek to extend their employment rights and influence within the company.

By contrast, the sheer weight and frequency of redundancies and the ensuing unemployment in the early 1980s, coupled with trade union legislation, led to a dramatic fall in the incidence of strikes and unofficial action. IR battles were more prominent in the attempts to force contraction of the old nationalized industries, such as steel (1980) and coal (1984–1985), than in the private sector.

The question for the 1990s is whether there has been a fundamental change in the behaviour of management and unions, which will counter the influence of the business cycle.

Managing the effects of technical change

If the 1980s have shown anything, it is that managing change presents personnel managers with a continuing challenge. Improving productivity has been, and is likely to remain, a constant preoccupation.

Daniel's (1987) study, however, derived from data from the 1984 Workplace Industrial Relations Survey, indicated that professional personnel managers played only a small role in bringing about major change in this period. They were involved in only 50 per cent of cases, and in these it was usually only later on and to manage organizational rather than technical change. Since organizational change typically involved issues like redundancy and demarcations between categories of manual workers, it represented traditional areas of work for the personnel function, to do with managing contracts, rather than a shift in focus.

The changing shape of industry and commerce

Accompanying these economic effects through the 1980s there were a number of structural changes to the shape of industry and commerce. The first was a growth in services at the expense of manufacturing. A second was the restructuring of companies through acquisition and diversification. A third was the emergence of the global economy and global company. Embracing these was also a fourth trend – decentralization – in order to manage increasingly complex organization structures.

Growth of services

The recession particularly hit manufacturing, producing a sharp acceleration in the long-run decline of manufacturing *vis-à-vis* services as a source of employment (Table 2.1). Among the major casualties were coal and petroleum products (down 32 per cent between 1979 and 1982), metal manufacture (down 35 per cent), clothing and footwear (down 29 per cent), textiles (down 34 per cent), and vehicles (down 29 per cent). In the same period, employment in insurance, banking, finance, and business services grew by 12 per cent. The result was to reduce employment in manufacturing, the primary industries (mining, agriculture, fishing), and the utilities (gas, water, and electricity) to just over 25 per cent by the end of the decade.

Table 2.1 Employment by sector (1974–1989)

	1974	*1979*	*1985*	*1989*
Primary & Utilities[a]	707	712	582	457
Manufacturing	7 722	7 107	5 254	5 080
Construction	1 223	1 201	994	1 057
Traded Services[b]	7883	8 518	9 049	10 252
Public Admin., Education & Health	4 357	4 742	4 720	5 009
All employees	22 297	22 638	20 920	22 134

[a] Comprises agriculture, forestry, and fishing; coal, oil, gas; electricity and water.
[b] Comprises retail and wholesale distribution; hotel and catering; transport, post, and telecommunications; and banking, finance, and insurance.
Source: *Employment Gazette*

In 1984, for the first time since the Industrial Revolution, Britain once again became a net importer of manufactured goods. This 'de-industrialization' had in fact been going on for some while. In the two decades from 1960 to 1980, the value contribution to GDP of manufacturing had already fallen from 32 per cent to 21 per cent (or, when measuring by volume and discounting price changes, from just over 30 per cent to just under 25 per cent between 1964 and 1981). By either measure the trend was already clear.

In the UK, however, the fall was both steeper and to a lower level than the average for the OECD countries. In the process, the British economy had begun to resemble the US economy, where services take an even greater share, rather than European countries like France and Germany. In further contrast, manufacturing in Japan had actually grown at the expense of services. Nevertheless, in all these countries, including Japan, employment in services had grown markedly, and during the 1980s continued to do so.

Apart from the economic questions whether this is a permanent trend and whether growth in services is capable of making good the shortfall in GDP and jobs, there is also the question, 'what kind of jobs are these?' Are service jobs good jobs? (Kirkland, 1985). One immediate response is that there is enormous diversity in what we mean by services. Services include the local authority sector and public administration; largely non-traded 'knowledge' sectors, such as education and medicine; traded services such as finance, travel, tourism, and leisure; 'producer' services to companies which support manufacture (such as all forms of equipment maintenance and business consultancy); the retail and distribution systems for all kinds of products; a wide range of personal services (from hair-dressing to psychiatry); and a host of domestic maintenance services for gas, water, electricity, and telephones. Conventional classifications of economic activity place these activities under a variety of headings which obscure their nature and range.

With this diversity in mind, the argument about the quality of service jobs is more an economic one than about intrinsic skill or interest. Gershuny and Miles (1985) have argued that the nature of economic advance has been to develop manufactured substitutes (or 'goods') for services. Washing machines and vacuum cleaners have replaced domestic servants; likewise, home entertainments such as television have been displacing the cinema (which before that itself killed off the music hall). What distinguishes economies like the Japanese, and more especially the companies within it, is that they have continued to be dynamic and innovative in searching out opportunities to create manufactured substitutes, whereas the UK and USA have become relatively moribund in this respect. The counterpart to this is that manufacturing gives greater scope to productivity gains. However, this would seem to discount the degree to which service activity, like retailing, hotels, medicine, and education, are backed by technology which improves productivity and standards of service (Kirkland, 1985).

With employment growing disproportionately in service industries, and the productivity improvements of the 1980s having been more concentrated in manufacturing, the recession of 1990–1992 is likely to have fallen more severely on services, where there remain larger efficiency gains to be made. Thus, sectors like banking and finance are looking to reap the benefits of the heavy investments in technology they made during the 1980s, and from which they have yet fully to gain the anticipated advantages.

The question is, how will management in services tackle such changes, given such factors as a lower incidence of trade unionism and different cultures from manufacturing? The diversity in services makes simple answers impossible, but the comparatively small size of operating units in many services outside the public sector has tended to make trade union organization difficult and to give managers greater power. The result may be more arbitrary management. On the other hand, according to Daniel's (1987) study of technical change, management in non-trade union settings tends to be 'relatively passive, conservative and even apathetic' (p. 273), and hence slower to react positively to economic pressure. Service organizations may therefore respond more slowly, even though they are more exposed than in the previous recession.

Acquisition and diversification

The second structural change of note has been the reshaping of companies that has taken place in many industries. This has been of two kinds. The first was rationalization as part of the recession in sectors like engineering. This took place through firms concentrating their own production into viable units or merging them with plant acquired from other firms, or both. Many firms thereby 'slimmed' down and simplified their organization. At the same time, many firms caught in declining sectors sought to break out and diversify into other areas with better growth prospects.

GKN is a typical example of a company changing shape in both these directions. In 1980, 15 per cent of its sales came from steel, 29 per cent from downstream products in low added value products like nuts and bolts, while altogether it had around 200 subsidiaries spread among a dozen product divisions. In 1989, none of the steel-making or processing was left. GKN instead had become a company based on three 'legs' – industrial services and defence, both almost entirely new, and automotive, an existing business which had branched out geographically and in product terms. Such changes radically alter the skill base of a firm, and demand changes in the structure of planning and control to accommodate the degree and kind of diversity in the business.

Beyond the recession, there was a major spell of acquisition and merger activity in the middle and late 1980s. This mirrored similar outbreaks of 'merger mania' in the late 1960s and early 1970s. Like those before it, this was stimulated by growth in credit from the banking system. In addition, there was the boost from deregulation of the Stock Exchange ('Big Bang') which encouraged 'deal-making' (with its lucrative commissions for merchant banks). In the UK, as in the USA, the mid/late 1980s became the era of the 'leveraged buyout', with takeovers based on debt rather than the predator's own equity value.

Motives and circumstances for mergers and acquisitions varied. In *banking and financial services*, in the lead up to 'Big Bang' in 1986, there was a widespread expectation of an enlarged market in sharedealing and corporate financing. As a result, banks outbid one another to put together comprehensive stockbroking and financial services. With too many expensively assembled businesses chasing too little business, however, there has since been a considerable shakeout, leading to closures and redundancies.

In the *computer industry* two strategies predominated. One was to gain economies of scale to sustain the levels of R&D necessary for long-term survival. The second was to merge telecommunications and computer firms in anticipation of a convergence in their technologies. Many who attempted the latter in fact failed, and have subsequently demerged. In the UK, ICL has been involved in both of these – being the subject of a hostile takeover by the telecommunications firm, STC, in 1984, and then, when STC gave up this strategy in 1990, being sold to Fujitsu as the pursuit of economies of scale in technological development reasserted itself (Lorenz, 1990).

Other sectors that have seen substantial merger activity are:

- *Publishing*, where family-owned houses have been absorbed into large international combines
- *defence electronics*, where falling sales and continuing technological advance have produced a situation similar to that in the computing industry, involving hostile takeovers and joint ventures
- *non-food retailing*. Here, the competition for vital high street outlets and new retailing formulae tends to produce periodic bouts of wheeler-dealing in which chains of outlets change hands and re-emerge in a new guise. This is often followed by the break-up of the new retailing empires when they are found to have over-extended themselves.

Restructuring in these various ways is nothing new, but typical processes in a capitalist economy. By and large, though, the 'unrelated' acquisition was less fashionable than it had been in earlier decades, with firms 'sticking closer to their knitting', as Peters and Waterman (1982) had urged – although two conglomerates, BTR and Hanson, thrived on accumulating diverse businesses.

Even so, acquisitions and mergers remain notoriously difficult to effect successfully, aside of the economic and financial doubts about the benefits they produce (Kitching, 1967, 1973; Cowling *et al.*, 1980). They present a major challenge to HRM, in its broadest sense, to be able to manage a great variety of interrelated changes in culture and systems (Cartwright and Cooper, 1990). There are also conflicting views about the impact on management behaviour from operating under the threat of takeover – whether it creates a discipline to run businesses profitably, or whether it induces short-termism. The failed attempt by BTR to take over Pilkington in 1986-1987 was something of a watershed in this respect, and brought hostile takeovers into temporary disrepute.

Internationalization

Such reshaping of firms and industries has been conducted in an increasingly international or 'global' economy. This is the third major structural change.

The UK economy has for a long time been more open than those of its nearest neighbours in the European Union, both to trade and to movements of capital. The abolition of exchange controls in October 1979, which allowed the free movement of funds out of the UK, encouraged British firms to invest overseas – in part to rectify their dependence on shrinking markets at home, in part to escape from a UK cost base to sources of cheaper labour. The result of companies building new plant abroad and

acquiring foreign companies has been the accumulation of foreign investments that represent around 23 per cent of GDP. This compares with 7 per
cent for France and Germany, for example (Directorate-General, 1990).

As a result, during the 1980s, there was a continuing and substantial shift
in the balance of employment in many British firms overseas, through job
losses in the UK combined with acquisitions/greenfield developments overseas. By 1987, for example, five British firms – ICI, GKN, Pilkington,
Turner and Newall, and Glaxo – had come to employ more than 50 per
cent of their workforce overseas, joining five others (BAT, before its break-
up, BOC, Lonrho, Beecham, and RTZ) already in that position (Hendry
and Pettigrew, 1992).

Another way of looking at this trend is that between 1979 and 1987 the
largest UK manufacturing firms had shed a total of 415,000 jobs in the UK
and gained 125,000 jobs overseas (*The Guardian*, 1987). This increase,
moreover, was predominantly in North America and Europe, indicating a
radical shift in British firms' competitive stance towards operating in the
more competitive markets of the world and away from the relatively
captive markets of the old Empire.

In addition, there has been an explosion in 'partnership' ventures which
fall short of full mergers. Sectors such as computer manufacture have been
using these since the beginning of the 1980s as a way of pooling product
development effort and providing a full product range through licensing
agreements (Sparrow and Pettigrew, 1988a). In the last few years, however, the impetus has come from the approach of the Single European
Market. Well-publicized, cross-border alliances have thus been taking
place in the pharmaceutical, food, and defence/aerospace industries. But
as Figure 2.3 shows, the volume of deals is both high and spread across
many sectors.

In anticipation of 1992, with its threat of an open market within, and
barriers without, American and Japanese multinational companies (MNCs)
have dramatically increased their inward investment in the EU, and in the
UK in particular. American investment of £30 billion in Europe in 1989,
for example, was three times that for 1988. In the process, through takeovers
of indigenous companies, European industrial restructuring is being
boosted by foreign capital.

This process is not new, of course. Britain has long been a favoured
target for US and Japanese companies wanting a European base, and this
process was tacitly encouraged by the government during the 1980s as a
way of introducing Japanese standards of management and efficiency into
British industry. Nissan in the North-east and Toyota near Derby are but
recent examples of a trend which has seen a variety of Japanese firms,
especially those in electronics, locate in South Wales. Equally, the UK has
been the location for MNCs, both UK-owned and foreign-owned for some
decades. Along with the USA and Canada, the UK is home to one of the
highest proportions of MNCs of all countries.

The completion of the Single European Market in 1992 was thus a
moment in a long-term process that has been accelerating in the past
decade. This process has involved British firms and the British workforce in
internationalization as a two-way process. On the one hand, British-based

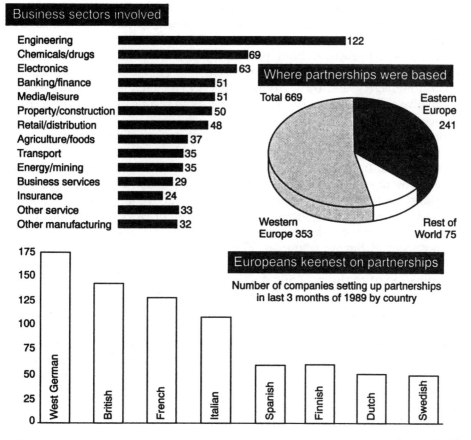

Business sectors involved

Engineering	122
Chemicals/drugs	69
Electronics	63
Banking/finance	51
Media/leisure	51
Property/construction	50
Retail/distribution	48
Agriculture/foods	37
Transport	35
Energy/mining	35
Business services	29
Insurance	24
Other service	33
Other manufacturing	32

Where partnerships were based

Total 669

Eastern Europe 241

Western Europe 353

Rest of World 75

Europeans keenest on partnerships

Number of companies setting up partnerships in last 3 months of 1989 by country

(Bar chart by country: West German, British, French, Italian, Spanish, Finnish, Dutch, Swedish)

Figure 2.3 *European companies entering into partnerships (1989). (Source: KPMG Peat Marwick McLintock)*

and British-owned firms have made acquisitions and built sites overseas, and entered into alliances with foreign firms. Managing an international organization and alliances across company boundaries in this way makes unusual demands – on companies' systems of strategic and operational control, on their management development systems, on their related systems of pay, and less tangibly on their culture. On the other hand, foreign firms have entered the UK by the same routes, taking over British firms and opening plants and offices. This imposes new demands on management in UK firms and exposes workforces to new styles of management from abroad.

Decentralization

The consequence of internationalizing and diversifying, in products and markets, has been that many larger firms have developed a wide spread of products, technologies, skills, and physical locations. Managing this complexity is a major organizational challenge. With the sharper focus on customers and the need for greater responsiveness of operating units to customers and labour markets, many organizations have responded by decentralizing.

This has happened in both private and public sectors. The National Health Service, for instance, first devolved cost responsibilities to hospital general managers; and then, from April 1991, the creation of trusts began to devolve responsibilities for output targets and resources across the health service generally.

Bringing about decentralization for many organizations meant a protracted effort centred on the dismantling of centralized collective bargaining arrangements. In the process, a wider range of other centralized personnel activities were truncated or abandoned. These included company-wide job-evaluation schemes, central recruitment, central training functions, and centrally orchestrated 'postings' for the purposes of career development. In due course, however, this has begun to raise issues about the corporate management of human resources. The result is that some avowedly decentralized organizations have begun to reinstate, in a modified guise, central coordination of recruitment and development (Hendry, 1990).

The interesting thing about this is that corporate headquarters has, as a result, become much more explicitly concerned with developing people. In other words, personnel activity in decentralized organizations has acquired a more distinctive 'human resources' focus. In contrast to what one might expect, there is evidence, too, that operational units in decentralized organizations have also begun to take the development of people more seriously.

The labour market

Changes in the labour market affect the work of personnel practitioners directly and visibly. These involve the bread-and-butter issues of industrial relations, training, development, and recruitment, which are at the core of the job.

Aside from purely political motives to do with curbing trade union power and bolstering the authority of management, government policy towards the labour market since 1979 was presented as improving the long-run supply side of the economy. This had two aspects, which we may colloquially refer to as 'loosening up' and 'smartening up' the supply of labour. Each, in their different ways, was intended to reduce supposed rigidities in the labour market. In addition, the structure of the labour market has been affected by demographic change.

'Loosening up'

Whereas the previous Labour government had relied on statutory and voluntary controls to contain wage demands, the Conservatives sought to make the 'free market' in wages work better by removing or weakening institutional 'distortions' to the market. This had three elements:

- Passing trade union and employment laws designed to reduce employees' bargaining power and protection
- Acting directly on pay levels by removing support for low wages
- Reducing the resistance to taking lower-paid jobs by weakening social security provision.

The 1980 and 1982 Employment Acts (amplified by the 1980 Code of Practice) limited the ability of trade unions to mount industrial action (1) by removing immunity from the common law for picketing other than at the place of work, and (2) by prescribing the conditions under which it should be conducted. Accordingly, unions became liable to legal action, injunctions, and prescribed levels of damages for unlawful action undertaken. Secondary action, and official action not approved by secret ballot, were also outlawed. The Trade Union Act 1984 and Employment Act 1988 placed further constraints through the holding of ballots – principally, the requirement to hold separate ballots at each place of work contemplating industrial action.

Trade unions' powers of recruitment were curtailed by limitations on the closed shop – the Employment Act 1988, for instance, making dismissal of non-members automatically unfair. The same Act also greatly extended the rights of individual members to take action against their union – for example, to avoid being 'unjustifiably' disciplined for not participating in or supporting industrial action.

Although there were some highly publicized cases in the early and mid-1980s (involving the TGWU, the NUM, and the NGA) of unions being heavily fined and having their assets sequestered for non-compliance, the 'new realism' among unions by the end of the 1980s had resulted in a more careful observance of the restrictions on industrial action. The effect of the new laws is reflected in the dramatic reduction in the incidence of strikes, from 2080 in 1979 to below 700 by the end of the 1980s. However, the impact of the laws themselves, separate from other factors, is disputed (Kelly, 1990). The sharpest fall in the number of strikes occurred in 1979–1980, before the new legislation took effect. Nevertheless, in recent years there has been a continuing consistent reduction (Table 2.2).

Equally, unions have turned the laws on ballots to their own account, winning around 90 per cent of all strike ballots (although it is possible they have been deterred from risking a ballot on other occasions when they thought they might not win the vote). This has had the unintended consequence of strengthening trade union legitimacy. Moreover, unions have begun to evolve strategies which turn legislation to their own advantage in conducting disputes. In the shorter working hours campaign conducted by the Confederation of Shipbuilding and Engineering Unions in 1989, site ballots became a potent weapon for bringing pressure to bear on strategically important individual employers.

Union influence, measured in terms of membership, has certainly declined, though. From its high point in 1979 at 13,289,000 members, membership had fallen to 10,475,000 by 1987 – a fall of 21 per cent – and by 1993 had continued its decline, to around 8.5 million members. Most establishments that recognized trade unions in 1979, however, continued to do so in

Table 2.2 Industrial stoppages in the UK (1976–1991)

	Number of stoppages beginning in period	Number of workers involved ('000s)	Working days lost in period ('000s)
1976	2 016	666	3 284
1977	2 703	1 155	10 142
1978	2 417	1 001	9 405
1979	2 080	4 583	29 474
1980	1 330	830	11 964
1981	1 338	1 499	4 266
1982	1 528	2 101	5 313
1 983	1352	573	3 754
1984	1 206	1 436	27 135
1985	885	643	6 402
1986	1 053	538	1 920
1987	1 004	884	3 546
1988	770	759	3 702
1989	693	727	4 128
1990	620	285	1 903
1991	357	175	761

1. In the four years, 1977–1980, metals, engineering, and motor vehicles accounted, respectively, for 6133, 5985, 20 390, and 10 155 working days lost.
2. In the two years of the miners' strike (1984–1985), mining and quarrying accounted, respectively, for 22 484 and 4 143 working days lost.
Source: *Employment Gazette*

1989, and membership density seems to have remained constant in these. Equally, however, there has been little advance in union recognition in workplaces that started out as non-union.

The greatest decline in overall membership clearly occurred as a direct result of manufacturing closures during the recession, and from the continuing contraction in industries like mining. Areas of growth in trade union membership – in banking (BIFU), post/telecommunications (NCU), and further/higher education (NATFHE) – reflected shifts in the economy towards services (although these trends may have been since reversed in banking and telecommunications). Explaining the continued erosion since 1984, when employment began to grow again, however, is difficult and complex, and involves a variety of cross-currents (Kelly, 1990).

Accompanying the changes to trade union law, individual employment protection has been reduced. The more significant of these changes include:

- The extension from six months to two years in the period of service necessary to be able to bring a claim of unfair dismissal
- A similar qualifying period for maternity leave, and for the receipt of redundancy pay
- Shifting the onus onto the employee to prove unfair dismissal.

In most areas of employee protection, rights are limited to full-time employees working 16 hours a week or more. However, decisions of the European Court of Justice, which in effect amend UK practice, are increasingly having an impact on access to benefits (sick pay, holiday pay, and pension entitlements) and on protection from dismissal, on the grounds of discrimination against women who in many sectors form a majority of part-time employees.

Protection against low pay has also been eroded by limiting the scope of wage councils covering sectors where trade union organization is weak (Wages Act 1986), and by abolishing those in sectors, such as road haulage, which were deemed to have developed adequate voluntary employer–employee organization. The effectiveness of wage councils in lifting rates of pay has been in doubt, however, for some time (Torrington and Chapman, 1983, p. 359).

Various measures were also designed to put pressure on people to accept lower-paid jobs or to stay in low-paid employment. School-leavers could not immediately become eligible for unemployment benefit; the qualifying period for benefit for employees voluntarily leaving employment was extended from six weeks to six months (Social Security Act, 1988); and levels of benefit were reduced with the abolition of the earnings-related element from National Insurance.

The combination of such measures affecting the employment market were designed to give employers greater flexibility in managing their employment levels and costs, and to be able to adjust these rapidly to market conditions. Critics, however, saw in this simply increased insecurity of employment. In Chapter 18, we will consider the implications of this policy for the creation of a 'secondary labour market' of low-skilled and low-paid workers, often in part-time and sub-contracted jobs (Campbell, 1991).

'Smartening up'

During the decade, there has been a general attempt to assert the importance of vocational education and initial training geared to the actual requirements of employers. In 1983, the then Manpower Services Commission (on behalf of the Department of Employment) tried to influence schools' curricula to become more technically and vocationally oriented by launching the Technical and Vocational Education Initiative (TVEI) for 14-year-olds. Beginning as a five-year pilot study, TVEI was extended into a national scheme, and by 1989 covered over half a million school children and three-quarters of all local education authorities. The Department of Education and Science subsequently introduced schemes of its own, including a Certificate of Pre-Vocational Education, which emphasized vocationalism.

This philosophy has been most prominently expressed in YTS (the 'Youth Training Scheme') – later known as YT ('Youth Training'). When this was conceived in 1981 it was intended 'to equip unemployed young people to adapt successfully to the demands of employment; to have a fuller appreciation of the world of industry, business and technology in

which they will work; and to develop basic and recognised skills which employers will require in the future' (Department of Employment, 1981, p. 7).

Initially launched as a one-year scheme in 1983 for all unemployed 16-
year-old school-leavers, it was converted into a two-year scheme from
September 1986. Its role in making young people more employable through
appropriate training was somewhat compromised, however, by the perception that it was a hastily conceived palliative for youth unemployment
(Keep, 1986), designed, moreover, to depress youth wages and thereby
wage structures generally. It could be argued, indeed, that its impact lies as
much in 'loosening up' the labour market by providing a cheap source of
labour, as in 'smartening up' new entrants to it (Bevan and Hutt, 1985;
Sako and Dore, 1986; Hendry, Jones and Arthur, 1991).

The merits and impact of government policy towards the education and
training of workers is dealt with more fully in Chapter 19.

Demography

Involuntary changes in demography, and social changes affecting the participation rate of different groups in the labour market, underly any government's policy in the labour market and provide a broad context for
organizations' employment policies. At the start of the 1980s, the unemployment situation was aggravated by the rising numbers of school-leavers just
coming onto the labour market. Through the 1980s, by contrast, the
number of 16–19 year-olds declined, and from 1989 through to 1995 the
numbers fall away dramatically. Between 1980 and 1992, for example, there
was a fall of 30 per cent, or 1.2 million fewer school-leavers coming onto
the labour market. Looking ahead, and using a wider definition of young
persons that allows for progress through higher education, the number of
16–24 year-olds in the labour force is expected to fall by 1.1 million
between 1989 and 2001. These trends are common to many countries in
Europe.

In 1988, the National Economic Development Council (NEDO) and the
Training Agency alerted employers to the implications of this in a report in
which they described an impending 'demographic timebomb'. Employers
needed to be weaned away from competing ever more furiously for this
dwindling group – especially as they were under the misconception (a
subsequent survey revealed) that the labour force as a whole was about to
decline. In fact, during the 1990s, it is likely to expand by nearly one
million. This depends, of course, on participation rates, as well as the
balance between young people joining and deaths/retirements.

Through the 1980s, the proportion of women entering the labour market
continued to rise, in keeping with the long-run post-war trend. As Table 2.3
shows, the effect of changes in economic activity and of company policy in
the 1980s was an increase in the absolute and relative numbers of women in
paid employment. This was particularly so of women in the 25–44 age
group (signalling, among other things, a greater readiness, or need, for
women to return to work earlier after child-bearing). Also noticeable is the
marked decline in the participation rate of older people generally.

Table 2.3 Participation rates of men and women in the labour force (%)

	1971	*1981*	*1991*
Males			
Under 20	69.4	72.4	75.8
20–24	87.7	85.1	75.8
25–44	95.4	95.7	94.0
45–64	93.2	65.6	79.7
65 +	17.6	9.2	5.6
All ages	80.5	76.5	73.1
Females			
Under 20	65.0	70.4	74.2
20 – 24	60.2	68.8	69.2
25–44	50.6	61.4	68.4
45–64	50.2	52.5	52.4
65 +	6.3	3.7	2.4
All ages	43.9	47.6	49.9
Males and females			
All ages	61.9	61.7	61.1
Total (in millions)			
Males	13.7	12.5	12.3[a]
Females	8.4	9.3	10.6[a]
(% of total)			
Males	62.0	57.1	53.9
Females	38.0	42.5	46.1

[a] These figures are for 1992.

Source: Adapted from Sisson (1989), Tables 2.4 and 2.7.

The answer to the 'demographic timebomb' put forward by most commentators was therefore for women to seek paid employment in yet greater numbers, while giving greater encouragement to older people and others, such as ethnic minorities, whose participation rate is also below average. This means changes in recruitment practices and conditions, including the provision of crèches, job-sharing, part-time work, and home-working. Banks, for example, have been among the leaders in devising schemes to attract and keep women, influenced by the fact that they have traditionally employed a high proportion of women. Equally, there is a general need to review policies which, for much of the last decade, sought to encourage early retirement.

In retrospect, the 'demographic timebomb' was overplayed. Even in 1988, there remained, after all, nearly 2 million unemployed according to the official definition, and the subsequent recession pushed that nearer to 3 million.

Beyond the crude exercise in numbers, however, there is the question of where jobs are likely to be created, according to geography and sector, and how the location and particular skills of people available match these. Before the onset of recession in 1990, skill shortages were being widely reported once again, with the South-west, South-east, and East Anglia at the top of the list. Moreover, the expectation is that the fall in the 16–24 age group will exceed the level of youth unemployment in all regions, but by twice as much in the South-east.

Interestingly, at the end of the 1980s, not only were difficulties in recruitment being reported in sectors that had remained buoyant through the 1980s – health, hotels and catering, and business services. But top of the list was engineering, with others like textiles, which had suffered excessively in the previous recession.

The inference from this is that the balance between demand and supply is a function not just of overall recruitment requirements which fluctuate, but also of the amount by which they do so, as a result of the business cycle and longer-term economic trends. Sectors and organizations which recruit consistently develop an image and reputation which attract young people. They are also likely to have put more prolonged effort into their methods of recruitment and in devising alternatives which mitigate shortages.

Thus banking, despite being a growth sector through the 1980s, has had relatively few difficulties in maintaining recruitment. On the other hand, sectors and organizations like engineering, which have suffered recent serious decline, have lost skilled people permanently and have acquired an image with young people of offering doubtful career prospects. Still other sectors, such as construction, which are used to reflecting the ups and downs of the business cycle, have developed relatively efficient ways of managing fluctuations in employment – although construction is usually also the first to register shortages in an upturn.

A further 'demographic' issue is how people with higher education match the types of jobs being created. Apart from the possibility of directly influencing the rate of participation in further and higher education – an issue which has risen in the political agenda since 1989 – it is important to note that the falling birth rate since the 1960s has been most pronounced among the working class. The middle classes have continued to reproduce and to send their offspring to university. The result is that the output of graduates rose until 1992, and was expected to fall away only marginally by the year 2000 (IMS, 1989). Since then, of course, government policy has encouraged a substantial expansion in student numbers. There may be better prospects therefore for meeting the demand for professional skills.

These trends in demography are not unique to the UK (DES, 1990). Most European countries, with the exception of Spain, followed the same pattern through the 1980s and do so to the year 2000. Spain only begins to dip from around 1995. Japan and the USA are different, though. In Japan, the number of young people entering the labour market rose steeply through the 1980s and peaked in .1990, after which it begins to fall back to 1982 levels by 1996. In the USA, the peak occurred in the mid-1970s, and has declined steadily since.

One can readily speculate what these comparisons mean for a country's economic dynamism, including the way the age of the population affects consumption patterns. Equally relevant is what an ageing workforce can do to organizations' pay and career structures. In the UK, for example, the number of 35–54-year-olds will rise by 2 million, and by 2001 constitute 47 per cent of the labour force. If systems of incremental pay are applied, total salary bills will be swollen. At the same time, people in this age group will be expecting to gain significant career positions.

The sectors of the economy and types of job likely to expand (namely, white-collar professional) are precisely of the kind to which these considerations apply. What will the effect be, then – inflated salary bills borne by other groups of workers? An inducement to organizations to contain employment growth in these areas? Attempts to restructure pay systems?

The political context

More than usually so, government economic and labour management over the past decade has been political, with policy across a wide range of areas united by a strong ideological thread. In the early years of Thatcherism this manifested itself in a variety of ways, although at first it was overshadowed by the preoccupation with inflation and the doctrine of monetarism. From around the middle of the decade, however, coinciding with the rise of Lord Young, this ideology coalesced around the theme of 'enterprise'.

The importance of this for organizations and for HRM is not just the particular measures associated with it, but the 'enterprise culture' it sought to promote. Arguably, the distinctive way in which management in Britain has changed, and consequently a particular feature of HRM in the UK, is in the influence of this 'enterprise culture'. Crudely summarized, it consisted of the assertion of free market liberalism, individualism, and the virtues of wealth-creation.

The market rules

From the outset, the government of Margaret Thatcher proclaimed the need for firms to be responsive to the market. In the recession of 1980–1982, the government steadfastly refused to intervene to support or bail out private sector firms in trouble. The constant message throughout the decade was that firms had to meet the needs of their customers, and were responsible for managing their own costs (specifically, their wage costs). Failure in either area would bring down the judgement of the market. It was thus an invitation to managers to manage and an assertion of consumer sovereignty against producer privileges. All employees should be aware that they owed their livelihood to their customers.

Alongside this was a preference for the private sector over the public, and for the individual over the collective. Both signified greater freedom and the release of initiative. The private sector was regarded as inherently more dynamic, while the share of resources public services had been absorbing in the 1970s was alleged to have produced an 'unbalanced economy', with too few people engaged in the productive, traded sector (Bacon and Eltis, 1976). The public service sector, moreover, had become highly unionized, and therefore reducing its size would cut into the trade unions' membership base.

Privatization

Under the guise of reducing the public sector borrowing requirement (PSBR) and curbing inflation, support for the nationalized industries was steadily cut (as was spending on social programmes). Nationalized industries were expected to submit increasingly to the financial disciplines of the market – if necessary, as in steel and coal, by drastic rationalization. Beginning in a small way with the sale of part of British Aerospace in 1981, this subsequently evolved into the policy of privatization. From 1984, with the sale of British Telecom, the assets of all the great public utilities (telephones, steel, gas, water, and electricity) have been transferred into private ownership, leaving only railways, coal, and the Post Office.

Although one of the avowed aims has been to promote competition, privatization, in fact, has served a number of objectives, some of them in conflict with one another. Since most of the former utilities, for example, remain monopolies or oligopolies, many argue that the discipline of the market has been muted. Certainly, it is difficult, at this juncture, to say what difference privatization has made to the operating cultures of these organizations, other than freeing managers from political interference. There have been some spectacular productivity improvements (British Steel) and transformations in image (British Airways). But the extent to which these are due to privatization, or to policies initiated by previous managements before privatization, has been disputed (Finniston, 1990). In other cases, such as Jaguar Cars, the transformation has been only half-complete, with Jaguar's fortunes declining as rapidly as they recovered and efficiencies improving less surely than quality. With Jaguar now taken over by Ford, however, this rather proves the point that privatization has exposed firms to market disciplines.

Opening up the public sector to competition

The public service sector has meanwhile been diminished by opening various areas of service to private competition, rather than by direct privatization. Refuse collection under local authorities and hospital laundries for example, were forced out to tender, while the monopolies enjoyed by other publicly run services such as city buses were broken up by deregulation.

In education and health, where there was already private sector competition and the wholesale privatization of assets touched too closely upon their core purpose, private sector market values have been introduced to improve efficiency and standards of provision. In education, this has taken the form of competition between schools for pupils and the introduction of local budgeting. In the NHS, it has involved the construction of an internal market through devolved budgets, and creating a structure of purchasers and providers who will regulate one another.

Putting professionals and producers under market discipline

In the same way that trade union power was seen as hampering companies from taking economically sensible decisions, impeding the free working of the labour market, and acting against the interests of the consumer, so the vested interests of professionals (such as teachers, doctors, and barristers) have been presented as acting against those of parents, pupils, patients, and public. Thus, on all fronts, there has been a concerted attempt to shift power away from the producer to the consumer – from the 'privileged producer' to the 'sovereign consumer' (Keat and Abercrombie, 1991). One direct consequence has been the rewriting of professionals' contracts, sometimes after protracted disputes such as that involving teachers. More generally, this represents an attempt to change the way people think about their jobs and their relationships with those they serve.

Private ownership of wealth

The immediate and direct consequence of privatization has been to create wider share ownership and make former nationalized industries directly answerable to shareholders. The result is that the number of individual shareholders (9.26 million in 1993) now exceeds the number of trade union members. Alongside the consumer, therefore, and ranged against the collective producer there looms also the shareholder. Again, the practical effect of this revolution is disputed. Holding shares in one or two utilities, sold at a discount, does not make someone a permanent member of a property-owning democracy, or make people entrepreneurial-minded. Moreover, the number holding shares has declined from its peak of 11 million at the end of the 1980s.

Private ownership and wealth-creation are, nevertheless, at the heart of the 'enterprise culture', and numerous measures of one kind or another aimed to foster this. Cuts in the basic rate of income tax gave people more discretion in spending their earnings. Personal equity plans (PEPs), introduced in the Budget of 1986, encouraged individual investment in smaller firms to help them grow. Profit-sharing schemes (introduced in the Finance Acts 1978, 1980, and 1984 – the first, incidentally, under the Labour government) gave employees an equity stake in their own firms and thereby encouraged identification with its success. Enterprise Allowances (from 1988) were one among a number of schemes introduced by Lord Young at the Department of Industry to encourage school-leavers and the unemployed to set up in business for themselves. Finally there were numerous measures to help small firms – tax incentives, reduced planning controls and employment regulations, and investment help.

An enterprise culture?

These were some of the initiatives taken by successive Thatcher governments to promote an enterprise culture, and the kind of claims made for them. The ideology, meanwhile, was given visible expression in the setting up of an Enterprise Unit in the Cabinet Office in 1984 and by the renaming of the DTI in 1988 as 'The DTI: the Department for Enterprise'. Embodying this philosophy was Lord Young who, in turn, headed each of these bodies, and under whom TVEI, with its aim of 'develop[ing] enterprise, initiative, motivation', was first conceived, when he was at the MSC, and then promoted nationally when he went to the Department of Employment in 1985 (Morris, 1991).

The extent to which Thatcherism in general, and the 'enterprise culture' in particular, have affected people's attitudes, even in the short term, is difficult to estimate, however. Despite the range and intensity of ideological pressure exerted, it was often opportunistic, and beset by internal contradictions, and policies given a convenient ideological gloss were liable to be dropped when they proved politically difficult to defend. Justifying increased pay differentials and the shift in incomes and wealth, for example, in terms of 'trickle-down' theory had a relatively short life in Britain, compared with the use made of it by President Reagan in the USA. Although the government was pleased to adopt successful business leaders as exemplars from time to time, the British people were less comfortable with the idea of the very rich as role models. Exceptional payments to top directors and chief executives sent out the wrong message, especially when, as things tightened again at the end of the decade, the government started to urge pay restraint on ordinary employees.

There is plenty of anecdotal evidence that the policies of Thatcherism influenced the behaviour of managers and employees to some degree. Certainly, they created a climate and the legislative means to devise individual incentives, promote wider pay differentials, develop anti-union strategies, and promote a more customer-oriented culture. The next chapter will consider examples of innovations in managing employment and what these mean for HRM. How enduring the political climate of Thatcherism and the 'enterprise culture' will be, however, remains to be seen. Certainly, the annual *Social Trends* survey seems to suggest a continuing attachment to the values of community and collectivism.

Summary

This chapter has taken a more extended and detailed look at economic change than is perhaps customary at this stage in a book about managing employment. Normally, the context is covered in a few gentle simplifications, before getting down to the 'real' meat about personnel technique and the problems of managing people. I have wanted to emphasize, however, the hard (mostly hard) economic realities shaping employment and against which HRM has to make its way.

The early 1980s saw the deepest recession in Britain since the 1930s, unprecedented international competition spilling over into domestic markets, and in consequence the second highest-ever level of unemployment. This was in the context, moreover, of the most right-wing post-war government, intent on rolling back employment rights and trade union power accumulated during the 1970s, and instilling anew the values of competitive individualism and market forces. As others have recognized, this is not a natural breeding ground for people-centred HRM:

> It is against this 'reality' that HRM emerged in Britain and its theoretical underpinnings and historical significance cannot be understood except in relation to the economic crisis of the early 1980s and the attempt to re-legitimise liberal individualist values and economic institutions as a solution to that crisis (Keenoy, 1990, p. 378).

In the next chapter we will trace the kinds of response in this situation, and assess how far, if at all, organizations in Britain have developed a new style of personnel management.

3
HRM in practice

Introduction

Against this background of economic, legal, political, technical, and social change, how have firms responded? How far, in the process, have they incorporated a new philosophy of HRM, either as a strategic model or as a philosophy? What, in other words, is the reality of HRM at the present time? Answering this question is not as easy as it may seem.

Fact and fiction

One problem is what we focus on. Within the changing 'workscape' described in Chapter 2, it is not surprising that many observers have detected significant change in the employment relationship. However, it is also clear that many of the traditional tasks of personnel management to do with economic efficiency remain relevant. This has given rise to a 'hard' and 'soft' perspective on HRM (Storey, 1989). 'Hard' HRM is concerned with managing headcount and pay costs; 'soft' HRM is concerned with processes such as leadership, motivation, and consultation. As Chapter 2 suggested, managing headcount and pay costs continues to be a perennial focus of concern for personnel and line managers alike. There is a tendency to ignore this reality in 'talking up' HRM as a new philosophy of management.

A second problem is that initiatives in personnel management occur within an ideological and motivational climate which colours interpretation. This means it is actually rather difficult to describe accurately changes that have taken place. On the one hand, personnel practitioners, chief executives, and consultants often tend to 'talk up' innovations in HRM, especially in over-emphasizing the 'strategic' quality of HRM.

On the other hand, there are those who hold on to what we may call 'the industrial relations orthodoxy', who see in such initiatives a fundamental and persistent weakening of employee power within organizations through the substitution of individualized systems for collective ones. For these observers, the issue of 'commitment' is critical, with 'flexibility' a secondary theme implying greater control over employees as organizational resources.

The ideological climate is, indeed, pervasive and operates at three levels. At one level, there is the fundamental question as to what ideology, or philosophy, HRM tends to promote (Legge, 1989). Does it represent more individualism? In Britain, the alchemy of Thatcherism in the 1980s does certainly seem to have given it this slant, and it has become associated with policies, in areas like pay, with increasing individual motivation. This is not what the Harvard group had in mind, however. The Harvard model is 'communitarian'. It attempts to reconcile individual, organizational, and community interests.

A second-level problem concerns employers' motives. An employer may take a policy like consultation, which is ostensibly designed to promote participation, with the intention of using it in a tokenist way to ward off real involvement in important decisions. In such circumstances, the employers' underlying ideology may remain individualistic – concerned with preserving exclusive property rights and the primacy of management decision making. The history of joint consultation in Britain is littered with schemes adopted as a last resort to ward off perceived greater evils (i.e. real power sharing) (Nightingale, 1980).

Finally, there are the ideological models with which others read employers' intentions. The great bugbear for critics of HRM who write from a perspective of adversarial industrial relations is 'integrationism'. Personnel strategies and policies that emphasize the individual against the collective institutions of trade unionism are 'bad' because they divide employees and enable the organization (i.e. top management, the employer, and shareholder interests) to rule them more easily. Equally 'bad' are policies and practices which seek integration directly, such as the promotion of 'corporate cultures'. Alongside this crude version there is the more sophisticated pluralist critique which sees the unitary organization as 'bad' because the denial of individual and group interests actually makes for a less effective organization.

The result of all this is a ready tendency to confuse motivations (or policy goals), human resource activities, and the performance outcomes from these (Guest, 1992). As Thomason (1975) noted some years ago:

> If we see personnel management as having developed from two diverse origins, the one paternalistically oriented towards the welfare of employees and the other rationally derived from corporate needs to control, we have a foundation for understanding the ambivalence so often associated with the function. This is reinforced in practice by the possibility of using similar methods to serve very different ends: a joint consultative committee might be established either to improve communication for the benefit of all involved, or to provide a barrier to the further development of independent associations of employees. Practically any activity which is or has been associated with the personnel manager's role could be characterized in each of these ways (p. 25).

Attempts to reflect change in personnel management and HRM are bedevilled, then, by people coming at the issue from different directions.

Strategy, commitment, flexibility, and quality: the key issues

In his 1987 article, Guest argued that HRM should be judged against four measurable goals – the development of employee commitment, the pursuit of flexibility, the achievement of quality performance through quality personnel, and the strategic integration of people policies. In practice, these represent measurable attributes of HRM. Evidence has accumulated around each of these themes, although two issues have attracted most attention within the context of HRM – whether organizations have become more strategic in their management of people and personnel systems, and innovations to promote commitment. We will now review this evidence, in the process distinguishing specific initiatives from supposed goals and actual consequences.

Developing commitment

As we indicated above, developing employee commitment is particularly subversive in a way that even increasing flexibility is not. Flexibility can be bargained over and resisted, but policies to promote commitment undermine the means and the will to resist. For this reason, policies with an individualistic slant designed to promote commitment have consistently attracted the ire of industrial relations specialists. This was linked with the general attack on trade unions during the 1980s and the weakening of trade union membership which we described in Chapter 2.

This theme was initially signalled in the American industrial relations literature in terms of a 'new industrial relations' (Kochan and Capelli, 1984; Kochan, Katz and McKersie, 1986) and quickly framed the terms of the debate in Britain when HRM began to make an appearance here in the mid-to-late 1980s. According to Guest (1987, 1989, 1992), HRM in this view can be antagonistic to trade unionism in one of three ways:

1 It can involve an aggressive anti-union stance, including derecognition in existing unionized environments.
2 Alternatively, firms may simply hope for trade unionism to wither or not take root, by pursuing policies which ensure superior terms and conditions and job and career satisfaction.
3 A third variant is to establish trade union arrangements involving single unions, no-strike clauses, and pendulum arbitration, coupled with careful attention to recruitment, selection, socialization, company-specific training, employee communications, team-working and so forth, to gain close control over the workforce.

What is the evidence that firms have actively pursued any or all of these strategies?

HRM as anti-unionism

The early 1980s provided a number of well-documented cases on the rise of 'macho-management' (Purcell, 1982), especially in nationalized industries such as British Leyland (as Rover then was) and the National Coal Board (British Coal). These instances aside, Mackay (1986, p. 25), on the basis of a wider survey, claimed that 'the macho manager is alive and kicking in a surprisingly large number of organizations'.

While Legge, in her 1988 review, repeated these observations, instances of a tangible anti-union stance in the form of derecognition, although capturing the headlines, have in fact been limited. Examples are mostly concentrated in provincial newspaper publishing (plus the case of News International at Wapping) and coastal shipping (Claydon, 1989). In newspaper publishing, there has been widespread incidence of regional companies dismissing (former NGA) compositors, terminating the collective agreements which covered their jobs, and recruiting new labour on revised terms without collective agreements. Many companies also repudiated collective agreements with the NUJ and introduced individual terms of employment for journalists (Smith and Morton, 1990).

This prompts two observations. First, the pursuit of a strategy of exclusion in newspaper publishing was the product of a fairly unique set of circumstances. According to Smith and Morton (1990):

> Union exclusion policies can constitute a viable option for companies characterized by stable and profitable product markets, access to capital resources, investment in new production facilities and systems, and a history of union strength overlaid by contemporary weakness (p. 120).

Otherwise, company initiatives to restructure work organization may be pursued within an existing framework of industrial relations and collective bargaining – as the case example in Chapter 17 illustrates.

Second, the attack on trade unions in newspaper publishing was triggered by the desire to restructure the wage–work bargain under the impact of the new technology of computer typesetting, photocomposition, and offset lithographic printing, and the potential for direct text input by journalists. In other words, it was a traditional head-on confrontation over who controls work. It had nothing to do with HRM in terms of creating commitment (despite the introduction of individualized pay structures for senior staff to counter the collective organization of the NUJ).

If HRM has any part in an overall anti-unionist strategy within an existing unionized environment, it is likely to be only feasible as a second stage to mend fences. Defined in terms of high commitment, HRM is fundamentally inimical to the behaviour exhibited in union derecognition disputes in the UK. By the same token, government confrontations with public sector workers have tended merely to reinforce an adversarial system of industrial relations and created widespread job dissatisfaction and distrust of management (Kelly, 1988; Millward and Stevens, 1986; Ferner, 1989).

In contrast, there has been some survey evidence in the USA of companies pursuing a strategy to keep themselves free of trade unions while making increasing use of employee-involvement techniques such as information disclosure and quality circle discussions (Freedman, 1985). Clearly, what is lacking in this respect is British research which takes a systematic look at employment innovations in companies specifically engaged in union derecognition.

HRM as non-unionism

An alternative strategy is for organizations simply to allow trade unionism to wither. The recession and the shake-out of labour in the early 1980s, coupled with legislation which has increasingly eroded the power of trade unions, has aided this process. The two main instruments in-company for helping this along have been:

- Systems of direct communication and consultation which bypass union channels and reduce their importance, coupled with
- A range of other 'progressive' innovations, in, for example, pay systems, which increase employees' sense of involvement and ownership.

While one of the lessons which managers took from the 1970s was their failure to 'communicate effectively' and their readiness to cede the responsibility for this to their trade unions, 'improving communications' is not the same as having a deliberate strategy to marginalize their trade unions. Once again, the test is to trace specific initiatives over time against levels of trade union strength and influence, together with evidence of how managers interpreted what they were doing. In fact, we have only a limited number of case studies which document the weakening of shop stewards and works councils in the workplace, alongside the introduction of management-controlled systems of communication (for example, Smith, Child and Rowlinson, 1991, on Cadbury).

What we do know is that a substantial number of organizations took initiatives to improve direct communications with their workforce outside union channels in the early 1980s (Millward and Stevens, 1986). At the same time, recent evidence from the third Workplace Industrial Relations Survey (WIRS3) documents a decline in formal systems of consultation through trade unions (Millward, *et al.*, 1992). On the other hand, the total number of communications initiatives in private manufacturing actually fell between 1984 and 1990 (although they increased substantially in the public sector), and a large percentage of the overall increase was accounted for by the adoption of quality circles. (A less comprehensive survey by Wood (1993), however, covering 135 manufacturing plants, found a dramatic threefold increase in team briefing methods (from 16 per cent to 48 per cent of establishments) between 1986 and 1989.) The evidence for a general drive by managers to develop novel methods of communication and employee involvement to displace trade unions is therefore mixed (Rose, 1993).

As to other initiatives, a relative minority of firms have used profit-sharing to increase commitment, involvement, and a sense of ownership. A survey of 1000 companies by Poole (1988) found that 21 per cent had a scheme covering all employees (with a further 9 per cent having discretionary schemes), while more recently Wood (1993) has found profit-sharing to be low on actual initiatives taken. The interpretation of motives, however, seems somewhat confused. In the survey carried out by Poole (1988), the most commonly cited reason for a scheme was 'to increase employees' sense of commitment to the company', and there was said to be a strong association with a consultative style of industrial relations and the use of other forms of employee involvement, most notably joint consultation. Yet in 90 per cent of cases such schemes were introduced by unilateral management action.

A more recent study (Poole and Mansfield, 1992), this time of management attitudes among members and fellows of the British Institute of Management (BIM), helps to clarify this. It suggests overwhelming support for the idea of profit-sharing schemes (both cash- and share-based) – but strictly within a unitarist rather than pluralist approach to employee participation. In other words, so long as it does not affect management control.

The corollary of such schemes and tactics to induce commitment is to consider the strength of trade union influence and organization in the face of these initiatives. There are a number of measures of this:

- Levels of trade union membership;
- The persistence of trade union organization structures
- The proportion of employees covered by collective bargaining agreements.

Until recently, the evidence seemed to suggest that although union membership in aggregate had fallen, union density had remained virtually the same in environments which were already unionized (MacInnes, 1987; Kelly, 1990). As we noted in Chapter 2, the (admittedly drastic) fall in total union membership was the result of the physical decline of industries which had been traditionally unionized, while employment growth, with some exceptions, had been in service sectors where union organization was already weak. Indeed, in those services where union organization was already well established and union density was high – such as entertainment/media, post/telecommunications, education, health, and banking – membership *and* density had increased (at least until the recent recession) (Kelly, 1990).

This picture must now be significantly revised in the light of the latest WIRS data for the period 1987–1990 (Millward *et al.*, 1992). Union density between 1984 and 1990 fell overall from 58 per cent to 48 per cent, and within the private sector from 42 per cent to 35 per cent. The presence of union members within all establishments fell from 73 per cent to 64 per cent, with recognition of unions falling from 64 per cent to 53 per cent between 1980 to 1990 (thereby requiring us also to review the case for overt anti-unionism above). The extent of this decline was especially marked in private manufacturing, where recognition fell from 65 per cent of establishments to 44 per cent (a fall of nearly one-third).

The second criterion – the persistence of trade union organization structures – suggests a greater stability and continuity. Thus, the ratio of shop stewards to members actually improved (from 1:20 in 1990, from 1:22 in 1984), and many more of these had some training for the role, with managers allowing them time off to train.

However, the third measure provides perhaps the most conclusive evidence of decline – namely, the proportion of employees covered by collective bargaining agreements. As few as 8.5 million employees – or 38 per cent of the British workforce – are now covered by such agreements. Even if such figures can be attributed to the disappearance of traditional workplaces, this is small consolation: institutional decline from structural economic change can be just as deep-rooted, if not more so. Millward *et al.* (1992) therefore conclude that trade union influence has been fundamentally eroded:

> Our findings showed that although the scope of union bargaining activity had been severely reduced, trade unions were still a core element of the system of industrial relations in Britain. By 1990 much of this had changed. Key elements of the system of collective representation had faded or been transformed (p. 57).

The BIM survey by Poole and Mansfield (1992) corroborates this in showing a marked reduction in managers' experience of collective bargaining, especially of informal contacts with union representatives.

One outstanding question in this is how far the structures of industrial relations have simply changed, in terms of the locus of bargaining and the resolution of job disputes. Where there is evidence of a concerted effort by managers to restructure industrial relations, much of this has been in the context of decentralization within large corporations. This leaves open the possibility that union power at the corporate level has been dismantled, only for conflict resolution and consultative structures to be reinforced at the local level. In the short term, indeed, the building up of local structures may lag behind the dismantling of centralized systems. Chapter 5 reviews this phenomenon.

In conclusion, then, has HRM stepped into the gap presented by the withering of trade unionism and joint regulation? The WIRS researchers suggest not. In non-union settings, for example, they found little attempt to institute a permanent alternative system. As Rose (1993) comments: 'The retreat of union representation, it seems, is leaving gaps filled mostly by piece-meal improvisation' (p. 303).

HRM as company-unionism

The third way in which an industrial relations strategy can interact with HRM is through the development of 'progressive' terms and conditions combined with unionism which is highly circumscribed. The archetype for this is the frequently cited example of IBM which has successfully prevented trade unionism taking root (Bassett, 1986). More generally, such a strategy involves a single union with limited functions.

In fact, the major clearing banks in the UK traditionally followed a not dissimilar strategy by building up their in-house staff associations to discourage employees from joining a recognized trade union. Nowadays, however, this strategy is associated particularly with greenfield site developments, involving foreign, especially Japanese, firms, notably Nissan, Toyota, and Toshiba, who have concluded single-union agreements of this kind (Wickens, 1987; Trevor, 1988; Kumon, 1992). American multinationals locating in the UK, on the other hand, have tended to maintain outright resistance to trade unions (Bassett, 1988), with none of the American firms locating in Scotland, for instance, during the 1980s becoming unionized (Guest, 1989).

The Japanese approach has been to reproduce the company union system with which they feel comfortable at home, although it is notable that they have not imported all elements of the Japanese system, such as elaborate welfare provisions and seniority-based pay and promotion:

> What they have brought is an approach to organization based on teamwork and devolved responsibility, careful selection procedures, extensive and intensive consultation and communications, appraisal-based pay, and employee relations systems designed to safeguard managerial prerogatives and minimize the likelihood of industrial action (Wilkinson and Oliver, 1992, p. 53).

Such employee relations systems allow

> virtually no independent role for shop stewards, and while the company does not intend to actively obstruct union activities, the mechanisms for representation are highly supportive of non-union participation (Crowther and Garrahan, 1988, p. 57).

The example of Fibres, an Anglo-American firm, in Chapter 13 illustrates many of these greenfield site practices.

Undoubtedly, the emasculated, company-union system goes furthest towards creating a unitarist form of commitment. However, there are a number of things to bear in mind. First, while greenfield sites provide an opportunity for a comprehensive restructuring of employment (Beaumont and Townley, 1985) and such issues have figured prominently on the agenda of many companies which have established them, the potential to restructure employment did not necessarily dominate the original locational decision (Preece, 1993). Second, greenfield site developments, involving substantial new capital investments, inevitably can only represent a small proportion of total establishments. On the other hand, however, and third, greenfield site developments may have a disproportionate influence – both as 'leading-edge' examples and through the direct influence they may bring to bear on suppliers. This is why the phenomenon of 'Japanization' is of particular interest, and one reason why the Thatcher government encouraged Japanese firms to come to Britain. Finally, we should distinguish between HRM as a generic label and 'Japanization' as a particular version.

Creating commitment though HRM

Running through the above analysis is a concern for the future of trade unionism. This is a legitimate issue for the interpretation of modern employment relations. Associating the attack on trade unions with the idea that HRM aims to create commitment, however, is, in many ways, a red herring. In particular, it greatly overplays the capacity of managers and firms to manipulate commitment, even supposing managers themselves operate such a policy. It is here that goals, initiatives, and consequences in practice diverge. A review of research findings by Iles, Mabey and Robertson (1990) draws attention to some of these discrepancies.

What is 'commitment'?

First, there is the confusion over what is meant by 'commitment'. Most empirical studies have concentrated on job-satisfaction variables rather than on the 'organizational commitment' which is of most concern in HRM. Commitment to the job, personal career, and the employing organization are not one and the same thing. Commitment to the work group and to the organization, for instance, are predicted ('influenced') by different variables. We should think, instead, of employees having multiple commitments. These will have affective, calculative, and alienative elements (Penley and Gould, 1988).

As a result, human resource innovations can have unintended consequences – for example, assessment centres can encourage employees to think about changing careers by highlighting career uncertainties. This is not a benefit normally advertised when introducing assessment or development centres (Iles, Robertson and Rout, 1989).

In particular, so-called commitment under 'Japanization' may, in reality, represent a system of control (with the potential for long-term negative effects). As Sewell and Wilkinson's (1993) account of human resource management at one Japanese firm, K-Electric, shows, the shopfloor reality is of work performance sustained by tight (team leader) supervision combined with electronic recording ('surveillance') of operator efficiencies and defects, backed by strict disciplinary procedures.

What influences organizational commitment?

Second, there is the issue of what influences organizational commitment itself. Perceived fairness over pay and promotion methods appears to be more important than, for instance, actual outcomes and levels of distribution (Ogilvie, 1986; Folger and Konovsky, 1989). Conversely, selection methods which candidates (even successful ones) feel are intrusive, insensitive, or inaccurate are likely to alienate, since they will be seen as symptomatic of how the organization treats employees normally (Herriot, 1989). With employees in mid-career, feedback, counselling, and the opportunity for development and reassessment can be important in retaining the commitment of those passed over for promotion (Rodger and Mabey, 1987). Such findings are therefore actually in line with the Harvard argument for 'mutuality' (that is, for shared influence) as the basis for commitment (Walton, 1985a,b).

Third, however, there is a lack of evidence that organizational commitment is actually associated with job performance. Policies designed to bind the individual to the organization through rapid promotion, high pay, and side benefits (such as health insurance, mortgage loans, and pensions) may encourage employees to 'stick', rather than stimulate high performance. This goes back to the issue of what we mean by commitment and how we measure it. There is some evidence that 'continuance commitment' – staying with the organization (hence low employee turnover) – is negatively associated with the 'affective commitment' that comes from high job satisfaction and high job performance (Meyer and Allen, 1988). Innovation, creativity, and adaptiveness is more likely to result from the tensions associated with people having differing types of commitment – to the organization, their jobs, colleagues, professional development, and personal careers (Coopey and Hartley, 1990).

These findings are supported in longitudinal research by Morris and Lydka (1992), who tracked a group of ninety-eight graduates through their first five years of employment. They note, for example, that commitment is given provisionally; commitment is transferable and cannot be taken for granted by one employer; commitment is short-lived ('contemporary') and cannot be relied on to survive changes in policy; and human resource policies do not have uniform effects, so that attention has to be given to individual needs.

Such paradoxes, discrepancies, and ambiguities highlight the fact that organizational life is beset by paradoxes, and that (mercifully) managers and organizations cannot get a handle completely on human behaviour.

Flexibility

Developments in flexible working through the 1980s have been a second major theme. Like the issue of commitment, it also bears on the role of trade unions, through the defence of working practices and job rights. Any of the three positions towards trade unions described above might equally, therefore, be accompanied by an organization pursuing a policy to increase flexibility as to promote individualized commitment.

Accounts of flexibility recognize four principal distinctions (Blyton, 1993) derived largely from Atkinson and Meager (1986):

- Task or functional flexibility (broadening established job boundaries and skill definitions, and thereby cutting across existing demarcations)
- Numerical flexibility (part-time working, contract labour, and sub-contracting)
- Temporal flexibility (shift-working, overtime, short-time working, flexitime, and annualized hours)
- Financial flexibility (performance-related pay, profit-sharing, fee-for service payments, individualized contracts, and young-person rates).

Numerical and functional flexibility have seen the most significant developments.

Numerical flexibility

Numerical and temporal flexibility are established ways of matching labour to demand conditions (although part-time working and sub-contracting have often been accompanied by inferior pay and conditions, and hence provided direct financial savings). The Price Waterhouse/Cranfield Project points to an increase in flexible working patterns of this kind on a European-wide basis, with part-time employment particularly prevalent in the UK, but concentrated in a few organizations (Brewster *et al.*, 1993). This may reflect recessionary influences, plus the growth of the service sector where part-time working is more common, rather than a concerted, long-term shift in employment practices (Pollert, 1988).

Earlier surveys, including ACAS (1988), reported in Blyton (1993) point to a more modest increase in numerical flexibility, with the use of sub-contracting most common in manufacturing, larger organizations, and parts of the public sector (such as health and the civil service). Job-sharing has made some advance in the UK where employers (in, for example, banking) have particular problems of balancing staffing and workload. Elsewhere in Europe (such as Germany and Scandinavia), legislation provides the driving force through legal rights for women to work part-time.

The phenomenon of numerical flexibility, with its overtones of core–periphery and primary–secondary labour markets, has attracted a deal of attention because of its implication of more precarious employment and more vulnerable employees. Alongside relatively marginal, 'peripheral' employees, 'core' employees can be managed through HRM practices designed to cement commitment to the organization. The core–periphery debate is thus critical to the employment systems perspective on HRM developed in this book and therefore will be dealt with more fully in Chapters 12 and 18.

In contrast, temporal flexibility, although producing flurries of interest from time to time, has seen only limited development.

Financial flexibility, similarly, is more talked about than practised. The exceptions have been over young-person pay rates (where YTS effectively created new minima below traditional apprentice rates), profit-sharing (encouraged by tax exemption), and merit pay (ACAS, 1988). Many organizations – for instance, in banking – that have wanted to get away from incremental structures and create a stronger performance orientation have introduced incentivized systems for senior staff. The problem, however, is then to find adequate and valid performance measures on which to base such schemes for middle and junior employees.

Functional flexibility

All four forms of flexibility are concerned with the 'effort–reward bargain', with pay costs and efficiency, and from that point of view represent 'hard' HRM referred to at the beginning of this chapter (rather than 'soft' HRM – the creation of commitment). Functional flexibility is no exception and it has been at the forefront of efforts to improve the productivity of British firms.

The two principal sources of information on the prevalence of increases in functional flexibility are the second and third WIRS surveys (Daniel, 1987; Marsden and Thompson, 1990, Millward *et al.*, 1992). WIRS consists of a nationally representative sample of around 2000 workplaces with twenty-five or more employees, covering most sectors of the economy, with data derived from interviews with employee representatives and senior managers responsible for industrial/employee relations (plus production managers in WIRS2). WIRS2 included specific questions on technical change and work reorganization, and WIRS3 repeated this in slighter form. (For example, the 1984 study (WIRS2) distinguished additionally between advanced change, involving microelectronics, and conventional technical change.)

The proportion of workplaces experiencing both technical and organizational change was substantial and in the two periods surveyed (1981–1984 and 1987–1990) increased from 47 per cent to 53 per cent (in workplaces employing manual employees) and from 63 per cent to 67 per cent (in workplaces employing non-manual workers). Since technical and organizational change tends to be more prevalent in larger establishments, the number of employees affected was somewhat greater (increasing from 60 per cent to 63 per cent in the case of manual workers, while declining slightly from 74 per cent to 73 per cent for non-manual workers).

Table 3.1 provides a breakdown between the forms of technical and organizational change. Among other things, it confirms the finding that technical change remains more common for non-manual employees. One other finding is that the rate of change has increased sharply among office workers in the public sector, whereas it was lagging behind the private sector in 1984. Above all, organizational change in the period 1987–1990

Table 3.1 Number of workplaces introducing different types of change in previous three years

	Manual workers (%) 1984	Manual workers (%) 1990	Non-manual workers (%) 1984	Non-manual workers (%) 1990
Advanced technical change	22	23	49	52
Conventional technical change	24	—[a]	20	—
Technical change of either kind[b]	37	40	57	55
Organizational change	23	29	20[c]	41[d]
Technical or organizational change[e]	47	53	63	67
Base: establishments employing 25 or more workers of the type specified				
Unweighted	1 423	1 401	1 547	1 581
Weighted	985	954	1012	1004

[a] Not asked separately in 1990.
[b] Some establishments adopt both kinds of technical change.
[c] Question asked only in relation to 'office workers'.
[d] Question asked in relation to all non-manual workers.
[e] Some establishments adopt both technical and organizational change.
Source: Adapted from Millward *et al.* (1992).

affected 29 per cent of manual and 41 per cent of non-manual workers. Even if we differentiate strictly, then, between organizational change involving true forms of functional flexibility (relaxing job demarcations and multiskilling), and technical change on its own, there has been a substantial effort to increase functional flexibility.

One of the key findings in the present context is that technical change has tended to be more common in unionized environments. Moreover, it has largely enjoyed the support of employees (Daniel, 1987), with shop stewards being more positive from the outset (Daniel, 1987; Millward *et al.*, 1992) – although resistance has been greater in larger establishments and in nationalized industries. In contrast, reactions were far more negative towards organizational change – that is, changes in work organization or working practices not involving new plant, machinery or equipment.

The explanation for this is fairly clear. Technical change is seen as progress. It provides clear benefits to employees; it increases job security; and it demonstrates an investment in the future. It may also involve training and new skills. Organizational change is often an admission of past failure, with implications of job loss and work intensification.

Marsden and Thompson (1990) draw on data from Income Data Services (IDS), the Industrial Relations Review and Report (IRRR), and the *Financial Times*, while reviewing also a number of other studies. Although they do not distinguish between technical and organizational change, they confirm the picture of substantial activity to increase functional flexibility. Among the studies they cite, the CBI Settlements Databank (Cahill and Ingram, 1988) identified 28 per cent of settlements between 1979/1980 and 1985/1986 involving some productivity concessions by employees in manufacturing – a figure remarkably close to the 29 per cent of manual employees directly or indirectly affected by organizational change between 1987 and 1990 in WIRS2.

Marsden and Thompson's own study looked just at cases in manufacturing where written agreements to change working practices were negotiated between an employer and a union (whereas the CBI count also included non-union situations). In the period January 1980 to August 1987, they found 137 examples, directly applicable to 2.3 million workers, of whom 380,000 were in manufacturing – representing around 10 per cent of all manual workers and $7\frac{1}{2}$ per cent of employees in manufacturing. Private sector engineering figured particularly in terms of number of agreements, although the bulk of workers affected were in public sector services. The agreements were primarily concerned with deployment, skill demarcation, and grading, especially as regards craft workers – reflecting, in other words, traditional issues for collective bargaining.

The fact that these issues continued to be negotiated suggested to Marsden and Thompson, as to Daniel (1987), that the institutions of collective bargaining up to 1987 were still alive and well. However, they note that equally significant, but necessarily unrecorded, will have been changes in working methods which fall outside such agreements. These often precede formal changes in agreed working practices. More recent data on the extent of negotiated settlements would obviously now be of considerable interest in the light of WIRS3.

Efforts to increase functional flexibility were fairly prevalent, then, reviving 1960s-style productivity bargaining that had degenerated during the 1970s into an exercise to avoid incomes policy.

Flexibility: fixation or fact?

However, taken as whole, we can either see flexibility occurring on a wide scale in one form or another (functional, numerical, temporal, and financial) or argue that the whole thing has been exaggerated precisely because it has been so disparate and lacking critical mass in any one area (with the possible exception of functional flexibility) (Pollert, 1988, 1991). More fundamental are the normative connotations that flexibility has. First, as we noted in connection with greenfield site practices (where flexible working has featured prominently), flexibility can mask increased control. Indeed, flexibility from a management's point of view means precisely increased control over deployment. Second, flexibility as a desirable practice in which employees with broad skills can adapt to changed conditions and/or be assigned to different tasks comes up against equally valid arguments for specialization and the desire (on the part of workers and management) for stability. Clark's (1993) account of flexibility at Pirelli in South Wales shows retreat from full flexibility in practice occurring for a number of reasons. Chapters 16 and 17 will develop this theme further.

There are inconsistencies and limitations, then, to the achievement of flexibility as an HRM goal. For these reasons, Blyton (1993) suggests flexibility is likely to become a more marginal aspect of HRM policy in the 1990s.

A more strategic approach?

The third criterion, and the most widely accepted manifestation of HRM, is the pursuit of strategic integration in personnel policies, systems, and practices, one with another and in relation to organizational strategy. The pursuit of 'functional flexibility' through technical change is relevant to this because it brings into focus the strategic integration of employment innovations and initiatives. Thus, it is widely recognized that a 'strategic' approach, involving changes in work organization, is necessary to get the full benefits from technical change (Buchanan, 1989; Bessant, 1991; McLoughlin and Clark, 1993). Or as Marsden and Thompson (1990) put it, 'their significance . . . lies in permitting changes in key working practices which enable further changes in workforce organization to be undertaken (p. 84).

The strategic integration of initiatives, however, is not the same thing as the strategic integration of personnel policies, systems, and practices – although it may be indicative of the latter. Failure to recognize this lies behind the curious discrepancy between normative representations of what HRM should try to do, and attempts to test whether firms are practising it.

Human resource initiatives versus strategic HRM

To illustrate this distinction, the various contributions to the seminal Fombrun, Tichy and Devanna (1984) book describe patterns of coherence between (1) systems like appraisal, development, and rewards and (2) the behaviours which the business strategy seems to require. The 'exemplary' cases of firms like the American General Electric and IBM then trace these linkages. In contrast, much of the effort to test whether firms are practising HRM has looked for evidence of coherence in the adoption of innovative techniques associated with HRM.

Guest (1990), for instance, adopts the 'innovative techniques' standpoint in his review of HRM in America, where he cites, for instance, Goodmeasure's (1985) survey on the use of twenty-one innovative work arrangements. In the UK, similarly, Storey (1992) has focused on the coherence of initiatives as a measure of an integrated strategic approach to employment. His finding of a piecemeal, 'pick and mix' approach, the sheer number of initiatives, and the lack of coherence is interesting (given that his sample firms are in the mainstream of Britain's large and even progressive organizations). But it is not surprising. As long as HRM is thought of as exemplifying particular techniques, it will not appear as a coherent phenomenon.

Storey's observation that there is a low correlation between the number of initiatives taken and financial performance indeed speaks for itself. The more initiatives taken in a short space of time, the harder they are to integrate. The more initiatives taken, the more indicative it is of a fixation with short-lived management fads, and the less likely they are to be thought through in relation to other things happening in the organization. There are other possibilities, too, such as under-performing organizations being inclined to thrash around for any panacea which will rescue them. Above all, though, as various people have noted, the field of personnel and HRM is particularly prone to flavour-of-the month ideas (Huczynski, 1993).

Conversely, what the sampling of 'innovative techniques' does not show is the coherence which may operate in day-to-day personnel policies, systems, and practices. Storey (1992) comments, for instance, that it is perhaps Smith and Nephew's conservative stance in the adoption of new human resource techniques that accounts for them being consistently a top performing firm in his sample. On one measure (the number of HR techniques adopted), Smith and Nephew are not practising HRM. On another, however (the integration of personnel practices with the requirements of the business), they may well be doing so.

We have, then, a fundamental problem in how we assess the extent of strategic integration as an HRM value. This is a problem at two levels. In the aggregate, there is the problem that simply counting innovative techniques may reflect quite the opposite of what is intended – namely, innovativeness equals incoherence. Asking, in addition, if the organization has a corporate plan and the role this plays in integrating people policies does not help much either, since answers to this kind of question are notoriously unreliable. The response in the large firm tends to be 'of course we have a strategic plan'; in the smaller firm it tends to be 'we don't have time for that, and we work to too short timescales'. However, neither is likely to adequately reflect what really goes on.

From this point of view, descriptive case studies that place human resource practices and initiatives in a business strategy context give a better picture. Examples of this kind include Norsk Hydro (Fox, 1988), the series of cases in Towers (1992), and the cases developed at the Centre for Corporate Strategy and Change at Warwick Business School (Hendry and Pettigrew, 1987, 1988; Sparrow and Pettigrew, 1988a,b; Sparrow, 1988; Pettigrew, Hendry and Sparrow, 1989). Other examples are to be found in the various chapters of this book.

Integration and performance

However, there is also a problem in assessing strategic integration at the level of the individual firm. While a plausible case can be made for the integration of policies, systems, and practices by means of description, the real test must be in actually trying to measure this. The ultimate test of 'fit' must then be the performance of the business.

There are two problems in doing this. One is in operationalizing the concept of 'fit' – what is 'fit' in one person's eyes may be disfunctional in the eyes of another. As Child (1977) some time ago observed, and as Pettigrew and Whipp (1991) have since shown, internal 'coherence' may be more important than external 'fit'. In other words, the two elements in a strategic model of HRM need to be separated. Thus, Nicholson, Rees and Brooks-Rooney (1990) found no association between the use of particular personnel practices and organizational success: 'This implies it matters not so much what methods are used, but how consistently they mesh with other organizational systems' (p. 530). The second problem is in being able to attribute organizational performance to human resource systems and practices. This presents formidable statistical difficulties.

Only one study (Fox, McLeay, and Tanton, 1990; Fox and McLeay, 1992) has begun to address these issues in any adequate fashion – first, by asking the right questions in relation to HRM; second, through a research design which standardizes for financial performance in a way that permits meaningful comparisons; and third, by combining qualitative and quantitative approaches.

The first point to note is that Fox and his colleagues consider human resource practices in relation to a specific group (the management team), rather than diffusely in relation to the workforce as a whole. This makes sense since the impact of management on the performance of the organization may be especially significant, as compared with that of manual, clerical, and technical employees. Most studies conflate the use of techniques regardless of to whom they are applied (for example, Storey, 1992), or, as in the commitment debate, implicitly treat HRM as a conspiracy against shopfloor workers. What is obviously necessary is a study which looks at the totality of human resource practices, discriminating where necessary between those applied to managers and those applied to the shopfloor. This will expose performance issues which derive from both the development and implementation of strategy.

Fox and colleagues then look at the development of the management team through a linked set of practices – recruitment and selection (RS), management education, training and development (METD), performance appraisal (PA), rewards and remuneration (RR), and company-level career planning (CCP). They then ask three precise questions:

1 How systematized were these HRM activities?
2 How integrated were they, regardless of how systematized or unsystematized they were?
3 How closely was the HRM function integrated with the business development and corporate strategy of the firm, regardless of the level of systematization and integration of practices?

Separating the question of systematization from integration highlights, for example, (1) which HR practices are most often systematized in relation to sectoral norms, and whether it matters, and (2) where integration between HR practices has most pay-off in feeding decisions affecting individual development and hence ultimate team development.

The third question also looks at the relationship of the HRM function to business strategy in a very precise way. The usual question is to ask whether or how human resource professionals contributed to competitive strategy. Instead, Fox and his colleagues looked at how human resource professionals contributed to the composition and renewal of the top team, and to shaping their thinking processes – in other words, to equipping the people who make strategy on a year-by-year basis.

They then applied this design to sixty companies in two main sectors (engineering and electronics) with a further twenty in an assortment of sectors (with a final achieved sample of forty-nine firms), selecting their firms on the basis of known performance data against industry norms. This enabled them to characterize individual companies according to whether they under- or over-performed their sector.

Two conclusions stand out. First:

> There is a significant positive relationship between financial performance and the integration of corporate strategy and HRM, a result which remains robust when other factors are added to the model (Fox and McLeay, 1992, p. 544).

Second, integration is the key to success – in other words, the 'hard' version of HRM is what matters, not the 'soft' one, which is concerned with issues like culture and communication.

A final reflection on this issue tangentially comes from WIRS where there were said to be constraints on altering work organization in 47 per cent of unionized environments, as compared with 15 per cent of non-union environments – in other words, unions act as a cultural constraint. Yet establishments recognizing some constraint were generally more efficient and performed better. As Rose (1993) comments:

> A non-union environment did not guarantee success. A unionized one did not exclude it. The operational incentive to work towards non-unionism is indeed far less strong than is imagined (p. 303).

Put another way, there may be less pay-off in 'soft' HRM designed to foster a unitarist commitment to the organization than there is in 'hard' HRM that focuses on developing people with strategy in mind.

A quality workforce

The fourth criterion that Guest (1987) applies to HRM is the achievement of quality performance through quality personnel. There are two ways of looking at this. One is the effort made to develop a quality workforce, especially through training and development. The second is the development of systems and ways of working which produce quality performance reflected in the quality of goods and services. A measure of this is the adoption of improvement programmes of one sort or another. Both aspects are closely related in fact, insofar as quality programmes invariably involve training in their implementation.

Training and development

As we noted in Chapter 1, when we speak of 'human resource management' the emphasis can fall on either 'human capability' or on 'managing people as resources'. The former implies that people are an investment; the latter that people are a cost, or commodity, to be minimized and to be efficiently deployed. If HRM is to have a distinguishing characteristic, however, which marks it out as a different way of managing, it has to be, as Keep (1989) argues, in focusing on the development of people. Human resource development (HRD) is the touchstone, the 'litmus test' (Keep, 1989, p. 125), and 'acid test' (Poole and Mansfield, 1992, p. 11) of any 'tight' definition of HRM, rather than, say, 'flexibility'.

This means, among other things, that we should look for evidence of increased commitment to and investment in training and development by firms. It also, though, includes the quality and integration of a range of other practices such as recruitment, selection, appraisal, and career planning, which sustain effective training and development. The achievement of a quality workforce cannot be dissociated, therefore, from other HRM goals such as 'the strategic integration of people policies, practices and systems', or, indeed, from 'employee commitment' since commitment is intrinsic to turning training into work performance.

Communication and consultation support training, for instance, not simply by 'inspiring motivation' but in 'providing direction' to people's efforts so that they can put their trained skills to effective use. Communication itself, moreover, can be a training strategy by facilitating on-the-job learning. Quality circles illustrate this very well in the opportunity they create for learning from one another through the act of talking about things in teams. As Keep (1989) observes:

> It is often hard to draw firm lines between new methods of training and new forms of communication. Team briefings are an example of management attempting to improve communications with their employees, but they can also be used as a training opportunity, and as a means of reinforcing the message of team-training exercises (p. 116).

The role of communication in the training process simply reinforces the argument for taking a strategic, holistic approach within HRM.

For the moment, however, we will focus on the evidence for training in the UK. Until the mid-1980s, certainly, the poor record of British firms on training suggested that a philosophy of HRM or HRD had not taken root in the UK. A series of studies for the Manpower Services Commission (MSC) and the National Economic Development Office (NEDO) high-lighted the comparative shortcomings of company performance on training (Hayes, Anderson and Fonda, 1984), the low absolute levels of training effort (IFF Research Ltd, 1985), and the negative attitudes of senior managers and directors towards training (Coopers and Lybrand, 1985). Other studies pointed out how the resulting lower levels of skill affected the business strategies of UK firms by encouraging production of cheap, mass-produced, low added value products, in contrast to German producers (Daly, Hitchens, and Wagner, 1985; Steedman and Wagner, 1987). At the same time, a series of studies pointed to the poor record of UK firms on management training (Mangham and Silver, 1986; Constable and McCormick, 1987; Handy *et al.*, 1987).

The MSC (and its successors – the Training Commission, Training Agency, and Employment Department) used these findings to mount a campaign to change attitudes, to stimulate employer training, and ultimately to reform the system of national training. In this, they were joined by industry which set up the Management Charter Initiative in 1988 to improve the quality of UK managers. (These reforms are described in Chapter 14.) In recent years, then, there has been an upsurge in the priority given to training.

What effect has this had? There are, of course, exemplary cases of organizations that invest in training and manage it well. The Investors in People scheme launched in 1991 had given recognition to around 250 organizations by mid-1993, with 3000 others ostensibly committed to gaining the standard. The aim of getting at least half the 6000 organizations nationally with more than 2000 employees qualified by 1996 seems therefore to be on course. Aggregate figures on training, however, are harder to come by and true comparisons between countries are difficult to establish.

Through 1987–1989 the Training Agency sponsored a series of studies to try to get a better picture of what training firms do, as well as of the factors which influence them. In the study which the Centre for Corporate Strategy and Change carried out we observed, for example, that

reported expenditure varies enormously, and both understates the true costs which can be attributed to recorded training and the activities which can be construed as training (Pettigrew, Hendry and Sparrow, 1989, p. 71).

The large survey study carried out by Deloitte Haskins & Sells/IFF (1989) tried to get round this by including estimates for (1) the opportunity costs represented by trainees' salaries and (2) on-the-job training (which is mostly made up of wage and salary costs). The latter alone almost doubled total reported expenditure, at £14.4 billion during the accounting year 1986/1987 (net of grants and levies), but is invariably not included in companies' own figures. Indeed, wage costs of one sort or another (for trainees, trainers, and line managers) were reckoned to represent 85 per cent of true training costs (with only trainers' costs normally included in company figures).

Notwithstanding this 'inflation' of the total compared with the IFF (1985) figure for 1984, it suggested employers were spending more in 1986/1987. However, this was near the peak of the business cycle when companies had more money to spend. There has since been no authoritative update, and in Britain we lack a system of constant reporting on training volumes and expenditures (just as we do on many other useful statistics as compared, say, with Japan).

When we add in the value of government grants less levies (at £3.6 billion) to reflect the true expenditure on training, we also find that average expenditure, at 1.2 per cent of national payroll, is not so different, for example, from the employer levy in France which has been fixed at 1.2 per cent of company payroll (Holden, 1991). However, there will be French firms which spend more than this. In general, meaningful international comparisons are difficult to come by for reasons which include institutional differences in who trains (companies or the State) and where training takes place (on-the-job or off-the-job). (Chapter 19 considers these issues in more detail.)

There appears, then, to have been some modest improvement in what employers are investing in training, and certainly in the importance which managers now give to it, As Poole and Mansfield's (1992) survey indicates, 'It is clear that this aspect of HRM has been incorporated into managers' attitudes and recent behaviour' (p. 15). Compared with many of the other facets of HRM discussed in this chapter, training and development is one area which seems to be gaining increasing attention into the 1990s.

Quality improvement

Commitment to quality has become one of the leading ideas in management in the 1980s, manifesting itself from Porter (1980), through Peters and Waterman (1982), and on through a series of techniques (quality circles, customer care, Total Quality Management (TQM) and quality gurus (Deming, Crosby, Juran, Feigenbaum, and Ishikawa). As we noted above, there was a large increase in the adoption of quality circles between the two WIRS surveys of 1984 and 1990, from nil to 23 per cent (Millward *et al.*, 1992). There was also an increase in related team briefing methods between

1986 and 1989 (from 16 per cent to 48 per cent of establishments) in Wood's (1992) smaller sample of 134 manufacturing plants.

However, the success of quality circles and customer care programmes has been chequered, to say the least (Wilkinson, 1993; Witcher and Wilkinson, 1992; Hill, 1991). A primary reason for this is the failure to integrate such initiatives with other human resource practices, and in particular to address the organizational culture into which they are introduced. The result is that quality initiatives are often short-lived or fail to meet expectations. Those programmes, like TQM, which purport to tackle culture, on the other hand, are often undermined in the medium-term as a result of being introduced as top-down panaceas. When their sponsors move on, the momentum falters and organizational cynics reassert themselves.

Quality programmes and the cultural change phenomenon, with their significance for HRM, are considered in more detail in Chapters 6 and 7.

Summary

In this chapter we have tried to assess the present state of HRM by looking at various measures with which it can be equated. In doing so, we adopted the premiss of certain commentators that it represents a new way of managing employment, characterized by a particular set of values or objectives.

As an alternative model, HRM in Britain has inevitably been measured by its impact on and consequences for formal systems of industrial relations. Implicit in this is the view of a British system characterized by pluralist control or joint regulation of employment in the workplace, in which organized trade unionism plays an important part. One irony, of course, is that union membership since 1960 has rarely risen above 50 per cent of the working population. A large number of employees have consistently worked within relatively individualized, non-union settings (notwithstanding the fact that the presence of a trade union in the workplace can also influence general terms and practices for non-union members).

The watershed years of 1979–1980, when union membership was at its peak, have tended to set the terms of the debate about HRM. Since then, government policy to roll back trade unionism has coincided with the import of HRM from a virulent anti-union environment (i.e. the USA). Defending the 'British system' of pluralist industrial relations therefore coloured the estimation of HRM in terms of its real or imputed values, while almost any innovation in employment has been arbitrarily labelled HRM. Not surprisingly, most observers see incoherent, piecemeal attempts to introduce 'HRM'.

However, the empirical evidence is that the driving force for HRM has had little to do with industrial relations. As Guest (1989) observes,

> rather, it is the pursuit of competitive advantage in the market place through provision of high quality goods and services, through competitive pricing linked

to high productivity and through the capacity swiftly to innovate and manage change in response to changes in the market place or to breakthroughs in research and development (p. 43).

Research at the Centre for Corporate Strategy and Change at Warwick University provides some of the clearest evidence for this. Firms that have introduced innovations in HRM have done so under competitive pressure. This pressure has taken a variety of forms, including competitive restructuring in the sector, decentralization to respond more closely to customers, internationalization, acquisitions and mergers as part of a rationalization process, pressures for higher quality, pervasive technological change, and new concepts of distribution and service (Hendry, Pettigrew and Sparrow, 1988). Some of these, such as decentralization, may have entailed a restructuring of industrial relations, but as a necessary byproduct, not as an end in itself. The result is not a drive to implement 'HRM' but the adoption of specific reforms which bring existing systems into better alignment with the competitive situation.

Guest (1989) acknowledges, then, that

> HRM is not necessarily anti-union. If the four central components of HRM [commitment, quality, flexibility, strategic integration] are considered, then neither strategic integration nor quality is in any sense incompatible with trade-union activity. On the other hand, flexibility is likely to pose a significant challenge to some unions, more particularly at multi-union sites. However, it is an issue on which the unions have shown themselves willing to bargain. The main challenge to the unions is therefore likely to come from the pursuit of employee commitment (p. 43).

As we have seen, however, the concept of commitment is highly problematic.

Rather than the demise of collective systems under the impact of HRM, it may well be that the challenge of the 1990s will come from the increasing accommodation and incorporation of HRM within collective structures as the UK comes into closer contact with Continental European systems of industrial relations and employment (notwithstanding the present government's opposition to the Social Chapter of Maastricht). This will mean remaking trade union-based industrial relations, not discarding it. We will attempt an assessment of the future in the final chapter.

For now, it is clear, in reviewing the elements of HRM, that strategic integration is the most consistent issue, underpinning the achievement of the more value-laden objectives. It is the *sine qua non* of HRM. In the following chapters therefore this will be the overriding theme, in both normative models and descriptions of actual practice.

Part Two
Strategy, Structure, and Culture in Organizational Change and HRM

4
Business strategy and organizational capability

Introduction

At the heart of HRM is the idea that it should serve the business strategy of an organization. As Fombrun, Tichy and Devanna (1984) put it in the quotation in Chapter 1: 'The critical managerial task is to align the formal structure and the HR systems so that they drive the strategic objectives of the organization' (p. 37). Underlying this simple proposition, however, are three questions to be answered:

- What is the nature of business strategy?
- What is the nature of human resources strategy?
- How are the two linked?

The way we answer these questions involves some basic assumptions about what makes organizations tick.

Some people take the view, for example, that there are various generic strategies and typical situations which organizations encounter. Suitable human resource strategies can then be spelt out which match the requirements of these strategies and situations. The result is a set of guidelines for designing human resource systems. This point of view emphasizes the positioning of an organization to achieve competitive advantage, and coping with predictable ups and downs that are part of the competitive life-cycle of firms.

If making business strategy itself were as simple as this, however, there would be no business strategy 'problem'. On the contrary, the problem of strategy continues to exercise countless practitioners and academics alike. This is aside of the known difficulties of implementation.

Critics argue, therefore, that strategy is not just about content but also about process. This is obvious in the case of implementation: there is many a slip between a plan and its implementation. Equally, however, making strategy can be a hesitant and halting process, in which a clear strategy 'emerges' only slowly. In contrast, defining generic strategies is to focus on immediate, definable, and simplified situations and on the solutions for dealing with these, and not at all on the process by which organizations decide which option to follow and how they then implement it. It is not just about what is the right strategic decision at a point in time, but having the organizational capacity to reach effective decisions, and the willing and skilled human resources to carry them through.

As a result, the relationship of people and HRM strategy to business strategy is not simply derivative. Instead, organizations need to look at their underlying requirements over the longer term. This perspective says sound strategies and their effective implementation depend on 'organizational capability' (Ulrich and Lake, 1990). Organizational capability, admittedly, has to be pursued with a view to what kind of organization its executives and major stakeholders want it to be; what is possible within various external and internal constraints; and in the light of broad strategic options. Nevertheless, the focus has shifted. 'Organizational capability' has moved into the spotlight, where it infuses, drives, and governs the development and implementation of business strategy.

The relationship has been reversed. Business strategy has become the output, or 'derivative', and organizational capability has become an input to strategy. This parallels, of course, the shift from viewing the employee as a cost centre to viewing an employee as a resource, which is the essence of the human resources idea.

So it is with people and strategy. We need to think of people's relation to strategy in exactly the same way and avoid elevating it over people as dumb instruments of the strategist. In particular, 'organizational capability' implies not just having sufficient of the right people in the right place at the right time (as manpower planning has traditionally put it). It is also about organizational learning – how information is drawn into the organization, filtered, and made use of, and how individual knowledge, skills, and learning are enhanced, shared, and mobilized.

In this chapter we will explore the nature of strategy and what this means for HRM, through the contrasting perspectives of generic models and organizational capability.

What do we mean by strategy?

First, some definitions. These can help us to understand two important dimensions in the relationship of HRM to the business and in the different kinds of contribution it can make. These dimensions are:

- The different levels at which HRM operates
- The timescale over which different kinds of contribution become effective.

Strategy according to level

The first set of definitions illustrates the question of levels. There are five terms frequently used in relation to strategy (Quinn, 1991) – goals (or objectives), policies, strategy (or strategic plans), strategic decisions, and programmes.

(1) Goals (or objectives)

All organizations have multiple goals. These range from broad sets of values that express the underlying purpose of the organization; through overall goals about the direction in which it is intended to progress; down to unit and sub-unit goals that define more immediate targets. At the pinnacle is an organization's mission statement (although not all organizations bother with one). For example, Boots' Optician business has produced a statement of 'Objectives, Values and Guiding Beliefs' which says: 'We aim to be the nation's most successful optician by providing excellent patient care and meeting the needs of our customers better than anyone else.' Such statements say what is to be achieved, and sometimes when. More often they leave the latter in the vague distance, and do not state how such results are to be achieved. Boots' Opticians has gone some way towards this by translating its mission statement into a detailed set of values for company–employee relations, customer relations, and for the delivery of its products and services.

Organizations vary in the seriousness with which they take a mission statement. The Pilkington company for a long time had written into its articles and annual report a statement that its business was in 'glass and allied activities'. To an outsider this statement might seem fairly innocuous: to an insider it expressed the fervent commitment to glass technology and to markets defined by glass as a material. It emphasized applications of glass, and the making of better glass. As a senior manager put it:

> There was a very long and rambling policy book that you could pick out maybe three sentences from, which directed Group strategy. And the key one referred to 'glass and allied activities', and 'allied' was asterisked. And that pretty well tied our hands. That policy booklet was sort of reopened for further consideration nearly every other year, but 'glass and allied activities' was never changed. And that was Board policy, clearly laid down (Hendry and Pettigrew, 1989, p. 126).

The upshot was that Pilkington's acquisitions and diversification strategy in the late 1970s and early 1980s was into products which contained glass (such as spectacles), rather than into other types of product defined by existing types of customer. In contrast, when BTR attempted a take-over of Pilkington in 1986, it claimed Pilkington's glass businesses in window glass and insulation would have synergies with its own interests in domestic building materials such as cement – a very different interpretation of what the business was about.

(2) Policies

Policies are rules or guidelines which express the limits within which action should occur. Like the objectives they support, organizations often have a hierarchy of policies, with departments having their own sets of policy guidelines. At a departmental level, the personnel function is fond of promulgating policy standards. An example would be the way many organizations now advertise themselves as equal opportunities employers. As the

Pilkington example indicates, the word 'policy' is sometimes used inter-changeably with 'mission' (or perhaps 'was', as the word 'mission' has become more fashionable).

(3) Strategy

The strategy (or 'strategic plan') 'is the pattern or plan that integrates an organization's major goals, policies, and action sequences into a cohesive whole' (Quinn, 1991, p. 5). It is the overall plan which holds together and gives purpose to special programmes of action (such as plant modernization) and departmental plans. What raises strategy in this sense above special programmes and departmental plans is the way it takes account (or ought to) of (1) internal competencies and shortcomings in the organization, (2) present and anticipated changes in the external environment, and (3) expected moves from competitors, and frames 'a unique and viable posture' (competitive position) in the light of these.

Strategy in the diversified organization can be further sub-divided into corporate-level strategy and business-unit level strategy. The latter may be heavily constrained, though, by the corporate level and the whole structure of goals and policies. Johnson and Scholes (1988) have framed these elements into a model of strategy analysis (shown in Figure 4.1).

As well as helping to construct strategy, strategic analysis gives rise to programmes. One consequence of looking at competencies to underpin a course of action, for instance, might be a human resources 'programme' to improve the skills of management.

(4) Strategic decisions

These are the decisions which determine the overall direction of an enter-prise. What Quinn begins to touch on here is the idea that there are a myriad decisions constantly being made in organizations which structure perceptions, entail resource commitments, and dictate what resources the organization will have available for tasks. These 'intimately shape the true goals of the enterprise' (Quinn, 1991, p. 5). This implies that 'strategic' decisions are not entirely distinct from 'operational' decisions, which focus on efficiency and getting things done through routines. In other words, strategy is not just a 'top-down' activity of managers who sit making strategy, although the contribution of those at the top can be decisive.

The notion of 'strategic decisions' emphasizes the processes which go into the making of a 'strategy' or 'strategic plan', and also how this con-tinues to produce adaptations to the general sense of direction set out in a 'strategy'.

(5) Programmes

Quinn (1991, p. 5) defines programmes as 'the step-by-step sequence of

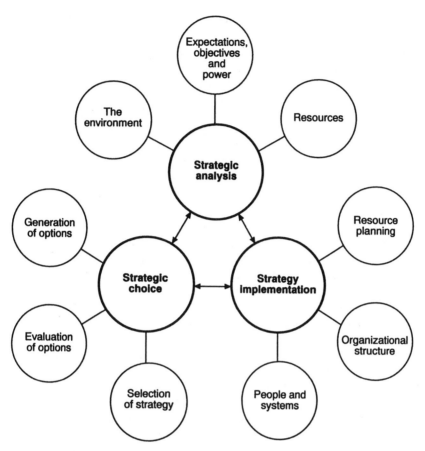

Figure 4.1 *Elements of a model of strategic management. (Reproduced with permission from Johnson and Scholes, 1988)*

actions necessary to achieve major objectives', involving the commitment of resources. Programmes provide the 'dynamic track' against which progress towards goals can be measured. An organization, for example, might embark on a programme of updating its computer systems to provide a better system of information collection and retrieval. Or it might modernize its manufacturing systems to improve quality, reduce waste, and cut direct labour costs. These are 'programmes' undertaken with commercial objectives in view.

Strategy and HRM

These definitions help us to get behind the bland use of the term 'strategy'. Usually, people just focus on the fourth of these definitions, the 'strategic plan'. By breaking 'strategy' down into its different elements we can begin to define the kind of contribution HRM can make through different levels of activity. For instance:

- *The goals and policies of the organization are sustained by values, culture and management style.* The direct influence of HRM on goals and policies might appear rather limited at first if we think of these as settled at the top of the organization. However, policies are only as effective as managers routinely 'behave' the organization's values – or 'walk the talk'. There is therefore a constant role for HRM and HRM specialists to propagate values. This can happen formally through training, management development, and the way selection is carried out. Or it can happen informally where a manager has an accepted role in keeping line colleagues up to the mark on standards of behaviour. In these ways, HRM is concerned with culture, values, and management style as the 'organizational glue' which holds an organization together.
- *Strategic plans and strategic decisions depend on the quality of management and the organization's decision-making processes.* HRM contributes to the quality of management through management selection and development over time. It also contributes to decision-making processes through organization structure and the way that affects information flow. This is perhaps a loose interpretation of HRM. On the other hand, traditional personnel texts have always tended to include job design and organization structure as relevant subjects for personnel. The point is that the personnel or HRM function may not have much direct influence over organization structure, but the latter has a strong influence on people's behaviour. Thus, organization structure affects decision making through formal communication processes and to the extent that it encourages (or discourages) politicking. Anyone concerned with the people processes of an organization needs to think about such issues, whether they are an HRM specialist or a line or general manager.
- *Strategic plans and programmes impact on the tangible aspects of HRM in terms of people as a resource and their skills, rewards, and motivation.* Strategic plans and programmes touch directly upon HRM in its role of getting, keeping, developing, and managing people. Programmes and plans typically involve changes in what is required of people and in the way they are managed, and therefore often mean adjustments in basic systems such as selection, training, pay, and appraisal. For managers, there are also specific skills in managing change, with which organizations often seem to have difficulty. These range from substantive issues of employee relations to process skills in handling the rate and pace of change and subsequent problems of motivation.

This hierarchy of HRM tasks is intended to indicate different levels and kinds of activity, in order to get away from the usual focus simply on 'resourcing'. Neither does it necessarily restrict HRM to what the personnel specialist does. In very large organizations there will also be a difference in focus between individual businesses and the group corporately:

Corporate strategy sets the agenda for HR strategy in the areas of culture, values, organization, performance and the management of change. It should not in itself be over-influenced by HR factors (HR strategies are about making business strategies work), but it must take account of key HR opportunities and constraints.

At the business unit level, strategic HR may be more closely involved in the cultural, organizational and resourcing implications of the business strategy (Cooke and Armstrong, 1990, p. 32).

Thus, the corporate director of HRM will obviously be concerned with different things from the personnel manager in an operating unit.

Strategy according to timescale

A corporate director and unit personnel manager will inevitably also think in terms of different timescales, since strategic focus tends to vary with level of responsibility. A second set of definitions highlights these differences in focus and timescale. Mintzberg (1987a) suggests five definitions frequently employed, although one (strategy as plan) has traditionally dominated explicit conceptions of strategy. The reader will recognize various overlaps with Quinn's (1991) definitions.

(1) Strategy as plan

This refers to a consciously intended course of action or guideline(s) to deal with a situation. This usage has two essential components: strategy is made in advance, and developed purposefully. An intended strategy which works out, or is 'realized', Mintzberg calls a 'deliberate strategy'. Not all intentions or plans, however, are fulfilled.

(2) Strategy as ploy

This refers to a specific aspect of conscious strategy, by which an organization tests out competitors and markets, in a way often intended to deceive.

(3) Strategy as position

Strategic position is what managers in a competitive market are supposedly striving for. It is about finding a 'niche', a 'product-market domain' (Thompson, 1967), which generates profits (or in economic terms, a 'rent'). The literature on competitive strategies and creating and sustaining competitive advantage (Porter, 1980, 1985) is all about defining viable positions. In addition, being able to sustain such positions depends on creating a match between the organization and its environment, through appropriate resources and organizational structures (Hofer and Schendel, 1978).

Mintzberg comments that a position can be achieved through intentional planning, or by an organization feeling its way. One would guess that a suitable organization structure is not likely to come about by chance. However, there are many instances of organizations in the same market domain operating with different structures.

(4) Strategy as a pattern

Instead of strategy being just what was intended, this definition incorporates the actions that follow and the resulting behaviour. Strategy is, then, the 'pattern in a stream of actions' (Mintzberg and Waters, 1985). From the outside, an observer often has to infer the strategy a company is following from the patterns he or she is able to piece together. Similarly, a manager sees a competitor's strategy by looking for patterns, and may, in the same way, have to try to make sense of what his or her own senior managers are doing.

It may be that even senior managers themselves are unclear about the direction in which they are going. The market may be uncertain or untried; the organization's ability to generate the necessary resources to sustain a particular course of action may be problematic; they may be distracted from what they want to do by the threat of takeover; and so on. The strategy may ultimately be what happens to emerge through various shifts and manoeuvres, and is defined by whatever consistency in behaviour develops. This may appear haphazard – in some organizations it may *be* haphazard. On the other hand, as Mintzberg says, there are times when it pays to manage the details and let the strategies emerge for themselves.

(5) Strategy as perspective

Where the previous definition looked outwards at the external environment, strategy as perspective is about an ingrained way of perceiving the world. The important thing about this is that it emphasizes the extent to which strategy is conceived in people's heads, and, moreover, that to influence action it needs to be shared. How such a shared worldview or common commitment to doing things comes about, and how preconceptions of this kind can then be changed, is of considerable significance. We refer to these issues through terms like 'organizational culture' and 'ideology'. Companies with distinctive cultures are often held up for admiration, and the creation of powerful organizational cultures to direct employees' behaviour in a united way was a dominant theme of the 1980s.

Time and HRM

Although Mintzberg did not intend his five definitions to be used in this way, and explicitly argued that a position can come about over time, they do capture an essential difference in perspective around time. 'Plan' and 'ploy' focus on a fixed point in time. 'Position', as the analysts treat it, also tends that way, although the more subtle ones like Porter emphasize 'creating advantage' as an ongoing process of innovation. It can therefore be seen as a bridging concept between the fixed point in time and extended periods. Perhaps, then, we should talk about 'position*ing*'. 'Pattern' and 'perspective', at the other extreme, suggest long timescales, continuity, and flux.

In the same way, HRM contributes to the functioning of an organization over long and short periods of time. Values and culture embody an ingrained way of perceiving the world ('strategy as perspective'). They are established over long periods of time and are slow and difficult to change. Likewise, managerial learning and capability are developed slowly. Strategy then emerges as managers 'feel their way' towards a tenable position ('strategy as pattern'). A 'strategic position' is reflected in the distribution of resources within an organization structure. Both can be changed, but take time to bed down, and managers have to be able to carry employees with them. That is why strategies often fail in implementation. Finally, a 'strategic plan' and specific tactics within that ('ploys') involve particular issues of employee resourcing, skills, and rewards.

While these facets of strategy can illuminate HRM, the terms themselves are not cut and dried. They tend to overlap and people use them in conflicting ways. Therefore, although it is useful to attempt clarification, it is even more important to accept ambiguity to shake ourselves out of thinking of strategy in simplistic ways. As Mintzberg and Quinn (1991) comment in their book which brings these definitions together: 'Upon completion of these readings, we hope that you will be less sure of the use of the word strategy, but more ready to tackle the study of strategy process with a broadened perspective and an open mind' (p. 4).

With this in mind, the following section now looks at the particular way HRM has used concepts from business strategy. More specifically, how it has narrowly dwelt on strategy in terms of competitive 'positioning'.

Strategy and HRM: matching HRM to strategy and situations

As we indicated at the beginning, a favoured approach has been to identify precise ways in which HRM can support specific business strategies and situations. The focus in doing so is on strategy as 'plans', 'positions', and (to a lesser extent) 'programmes'. (Since this approach tends to be over-generalized, it usually does not get down to the level of detail implied by 'programmes'.) In trying to match HRM to strategies and situations, three frames of reference are often used:

- The model of generic strategies for achieving competitive advantage, which derives from Porter (1980, 1985)
- The life-cycle model, with its stages of start-up, growth, maturity and decline (sometimes arrested by turnaround), as expounded, for example, by Hofer and Schendel (1978)

- Portfolio models for evaluating the growth prospects and investment requirements across a number of businesses within a diversified corporation, the most well-known example being that of the Boston Consulting Group (see Hedley, 1977).

These frameworks have been used to identify specific requirements for employee and management behaviour; consequent strategies for employee resourcing; and different priorities for personnel and HRM managers, arising from what Schuler (1989) calls the 'imperative for specific HRM practices for organizational effectiveness'. Thus, Schuler (1989) has developed characterizations of HRM strategy from generic strategies and the life-cycle; Fombrun and Tichy (1983) have related HRM strategies to the life-cycle; and Szilagyi and Schweger (1985) have adopted the portfolio model.

The lure of frameworks like these for establishing 'a problem- and market-oriented approach' (Baird, Meshoulam and Degive, 1983) towards HRM is considerable, but simplistic and dangerous. Their popularity, however, means that we need to provide some exposition of them, but we will do so critically.

Generic strategies and HRM

Schuler (1989) draws together and summarizes the large number of studies that are based on Porter's (1990) generic strategies framework – cost leadership, differentiation, and focus. The first of these is self-explanatory. A firm aims to maintain a *cost advantage* over competitors in order to undercut them on price. The benefits come from the achievement of higher volumes, which in turn stimulate efficiency from doing things on a large scale. High profits come from lots of products/services delivered at low margins.

The second (*differentiation*) trades on the distinctiveness of the product or service. This means superior quality or originality. Instead of price being the dominant concern, premium prices can be charged and profits come from high margins.

The third (*focus*) is essentially either of the first two, but directed at a more narrowly defined target audience or market segment. This is the niche strategy which avoids direct competition with others who may have stronger resources at their disposal.

What does Schuler say are the implications for HRM of the two contrasting routes – cost leadership and differentiation through quality?

Cost leadership (or cost reduction)

According to Schuler, this strategy means that control is centralized at the top of the organization and exercised through close design of the workflow. The emphasis is on productivity, by minimizing output cost per person. This means downward pressure on numbers of employees and on wages.

Cost reduction is also likely to be pursued in a number of other ways – through the use of part-time employees, sub-contracting, work simplification and work measurement, automation, and flexible deployment in the workplace. This (says Schuler) implies that employee behaviour needs to be:

- Relatively repetitive and predictable
- Predominantly short-term in focus
- Stressing individual activity
- Only moderately concerned with quality
- Giving heavy emphasis to quantity of output
- Focused on results
- Low in risk-taking
- Comfortable with stability.

HRM is therefore concentrated on:

- Writing explicit job descriptions that leave little room for ambiguity
- Narrowly designing jobs and career paths to encourage specialization, development of expertise, and efficiency
- Administering results-oriented appraisals, focused on performance in the short term
- Closely monitoring pay comparisons externally in deciding pay awards
- Providing minimal levels of training and development.

Schuler could have added, but did not, that there is likely also to be tight control of industrial relations to control pay and work discipline.

How valid is this portrayal of the HRM implications of a cost-reduction strategy? While the description of employee requirements and the general controlling approach to employees could be reasonably applied to many small engineering firms, it stands up less well in other technological settings. Specific HRM practices can vary considerably according to the technological environment and local custom. The West Midlands engineering industry, for instance, has traditionally relied on payment by results schemes to exercise control and motivate for output. Job descriptions thus belong to a different production environment. Equally, shopfloor appraisals are foreign to the British industrial environment.

It might be possible to substitute more accurate HRM 'contingencies', but already we can see there is a problem that the cultural and technological context of firms pursuing a cost-reduction strategy can vary.

Differentiation (or quality enhancement)

In his description of what he calls a 'quality enhancement' strategy, Schuler (1989) adopts Porter's ideas on the value chain within the organization and its extension out into the industry, and emphasizes cooperation across departmental and external organizational boundaries:

[Q]uality enhancement efforts are targeted at suppliers and customers as well as the organization itself. Suppliers are brought into the picture to ensure that they know how to produce quality products. If they don't know how, then the organization itself trains the supplier in methods to ensure high quality. From customers, information is sought as to what is desired ... [M]anufacturing organizations become like service organizations: they listen to their customers and what their customers want, and deliver it when they want it ... Regardless of the type of organizations then, quality enhancement depends upon the close cooperation of all segments of the organization and the industry chain ... In many respects with quality enhancement, the distinction between manufacturing and nonmanufacturing organizations becomes very blurred (p. 169).

Employee behaviour in a quality enhancement/differentiation strategy, Schuler says, needs:

- To be relatively repetitive and predictable
- To have a long-term or intermediate focus
- To engage in a certain amount of cooperative, interdependent behaviour
- To have a high concern for quality, a modest concern for quantity of output, and a high concern for the way goods or services are made and delivered
- To be low in risk-taking
- To have high commitment to the goals of the organization.

HRM aims to promote these behaviours through:

- Relatively fixed and explicit job descriptions
- High levels of employee participation in decisions relevant to immediate work conditions and to the job itself
- A mix of individual and group criteria in performance appraisal with a mostly short-term and results-oriented focus
- Egalitarian treatment of employees and the provision of some guarantees of employment security
- Extensive and continuous training and development.

How do these prescriptions match up to reality? Again, there can be significant variation in HRM practices according to the technological and cultural context. For example, Japanese firms pursue quality goals while mostly avoiding all forms of job description. Instead, they emphasize the development of broad skills, appreciation of the overall work process and final product, and cooperation with colleagues as the essential underpinning of product quality:

Practically, there is no job description for individual employees. Instead, a simple notice called a *jirei* (assignment notice) is issued for each assignment, including a transfer and promotion. 'It states: 'To Mr so and so. On this date, you are assigned to section, (and your salary grade is grade 1 rank 2),' without any further specification of job content, accountability, responsibility, and period of such an assignment (Inohara, 1990, p. 36).

This philosophy of flexibility is followed by many new British firms in manufacturing and services, influenced by successful Japanese companies.

Other HRM practices outlined by Schuler are plausible, although there are technological environments, such as process manufacture, where participation is often relatively low. There are also alternative (though less fashionable) quality philosophies to the one described which put less emphasis on collaboration with the supplier.

The value of generic strategies to HRM

Looking at the generic strategies approach to HRM as a whole, then, how useful is it? Does it provide accurate descriptions and prescriptions? And even if it does, are they useful? The answer is, it does provide plausible descriptions up to a point, but falls down on details by not sufficiently distinguishing different contexts. As a result, the model is so schematic that it is of limited use in practice. Any HRM practitioner developing the details of HRM in order to implement a business strategy – even one closely approximating to either of these generic types – is thus better off working through the detailed implications of the strategy in the light of the organization's particular circumstances. Which is, of course, what happens.

Going back to Porter, we can see that there are two other important features of his analysis which are left out. Generic strategies are only the foundation stone.

The second key concept is of a firm as a value chain of activity, from production through to sales and after-sales service. These are backed by various support activities – procurement of materials, finance, technology development, and human resources. Competitive advantage can come from particular strengths in any of these areas, or, more likely, from the way a firm links them. Activities within the value chain also vary in importance in different industries. The idea of the value chain makes clearer than Schuler does that employee role requirements and HRM practices may need to differ across the firm, and often do. In theory, of course, this could simply mean creating a more refined contingency model.

The third key idea of Porter's, however, is that firms gain competitive advantage by perceiving or discovering new and better ways to compete, and that this usually grows out of some discontinuity or change in industry structure. Perceiving and acting on this knowledge before others is a critical source of advantage. Innovation and organizational learning are thus key processes. Schuler, by contrast, describes the innovation process as if it is a third, alternative strategy, rather than as a process that can be pervasive and ubiquitous. Competitive advantage, in other words, is the act (or many acts) of grasping opportunities, rather than something static and achieved. If HRM fixes on the competitive position taken, therefore, it misses half the game.

Organizational life-cycles and HRM

The second strategy framework to influence HRM is the idea that organizations go through distinct stages of a life-cycle. This originates with the work of Greiner (1972), and has been developed, for example, by Churchill and Lewis (1983) who identified five stages. Hax and Majluf (1984) identify four stages – entrepreneurial/start-up, growth, maturity, and decline – while Grinyer, Mayes and McKiernan (1988) emphasize a fifth possibility, 'turnaround'. Schuler (1989), following Lorange and Murphy (1984), condenses these to three – the entrepreneurial/growth stage, the mature/decline stage, and the turnaround stage.

The important thing to realize is that the organizational life-cycle is largely a reflection of product life-cycles (Hendry and Pettigrew, 1992). The product life-cycle (Levitt, 1965) describes the way sales, costs, and profits vary over time as the requirements for developing, promoting, and sustaining a product/service alter as it gains consumer acceptance. As Figure 4.2 shows, initial sales of a successful product follow an upward line, but profit lags as high development and promotion costs are absorbed. Once established, sales generate revenues that exceed costs. Costs also fall as production efficiencies are found and marketing expenses reduce proportionately. The result is profits. Eventually, consumer interest may wane as substitute products come onto the market or the market becomes saturated. Competition through very similar products may also intensify. All these factors produce a levelling out and then a fall in sales; profits are squeezed; and ultimately the product is withdrawn.

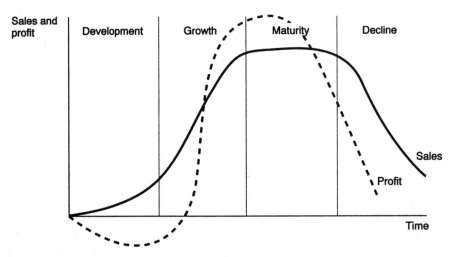

Figure 4.2   *The product life-cycle*

The early phase is also likely to be characterized by efforts to 'differentiate' the product from what is already available, and the later phases of maturity and decline are likely to be characterized by efforts to keep up profits by 'cutting costs'. Cost-cutting may fall on a number of targets, but production will be a prime candidate, especially as experience with the production process will steadily identify increased efficiencies and process improvements. In other words,

business [organizational] life-cycle stages are anchored in critical cost and market conditions. [Conversely], the appropriateness of competitive strategies is likely to be influenced by the life-cycle stage of the firm (Schuler, 1989 p. 173).

There are likely to be parallels, then, between life-cycle stages and generic strategies in the requirements for employee behaviour and HRM strategies and practices. What are these requirements and strategies?

Entrepreneurial/growth stage

In its early stages of growth, according to Schuler, the new firm needs technical talent to transform an idea or technology into a marketable product (Kochan and Chalykoff, 1987). Since such talent is critical and assumed to be in short supply, the attraction and retention of such individuals is paramount. Scarcity will ensure high pay, and labour costs will tend to be given low priority. Retention is likely to be managed additionally through innovative HRM practices, including high levels of employee participation and employment security – the latter achieved by the use of part-timers and sub-contract staff to protect core staff against fluctuations in activity. To facilitate an entrepreneurial/growth strategy, employees need to be innovative, cooperative, oriented to the longer-term, risk-taking, and willing to assume responsibility. These characteristics correspond in large degree to those Schuler defines for an 'innovation strategy'.

Mature/decline stage

By this stage, firms are assumed to have developed an internal labour market and extensive training and development programmes. Attracting highly skilled individuals is no longer a priority, and high wages are the exception. There is more emphasis on job classifications and cost of living comparisons for determining pay. Jobs are more narrowly defined, employee participation is limited, and there is more use of collective bargaining for resolving grievances. Economic downturns are handled by lay-offs.

As product prices are driven down, attention turns to more cost-efficient ways of operating. Employees need to focus on quantity and efficiency, short-term performance factors and results, with less risk-taking or creative behaviour. It is assumed that this requires or will produce less identification with the organization, as the organization treats the workforce increasingly as a cost to production to be varied at will.

There are clear parallels here with the cost-reduction strategy described earlier.

Turnaround

Faced with extinction, the firm will continue to give high priority to reducing costs, through layoffs and even pay cuts. This is unlikely to be sufficient, though. To regain customer loyalty and market share, product quality must be enhanced.

This implies similar requirements to the quality-enhancement strategy described earlier.

The value of the life-cycle model to HRM

Stating the requirements for employees and HRM in an idealized way like this is clearly unsatisfactory, for the same reason that defining them as contingencies of generic strategies is unsatisfactory. First, it assumes that all new firms are high-technology product innovators, whereas many come into a market someone else has already defined. If we remove this assumption, many of the HRM assumptions and prescriptions fall – such as a scarcity of skilled labour, the overriding importance of skilled labour, and the new firm's relative indifference to labour costs. Many new service firms have been formed, for instance, to perform low-cost services as large firms have contracted-out tasks like security and cleaning. In general, also, new firms are not indifferent to wage costs: the marginal cost of employing extra people is a major preoccupation of the small firm.

Second, the picture presented assumes that a new firm starts small and becomes large – developing an internal labour market in its mature stage, for instance. On the contrary, many small firms stay small and die small. In other words, Schuler confuses size and growth characteristics.

Thus, major contextual or contingent factors such as size and product-service characteristics need to be taken into account in projecting likely HRM practices. However, even then it is not simply a matter of devising better descriptions of HRM contingencies. There are also rather fundamental objections to the life-cycle idea of organizational growth. For example, many commentators have found little support for the notion that organizations move sequentially from one predictable stage of growth to another. Instead, they see recurrent patterns of crisis and renewal (Birley and Westhead, 1990; Hendry, Arthur, and Jones, in press).

By representing organizational change in terms of a life-cycle, writers on HRM simply reproduce certain fallacies, which Porter (1980), among others, has exposed. The idea of a life-cycle encourages a fatalism about a product's 'shelf life' and does not answer the important practical question, 'how do you know when you are moving from one stage to another?' The maturity stage, for instance, can be prolonged considerably and frequently by repackaging and modifying a product. Innovation and creativity thus continue to be at a premium.

There is also the problem of disentangling the effects of boom and recession in the wider economy from product life-cycle effects. From the organization's point of view, these can have a far more serious impact. Recession frequently exposes weaknesses in companies' financial structures which cause them to fail. Product life-cycle is not therefore the be-all and end-all in company success and failure. Recession in particular can seriously foreshorten the company life-cycle even though it may have sound products (Hendry and Pettigrew, 1992).

Despite these criticisms, the idea of an organization passing through distinctive stages of development has a persistent appeal and fits with much common observation. It can, for instance, account for and predict what activities will dominate organizations at different times. Firms can be relatively easily assigned to phases of evolution and their HR practices compared. Jackson, Schuler, and Rivero (1989) have done some empirical work contrasting organizational practices in this respect, highlighting in particular differences in treatment of hourly paid and other employees which belie earlier generalizations. The life-cycle model is also especially useful in focusing problems firms have in managing the shift from one stage to another. The Barclaycard case in Chapter 7 and the Pilkington case in Chapter 8 illustrate these shifts, through one firm going from a high growth stage to maturity, and another going from maturity and decline through a process of turnaround.

The life-cycle model helps, finally, to understand the tendency for firms in the same industry to behave in a similar manner. When a market is first created for a new line of products, firms put a lot of emphasis on distinguishing their own offering. As consumer preferences begin to settle on certain standards and qualities, differentiation behaviour begins to give way to a general emphasis on standardization and cost cutting. As the industry becomes increasingly mature and market growth starts to tail-off, cost-cutting behaviour becomes more intense. The result is that firms in the same stage of an industry's life-cycle tend to display similar characteristics and have a use for similar kinds of HRM. These similarities extend across different industries.

Portfolio models and HRM

The third model used to chart and prescribe employee characteristics and HRM activities, the portfolio model, extends the thinking behind the life-cycle idea. The basis for this is the observation that many firms do not depend on just one product but make and sell many different ones. The more these differ and are organized into distinct product lines with different manufacturing and marketing requirements, the more scope there is for managing them in entirely different ways.

To understand the use of portfolio models, it is necessary to look at the recent history of large firms. During the 1960s and into the 1970s, a new form of highly diversified company began to emerge, first in the USA and then in the UK (Channon, 1972). These developed mainly through acquisition of other companies. The acquired units tended to be managed from head office through tight systems of financial planning and control, leaving product divisions to manage operations. At the same time, during the 1970s, many US companies diversified their activities internationally. This added a further level of complexity, as overlapping geographic divisions were introduced. For a time, the idea of matrix management was in vogue as a way of reconciling the competing claims of products and geography. However, the greater the degree of product diversification, the more product divisions tended to dominate, and in the USA the relative size of the domestic market tended to overwhelm overseas operations and bias investment decisions (Channon, 1991).

What was needed was a form of organization and a way of evaluating the prospects of different businesses in a rational way. The solution was the 'strategic business unit' (SBU), pioneered in the USA by General Electric in conjunction with McKinsey, the management consultants. The SBU is a way of dividing the diversified corporation into a series of separate businesses, each with its own set of customers and competitors, functional skills, and profit-centre status. These are linked by an investment philosophy which says that the corporation as a whole should have a mix of businesses at different stages of their life-cycle.

The status of businesses is then assessed on the basis of two variables derived from the Boston Consulting Group's PIMS programme – (1) the attractiveness or potential of the market for growth, and (2) the SBU's relative competitive position in terms of current market share. The basic premise of the PIMS model is that market share equates with profit because it gives economies of scale and raises the experience level in all aspects of the particular business.

Taken together, these two variables signal the relative needs of SBUs for investment to improve market share and profitability, as against the ability of other SBUs to generate cash. The ideal is a balance or mix of businesses: there should be enough of the latter to fund growth, and enough of the former to provide that future growth. Thus, mature businesses with a strong competitive position, but slow growth, can be used to provide cash flow for new businesses with high market share in growing markets, or to raise market share in a growing market from a low level. In the jargon, mature 'cash cows' are 'milked' or 'harvested' in order to build potential 'stars'. Meanwhile, those businesses with small market share in unattractive markets ('dogs') are divested for a quick return of cash.

General Electric plotted these and other options on a nine-square, three-by-three matrix, while Hofer (1977) suggested a twelve-square model which related competitive position to the five stages of the product life-cycle. The most common version was that of the Boston Consulting Group itself, which highlighted four options (Figure 4.3).

The portfolio model has been used within HRM to suggest specific requirements for managerial behaviour and employee resourcing, especially the choice of general manager of the business unit. For example, the business intended for 'milking' to fund growth elsewhere requires tight cost control and an ability to 'make assets sweat'. Managers can either be carefully selected for their personalities, styles, skills, and experience in this style of operation (Szilagyi and Schweger, 1985), and/or by setting the right framework of rewards (Kerr, 1982). As General Electric's former chief executive, Reginald H. Jones, observed:

> When we classified . . . [our] . . . businesses, and when we realized that they were going to have quite different missions, we also realized we had to have quite different people running them. That was where we began to see the need to meld our human resource planning and management with the strategic planning we were doing (Fombrun, 1982, p. 46).

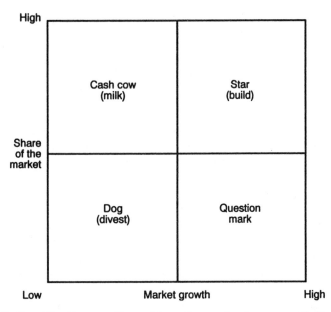

Figure 4.3   *The Boston Consulting Group business portfolio model*

The value of the portfolio model to HRM

Matching managers to strategies has obvious intuitive appeal. However, there are counter-arguments which have a bearing also on the general principle of personnel selection and testing. These arguments, for and against, were well set out by Gupta (1986).

On the one hand, managers differ in their education, experience, and personality, and these backgrounds predispose them towards different types of strategic activity. The universalistic general manager who can turn his or her hand to any situation, in other words, is a myth (Kotter, 1982). If different skills and orientations are needed for the effective implementation of different strategies, systematic matching of managers to strategies can therefore be expected to yield superior performance. There is some evidence to support this (Gupta and Govindarajan, 1984).

The counter-argument has a number of elements. First, there is the assumption that strategies are clear-cut. On the contrary, if a business situation and its prospects are uncertain, flexibility is more important than trying to match skills and background against a specific strategy. This touches on an underlying weakness of the portfolio model and of the life-cycle model on which it rests. This is the problem, already referred to, of predicting the eventual death of a product or business. The case of the radio is salutary: whereas American manufacturers wrote it off, the Japanese firm Sony turned it into the 'Walkman' (Ohmae, 1982).

In reality, therefore, there may be a whole range of options from 'build' through 'niche-based repositioning', to 'harvest' and 'divest' (Harrigan, 1981). The portfolio matrix can simply become a self-fulfilling prophecy

(Wensley, 1982), stifle organizational renewal (Chakravarthy, 1984; Porter, 1987), and damage the wider economy:

> [Product portfolio management], which was originally conceived as a device for determining priorities for an investment portfolio, has been perverted into a device for killing certain businesses and boosting others, purely in order to maximize the corporation's financial results (Ohmae, 1982, p. 142).

Flexibility may also be an increasing requirement at other stages in the product life-cycle, as product life-cycles become shorter and the transitions between stages become more unpredictable. The ability of a manager to handle the current or intended strategy becomes less important than his or her ability to adapt to changing situations.

The second objection to matching managers to strategies is the need to develop future top managers who can encompass a variety of business types and situations. Career development requires sometimes *mis*matching. Such breadth of experience contributes to the strategy-making process, since people in unfamiliar situations can bring a fresh perception. It also helps with linkages and the exchange of ideas across SBUs. This can be important because the SBU structure otherwise discourages the identification and exploitation of synergies.

A third objection is the effect on managers' motivation of being pigeon-holed as a particular type of manager – especially as a risk-averse 'harvester' of businesses that are going nowhere. It is those who acquire reputations as 'builders' of growth businesses who tend to become the organizational 'stars' and get the top promotions. One suggestion here is that older, plateaued managers should be reserved for the task of harvesting.

The final objection rests on whether the choice of a general manager makes any difference. Research on this question ranges from those which suggest that leaders make relatively little difference (Lieberson and O'Connor, 1972), to those which report evidence of significant impact (Weiner and Mahoney, 1981; Smith, Carson and Alexander, 1984). These viewpoints can be reconciled by reference to the contingencies which affect performance (Hambrick and Finkelstein, 1987). These include:

- External factors (such as constraints on a manager's freedom of action from industry regulation, and powerful suppliers and customers)
- Organizational factors (such as the availability of resources to pursue a strategy, and the constraints of superiors and organizational culture)
- Personal factors to do with colleagues.

In other words, as the contingency theory of leadership would lead us to expect, leader effectiveness and impact depends upon the interaction between variables associated with the leader, the situation, and followers (Fiedler, 1967; Stogdill, 1974).

The implication of these arguments for HRM lies in the relative emphasis that should be given to rigorous selection according to preconceived criteria (especially those embodied in testing procedures such as psychometric testing) – as against using training and other means of personal development (such as job rotation and job assignments) and appropriate reward systems, to develop and direct a manager's repertoire of skills. A second implication is how far selection should be focused on the single leader or on the team.

These issues are fundamental not just to matching managers to portfolio situations but to the whole project of personnel management and HRM insofar as they attempt to channel employee behaviour through various techniques and tools. Among these tools, job descriptions, incentive pay schemes, and psychological testing are based on differing suppositions about the rigidity versus the malleability of human behaviour. Subsequent chapters will explore options, limitations, and preferences in the use of these tools.

Strategy and HRM: a process view

In analysing the application of these three widely used models from business strategy to HRM, we end in each case in something of a cul-de-sac. Each time, we come up against some fundamental objection, either inherent in the strategic model or occurring in its translation into usable HRM prescriptions. We have to conclude that they help with thinking, but are limited in practice.

The problem lies in how we look at strategy and how, in consequence, we interpret HRM. The perspective on strategic management contained in the models analysed above sees human resource management as a derivative – something implemented downstream from decisions about corporate strategy. While this may be true at a lower level in relation to specific business plans, the relationship is not so straightforward in other respects. It shows a confidence in (and lack of realism about) the way corporate strategy itself is arrived at, which is no longer shared among strategic management theorists themselves.

Strategic management was born out of a post-war belief that the external business environment could be controlled by planning mechanisms (Ansoff, 1965) – just as earlier management theorists in this century concentrated on developing systems for controlling what went on inside the organization, especially the people (Knights and Morgan, 1991). The consequence of this philosophy was the development of rational, analytic models for formulating strategy. The 'strengths–weaknesses–opportunities–threats' (SWOT) model was one product of this thinking; the PIMS portfolio methodology was another; and Porter's (1980, 1985) generic strategies and competitor analysis models have become the dominant contemporary example. Embodied in these, moreover, is the belief that strategy making should be explicit, deliberate, conducted by strategists, and therefore top-down.

Critics argue, in contrast, that strategy is often 'emergent', or 'realized' after the event, rather than 'deliberate' (Mintzberg, 1978). Indeed, it is often best kept 'fuzzy', both to preserve latent options and to build support (Pettigrew, 1985). It does not fall into discrete stages of formulation and implementation, but is a continuous and iterative process of 'crafting' strategy (Mintzberg, 1987b), and is most effective when managed in this way. Likewise, there should not be a rigid distinction between strategy and operations (Wissema, Brand, and Van der Pol, 1981; Pettigrew and Whipp, 1991); nor between top management, as strategists, and those lower down the organization who may initiate ideas or, by dint of the commitments of resources they make, predetermine strategic options (Gluck, Kaufman, and Walleck, 1980; Kanter and Buck, 1985; Kanter, 1989). Finally, there are two particular problems which defy a purely rational approach – how to shake an organization out of its attachment to particular strategic recipes even in the face of failure (Huff, 1982), and difficulties experienced with implementation.

The conclusion of these arguments is that the process of strategy is as important as the content. Deriving HRM prescriptions from strategic models, in the way described in this chapter, is at best partial, at worst, misconceived. By recognizing strategy formation as an incremental, trial-and-error, learning process, HRM becomes not simply an accessory to an implementation process but a contributor to organizational learning and innovation. HRM helps in the realization of new business directions – most obviously through the long-term development of people, including managers as decision makers, but also in more subtle ways in creating a climate and capability for continuous development and improvement.

Organizational capability as the source of competitive advantage

This view has begun to command considerable support among strategic management theorists themselves. Rumelt, Schendel, and Teece (1991), for instance, comment that:

> Both theoretical and empirical research into the sources of competitive advantage has begun to point to organizational capabilities, rather than product-market positions or tactics, as the enduring sources of competitive advantage (p. 23).

The point is pressed home by Nelson (1991) and by Porter (1991), who argue that differences in firm performance derive from their capabilities to innovate and the search and discovery processes that are part of this.

Developing this theme, Ulrich and Lake (1990) refer to the focus on organizational capabilities as 'competing from the inside out'. They contrast this with deficiencies in the traditional approach which assumes a rational process of strategic analysis, a static view of competitive advantage, neglects implementation of strategy, and treats the generation of commitment from employees as an afterthought of the financial, strategic, and technological planning process. They therefore propose a new model which puts the building of competencies and the generation of employee commitment at the centre. Organizational capability then becomes a fourth source of uniqueness for achieving competive advantage (Figure 4.4).[1]

Underlying this general shift in perspective within strategic management is a concern with short-termism, associated with pressure for short-term

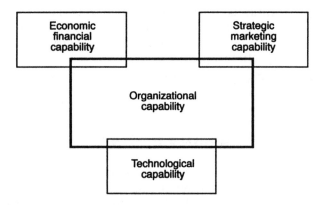

Figure 4.4 *Organizational capability as a critical source of competitive advantage. (Reproduced with permission from Ulrich and Lake, 1990)*

financial returns. Hayes and Abernathy (1980) pinpointed this at the beginning of the 1980s, citing the popularity of portfolio theory and profit-centre management as culprits. A decade later, with the experience of leveraged buy-outs and corporate break-ups in the USA and UK fresh in the memory, Channon (1991) echoed the sentiment. The concept of shareholder value and return on equity had become important determinants of corporate strategy in the 1980s, as banks and institutional fund managers in North America and the UK applied greater and greater pressure on industrial companies to produce maximum financial performance:

> Many industrial company managements thus found themselves under pressure to achieve short term financial performance, sometimes at the expense of a long term balanced programme of investment or to dismember themselves by divesting of important businesses in their portfolios . . .
> Many western institutions that had earlier adopted the divisional, and subsequently strategic business unit system of management in the 1970s and 1980s, were under pressure to maximize their short term profitability irrespective of portfolio balance and short term versus long term perspective (Channon, 1991, pp. 6–7).

The result has been an ever more visible failure of British and US business competitiveness, relative especially to Japan.

While Channon uses this to argue for a change in the relationship between financial institutions and companies and more planning by governments, its general significance is the increasing reaction it represents to the 'market-driven' assumptions on which HRM has been based – and specifically against certain of the concepts HRM has adopted from business strategy.

In conclusion, therefore, more useful for the HRM practitioner than having an understanding of types of strategy is understanding the roots of strategy. (The strategy models outlined in any case are not hard to grasp.) As Porter emphasizes, competitive advantage comes from innovating, and this places organizational learning and organizational capability at the heart of the issue. How to stimulate, organize, and capitalize on learning, how to build capability, and how to mobilize capability for innovation are the key tasks. While HRM practitioners have to be concerned with implementing particular strategic plans, they should therefore also be concerned with building capability.

Decoupling human resources strategy

This means to some extent 'decoupling' human resources strategy from business plans. The process of developing HR strategy should mirror the way business strategy itself is evolved and adjusted. Strategy is not just how

Table 4.1 Questions for developing human resources strategy

Business	*Human resources*
What business are we in?	What sort of people do we need in the business?
Where are we going, and how are we going to get there?	What sort of organization do we need?
What are our business strengths and weaknesses?	To what extent are those strengths and weaknesses related to our human resource capability? How do we remedy them?
What opportunities and threats do we face?	What opportunities do these create for developing and motivating employees?
	What are the threats to growth through skill shortages and the retention of key staff?
	What are the threats from decline in holding the skill base of the organization together?
What are the main strategic issues facing the business?	To what extent do these issues involve organizational and HR considerations?
	Do managers recognise the HR implications?
What are the critical success factors which determine how well we achieve our mission?	How far is business success helped or hindered by the quality, motivation, commitment, and attitudes of our employees?
	How can high performance be encouraged?

Source: Adapted from Cooke and Armstrong (1990).

to manage particular situations, but identifying changing competitive forces over the medium to long term and developing an appropriate response. This means constantly asking the simple questions outlined in Table 4.1 in 'a continuous process of analysing what is happening to the business and where it is going' (Cooke and Armstrong, 1990). By asking these questions, the human resources 'strategist' responds to the needs of the business in terms of the different levels of activity across different timescales, delineated at the beginning of this chapter.

Summary

This chapter has reviewed HRM's relationship with business strategy by considering, first, what we mean by strategy. By breaking down 'strategy' into different elements – goals, policies, plans, decisions, and programmes – we were able to define the contribution of HRM in terms of different levels of activity.

Overall goals and policies, we suggested, are sustained by values, culture and management style. These give direction and coherence to an organization through a set of underlying values, norms and rules. We tend to sum up all this as 'culture'. HRM is involved in the process of culture building through changing structures and organizational systems (including human resource systems), and the promotion of behavioural norms and values. Culture is a 'strategic' issue.

At another level, the capacity of an organization to make effective corporate strategies depends on the quality of management and decision making. HRM contributes to this through management selection and development over time, and through organization structure, with its impact on information flow. HRM should be concerned with the process of learning which leads to the formation of better corporate strategies.

Coming closer to the present and the level of activity usually associated with HRM, plans and programmes generate a wide range of activity concerned with employee skills, rewards, and motivation. This is HRM in its role of getting, keeping, developing, and motivating people. This is HRM at its most focused, and in its functional guise.

The major part of the chapter then considered the value and use of general strategy models. First, we outlined the implications of two generic strategies (cost leadership and differentiation). The parallels of these with life cycle patterns and the resulting differences of emphasis in HRM at different stages of an organization's growth, maturity, and decline were explored. We also considered a third framework (portfolio modelling) which differentiates relative life-cycle prospects of businesses in large, diversified conglomerates, to suggest different managerial attributes across different types of business.

We concluded that the development of business strategy and the HRM response work at a much greater level of detail and subtlety, and that therefore it is more important for HRM practitioners to think strategically than to make use of generalized models. Chapters 4 through to 13 are all about enhancing this capability in the human resources professional.

We then outlined a processual approach to strategy, concerned with the making of strategy, not just its implementation. HRM has a role to play in this through its contribution to innovation, learning, and 'organizational capability'. The last is a somewhat elusive quality, difficult to illustrate and describe in tangible ways. However, it is increasingly agreed by commentators and analysts both of strategy and HRM that organization capability is central to success and to the contribution of HRM. We will develop this notion further in Chapter 10.

Note

1   For a more detailed discussion of 'organizational capability' in terms of resource-based theory, see Hendry, Arthur and Jones (in press), especially Chapter 2.

5
Organization structure and human resource management

Introduction

Organization structure is an HRM issue because it is about the way people are grouped and their work coordinated and controlled. This influences individual motivation through the feelings of discretion and control people feel over their own work; their sense of direction; and the opportunity to interact and participate in teamwork with others. It also affects performance through the barriers or otherwise it can create to communication. Organization structure has other indirect HRM implications through the opportunities for promotion and personal development it creates.

While we tend to think of organization structure in terms of the overall view of the organization, these HRM themes have an obvious counterpart in the design of individual jobs, through the levels of specialization pursued. For example, a high degree of specialization tends to generate multiple levels of supervision, and therefore a tall hierarchical structure.

Changes in an organization's structure can be an essential step in bringing about strategic change. An organization's structure should fit with its strategy, to ensure that the strategy is effective and the organization is efficient. Specific HRM processes and systems then need to be brought into line to support both of these. Strategy, structure, and HRM are necessarily linked:

> Just as firms will be faced with inefficiencies when they try to implement new strategies with outmoded structures, so they will also face problems of implementation when they attempt to effect new strategies with inappropriate HR systems (Fombrun, Tichy and Devanna, 1984, p. 37).

In this chapter we will explore the relationship between strategy, structure, and HRM. In particular, we will look at the tendency, prevalent through the 1980s and into the 1990s, to decentralize responsibilities and focus activities on smaller units in order to increase motivation and entrepreneurialism, while sharpening up efficiency. We will look at how decentralization affects:

- Structures for pay bargaining and industrial relations
- The operation of internal labour markets
- Corporate culture
- The organization of the personnel function.

Finally, we will consider how firms have tried to manage the conflicts between centralization and decentralization in recruiting, retaining, and developing people, and in managing their overall resourcing needs.

Strategy and structure in large organizations

Alfred Chandler (1962) began the interest in matching structure to strategy when he described how American firms in the twentieth century had developed new models of organization to manage increasing diversity in their business. In particular, he identified the evolution of a much looser, multi-divisional form ('M-form'), coordinated by a General Office, with operational responsibilities located lower down. This began to replace the functional form of organization ('U-form'), where a single line of authority culminated in the functional heads sitting round the chief executive. The 'U-form' worked where an organization was vertically integrated, but once it started to become more diverse, strategic issues got crowded out by operational ones. A number of American corporations developed innovations of this kind in the 1920s and 1930s, including General Motors, Du Pont, Standard Oil of New Jersey, and Sears.

Increasing complexity in firms has resulted in the dominance of the 'M-form' organization. As large companies diversify they typically move from a functional structure to a divisionalized one. In the process, responsibility is pushed down to business units and profit centres, headed by general managers (Salter, 1973). The result is a decentralization of responsibility and decision making. At the same time, large companies have to try to hold this in check somehow. As they become larger and more diverse, they may introduce sub-grouping of businesses within the whole structure and intermediate levels of control, each with their own level of general management responsibility.

Various writers have described this pattern of evolution in terms of how far a firm's product portfolio is dominated by one or more products, and whether these are related or unrelated (Wrigley, 1970; Scott, 1971; Channon, 1972; Salter, 1973). Channon, for instance, defines firms according to four categories of product-market strategy:

- Single product (where one product line accounts for at least 95 per cent of sales)
- Dominant product (where secondary activities make up no more than 30 per cent of sales)
- Related product (where products are related by technology, markets, or vertically, but no one product line accounts for more than 70 per cent of sales)
- Unrelated product (where products are unrelated by technology or markets *and* no one product line accounts for more than 70 per cent of sales).

Thus, Barclaycard, which is described at length in Chapter 7, was a 'single product' organization from 1966 until around 1982, with its business based almost entirely on the 'classic' Barclaycard. Pilkington, described in Chapter 8, was more diversified. Nevertheless, two vertically integrated businesses, flat and safety glass, contributed 95 per cent of UK profits and sales until the early 1980s. In terms of the above categorization, it was a 'dominant product' type of organization (with the former supplying raw material to the latter). Both Barclaycard and Pilkington were managed in the 'U-form' way, through strong functions. In contrast, two other companies that feature in this and other chapters, IMI and GKN, were considerably more diversified and managed as multi-divisional (M-form) organizations.

The metals and engineering company, IMI, was, and is, a 'related product' organization. Although no single division accounted for more than 30 per cent of sales, there was a natural affinity and cohesion between the various businesses, the Group having grown, as its flotation documents in 1977 put it, 'by logical extension of its activities' around the use, in the main, of copper in metals processing and engineering.

At the furthest extreme, GKN in the late 1970s was a good example of an 'unrelated product' organization. As it moved away from its roots in steel-making and the downstream processing of steel during the 1970s, it went through what Sir Trevor Holdsworth, who later took over as Chairman, called a period of 'unfettered diversification'. As he put it in 1977: 'We have a miscellany of engineering and construction businesses . . . there is little cohesion between them and we have far, far too many of them.'

The significance of a firm's product portfolio is the degree of administrative complexity it produces and the demands such complexity creates for managers in trying to control the business as a whole. Simpler businesses can be managed in relatively centralized ways. The more diversified and complex, however, the greater the pressure for decentralization so that the individual businesses can react more effectively to their different markets.

As simple and dominant product organizations, respectively, Barclaycard and Pilkington tended to be managed in centralized ways until the early 1980s. GKN and IMI, on the other hand, had a strong attachment to decentralization. During the 1980s, however, Barclaycard and Pilkington also began to diversify and decentralize. In this, they were part of a general trend to push more responsibility down to operating units. In the process, for reasons which we will explore, HRM has become particularly associated with the supposed virtues of decentralization.

The trend towards decentralization

There are a number of reasons why firms have pushed for decentralization in recent years. Partly it is the result of increased diversity, partly it relates to the desire to reduce costs. Both have their origin in the increased competitive pressure all organizations have been experiencing. Figure 5.1

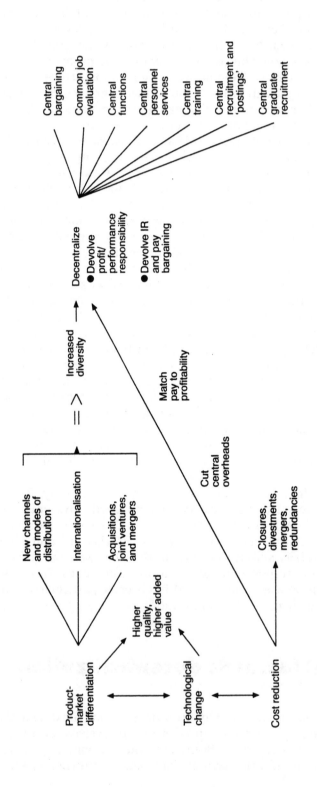

Figure 5.1 *The origins and consequences of decentralization*

outlines these influences for decentralization and the consequences for HRM. This shows four things.

First, during the 1980s, firms reduced their dependency on UK markets and commodity products through greater product-market differentiation. This was largely achieved through acquisitions and mergers, but also by internationalization. Following the bouts of 'merger mania' in the early 1970s and again in the late 1980s, the UK has thus gone from having the highest percentage of companies of the single and dominant business kind to having the highest percentage of companies in the related and unrelated (or conglomerate) categories (Channon, 1982; Constable, 1986). As a result, the UK economy is now exceptionally dominated by large, diversified companies, and the modern corporation in Britain is increasingly a multi-product, diversified organization.

Second, allied to the overall reshaping of businesses, firms looked to technological change to create higher quality, higher added-value products and services as part of a general effort to focus more sharply on different customer groups.

Third, the 1980–1982 recession saw a dramatic effort to cut costs, through closures, divestments, rationalization (through mergers and acquisitions), and redundancies. Technological change also contributed. In addition to the impact on operating units, cost-reduction also created pressure to cut central staff overheads.

Finally, a by-product of centralization had tended to be standard rates of pay for employees on the same grade throughout large organizations, regardless of where they worked or how profitable their part of the business was. Common rates of pay were therefore seen as contributing to business unit costs. This created a desire on the part of managers to break away from central pay and grading structures.

The first two processes led to large organizations encompassing a range of businesses distant in geography, product, technology, and skills; while the second pair of factors involved employment costs. Together, they created considerable pressure for decentralization. The result was a devolution of profit and performance responsibilities to individual businesses, and the break-up of centralized industrial relations and pay bargaining. The outcome was a well-documented trend during the 1980s towards smaller organizational units, less hierarchical structures, and more flexible styles of management (Kanter, 1989; Handy, 1989). In the process, many companies looked long and hard at their central personnel activities, including pay bargaining, common job evaluation, central personnel services and training, centrally administered systems such as recruitment (including graduates), and centrally orchestrated career 'postings'.

Centralization versus decentralization

While decentralization has attracted more attention, in fact at any one time there are likely to be as many instances of centralization occurring (Lester, 1991). A particular catalyst in recent years has been mergers. Rationalization in the building society industry, for instance, has meant increasing centralization as merged societies reconcile their computer systems and operating procedures, and standardize personnel systems. For a time, at least, this means a stronger role for the centre.

Over time, however, decentralization tendencies may reassert themselves. The TSB Group, for example, over the last ten years has gone through successive phases of centralization–decentralization–centralization, as different performance imperatives have come to the fore. In most organizations, in fact, there is a constant tension between centralization and decentralization, with the balance between the two tending to shift backwards and forwards over time.

Apart from the immediate pressures to decentralize described above, four factors affect this balance, and hence the degree of decentralization or otherwise of personnel and HRM activity. These are:

- The kind of business environment(s) the corporation faces, and its pattern of growth
- Patterns of interdependence between its parts, occasioned by the physical technology and product/service transactions
- Labour market characteristics
- Company philosophy, managerial beliefs, and recent history – this includes views about the desirability of maintaining a corporate culture.

We will briefly look at each of these.

The business environment and pattern of growth

The pattern of growth determines the degree of product-market diversity in the firm, which we described above in terms of single, dominant, related, and unrelated products. Goold and Campbell's (1987) typology of business growth strategies, in terms of 'core', 'diverse', and 'manageable/financial control' businesses, helps to explain the degree of diversity and how the range of businesses resulting are strategically managed and controlled.

One additional consideration that is often overlooked is the amount of internal integration necessary where a business has a number of sites, possibly in different parts of the world. IMI's division manufacturing drink-dispensing machines, for example, fronts up to world customers like Coca-Cola on a global scale, while, at the other extreme, it has a clutch of specialist small engineering businesses operating in niche UK markets. The organization of the customers each type of business is dealing with produces different patterns of integration and centralization. Dealing effectively with the Coca-Cola Corporation, for instance, dictates centralization in IMI's Drinks Dispense business, but a much looser structure in Special Engineering.

Interdependence between businesses and technologies

The impact of product-market diversity may be reduced by transactions between operating units. The more technological and business links there are, the greater the tendency towards centralized systems and control (Scott, 1971). A vivid way of looking at this is through Thompson's (1967) characterization of three types of interdependence – pooled, sequential, and reciprocal. All these are found in the traditional core flat and safety glass businesses at Pilkington.

Figure 5.2 provides a simplified view of the overall business in the late 1980s, with the major companies in flat and safety glass in the UK (PGL), Germany (Flachglas), and USA (LOF). Expertise in 'basic' (flat) glass production is 'pooled' through Group Engineering, which manages the international licensing of 'float' glass technology and acts as a channel for technical information between the country and regional divisions. On a more *ad hoc* basis, product developments are managed through project groups (reviewing, for example, the use of safety glass by the world automotive industry). These draw in ('pool') staff from major operating companies within the Group. The dotted arrows in Figure 5.2 indicate a series of 'sequential' supply relationships between 'basic' glass plants and downstream processing for the safety glass and architectural markets. Finally, the two 'basic' glass plants in St Helens have a 'reciprocal' relationship insofar as there is product overlap and joint scheduling.

Company labour market

Physical and technical links between parts of a company arising in this way lead to familiarity with each other's businesses among managerial and technical groups. This in turn creates scope for people to move between plants and businesses and for the development of common sets of skills. In other words, it encourages development of an 'internal labour market' (ILM). Close geographic proximity of plants, as in Pilkington's case in St Helens, reinforces this. Close proximity of plants and businesses, even though these may be quite different, creates pressure for convergence of many other personnel/HRM practices – in particular, for centralized pay bargaining.

Historically, the concentration of much of Pilkington's employment in St Helens created strong pressures for centralization. As the company expanded further afield and reduced employment in St Helens, however, the balance shifted towards decentralization.

Company philosophy, managerial beliefs, and history

The last factor in many ways should actually be the starting point for understanding pressures for centralization/decentralization. Company philosophy, managerial beliefs, and history explain much about the pace and vigour with which decentralization is pursued. Three of the companies already mentioned provide striking contrasts in this respect.

When IMI began the process of separation from ICI in the 1960s, it asserted its independence in a powerful reaction to the centralized ICI way of doing things. The large central functions of engineering, research, and

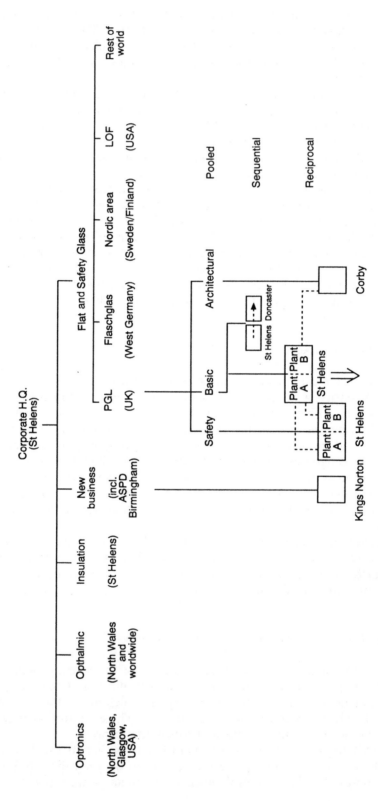

Figure 5.2 *Patterns of interdependence among Pilkington's businesses (simplified)*

personnel were all dissolved by the end of the 1960s, and the central site services at its Witton (Birmingham) headquarters were dismantled at the beginning of the 1980s. Decentralization as a philosophy was therefore entrenched within IMI.

In contrast, Pilkington's conversion to decentralization was more tentative, a product of the 1980s. Engineering and R&D, for example, are still retained as central functions, although they are now smaller and have a more specialized remit.

In the third company, GKN, there was a strong historic attachment to the philosophy of decentralization. This was overlain, however, by the creation of sub-Group head offices from the mid-1960s onwards, coupled with weak corporate control. Meanwhile, a powerful Group personnel function emerged through personal links with the Group chairman and sub-Group personnel administrators. During this time, central graduate recruitment and management development flourished, although anything which tended towards centralized industrial relations was always resisted.

With the dissolution of sub-Groups in 1978–1979 the intermediate layers of administration were removed. This had two paradoxical effects. On the one hand, it allowed the reassertion of corporate control over strategy, but, on the other, gave more latitude to operating companies. The central personnel function then began to wither as its tentacles through the sub-Group offices were cut off.

The implications of decentralization for personnel and HRM

Pressures for centralization versus decentralization create a number of choices for personnel and HRM. Ahlstrand and Purcell (1988) have defined these choices in four areas:

- What the structures for pay bargaining and managing industrial relations should be
- What kinds of internal labour market should operate, and how
- Whether or not a corporate culture should be promoted through the above (and other) means
- How the personnel function itself should be organized, as between corporate head office, the division, and plants.

Structures for pay bargaining and industrial relations

Changing industrial relations structures have been in the forefront of decentralization. Indeed, industrial relations specialists have tended to see decentralization primarily in terms of the restructuring of collective bargaining arrangements. A number of research studies have mapped these changes through the 1980s (Kinnie, 1987; Marginson *et al.*, 1988; Purcell, 1989). Arising from this, Purcell (1989) provided a set of guidelines for judging whether industrial relations should be decentralized or centralized (Table 5.1).

Table 5.1 Decentralization planning checklist

Industrial relations factors [a]	Tending towards decentralization	Tending towards centralization
Is the same union recognized throughout the company?	No, wide variety in recognition practices	Yes
Does the main union have a significant percentage of its members in the company?	No, unions are mainly general	Yes, it is an industrial/company union
Does the main union have a tradition of head office control?	No, dispersed full-time officers	Yes, head office-based full-time officers
Who does the company prefer to bargain with?	Shop steward, lay officials	National full-time officers
Is there a tradition of shop steward combined committees?	No, weak or non-existent	Yes, they are well organized
Past policy on information disclosure for collective bargaining	Restricted to local issues	Centrally controlled, local profit figures not provided
Past arrangements for bargaining in the company	Some local bargaining and bonuses, local rates	Exclusively at corporate level
Consultative committees	Well developed at local levels	Only at corporate level
Is there a history of interplant pay comparisons and coordinated industrial action?	No	Yes
Where is the final stage of internal disputes procedures?	Local level	Corporate/major division level
Do fringe benefits and conditions of service vary between units?	Yes	No, common standards apply
Are there wide variations in actual earnings and hours of work between units?	Yes	No, standard pay rates and hours of work apply
Payment systems	Numerous and complex	Simple/unified
Job evaluation	Locally based in business units	Company-wide
Are there wide variations in labour productivity between plants or areas?	Yes	No
Is there a perceived need for bonuses or incentive payments?	Yes	No
Is the corporate or major division personnel department well staffed?	No	Yes
Negotiating skills	Diffused and widespread	Concentrated

[a] Many of these factors will need to be changed with bargaining realignment.
Source: Reproduced with permission from Purcell (1989).

Changing bargaining structures, however, is fraught with difficulty because of the entrenched interests involved, and hence has often been slow to
work through. In a company like Pilkington, for example, it took the best
part of ten years from getting management committed to implementing it
across all its UK plants.

An internal labour market?

Of the four issues or 'choices', the least discussed, but the one requiring
perhaps the most subtle and skilful management, is how far an internal
labour market should operate and how it should be managed. How a firm
answers this can undermine decentralization in other areas, such as collective bargaining, while determining whether an organization gains managerial and operating synergies from its multiple parts.

Arguably, the biggest failure of diversified organizations has been in
achieving such synergies. Many companies have been more concerned with
financial synergies – that is, moving cash and capital around the organization, rather than moving people and ideas (Goold and Campbell, 1987).
Managerial and operating synergies, however, are vital in achieving organic
business growth.

An internal labour market (ILM) implies habitual patterns of movement,
vertically and laterally, within and across business and departmental boundaries, to meet promotion needs and skill requirements. Such moves themselves contribute to employee development and may be actively supported
by training programmes. Chapter 11 analyses the ILM in detail in relation
to other types of labour market. Here, it is enough to note that an ILM
implies:

- Limited points ('ports') of entry
- A well-defined job ladder
- Pay set by internal criteria which diffuse market forces
- Job-security rules
- Training that is firm-specific and on-the-job (or, more accurately, 'in
  post').

Two sub-types of the ILM can be distinguished, according to differences
in the level of security and job size. Osterman (1982) calls these sub-types
the 'industrial' and 'salaried' sub-systems. The one broadly applies to blue-
collar, manual workers and to clerical grades; the other to managerial and
technical employees. An ILM can be orchestrated by central Personnel, or
it may operate implicitly. The important thing is that the rules governing
the ILM are set within the organization itself.

In contrast, an occupational, or 'craft', system regulates training, grades,
and qualifications through external bodies – traditionally, the professions
and craft trade unions. Through these means, they also influence pay. The
point of reference in these matters therefore lies outside the organization.

It is interesting to note how companies have sought to restructure their
employment systems over the last ten years in terms of internal labour

markets and craft/occupational systems. At one level, some have tried to convert externally regulated occupation/craft systems of employment into internally regulated 'industrial' and 'salaried' arrangements. That is, jobs have been detached from external systems and sources of reference for determining pay and the acquisition of skills. A typical instance of this process is the shift away from apprenticeships to firm-specific training programmes. Related to this is 'multi-skilling'. Multi-skilling breaks down craft demarcations by adding other skills specific to the work processes of the firm. If those who are multi-skilled are non-craft workers in the first place, the shift to an 'industrial' ILM system is even more pronounced. In this way, a company gains more control over the supply and price of skills.

At another level, firms have used decentralization to loosen common rates of pay and grades by the dissolution of corporate-wide job-evaluation schemes and central bargaining. In this case, they are moving away from an ILM at the corporate level. At the same time, however, they may well be trying to create a stronger ILM at a lower level. The issue is therefore one of scope. Thus, it is necessary to distinguish between internal labour markets at the corporate, divisional, and plant level. Put another way, should employees be considered as a corporate, divisional, or plant resource?

Company policy in the 1980s turned against the corporate ILM because in recessionary conditions it reduces the flexibility and raises the costs of operating units. But an ILM at plant level is often favoured for the very same reasons, as a source of employee flexibility, cost-effectiveness, and a predictable labour supply (Osterman, 1987). Many firms have therefore become keen to draw their whole workforce into an 'industrial' form of ILM employment at plant level.

Apart from these broad trends, different employee groups can in fact fall within different ILMs. There may be a corporate ILM for managers and technical/professional staff, co-existing with plant-level ILMs for craft workers and technicians (with other low-skilled groups excluded altogether). The difficulty lies in sustaining the two systems, while keeping them separate. As we describe below, problems arise in the knock-on effects which a corporate-level ILM for one group can have on other groups, especially over pay.

ILMs are thus closely bound up with pay bargaining structures and the ability of groups to act in concert in industrial relations – as the IMI example that follows illustrates.

Transforming a craft system into an industrial ILM at IMI

'Craft' organization was entrenched at IMI on its heartland site at Witton (in Birmingham) until the early 1980s. Most of the trades were organized into a single central services department of 1200–1500 employees, serving the various businesses on the site, which the operating businesses paid for through a central budget.

Increasingly, as business conditions deteriorated, the operating units saw this as a tax or overhead. An attempt to settle pay with the trades at different rates was defeated in an eight-week strike in 1974, while their links with other craft groups on site (such as toolmakers) posed a constant threat of sympathy action in any local dispute.

When decentralization occurred between 1980 and 1983, aided by the recession, it meant breaking up this department, transferring staff into operating companies, and into one or two newly formed service companies with a specific focus (such as transport). The latter were constituted as subsidiary companies, and therefore had to earn their way by charging other IMI companies for their services. In 1983–1984 the Witton Site Joint Negotiating Council was wound up and the system of central pay negotiations was dissolved.

In this way, 'craft' arrangements were converted into 'industrial' and also 'secondary' ones through limited sub-contracting. Unlike many other organizations in the 1980s, however, IMI stopped short of fully contracting out services – retaining, for example, catering, cleaning, and certain site-maintenance functions in IMI Witton Services. Other IMI companies away from Witton, however, did choose to contract these out. In these ways, IMI operating companies gained closer control over their own pay costs, related to their own market situation.

A corporate culture?

The third area of choice around centralization and decentralization concerns corporate culture. The idea of corporate culture is itself contentious. It is dependent on things like the existence of an internal labour market, but has often been represented as if it can be waved into existence through a chief executive's 'vision'. Since Peters and Waterman (1982) popularized corporate culture as a manageable phenomenon, there has been a lot of largely speculative treatment of it in the context of decentralization (Devanna, Fombrun and Tichy, 1984; Miller, 1989). To understand the issues properly, therefore, we need to take a critical look at the whole idea of corporate culture. This we will do in Chapter 6. For now, it is interesting to note that Shell – a company noted both for its decentralization and a strong corporate culture through which it holds decentralization in check – was recently reported as having second thoughts about decentralization:

Shell UK pulls responsibility back to the centre

[Shell has] discovered that pushing decision-making down to small groups and individuals, in line with 'fashionable human resource management ideas' in the late '80s, diluted the traditional corporate culture which had proved successful in the past.

Communications suffered as business units, given more independence, became too cut off from each other and from expertise at the centre.

Shell's response over the past year has been to improve the lines of communication between business units, making them more accountable to each other and more guided by a central company culture, while keeping the basic decentralized culture.

Speaking at an *Economist* conference, John Wybrew, Shells's public affairs and planning director, said a conflict had emerged between professionals, such as accountants and engineers, and generalist executives who were concerned with fast decision-making and 'getting things done'.

In a small team, it was too easy for the professionals who represented the 'Shell way' of doing things, to find themselves losing influence.

Wybrew said that Shell started to experience over-runs on some major projects and deteriorating operational reliability.

'When we tried to get a deeper understanding of this, we began to realize that to some extent, while we had adopted some new ideas with the best of intentions, it was working against some of the fundamental principles on which our business success is based. There was a need to reassert professionalism and integrity.'

Wybrew added: 'In adopting fashionable personnel management ideas, for which there are very good reasons, you have to be careful how you integrate them into the business' (Pickard, 1992, p. 1).

Organization of the personnel function

The final issue concerns the way the personnel or HRM function itself is organized. The structure. of personnel is partly a function of changes elsewhere, in business organization and industrial relations (Sisson and Scullion, 1985); and partly an issue in its own right. Shifting the centre of gravity of the personnel function can be a difficult process (1) because a lot of the instincts of the personnel professional are towards order, equity, consistency, control; and (2) because the function's influence (especially in the industrial relations sphere) has often depended on having information, which decentralization deprives it of. As one chief executive put it: 'Personnel is one of the last remaining centralizing forces.'

Nevertheless, decentralization has had a marked effect on the role and structure of the personnel department. Torrington, Mackay and Hall (1985), for instance, believe that decentralization has tended to polarize ('attentuate') roles and activities, between senior level directors of personnel and plant-level personnel officers. Tyson and Fell's (1986) characterization of personnel management in terms of three models, or types, implies a similar difference of focus. Thus, the 'architect', 'contracts manager', and 'clerk of works' differ in their degree of involvement in strategy as opposed to routine personnel administration. Although organizations may operate just one type of personnel role, the high-level 'architect' role can also obviously co-exist with the low-level 'clerk of works' role in the same organization.

Fowler (1992a) sets out a similar set of options, which take into account the effects of decentralization and the related processes of 'delayering' (removing layers of management and specialisms). These trends have led to a certain amount of operational personnel work being devolved to line managers. As a result, the personnel/HR professional may adopt one of three possible roles:

- To undertake a wide range of *detailed* day-to-day *operational* personnel work on behalf of line managers (a role that has declined in the
  last few years)
- To provide largely *administrative support* to managers who handle
  their own operational personnel work
- To *set quality standards* for line managers' operational personnel
  activities, provide support to managers to help them meet these
  standards and monitor the results.

The last tends more towards the strategic and is more likely to mean that
the head of the HR function will be a member of the top management
team.

A further aspect of this is the degree of specialization within the function,
and how such specialists are organized. Fowler (1992a) distinguishes three
options:

- To retain personnel *specialists at the centre*, but allow operational
  divisions to negotiate the range and cost of personnel services they
  use through service-level agreements
- To keep personnel specialists executively responsible to the central
  personnel manager, but *outpost* them to work within operational
  divisions where they establish close links with line managers
- To maintain a *small central* department dealing solely with *strategic*
  (or organization-wide) issues, while operational divisions employ their
  own personnel specialists.

The first of these has been widely adopted in local government, while the
third has been the most common pattern to emerge in the private sector.
However, this bifurcation of functions within personnel can lead to three
problems. The first is how to avoid the local personnel manager/officer
seeing head office as a threat to be kept at bay. The second is how to
maintain professional standards and avoid professional isolation for those
in operating divisions or companies. The third is the difficulty in managing
career development. These problems are signalled in Torrington, Mackay
and Hall's (1985) diagnosis of 'attentuation' in the personnel role under
decentralization.

A further set of design options arise in relation to the various specialisms
(such as management development, remuneration, and industrial relations).
Fowler (1992a) identifies four different approaches:

- The *fully generalist* approach, where each division has one nominated
  central contact for all purposes
- The *fully specialist* approach, where a top central personnel team
  consists of a series of experts in different aspects of personnel (GKN
  in the past followed this model)
- A *mixed* structure, with generalists acting as the first points of contact, with some specialists they can call on for particular issues
- *Combined generalist–specialist roles* in the one person, with each
  central personnel professional providing a general service to part of

the organization, but acting additionally as a specialist on a particular subject across the whole organization.

IMI has followed the last model. A small number of central staff are responsible for a particular 'parish' (that is, a group of businesses), while each maintains also their own specialisms – in industrial relations; job evaluation/ senior remuneration/redundancy policies; management development/succession planning/staff appraisal/graduate recruitment; and external recruitment/ expatriate staff. Training, pensions, and occupational health, meanwhile, are run as separate functions.

Overcoming decentralization without overturning it

A recurring theme when considering the pros and cons of centralization and decentralization is how to offset the incipient fragmentation which decentralization brings. We have seen Shell backing away from decentralization to some extent over corporate culture, because that is one thing which holds the Group together. It also arises as an issue over whether firms should maintain group-wide, corporate internal labour markets. As we noted, by fragmenting a firm's internal labour market, decentralization can deny an organization the managerial and operating synergies on which organic growth depends.

Awareness of this as a problem has tended to be triggered by concerns over top succession (Pfeffer, 1985), and doubts over whether a company has adequate 'strength in depth' in its management to feed the top posts. In the UK, such concerns began to surface in a number of companies during the renewed growth of the late 1980s, following the heavy de-manning that had preceded it during the 1980–1982 recession.

The extent and impact of these outflows can be gauged by the example of the three companies referred to earlier – GKN, IMI, and Pilkington. Thus, GKN, in the period 1979–1987, lost over two-thirds of its 70,000 UK employees, and saw world-wide numbers drop from 105,000 to 40,000 employees. IMI and Pilkington both almost halved their UK numbers (although at Pilkington this was offset by a doubling of employees world-wide through overseas acquisitions). Such outflows included a massive haemorrhaging of management and technical skills.

As these companies then moved into an era of more confident growth and diversified into new areas, they then found they had to review the whole range of their human resource policies. Diversification and internationalization focused the need for a general management cadre with experience of more than one company, sector, and country to hold the Group together and provide succession at the very top. To support this, any corporate ILM has to begin at a much lower level. In these companies, therefore, sustaining a corporate management cadre became an active strand of Group policy from the late 1980s onwards.

In sum, therefore, the challenge such firms face is how to develop corporately inspired (and, in many cases, corporately managed) solutions which do not negate the benefits of sharper management accountability and employee motivation, which are at the heart of the decentralization philosophy. The rest of this chapter will consider the tactics firms might use to do this.

Reconciling centralization and decentralization in HRM

Table 5.2 summarizes some of the tactics employed in GKN, IMI, and Pilkington. Each of these relates to an area of personnel activity which came under close scrutiny during decentralization, and is an attempt to recover some of the benefits that accrued from centralization. The list also reflects to some extent the sequence in which these issues seemed to re-emerge. Certainly, this was the case at GKN and IMI, where the succession issue led to a revision of succession planning, management development, recruitment, and retention practices more or less in that order. At Pilkington, however, management development and recruitment strategies were

Table 5.2   Tactics for reconciling centralization and decentralization

---

Group contracts

Restrict numbers

Cap pay locally by building in 'headroom' below a centrally evaluated handful of jobs

Succession planning

Standardize appraisal practices, and compile management development register

Identify pools of talent and pools of jobs

Establish brokerage role

Management development roles

Recognize and exploit seedbeds (functions, units, lead companies, bedrock roles)

Exploit the structure of general manager roles

Rotate high flyers through career-development roles

Management development programmes and processes

Sponsor task-centred action learning

Encourage organizational learning through projects, *ad hoc* teams, and routine management contacts

Graduate recruitment and retention

Recruit into lead companies and centres

Restore limited graduate sponsorship and promote central programmes to achieve a 'settled connection'

Redefining skills

Identify common, transferable skills

---

more to the fore, because of the concern to develop a more entrepreneurial management style in a decentralized environment. The following sections consider each of these headings in turn.

Group contracts

Often when a company starts to decentralize it is careful to retain some staff on Group employment contracts held at the centre. Group contracts represent a degree of residual centralization. Their creation is an attempt to retain key managers and to create a pool, or 'cadre', from which top jobs can be filled. A limited number of managers are therefore held on a centrally determined pay structure, based on centrally evaluated jobs.

IMI, for instance, adopted the principle of Group contracts in 1974, when it started to acquire new businesses and wanted to regularize terms and conditions so that it could move staff between old and new businesses. After three years developing a job-evaluation structure and common pension arrangements, around 300 managers were offered Group contracts. GKN adopted a similar principle of a 'cadre contract' in 1978, initially with 180 staff, following the dissolution of 'sub-Groups'. At Pilkington, however, all middle and senior management (the 'B' list of 750 and 'A' list of 250) remained on centrally negotiated terms through the 1980s. The number of employment contracts held centrally in this way is thus a useful test of a company's commitment to decentralization.

The important thing is to limit the numbers on Group contracts. IMI, for instance, in 1989 had fewer than 150 such contracts for 21,000 jobs world-wide, and GKN had less than 100 out of 40,000 employees. In 1985, in fact, IMI had taken the deliberate step of raising the number of Hay points necessary to qualify for a Group contract (from 800 to 1000), thereby signalling its determination to remain decentralized. This reduced the number on Group contracts at that time from 285 to 176.

One hidden effect of operating group contracts is that, by building in a percentage differential ('headroom') between group-evaluated jobs at the top in any operating subsidiary, staff salaries locally can be effectively capped without any seeming central intervention in pay negotiations. As a manager in one company put it:

> It was felt there were many ways of skinning a cat if you wanted to control our pay structures. If you control those at the top, automatically you put a lid on pay levels. If you say to a managing director, 'you cannot pay your commercial director more than x', that commercial director is hardly likely to pay a national sales manager more than himself.
>
> When we made the decision not to use job evaluation for everybody, but confined it to the senior group, I think by then the realization had come that it was a method of control. And without stating it very explicitly at the time, it was there nevertheless – that we would control the pay centrally of the senior group, and there had to be a reasonable differential between that group and the locally employed people.

Succession planning

Thereafter, the first cracks in decentralization in these companies occurred when the inheritance from past centralization policies and from the pool of people redeployed during recession and from acquisitions started to dry up. IMI, for example, continued to benefit from recruitment into central functions carried out when it was still part of ICI long after these were disbanded and it was cut loose from ICI. Its acquisitions also brought a lot of new talent into the Group. An expanding company also has expanding needs, however, as it found when it began to encounter difficulties in making senior appointments. The immediate response, at IMI as in other companies, was to beef up succession reviews at the different levels in the organization by giving the process a stronger thrust from the centre.

In fact, IMI had a well-established system for reviewing management development and succession which it had formalized back in 1974 when it first started to decentralize. Appraisal practices were standardized and information on shortfalls and surpluses were compiled into an annual management development register which the main Board reviewed. After 1985, when signs of strain started to appear, it changed its approach by concentrating less narrowly on identifying cover for specific jobs on a one-to-five-year time horizon. This style of succession planning tends to be overtaken by events, as people leave, die, or are promoted elsewhere in the organization, and it therefore lacks credibility.

Since 1985, at IMI, pools of people are related to pools of jobs at various levels in the organization. This encourages more of a 'supply side' approach. It has more of an emphasis on action and is more likely to encourage active development of people, beyond the formalities of succession planning.

GKN began to compile a similar review in 1986, but it started from a much less developed base. Succession at GKN had tended to be managed in a highly informal way through social networks, with the Group personnel function struggling against the autonomy of operating companies. It was thus at the other extreme in managing succession, with an absence of planning. In a small organization this may work – at least people are known to one another. But in a large organization it relies heavily on social and political networks for people to be sufficiently known.

The other side to this is making sure that planned moves actually take place, in the face of pressure from operating units and divisions to hold onto their own. This is a real problem in a decentralized organization. In addition, recession encourages a tendency to block staff moves, since units that are run lean are more reluctant to see a temporary gap open up in their staffing. Recession can also encourage external recruitment of people of proven experience, in preference to taking a risk by promoting someone internally and having to wait for them to learn the job. This may, of course, be beneficial in bringing in people with outside experience and providing a leavening to an inwardly focused management development system.

In a centralized company a central personnel department often manages staff moves in a coordinated way with both their career development and the long-term needs of the organization in mind. In the absence of this kind of central 'postings' culture, ensuring that moves take place depends on a high-level 'brokerage' role being created. Both IMI and GKN found that such a role was necessary to overcome the 'baronialism' of operating units under decentralization.

A brokerage role is necessarily a task for a main board director. It cannot be done by a more junior person, and not easily by someone in the personnel function – especially where (as in both IMI and GKN) directors are active in driving the different divisions and therefore have a personal interest in the success of these. How far directors in general are absorbed into the executive role of driving businesses is therefore important in determining internal mobility overall. Another factor is the closeness and stability of the top team. Where executive directors have worked closely together as a team – as they had at IMI and GKN through the difficult early 1980s – it makes for decisions taken in the interests of the wider business. In the old GKN, with a board of seventeen in the late 1960s – more than half of whom represented operating divisions – such cohesion was lacking. The trend during the 1980s generally towards much smaller boards and mixed portfolios among directors is likely to reduce similar 'baronial' tendencies.

Management development roles

Implicitly and explicitly, centralized companies make use of certain key roles and points of entry into the organization to develop managers' experience. In the past, large specialist central functions such as engineering, R&D, and management services have fulfilled this role. With their demise, management development depends on other 'seedbeds' to provide basic learning and broadening experiences.

Some smaller central units, such as central audit and strategic planning, may still remain, allowing relatively junior personnel to gain a wider and more intense exposure to a diversified Group early in their career. In a large Group there are often 'lead' companies which, because of their own recruitment and developmental practices, provide a regular source of outward promotions, especially to strengthen or head up new acquisitions. In every company there are also 'bedrock' roles where the essential tasks of the organization are learnt and from which promotions into other areas can be made.

In addition to recognizing and exploiting these, decentralized organizations have the great advantage that they generate many more general management roles. Throughout IMI, for instance, the creation of profit-responsible roles at relatively junior levels in the organization, in companies of various sizes, is seen as a particular strength to prepare people for larger general management roles. GKN's Industrial Services division has a similar structure, with a number of companies each with many field units run as little businesses. In other companies (such as Unilever and Barclaycard) the role of brand manager performs a similar function, although not necessarily with the profit responsibility. In each case, there is a ladder of opportunity to support management development.

At the top of the ladder some organizations are defining senior positions as general manager roles in what have previously been career specialisms, and rotating high flyers through these. Interestingly, the human resource function is beginning to be used in this way by a number of companies, including GKN.

Management development programmes and processes

In-house management development has tended to become more focused on the actual problems of a business. This helps to 'contextualize' learning and make it relevant and applicable. In this way, the theory and methodology of management development, as of training generally, happen to coincide with decentralization. Paradoxically, this can also help to overcome the fragmentation effects of decentralization.

'Task-centred action learning' illustrates this point well. This is based on the idea that significant learning comes from challenging experiences (Mumford, 1987) – hence the importance of management development roles themselves which we discussed first. Learning is therefore focused on the tasks of operating units and real problems. However, it also incorporates the original concept of action learning, that the manager should work on problems in another organization outside their normal sphere of experience (Revans, 1982). By assigning people in teams to projects outside their normal area of operations, the 'task-centred action learning' process helps to transfer knowledge between parts of the organization, promotes an organizational perspective, and aids cohesion.

Pilkington has been particularly innovative in its programmes in this respect. IMI and GKN, on the other hand, have favoured short educational inputs, in line with their view that most development occurs on the job. All, however, encourage organizational learning through projects, *ad hoc* teams, and routine management contacts, in preference to the more formalized 'bureaucratic' working parties once in vogue. Real tasks are thus seen as a vehicle for learning, and are tackled in such a way as to take people across organizational boundaries. Synergies through the movement of ideas may therefore not be so dependent on people moving jobs, as we implied earlier. Certainly, many organizations take the view that short assignments are more economical and just as effective as orchestrating large-scale job mobility.

Graduate recruitment

As companies face greater competition for skilled people and find their feedstock is no longer adequate for new growth, attention is also likely to turn to initial recruitment and the retention of younger employees. All three companies described here made severe cuts in graduate recruitment during the recession of 1974/1975 and then again during 1979–1985. GKN (in 1975) and Pilkington (in 1984) abandoned recruitment of graduates into centrally administered schemes which had combined general training with degree sponsorship. IMI, on the other hand, against all its decentralist instincts, retained two such schemes from the early 1960s when it was part of ICI, before dropping one, in 1986, after a review of its cost-effectiveness.

With graduate recruitment, one problem a decentralized organization can face is the lack of a coherent, strong, corporate image, as operating companies recruit only for their own perceived immediate needs. By taking on the role of a central agent in managing UK graduate recruitment, Group personnel in all three presents something of a corporate image. However, companies in GKN, for example, can still make their own arrangements.

A second problem is how to meet long-term needs against the understandable reluctance of operating units to carry excess costs in the interests of the greater good. After a short lapse, Pilkington re-established initial graduate training, but at divisional level, thereby bringing the responsibility closer to operating level – but not too close. It also retained a modified centralized scheme for engineering graduates. Divisions pay for sponsorship of engineering students while Group engineering trains them. The reason for this is that Pilkington is not a large user of engineers and they are thinly spread among units. It is therefore easier to attract and train graduates at Group-level. Centralization thus provides economies of scale.

Such solutions will be specific to the special circumstances of companies. Thus, at GKN, a heavy concentration of graduate recruitment in two locations – its Automotive division technology centre and at Chep, its leading company in the Industrial Services division – has helped to avoid the problem that individual companies may not recruit to the Group's long-term needs. Graduate development programmes are therefore now focused on each of these, and both are used to drip-feed experienced people into other parts of each division.

Graduate retention

A related problem is retention within decentralized businesses having short career ladders. As indicated above, this has been a problem at Pilkington with engineers. Group engineering has therefore taken on the role of monitoring engineering graduates' career development, as well as providing leadership on professional standards.

At the other end of the scale, in a business based on engineering, IMI introduced an engineer development scheme to take selected graduates between the ages of 23 and 28 through to a 'settled connection', at which point they might expect to attain a significant management appointment. The key to retention here, apart from centrally organized assignments to jobs, is enhanced salary rates centrally determined but paid by the local unit. This gets round the connected problems of locally uncompetitive rates in a national market; the need to pay similar rates to people on the same centrally managed scheme as they pass through two or three different jobs; and the reluctance of operating companies to distort their own pay structures by adhering to these. While the operating unit pays the full wage costs, the assignee is effectively kept out of its grading structure.

Redefining skills

Underlying many of the remedies proposed above is the task of redefining the skill base of the organization – preferably in a way that emphasizes flexibility. In most organizations there is an implicit sense of the key skills on which success depends. During a period of change, this may also, at some point, become explicit. This is important in coping with decentralization because it can help to identify common, transferable skills which effectively provide the basis for a corporate internal labour market.

GKN and IMI have not only faced large population outflows; both have also been active in making acquisitions in new areas. Together, these have moved them away from a metallurgical to an engineering skill base. Elsewhere, growth in industrial services in GKN also represents an entirely new kind of expertise in the company, based on systems and interpersonal skills. Interestingly, both engineering and interpersonal/systems skills are inherently more flexible than metallurgical ones. At the same time, the greater emphasis on general manager roles in these organizations involves the development of commercial skills, which again are inherently flexible and enable people to adapt to shifting products and technologies and to move across boundaries. Other kinds of technical skill have a similar broad currency in other sectors, while general business skills involving the management of money, resources, and people are the *lingua franca* of modern business.

Understanding such commonalities, involving transferable attributes and aptitudes among individuals, and common organizational philosophies and work systems, effectively enlarges the internal labour market that can be mobilized for promotions and new projects. This should be a critical focus for manpower and human resource planning, and is fundamental to HRM. We will take up this theme in Chapters 9 and 10.

Summary

In this chapter we have identifed decentralization as a dominant trend in organizations in the 1980s. There is little sign of any serious reversal of this in the 1990s. We traced its origins, the choices it presents, some of the problems it can give rise to, and ways of mitigating the consequences. Thus, decentralization impacts on HRM in terms of:

- The structures for pay bargaining and industrial relations
- The operation of internal labour markets
- The existence of a corporate culture
- The organization of the personnel/HR function.

The loss of some central tasks through decentralization, such as the orchestration of central bargaining, and management of pay structures and job evaluation, along with the strengthening of others associated with staff development has produced a significant shift in the corporate personnel role.

One way it has done so is simply by freeing up time from administrative tasks to allow for developmental issues to be addressed. At IMI, for instance, simply cutting down the number of people on centrally held Group contracts reduced the time spent by Group Personnel and the Board in servicing and monitoring these contracts, while it gave the Board more time to address substantive issues of staff development. Time could be spent making succession planning work. The focus shifted from a routine paper exercise to take a broader view of the whole management population against future needs dictated by the changing shape of the business.

Decentralization can thus affect the orientation towards human resource management in both the personnel function and among senior managers. Other elements enter into any comprehensive definition of HRM, but the high-level combination of manpower planning, training and management development, supported by top-level board attention to these issues, are key components. To this extent, decentralization supports the emergence of human resource management.

However, the legacy of personnel management through an era of decentralization also determines the ability of a corporate (or divisional) function to develop a new role. It matters very much what structures and staff it retains; the systems and procedures created in the past; and the reputation it carries. Despite its role and staffing being considerably reduced, for example, the Group personnel function in IMI enjoyed exceptional stability in terms of staff, backed by a similar stability among Board directors. These have given continuity in key areas of staffing policy. The result was a survival of central personnel systems within a culture of local management accountability. The personnel function in other companies may lack this authority and continuity, and therefore the ability to devise and implement effective solutions to the strains from decentralization.

Finally, decentralization and HRM have come to be associated in two other ways. First, they share a common concern with a sharper performance focus. In many cases, decentralization has provided the structural opportunity for HRM to build on. Second, and quite simply, decentralization has shaken up entrenched systems for managing people and has created the opportunity for reinventing them anew. Having to do this wholesale is an encouragement to take a broad 'strategic' view of employment practices, and makes it possible to create them coherently. Decentralization has thus helped HRM to realize its twin goals of strategic integration around business objectives and internal coherence. Widespread decentralization over the last ten to fifteen years thus has played a major role in bringing HRM into being.

6
Corporate culture and the management of organizational change

Introduction

In the early 1980s four books were published which suggested that 'corporate cultures' could be the means to competitive advantage. Ouchi (1981) and Pascale and Athos (1981) argued that the financial success of the best Japanese and American firms depended on a strong culture which emphasized humanistic values. Peters and Waterman (1982) produced a list of eight distinctive traits which they said characterized sixty-two successful firms. Deal and Kennedy (1982) characterized corporate cultures for product-market strategies in different operating environments, emphasizing the power of values and the value of strong cultures. These key publications seemed to suggest that:

- Corporate culture matters and the right culture can lead to better performance
- Corporate culture as a tangible phenomenon can be changed.

The significance of this to HRM is that culture is clearly to do with people and is formed by things that the HR function can influence. Recognizing this, Fombrun (1983) introduced culture (in the form of a 'dominant value') as an output variable into the model of the human resource cycle.

At the same time, many organizations have been encouraged to try to change their cultures to embody ideals such as customer service, quality, high performance, and (most recently) continuous learning. As a result, there is a developing body of experience as to the best ways to bring about organizational change. One lesson from this is that corporate cultures are hard to change. It is important therefore to be clear about what culture is, so that we know what we can change, what we need to change, and what may be relatively impervious to change.

With this in mind, this chapter will consider four themes:

1 What is the evidence that the 'right' corporate culture leads to measurable success in performance? – More bluntly, does corporate culture matter?
2 What do we mean by culture, and what does it consist of?

3 Can corporate culture be changed?
4 What do we know about how to create cultural change?

Does corporate culture matter?

Before we even define an organizational or corporate culture, it is useful to ask first, 'does culture matter?' Can it affect performance? In what way? How can we know? Although this might seem a back-to-front way of proceeding, it throws up some fundamental issues about the nature of culture itself. Siehl and Martin's (1990) critique of research on the culture–performance link (in a paper entitled 'Organizational culture: a key to financial performance?') is a good starting point. Their comments are worth summarizing, not only because they throw doubt on the link with performance but because they allow us to see how complex and difficult changing an entire organization's culture is likely to be.

First, when people do research on culture, there are three things they look at:

- Formal practices (such as structure, job descriptions, and written policies)
- Informal practices (for example, behavioural norms)
- Artifacts (such as rituals, stories, jargon, humour, and physical arrangements, including the way people dress, external architecture, and interior design).

Mostly, researchers tend to focus on one of these and ignore the other two. Such research is 'specialist', rather than the 'generalist' research which tries to capture a wide range of features that express a culture.

Second, researchers typically try to describe cultures in terms of content themes, especially if they are trying to compare organizations in relation to success criteria. Thus, a formal practice like team structure may be seen as expressive of an egalitarian culture. It may be supported by informal practices, such as the use of first names between boss and subordinate and open expression of differences, and by artifacts like a single canteen. However, the choice of content themes is usually relatively superficial and value-laden (according to Siehl and Martin), centring on themes such as the need for innovation, egalitarianism, a holistic concern for employee well-being, or the importance of 'bottom-line' profitability.

Third, there is a big difference between what people say they do or think, and what they actually do (Deutscher, 1973). It is important to get below the surface, then, of people's 'espoused' views, to see culture 'enacted' in behaviour. This points to the need for in-depth study in which the researcher gets close to the organization over a period of time. Although this adds to the general criticism that much observation of culture is relatively superficial, those who belong to a particular organization do, of course, have such in-depth knowledge already. On the other hand, senior managers often have remarkably distorted views of what people lower down think and how they behave, and vice versa. In this sense, we are all 'researchers', and all encounter perceptual barriers to knowing what really goes on.

Fourth, and most important of all, there is a tendency among many researchers to take account just of those cultural features which are consistent with one another. The result is to present an organization as if it has a single, unambiguous corporate-wide culture. This is all the more likely to happen if the researcher has started out by measuring culture in terms of some limited value-laden categories like innovativeness or performance-orientation. This leads to stereotypical portrayals of 'innovative cultures', performance cultures', and so forth.

An entirely different stance is to question the existence of organization-wide consensus and treat an organization as a series of distinct sub-cultures that develop round functions, occupations, hierarchy, and even friendship groups. All of us have multiple affiliations, including those we bring from outside. Any factory or business with strong local ties will recognize this. Managers in such firms will be acutely aware of how differently 'people round here' behave, and how employees loyalties may be divided between company and community. Recognizing sub-cultures allows for the exploration of conflicts and inequalities, and understanding how differences of perception occur.

These two standpoints reflect, respectively, an 'integration' and a 'differentiation' perspective. Siehl and Martin also describe a third (the 'ambiguity' paradigm) which challenges the very idea of culture as a coherent phenomenon at either the corporate or sub-cultural level. In practice, researchers (that is, outsiders) tend to adopt just one of these viewpoints, when in reality an organization might exhibit some organization-wide consistency and consensus, some inconsistencies and sub-cultural groupings, and some inescapable ambiguities.

Culture and performance

Against this background, Siehl and Martin then go on to review what we know about the link between performance and culture. Most of the research that claims to have found such links is limited in various of the above ways, especially in adopting a view of the organization as one culture (the integrationist perspective). The two things to note are how studies differ on the nature of the culture–performance link, and the validity of the research methods used.

'Strong' cultures

The four studies by Ouchi (1981), Pascale and Athos (1981), Peters and Waterman (1982), and Deal and Kennedy (1982) all argue that the key to success (defined in terms of financial profitability) is a 'strong' culture – one where all employees share the same view of the firm. For Ouchi and Pascale and Athos, this is a culture which is strong on certain humanistic values, such as consensual decision making and treating employees well as a long-term investment for the business. Peters and Waterman (1982, p. 89), on the other hand, include both humanistic values and values related to the market in their 'eight attributes of management excellence' (see Table 6.1).

Table 6.1 Eight attributes of management excellence

Managing ambiguity and paradox
A bias for action
Close to the customer
Autonomy and entrepreneurship
Productivity through people
Hands-on, values-driven
Stick to the knitting
Simple form, lean staff
Simultaneous loose-tight properties

Source: Peters and Waterman (1982).

The Peters and Waterman study used a fairly large sample of sixty-two financially successful firms across six industries that were considered to be excellent but did not attempt any comparison with unsuccessful firms. We therefore do not know whether unsuccessful firms might have had the same kind of cultures. They relied on interviews, and therefore captured 'espoused' values rather than behaviours, and they talked to managers and to employees largely selected by management. It is therefore very possible they got a picture of how top managers would like to see their organizations rather than the way they actually were. These methodological weaknesses may account for the fact that many of the sixty-two firms have since fallen from favour in the public eye and suffered a decline in performance (*Business Week*, 1984; Hitt and Ireland, 1987; see also Wilson, 1992, pp. 72–78).

Another study (Denison, 1984), using a more stringent methodology, also argued for the benefits of a 'strong' culture specifically characterized by a high degree of participativeness. This study claimed that such a culture was effective regardless of the state of the business environment or strategy being pursued. However, in a follow-up study with the same thirty-four firms, long-term performance had suffered in those with strong cultures (Denison, 1990).

Most of this work is American, and the values claimed to enhance performance are ones which have been trumpeted by American management gurus for many years. One rare European study that attempted to find a correlation between particular sets of values and performance could find no association (Calori and Sarnin, 1991).

'Congruent' cultures

The Denison (1984) study flies in the face of one of the dominant ideas in the management literature of the last thirty years – that successful organizations develop a structure (and a culture which the structure generates) which is contingent upon the nature of the external environment (Burns and Stalker, 1966). Often, this assumes that an appropriate strategy is also being pursued, so that strategy becomes a mediating variable between environment and structure–culture.

In studies of culture and performance, there are two main variants of contingency theory, (1) those which claim higher performance where a firm has a culture that is congruent with its strategy, and, less commonly, (2) those which address the relationship between culture and environment directly. The strategic approach to HRM analysed in Chapter 4 and typified by Fombrun, Tichy and Devanna (1984) and Schuler (1989) is built upon the assumption that culture, through HRM, should be congruent with business strategy. Similarly, Harrison's (1972) and Handy's (1976) well-known characterization of organizational 'ideologies' or 'cultures' argues that there are appropriate cultures for different operating situations. The case example featuring Don Valley Joinery at the end of this chapter outlines three of these – the power, role, and task cultures.

Unfortunately, evidence that 'congruent cultures' matter is mostly confined to short, anecdotal case studies of single organizations. One study with a large sample of seventy-two organizations, undertaken by Siehl and Martin themselves, found no evidence at all to support a contingency relationship between culture and financial performance (Martin, Anterasian and Siehl, 1988).

Does culture not matter, then?

It might appear from this, if the evidence for a culture–performance link is weak, that organizational culture does not matter. This does not follow, however.

Culture matters, but not as we know it

First, in defence of the claims above, we should note that Fombrun, Tichy and Devanna (1984) only argue for culture and HRM being aligned with strategy in very general terms. They do not say *what* form this should take. Although Handy (1976) is more specific, his is a 'pragmatic' and descriptive model only intended to indicate in broad outline a tendency for certain patterns to occur. Its appeal is due to the 'face validity' these patterns have for many people (that is, we recognize these patterns from our own experience).

Second, there are other versions of the contingency argument which may be valid. Barney (1986), for instance, suggested that organizational culture may be a factor in competitive advantage only when it is different from that in other companies, and difficult to imitate. A moment's thought will show the sense of this. If there is a 'one best way' culture (as Peters and Waterman suggested), what happens if every firm succeeds in adopting it?

A business sector can only support so many firms, so 'excellent' firms must also fail. Although Peters (1988) subsequently argued that there is no one best way to be excellent, other than to 'thrive on chaos', this also is a cultural value, and only so many imbued with this can succeed.

The theory of congruent cultures leads in the same direction. Business sectors tend to converge round similar strategic 'recipes' (Grinyer and Spender, 1979; Huff, 1982) – competing on price, for example, as the industry matures. This would imply that firms' cultures will emphasize similar values. In practice, however, sectors are characterized by 'strategic groups', with some firms deviating from the majority. Within these, there will also be 'lead' firms which are more successful. This is likely to be due not to the particular strategy, structure, or culture, where there are pressures for convergence at either the sector or sub-sectoral level, but to the unique combinations which particular firms have put together. Success, in other words, is due not to external 'congruence' but to internal 'consistency' (Child, 1977, 1984; Pettigrew and Whipp, 1991).

There is also a third possibility that a 'strong' culture will matter more under certain conditions, to hold an organization together in the face of difficulties. Conversely, a strong culture can create 'organizational myopia' which stops members perceiving dangers or opportunities in the external environment. Ultimately, strong cultures are their own ruin (Dennison, 1990). IBM may prove to be a spectacular instance of this. The proof that culture matters is when people can clearly see that the organizational culture is getting in the way of needed change.

Understand culture, but don't think you can measure it

Culture matters, then, but not necessarily as we are accustomed to seeing it, and not as performance studies try to measure it. The big mistake, according to Siehl and Martin (1990), is the very idea that we should be trying to measure culture against performance. The problem is a practical one, that it is almost impossible to test such a relationship. Testing culture against performance requires:

- A large sample of organizations to develop proper comparisons
- Attention to formal and informal practices, including behaviour, and artifacts
- Exploring these in some depth to reveal the complexity in culture, and cultures
- Going beyond just what people say.

The quantitative measures which some researchers have developed (among them, Martin and Siehl) for comparing organizations lack the necessary breadth, depth, and richness.

On the performance side, also, a wide range of factors rarely controlled for (such as market structure and competitiveness) should be taken into account. Even then, to establish any causal link between culture and performance would need longitudinal study. It is quite possible, for example, that humanistic cultures are a result of financial success, rather than the other way round. Short-term measurement of performance, moreover, is liable to miss the impact of longer-term cultural processes that encourage innovativeness.

Gathering data to this extent is simply too demanding in time, people, and money. Unless we recognize these problems, we are simply not taking culture seriously enough. Part of the problem is, indeed, that people want an easy and quick handle on culture because they see it as a way of controlling other people without appearing to. Culture is treated as a 'soft' form of control. Research which derives its view of culture simply from the ideologies espoused by top managers is thus doing no more than pandering to an ideal of managerial control. In the end, however, because it is superficial in its grasp of culture, it is unlikely to be able to deliver real cultural control:

> An implicit managerial bias leads many researchers to continue to advocate and pursue this relationship in spite of a glaring lack of empirical support and potentially insurmountable difficulties in getting reliable data (Siehl and Martin (1990, p. 274).

Corporate culture does matter then, but precisely how it affects performance is difficult to demonstrate or even be sure of. Above all, it is a complex phenomenon which is not changed by one-dimensional approaches.

What is corporate culture?

If culture is a complex phenomenon what does it consist of? Unfortunately, culture tends to be one of those rag-bag terms that all sorts of things get dumped into. Smircich (1983) has gone so far as to call it 'a metaphor for organizational life' because it is so all-embracing.

It is useful to see culture as existing at a number of levels – from core beliefs at one extreme, to a range of visible manifestations such as the artifacts Siehl and Martin (1990) refer to. Behaviour comes somewhere between these. Different writers emphasize different aspects. With this goes a stress on the different functions that culture performs.

Culture as basic assumptions

Edgar Schein (1983) uses a restrictive definition, arguing that:

> Culture is not the overt behaviour or visible artifacts that one might observe if one were to visit the company. It is not even the philosophy or value system which the founder may articulate or write down in various 'charters'. Rather it is the assumptions which lie behind the values and which determine the behaviour patterns and the visible artifacts such as architecture, office layout, dress codes, and so on.

This perspective emphasizes the basic assumptions that drive and guide behaviour. It has the virtue of being focused on what produces action and outcomes, rather than on extraneous external features. Above all, basic assumptions reflect past learning about how to deal with problems, outside and inside the group, in order to cope and adapt. Culture in this sense provides a short cut to action. In business strategy, for instance, where many problems are novel and ill-structured (that is, present themselves obscurely and opaquely), 'cultural products mediate or substitute for rationality in strategic decision making' (Shrivastava, 1985, p. 105).

According to Schein, the learning that is embodied in culture comes about either through dealing with threats (the 'trauma' model) or through 'positive reinforcement' of successful behaviours. The resulting assumptions become embedded and develop into habitual behaviours. Individuals, groups, organizations, and whole societies can develop assumptions and habits. The primary significance of a culture from this point of view is what it is about – the attitudes, values and beliefs that people hold:

> All social groups have to deal with issues about what they are trying to do together, who has power, authority, responsibility etc, how different roles will be done, what rewards and sanctions will apply and for what values, behaviours etc, and ultimately they have to deal with why these purposes and social processes are the ones to value and adopt (Payne, 1991, p. 28).

It is understandable, then, why the type of organizational culture is of such interest, in terms of basic themes such as how egalitarian, how democratic, how humanistic it is.

Culture as the communication of meaning

A second group are concerned with the symbolic properties of culture. They emphasize what Pettigrew (1979, p. 574) has called 'the expressive social tissue' that gives meaning to activity. The focus here is on symbols, the language used in organizations, beliefs, ideologies, visions, stories, rituals, ceremonial acts, people as role models even, and myths. All these emphasize the person as 'a creator and manager of meaning' (Pettigrew, 1979, p. 572). These are not incidental or trivial, but recognize the powerful role which symbolic expression plays in human society in promoting values and emotional attachments (Deal and Kennedy, 1982).

For example, myths and stories reinforce the solidarity and stability of a system by linking current situations with the past, offering explanations, and giving legitimacy to social practices. They help to preserve the assumptions and beliefs that Schein talks about. Ideologies provide justifications and thereby link attitudes to action. In their different ways, these symbolic processes provide a set of 'cognitive coping mechanisms' (Johnson, 1990, p. 186). Culture gives people a 'cognitive map' with which to understand and influence behaviour, and a social justification for what they are doing through shared beliefs. Such processes, moreover, by helping to express and sustain values have a close affiliation with political processes.

The 'interpretive' perspective (Risto, 1990; Silverman, 1970) on culture is concerned, then, with two key themes:

- With the way people interpret and legitimize their behaviour to themselves and others
- With the processes by which culture is communicated and shared.

Attention to these makes us aware that culture is a communal thing; that individuals are partly created by the cultures they participate in, but also recreate that culture and can change it. Culture (and society) in the last resort is people. Culture can therefore be contested, negotiated, and changed.

As a result, this perspective has important things to say about the processes of change in organizations – for instance, how people can be made conscious of the need for change; how energy and purpose get mobilized around objectives and strategies; and how systems of management and leadership are overturned or established (Pettigrew, 1979).

Culture as structure

A third group pays particular attention to the structural elements of organization (job roles, organization structure, planning and information systems, written policies, human resource systems) because of their capacity to constrain and channel behaviour. Handy's (1976) 'cultures and structures' model is an example of this, while HRM is naturally drawn to the potential of HR systems for creating cultural coherence.

Whereas the emphasis was previously on creating legitimacy, the emphasis here is much more on the power of culture to exercise control. Part of this lies in the recognition that many structural elements are both normative and coercive. They involve real material sanctions and rewards, alongside attempts to foster willing identification (Child, 1977, 1984).

An holistic view of culture

Johnson (1990, p. 187) has combined the elements from these three perspectives into an overall model representing 'the cultural web of an organization' (see Figure 6.1). The 'interpretive' and 'structural' elements on the outside (Risto, 1990) contribute to, hold in place, and reproduce the central set of beliefs, or 'paradigm', which corresponds to Schein's 'basic assumptions'. Together, they provide the normative glue that holds an organization together. An obvious implication is that changing fundamental beliefs is likely to mean tackling more than one factor, and doing so on a number of levels.

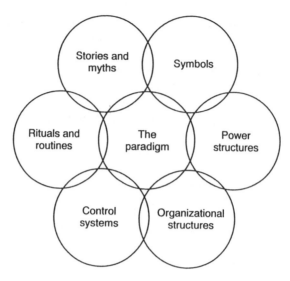

Figure 6.1 *The cultural web of an organization. (Source: Johnson, 1990)*

Can corporate culture be changed?

Can corporate culture be changed, then? In many ways, the very idea of organizational culture is peculiarly American, and the idea that you can change it even more so (Adler and Jelinek, 1986; Laurent, 1986). It embodies American cultural norms of dominance and freewill, and the belief in being able to control and manipulate the natural world:

> Fundamental to the organization culture concept is the belief that top management can create, maintain, and change the culture of an organization . . . Management's influence is seen as capable of changing or erasing other influences on employees' behaviour . . . work environment influences are seen to dominate private life conditioning . . . Moreover, employees are seen as capable of changing; and change, in and of itself, is basically good (Adler and Jelinek, 1986, p. 82)

In the UK and other European countries, by comparison, 'tradition' counts for more, and external affiliations may have a greater influence on individual behaviour than in the more culturally diverse and less recently stabilized US society (Thomas, 1985).

In recent years, this issue has come to the fore with the idea that multinational companies can create an international corporate culture which transcends national differences. On the one side there are those who suggest it is possible and desirable (Evans, Lank and Farquhar; 1989; Bartlett and Ghoshal, 1989; Barham and Oates, 1991). On the other, there are those who regard it as undesirable and unachievable (Hofstede, 1980, 1991; Laurent, 1986). Both the latter have conducted extensive empirical studies which show the persistence of national characteristics even among managers who are most exposed to the cosmopolitan influences of large multinationals.

This debate is part of a more general one about the relative impact on behaviour of societal culture compared with factors such as organization structure, technology, and size. The conclusion in each case is likely to be somewhere between – that organizational culture can moderate the influence of society on individual behaviour.

The ethics of corporate culture change

There is one more fundamental question that we should ask, however, before looking at examples of culture change and some lessons for managing change. Should culture be a focus of deliberate attempts to shape it? As citizens and employees, we should all have an interest in the ethics of culture change. The new interest in corporate responsibility and governance makes this a legitimate public question once again.

In a polemical piece, Willmott (1993) argues that the idea of corporate culture and culture change is dangerous because it seeks to erode the ability of individuals to assess the meaning and worth of a range of competing value-standpoints. A 'strong' culture is one which excludes rival ends or values which could result in a mis-direction of employees' efforts. This is bad for individual autonomy and sense of identity, and if successful results in employees being 'trapped in a vicious circle of cynicism and dependence' (p. 518). Thus, the offer of 'meaning as well as money' (Peters and Waterman, 1982, p. 323) is an attempt to subsume personal identity in the organization:

> Culture Excellence is a struggle for identities, an attempt to enable all sorts of people, from highest executive to lowliest shop-floor employee, to see themselves reflected in the emerging conception of the enterprising organization and thus to come increasingly to identify with it (du Gay, 1991, pp. 53–54).

At root, it is a way of managing the indeterminacy of people as employees – much as Taylorism sought to do but by different (normative) means. It is notable, for example, that the cultural excellence phenomenon has been inspired by Japan which is seen (admired?) as a highly disciplined society.

Finally, certain of the favourite values espoused in the corporate culture movement operate through a kind of Orwellian 'doublethink' and 'new-speak'. Thus, values like 'respect for the individual' involve a simultaneous affirmation and negation of autonomy. Since respect for the individual is equated with the values of the corporate culture, such a value cannot be challenged by the individual, and hence infringes autonomy. This is the way totalitarianism works.

Willmott's may be an unduly pessimistic view. The issue of autonomy versus control, as we have noted previously, is fundamental to organizations and there is liable always to be ambivalence about any corporate value which professes to elevate or 'empower' the individual. There is also inevitably an uncertain dividing line between legitimacy and control. One person's legitimation is to another person an attempt to control.

The objective of firms when they seek employee commitment is to gain it willingly. A 'strong' culture is effective in controlling people precisely because it is willingly shared by the members themselves (Payne, 1991). It relies on self-control (supported by peer-group control), rather than on an imposed set of values. Much of the interest in corporate culture is thus its ability to gain general employee commitment.

Equally, however, people will often disagree about the best way to achieve common goals. They will engage in attempts to gain legitimacy for their own view of how things should be done. An organization may, of course, have a culture which legitimizes dissent and constructive disagreement. On the other hand, one which has such a strong culture that few people feel inclined to dissent may be better off in the long run without that corporate culture. A 'culture' is therefore double-edged if it totally absorbs people and produces a high degree of conformity, because in the end it is self-defeating.

We can take heart from two facts. First, a system of ideology and rewards as strong as Communism was supposed to disintegrate virtually overnight. Second, the view of culture as a system of meaning subject to legitimation practices means corporate culture can be contested, negotiated and changed – from within, from without, and from below. More powerful than culture as a system of values in many ways is the system of overt rewards, punishments, and controls.

Managing cultural change

By now, we should have a realistic sense of how far cultural change is possible. Nevertheless, in recent years, inspired by 'corporate excellence' prescriptions, many organizations and their chief executives have embarked on cultural change programmes at great cost and no little disruption. HR functions have often been willing accomplices in spearheading these programmes. In this final section we will review the issues in cultural change programmes and summarize some of the more general lessons in managing the dynamics of organizational change.

The fallacy of programmatic change

One American study conducted over a number of years which compared approaches to organizational change describes the 'fallacy of programmatic change'. Programmatic change typically is initiated and led from the top, and from corporate HQ. It focuses on attitudes and values, and tries to change them directly. When one programme doesn't work, senior managers will try another:

> Buzzwords like 'quality', 'participation', 'excellence', 'empowerment', and 'leadership' become a substitute for a detailed understanding of the business (Beer, Eisenstat and Spector, 1990, p. 161).

Such programmes become a kind of 'magic bullet' to spread change rapidly through large organizations. The problem is that they drain energy away from efforts to solve core business problems. The succession of these programmes, moreover, inhibits change in the long run by promoting scepticism and cynicism:

> Most change programmes don't work because they are guided by a theory of change that is fundamentally flawed. The common belief is that the place to begin is with the knowledge and attitudes of individuals. Changes in attitudes, the theory goes, lead to changes in individual behaviour ... According to this model, change is like a religious conversion experience ...
>
> This theory gets the change process exactly backward. In fact, individual behaviour is powerfully shaped by the organizational roles that people play. The most effective way to change behaviour, therefore, is to put people into a new organizational context, which imposes new roles, responsibilities, and relationships on them. This creates a situation that, in a sense, 'forces' new attitudes and behaviours on people (Beer, Eisenstat and Spector, 1990, p. 159).

The authors are alluding here to a long-standing debate in the change literature – which is more effective in creating organizational change, a techno-structural approach (focused on organization structures, technology, and systems) or a socio-cultural approach (targeted on attitudes, perceptions, and values)? In fact, they recognize that structural change on its own is also not enough. Programmatic change does not work because it typically fails to tackle three interrelated structural-cum-attitudinal factors – the requirement for coordination through teamwork, the need for commitment, and the need to develop new competencies. Company-wide change programmes address one only or, at best, two of these. Culture change programmes in particular dwell on the creation of commitment, but only at a very superficial level.

These criticisms are echoed by Pettigrew (1989). The weakness of programmatic change is that:

- It starts with 'global', often long-term issues that are not on the 'critical path' of the business
- It tends to rely heavily on educational and training interventions which create unrealistic expectations
- It encourages representational learning (through language) rather than behavioural learning (through doing)
- It is often driven by an exclusive project team, rather than ownership being spread to the organization at large
- It is insensitive to sub-unit differences and cultures
- It sets up a tension between what people say and what they do, and encourages cynicism
- It is vulnerable to changes in the business environment and changing priorities
- It is vulnerable to changes in personnel, as sponsors move on and cynics reassert themselves.

Quality change programmes

Among programmatic approaches in recent years Total Quality Management (TQM) has been a particular favourite. It tackles quality on an organization-wide basis by seeking to instill an obsessive concern for quality service to outside customers, coupled with a philosophy that each function is both a supplier and a customer to other functions within the business. There are a number of variants, each with its own guru – including Deming (the father of the quality movement), Crosby, and Juran. The principles are often wholly admirable and the techniques on their own often provide a solid foundation to improved performance.

Deming's use of statistical process control (SPC), for instance, provides a sound methodology for identifying and analysing variance in quality, and has been widely adopted in its own right. His insistence on respect for the human being and allowing the knowledge and skill of people full play remains a refreshing message:

> The system must have an aim; everybody must know about it. Who depends on him, whom he depends on. That's the joy in work ... [They've] done a good job, and have a chance to do it. That's all people ask for (Deming – the video).

Deming's core message – the need to drive out fear in the workplace and make use of people' instinct to cooperate – is attractive and consistent. It leads, among other things, to a deep opposition to performance-based pay, which he sees as divisive and illogical. There will always be variations between people, with someone at the top and someone at the bottom, especially in a reward–appraisal system which ranks people. The aim must be to enhance the performance of all, not of the few. Together, Deming's fourteen principles (see Table 6.2) provide a coherent programme of action.

Table 6.2 Deming's fourteen principles

1 Constancy of purpose
2 Adopt the new philosophy
3 Cease dependence on mass inspection
4 Cease doing business on price tag alone
5 Continual improvement of process
6 Institute training on the job
7 Institute leadership
8 Drive out fear
9 Break down barriers between departments
10 Eliminate slogans, exhortations, and targets
11 Eliminate numerical quotas
12 Eliminate all barriers that inhibit the worker's right to pride in workmanship
13 Institute a programme of self-improvement
14 Do it

Many have been widely adopted and have transformed the approach to quality in manufacturing. Moreover, he stresses that there is no quick fix. Quality is a way of thinking which cannot be attained overnight.

The problem with TQM is not so much its message as the manner in which it gets implemented. Deming's principles imply a long-term effort – 'constancy of purpose' is his first principle – and the implication that development needs to start from within. In the hands of consultants, however, it can easily acquire a top-down, quick-fix character. Some commentators have also criticized the tendency to rely too much on 'leadership' to instill these new virtues, and too little on building in structural and procedural change (Wilson, 1992, pp. 96–103). In this respect, a comparison between TQM and the BS 5750 route to quality is instructive:

> At the risk of over-simplification, it can be said that TQM is concerned with culture, while BS 5750 is about systems. TQM emphasizes the importance of attitudes: the generation of enthusiasm and commitment to quality from top to bottom of the organization. BS 5750 (or ISO 9000 to quote the international standard) places the emphasis on effective, documented systems and procedures. At the extremes, TQM enthusiasts criticize BS 5750 for the bureaucracy of its documentation and certification criteria, while BS proponents dismiss TQM as little more than missionary zeal. A more balanced view is that enthusiasm without a framework of procedure is as likely to be as ineffective as systems operated without commitment (Fowler, 1992b: p. 30).[1]

TQM thus illustrates the criticism of Beer and his colleagues (1990) of programmatic cultural change which begins with the attitudes of individuals. Where the method of introducing TQM relies also on a 'big bang' educational approach, it also exhibits many of the weaknesses listed by Pettigrew (1989) above. The critical factor must be how closely such an initiative is tied into core business issues of the moment – that is, whether it is on the 'critical path'. The case study featuring Barclaycard in Chapter 7 describes how one organization implemented TQM programmatically.

Managing change through the 'critical path'

Drawing on case examples of successful organizational change, Beer, Eisenstat and Spector (1990) identify six steps (which they call 'task alignment') that avoid the shortcomings of programmatic change. These are:

1 *Mobilize commitment to change through joint diagnosis of business problems.* The emphasis is on 'business problems'. In this way, change will make a tangible difference and any initiatives resulting will be seen as relevant. The joint diagnosis ensures that problems identified are 'owned' by a core group of people, and therefore that any commitment to action has more chance of taking off.

2 *Develop a shared vision of how to organize and manage for competitiveness.* The point of this is to start to prepare people for new roles and responsibilities, but without prematurely defining these and creating resistance. The aim is to start information flowing in new ways and more freely within an *ad hoc* structure, so that when new roles are

defined, people have already begun to get accustomed to new patterns of communication.

3 *Foster consensus for the new vision, competence to enact it, and cohesion to move it along.* Strong leadership at the top now comes into play to maximize commitment. Roles, responsibilities, and relationships in the core group are now more clearly defined, and help to foster new skills and attitudes. Specific skill development may also be required. Now, but not before, is the time to replace those managers who cannot adapt.

4 *Spread revitalization to all departments without pushing it from the top.* This is the stage in which the details of new roles are worked out, function by function. The important thing is to let each department work out its own structure within the overall framework.

5 *Institutionalize revitalization through formal policies, systems, and structures.* Institutional systems like IT, planning, and financial reporting can now be adapted to the emerging work organization.

6 *Monitor and adjust strategies in response to problems in the revitalization process.* This ensures that change prompts continuing learning. Like the process at the beginning, monitoring too should be a shared activity.

This process is a generalized one. It might seem unrelated to cultural change, but the point is that the authors see cultural change as a consequence of structural change, never as a stand-alone strategy. Culture cannot be usefully targeted for change in isolation. Embracing these six steps, the key lessons for large-scale organizational change are:

- Start at the periphery in a plant or division away from corporate headquarters, so that change begins at the grass-roots
- Focus energy for change on the work itself, not on abstractions
- Create *ad hoc* organizational arrangements to solve these concrete business problems
- Recognize that the role of senior managers initially is limited to
  (a) creating a climate for change (by setting exacting standards, and holding managers accountable for fundamental changes in the way they use human resources); and
  (b) spreading lessons from successes and failures (while giving support to units that are innovative and offer the best prospects of success)
- However once grass-roots change reaches a 'critical mass', senior corporate managers need to be active in bringing organization-wide systems into alignment
- In this way change starts at the periphery and moves steadily towards the core of the organization.

This model of change, then, is a step-by-step, incremental one, relying on commitment developed from the bottom-up, and the development of role models to spread it. Change is cemented locally by structural means, and protected corporately by the alignment of systems.

Other writers on change stress many of the same features – role modelling; the 'coercive' power of redefined roles and responsibilities in getting people to work differently; bringing reward systems into alignment to support new definitions of role; etc. (Beckhard and Harris, 1987; Tichy, 1983).

The political and cultural management of change

In our earlier discussion of culture we distinguished the idea of 'culture as structure' and 'culture as the communication of meaning'. The prescriptions for change set out above clearly belong with the 'culture as structure' approach. In some ways, however, it is a rather narrow view of the change process. It is focused on putting change into effect (the implementation phase), rather than on getting it going. If we look at the process of change in its fullest sense, changing attitudes and perceptions plays an important part in starting the process off and moving it along.

Change is not just about better or worse ways of doing things but about ideas, interests, and commitments. Any change has to dislodge existing patterns of these. This may well involve a competition to legitimate one's own ideas and actions and delegitimate those of opponents (Pettigrew, 1987). There is often therefore an important phase which precedes any ostensible change, in which existing assumptions are challenged and questioned. The father of change theory, Kurt Lewin (1952), described this as the 'unfreezing' stage.

Johnson (1990) and Pettigrew (1987) relate various strategems for shaking confidence in the existing 'paradigm' and eroding set beliefs. These involve a mix of symbolic events and activities (like ridiculing the dominant culture) and 'structural' innovations (like shuffling people and portfolios). Johnson (1990) has extended this symbolic and political view of change and identified other behaviours appropriate to the second and third stages of Lewin's three-stage model of the change process – unfreezing, change, and refreezing.

As it is concerned with meaning and how people perceive things, the 'symbolic' perspective on culture helps to focus attention on the uses of communication in change. It draws attention to such things as the role of opinion formers and the value of converting them early on; the messages that can be conveyed by acts and objects that enter organizational folklore; and the need to 'walk the talk' to reinforce what people say by what they do.

The role of visionary leaders

It is impossible to talk about the symbolic and political management of change without considering the role of leaders. Many writers have commented on how leaders play an important symbolic role, not only in getting change going but also in sustaining organizational cultures. In the America of the 1980s, this translated into the idea of 'transformational' leaders who created strong corporate cultures with values in their own image. The implication (made explicit in the writings of people like Tom Peters) was that heroic leaders were needed to break the mould of bureacracy and management method into which American organizations had sunk.

Deal and Kennedy's *Corporate Culture: The Rites and Rituals of Corporate Life* (1982) (incidentally dedicated to Tom Peters) captures this mood:

> If values are the soul of the culture, then heroes personify those values and epitomize the strength of the organization. Heroes are pivotal figures in a strong culture. Like a John Wayne or a Burt Reynolds in pinstripes, they create the role models for employees to follow . . . They do things everyone else wants to do but is afraid to try. Heroes are symbolic figures whose deeds are out of the ordinary, but not too far out. They show – often dramatically – that the ideal of success lies within human capacity (p. 37).

And again:

> It is time American industry recognized the potential of heroes. If companies would treat people like heroes even for a short time, they might end up being heroes. Employee motivation is a complex science, but its foundations rest on the simple recognition that we all need to feel important in some phase of our lives . . . Quality circles, management by objectives (MBO), organizational charts, and concepts are useful, but they cannot influence behaviour the way a hero can (p. 57).

This kind of writing and view of management has been criticized and lampooned. For most of the time, management is not exercised in symbolic ways, even during periods of change. Tushman, Newman and Romanelli (1985), for instance, see leadership being more concerned with symbolic activities when change is *less* abrupt, and more immersed in the detail when radical change occurs. Simons (1991) likewise emphasizes the obvious but overlooked fact that new chief executives will seek to get their hands round the control systems of an organization as quickly as possible in order to impose their way of doing things. On the other hand, as we saw, Beer, Eisenstat and Spector (1990) describe top management becoming more active in details later on, after early climate-setting (although part of that climate-setting is to set standards and establish accountabilities).

The point, though, is that Deal and Kennedy are writing not about management but about leadership. A person may operate in both ways. What they are saying is that there is not enough real leadership and not enough appreciation of symbolism in organizations. They remind us that corporate culture is also fun. The deeds of heroes and their values are perpetuated by stories. People who tell stories gain power and influence because they can change reality. The vitality of working groups is marked by the rites and rituals they invent (although these can become a trap if they become sterile or people try to transplant them into other cultures).

In many ways Deal and Kennedy (1982) come closer to the patterns of behaviour which we most readily recognize in organizations. Their types of culture – like the 'tough-guy macho culture' to be found in police departments, construction gangs, advertising, sports, management consulting, venture capital, and so on – are ones we recognize (if only from the television). They reflect the vast range of organizational settings that exist. Above all, they put their finger on two factors which determine the dynamism of a culture and organization – the degree of risk associated with its activities, and the speed with which the organization and its employees get feedback on whether strategies and activities have been successful. They start with market realities. In contrast, more formal typologies, like the 'cultures and structures' model, begin with internal structures and power distribution, and only end with what this means in the market or environment (see, for example, Handy (1976, Chapter 7)).

Diagnosing the culture

Culture change remains, nevertheless, hazardous and unpredictable. The focus on culture is valuable above all if it causes companies to temper their expectations about implementing strategic change. Sometimes an appreciation of corporate culture lies simply in recognizing how much it might prove an obstacle to specific strategic plans. A judgement may have to be made then as to whether to change the strategy to fit the culture, or the culture to fit the strategy, depending on the degree of compatibility and level of risk (Schwartz and Davies, 1983).

This applies particularly to mergers and acquisitions. A high proportion of mergers and acquisitions miscarry and half fail to come up to financial expectations. Cartwright and Cooper (1993) suggest that mergers and acquisitions should be viewed therefore rather like a marriage, in terms of the compatability of the partners. The first requirement is that the partners recognize specific differences; the second is that they are able to negotiate and accept these differences. To help this recognition process, they suggest using Handy's (1976) typology of cultures to test for likely compatibility.

Ideally, this process should take place before prospective partners get into bed, through a 'cultural audit'. Like marriage, though, this often does not happen until later.

A clash of cultures

The failed attempt by the Leeds Permanent and National & Provincial building societies to merge in 1993 illustrates how important corporate culture can be, and how differences are often not fully recognized until late in the day while senior managers are focused on the strategic issues. This is how the *Financial Times* (1993) reported the decision to call off the merger:

A very British clash
Chris Tighe on two society cultures that refused to gel

However sudden the abandonment of the Leeds Permanent–N&P merger may have seemed, it came as no surprise to many employees in Yorkshire's close-knit building societies.

From the outset the proposed deal was viewed with scepticism locally. How, one employee of a rival society asked this week, could the conventional Leeds ever have merged with a society which allowed a middle-ranking employee to buy a four-year-old Porsche, using a company scheme?

'Most Yorkshire societies,' he said, 'would very strongly dissuade the employee from it.'

Some of the financial gossip in Yorkshire may be a little extravagant in describing the yawning gap between the two societies' management styles – 'feudal' and 'off the wall' were among the epithets used to characterize, respectively, the Leeds and N&P.

But there is no disguising the glaring difference between the sober culture of the Leeds, said to be 'hierarchical', by one employee, and the more innovative approach of N&P, where staff are 'players', the executives are the 'direction management team', the marketing department is called the 'customer requirements process' and meetings are styled 'events'. N&P has three 'role levels' of staff; Leeds has 15 grades.

N&P's unorthodox management style has even fostered a witticism. 'At these events, they go on talking until there are no more challenges to proposed changes,' says one insider. 'It gives a new meaning to 'three day eventing'.'

'It's just not British. It's an American-based system of equality,' says Yorkshire Building Society's communications director. 'A lot of the stuff seems like gobbledegook science fiction. We all know the realities of working for large organizations.'

He adds, however, that Mr David O'Brien, N&P chief executive, termed 'messianic' by some rivals, has created a strong body of disciples among his staff, committed to his approach. 'The people who work there find it invigorating,' says Mr Holmes.

At the Leeds' imposing new headquarters many employees including middle management – a level N&P calls 'managers of implementation' – were evidently not ready to follow a new messiah. 'There were a lot of people celebrating in the pub on Tuesday night,' says a Leeds middle manager.

'When I heard the merger had been called off, I had mixed feelings,' says one Leeds HQ employee. 'It was good news because it was 1,600 jobs saved, and that's 1,600 families. But on the other hand the merger would have made us stronger and better able to compete against the Halifax.'

At N&P, the staff association chairman, Ms Janet Wojtkow, says 'players' were relieved, although some were disappointed too, having seen in the merger the opportunity for career progression.

Among other features, the reader will note how the structural differences between the societies (the number of hierarchical levels and differences in role behaviour) are reinforced by the symbolism of organizational stories and jokes. Also conspicuous is the political consideration of jobs and careers which was not far from people's minds.

Models for diagnosing the culture

In such situations what is needed is some model to diagnose culture and open up a dialogue about it. Johnson's (1990) model of cultural elements can be very useful in this respect. It can help managers to map their organization in terms of its dominant strategic 'paradigm' and the structural and symbolic elements that support it. They might then consider questions like 'what needs to change if the paradigm needs to change?' or 'where is there a lack of coherence and conflict which undermines the central paradigm?' Or the two parties to a proposed merger can compare their self-perception and perception of the other in a form of intergroup exercise, to draw out their stereotypes of one another and agree real areas of difference which they can then decide to work on (or not).

The value of models in the social sciences lies often in pragmatic qualities like this – that they help to stimulate action and debate.

We end this section with an example from a consultancy report I wrote some years ago where I used Roger Harrison's 'organizational ideologies' model (since popularized in Handy's 'cultures and structures' typology) to highlight problems of management style among senior managers in a manufacturing organization. The point of using it was to represent the behaviour of the production director (to whom the report was directed) in a way which might allow him to address it more objectively. The extract on 'climate' indicates the problem, while other sections, not reproduced, dealt with a range of specific themes and role issues at different levels.

Don Valley Joinery[2]
Communications in No. 1 Factory
A Report to the Production Director and
Production Manager

Climate

Studies of communication in organizations have shown a relationship between the use of punishments, threats and close control over people and counter-productive behaviour by subordinates. Where punishment and threats are a feature of the way control is exercised, not surprisingly concern for staff as people is low. The prevailing atmosphere in such organizations is one of 'crisis-management', with managers reacting over-emotionally towards subordinates when something goes wrong. To protect themselves against the consequences of mistakes, subordinates behave cautiously and act restrictively. The signs of this are lowered initiative, lack of flexibility in the organization and frustration among those affected by restrictive behaviour.

[*There then followed a number of examples of such behaviour at Don Valley.*]

Stages in the development of a company

The way a company grows is complex. Its development will involve how it responds to crisis. At Don Valley, a certain pattern in recent years can be discerned. I will illustrate this by reference to two types of organization.

Companies invariably begin life as the creation of one strong leader (or they are rejuvenated at a time of crisis or stagnation by such a person). As they grow, they become too big for one person to control single-handedly, and it becomes necessary to create a system of roles to deal with all the work. When a company (or department) is dominated by one person, it is characterized as having a 'power culture'. With increase in size and complexity of business, development of a system of specialized roles becomes necessary. Authority is delegated to the individuals in these roles, and, although power ultimately derives from the person at the top, it is more dispersed than in a 'power culture'. This kind of organization is characterized as having a 'role culture'.

Typically, in a 'power culture' the leader is closely involved in all affairs, either personally or through lieutenants, and has a close hand in all decisions. Their word is law, and the organization carries their stamp. However, the very success of such a form of organization leads eventually to pressure for change as it grows in size and is forced to take on specialists. The larger organization makes greater demands on coordination, and specialists bring with them different backgrounds, styles and expectations which clash with prevailing norms.

The organization which emerges relies on clearly defined roles, separate functions, clearly understood procedures for communications, and rules (governing, for example, the settlement of disputes). In this way efficiency and predictability are achieved in the working of the organization. Emphasis is on rational allocation of work and responsibility rather than on individual personalities.

Each type of organization has particular strengths and weaknesses, and is successful in particular environments. One with a 'power culture' is good at forging a market for its products and can respond to threat or changes in the environment: whilst an organization with a 'role culture' is better adapted to an environment that is relatively stable and to consolidating growth and improving its efficiency.

The recent history of Don Valley exemplifies this process. Thus, the rationalization of planning and control systems, the creation of professional functions such as work study, and the introduction of cost accounting methods represent an attempt to develop more rigorous and systematic methods in planning, organizing and evaluating work.

Although I have confined my study to the Production Department, I understand that other departments have undergone an overhaul in the past two years, with the creation of additional levels of management below director level and the introduction of specialists, in order to reduce reliance on directors in all things and provide a broader management capability. A process of moving from a 'power culture' to a 'role culture' can therefore be observed throughout the company.

The decision to change from mainly contract work (in No.1 Factory) to producing for stock, and the switch from batch to a flow-process system, is part of the same process, making production more efficient, predictable and regular, by directing sales at a more stable and predictable market.

Although the trend at Don Valley is therefore towards achieving efficiency and predictability through more rigorous and systematic organization, and the evolution of a system of roles with clearly differentiated duties and authority is an essential part of this, the problems I have indicated in the preceding sections suggest two things:

1   the prevailing management style is still characteristic of a 'power culture' and prevents the emergence of an effective organization based on properly defined roles and adequately differentiated authority;
2   the roles that exist, from chargehand to production director, have not been systematically conceived.

[*There then follow some specific recommendations. A final section then 'endorses' a further pattern of behaviour, in which power is even more distributed, which was becoming attractive to a number of people in the company.*]

A task (or team) culture

Whilst the general tendency is towards clarification of a system of roles, there is a third kind of organizational culture which is also becoming more important at Don Valley. This is characterized by the existence of work teams, joint problem-solving activities, and cooperation, and is known as a 'task culture (or, alternatively, 'team culture').

In a 'task (or team) culture', the emphasis is on getting the job done, with sharing of responsibility through greater dispersion of power than in either of the other two cultures described. Resources are given to individuals or teams, and they are left to get on with their tasks. Consequently, they experience a high degree of control over their work and are judged on results. This is the culture said to be preferred, as a personal choice to work in, by most managers. An organization with a 'task culture' is flexible and adaptable to different environments.

'Task culture' can be seen generally at Don Valley in the changing character of meetings, where different levels of management can discuss problems with a view to solving them, and come together specifically to do this. 'Task culture' can also be seen in the way work in the factory is done through groups supervised by chargehands. It is more conspicuous in certain parts of the factory than in others, due partly to differences in tasks and technology in use.

The introduction of a fully operational flow-process system, by linking machines and unit-operations together, will create a system where factory operations are more dependent than now on successfully functioning work-teams. This means recognizing what will make these work-teams effective and taking steps to encourage team behaviour. Above all, it means that a management style based on a 'power culture', being essentially at odds with a team or task culture, would be likely to evoke all the negative and restrictive behaviours that cohesive groups can employ.

This kind of shift in cultures is not unusual. It corresponds to stages in the growth of an organization (Greiner, 1972) and, historically, to the emergence of product-line and divisionalized structures (Chandler, 1962). Figure 6.2 maps these crudely onto one another.

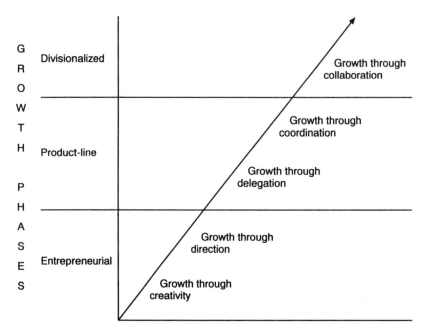

Figure 6.2 *Organization culture and patterns of growth. (Based on Chandler, 1962, Greiner, 1972, and Harrison, 1972)*

In practice, the development of culture will be influenced by a range of factors other than just size. In the case example of Don Valley Joinery, technology was influential. Business environment factors (such as the maturity of the industry and attempts to rejuvenate old-established businesses) also play a part. Since different functions are often exposed to different sets of technological and environmental contingencies, they tend, of course, to develop distinctive cultural traits (Lawrence and Lorsch, 1967).

It is worth noting that the 'high commitment' system (Lawrence, 1985) and Harvard perspective on HRM (Beer *et al.*, 1984), with its 'task/team' cultural orientation, is based on this kind of evolutionary view of the technological and business environment (plus the influence of social environmental factors). Technological and business environment factors continue to exercise a powerful influence in spreading task/team culture. Chapters 15 and 16 will describe this in terms of (1) the general trend towards taking out levels of management and supervision, and pushing substantial responsibilities down onto the shopfloor (Chapter 15), and (2) cell manufacture (Chapter 16).

Summary

This chapter has considered corporate culture through four questions:

1 Does corporate culture matter? Is there any evidence that the 'right' corporate culture leads to better performance?
2 What do we mean by culture, and what does it consist of?
3 Can corporate culture be changed?
4 What do we know about creating cultural change, and, more broadly, about how to create large-scale organizational change?

In answer to the first question, we have to say that the evidence for a culture–performance link is weak. The message from this is not that culture does not matter so much as that trying to measure it is a diversion from the real job of trying to understand it.

To help us with this, we should think of organizational culture as operating at three levels – as basic assumptions (or a set of underlying values); as the multitude of symbolic ways in which meaning and significance are developed and communicated; and as the various structural ways by which behaviour is channelled. The second and third of these complement one another in upholding the central set of values about organizational purpose and direction, and maintaining stable patterns of culture. In other ways, symbolic communication can play a special part in beginning a process of cultural change; while the structural expression of culture tends to 'fix' behaviour.

HRM is largely preoccupied with the latter – with defining job roles, writing policies ~~~ ~pplying systems such as selection, pay, training, and develc~ ~d or not, such systems are liable to send out able and desirable behaviour. Many of the :er in trying to implement business strategies ire not projecting appropriate values or are

:e systems provide direction and control has [can deliver desired cultures. However, can \nd, as important, should it? The idea of an :e from and dominant over individuals and nized as peculiarly American, as is the idea will. Cultural change raises issues of ethics then so does the very existence of large ; to be addressed within a much broader >vernance of private companies, alongside

:onsidered two approaches towards creating change, and managing change through the re chance of working because it starts from ; perceive as real problems related to the tries to tackle values head-on while 'critical path' change sees the development of new roles as the determining force. That is not to say, however, that this also excludes 'critical path' change as a political and symbolic process. The whole rationale for starting off change in a localized way is to gain legitimation for new ideas where they will not meet immediate resistance from central power sources. As piloted change is successful, it can then be used as demonstration or role model by its corporate sponsors (which, of course, it must have). Chapter 8 gives an example of this, while Chapters 7 and 8 offer various contrasts around the theme of programmatic versus 'critical path' change.

After a brief diversion onto the subject of visionary leaders and their role in creating change, we concluded with some comments about the importance of diagnosing corporate culture. Corporate cultures above all cannot be taken off the shelf or made to order, and culture change remains risky and slow. At the very least, at times of change, it is useful to reflect on the characteristics of one's corporate culture, how it may need to change, and how difficult that may be. We considered some ways this might be done. In practice, the value of models in the social sciences lies in their pragmatic qualities in being able to stimulate action and debate, rather than in any claim to give answers.

The final impression we hope this chapter has left, through the different ways of looking at culture and cultural issues, is one of sheer diversity. The essence of culture after all, corporate or otherwise, is that it is a unique combination of many things. Any kind of organizational change needs to begin with the particular context that has formed the culture and holds it in place.

Notes

1 A research report on the human resources dimension of quality management, undertaken by Mick Marchington and colleagues at UMIST, was recently completed for the IPM, and is available as IPM (1993). *Quality: People and Management Matters*, London: IPM.

2 The strategic background to this report can be found in a case study, subsequently published as Hendry, C. (1985), 'Don Valley Joinery' in *Marketing in Action*, Open University Press, pp. 27–36. The company name is, of course, a pseudonym.

7
Strategic change and HRM at Barclaycard: from rapid growth to maturity

Introduction

This is the first of two cases which describe the process of developing and implementing strategy through HRM, with the structural and cultural changes accompanying it. In Chapter 4 we described the concept of organizational life-cycle and what this means for employee behaviour, skills, and HRM practices. This chapter describes the changes one organization went through at a particular stage of its life-cycle, having experienced a period of rapid growth and then having to face greater competition and a more saturated market. It will be obvious from this that it does not perfectly fit into the simplified view of stages of growth, nor match the prescriptions for HRM derived from that.

Equally important is the process of change itself. It is one thing to say an organization is likely to be characterized by certain behaviours and human resource practices at one point in its life. How it gets from one set of behaviours to another, however, is quite a different thing. The case shows how the personnel function itself must evolve to help bring this about. In this example, it means the transformation of a traditional personnel function into an HRM function.

Business and human resource change at Barclaycard[1]

Barclaycard is a relatively young organization. It was formed in 1966, as a division of Barclays Bank, enjoyed rapid growth and success from the late 1970s, and celebrated its twenty-first anniversary in 1987. It pioneered the use of the credit card in Britain, following the example of Bank of America in the United States, whose operating systems it adopted under licence.

This growth was to be seen in the number of its customers (on the one hand, credit card holders and, on the other, the outlets (merchants) who accepted cards), in the value of its cardholder turnover, and in its profits (see Table 7.1). These periods of growth fall into two or three stages, depending on whether we focus on volume or profits. In terms of absolute

Table 7.1 Product and organizational growth at Barclaycard

	Number of cardholders (000)	Annual cardholder turnover (£m)	Number of merchant outlets (000)	Profits (£m)
1966	1 000	4	35	(loss)
1967	1 100	10	38	(loss)
1968	1 200	14	41	(loss)
1969	1 116	23	43	(loss)
1970	1 350	42	46	(loss)
1971	1 740	76	50	(loss)
1972	2 060	118	62	(0.3)
1973	2 440	166	78	(loss)
1974	2 890	236	84	(loss)
1975	3 310	340	89	(loss)
1976	3 500	451	94	(loss)
1977	3 800	585	102	6
1978	4 135	779	116	n/a
1979	4 991	1 009	134	n/a
1980	5 519	1 355	156	n/a
1981	6 108	1 704	180	n/a
1982	6 634	2 179	197	27
1983	6 840	2 712	202	35
1984	7 380	3 370	216	62
1985	8 010	4 413	235	75
1986				92
1987				97

Source: Barclaycard Factfile and Financial Records

volumes, growth accelerated in three phases – 1966–1969, 1970–1977, 1978–1985 – as the credit card gained in public acceptance. Two key events that helped this were the launch of the rival Access card by Lloyds, National Westminster, Midland, and Williams and Glyn's banks in 1972, accompanied by heavy advertising, and the formation of the world-wide Visa organization which Barclaycard joined in 1977.

For the first eleven years, however, up to 1977, Barclaycard reported losses. This is an accepted pattern for a new product during the launch and development stage, although much longer than one would normally expect. Profitability would have occurred sooner but for the credit squeeze imposed by the Bank of England in 1973. After 1977, however, with critical mass achieved, profits rose rapidly, helped by the removal of credit restrictions in 1980/1981 and of exchange controls in 1980, and periods of lower interest rates in 1982–1984. By 1985, Barclaycard was producing 10 per cent of Barclays Bank's world-wide pre-tax profits, and was the second most profitable part of the Bank after the branches. At that time, then, Barclaycard was still on a growth curve, and this even accelerated in 1986.

Business growth promotes recruitment activity

This success generated massive growth in employee numbers – from 297 in 1966, to 5343 full-time equivalents in 1987 (or over 7000 actual employees, plus over 700 additional agency staff and students at peak times). Apart from two years in 1976 and 1977, the numbers increased year-on-year, and in the ten years from 1977, for instance, multiplied 240 per cent. The personnel function in Barclaycard consequently grew on the back of the need to recruit.

Employee profile and skills

Over 90 per cent of employees in Barclaycard were clerical staff engaged in data preparation and processing tasks, telephone authorizations, and servicing the cardholder and merchant customer base. Most of these staff were female. On the other hand, the total number of 'appointed managers' (at grade GG8 and above) was only 427 in 1987, compared with 4916 keyboard/secretarial/clerical staff. Many of these 'managers', moreover, were specialists in functions such as finance, sales/marketing, and systems (transferred to Barclaycard in 1987). Barclaycard was thus heavily oriented towards routine operations.

Personnel as administration

Because of the sheer numbers required to perform routine tasks to a high degree of accuracy, coupled with the inevitable turnover (anything between 200 and 400 employees annually), recruitment carried with it a heavy load of administration. Until the mid-1970s, in fact, the function was designated 'personnel administration'. This included responsibility for premises, since the growth in staff had direct and severe implications for accommodation. In Northampton, for instance, where the business had its headquarters and many of its operations, the 3300 staff in 1987 accounted for 3 per cent of the labour force. Future growth at that point was therefore being channelled into other locations (Liverpool and Birmingham) where there was unemployment.

The function's credibility, as a result, rested on being able to meet the demand for new employees, while maintaining tight control over its own staffing levels. To support this, it operated a conventional system of manpower planning, with a five-year rolling horizon. However, since volume growth constantly outstripped forecasts, and because commitments to new products and systems developments tended to occur with inadequate warning, the credibility of the personnel function in delivering the necessary people tended to suffer. In other words, weaknesses in strategic planning generally forced the personnel department to be reactive to demands placed upon it. As one manager said:

> The personnel function was reactive. It reacted to other people's wants, desires

and wishes. When new business came in, the last thing anybody considered was the number of people required to fill it. They were blissfully unaware of the lead-times. This division is rapidly evolving and nobody has yet said to Personnel, 'Here are the plans for what we want to do, that's where we're going – Personnel, can you cope with it?'

Or as a manager in another function put it:

There was little strategic planning – there was a process that was gone through, but nothing really to get a hold on, other than to say it would tend to be market-driven. It was not a declared policy, but in fact that is what it tended to be. It was always 'a market window opens on Monday and we have got to be there'. It was constant surprise, surprise, surprise. On the other hand, it is a very rapidly changing market, and so saying where you want to be three years out, in any sort of practical terms, is very difficult.

An emphasis on technical training

The numbers of staff entering the organization resulted in a heavy, but highly efficient and cost-effective, investment in training for clerical, key-board, and secretarial staff. This included a strong commitment to computer-based training (CBT). This began in the mid-1970s to cope with three related developments:

- Dispersal of staff to regional locations
- The restructuring of operations around a self-contained unit (the 'muster') in which the whole range of customer activities (issuing cards, setting credit limits, dealing with cardholder queries, monitoring repayments, chasing late payments) for some 200,000 accounts were devolved to a work group of thirty to thirty-five staff
- The introduction of on-line VDU screens to deal with authorization enquiries.

CBT thus offered an efficient way of dealing with a dispersed population; fitted with a prevalent technology in the organization; and its introduction to train for the 'muster' system visibly justified itself in substantial savings in training time (around one-third) and in trainer and travel costs. Since then, CBT has enabled the training function to cope with rising and fluctuating numbers of employees and system enhancements. By the mid-1980s, it provided a third of all training activity.

Up to this point also, training in general was geared to specific requirements for technical knowledge and skills. Reflecting the prevailing functional form of organization, it was kept separate from other mainstream personnel activities such as recruitment. Unlike other areas of personnel, however, it had a close relationship with the operations side of the business and had been closely involved from the outset in the development of new work systems. From that point of view, it enjoyed a high reputation. On the other hand, its status was tied to servicing skills in the lower grades, a fact reflected in its staffing through trainers drawn predominantly from clerical grades.

Management training has a low priority

Alongside this stress on routine job skills, the distinctive character of the management role was hardly recognized. Management training and development were formally the responsibility of the parent organization, Barclays Bank, and were geared to jobs, skills, and promotion routes in the branch network. Branch banking skills and the unit of organization, however, were very different. Whereas a branch manager might be responsible for twenty to twenty-five staff, operations managers in Barclaycard might have 450 people working for them.

Appointments to management positions had to be approved by the central personnel function in London so that an internal trawl of the bank could be first made. Similarly, Barclaycard depended on the central graduate recruitment scheme for graduates, although it was rarely the first choice of a graduate who was looking for a career in banking. The result was that Barclaycard had only sixteen managers with degrees in 1987, or 4 per cent of the managerial stock, and many of these had transferred with the systems function early in 1987.

By the mid-1980s, the dependence on the Bank was becoming particularly troublesome in the slowness of the central job-evaluation system to cope with the creation of new management jobs and specialisms that fell outside existing job definitions and gradings adapted to the branch network. Unfortunately, this discontent tended to rebound on Barclaycard's own personnel function.

The onset of competitive threats and the strategic response

Until the early 1980s, then, Barclaycard was a relatively simple, although large, organization. Its success had been based on a single product – the classic Barclaycard – and until 1982 it remained essentially a single-product organization. It was organized on functional lines, and was dependent on its parent organization for certain key activities such as computer systems support and development, and management development.

In the early 1980s, however, Barclaycard began to experience resistance from buyers in the two key areas from which it gained revenue – retail merchants who paid a fee to belong to the Visa organization, and the cardholding public who were beginning to respond to interest charges by settling their accounts earlier. In addition, entry barriers in the industry were being lowered by the availability of electronic processing which circumvented the need for a branch banking system to collect merchants' vouchers. Nevertheless, at this point such threats were still only just on the horizon. On the other hand, the dependence on a single product was seen as increasingly risky:

> We started talking about 'closing windows of opportunity'. And so the first emphasis was to maximize our growth, and then to start looking for additional revenue streams.

Barclaycard's initial response was a classic case of adapting within a dominant strategic frame (Tushman, Newman, and Romanelli, 1986):

- Some marginal diversification by developing specialist card facilities for certain target populations
- An effort to differentiate the 'classic' card itself by various 'add-ons'
- Combined with a change in the charge structure for cardholders
- More active marketing towards merchants.

Out of this last initiative, however, came the realization that merchants themselves represented a second major stream of service activity. As one manager put it, 'if you ever mentioned a customer until then, it was a cardholder'.

Thus, Barclaycard's diversification began in a small way, from around 1982, through enhancements to the basic credit card and variants on it. In 1983, however, arising out of its first formal strategic review, the idea of the merchant side as a second mainline business and source of profit in its own right began steadily to gain ground. Following on, in 1985, the Bank carried out a broad strategic review of its own, and redefined Barclaycard's role as a centralized provider of banking services (renaming it Central Retail Services Division, or CRSD), with special skills in handling large-volume activity delivered from a central point. As a result, it began to be seen not simply as a credit card business. Shortly after, it was given charge of the Bank's travellers' cheques business; acquired responsibility for a centralized mortgage scheme; and was made jointly responsible with the Bank for development of the debit card, Connect, launched in 1987.

By the second half of the 1980s, Barclaycard/CRSD had four major businesses, and these began to assume more importance as the set of competitive threats to the credit card began to intensify:

- Electronic technology continued to advance, opening up the prospect for other financial institutions and non-banks to operate credit cards, without having to have branch banks to act as collection centres for payment slips
- The major high street banks separately applied for dual membership in the Visa and Mastercard organizations (the two world-wide organizations which backed Barclaycard and Access, respectively). This introduced competition into the merchant side of the business where Barclaycard and Access had formerly each enjoyed an effective monopoly in their own domain, and thus threatened income from commissions
- Resistance from merchants to charges became more vociferous and effective
- A Monopolies and Mergers Commission investigation, announced in May 1987, threatened to cut income from both cardholders and merchants
- Finally, the introduction of debit cards from 1987 began to undermine the economics of credit card operation.

By 1988, the threats which only a few had perceived in 1983 were becoming a crescendo that could not be ignored. In its response, Barclaycard/CRSD had broadened its base, moving from a single-product division of the Bank to become a genuine multi-product business. To do so, it had taken actions spanning all three of Porter's generic strategies and various forms of product-market development – thus illustrating the complexity of a company's response when wanting to hold onto a high market share. It had sought out special *niches* for new forms of the credit card (focus); sought to *differentiate* the classic card by add-ons and a faster service at retailers through on-line terminals; and was making a concerted attempt to *reduce costs* in the business. It had also substantially *diversified* through new lines given it by the parent bank.

Structural change follows strategy

To manage this increasing diversity more effectively, and to drive the development of these separate lines more vigorously, Barclaycard/CRSD was reorganized into a series of product centres in 1987, with revenue and cost responsibilities vested in what were in effect, though not in name, managing directors. These profit centres (named 'strategic business units') were served by support services, termed 'centres of excellence'. Although the new arrangements stopped short of a full transfer pricing system, the intention was to replace a functional, bureaucratic structure with one modelled on customer–supplier relationships between 'departments'. The aim was twofold:

- To promote stronger development of fledgling products
- To achieve better resource management, through closer control of costs in a tighter competitive climate, with better decisions on resource allocation to new projects.

To this end, the 'strategic business unit' (SBU) structure was supported by a newly devised strategic planning process. This required managers to develop plans and budgets in four key areas (people, premises, computer systems, and capital expenditure), with profit/loss projections for each individual business. The resource needs for new projects would then be determined in a quasi-competitive situation and managed on more of an arm's-length basis.

New perspectives on recruitment and training to meet changing task, skills, and knowledge requirements

These changes in the strategy, structure, and operating disciplines of the business in turn demanded new skills and standards in a wide variety of jobs. These were met in some cases by specific retraining. For example, the sales force had fallen into an easy routine of visiting existing outlets simply to stock up their supplies of vouchers and promotional material, and quoting rates of commission from a standard formula. Many had been with the organization from the beginning, and were into their mid-40s. They had ceased to be salespersons. As the launch of the debit card, Connect, illustrated, however, dealing with merchants required a much more professional approach to sales negotiations, as these were increasingly conducted at a higher level and required more initiative and discretion on the part of salespersons.

The first step was to restructure into fewer areas and territories, and cut out the amount of hierarchy and numbers of managers. The second was to create a training programme to put across the new sense of direction, to remotivate the 190 salespersons, and to develop genuine negotiating skills so that they could deal with merchants who were becoming tougher in their negotiating stance.

The approach to this training, however, was novel within Barclaycard/CRSD, and significant for the kind of change that was coming over the organization. The key to the programme was to make it highly participative, to get the salesforce's commitment to their changed role and overcome their natural anxieties about being able to live up to it. An outside sales consultant was briefed, along with the staff, on the objectives for the sales organization, and they were then left to design the programme together. The novelty of the successful programme that resulted was that staff for the first time were not waiting to be told what to do or being spoon-fed training designed for them.

In other areas of Barclaycard/CRSD, a leavening of external recruits were brought in from outside the Bank, to introduce or add specialist skills – for example, in marketing, business research, and computer systems. This was also counter-cultural, in that the whole style, not just of Barclaycard/CRSD but of the Bank, was to recruit generalists and develop them at various stages in their career to work in specialist areas. Even so, this intake was limited – comprising just 8 per cent (three staff) of new managerial appointments in the first quarter of 1987, as against 11 per cent (eight staff) transferred from the bank, and the rest promotions and internal moves within Barclaycard/CRSD – almost the same proportions as in the previous full year.

Management development for a more complex environment

Apart from new skills in specific areas, the major shift was in the demand for more developed management skills – and more people with these skills – across a broad swathe of the organization. In the first six months of 1987, for instance, some 500 promotions were made in all grades, including 100 in management positions (almost a quarter of the total). This put tremendous pressure on internal sources of supply – the feedstock for which was ultimately the general clerical intake (with four to six O-level/GCSE passes). In 1986 a review of junior managers (grades GG8-GG11) highlighted the impending problem in rating 75 per cent of this group – almost half the management population – as having no further promotion potential.

To respond to this demand in quality and quantity, there were a number of initiatives, which in turn began to establish management training and development as an in-house responsibility:

- A four-year Management Training Programme was established in 1984 to take new entrants of two to three years' standing through to their first management appointment, through experience in a variety of jobs while they completed formal qualifications (the Credit Card Certificate and Associate of the Institute of Bankers Diploma)
- A career development manager was appointed in 1985
- A graduate recruitment and training programme exclusive to Barclaycard/CRSD was established in 1987
- An Accelerated Training Programme was introduced to improve the stock of young managers, following the 1986 review
- More refined profiles of jobs and of the people to fill them were developed, in place of the crude 'job-banding' system, including psychometric testing in 1987 of some 250–300 staff in lower management grades
- From 1987, staff-appraisal reports were computerized to assist the identification of candidates for promotion.

In addition to these developments in structure and provision, a training consultant from Bacie was employed in 1988 to help the newly formed management development team develop a facilitative training style along the lines of that recently used to reorient the sales team (see Arkin, 1993).

Reorganization of the personnel function – from personnel to HRM

Capping this development in personnel activity, the personnel function at Barclaycard/CRSD was radically reorganized in 1987 into a 'human resources' function. The principal features of this were:

- Greater emphasis given to management development
- A more 'strategic' approach by relating recruitment, training, and career decisions more closely to resource planning (not just through organizational lines and through the planning system, but by physically relocating the training function into the same building as personnel for the first time)
- Greater autonomy in its resourcing from the Bank's central personnel systems (with the latter also reviewing its own activities).

Figure 7.1 shows the new departmental structure for personnel and training.

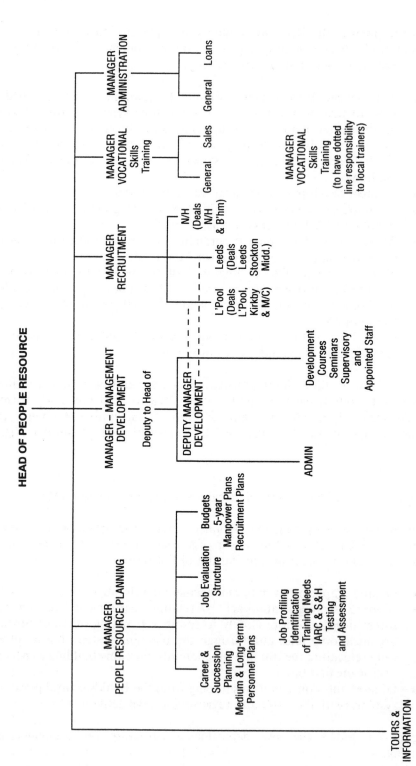

Figure 7.1   The new personnel and training organization (1987)

Programmatic cultural change

To make the structure work required wide-ranging changes in people's roles, in their outlook and motivation and in their skills. The delivery of services from 'centres of excellence' to product managers in SBUs, for instance, had enormous cultural implications for how departments delivered work and services to one another.

In particular, it involved a new attitude to the 'bottom-line'. How to create this posed a challenge to policy and practice in a number of areas of personnel management. For instance, performance-related pay and dismissal for non-performance were extremely counter-cultural for the bank (although incentives for senior managers were under consideration). It was also difficult for training to contribute to the development of entrepreneurial attitudes, (1) because of the type of recruit into banking and (2) because of the image and expectations people had of training. It was bred deep into banking culture that training represented a series of landmarks in a career, allied to clear steps up the promotion ladder, both of which – training and promotion – were determined by other people:

> I do not think training, as we are running it at the moment, can contribute that much. In this culture, people expect training to be given to them. Once in a while they will be sent on a formal course; once in a while something will be spoon-fed to them. You have to make people recognize that training and personal development is as much your responsibility as an individual as it is for a training department. I suspect when you mention training and development, people at the moment would think in terms of being chicks in a nest, months open, waiting to be spoon-fed. That sort of training can't deliver what we are looking for.

About this time (although in fact it started before the reorganization into SBUs took place), Barclaycard/CRSD embarked on a major training programme, embracing all employees, to promote the idea of quality. However, while improving quality was the ostensible focus of the programme, intentionally or not it directly addressed the kind of relationship and attitudes identified above that needed to be forged between 'centres of excellence' and SBUs. The sequence of events in this case shows the 'loosely coupled' relationship that may often exist between strategic, structural, and cultural change.

Under the banner of 'Quality 1st', this commitment originated in the attendance of the Chief Executive at a course at Crosby Associates 'Quality College' in Florida, in 1985. Senior personnel staff then followed, and in March 1986 the Head of Personnel moved into the post of Head of Quality Coordination, and began visiting other companies to see how they had approached similar programmes. A programme was devised with Crosby Associates, and in mid-1986 this was discussed with BIFU and Barclay's staff association. Since Barclays Bank was itself engaged in a 'customer service programme' for branch staff from 1985, it was a favourable time to get Group support for the heavy investment involved (at around £600,000 exceeding the annual cost of all other training).

The programme was in two phases:

1 The first phase involved direct training to impart basic concepts. This was cascaded down to all employees, beginning with the top 110 managers. Through early 1987, another 1200 employees in supervisory and management roles participated, with the remaining 4000-plus staff following in March-September 1987. The first phase of training for 110 senior staff was carried out by Crosby Associates off-site, and then fourteen of these managers received additional instruction in training technique and the use of course materials before going on to train the next group.

2 The second phase came into effect in the latter part of 1987, and involved the creation of 'Quality Improvement Teams'. Again, the top 110 managers were central in identifying problems and unnecessary costs, while the teams formed were intended as a forum for staff to refer problems they were unable to get action on through normal management channels. In mid-1987, it was estimated that something like 15–20 per cent of all documents circulating within Barclaycard/CRSD related to the Quality programme.

Overall, following Crosby, it was presented as:

> a long-term process to change the culture of the organization – a continuous, long-term process . . . to eliminate problems and the unnecessary, wasteful expense they cause . . . which emphasizes the individual contribution every member of staff at every level can make . . . [and] gives greater responsibility to managers and staff at all levels (*Quality 1st: An Introduction for Staff*).

This took the concept of the organization as a work chain in which 'each of us receives work from other staff (our suppliers) and delivers to other staff (our customers)'. It aimed at correct performance of tasks 'first time', so that 'internal Quality creates external Quality'.

Central to this, in the Crosby approach to quality was the notion of 'conformance to requirements' – clearly and precisely defining requirements, as a fundamental work discipline. As one manager put it:

> It is very common for loose and unstructured instructions to be given to people. The key things are adequate specification of requirements and performing to requirements. The philosophy of 'that's close enough' isn't good enough.
>
> Everybody claims that it isn't new, because all it has done is professionalize the management process, and everybody claims to have been doing it all along. But I haven't, and I think it's focused a lot of interface problems between different bits of the organization.

Considerable effort went into structuring the whole process to gain commitment. It was initiated at the very top; training began with the most senior staff; and senior line managers were given a central role in the training/cascade process. Their commitment was thus intended to ensure that the programme was embedded in the work of the organization, and this was carried through in the formation of 'Quality Improvement Teams'. Although the programme was managed by a 'product champion' outside the Training Department (the former Head of Personnel), the full-time staff of five was kept small to ensure that effective ownership remained with the line. Thus, the fourteen senior line managers responsible for cascading the training remained a core group of 'disciples' for the whole programme.

On the other hand, it had to overcome initial scepticism because of previous experience with abortive programmes – in particular, an attempt to found quality circles in 1983, with a lot of hype, limited achievements, and lack of support from management. By the middle of 1988, 'Quality 1st' was beginning to face problems of sustaining commitment, and the departure then of the chief executive (to TSB) took a lot of the steam out of it.

Nevertheless, management training continues to emphasize the need for a change in culture. As elsewhere in the banking sector in the late 1980s and early 1990s, the focus is on people taking more responsibility for their own development (Hendry, 1987; Hendry and Pettigrew, 1987). Instead of staff expecting that career progression and job training will be handed down to them there is a perceived need for a culture of self-development. A fast-changing business means that career opportunities and job requirements cannot be as readily forecast or assured as in the past. In Barclaycard/CRSD uncertain future growth means there can be less expectation of promotion happening as a matter of course, compared with the years of continual expansion, when, as one manager put it, 'staff went up with the lift'. The requirement, in a newly competitive sector, is the revival of entrepreneurial attitudes.

Employee relations – *a footnote*

In these changes we have said little about the quality of employee relations or how these were managed. In a sense, this is a footnote because employee relations posed few problems. This was one area where the bank's central personnel function had ceded more decentralized control earlier (although retaining control of pay negotiations). Barclaycard/CRSD had then managed its employee relations in a more participative way than was probably common in the bank.

This stemmed from the sense of common purpose forged from the beginning in launching the business. It then carried through in the habit of close consultation with clerical and keyboard staff over changes affecting their work, reflected also in the early involvement of training staff in designing appropriate training. On the few occasions when jobs appeared to be threatened, considerable effort had gone into consultation and reassuring staff – for instance, when first TSB (1982–1984) and then the Bank of Scotland (1985–1987) took over the processing of their own cardholder operations:

> At all levels we were determined to talk to the unions, and to talk with people on a one-to-one – well, not one-to-one, but one-to-120 – basis. When it comes to talking to the staff, it is seen as better to do it through me because I have the relationship with the people as the senior operating manager, than through a personnel man who might not be quite so well known. The AGMs [Assistant General Managers] try to have a programme of walking the floor so that they're seen as well.

Finally, growth provided a cushion, while natural wastage alone meant that 200–400 new staff had to be taken on each year. The cost-saving measures being introduced at the end of the 1980s, through greater use of computer technology, were likewise expected to be absorbed in the same way. In fact, however, the end of growth and the consequent pressure to contain costs has resulted in Barclaycard/CRSD announcing some 400 redundancies in 1993.

Barclaycard today

The tougher climate that was foreseen has come about. The squeeze on profits has happened, with a substantial drop in published profits in 1989 from £99 million to £42 million (and a loss in 1990). Barclaycard continues, however, to evolve its human resource systems and commercial strategy along lines defined in the mid-1980s, and by 1993 had substantially recovered, with profits of around £150 millon.

An obvious lesson in this is that neither personnel nor HRM can be the be-all and end-all in company success. HRM can make a contribution. On the other hand, the timescale for having an impact through the quality of people recruited and developed is bound to take some little time. The challenge is being able to anticipate needs. This is the problem in saying that HRM should be driven by the needs of the business: too often, these are not recognized or articulated until too late in the day.

Summary

Barclaycard/CRSD shows an organization moving through a period of transition. Fortunately, it was able to do so at the top of its growth cycle. However, that itself involves problems. A period of seemingly endless growth breeds an attitude that it will continue for ever. Success tends to reward existing incumbents, who consequently rise with an expanding organization, like currants in a dough. In banking, this tendency to inbreed is exacerbated by traditions of internal promotion.

The result is double-edged. People have a very firm understanding of the industry they are in, and a grasp of the rules for competitive success in that industry. When the environment begins to change, however, these rules begin to lose their efficacy. However, because people are steeped in an existing success formula and a view of themselves as pre-eminent in the business it is harder for them to recognize the warning signs. As a result, at Barclaycard/CRSD it took some years of pressing the argument for change and building a convincing case from accounting data to persuade the management team as a whole of the need for change.

Strategy can thus take some time to form – three to five years to emerge in a clear form here and much longer to implement effectively. An essential step in bringing about strategic change is often to make the structure compatible. This was the case at Barclaycard/CRSD. The task, then, was to develop the necessary skills and behaviours to make the new strategy and structure work. A further element in the process was to change the culture:

- First, to change the way people related to one another by seeing others in the organization as customers for their work output, and hence to give attention to quality in everything they did
- Second, to become more proactive, in taking responsibility for their work and for their personal development.

In this respect, the Barclaycard/CRSD case follows a predictable pattern of strategic, structural, and cultural change. It shows how changes in an organization's structure can be an essential step in bringing about strategic change. The creation of 'strategic business units' provided a new focus of activity, aiming to release entrepreneurial energies while increasing the concern for efficient resource allocation. This broke down a large organization into smaller units to give a stronger focus to different products and strengthen people's identification with the strategic objectives for these.

It illustrates, then, the general point that an organization's structure should fit with its strategy, to ensure that the strategy is effective and the organization is efficient. Specific HRM processes and systems then had to be brought into line to support strategy, structure, and cultural change. The Barclaycard case shows a firm taking to heart a central tenet of HRM:

> Just as firms will be faced with inefficiencies when they try to implement new strategies with outmoded structures, so they will also face problems of implementation when they attempt to effect new strategies with inappropriate HR systems. (Fombrun, Tichy and Devanna, 1984, p. 37).

The personnel function itself, however, had also to evolve to help bring this about. Influenced in part by new ideas circulating in the late 1980s, a traditional personnel function was remodelled as an HRM function. Most important in driving this transformation in the orientation and status of the personnel function was a higher priority for management development as part of the need to manage a more complex environment, both inside and outside the organization, and with this, the need to manage continuing change into the 1990s. Management had to develop a more 'strategic' outlook and style; and personnel had to become more 'rounded' in its role and activities. The sequence of these changes and the HRM response are summarized in Figure 7.2.

One final observation. The case describes an organization having to adjust to a levelling out of growth. Instead of acquiescing in this, and instituting policies associated with maturity (as Schuler in Chapter 4 implies), Barclaycard/CRSD sought to reinvigorate itself – as, of course, organizations do. Despite growing rapidly, the problem it diagnosed was that too many managers had already plateaued. In that sense, behaviours and personnel practices are likely to stultify before this becomes apparent in falling organizational performance. The promise of HRM is supposedly that it can revive an organization by stimulating higher levels of performance.

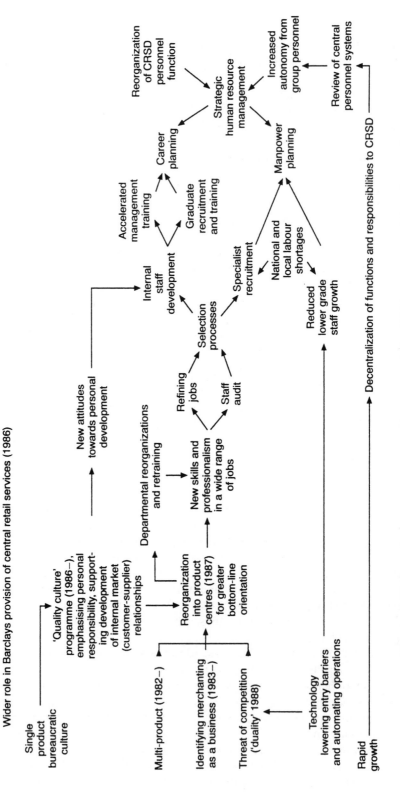

Figure 7.2 *Corporate strategy change and the HRM response at Barclaycard*

Note

1   This case is derived from Hendry, C. and Pettigrew, A. (1989). *Strategic Change and Human Resource Management in Central Retail Services Division, Barclays Bank* (*'Barclaycard'*), CCSC, University of Warwick. A version of the case appears in Hendry, C. and Pettigrew, A. (1992), 'Patterns of strategic change in the development of human resource management', *British Journal of Management*, **3**, 3, 137–156.

8
Strategy, structure and cultural change: managing retrenchment and recovery at Pilkington

Introduction

The Barclaycard case in Chapter 7 described an organization having to adjust to a levelling out of growth, but trying nevertheless to reinvigorate itself. A second pattern is that of severe retrenchment in conditions of market decline, followed (hopefully) by renewal. This is the story of Pilkington, the UK glass company, in the 1980s.

During the recession of the early 1980s, many UK manufacturing companies were forced into this pattern by the belated attempt to get out of declining product areas and to lower their costs. Mostly, this centred on reducing the number of employees and changing terms and conditions. As a result, unlike the Barclaycard example, industrial relations issues were prominent.

At the same time, Pilkington was one of a number of companies that sought to invigorate themselves by pushing more responsibilities out from the centre to operating managers – in other words, to decentralize. Decentralization was thus a key part of change at Pilkington. As managers saw it, decentralization made possible many of the other changes for turning the company around, including the achievement of more efficient operating units.

Like the structural changes at Barclaycard involving the creation of strategic business units, decentralization was intended to make people both more market-oriented and cost-conscious. There are thus strong similarities with Barclaycard in the part played by structural and cultural change, although precise details and the approach differ. The two cases therefore provide a contrast around some of the issues described in the chapters on organization structure and culture.

Finally, the personnel function was closely involved in the changes at Pilkington. During the first half of the 1980s, the focus was on negotiating structures, pay bargaining, job evaluation, pay systems, and job demarcations, all in a highly unionized environment, therefore giving personnel activity a strong industrial relations focus. In the second half of the 1980s, however, from around 1987, other themes began to assume greater prominence as changes in these areas were pushed through and as Pilkington moved out of decline into renewed growth. Skills, recruitment, training, and management development began to move up the agenda as the company started to focus on the people and skills it needed for the future. A shift therefore occurred through the 1980s from IR to HRD as the core of personnel activity.

Strategic and human resource change at Pilkington Glass Limited (PGL)[1]

Recession and business decline

Pilkington is one of the oldest industrial companies in the UK, having been founded in 1826. In 1959, while still a private, family-owned company, it had transformed the production of glass by the invention of the 'float glass' process. The royalties from licensing this had enabled it to build plants in the secondary markets of the world (particularly old Commonwealth, and South America), and in due course, in the 1980s, to take over two of the largest world producers in Germany and the USA. These acquisitions propelled it into the number-one position in the world in flat glass production ('flat' as opposed to shaped glass as in goblets).

From 1979 until the mid-1980s, however, it experienced severe pressure in its core UK business in flat and safety glass, and in other UK businesses such as glass fibre insulation. This was brought about by a number of factors. First was the impact of recession on two of its major markets – window glass to the building industry, and windscreen glass to the car industry. Second, changes in the distribution of building glass were passing Pilkington by, as sales developed through channels other than the traditional merchant (for example, via double-glazing manufacturers who were more willing to shop around for their supplies). Third, sales of safety glass to the motor industry were in serious decline as sales of British cars plummeted from the mid-1970s.

Despite these pressures on demand, however, the total market for flat glass actually grew from 1978 (briefly falling back in 1980, before soaring through the 1980s). Pilkington's own sales and share of the UK market, however, fell drastically, as Figures 8.1 and 8.2 show – from 74 per cent in 1979 to 50 per cent in 1982/1983. Two of the causes lay outside Pilkington's control; the third they could do something about.

First, there was the impact of the high interest/high exchange rate policy of the British government. This progressively cheapened imports from Pilkington's Continental rivals, such as the large French company, St Gobain.

Second, importers were able to take advantage of the revolution in roll-on, roll-off ferries which allowed UK double-glazing firms in the South-east to take supplies more conveniently from the Continent. The considerable overcapacity in plant which then built up among European producers

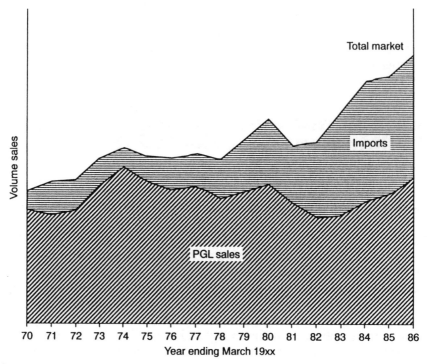

Figure 8.1 *Volume sales of Pilkington's flat glass to the UK market (1970–1986). (Source: company records)*

from 1980 through to 1986 provided a strong motivation to Continental firms to invade the UK market.

The third key factor was Pilkington's own labour costs. This was due, on the one hand, to high wage inflation during the 1970s which persisted at over 10 per cent per annum almost continuously from 1970 through to 1981. On the other, it was due to Pilkington's own overmanning. In part, this was a result of the survival of outdated sheet glass works (the last one in St Helens closing only in 1980). Largely, however, it was due to the fact that Pilkington had been the first to lay down new float glass facilities, which were ageing by then, while rivals who built later were able to incorporate the latest developments and achieve more efficient working.

The result was that Pilkington's UK business made a loss in 1981 for the first time in sixty years, and continued in this position for four years through to 1984. Only continued licensing income and profits from its overseas businesses kept the Group in profit.

New directions

Whereas other companies around this time transformed themselves by getting out of low added-value commodity products, Pilkington had a technological leadership in the production of flat glass which it was commit-

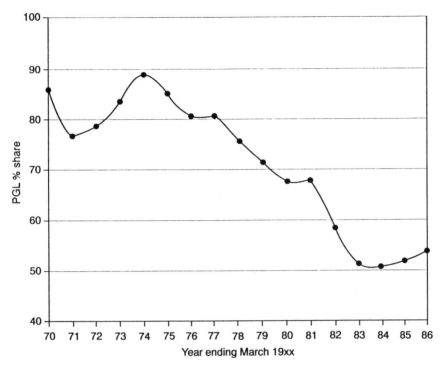

Figure 8.2 *Pilkington's share of the UK flat glass market (1970–1986). (Source: company records)*

ted to retain. It still wanted to be a world leader, and in the UK was in any case dependent on flat glass for 80–90 per cent of its sales volume. World-wide, the Group had continued to build up its position in flat glass and in downstream safety glass products by building plants outside the UK during the 1970s. Its commitment to its traditional product line was thereby reinforced. Within Europe its strategy was directed at securing cost leadership, and the process of turnaround in the UK focused therefore on cutting labour costs through new work practices and shedding jobs.

Alongside this strategy, the Group pursued product diversification in glass-related products, such as ophthalmics and electro-optics, through a series of acquisitions in the 1970s and 1980s. In 1986, this had materialized into an objective (set out in the Annual Report) to have a third of sales and profits in these newer, non-core businesses. In practice, however, this proved difficult to realize, and by the early 1990s the focus on the traditional flat and safety glass businesses had reasserted itself. This goes to show how strong the core business was in the Group psychology. On the other hand, considerable progress was made towards the goal of a higher proportion of sales and profits in North America, Continental Europe, and the Rest of the World, by the acquisition of the German company Flachglas, in 1980, and the glass interests of the American company, Libby-Owen-Ford, in two stages, in 1982 and 1986.

Redundancy and recovery in the UK

In the UK, meanwhile, turnaround centred on cost-cutting. The result was a steady reduction in total UK numbers employed throughout the 1980s, even though employment across the Group grew considerably. The graph in Figure 8.3 shows these changes in employment against sales and profits.

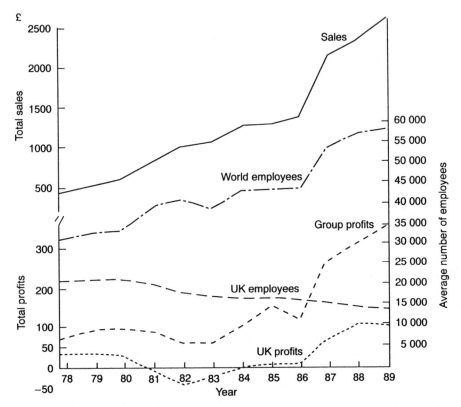

Figure 8.3 *Business performance and employment at Pilkington.* (Source: *company records*)

The picture is slightly confused by the inclusion of electro-optics and ophthalmics businesses in the UK figures. However, if we look at employment in St Helens (Table 8.1), where the company had its headquarters and where most of its UK employment was concentrated, we can see that these job cuts in the core businesses were (1) severe and (2) disproportionately felt in St Helens. Thus, whereas in 1960, 60 per cent of all employees in the

Table 8.1 Employment in St Helens

	1970	*1975*	*1982*	*1987*	*1989*
St Helens	17 011	12 968	10 100	6 700	5 700
Total UK	25 895	20 525	18 250	15 200	13 500

company had been in St Helens, and still constituted just under a quarter in 1982, by 1989 company employment in St Helens amounted to only 9 per cent.

In 1980, however, the company's heart was still in St Helens. Despite the jolt to its image as a paternalistic, family company from a seven-week strike in 1970, and the fact that it had gone public in 1970, it retained the instincts of a community-based, family company. As a result, it took pains to minimize the impact of redundancy. The redundancy programme was spread out over a longer period than it might have been (from 1980 to 1987), and without compulsory redundancies. Altogether, in the period from 1981 to 1987, £103 million was paid out in redundancies.

At the same time, to help with job creation outside the company, Pilkington set up the 'Community of St Helens Trust'. This in turn led to a number of infrastructure developments (Rainford Venture Capital, INDEX to promote youth training, a company to help small businesses find accommodation, and NIMTECH to facilitate technological transfer from large to small–medium companies). Between 1978 and 1985, it is reckoned the Trust helped to generate 6000 jobs in small businesses and to help over 2600 small businesses in the St Helens area (Fazey, 1987).

The end of this process saw Pilkington's UK (and European) profits reviving, with the benefit of a 'window of opportunity' between 1986 and 1990, when demand for glass once again exceeded capacity after the period of very low utilization and price wars of the early 1980s.

Decentralization

While job cuts lowered operating costs, an integral part of the whole turnaround process was decentralization. Decentralization challenged deeply established management practices and assumptions and the whole structure of industrial relations, and had a direct bearing on the way new working practices and redundancies were managed. It represented an interweaving of strategic, structural, cultural, and attitudinal change which transformed personnel work. It was part therefore of the evolution of personnel management towards HRM.

Decentralization was a 'catch-all' term used by people within Pilkington to describe a process they recognized was of fundamental significance to the company's development. It had a number of strands, covering:

- Structural changes in the composition of the main board, whereby the chief executives no longer sat on the board as of right, and divisions and functions were represented by 'sponsoring' directors
- The regrouping of individual businesses within a merged 'flat and safety glass' division (subsequently 'Pilkington Glass Limited', or PGL)
- New profit and loss responsibilities for these individual businesses which affected their standing *vis-à-vis* one another and Group Headquarters

- A reduction in the size and role of centrally provided services
- Plant bargaining and productivity packages agreed at local level.

The overall intention and effect of these changes was to give individual businesses fuller control over their own operations. In the words of a main board director: 'Decentralization was aimed at pushing responsibility and authority for business performance down the line.'

One aspect of this was to make the businesses more responsive to their markets. The flat glass side of the business consisted of four large tanks, based at the Cowley Hill works in St Helens, which poured out flat glass. Beyond these, there were a number of units which processed the basic glass in various ways – for architectural and motor vehicle use, for example – and other units which used a different raw material, such as glass fibres. These downstream units needed to become more marketing-oriented, and indeed think of themselves as stand-alone businesses.

A second aspect was to give the different plants better control over their own costs. Pay, conditions, and working practices were critical in running the individual businesses – whether conceived as single plants, groups of plants, or the whole flat and safety glass division. Historically, these had been determined centrally, and geared to parities among the workforce in St Helens, where, as we noted, the majority of employees were located into the early 1980s.

Decentralization as a structural process was therefore closely bound up with the turnaround strategy of making the UK plants cost-efficient by world standards, in that it established local bargaining and terms that could diverge between different units. This involved:

- A massive dismantling of central structures for determining job grades and wage rates
- The building of a local capability, among line managers and personnel specialists, to take over responsibility for negotiating grades and pay.

This could not be tackled in one fell swoop, simply and directly, though. The process by which it was done is especially interesting for the way structural and cultural issues were linked over a number of years. In macro terms, the ability to bring about change at plant level depended on first being able to clarify the strategies and structures of the different parts of the business, or, in the case of the central functions, their role in the Group. This likewise depended on being able to weaken the functional structure.

At a more micro level, the process of negotiating local terms on jobs and pay, to secure productivity improvements, provided an object lesson in decentralized decision making. Managers gained confidence to manage things at a local level, and both managers and employees started to focus on the local operating and market environment. In the best traditions of productivity bargaining, it thus had immediate practical benefits and longer-term cultural and attitudinal ones. Decentralization, then, was not only, or simply, about establishing site negotiations.

Decentralization as a cultural and structural process

The structural–cultural problem was fourfold:

- An 'horizontal' affiliation to employees in the same bargaining group across the company, reinforced by separate centralized bargaining for each group
- The concentration of employees in St Helens with elaborate family networks across the four plants (plus head office, plus the R&D centre), which made it difficult to sustain different terms and conditions across sites in close proximity
- A highly functionalized, hierarchic decision-making structure, at the top of which sat main board directors wearing functional hats, while relying on cross-functional committees at senior level to settle intractable problems
- The technological dominance of flat glass manufacture (operating through this functional structure) over the other businesses (safety glass, insulation and reinforcements, ophthalmic, and the electro-optics).

These features all tended to cut across the businesses as entities in their own right and contributed to the lack of market orientation within the operating units.

An initial important change was in the strategic and structural framework of the Group and Divisions. In 1983, to bring the business into line with similar companies elsewhere, the UK Flat and Safety Glass Divisions were merged. Although ostensibly an act of centralization, this allowed a regrouping of units into three constituent businesses, and a clearer definition of their strategies and relationship. Nevertheless, resolving this satisfactorily continued to be a problem through the 1980s. The influence of the functions was then reduced through changes in the structure of the main board from 1984 to 1986.

Changing the 'horizontal' affiliation of employees and undoing centralized bargaining, however, surfaced as an issue much earlier, but also took much longer to complete.

Undoing centralized pay bargaining

Until 1984, there were separate systems of negotiation across the UK for five major groups of employees – process workers, craftsmen, foremen, clerical staff, and middle management/professional/technical staff (the 'B' list). Group-wide schemes of job evaluation reinforced these 'horizontal' affiliations centred on pay bargaining.

Breaking down this system took a long time to bring about. Decentralization was talked about in the 1970s, but only began to crystallize into a strategy in the period 1978–1982, when senior managers in the personnel function started to see the central management of pay and grades becoming unmanageably complex, ineffective, and costly. It was estimated, for instance, that the centralized job evaluation system added 5–6 per cent to wage costs through administration and wage drift.

With new acquisitions during the 1970s being held outside the central system, however, the whole structure began to lose coherence and to creak with anomolies (Figure 8.4). As the squeeze on the UK businesses mounted from 1979 onwards, line managers began to add their voices of complaint about costs that were being imposed on them by centrally determined agreements. Those operating in more than one location – like the safety glass business, Triplex, with plants in St Helens and in Birmingham, partly in the central system and partly out – were particularly vociferous. As a result, the personnel department began to float the idea of greater local autonomy in a series of conferences with union officials in 1979, and in 1980 guidelines were laid out for developing local agreements.

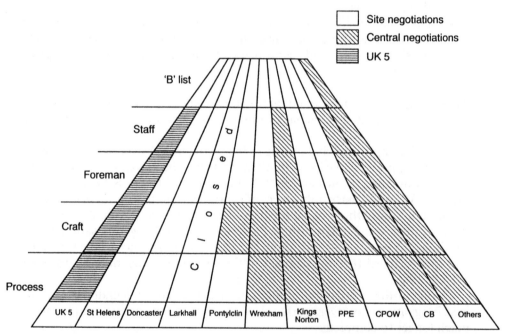

Figure 8.4 *Centralized and site negotiations at Pilkington in 1982. (Source: Group Personnel)*

The personnel function, then, was among the first to recognize the need for decentralization, and the first to try to do something about it. Not only were personnel managers nearer to many of the issues, but their perception of these was helped by their affinity with line managers. As a senior personnel manager put it:

It was the personnel function that picked up the ball and ran with it. And that was maybe because in the personnel function we'd had a policy of bringing through people who'd had significant line experience – who'd come from the businesses and had an orientation to the businesses in their thinking. They started to press the board, and to say, 'you really must look at the way we're organized in the UK – it's not appropriate – we must change'. And so the debate started.

Piloting change at Greengate (1979–1981)

Meanwhile, between 1979 and 1981, terms and conditions were being worked out for the first completely new float plant (Greengate) to be built by Pilkington in the UK since the company had developed the float glass process in the 1950s. This was sited in St Helens but was held outside the central system. It was designed to achieve Continental levels of efficiency by putting into effect lessons in plant design and working practices achieved in a similar investment in Sweden in 1975. As these were being evolved at Greengate, they became a model for what might be achieved elsewhere.

Policy and implementation (1981–1988)

Decentralization only became a policy adopted by the main board, however, with the continuing deterioration of the commercial situation; the accession of a new chairman (Anthony Pilkington) in 1980; and the growing difficulty for the board in centrally controlling diversification and overseas expansion (especially with the acquisition of the German-based Flachglas company in 1980). The board set out its commitment to move towards decentralization in 1981, but despite talks between the company and its unions through 1982–1983, no agreement could be reached. In late 1983, the company gave notice of terminating its central agreements (from 1 January 1984) and its intention to negotiate separate site agreements.

The actual process of doing so, however, was effectively to occupy the next four years, until 1988, as separate packages were negotiated, one by one, across each site and in the major central facilities of engineering and research and development.

Although differing in detail, they embraced many of the same principles first laid down in 1980 as the Greengate model took shape:

- Multi-union negotiations
- A single, simple, salaried reward system, with no extra payments (other than for shifts), including no bonus payments, and a standard week
- No paid overtime
- Involvement through participation in workplace decision making and an open style of management, to promote team effort
- High productivity
- Flexibility between crafts, and to a limited extent between operators and crafts, including job rotation, to promote efficiency and job satisfaction
- Employee commitment, through
  (a) Identification with the aims of the site;
  (b) Each individual being responsible to the work team by limiting sickness absence, planned time off, and ensuring continuous cover for a full 168 hours a week);

    (c) Company and employees recognizing that training continues for life.

(*Principles for Decentralized IR in Pilkington*, 1980)

Changes along these lines, from plant to plant, were intended, in the words of a senior personnel manager, 'to turn people's heads around', to focus them on the plant, rather than on the division or the company.

Precise terms differed from plant to plant. At one of the safety glass plants (Eccleston), for instance, annualized hours were adopted to cope with the peaks (May/June) and troughs (October/November) of supplying the motor industry. A new contract of employment required each individual to work a set number of 222 days/shifts over the year. Management could then vary the distribution of these according to the volume of business. The scheme devised at Eccleston also had another aspect, to control the high level of 'sickness' absence. In 1987, this was running at an all-time high of 11 per cent (compared with 8 per cent at two other works and 4 per cent at Greengate). Traditionally, management had tried to control this by disciplinary measures. Annualized hours represented a different approach. By scheduling only 213 shifts out of the 222 contracted, it left each individual nine shifts in reserve to cover the sickness absence of colleagues. If these were not called in, it effectively reduced their working hours from 39 to 37.5 per week. In this way, management put the onus on the workforce to control colleagues' sickness absence.

The approach at each site in developing and introducing its productivity package also differed. Some approached it in participative manner; some adopted a unilateral, management-directed approach. Some attempted radical, all-in-one-go change; at others it was more incremental and drawn out. A key factor was the history of industrial relations and the degree of trust existing on the particular site. Some, for example, were recognized as particularly difficult IR sites, with a history of conflict.

The following example describes the process of change at the St Helens site of Cowley Hill in order to illustrate a radical, participative approach, and the role of outside pressures in pushing this through.

The site agreement at Cowley Hill *(1984–1985)*

The float glass method had been pioneered at Cowley Hill. By 1972, four lines had been converted to float glass operation. The smaller of these were then phased out, however, and with the opening of Greengate in 1981, Cowley Hill was down to two float lines, or 'tanks' (on which the molten glass was 'floated'). As the figures show, de-manning had been going on gradually since 1978 in an effort to cut costs as Pilkington began to lose market share, and as Cowley Hill suffered from the decline in demand for its own thicker glass (4–5 mm). A sharp drop occurred in 1981–1982 through the closure of one of the original lines, while changes in glass handling and cutting had a further impact. All told, from April 1979 to 1984, the number of employees halved from 2906 to 1416 (see Table 8.2).

Table 8.2   Numbers employed at Cowley Hill (at 1 April)

1978	*1979*	*1980*	*1981*	*1982*	*1983*	*1984*	*1985*	*1986*
2938	2906	2832	2435	1813	1621	1416	1280	1055

These manning reductions enabled Cowley Hill to raise productivity from 2 tonnes per man per week to 4 tonnes. Further improvements in efficiency, an upturn in orders, and better loading of plant increased this to six tonnes in 1984/1985. However, these improvements and job cuts had not been accompanied by any fundamental change in working practices, outside the cutting area which had been automated.

In 1984, the periodic repair of furnaces on one of the two remaining float lines created the opportunity to push for fundamental change.

Furnace repair

Furnaces have a life of between five and ten years, varying according to the conditions of use. When in use, during the period of the glassmaking 'campaign', the priority is to keep the line running, since it is an expensive item of capital equipment, and it was always feared that damage would be done by letting furnaces cool. This allows only incremental improvements in efficiency at the 'hot' end. Every five years or so, however, the line shuts down and the furnaces are rebuilt, at considerable cost – £7 million in 1984. The implied threat that this investment would not be made allowed the company to seek changes in working practices and conditions, in line with those in operation at Greengate:

> You were into the classic situation of needing a crisis to get change, whether real or manufactured. We had the real one – a lot of investment was hanging on Cowley Hill, and whether we would be a one-tank or two-tank operation. We would not have been a two-tank operation if we had not had agreement in principle to go down the package route.

The physical proximity and technical similarity of Greengate, moreover, meant that it provided a very close model – as one manager put it, a 'whipping boy' to get similar manning levels to Greengate's design head-count of 404 employees.

A number of additional factors helped the process – some transfer of managers from Greengate to Cowley Hill; guidance from PGL's central personnel function; a long-standing rivalry with Greengate; and, above all, the prospect of a £1000 pay increase and pay parity with Greengate, when the new grading structure was accepted. Cowley Hill was, however, a tougher proposition than Greengate. First, Greengate had been established as a 'greenfield site' and its terms and conditions worked out before recruitment began. As a functioning plant, there was the difficulty of getting managers at Cowley Hill to turn away from their day-to-day problems to support radical, fresh solutions. Second, although managers were individually respected and had high personal credibility from having come up through the ranks, they were (1) unaccustomed to working as a team and (2) relied on a traditional dominating style to get things done in an adversarial IR environment. As a former works manager described it:

> The style at Cowley Hill was continual conflict. You expected every decision you made to be challenged. Everything would be put through the disputes procedure, and you conditioned yourself to managing in that sort of environment.

Third, as the oldest float plant in the company, the unions had a well-established power base. Attempts to crack down on working practices in 1982 had soured relationships, while the instability of the top management team (with the illness of the works manager in 1982) held back concerted change in working practices and terms. The coming together of a more stable management team in 1984, combining established insiders and new-comers, set the scene for the successful introduction of Cowley Hill's 'package'.

Planning and consultation

As at Greengate, the whole process depended on management spending time carefully working through principles, objectives, and tactics, and working indirectly on their own team development. In the light of what has been said about the functional loyalties and barriers which existed in Pilkington, this was important in encouraging managers out of their functional mind-set. The process began with a two-day planning meeting off-site, and the management team continued to get together throughout 1984–1985 for half a day a week off-site to talk through the major issues arising:

> We were very clear on our principles and spent hours testing things against our principles – 'could we accommodate that suggestion in terms of what our principles were? and if we couldn't, could we challenge the unions on it?'

In this respect, it helped to have outsiders on the team, without any ownership of the past, who could accept concessions which did not infringe underlying principles. A key figure in this respect was the new personnel manager, who had had experience of a similar change process at Esso, and could anticipate what might arise:

> The process I was looking to use was very similar to what we used at Esso. It was all the things to do with 'What is the mission? What are the standards? Why don't we have standards? How do we establish them? How do you establish management credibility?' And then, 'How do we involve people and get commitment?'

Thus, an early initiative was to take senior managers on a three-day course in the management of change to expose them to the concepts of 'establishing mission, establishing values, recycling the debate, testing as you go along, challenging everything, and, above all, being consistent in your message' (site personnel manager). The other critical part of the process was to develop trade union commitment to the basic objective of change, and to develop a consultative, problem-solving approach to working out the details. The character of the shop stewards at Cowley Hill helped here:

> Because historically Cowley Hill was the largest workforce, it tended to have more experienced stewards. So we had senior stewards who were, in the main, mature in their approach and understood the realities. The GMWU in particular were a very positive union, with a lot of very mature stewards.

A joint consultative committee of unions and works management (seventeen people) was formed in 1984, and discussions began in August 1984 after the annual pay deal was concluded. The objective was to devise a productivity–pay agreement before the next pay settlement, and implement this by the end of 1985. The furnace repair would then take place between June and September 1985.

Building relationships and trust

The first two to three months in autumn 1984 were spent effectively on relationship building; exploring the issues, difficulties, and problems; briefing and sharing information; and gradually sharing perspectives. Alongside this, the workforce as a whole were kept informed through a series of videos:

> It was a building process, and all the way through we played the same tunes in simple words – 'we are going to make mistakes, we need to work together, we need to make things happen'. In each video we made sure that whatever we put in, we had done before the next video. So, in the new video we said 'last time we told you about this – it has been done – now we will tell you about this'. So when we came to September, we could say 'the repair has been done and completed, everybody has made a great effort, now we need to do . . .' And I think it was believable. Each one was simple and reinforced the one before (Cowley works manager).

In this way, a sense of the timetable, clear stepping stones, and achievable targets were established in people's minds.

Negotiated terms and conditions

One of the earliest hurdles to be cleared was the level of job cuts. Management declared the manning levels it would be seeking in December 1984 – around 400 out of a then total of 1320. The enhanced terms for voluntary redundancy were put to the workforce in February 1985, and accepted. The next stage, evaluation of new job grades, went ahead in the summer, and the outcome of this was voted on by each of the four union memberships separately in September 1985. The full deal concluded in November 1985 (with the pay benefits backdated to 1 July) consisted of:

- Considerable reduction and simplification of the grading structure (drawing on the Greengate model) to ten non-management grades (where previously there had been 26 craft job grades alone), to be determined by a joint evaluation process, with cleaning services contracted out
- Consolidation of bonus payments and buying out of overtime, and an additional cost-of-living increase applied to the new grades
- Flexibility within broad categories ('glassmaking' and 'warehouse', in production, and 'maintenance', 'electrical', 'building', among craft employees)
- Training by October 1986 to enable all production employees to perform at least four or five jobs in their area (though not necessarily to be proficient in all jobs), with similar training for broader skills and job flexibility for other groups
- Elimination of labouring jobs
- Greater responsibilities for supervisors and a large number of new posts (as a result of vacancies created by voluntary redundancies), with selection using aptitude tests
- Harmonization of hours between staff and manual workers, and the abolition of overtime
- A supplement on the shift allowance for disruption to the engineering team, with continuous shift patterns otherwise already in operation (three patterns involving four-, five-, and six-member crews, and a double-day shift)
- Multi-union bargaining and four multi-union committees for each main area of the plant, in place of separate negotiations with the eight existing unions
- Further voluntary redundancies to bring numbers down to a target figure of 864, with the basic Pilkington redundancy payments scheme enhanced by an additional lump sum of £5000 (as part of the enhanced redundancy scheme introduced to bring the process across Pilkington to a more rapid close, and adopted already at another adjacent works).

In the event, the take-up of these terms exceeded requirements, and by 1987 employment had stabilized around 820 employees. Since this was below what had originally been envisaged and agreed, it had the effect of keeping in view the prospect of continuing change. As Income Data Services Ltd (IDS) reported on the Cowley Hill experience:

> Although the changes in bargaining, pay structures, employment and working practices are clearly related, they were not presented by the company as a package. Pay rates were only tabled after job relativities and numbers had been agreed in principle. The most important thing from the company's point of view was the commitment to on-going change, which has been reflected in changes made since the introduction of the new package (IDS Report 485/June 1986).

In other words, IDS recognized that the precise details were only presented and agreed, step by step, even though the outcome as a whole was a comprehensive, radical, and fairly quickly conceived 'package'.

From industrial relations to human resource management and HRD

As the Greengate and Cowley Hill episodes show, the aspects of personnel management at the fore in site-level changes during the early-to-mid-1980s were.negotiating structures, pay systems, job grades, and job cuts. Other areas, such as graduate recruitment and training/management development, however, also underwent significant change in keeping with decentralization.

At first, this was largely in the form of a winding-down of recruitment and training, as the Divisions took over responsibility from central Personnel for managing and paying for them, and consequently geared their recruitment and training to their own reduced requirements as decentralized units. In the second half of the 1980s, however, these became important once again, as corporate and divisional issues, as the problems of survival and restoring competitiveness were steadily overcome, and as organization structure and strategy were clarified.

A number of initiatives illustrate this shift towards greater preoccupation with employee skills and competences:

1 *Craft and production training* was reformed to broaden skills and promote flexibility, using training modules through which 'competences' could be developed over a lifetime. This included a revolutionary scheme, introduced in 1986, to provide production training in a common programme with first-year craft trainees. In parallel with this, the Youth Training Scheme (YTS) was adopted as the basis for all initial training for 16–18-year-olds, as part of a broader process of moving towards standards-based certified training.
2 From 1982 onwards *supervisory skills* were redefined; standards of recruitment were raised; training started to make use of formalized manager–supervisor coaching to promote personal role development; and supervisory courses from 1986 were given a higher technical and business content.
3 *Graduate training* and *management development* were given a stronger business focus, instead of simply developing functional specialists. The cornerstone of this was a new 'business development programme' launched in 1987 (specifically not a 'management development' programme), which was targeted at the 200-plus middle managers in the UK Flat and Safety Glass Division (PGL). This used team-based project/action-learning (and is described in Chapter 14).

In these ways, skills and competences at a number of levels were developed to support the requirements of decentralization for more performance-oriented management. This shift in priorities and focus is reflected in Figure 8.5.

Figure 8.5 *The process of organizational development at Pilkington Glass Ltd since 1979. (Source: PGL Personnel Department)*

This diagram, in use from 1987 onwards within the Flat and Safety Glass Division (PGL), was used to focus on the need in the late 1980s to address issues of human resource development. The words of the Personnel Director provide an apt comment on how the subsequent attention to HRD depended on first resolving the complex of other issues to do with strategy, structure, and industrial relations:

> The early 1980s were very much characterized by cost competitiveness anxieties, and it was essentially a period of slimming down and economizing. We then moved to a recognition that we needed to focus ourselves better – to organize ourselves better, and in our case we merged the Flat and Safety Glass Divisions in 1983. But even then, we were still in the process of defining our businesses – was it one business (basic glass), or three businesses (float, rolled, and polished wire), or businesses associated with customers? It's taken us a long time to sort that out in our minds, and only then could we start talking about business goals and how to meet them.
> And it's only at that point that you could start talking about what people you want – how many? what skills should they have? And then you can start talking about performance standards, and development.
> The early 1980s were very much in the top half of this diagram, bouncing up

and down, not going through a complete stage but keeping going back and refining things. And we're now in the bottom half, again bouncing back up and down, now using the word 'development' very much more today than we were five years ago.

A human resources function?

At Pilkington, staff see what they have done as good personnel work, and tend not to use the label 'HRM'. Nevertheless, changes were pursued with a very clear eye to the requirements of the business, while the actual shift in preoccupations was very obviously from industrial relations to HRD. Up to that point, the wheels of Personnel tended to grind on, maintaining the traditional apparatus of pay bargaining and job evaluation, and delivering centralized training schemes that were increasingly outdated and unrelated to demand.

The Pilkington case thus provides an opportunity to go beneath the label of HRM. Some of the best examples of a strategic HRM approach – such as Pilkington and Hardy Spicer in this book – eschew the label; while others who adopt it, don't practise it.

This transformation was intimately bound up with decentralization. Decentralization has been seen as weakening the personnel function – producing an attenuation in roles between senior and junior staff, and transferring responsibilities to line and general managers (Torrington, Mackay and Hall, 1985). This does not seem to have been the case at Pilkington.

First, there was the effect of dissolving collective bargaining arrangements at corporate level. Simply from the point of view of the preoccupations of senior management, this permitted a shift in attention from IR to HRD.

Second, the state in which the personnel management function survives an era of decentralization will depend on its standing at the outset. In Pilkington, the central and divisional personnel functions promoted decentralization, and they held the ring while line management and personnel managers at plant level developed their local industrial relations packages. The function at senior levels thus came through decentralization with its prestige and influence in the company at the very least intact.

Third, the personnel role at plant level in Pilkington was strengthened, and, in the course of devising and implementing productivity packages, plant management as a group also acquired more sophistication in HRM. They had to review the whole range of employment and work practices in line with business plans, and then give attention to the process of implementation and to maintaining a culture of change in the longer term that went beyond a one-off package of change.

Fourth, the training function shifted onto a new footing, with the central function put onto a profit centre or 'break-even' basis. This encouraged training that was sensitive to the needs of operating units, in both content and form of delivery.

Pilkington, however, also exemplifies another aspect of HRM, more rooted in its past, that is, a pervasive set of values to do with the company's responsibility to its employees and the community. The attempted take-over by BTR highlighted these.

The BTR bid and company social responsibility

In November 1986 BTR launched a £1.16 billion hostile take-over bid. The performance of the Group, with its depressed share price, had made it a rumoured candidate for such a bid for some while. When it came, it was twelve months too late, since the hard work of cutting costs had been done.

This had not yet shown up in company results in 1986, partly because accelerating the redundancy programme to bring it to an end had loaded additional redundancy payments into the accounts (totalling £21.1 million). Along with much-improved trading conditions, however, with demand for glass within Europe once again exceeding capacity, there was a significant recovery in UK and Group profits and sales in the half-time figures for January 1987 and a full-year forecast for 1987 to double profits. Pilkington mobilized public and City opinion against BTR; marshalled the 20 per cent of the equity the family and its army of pensioners still controlled; and forced BTR to abandon its bid.

Pilkington versus BTR was widely recognized at the time as a clash of very different corporate cultures, each of which in its way had been very successful. BTR was the corporate raider which had increased profits from £24 million to £362 million in ten years and earnings per share in that time from under 5 per cent to nearly 25 per cent. It had done so by introducing tight financial management into acquisitions and turning round what it unashamedly termed 'rust bucket companies' in mature industry sectors. The short-term perspective which this implied was fundamentally at odds with how Pilkington saw itself – an increasingly high-technology company relying on long-term investments and a strategic perspective on its markets.

The BTR bid at this particular time of frantic merger activity in 1986 crystallized for many, including CBI members, the issue of long-termism versus short-termism – or 'Industry versus the City'. As Anthony Pilkington put it in the formal defence document:

> This bid is about the future of *all* British companies who believe in the creation of wealth and the pursuit of excellence that leads ultimately to world leadership – rather than the poverty of cashing in the future for short-term gains.

At the same time, in its defence documents, Pilkington stressed its social philosophy – cooperation with employees, social responsibility, the creation of wealth which benefited a wide range of groups, and the need to balance the conflicting claims of stakeholder groups (and not just act for shareholders). Managers brought up in the traditions of the company echoed this:

> The basic question is, 'is the boundary of the organization's responsibility for employment and unemployment simply the boundary of the organization itself, or is it broader than that, encompassing the community?' And how does the organization handle the difference between the two?

And again:

> We have a company which introduces new technology and as a result it alters its labour requirements and has an impact on the local labour market. It can either walk away from that problem, or it can accept the problem. And here you have a company who have accepted the problem.

As a result, Pilkington was able to draw upon the credit it had built up with employees and the community to gain their active support against a company that was perceived as likely to initiate far worse job cuts than anything Pilkington had made.

The failure of the BTR bid was recognized as something of a watershed in the attitude to company take-overs. However, since then a second recession and the addition of further capacity in the European glass industry have brought renewed pressure on Pilkington's profits (aggravated by difficulties in the electro-optics ('optronics') business from defence industry cutbacks). So far, tight financial conditions and high interest rates after 1989 have tended to depress further hostile acquisitions.

Summary

The ingredients of retrenchment and turnaround at Pilkington were perhaps unique to the period of the early 1980s. Many sectors of manufacturing industry were forced to tackle what were seen as accumulated problems of overmanning, poor work practices, and loss of control to trade unions. Industrial relations issues were therefore at the heart of change in the early 1980s. By the time of the recession of 1990–1993 employers were generally on top of their industrial relations and trade unions, helped by the anti-union legislation of the 1980s. Manufacturing also had largely overcome its deep-rooted problems of overmanning.

The 1990–1993 recession has therefore had a rather different impact. Nevertheless, the lessons of retrenchment and turnaround from the 1980s still have relevance, albeit with less force and in different sectors. They now apply more especially to the service sector, the privatized utilities, and in relatively protected industries which the Single European Market will increasingly open up to competition. Moreover, the business cycle will continue to repeat itself, and there will always be organizations that let things drift until a crisis looms.

Looking ahead, the case also addresses wider issues for HRM than simply company strategy, success, and survival. Pilkington has long had an image as a company that takes its social responsibilities more seriously than most. Although this has declined in recent years, the case articulates a key issue about a company's social responsibilities. During the 1980s, the interest of employees and community tended to be entirely subordinated, in public rhetoric, to shareholders and customers. In the 1990s, the interests of this broader set of stakeholders, through corporate responsibility and governance, are gradually coming more into public view again, in the wake, among other things, of scandals such as the Maxwell affair, Barlow Clowes, and the Guinness trial.

Finally, this chapter reinforces the message about aligning HRM to the strategic and structural drives of the organization – 'aligning', not simply 'following' – and the effect of changing perspectives and behaviour. Managers often talk, for instance, about bringing about cultural change, as if this can be achieved in a vacuum. Certainly, there are all sorts of ways HRM can tackle this directly, usually focused on training (as in Barclaycard's 'Quality 1st' programme). HRM, as a force for cultural change, is far more potent, however, if it is associated with real business issues, and with structural changes that aim at a better alignment between business goals and organization. The case of Pilkington thus exemplifies the notion of change along the 'critical path' of the organization and its strategic business concerns (Beer, Eisenstet and Spector, 1990).

Note

1   This case is derived from Hendry, C. and Pettigrew, A. (1989). *Strategic Change and Human Resource Management in Pilkington PLC*, CCSC, University of Warwick. A version of the case appears in Hendry, C. and Pettigrew, A. (1992), 'Patterns of strategic change in the development of human resource management', *British Journal of Management*, **3**, 3, 137–156.

Part Three
Basic Concepts for an Employment Systems Perspective

9
Manpower planning

Introduction

A key message of this book is that a strategic approach to employment has to operate at a number of levels. A human resources strategy cannot be confined to a written document. It consists of many things. In Chapter 4, we described strategy in terms of goals, policies, plans, decisions, and programmes.

Goals and policies involve the long-term creation of an organizational ethos (or culture) in which appropriate behaviours and motivation can flourish. Plans and strategic decisions determine the broad direction of an organization and within that specific activities and resource commitments in the medium term. Programmes are specific initiatives to implement plans or secure improvements in aspects of the organization's work in the short to medium term.

The chapters in Part Two provided various illustrations of this multi-level, variable timeframe activity. Chapter 4 looked at the implications for HRM of organizational growth and the firm's competitive posture on price, quality, and innovativeness; Chapter 5 considered the impacts from organizational structure change; while Chapter 6 explored the theme of organizational cultures and the problem of culture change. Each chapter, and especially the case studies in Chapters 7 and 8, provided examples of thinking and activity involving goals, policies, plans, decisions, and programmes. Each showed organizations attempting to align human resource activity in a coherent way.

One characteristic of HRM in all this is the way a single activity or initiative can have an impact at a number of levels. For instance, capping a payment-by-results system to reduce the overall paybill (a programme) might lower output in the short term and cause employees to leave the company for better-paid work elsewhere. If labour turnover is severe, this could jeopardize the achievement of the strategic plan in the medium to long term. At the same time, there might be a short-term impact on the culture (involving loss of motivation and resentment against management) and a longer-term shift from an output focus to a concern with quality and wastage. The various objectives which such an action might serve and the possible impacts all need to be thought through.

A strategic approach thus involves, above all, a way of looking at things which takes account of multiple impacts and interconnected activity. The chapters in Part Two did this also by emphasizing the links between strategy, structure, and culture. For a long while, corporate strategy has been concerned with models of growth which link business strategies to types of structure. Although we criticized the prescriptive use of such models, they have a role to play in identifying patterns and options, and sensitizing the practitioner to the organizational implications of growth. By understanding how organization structures differ and the dynamics which determine the balance between centralization and decentralization, the practitioner can anticipate the areas of HRM that might be affected and the options for managing adverse consequences. Likewise, various authors have linked patterns of strategy and structure to organizational culture – for example, Harrison (1972), Handy (1976), and Mintzberg (1979). Models like these combine elements of corporate strategy and organization behaviour.

In Part Three, we turn to the tools and frameworks for a strategic perspective which HRM can provide from within. If the distinguishing feature of HRM is 'strategic integration', manpower planning has to be near the heart of HRM in practice. The aim of this chapter is to outline how manpower planning works and to describe some of the models and techniques in its repertoire.

Manpower planning, however, has often failed to live up to expectations, largely because of an over-quantitative approach and the difficulty in an uncertain environment of forecasting an organization's demand for labour. For this reason, there has been an attempt to recast it as 'human resource planning' (HRP). In Chapter 10 we will therefore look at developments within manpower planning which give it a broader character.

One outstanding weakness in the whole project, however, remains the focus on stocks and flows of people, and the relative absence of any concept of skill as the basis for work performance. Indeed, this has been a curious deficiency in the theory of personnel management generally (Hendry, 1990). At a fundamental level, HRM is about skills – their acquisition, utilization, development and retention (to paraphrase the objectives of manpower planning) – and the core task of HRM is the development of a skill supply strategy to realize the aims of the corporate strategic plan. It is an organization's skill supply strategy, with its overtones of deliverable performance, which turns business strategy into reality.

In Chapter 10 we will therefore introduce the idea of skill into human resource planning, along with the alternative concept of 'competency', and look at the methodologies for analysing and describing skills and competences.

A framework for manpower planning[1]

Manpower planning arose out of the same rational belief in being able to manage the business environment that animated post-war corporate planning. Each was sustained by the long boom of the 1950s and 1960s, and by relatively stable, centralized organizations which made planning possible and feasible. Many of the early examples of manpower planning and developments in manpower forecasting were thus in large, centralized public sector organizations such as the Civil Service, the National Coal Board, and the armed forces.

The preoccupation with forecasting labour supply can also be traced to the economic circumstances of that time when unemployment was low and the problem facing many organizations was to ensure a predictable supply of labour coming through the organization. Increasing uncertainty in the economic environment (on the demand side) has meant that manpower planning has often failed to live up to its promise. Corporate planning has faced the same problem and has moved away from the mechanics of computing numbers to adopt more creative approaches to the future (like scenario building).

In this chapter we will outline some of the main elements of 'best practice' in manpower planning, before considering how human resource planning improves upon it. Manpower planning has five essential elements:

- Analysing the current manpower resource
- Reviewing labour utilization
- Forecasting the demand for labour
- Forecasting supply
- Developing a manpower plan

While these can be seen as sequential steps (Bennison and Casson, 1984), in practice thinking about manpower can begin with almost any of these. This is what makes manpower planning a dynamic process. For instance, a manufacturing function might want to introduce new machinery that will do a job to a better standard and more quickly. To justify the expenditure, the manufacturing manager will be expected to show a saving on labour, which may translate into fewer people. In another case, a downturn in business may provoke an urgent drive to reduce overheads and cuts in office staff. The point is that manpower decisions have been triggered outside the personnel or HRM function, and most certainly outside the hands of anyone who carries the title of manpower planner. The job of everyone concerned with such decisions is to think through the implications in these five areas. Also because of this, it is better to show it as a circular process (as in Figure 9.1), rather than in a linear way, as is usually the case.

The other point that the two examples highlight is that planning can have a short-, medium-, and long-term aspect (Bramham, 1975). The long term is necessary to provide a framework for managing broad trends. Long-term planning should be done regularly and systematically, and plans kept under review. The short to medium term, however, is what matters to most managers. But this does not excuse them from planning. The emphasis in planning simply changes – from writing formal plans to thinking things through. Failure to distinguish the process of planning from the writing of a plan is one of the biggest misconceptions in management. It is also what has kept manpower planning as a backroom function, as the custodian of plans.

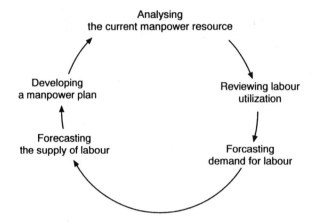

Figure 9.1   *The manpower planning cycle*

Analysing the current manpower resource

The starting point for planning is to have proper records of existing employees. The advent of relatively cheap personal computers (PCs) and software specially designed to hold such records has transformed this activity for the smaller firm. For larger organizations and for more sophisticated tasks, however, a PC will be inadequate. Setting up a system also remains a major task. Basic records cover:

- *Personal data* – including date of birth (age), qualifications, special skills, and training record
- *Position data* – including current job and work history in the organization
- *Financial data* – including current pay, how this is made up (for example, overtime and shift premia), incremental scale, and pension rights.

Many of these details will traditionally be kept for payroll purposes. When introducing a personnel system it may be simpler and cheaper to extend a payroll system. On the other hand, this will be less focused and less flexible for the kind of analysis the personnel/HR function might want to carry out. This analysis will comprise both an 'inventory' of employees (who they are) and an on-going 'audit' (what is happening to them). Such analysis may include:

- *Headcount analysis*, by age, service, skills, grades, and department. The overall profile of the workforce generated in this way is basic to any manpower planning system, and a vital aid to management decision making on things like redundancy. It can highlight impending problems, such as the retirement of a whole cohort of employees, and the need for fresh recruitment and training. One development is the way accreditation schemes like BS 5750, NVQ, and IIP are bringing greater formality to the analysis of training (how many employees are trained, and to what standard). This may tend to push organizations towards a more human resource-oriented style of planning

- *Employee turnover*, using data on joiners and leavers over a year. Along with headcount analysis, this is basic to forecasting supply. It may also identify problems – for example, particular jobs where there is high turnover – and stimulate corrective action

- *Absenteeism and sickness*. This will be especially geared to alerting management to problems and the need for corrective action. It will interact with other indices concerned with productivity (such as the amounts of overtime that are incurred simply to provide cover for absenteeism and sickness). Like turnover data, this information clearly needs to be generated on an on-going basis, as distinct from basic records (the 'inventory'). It is likely to be a natural product of payroll data and the subject of regular reports from line functions (similar to the analysis of pay below). The introduction of Statutory Sickness Pay (SSP), which put the onus on employers for paying out benefits to employees and claiming back from the Department of Social Security, has encouraged employers to maintain more rigorous records

- *Overall structure of the paybill*, including how salary costs will rise with increments and reduce with new entrants at lower points in a scale

- *Actual paybill against budget*, with areas of variance.

Analysis in these various ways can identify significant issues of performance and productivity, and imbalances that may need to be corrected. It underpins the shift in manpower planning from macro-forecasting towards the more problem-centred approach advocated by Armstrong (1979).

Reviewing labour utilization

The audit activity described above may be supplemented from time to time by data from other sources concerned with how efficiently people are being used. Whether this is part of a normal auditing process will depend from company to company. Data on and analysis of manning ratios ('directs' to 'indirects') is a case in point. This may come under review only when cost pressures or the example of a competitor cutting indirect staff focuses attention on labour costs. Many large organizations have permanent staffs using work study and O&M (organization and methods) techniques to undertake periodic reviews of working methods and the efficiency of staff levels.

Forecasting the demand for labour

At first, forecasting the demand for labour might seem straightforward. Unfortunately, it is not. The problem is how to convert volumes of work into numbers of people. Two of the favoured means for doing this are ratio-trend analysis and the use of work study standards.

Ratio-trend analysis

The basic principle here is to say if it takes six people, for example, to perform an existing amount of work, it will take twelve people to do twice as much. Organizations measure activity levels in a variety of different ways. Telecommunications companies, for instance, apparently use the number of telephone lines as the critical measure for the volume of activity. Year-on-year growth or decline in this can be translated into likely numbers of employees. With increasing competition in the world's telecommunications markets, companies like BT are paying particular attention to the 'numbers of employees: number of telephone lines' ratio of major competitors like AT&T. Aggregate figures can then be broken down into the implications for different functions, according to the historical ratios between them. The ratio between 'directs' and 'indirects' in manufacturing is a classic one, with sub-divisions into foremen/chargehands: direct workers and inspectors: direct workers.

Individual departments in an organization also will have their own rule-of-thumb measures. A sales department, for instance, may have an idea of the number of customer calls a salesperson should make in a week, and, indeed, use this as one criterion for monitoring sales efficiency. If the business plan projects an increase in the number of new customers, this can be translated into a proportionate increase in the sales force.

The problem with measures like these is that they are crude. They take no account of economies (or diseconomies) of scale which affect efficiencies; nor of local conditions; nor of the potential of new methods and technology to increase efficiencies. For example, getting new customers in an undeveloped market where there may be many new prospects close together is a lot easier than in a relatively saturated one where each additional prospect may require travelling greater distances. A new approach to work may completely undermine traditional ratios. In many firms, for instance, the new philosophy in quality, whereby direct employees are responsible for managing their own, has eliminated the inspection function. It is thus a great mistake simply to extrapolate from the past.

What ratio-trend analysis can do is to provide ballpark figures, which then focus attention on ways of improving efficiencies and a closer look at the underlying implications. In the example described in Chapter 7, continuing staff growth at Barclaycard at the level seen through the 1970s and 1980s was regarded as untenable in view of the local labour market and limited office space in Northampton. In the short term, this encouraged a policy of devolving activities to regional centres, and in the longer-term the development of technology to replace people. Accompanying this, a diversification into new lines of business showed up the need for a higher proportion of management staff to manage a more complex business. In the process, more complex ways of measuring activity levels had to be developed than 'numbers of cardholders', 'cardholder turnover', and 'number of visa merchant outlets'.

Work study

Work study is a more systematic method, but limited to manufacturing, certain other areas of manual work (such as in local authorities), and large clerical functions. For it to be worth while and do-able in the first place, an activity has to be repeated sufficiently often to generate a reliable standard and justify the cost of measuring it.

The time taken for an experienced person to perform an operation is assessed through observation, and a work standard established. Allowances for rest breaks, fatigue, and idle time are then factored in. If a product goes through a number of operations, as is likely, the separate standard times are totalled to produce a standard hour figure for how long a job should take. A manufacturing or similar budget can then be built up which converts planned output for the year into total hours required. This is then divided by a figure representing the average hours one person works in a year, to give the number of direct production workers required.

There is a strong tradition of measuring repetitive work in manufacturing. As factory work engages direct workers in more sophisticated tasks, however, work study becomes less useful. This highlights a problem demand forecasting in general has. It needs a reliable base-line and a relatively unchanging world. In the absence of these conditions, there is no simple direct path from the corporate business plan to quantifying manpower requirements. Managerial judgement has to be applied. This is apart from the fact that agreeing changes to existing manpower allocations is liable to be a political process (Wilensky, 1967).

Forecasting supply

Forecasting supply has two components, internal and external. Forecasting external supply means understanding the impact on recruitment and retention of such factors as:

- Demographic patterns
- Levels of unemployment
- Developments in the local economy, transport, education, and housing
- The pay policies of other employers, locally and nationally, and their plans for growth and contraction.

While the HR or personnel function should be keeping a general eye on these as a matter of course, they are likely to receive closer attention when there are specific plans to grow a business and there is a perceived gap between requirements and existing skills and numbers of employees ('the manpower gap').

The origins of manpower planning in operational research (Bryant, 1965; Lawrence, 1973), however, have meant that the main focus has been on developing models for understanding internal supply. The central concern here is with what is happening in terms of leavers and joiners, and the changing shape of the workforce in terms of age, grades, numbers, length of service, and location. This links back, then, to the basic 'manpower inventory' and its analysis.

There are a number of simple ways of reflecting people leaving and joining:

- *Crude labour turnover rate (or wastage index):*

$$\frac{\text{Number of leavers per period}}{\text{Average number employed during that period}} \times 100$$

  This shows the percentage of employees leaving over a period of time (say, in the course of a year). This rate can be then compared over time and with that of other organizations. It fails to discriminate, however, between the same job turning over frequently and a general pattern of turnover. Thus, many organizations will have 'hot spots' where it is hard to retain people for long in particular jobs. The job itself is perhaps unattractive, or the type of recruit is in great demand. To overcome this, Bowey (1974) developed the stability index.

- *Stability index:*

$$\frac{\text{Number of employees with one or more year's service}}{\text{Number employed one year ago}} \times 100$$

  This will show whether the workforce is generally stable or volatile. In conjunction with the crude turnover rate, it can help to focus problems. These may include whether the organization is failing to bring in new blood because of low turnover.

- *Wastage/survival curves:*
  Having a picture of wastage patterns over time is a major help to an organization in:

  - Planning recruitment and training to renew skills and experience
  - Developing policies and practices to minimize the loss of valuable trained people
  - Managing career progression
  - Managing outflows through pension arrangements, and, if necessary, encouraging people to leave to make it possible to bring in new blood.

Wastage can be plotted in a number of different ways: for instance, to show when people tend to leave and at what rate according to length of service. This can be expressed either in actual numbers (as shown in Figure 9.2) or as a percentage of joiners. Alternatively, by showing the cumulative impact of turnover, as in Figure 9.3 (again either in numbers or in percentage terms), we can see who remains from a diminishing population of original entrants (the half-life index is a variant of this, showing how long it takes for a cohort of new entrants, such as graduate trainees, to reduce to half).

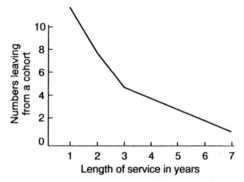

Figure 9.2 *Frequency distribution of leavers by length of service (in numbers)*

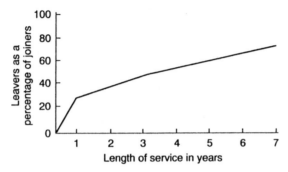

Figure 9.3 *The cumulative impact of labour turnover in a single cohort*

The expectation is that such curves will reveal regularities in overall behaviour. Early work on the psychology of labour turnover (Rice, Hill and Trist, 1950) suggested that there are three major phases in people's attachment to an employer:

1 *An induction crisis*, when the relationship is weak and people either promptly leave or take a 'wait and see' attitude having invested some commitment in joining already. The latter was seen as more typical of skilled and professional workers who are likely to put more effort into assessing a job before taking it. The induction crisis may therefore be delayed for this group, with wastage starting at a lower level than in Figure 9.3 before bounding up for a short period. High unemployment may have changed this pattern, however.
2 *Differential transit*, when wastage declines and people think about settling or steel themselves to leave.
3 *Settled connection*, when people have decided to stay (or inertia has set in), and wastage is consequently low or intermittent.

In addition to these simple indices and principles, operations research has contributed a variety of mathematical techniques for analysing labour force renewal (see, for example, Bartholomew, 1969), and models for representing internal supply as a series of stocks and flows. In essence, what such models attempt to do is 'map' the organization as an employment system and describe or account for its behaviour in one of two ways:

- One in which people leave, vacancies occur, and people can therefore be promoted (a 'renewal' or 'pull' model) or
- One where the defining factor is length of service, and promotion is driven by the numbers in particular grades with an equivalent length of service (a Markov or 'push' model).

Such an approach is central to manpower planning in the work of Bennison and Casson (1984) and that of the Institute of Manpower Studies. First, you draw a 'map' of the employment system to show how the organization manages manpower movements; second, you identify problem areas, using data on manpower stocks, flows, age distribution, length of service, etc.; and third, you take account of the rate of loss and types of wastage. Action plans are then geared to specific problems and estimated labour demand from developments in the business.

A 'systems' approach readily lends itself to understanding and controlling for career progression. For this reason, although it comes out of the tradition of manpower planning, it begins to shade into the more qualitative approach associated with human resource planning. Figure 9.4 shows the 'manpower system' for a retail financial services organization.

Employees are placed in 'career groups' generally comprising more than one grade. Groups are distinguished where there is a significant change in the nature of the job or in status. The size of each box indicates the number of employees in that group. The relative sizes of the different boxes can suggest problems likely to arise in the dynamics in the whole system. For instance, the small number of supervisors in the middle is a serious bottleneck.

The arrows marked 'R' show entry points into these groups from outside the organization; 'P' shows promotion routes; and 'T' lateral transfers within the organization. In this example, typical of finance companies, the main entry route is into junior clerical grades, from which most management grades subsequently come. 'L' represents losses from the system. Wastage patterns can be readily shown by putting actual numbers against this for each group. Similarly, numbers for promotions and transfers, in conjunction with the changing composition of career groups, will show pressure points in the system. Other information, such as the male/female split at each level, will highlight selection processes in the career system.

Visual representation of the employment system in this way can then be used to highlight and challenge the beliefs that underpin it, the practices which sustain it, and the consequences it can breed. For instance, as Hirsh (1984, p. 50) notes, the tendency to draw management from the clerical intake, which has been typical for most of the financial sector, was based on the following suppositions:

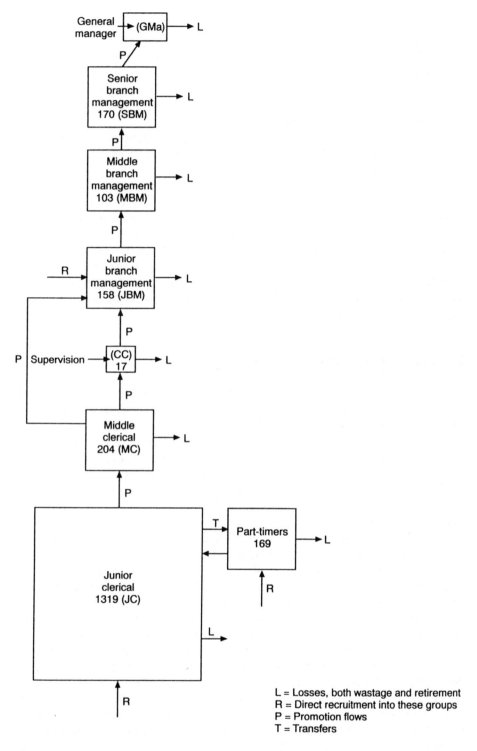

Figure 9.4 *The manpower system in a financial services organization. (Reproduced with permission from Hirsh, 1984)*

- A trustworthy workforce in finance is paramount, and therefore socialization into steady habits from an early age is important.
- Managers' jobs in the past were a development of clerical skills and they acted as 'super-clerks'.
- It was possible to recruit young people into banking and finance in this way because there were enough who were attracted by the job security and 'clean' work.
- The lack of technological expertise in management made it unnecessary to recruit more highly educated people (such as graduates) and specialists from outside.

The conditions on which these beliefs were based have, of course, been rapidly eroded in the last ten years (Hendry, 1987; see also the Barclaycard case in Chapter 7). Nevertheless, career systems tend to institutionalize outmoded beliefs, and through the cumulative effect of recruitment and selection practices they embed obsolete skills and experience. To make matters worse, promotion systems also tend to perpetuate themselves. As we note later, the problem of 'inheritance' is one of the critical issues a skill supply strategy and HRM has to address.

Developing a manpower plan

The various forms of analysis described above may already have identified problems that require action. Specific plans to grow or shrink a business, or to introduce technological change, will demand coordinated action in a number of areas affecting headcount and skills. This may involve recruitment, training and development, retention, or redundancy. Each of these can involve a further set of human resource initiatives – with retention problems, for example, typically exposing issues of pay, career opportunities and selection, and working conditions. However, while descriptions of manpower planning talk grandly of 'the manpower plan', and may then break this down into 'a recruitment plan', training plan' and so on, the problem is often the failure at this point to take coordinated action.

Failures of planning have complex causes. One reason may be that the responsibility for manpower planning is detached from the management of recruitment, training, and other areas like pay. Therefore there is insufficient commitment to 'the plan'. A second reason may be that these latter activities are themselves uncoordinated. This also is not unusual. A third reason is simply that we invest too much confidence in systematic planning. Unexpected events overtake intended plans and force them to be changed; adjustments in different activities move at different rates which were not foreseen; actions do not produce the outcomes we intend. Plans therefore need to be broad in intent and flexibly implemented. Our earlier distinction between (broad) plans and (detailed) programmes is relevant here.

The other basic lesson should not be ignored either. A coordinated or strategic approach to manpower (HRM) is also an organizational issue (as the example of Barclaycard in Chapter 7 shows). A lack of integration and overdetermined (or unreal) plans explains why the practice of manpower planning has often been very different from the theory.

The following are some areas a manpower plan may seek to address:

Recruitment:
- How many and what types of people are required?
- Should recruitment or internal development and transfer be preferred, and why? For instance, are there imbalances where transferring people would avoid a redundancy problem and solve a recruitment one?
- What problems exist with recruiting, and how might these be overcome? Might less conventional contracts (such as job-share) tap new sources of recruit?
- What is a realistic/necessary timetable for recruitment, and how should it be done?

Training and development:
- Given the number and types of people required, how desirable is it that they should be trained from within, and what is the capacity of the training and development system to deliver them?
- Where will trainees come from – from among existing employees, through those already in the pipeline, or new recruits who will first have to be recruited?
- How will trainees be selected, either from within or without?
- What kind of training programme is required, what are the implications of taking people off-the-job, who will run it, how will it be resourced, what will it cost?
- What are the requirements for developing people, such as managers, over the longer term?
- Is the organization making full use of the potential of all employees, such as its women, in training and development?

Retention:
- Is the problem retaining people too long or losing them too soon? Are skills and experience being lost or getting stale?
- Is pay too low, compared with the competition?
- Are there inequities in the pay for different groups?
- Is the career system holding people back and frustrating them? Is promotion unnecessarily slow?
- Are people being passed over in favour of outsiders because they are not being prepared for promotion through training?
- Is the organization recruiting too many high flyers, all of whom it cannot hope to satisfy?
- Are new recruits being given realistic information about the organization and their prospects?
- Are selection processes recruiting the right people?
- Are new recruits being given adequate initial training?
- Are working conditions satisfactory? (There may be an allied problem here of health and safety practices that shows in sickness and absence figures – like turnover, sickness and absence represent a leakage of resources.)

- Is conflict a problem, and does the organization have effective procedures for consultation, communication, and grievance handling?

Redundancy:

- How far can people be lost through natural wastage or redeployed?
- What do the organization's agreements say about the procedures for handling redundancies? For example, does LIFO ('last in, first out') limit the organization's choice about who goes?
- How and when should it be announced, with how much consultation?
- How is redundancy pay determined?
- Who should be selected, how, and when?
- How far can redundancy be managed voluntarily, and does the organization want to place any restrictions on this to avoid losing key people?
- What can and should the organization do to help people to find new jobs?
- What do the redundancies mean in terms of reorganization to secure cover for work, and are there training implications for employees who remain?
- How long before the redundancies pay for themselves in salary and wage costs saved?

The Hardy Spicer example in Chapter 17 shows how one company identified and tackled many of these issues, both as a set of problems that had to be managed in the round and as actions which had to be implemented sequentially over time.

Presented like this, the 'manpower plan' is less a detailed written document, than a process set in train to deliver (or discard) specific numbers and skills. The 'plan' may set targets and an outline timetable, but the detail will be filled in as people work through the implications asking questions such as those above. At this stage, it is vital then that proposed actions in one area are continually tested against those in others to ensure a coherent, integrated response. This is a social process of people talking to one another, not a backroom analytical process.

Manpower planning at IBM: a case example

In this discussion we have emphasized the action focus of manpower planning, whether the plan has a five-year horizon (as at Hardy Spicer) or has to deliver much sooner. In 1990, IBM, a company renowned for taking the long view in its employment policies, was faced with having to make large and rapid reductions in its UK workforce (Peach, 1992)[2]. How it went about this is a good illustration of what manpower planning in practice can involve. The student can compare this with the processes and analysis described above.

Towards the end of the 1980s, equipment costs in information technology continued to fall and the performance and power of hardware continued to increase. The erosion in profit margins meant that IBM had to reduce the number of support staff in relation to those directly earning revenue. In 1989, 55 per cent of all its 10,600 employees in the non-manufacturing area were classed as 'support'. A review of strategy concluded that a more satisfactory ratio would be 35 per cent in support, with 65 per cent revenue earning.

In addition, the software and services side of the business offered greater growth opportunities and higher margins than hardware sales – the traditional core of IBM's business. In addition to reducing employment, therefore, there also had to be a transfer of resources into this side of the business. When the decision was taken, therefore, a target of 8700 total employees (excluding manufacturing and laboratories) was set, although this was subsequently revised down to achieve a total of 8450 by mid-1992.

On a previous occasion, in the early 1970s, with labour turnover running at 10 per cent, it had been possible to reduce the permanent workforce by 1000 by not filling vacancies and internal transfers within IBM internationally. In 1990, labour turnover had fallen to 2 per cent, while IBM overseas was also cutting back. The timescale for change was also getting tighter, with the plan to phase change over three to five years having to be accelerated to twelve to eighteen months in the face of a deepening recession. The necessary reductions, moreover, had to be implemented against the background of IBM's renowned policy of putting employees first and implied policy of lifetime employment. As Sir Leonard Peach (1992) commented: 'Having spent much of our lives winding golden and silver chains around IBM employees, the personnel group had to set about the task of unravelling them' (p. 41). It was clear they would have to resort to voluntary redundancy. This meant constructing a package of incentives to encourage volunteers, targeting those whom the company wanted to leave, and ensuring that those with scarce skills stayed.

The details of the package need not concern us here. Essentially, it consisted of a lump sum, calculated on present pay, and an enhanced pension (paid for by the company out of income, not by transferring ('raiding') surpluses in the existing pension fund). Once someone had decided to leave, they would also be allowed paid leave of absence to find another job, and given help from an outplacement service. A later refinement was to spin off certain support activities (such as property services, and management development) into new companies with their IBM staff where this would reduce costs by 30 per cent or more.

Analysis of the company's employment profile meanwhile showed a distinct bulge in the 40–50 age group (see Figure 9.5), reflecting the heavy recruitment and expansion of the 1960s and later high retention. This group were a natural prime target in the reshaping of the company, along with other senior staff on high pay.

The presentation of the package (termed the 'Career transition programme') had then to be geared in such a way as to attract people from the target groups, while phasing the process to minimize disruption. Accord-

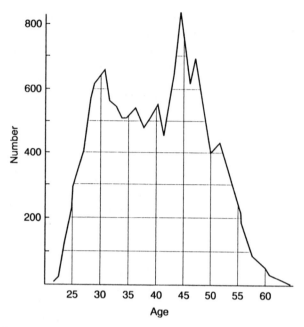

Figure 9.5 *IBM UK's total company demographics in 1990. (Reproduced with permission from Peach, 1992)*

ingly: 'A great deal of modelling on skill and age profile was undertaken to ensure that scarce skills were preserved and to try to forecast an appropriate take-up by the groups chosen' (Peach, 1992, p. 42). The eventual programme comprised five phases during 1991 and 1992, with the package put to different target groups in the various locations, according to age, grade and function.

The proposals and offers were communicated at each stage through the quarterly meeting of the company's top 150 managers and cascaded down, with other information supplied in the normal way through IBM's well-developed employee-communications system (see also Chapter 13). Briefing sessions for eligible groups then followed. At the outset, it was made clear that certain departments were wholly excluded, along with individuals with important skills, while offers could be withheld in the light of the level applications. Again, in accordance with normal company practice, the impact of the programme on morale was monitored through periodic opinion surveys.

The result was to reduce the number of employees in support and non-support areas by around 2000 (taking account also of other sources of wastage), and to reduce the number of employees in IBM UK (including manufacturing) by 2334 (just over 13 per cent), with a further 2 per cent reduction from normal turnover. The cost of the redundancy programme averaged around two years' pay per head, but led to the departure of a large number of senior staff earning in excess of £40,000 per annum. The savings this represented meant that the costs of the programme were recoverable in eighteen to twenty months.

While the objective was to shed staff, one final feature worth noting has been the way IBM has retained the services of some staff through Skillbase, the consultancy company it helped set up and in which it holds a 40 per cent equity stake. Former employees joining Skillbase are guaranteed a certain amount of part-time work with IBM, while being able to sell their services to others outside. While easing the difficulties of separation for staff, it thereby becomes an extension of IBM's own customer services.

Summary

In this chapter we have introduced manpower planning as one of the key planks in a strategic approach to employment. This consists essentially of five elements or stages:

- Analysing the current manpower resource
- Reviewing labour utilization
- Forecasting the demand for labour
- Forecasting supply
- Developing a manpower plan.

Thinking about manpower can begin with any of these, even with a review of a previous manpower plan. This is what makes manpower planning a dynamic process. Nowadays, the trend within firms is to focus on action planning in the short to medium term, rather than to hatch grand plans for the long term. Above all, manpower planning should not be seen as the exclusive responsibility of the personnel or HRM function, and certainly not of a manpower planner. It is the job of everyone to think through the implications of business and employment decisions in these five areas, even if they look to the specialists for expert information and advice.

The problem manpower planning has is often the failure after conceiving plans to take coordinated action. Among the reasons for this are:

1 The responsibility for manpower planning is detached from the management of recruitment, training, and other areas like pay, so that there is insufficient commitment to 'the plan'.
2 These activities are themselves uncoordinated.
3 We expect too much from systematic plans, ignoring the possibilities of the unexpected.

A lack of integration and unreal plans explains why the practice of manpower planning has often been very different from the theory.

In conclusion, we described an example of how the techniques and process of manpower planning can be used to good effect.

Notes

1 The original term 'manpower planning' is retained, despite its sexist connotations which HRM/personnel practitioners would now seek to avoid.
2 I am indebted to Sir Leonard Peach, formerly director of personnel and corporate affairs of IBM UK Ltd, for permission to use this material.

10
From manpower planning to human resource planning

Introduction

The presentation of manpower planning in the previous chapter has come close to the philosophy of HRM itself. Numbers and skills are derived from a business plan, and the implications are worked through in a coherent way across the various systems for 'getting, keeping, developing, and using' employees. The extension of manpower planning into career management also introduces a qualititative element, thereby getting away from the over-quantitative approach for which it has sometimes been criticized.

A fully strategic approach, however, is still limited by a number of things in practice. First, there is the linkage of people planning to corporate strategy. It does not help that the HR or personnel function still does not play an active role in the development of corporate strategy in many organizations. In the Price Waterhouse/Cranfield survey which obtained some 2800 questionnaire responses from HR specialists and chief executives in the UK, only in half the cases was the HR specialist involved in developing corporate strategy from the outset (Brewster and Smith, 1990). Interestingly, in finance and professional services, and in building and construction, this was down to a third, compared with the distributive trades where it was nearer 60 per cent. In Europe (for example, in France and Sweden), early involvement was generally higher. The problem exists on a similar scale in the USA, the home of HRM (Greer, Jackson and Fiorito, 1989).

Second, there is the extent to which organizations have personnel strategies or do manpower planning. In its 1988 survey, the IPM reported a high level of HRP activity on the basis of replies from 245 corporate members – indeed, 'surprisingly high' (IPM, 1988, p. 12). The regular surveys which Colin Richards-Carpenter of the Institute of Manpower Studies carries out for the IPM likewise reflect the increasing prevalence of computer systems to support HRP. On the other hand, the much larger and more representative Price Waterhouse/Cranfield survey found that only four out of ten UK organizations had a written HR strategy, with another three out of ten claiming an unwritten strategy. However, they doubt the substance of the unwritten strategies, and note that:

> This scepticism is reinforced by the somewhat startling findings that around a third of the companies responding to our survey were unable to say what percentage of their turnover was accounted for by labour costs (Brewster and Smith, 1990, pp. 39–40).

An even larger proportion (40 per cent) could not say what percentage of labour costs were spent on training.

Third, there is the way companies conduct their business planning. Styles of planning vary markedly. As we noted at the outset, manpower planning had similar origins to corporate planning, being a feature of large organizations in relatively stable environments. Increased turbulence in external environments has meant that corporate planning has had to become more flexible. At the same time, many large organizations have increasingly diversified, and then recognized that to respond effectively to turbulent environments they need to decentralize responsibilities. This too has encouraged a more flexible style of planning, with less emphasis on detailed, top-down plans.

The first two factors suggest why organizations often fail to achieve a strategic approach in planning for people. They are the kind of concerns which preoccupy personnel practitioners. The third factor, however, suggests a failure to take account of the wider context of business planning itself. In the light of this, manpower planning has limitations. In contrast, human resource planning is a broader approach which adapts people planning to a more flexible style in business planning.

Styles of business planning

Styles of business planning vary a great deal. The trend towards greater flexibility can be illustrated by the change in the way Pilkington PLC conducts its planning:

> Corporate planning was introduced in 1964. In keeping with common practice then, a ten-year plan was developed, based on extrapolations for sales growth from the various businesses. Typically, as people now acknowledge, these projections were invalid by about the third year of the plan. In 1974, a planning executive was set up under the Group Deputy Chairman, with the divisional heads and heads of Group functions. The divisional heads each presented their case for capital to this group, while the Group planning unit (comprising just two persons) would provide background analysis. Funds were then allocated and the businesses then adjusted their financial and other plans accordingly.
>
> This worked well until the profits crash in the UK in 1981–82, and as long as the Group operated within a tight sense of strategic direction, defined as 'glass and allied activities' in the statement of company policy which was annually endorsed. In the early 1980s, however, Group planning began to argue for the building of a new 'high tech' leg to reduce dependence on 'flat and safety glass', and a stronger geographical spread away from the UK. The result, following detailed studies by consultants, was an explicit strategic commitment in both these directions, including major acquisitions outside the UK.
>
> In 1984, the central planning function was increased to seven people; the structure was revised; and the Group Chairman took over control of the process. With the company by now committed to decentralization [see Chapter 8], each division was allowed to develop its own planning system within an overall framework. 'Account executives' from the central unit helped the divisions to develop their strategy at the beginning of the calendar year. These were then

submitted in writing in July for analysis. The divisional chief executives then formally presented their strategy at a meeting in September, and gained 'outline planning consent' for their capital requirements. Following this, the overall impact of these strategies were reviewed by the main board in November in relation to their top-down view of Group strategy.

The resulting Group strategy was communicated to the chief executives during November-December, with areas for improving performance identified. Detailed budgets were then developed through February-April in conjunction with the Finance function. During the year, implementation was reviewed by the 'account executives', and formally at the next November strategy review by the board.

The system since the mid-1980s has thus tried to build in a greater degree of bottom-up planning and make it responsive to changing business circumstances in the short-term. Further international development of the Group has more recently led to other changes designed to consolidate and simplify business unit planning. One final feature of the process, however, is significant, and much favoured in modern strategic planning [Goold and Quinn, 1990]. This is the formulation of 'milestones' during the strategic review. These are tasks the board sets to improve performance or to develop innovations to be completed within a certain time. More generally, companies use these to set goals which can then be monitored – covering, for example, market share, headcount reductions, new product introduction, or customer satisfaction. At Pilkington, 'milestones' are more typically projects or studies conducted at Group and/or divisional level with medium- to long-term implications for Group development.

What we see here is a move away from centralized 'corporate planning' to a more 'strategic' style. Indeed, the style Pilkington has evolved comes fairly close to what Goold and Campbell (1987) refer to as a 'strategic planning' style:

> The centre works with the business unit managers to develop strategy. It establishes extensive planning processes, makes contributions of substance to strategic thinking, and may have a corporate strategy or mission guiding and coordinating developments across the business units. Less attention is devoted to the control process. Performance targets are set in broader, more strategic terms such as 'become the leading supplier' or 'establish a position in'. Annual financial targets are seen as being less important than the longer term strategic objectives (p. 42).

Other companies with a less centralized history and a more diversified business portfolio work less closely on inputs to planning and rely more on monitoring the performance output. Goold and Campbell (1987) refer to this as a 'strategic control' style:

> The centre prefers to leave the initiative in the development of plans to business unit managers. The centre does review and criticize the plans, but it uses reviews as a check on the quality of thinking of business unit managers, rather than as an opportunity to give direction. The control process is an important influence mechanism for the centre. Targets are set for strategic objectives (such as market share) as well as financial performance, and managers are expected to meet the targets. Budgets can only be missed when important strategic objectives are at stake. Strategic Control companies combine moderate planning with tight strategic controls (p. 43).

The diversified engineering company, IMI, is a good example of this kind of approach:

I leave it largely to the executive directors to develop their own businesses. I review strategies in financial terms, and I pick on certain parts of the businesses and say, 'will you do us a strategy paper about where this particular business is going, because I have lost it a bit, I can't see where it's going'.

IMI treats companies exceedingly lightly in terms of financial reporting. It's a feature of decentralization. Monthly reports are on one piece of paper. They're incredibly thin. At GEC, for example, they have to supply all the figures and a two-page MD's report, highlighting all the negatives and the action they intend to take to put it right, every month, and to a strict deadline. At IMI, all monitoring is left to individual MDs – though they are tough on annual results. Fall down on your forecast one year, and repeat it the next, and your chances of promotion have slipped greatly. Performance is constantly monitored (IMI, Group Managing Director).

As this quotation suggests, GEC is an exemplar of a company that combines an even more hands-off approach to developing strategy with yet stricter financial controls – what Goold and Campbell (1987) describe as a 'financial control' style:

The centre's influence is exercised mainly through the budget process. Corporate management's role in developing strategies is limited, and long-term plans are not formally reviewed by the centre. Instead, the centre focuses on a close review of the annual budget. Profit targets are set when the budget is approved, and careers are at stake if budgets are missed. Financial control companies combine a low level of planning influence with tight financial controls (p. 42).

Styles of planning and the implications for human resources

What can we deduce about human resource planning from these forms of corporate planning (bearing in mind that they are in fact just three, albeit the most distinctive, among eight planning styles which Goold and Campbell (1987) describe)?

First, there are those, like the 'financial control' companies, that appear not to treat human resources as a strategic issue. The emphasis on budgets is nevertheless likely to encourage the use of quantitative techniques in relation to short-term manpower needs and utilization.

Second, those who operate as 'strategic planning' companies do not generate corporate-level plans with the kind of detail from which demand forecasts for labour can be readily derived. Nevertheless, the operating businesses will do this within the budgeting process. Meanwhile, the corporate centre will focus on broader human resource concerns (such as the future supply of managers, engineers, and other professionals) as part of its larger strategic reviews and on-going dialogue with business units.

Finally, 'strategic control' companies may not be dissimilar. Indeed, the more selective role the centre plays in sharpening up strategy may allow it more time to force business units to think about human resource issues in the medium term. Moreover, by not involving itself in the detailed work of drawing up business plans, the main board has more time to address the strategic development of human resources. As we saw in Chapter 5, this is exactly what happens at IMI where management development and succession planning are periodically reviewed by the board.

Taking these three types together, we have a curious paradox. The more explicit the business plan, the more it encourages just the mechanical aspects of manpower planning in which labour demand is derived from the business plan. Meanwhile, the more strategic the style of planning, the less formally 'integrated' people planning is into a 'business plan' and the more fluid 'human resource planning' has to be. 'Financial control' companies notwithstanding, the trend in corporate planning has been towards a more 'strategic' style.

Towards human resource planning?

Business planning styles set the climate and context for people planning. The evidence suggests that large companies have tended towards a looser, strategic style which allows more attention to be given to broader human resource issues. 'Integration' with the business plan is *less*, rather than more, exact. This runs rather counter to the glib assertions that have tended to characterize HRM from its early days. For instance: 'Every personnel programme will be linked to each other and all such programmes will be related to the organization's workforce forecasts and plans' (DeSanto, 1983). Statements like this were often no more than a traditional plea for better manpower planning, which in the USA, as in Britain, was undeveloped and in decline (Rowland and Summers, 1981; Angle, Manz and Van de Ven, 1985; Mills, 1985).

With some few exceptions (for example, Cook and Ferris, 1986), the evidence from the USA, where more such studies have been carried out, is that a looser, more informal linkage is characteristic of more sophisticated organizations where HR issues are a top-level concern (Golden and Ramanujam, 1985; Mills, 1985), *and* that this looser linkage is associated with higher company performance (Nkomo, 1987; Baird and Meshoulam, 1988; Buller and Napier, 1993). For instance, Mills (1985) found that: 'Companies that do the best job of people planning usually avoid these problems by keeping the process as informal as possible and leaving the responsibility in the hands of line officers' (p. 99). Similarly, Golden and Ramanujam (1985) describe four types of linkage between HRM and strategic business planning in a sample of ten companies, and conclude that the most developed form achieving closest real integration is where the relationship is informal and interactive:

> Integration describes a dynamic, multifaceted linkage that is based on an interactive . . . relationship. From both a formal and informal organizational perspective the HR executive in this phase is considered an integral member of senior management. Informal, however, appears to be the operative word. Such a relationship is critical for the HR function if it is to become truly strategic. For, as has been noted elsewhere, much of the time organizations use informal processes in addition to the formally established procedures to develop their

strategies [Quinn, 1977; Dyer, 1983]. Participating in an interactive relationship with other senior management enables the HR executive to be regarded as a team member who, while specializing in HR-related areas, provides input and makes decisions on business strategies not directly involving human resource considerations. In this regard, the HR executive has the opportunity to impact the organization over the long term (p. 439).

A picture emerges, then, of how human resource planning differs from manpower planning.

1   Human resource planning makes greater use of more qualitative techniques for assessing future manpower requirements.

While the basic armoury of manpower planning still has a very important place, there is little use for the more mathematical techniques (Greer, Jackson and Fiorito, 1989; Timperley and Sisson, 1989). This may include the use of more imaginative forecasting techniques for an uncertain environment derived from corporate planning, such as scenario planning. This can be tied into quantitative analysis through the use of 'what if' questions applied to computerized manpower databases.

2   Human resource planning makes an input into strategy.

It can do this by forewarning of problems which may come about – for example, from changing demographics or people's expectations about jobs and work. Or, more boldly, it may seek to pinpoint resource advantages in the people and skills the organization has, and the opportunities for building business strategies on these (Porter, 1985). The latter may seem an inflated claim or ambition. However, within the corporate strategy literature itself, as we noted in Chapter 4, there has been a shift in thinking towards a 'resource-based' perspective, with skills and 'organizational capability' key themes. Moreover, if we get away from the idea that human resource management is merely the preserve of specialists, we will begin to see line managers regularly making these kinds of assessment about the capabilities of employees and the opportunities and limitations these create.

3   Human resource planning is concerned with developing people with the long term in mind.

The problem-centred approach to manpower planning in contrast tends to be reactive, as it has shrunk from the uncertainties of long-term planning.

4   *Human resource planning is flexibly linked to business strategy.*

This has two aspects:

- The head of the HR function (though not necessarily the leading HR professional) is part of the top team. This ensures a dialogue about people and strategy.
- There is no pretence that all HR programmes and systems equate with specific business plans. It is easier to represent the antithesis of this. The most mechanistic form of linkage described by Golden and Ramanujam (1985) is what they call 'administrative'. This is focused on day-to-day concerns. HR staff in such situations recognize the limitations of this and say things like 'we haven't tied employees to the business'.

    A sure sign of an underdeveloped HR function, that is not well tied into the business and has a history of being unregarded, is where the HR professionals start to describe their 'strategic' orientation in terms of elaborate systems and programmes they have put in place, to show how they are 'tying employees into the business'.

    A good illustration of HR programmes and systems not equating with specific business plans is the way IMI has come to manage succession. Instead of the old way of (forlornly) trying to match individuals to particular positions through detailed plans business heads had to submit, it now tries to balance pools of people against groups of jobs. Attention can then be given to the broad business development and management education of populations of managers at different levels. In this way, the flexible approach links back to the idea of HRP making an input to strategy and to developing people with the long term in mind.

Skill and skill supply strategy

The characterization of human resource planning above makes reference to one element that is curiously almost entirely absent from manpower planning, that is, the concept of skills. Manpower planning deals with people in the aggregate, not with what the qualities they have and what they actually do. HRP and HRM, in contrast, are fundamentally about skills – getting, using, developing, and keeping them. Central to a strategic perspective on HRM is the idea of a skill supply strategy that realizes the aims of the corporate strategic plan. It is an organization's skill supply strategy, with its overtones of deliverable performance, which turns business strategy into reality.

Skill, however, is a difficult thing to specify. Everyone has a view on it; a lot of effort is expended trying to define it; but much of this is unsatisfactory. For example:

One has only to mention the word 'careers' in most organizations to unleash a flood of conversation about 'skills': what kinds of people they need or want, whether current recruits are of high enough 'quality' or not, whether existing staff can adapt to new technology and so on. For years management development specialists, amongst others, have been trying to describe the knowledge, skills and personal qualities needed for certain jobs or possessed by individuals (Hirsh, 1984, p. 63).

However, as Hirsh goes on to observe, selection and appraisal processes (not to mention job descriptions) have a habit of representing skills in ways which most people in the organization would instinctively say 'felt wrong'. Jobs tend to be defined in terms of activities; these activities often have little to do with how the competence of the individual will be judged in performing the job; and the skills defined as necessary for doing the job may be poor predictors of success. In the longer term, it is very unlikely that these 'skills' will be appropriate to the series of job changes a person goes through in the course of their career.

Attempts to specify skills in the traditional way meanwhile, through job analysis, are unsatisfactory because job analysis

- Is backward looking, being concerned with the way a job is done now
- Fails to reflect the necessary progression from job to job, and what skills are therefore common and generic, and what are job-specific
- Is inflexible, failing to differentiate between different interpretations of a job by different job holders
- Concentrates on differences between jobs rather than similarities
- Is based on the idea of 'matching' a person to the job, thereby denying the possibility and desirability of a person learning within it.

A forward-looking view on jobs and skills is vital because both nowadays are liable to continuing change. The aim of a skill supply strategy is to equip the organization to fulfil its business strategy *now and in the future*. Indeed, it is more realistic to think of an organization having actual and nascent business and technological strategies. Someone, somewhere in the organization, may already be doing something which will lead it in new directions. Thus, five years on, it is very possible that an organization will be trying to do rather different things.

How managers and employers see skills

Skills are therefore important, but we still lack an adequate vocabulary to talk about them. A study of skill supply strategies in three high-technology organizations confirms the difficulty managers have, to which Hirsh earlier referred:

> Most of the managers interviewed had to be prompted repeatedly to discuss the strategic importance of skills. They lacked a vocabulary to articulate their skill needs and concerns. They often relied on indirect indicators of skill such as formal education, experience with a particular technology or computing language,

and project management experience in a specific area. They discussed skills indirectly by attending to the work organization and by their frequent reference to the need to grow skills (LeBrasseur, 1994).

A second problem is that definitions of skill tend to be very 'slippery'. Rather than specify 'skills', employers and recruiters will often specify their requirements in terms of 'personal qualities'. This was especially apparent among small–medium enterprises in a study carried out by the author and colleagues at the Centre for Corporate Strategy and Change (Hendry *et al.*, 1991). In part, this reflected the fact that new, growing, and small firms require people who are flexible, and some small organizations are actually having to invent the skills they need and cannot yet define them. In many low-technology organizations and menial jobs, also, skill may not count for much (Marsh, McAuley and Penlington, 1990).

On the other hand, emphasizing personal qualities may simply be a way of saying 'when other more tangible skills and knowledge have been taken into account . . .' The way employers define skills in public may therefore mask more complex criteria they operate in practice. This would correspond to the fact that managers, and people in general, often have fairly elaborate ways for distinguishing their preferences between things. Mostly, though, they do not articulate these, and may well have difficulty doing so. The criteria they apply are 'tacit', even to themselves.

What this discussion, nevertheless, shows is that employers rate performance above skills, even if skills are a factor in that.

The competency approach

The difficulties in defining skills and the sense that definitions do not capture the element of 'effective', or even 'exceptional', performance has created considerable interest in recent years in the idea of 'competences'.

Defining 'competency' is itself something of a minefield. As Sparrow (1992) points out, different models emphasize either characteristics in the individual (Boyatzis, 1982; and the McBer approach) or standards of performance in the job or occupation (the vocational qualification approach associated with NVQs in the UK). The essential thing to hold on to (according to Woodruffe, 1992) is the distinction between the behaviours or personal qualities a person needs to do a job properly, and the outputs, tasks, or 'deliverables' which result. Jobs are normally defined in terms of the latter, while pyschologists tend to emphasize behaviours: 'Competences are behavioural repertoires that some people carry out better than others' (Woodruffe, 1992, p. 17). Unfortunately, lists of competences often confound the two.

The competency approach has two initial stages – identifying or analysing competences, and assessing competences. The first is concerned with what competences are used in a job, the second in measuring the extent to which existing employees (or would-be recruits) possess them. This information can then be used for making better judgements in selection and recruitment, career development, promotion, and pay.

Table 10.1 An example of a simple job analysis interview

1 What do you understand to be the purpose of this job? What role or roles do you carry out?
2 What are the main activities you are involved in and what is your estimate of the percentage of time involved in each one?
3 Which of these activities do you consider to be most important and why?
4 What do you consider to be the most difficult things to achieve in your job and why?
5 How can you, or others, tell if your role is being satisfactorily carried out?
6 What do you consider to be the most important knowledge, skills or other attributes that are required for successful performance of this job?
7 What are the main challenges facing you now and in the immediate future (i.e. within the next two years)?
8 What are the main challenges facing you in the long term (i.e. 3–5 years)?

Source: Based on Kandola and Pearn (1992).

Identifying and analysing competences

Much of competency analysis is a refined form of job analysis. It uses a variety of methods, which should be employed in combination with one another rather than relying on one alone (Pearn and Kandola, 1988; Kandolo and Pearn, 1992):

- *Systematic observation.* This will provide information on the general job context, tasks, areas of difficulty, etc. Ideally, it should observe differences in behaviour between good and less good performers. It is best carried out using a structured rating scheme to record observations.
- *Diaries.* Job-holders themselves completing diaries can yield a lot of information economically. While this can get close to what job-holders regard as significant, the risk is they describe tasks rather than behaviours. As with the observers above, job holders should have some training or instruction as to what to look for.
- *Interviews.* This is probably the most common way of gathering data. It is more removed from the actual job, but this can be reasonably overcome by sampling the views of both selected job-holders and their supervisors. Group discussion is an alternative. The advantage is the interview's flexibility in being able to explore aspects of the job which may be critical to performance. Table 10.1 shows the kinds of question a simple job analysis interview might cover.
- *Critical incident technique.* This technique relies on job-holders, supervisors or others being able to generate accounts of observed

behaviour or activity which can be shown to be critical to either effective or less effective performance in a job. Data generated from interviews can then be content-analysed for types of incident and relevant behaviours for managing them. Boyatzis (1992) used a variant of this called 'behavioural event interviewing' in his original work on management competences. A subjective leap still has to be made, however, from a list of behaviours to categorizing underlying competences.

- *Repertory grid.* This method attempts to go straight to the underlying behaviours which make for effective and less effective performance, but does not provide a systematic picture of a job. The essence of the method is to ask how any two workers are similar to each other and different from a third, and to keep repeating this with different combinations of people. This generates a list of the important 'constructs' which distinguish performance. The interviewer then asks for examples of observable behaviour which allow someone to make these judgements.

In addition to these methods, there are a number of checklists and inventories which provide detailed, standardized ways of analysing either jobs or workers. The most well known of these are the Position Analysis Questionnaire (PAQ), the Job Components Inventory (JCI), and the Work Profiling System (WPS). The first of these is backed by a large database which allows comparison with thousands of other jobs, but requires specialist training to use it.

Assessing competences

Having identified what behaviours matter in a job, the next task is to assess whether employees (or potential recruits) possess them. Smith and Robertson (1992) provide a comprehensive review of the methods commonly employed to do this. The main forms they describe are:

- *'Analogous'* approaches, where the aim is to simulate elements of a job. Any such method therefore has to sample work activity in a detailed way so that there is a 'point-to-point correspondence' between the test and the job. Examples include:
    Group exercises
    In-tray exercises
    Role plays
    Presentations
    Written reports
    Psychomotor tests
    Trainability tests (or the ability to learn new things)
Presentations and written reports, for example, would be used where either of these was a regular and important part of a job. The problem with such methods generally, however, is that assessors find it difficult to make independent, consistent assessments of detailed

competences displayed. If a limited number of clearly defined competences are used, however, such methods can provide a reasonable guide to job performance.

- *'Analytical'* approaches. These are various tests, covering mental and physical ability, temperament (the so-called 'personality tests'), and motivation. The problem with such tests generally is their validity. As Smith and Robertson (1992) observe, 'a good test used for a stupid purpose has no validity' (p. 64). Their use must depend therefore on how satisfactory the identification of competences has been in the first place.
- *'Reputational'* approaches. These include references, supervisors' assessments, and assessments by colleagues or peers. Their advantage is that they make use of the everyday knowledge people have of one another. Equally, however, such judgements are susceptible to forms of bias, and references in particular are of questionable validity.

How useful is the competency approach?

In Chapter 14 we will look at the application of the competences approach to management jobs. Before that, however, there are some basic reservations we have about the utility of the competency approach as a strategic tool in human resource planning.

1   It excludes the specific technical skills, knowledge, and abilities that are required in a job.

Woodruffe (1992) argues that skills and knowledge should be kept out of the picture: 'Calling these "competences" is likely only to muddle the definition of a competency again' (p. 19). However, any strategy for getting people to perform work which neglects knowledge and skills is likely to be pretty empty. 'Competency' definitions can only then be an add-on to distinguish the effective performer from the less effective one. The fundamental strategic activity is to have a 'skill supply strategy', not a 'competency supply activity'. Put another way, the focus of HRM and HRP is to have a strategy for 'skills', not a strategy for 'competences'. Too often, the term 'competences' seems to be used as a way of avoiding the more concrete word, 'skill' – a kind of white-collar word, in preference to a blue-collar one. In fact, Boyatzis (1982) defines a job competency more inclusively to cover knowledge as well:

> A job competency is an underlying characteristic of a person in that it may be a motive, trait, skill, aspect of one's self-image or social role, or a body of knowledge which he or she uses.

2   *The fact that people have difficulty in agreeing on what they mean by 'competences' suggests that the term may be inherently imprecise.*

On closer inspection, competences look very like other discredited labels psychologists have invented to describe behaviour, with the likelihood that they will meet the same fate:

> Competences are indeed the same as aspects of personality such as traits and motives, but those terms are so poorly understood and agreed that to say that competences are, for example, traits risks competences inheriting the confusion that surrounds traits (Woodruffe, 1992, p. 19).

or as Sparrow (1992) puts it,

> A competency analysis ... taps a wide range of psychological areas (personal traits, motives, attitudes, skills and aptitudes) and summarizes them at a descriptive level (p. 8).

3   *There are serious practical problems in identifying and assessing competences.*

Much of this comes down to the trade-off between precision and cost. This in turn involves the contentious issue of generic versus organization-specific competences. Such competences are more precise and are more likely to capture behaviours that are specific to culture and technology. But to produce a valid list requires close analysis, which is costly. An off-the-shelf generic list, meanwhile, is liable to be so generalized and bland that it is practically useless:

> The cost of using a method often depends on the number of analysts that are required, the time it takes and level of computer-processing costs. Once again, the advantage of proprietary systems is that they are relatively cheap compared to the benefits derived.
>   This has to be offset against the efficiency with which they would identify the particular and precise needs in a given situation. A typical study could range in cost from a few thousand pounds to well in excess of £100,000, depending on the size of the project and the particular methods that are employed (Kandola and Pearn, 1992, p. 34).

Do the pay-offs justify the elaborate methodologies required to develop a valid analysis? As Kandola and Pearn (1992) put it, 'many of the methods give the appearance of using a sledgehammer to crack a nut' (p. 34).

Ultimately, competency analysis and assessment has to answer two basic questions:

- How readily available in a normal population are the personal qualities sought in a job?
- How readily are the necessary behaviours likely to be acquired through on-the-job experience and formal training?

The view taken here is that for most jobs the answers are likely to be 'readily available' and 'readily acquired'.

The possession of requisite skills and knowledge is more often what separates out people (although 'behaviour' is a more significant factor in many services jobs (Bowen and Schneider, 1988)). If a job demands unusual behavioural qualities, these are likely to be so obvious as to require little analysis to identify them. Where effort can then be usefully expended is in developing reliable indicators of such behaviour. Competency analysis and assessment is then best applied in a focused way. The recruitment process resolves the same question by using less sophisticated filtering procedures where a job is relatively undemanding and unique, and/or there is a large population of people capable of performing it.

The second question concerns the ability of people to develop and learn – or the 'plasticity' of personality. The use of competency analysis often betrays questionable motives to control behaviour (by closely specifying it and fitting the individual to the job) and an unwillingness to allow that people will develop appropriate behaviours for themselves according to the demands of the situation. The problem of behaviour is more often to do with the contexts in which people work. This leads into the fourth issue.

4   The issue is 'better performance'. This may lie, not in individual 'competences', but in an organization's systems and in how people work together in teams.

Although Woodruffe (1992, p. 17) argues that it is important to differentiate 'competency' from 'competence', it is really 'competence' – or how effectively objectives are achieved – that counts. The work context, the systems of the organization, the motivational effect of human resource practices, and working in teams may be at least as significant as individual competences (although, of course, the ability to work in teams may itself be a recognized competence). Two people may also achieve success by different means. 'Competences' looks suspiciously, then, like a 'one best way' approach.

5   Competences are concerned with the past or present, not with the future.

Most behavioural analysis of competences is limited to what already is, not what might be. Like job analysis before it (on which much of its methodology is based), it can be just as backward-looking. As Morgan (1989) has observed: 'In developing managerial competences we must do more than drive through the rear view mirror.'

Beyond competences

Acknowledging some of these problems, Sparrow and Boam (1992) seek to make the competences approach more useful and 'strategic' by (1) suggesting ways for projecting required behaviours in the future and (2) considering competences in group situations. For instance, competences at the organizational level can be distinguished according to whether they are likely to become more important in the future for that organization, less important, temporarily important during a transitional phase of development, or remain enduringly important. A method for doing this is 'visioning' workshops, where groups of employees focus on questions like 'what aspects of people's work and roles has changed/will change?' and then to identify success criteria for managing the changed state. While this is a useful activity, it clearly dilutes competency analysis as a rigorous methodology. At its worst, it can lead to vacuous wish-lists around imprecisely defined objectives such as the ability to manage change.

This brings us back, however, to the fundamental question: 'which matters more – skills and knowledge, or competences?' A sure lesson from the past is that the future will mean massive and continuing change in skills and knowledge in the workplace. This does have important implications for behaviour, in terms of management style and the need to work in teams, which are partly based in technology and partly in social attitudes. The latter are broad trends, readily identified. Skills and knowledge, in contrast, are specific and detailed. The pay-off will be far greater from effort spent in identifying these, and understanding the ways skill and knowledge are developed and applied in work situations.

Skill and knowledge in work situations: 'tacit skills'

The critical factor in superior competitive performance often lies in relatively unremarked ways of doing things. For instance, American managers were often surprised to find no obvious differences in manufacturing or magical explanations for the better performance of the Japanese firms they encountered in joint ventures (Hamel, 1991). The answer lies in what has been called 'tacit skill'.

Tacit skill differs from formally developed skill in that it is generally difficult to articulate and is developed informally. It is a kind of 'practical knowledge' gained through daily experience. Such knowledge is typically:

- Untaught
- Increased by experience in the job
- Possessed in larger quantity by successful personnel
- Largely context-dependent
- In the form of simple 'if – then' rules, such as 'if the telephone rings, then pick up the receiver'
- An automatic, often unconscious, action in response to specific conditions (Myers and Davids, 1992, p. 46).

It is, moreover, rarely reflected in the prescribed skills for a job, but is essential in working effectively (Orr, 1990).

As LeBrasseur (1994) cogently describes, the term, 'tacit skill', was coined by Polanyi (1966) to distinguish between two necessary, inseparable components in the practical application of knowledge and skill – one explicit, the other implicit. Before him, Hayek (1945) had distinguished between systematic and codified knowledge, and unorganized knowledge of particular circumstances of time and place, arguing that too much reliance was placed on the former. The latter 'embedded' knowledge does not lend itself readily to codification. Argyris and Schon (1974) and Schon (1987) developed this pragmatic view of skilful performance, or 'knowing-in-action', with ideas about 'organizational repertoires' and the learning relationship between a skilled coach and an apprentice learner.

Embedded or tacit knowledge can then be viewed at the individual, group, organizational, and even inter-organizational level (Badaracco, 1991). Tacit skills are thus integral to 'firm-specific assets' (Williamson, 1975). In any one organization there will be a variety of technologies and work processes, with varying levels of tacitness in knowledge and skill (Dosi, 1988). An important final linking concept is that of 'routines' (Nelson and Winter, 1982), since routines are the means by which individual skills are harnessed to organizational activity. Routines should be among the more observable phenomena, but have been an underdeveloped part of the theory (see however, Hendry, Arthur and Jones (in press) for an exploration of some of the forms routines can take).

The theory apart, tacit skills are important for a number of reasons. First, they are critical to the way trainable skills are actually used because they make the link between the general skill formally acquired and the particular context in which it has to be used. Second, while individuals develop their own fund of tacit knowledge, which enables them to get round problems, tacit knowledge is especially bound up with the way groups of people work together. They learn together, in 'communities-of-practice' (Lave and Wenger, 1990; Brown and Duguid, 1991), and adjust their working habits to one another. Tacit knowledge and skills are 'shared'. This is an organizational strength which is easily dissipated if people leave and is difficult for outsiders to copy because it is not very visible. Interpersonal and teamworking skills – what otherwise one might call 'competences' – are obviously then of considerable importance, but are themselves bound up in a tacit developmental process. Third, tacit skills represent a reservoir of knowledge and ability which an organization may fail to tap, and can readily frustrate, because of the systems it imposes on people.

Tacit skill, in other words, represents continuing learning beyond the knowledge and skills that are formally acquired and communicated. Creating the conditions for this learning to occur is therefore vital for continuous organizational development. Japanese production systems recognize this in the philosophy of *kaizen*, or continuous shopfloor-led improvement, as does the notion of employee 'empowerment'.

The emphasis in these philosophies is not to try to control for competences but to give employees the technical skills to do a job and create the social conditions to use them and to innovate. In this way, true 'competence' comes into play by providing the right motivational and learning environment.

Formulating a skill supply strategy

We embarked on this discussion of skills, competences, and tacit skills in the belief that a skill supply strategy is fundamental to HRM and an essential part of human resource planning. It is the means to realizing present corporate strategy, and can contribute to the development of strategy by identifying problems and opportunities deriving from the skills of people in the organization. We noted, however, that 'skill' is a concept that gives some problems. We concluded that effort should go into developing skills and knowledge at two levels – a specific technical level and a tacit level. The former can be analysed and learnt through formal education and training. The latter occurs on the job, and depends on learning opportunities from new tasks and situations, employee interaction, and the climate for learning in the organization.

A skill supply strategy will therefore consist of two things.

1   Understanding and monitoring the existing and emerging knowledge and skill base of the organization, in broad terms

Many organizations are dominated by particular skills. Insurance firms, for example, have traditionally been run by those with actuarial skills, training and experience, but this is changing. IMI, which now presents itself as an engineering firm, was formerly the Metals Division of ICI and its expertise centred on metallurgists. Business circumstances change, however, and IMI gradually developed into an engineering company through a deliberate strategy of reducing dependence on metal processing because of the market volatility. In the process there was an outflow of metallurgists and an inflow of engineers. At the same time, decentralization into smaller profit centres, and the competitive nature of its markets, required many more general managers and greater entrepreneurialism. The result was a change in the knowledge and skill base, and, indeed, in the development of new behavioural competences.

Such a shift in the technical base was brought about by many individual recruitment and redundancy decisions, and especially by divestments and acquisitions. Meanwhile, new behaviours and general managers were developed by giving people broad responsibilities early on in their careers and putting people into progressively larger general management jobs. In some ways, the shift in the skill, knowledge and competences base at IMI was not managed as an explicit skill supply strategy but was driven by cumulative decisions on business strategy. Opportunities for general management development were a byproduct of decentralization to bring businesses closer to their markets; engineers came in with acquisitions and metallurgists went out with divestments. In these circumstances, the need is for some broad monitoring of the knowledge and skill base.

At IMI, the executive directors, sitting as the 'management development committee', performed this function by monitoring graduate recruitment to ensure that sufficient numbers of engineers were being taken on, and by a comprehensive annual review of the management stock. In the course of time, they found that this worked best if they approached the problem in terms of 'pools of skills'.

At one level, therefore, it is possible to overcome the difficulty in specifying skills and competences by relying on fairly broad definitions. The HR function ensures there is a sufficient population of people with broadly defined skills and experiences – such as 'engineers' at IMI – who can then adapt to a range of specific jobs as needs arise. This is similar in principle to the employment systems approach to manpower planning described in the previous chapter, which treats 'career groups' as the units of analysis.

2 Specific initiatives to remedy 'skill gaps'.

As we have just indicated, a skill supply strategy often involves many individual decisions on recruitment, training, promotion, and redundancy. In this way, many managers can contribute to a 'skill supply strategy' without knowing it, and firms end up with a strategy whether they intend it or not. The result is that skills strategy is often 'emergent' rather than 'deliberate', in the same way as a business strategy can be (Mintzberg, 1978; and see Chapter 4). This is especially liable to happen once the broad character of a business is laid down. On-going recruitment and training will then tend to perpetuate the skill base. The more integrated the different elements of the employment system (or the more 'strategic' in HRM terms), the more the organization develops a distinctive set of skills and fixed patterns of behaviour.

Inevitably, however, a skill supply strategy and employment practices that are a matter of habit get overtaken by events and by shifts in business strategy (although organizations which have deliberate skill supply strategies can also get caught out). Sudden change is liable to reveal 'skill gaps' and too many of the wrong skills. The last decade and a half has been a time of such quantum change, in which many companies have had to make major adjustments in their skill base. Competitive pressure has forced firms to radically change their product-market strategies and/or introduce technological innovations to improve competitiveness. These in turn have created visible skill gaps, and during the mid-1980s this provided a major stimulus to training activity among firms (Pettigrew, Hendry and Sparrow, 1989). Figure 10.1 illustrates this process. The interest in human resource manage-

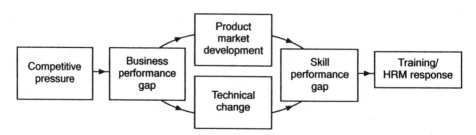

Figure 10.1 *Competitive pressure and the HRM/training response*

ment can also be attributed to the need to bring about large-scale change in skills and in the way firms use them by altering the set of employment practices, instead of just relying on training.

The essential point about this process is that firms' attention tends to become focused on an issue as result of powerful external forces. When that subsides, their attention and effort relaxes too. The result is that a skill supply strategy is often sporadic and episodic. This pattern was very evident in the twenty firms in the 'Training in Britain' study referred to above (Pettigrew, Hendry and Sparrow, 1989), and more recently has been confirmed by LeBrasseur (1994):

> Skill issues rise to the surface of the management agenda as an episode. Once a solution is found and implemented, strategic attention to skills disappears.

The second form which a skill supply strategy is likely to take, then, is as specific initiatives to remedy a skill gap. Such initiatives attend to visible and specific technical skills.

Once this kind of change has been accomplished, attention to skills then becomes less overt. Skills will nevertheless be subject to continuing adjustment and change through localized modifications in work processes and technology, including on-the-job developments as major change beds down. In other words, there is continuing development of tacit skills:

> While specific skill requirements may be provoked by external circumstances (skill shortages, new customer service), the chosen solution quickly becomes part of the existing work organization and systems, and becomes relatively invisible. The episodic nature of SKISS [skill supply strategy] operates from a background of regular attention to the embeddedness of skills. Thus the apparently discontinuous attention to skill issues masks the on-going adjustments of the work organization where a skills-related topic, such as technology and management systems, predominates (LeBrasseur, 1994).

What a consciously strategic approach requires at this point is on-going monitoring of the knowledge and skill base, as described in (1) above, combined with the on-going monitoring of recruitment, training, and development by which recognized skill requirements are replenished.

Summary

In this chapter we have presented human resource planning as an approach that is better adapted to the more flexible style of business planning that many large companies have adopted. This looser, strategic style actually allows more attention to be given to broad human resource issues. We outlined four ways in which human resource planning therefore differs from manpower planning:

1 HRP makes greater use of qualitative techniques for assessing future manpower requirements.

2 HRP makes an input into strategy.
3 HRP is concerned with developing people with the long term in mind.
4 HRP is flexibly linked to business strategy (a) through the way the head of the human resources function participates in discussions about strategy and (b) by getting away from the idea that all HR programmes and systems necessarily equate with specific business plans.

In addition, however, a strategic approach to people planning needs to incorporate thinking about skills. A skill supply strategy is fundamental to HRM, and an essential part of human resource planning. It is the way in which corporate strategy is realized. 'Skill', however, is a concept that gives some problems. People have difficulty in saying what they mean by it, while employers rate performance above skills. The current interest in behavioural competences is an attempt to address both of these.

We concluded, however, that rather than investing in the identification and assessment of competences, effort would be better spent on developing skills and knowledge at two levels – a specific technical level and a tacit level. Instead of trying to control for competences, it is more fruitful to ensure that employees have the technical skills to do a job and the social conditions that encourage use of, and innovation in, skills. True 'competence' comes about by providing the right motivational and learning environment.

This suggests that a skill supply strategy will consist of two things:

1 Understanding and monitoring the existing and emerging knowledge and skill base of the organization, in broad terms.
2 Specific initiatives to remedy 'skill gaps'.

In this way, specific skill needs are met by programmes, within a framework which allows for the continuing development of tacit skills.

11

Employment systems: recruitment, pay, and careers

Introduction

In this chapter we develop the idea of 'employment systems'. This is a core concept in our approach to HRM. It provides a framework for understanding how recruitment, pay, training, and career practices hang together and form a coherent pattern, or ought to. It explains why these differ between organizations and often between groups within the same organization. It provides a focus for understanding changes in the way firms have managed employment over the last decade. Lastly, and most important, it highlights the fact that implementing business strategy has to confront the 'inertia' of established employment structures and processes.

Without an understanding of a firm as an employment system, human resource practices and HRM cannot be considered 'strategic'. This chapter looks at the broad differences between organizations as employment systems and the internal and external influences on them. We consider four types of employment system, along with HRM (or the 'commitment system') as potentially an emerging fifth type. The four types are:

- The 'internal labour market' (ILM)
- The 'open external labour market' (ELM)
- The 'occupational labour market' (OLM)
- The 'technical/industrial labour market' system (TILM)

Each represents a different way of trading off between two strategic imperatives – (1) the need to secure and gain control of necessary knowledge and skills against (2) the need to manage the costs of this efficiently. While each type, especially with their variations, is the result of a wide range of external and internal factors, these two imperatives are at the heart of the conceptual distinctions.

Organizations are often made up of a number of employment systems, and apply different criteria and practices to different groups of employees. This chapter provides a lead-in, therefore, to Chapters 14–19 which look in detail at the ways organizations manage different groups of employee and at changes in employment practice in recent years in relation to these.

An ancillary aim in this chapter is further to point up the contradictions within HRM as a coherent model. Sometimes it seems to be equated with the careful nurturing of employees associated with the creation of an internal labour market. At others, the emphasis on managing employees strategically and on performance implies a more open market approach. Both patterns are evident in the examples used in this chapter. The contrast between these is central to HRM as a distinctive philosophy of personnel management.

The internal labour market

The pioneering work on employment systems (or 'labour market types', as they are elsewhere called) was done by Kerr (1954) and Doeringer and Piore (1971). Kerr set out to describe the 'internal labour market' (ILM) as an empirical type that had developed in the post-war period, to contrast it with the economist's image of a competitive labour market where all workers are assumed to be competing for all jobs all of the time.

In crude terms, an ILM refers to the structure of jobs within an organization in which there are few points of entry (or 'ports of entry' in the jargon), other than at the bottom, and promotion is then via a fairly well-defined career ladder. Such movements are linked to seniority, as consequently is pay, and there may be a system of annual increments which reinforces this. Employees tend to stay with the organization a long time, and in due course are rewarded with a pension. In return, the organization gains the loyalty of staff, turnover is kept to a minimum, and recruitment costs are minimized.

An important feature, often used to explain the creation of an ILM, is the development of firm-specific skills through on-the-job training provided by more experienced workers. This has the effect of making employees more valuable to the organization because an important part of the organization's capital lies in their special knowledge and expertise, and this cannot be readily acquired on the open market without a further period of in-company training. Equally, however, firm-specific skills can restrict the individual's marketability outside, because a large part of their 'skill' lies in knowing the systems and working methods of the particular organization. (Of course, if that includes familiarity with a documented system or production process which can itself be transferred or bought outside, the person's marketability increases. Experience with quality procedures such as BS 5750 is a good example of this at present.)

The result of these various factors is supposedly a workforce which is more reliable and effective. Employees know one another and know the organization's philosophy, and they develop behaviour and work characteristics which ensure dependability. This provides an environment or 'culture' which reduces the need for direct supervision. In return, the organization manages work relationships through bureaucratic rules and procedures which ensure fairness. Thus, there are likely to be clear, written grievance and redundancy procedures to provide the protection of 'due process' for individuals, and grading based on job evaluation to ensure parity and equity between all employees.

Obviously this is an 'ideal typical' case. The actual form enterprise-based

ILMs take varies considerably in practice. Japanese ILMs, for instance, like the traditional British civil service, tend to be based on broadly defined jobs, while American ILMs are said to be organized around more exact differentiation of tasks (Koike, 1984). In fact, these differences are sufficiently distinctive to warrant separate labels. Lawrence (1985), for instance, distinguishes the 'career system' from the 'technical system', while Osterman (1987) refers to these respectively as the 'salaried (sub)-system' and 'industrial (sub)-system'. We will elaborate on the 'technical/industrial' system later.

As we shall see, there are often also significant differences between the treatment of different groups of employee. The important point is that the ILM describes a system in which employment is regulated within the organization, rather than leaving it simply to external market forces. The ILM attempts to insulate the organization and its employees from market forces.

The open external labour market

In contrast, other types of organization are much more open to the external labour market. The epitome of this is the classical economists' model of a competitive labour market (to which Kerr, 1954, was reacting) where all workers are assumed to be competing for all jobs all of the time and where firms take immediate action to adjust the numbers employed to the level of business activity. Dockwork used to be the classic form of this kind of employment, with a 'spot market' for jobs operating each day at the dockside.

Such examples are harder to find nowadays. Nevertheless, relatively open employment systems can be found in (1) the kind of organization which hires and fires from a pool of unskilled or semi-skilled people and (2) where extreme fluctuations in business encourage casualization. The two may go together: the key factor is how business levels fluctuate. In many industrial situations, relative stability in production makes it desirable to keep the workforce together, although they can be fired at short notice and can be replaced quickly if they leave. Construction, on the other hand, operates with many more skilled people, but for various reasons has a more casualized system of employment.

We will look at an example of construction in the next chapter because it challenges some of the assumptions about the way employment systems work, and because it illustrates the range of influences on the form they take. For the moment, we can illustrate the idea of the open external labour market system (ELM) with an example taken from a study carried out by the author with Alan Jones and Mike Arthur from the Centre for Corporate Strategy and Change. Among the seven types of employment system identified in the sample of twenty small–medium enterprises was one the authors termed 'unskilled mass' (Hendry, *et al.*, 1991, pp. 43–44; see also Hendry, Arthur and Jones, in press).

In this kind of firm, 'skill' and 'training' are relatively superfluous concepts. The mass of employees do monotonous work, in an unpleasant environment, with training consisting of a brief induction of a few hours. Pay is highly incentivized, with a reliance also on direct discipline. Most employees are locally recruited. Because they come to work almost exclusively for the money and lack specific skills, they move elsewhere readily for more money, or having put something aside, leave for better things. Such firms are therefore subject to considerable 'leakage' of employees into unrelated industries. The business relies on a narrow spectrum of skills at the top, on whom all training tends to be concentrated. Because this group is itself small, with few opportunities for internal advancement, these firms have difficulty in attracting and keeping specialists in areas like engineering maintenance.

Bread Products[1]

The employment profile of the company called Bread Products illustrates this situation. It comprises:

Directors	5
Managerial (foremen, office managers)	12
Clerical/administrative	40
Fitters and trained bakers (skilled)	25
General unskilled	233
Van drivers (sales)	35
	Total 350

Seventy-five per cent of the workforce is Asian. All these are male and mostly classed as 'general unskilled'. The skilled, semi-skilled, and managerial grades are all white, male, and over 40. The exception are the foremen, who are mostly Asian, which ensures a line of communication with the general workforce whose English in many cases is poor. The semi-skilled include the van drivers, who are all over 50 and all relatively long serving (ten to fifteen years). Having come originally from the shop floor, they are the nearest to an internal labour market system in the company.

With two exceptions, the directors and managers orginally came from larger bakeries, although most have now been with the company for many years. They are part of a very small national labour market in a highly concentrated industry, and their knowledge, experience, and skills is paramount. Between them and the rest of workforce there is a marked status-divide. There are only two graduates in the firm, and three with any kind of technical qualification.

Long hours, shifts, noisy conditions, and boring work, following the introduction of automated production, make the bakery an unattractive place to work. Anyone who can will readily choose to work elsewhere in an area which has, until recently, had low unemployment. As a result, the company has difficulty in recruiting and keeping white workers in the bakery, and the proportion of Asians far exceeds that in most other local firms. At the same time, the Asian workforce is attracted by the possibility of high earnings. With unsocial hours premia and high overtime, the basic pay of £123 per week can be boosted to £20 000 per annum, and many earn this. Not surprisingly, such a workforce shows little inclination for out-of-hours training, and (the directors complain) little interest in the company. Turnover among this group consequently runs at around 30 per cent a year. The labour market for this kind of firm can be represented pictorially as in Figure 11.1, as a series of simple flows in, out, and within.

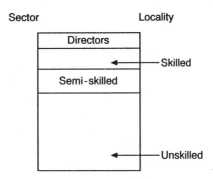

Figure 11.1   *The open external labour market at Bread Products.*

The occupational labour market

The internal labour market system clearly differs from the open external labour market in terms of job security, pay structure, attitudes to and levels of training, attachment to the organization, and so forth. Definitions of skill are also certainly more favourable to those in the ILM, regardless of whether they possess skills which the outside world would recognize and value. However, there is another kind of employment system which is also externally oriented but where employees have recognized skills, job security, comparatively high levels of pay, and favourable attitudes to training. This is a market, but one which is regulated, rather than a free-for-all. The term we use to describe this is the 'occupational labour market'.

Kerr (1954) called this the 'guild or craft-based labour market'. When he wrote, the features of the craft system were more in evidence. In Britain, however, manual apprenticeships and craft-based trade unions over the last decade have undergone considerable change. Moreover, the characteristics of the 'craft system' apply as much, if not more, to professional labour markets. For this reason, the broader description, 'occupational labour market', is preferred. Others such as Althauser and Kalleberg (1981) slightly confusingly use the term, 'occupational internal labour market'.

What all these terms refer to is a labour market that is relatively orderly and structured, but outward-facing. Thus, Kerr contrasted the internally ordered ILM with an equally ordered external employment system.

In the 'occupational labour market' (OLM), the craft or profession has much more influence in controlling the development of skills, access to jobs, and levels of pay, whereas in the ILM these are largely determined by the employing organization. An important instrument in this is certification of those who complete a specified period of training at the beginning of their career, so that only those who have such qualifications can practise the trade. Since the content of this training is largely controlled by the occupation itself, the real level of skill required to do a job may be exaggerated. As important, the period of apprenticeship involves the acquisition of norms and practices which create a social identity with others in the craft.

In the craft-based system, more of the benefits of training accrue to the individual, and their first loyalty is often said to be to the craft, occupation, or profession, rather than to the organization. Such workers look for new jobs and self-betterment by moving between organizations via the external labour market for craft skills, rather than through vertical moves within an organization.

Skilled manual crafts and white-collar professions, such as law, architecture, and medicine, are the classic examples of this system, their interests and employment conditions being protected by craft trade unions and professional associations. In contrast, unions and levels of unionization are weak where open external labour markets prevail, such as in 'Bread Products'.

Hendry *et al.* (1991, pp. 39–45) provide examples of both blue- and white-collar OLMs, although these also show how real-life examples diverge from the simplified 'ideal type'.

Aerospace Engineering

Aerospace Engineering is a specialist engineering workshop making products for the aerospace industry. Its source of skills has traditionally been people who have completed engineering apprenticeships. It has a high proportion of time-served machinists (that is, they have completed formal apprenticeships), and support staff in areas like inspection have a similar background. Although small (sixty-one employees in 1990), it has continued to train its own craft apprentices at one a year for the past fourteen years. More recently, however, as a cost measure, it has also taken three young people from YTS/YT and one adult trainee into the machine shop.

Working in unusual metals and producing complex shapes requires a high level of skills. The men work independently to exacting product specifications and have acquired knowledge and skills specific to the kind of product. As a result, it is reckoned to take another six months for a qualified man to become proficient in the machine shop. At the same time, Aerospace Engineering is one of a small group of companies making similar products for a limited number of customers, so that there is a common pool of expertise which transcends any one of half a dozen small companies.

People move between a handful of firms well known to one another, and gravitate towards those like Aerospace Engineering which supposedly do the highest quality work. Thus, fourteen of the present employees did apprenticeships at other of these companies, while nine were apprenticed at Aerospace Engineering itself. Moving around between these in the course of a career does not seem to be a barrier to returning to an earlier employee, although progression into a production management role is more likely for someone who stays with the one firm.

Since the industry has tended to settle in particular localities, pay is highly sensitive to competitors' rates. According to the quality manager:

> We know which firms are reputable, which is why people tend to move between the same companies. People know you're qualified. The only question is how long you were there. When R... put up their rates, it affects us. The grapevine reacts very quickly.

For such firms, the industry/sectoral network is also more significant for recruitment than is the locality as such, although local concentrations of firms tend to obscure this fact. The existence of these within-industry networks means a lot of recruitment is by word of mouth. For Aerospace Engineering, its radius for recruitment for all grades is 25 miles ('this community and a bit more'), which takes in three or four similar companies. This same pattern of similar types of firm in local sectoral clusters can be found in many other industries. The specialist valve industry west of Huddersfield ('Valve Valley' as it is known locally) is an example.

Here, then, is a blue-collar OLM where the company is fairly open to its external labour market. This is also orderly from both the company and employees' point of view, although not appreciably governed by active trade unionism. The company can and has suffered from losing skilled workers, but there is also a considerable degree of employee loyalty and stability, generated by personal friendships and job satisfaction. An important recent initiative was to introduce a new bonus system, especially to improve incentives for productivity and quality, but also to produce higher

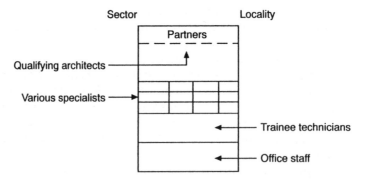

Figure 11.2 *The occupational labour market at Architectural Services*

earnings to ensure retention. There are thus tangible financial rewards and intangible psycho-social ones which maintain stability in this employment system. The elements of an occupational labour market show up even more clearly in the second example featuring a professional organization.

Architectural Services[2]

In Architectural Services, there are two major groups – architects (fourteen) and technicians (or architects' assistants) (thirteen) – with little differentiation in status within each group, no attempt at career progression between the two, and no attempt to develop career lines between the technicians and professional administrative jobs such as contracts management or programming. In fact, this is not entirely typical, and some architectural practices make more effort to provide careers and expand jobs for those not qualified as architects (that is, to create a semblance of an ILM). In consequence, the company (or, more strictly, the 'partnership') suffers high turnover among technicians. As Figure 11.2 shows, Architectural Services is also characterized by an exceptional range of specialists without any career lines associated with them.

Architects are recruited from a national labour market, although in practice many come from two schools, Newcastle and Sheffield Universities, with which Architectural Services maintains a special relationship (one of the partners being an external examiner to Newcastle). Technicians are recruited locally. Architects have already completed three years of study when they first come for a year's practical experience, and then return for a further two years to Masters level. They then spend their first year in full-time professional practice completing their training. The partnership (that is, other professionally qualified architects) give special attention to recruitment because the quality of recruitment is critical to the image and reputation, as well as competence of the firm.

Technicians, on the other hand, spend four years working towards ONC/HNC through day-release and evening classes, with two more years of formal work experience and a final oral exam. Their training, therefore, runs parallel with their employment from the beginning. The partnership then expects to lose most of them after they have completed their training, but regards this as healthy for the individual and the firm. Paradoxically, but perhaps not surprisingly, they have much more success in retaining qualified architects. Part of this is because on-the-job development is focused on the younger, rising architects, excludes the technicians, and involves close, personal mentoring by one of the leading partners.

Both groups, and the many specialists in areas like graphics design, thus belong to occupational labour markets, but with different levels of incentive to tie them to the organization. The wider profession in each case structures the labour market through formal qualifications and entry standards, which are externally validated (by RIBA, the Royal Insitute of British Architects, and BIAT, the British Institute of Architectural Technicians). They both also exercise some influence over pay levels through the profession's fee structure. Architectural Services deviates from normal practice, however, in that it pays overtime (introduced as a means of retaining some pay flexibility and avoiding the permanent ratchet effect of paying discretionary bonuses).

The technical/industrial labour market system

Paul Lawrence (1985) has described five basic employment systems in the American industrial landscape – the craft, market, technical, career, and commitment systems. Each emerged as part of an historical process of change in the economy and society: 'Each system grew from specific technical, social and economic preconditions, and each had certain human and economic consequences' (Lawrence, 1985, p. 16). The development of the remaining two types of employment system – the 'technical' (or more fully, the 'technical/industrial labour market' system) and the 'commitment system' (or HRM) – can best be understood against this historical background.

The *craft system* Lawrence describes is the pre-industrial guild system where a master craftsman, such as a shoemaker or cabinetmaker, operated in a small workshop with a number of apprentices and perhaps a journeyman or two as a middleman. It is therefore not precisely the craft system that Kerr (1954) and others talk about in the modern economy, although certain elements of it survive. In industrial society, the craft system (or 'occupational labour market') was recreated by new technologies (such as in metalworking) and by the success of craft unions in protecting their members' status.

The craft (guild) system was rapidly displaced by the *market system* during the early stages of industrialization (from 1800 onwards in the USA, slightly earlier in the UK). This description is appropriate in that the two processes driving it were:

- The expansion of product markets, as a result of transport improvements and wholesaling arrangements and
- the development of a labour market of surplus, unskilled workers.

In the USA, such workers came from mass immigration as the nineteenth century wore on, while in Britain they came initially from displaced agricultural labourers. These processes were accompanied by technological developments in machinery which made possible the concentration of activity in factories. The conjunction of economic, social, and technical factors is thus clearly apparent.

As in Britain, the system first emerged in North America in textiles. Unions also grew up to counteract the power of employers, first among the old crafts and then among the new industrial workers. In the USA, however, neither kind of union was able to achieve the same foothold as in Britain, and the non-craft unions were almost wiped out at the end of the nineteenth century. Lawrence estimates that up to one-third of all employees in the USA still work under this kind of system. It survives in the UK in the guise of what we termed the 'open external labour market'.

The *technical system* then arose in the changing social and political climate after 1900, when people wanted to get away from the endemic and escalating industrial conflict and to alleviate the hardship among workers which fuelled it. As with the shift to the market system, this was accompanied by economic and technological developments which made a new order possible. In the USA, the economic trigger was the further expansion of markets onto a national basis, as transport and communications improved through intercontinental rail and road networks and intercity telephone lines. This made mass production viable, and Henry Ford then contributed the required technological development with the invention of the assembly line in 1914 at Dearborn.

The innovatory character of the technical system as an employment system lay in the minute division of labour, machine-paced work, and the payment of high, regular wages:

> The foreman no longer needed to be a pusher; that role was built into the moving components of the machine... Once pace was determined, pay could be set at an hourly rate, so that employers could avoid piece-rate disputes and could even afford to be generous with workers who accepted the discipline of machine pacing. Improved wages reduced turnover, and the remaining turnover was less costly, since the fine division of labor permitted workers to acquire quickly the necessary knowledge and dexterity (Lawrence, 1985, p. 25).

In a very short time, this became a prevalent model for organizing work in many other industries outside automobiles. With variations depending on (1) the scope for applying assembly-line techniques and (2) the degree to which trade unions have been able to circumscribe management powers to lay off and move employees around within the firm, the technical system is still widely used. Lawrence estimates that a third of the US workforce is still managed under some form of it.

Osterman (1987), again from an American perspective, puts its wider development in the context of the spread of unionization during the 1930s Great Depression and post-Second World War prosperity. Work, in what he calls the 'industrial model' or sub-system, is organized into tightly defined jobs with clear work rules. Wages are attached to jobs and vary exactly according to the job grade. The definition of grades and the prerogative of management to move people between jobs is therefore a focus of union attention, since this is a major influence on members' living standards and security. Management–union relationships tend, therefore, to be focused on the minutiae of day-to-day decisions on grades and job relocation in the workplace. Typically, workers are required to accept movement between shifts and management retain the right to make lay-offs. But management power is constrained by the fact that promotion and lay-offs are determined by seniority, as in last-in, first-out (LIFO) rules for redundancy.

In the context of our earlier discussion, the technical/industrial system is thus seen by some as a kind of internal labour market system, insofar as there are internal regulation, procedures, and job structures. However, it lacks the dimensions of significant job security and personal advancement. It is therefore a distinctive fourth type, alongside the ILM, OLM, and ELM systems described earlier, and we shall refer to it as the technical/ industrial labour market (TILM) system.

The social and behavioural drawbacks of the TILM system, or more generally 'Taylorism', are well known from the critiques of writers like Braverman (1974) and Rose (1975). As Lawrence notes, it reduced levels of industrial conflict through collective bargaining, and, of course, made possible the production of large volumes of standardized goods at low cost. However:

- It has built-in rigidities in deployment and job classifications that make it difficult to adapt to the changing demand for more customized, higher-quality products, and to changing technology
- It has serious motivational penalties in the form of boring work
- Considerable management time is absorbed in resolving shopfloor disputes
- There has been a tendency in good times for management to buy off disputes with higher pay, which raises wage costs that then rebound when competition gets tougher.

These disadvantages became increasingly apparent in the changing competitive climate of the late 1970s and early 1980s, especially when competitors to American and British manufacturing industry, like Japan, operated a much more flexible employment system, based on ILMs in their major companies and ELMs in the smaller firms supplying the larger ones. As Katz and Sabel (1985) argue, there was little difference between American and Japanese or German ways of organizing work and developing skills in the 1950s and 1960s, so long as technological change was limited to incremental improvements. Until that time, the American system had retained certain cost advantages, such as reduced training requirements. In the face of changing patterns of demand and new technological possibilities, however, the disadvantages of inflexibility became apparent.

As a result, the TILM system has been at the centre of efforts to create a new kind of employment system. In the 1960s and 1970s, this centred on experiments in job enrichment and the 'Quality of Working Life' movement. In America in the 1980s this turned into an interest in HRM as an emerging new system. Beer, Eisenstat and Spector (1990) thus set out to study HRM as an emerging system in the older 'smokestack' industries where the TILM predominates, while Lawrence (1985) identified a number of industrial firms, including General Motors and Ford, that were experimenting with the new approach, which he called 'the commitment system'.

To a large extent, therefore, HRM, as a distinctive approach to organizing and managing employees, is about reforming the technical/industrial system of employment. Chapters 16 and 17 provide examples of this.

The commitment system (or HRM)

The fourth type of employment system in Lawrence's classification is the *career system* – or what we have called the internal labour market. Lawrence locates the origins of this in the electronics/computer industry, which grew rapidly after the Second World War. Again, the system was a response to a combination of economic, social, and technical factors. Fast economic growth in the USA created unprecedented opportunities for career advancement, and this meshed with the career expectations of the large numbers of college-educated workers which these industries required. There was also a social dimension in that management in this developing industry wanted to avoid unionization, partly as an end in itself but also to maintain flexibility in a fast-changing technology. In terms we will by now be familiar with, Lawrence (1985) describes the career system as follows:

> The hallmark of the career system is its flow policies [i.e. the movement of people in, up, and out of the organization]. People are recruited for positions that are spelled out with explicit, detailed attention to duties and rights. Every position is linked to a career ladder, so that every worker has the opportunity for some upward mobility. Thus, the firm is in effect offering an employee not just a job but a career as well. Longer-term employment is encouraged, and layoffs are used only as a last resort. If layoffs are necessary, both seniority and merit are commonly taken into account in some orderly fashion (p. 28).

Payment is typically in the form of salaries (hence, Osterman, 1987, refers to this as the 'salaried' internal labour market model), and progression, like lay-offs, is determined by a mix of seniority and merit considerations. As both Lawrence and Osterman note, the career/salaried/ILM system often embraces both white- and blue-collar employees in the firm (or, in the public bureaucracies, employees at all levels). This helps the creation of an homogeneous work culture throughout the organization, and discourages adversarialism and trade unionism.

While computer firms like IBM were the leaders in establishing this system in the USA, it emerged also in other sectors like pharmaceuticals in both the USA and the UK. It is also obviously the system which for some while previously governed many public service organizations, especially the middle and upper reaches of the British civil service and the major banking institutions. The difference between the way these organizations manage employment lies in the relative emphasis on individual employment contracts and personalized decisions on promotion and pay (IBM) versus published grading structures and bureaucratic procedures for determining the latter (government). In the longer term, the risk is that the bureaucratic element gains the upper hand, especially in organizations operating in a competitive environment, so that their flexibility is reduced.

What the civil service, as the classic form of bureaucracy, banking, electronics and pharmaceutical industries all had in common, at least until the 1980s, was a product-service environment which was fairly benign, stable or growing. As a result, they could offer employees protected employment and long-term careers, while drawing upon accummulated employee knowledge for incremental product-service change. In the 1980s, however, radical changes in the competitive environment changed the scope for job security and the need for continuity in 'old' skills in all except pharmaceuticals. Radical discontinuities in technology, products, services, knowledge, and skills have thus put the career system under strain.

In the same way that others have turned away from the technical system, Lawrence sees organizations who have had to face up to the inflexibilities of the career system also beginning to invent the *commitment system*. The key elements in this are new forms of work organization which put greater responsibility for work performance on the work group itself, and new forms of employee representation which give employees a stronger voice:

> The new approach draws upon a variety of experiences: earlier programs in American industry centering on job enlargement and job enrichment; the British experience with sociotechnical planning; the quality-of-worklife approach; the Scanlon Plan and other gain-sharing programs; the European experience with work councils; and the Japanese model for human resource management, which makes use of enterprise unions, quality circles, and lifetime employment policies (Lawrence, 1985, p. 30).

The commitment system, or HRM, is a response, then, both to defects in the technical/industrial labour market system and to the breakdown of the career (ILM) system. The career system, which until recently dominated modern consciousness of employment and characterized leading-edge research-intensive industry, has begun seriously to erode. From this point of view, HRM is an attempt to rescue elements of the white-collar career system, while overcoming the demotivating features of the TILM. While this may lead towards a system combining features of each – including similar access to job security (and insecurity) and discretion in work – equally it is not surprising that there are tensions in any such emerging model.

Lawrence looks to Japan and Germany as exemplars of his 'commitment system'. At various points, this book looks at these and other innovations that may be producing a new, distinctive model of employment. However, central to our perspective is that no innovations or single system is likely readily or entirely to supplant other existing types. Each type of employment system in this chapter has been brought about and is sustained by a particular combination of factors. As Lawrence (1985) says:

> Each new system has historically emerged without totally displacing the earlier ones. There are still large numbers of people working under the market and technical systems. History indicates that newer systems, even if they come to dominate the employment scene, do not by any means totally displace earlier systems. It seems true, however, that firms that led the way into each new system, such as Ford and IBM, did experience a significant competitive advantage (p. 34).

A general model of factors influencing employment systems

Lawrence described the evolution of different employment systems in terms of specific technical, social, and economic preconditions at different periods. Other writers extend and elaborate on this list. Writing about skill formation, Curtain (1987) refers to the influence of a firm's production process, product markets, the availability of labour, the nature of firm-level and national-level industrial relations, and also to the role of government and individuals. Peck (1989) identifies an even fuller range of influences:

- *Labour demand factors*: for example, the technical requirements of different labour processes; the stability of different product markets; the labour control strategies used by employers; and the effect of industrial structure
- *Labour supply factors*: for example, the role of the household division of labour in shaping labour market participation; the stigmatization of certain social groups as secondary workers; the processes of occupational socialization; and the influence of trade unions in restricting the labour supply to certain occupations
- *The role of the State*: for example, the structure of welfare provision and its eligibility rules; support for the training system; and differentiation within the education system.

Peck's focus is on people and the way they fall into and get trapped in different labour markets. This is the theory of labour market segmentation (see Chapter 18). The value of this perspective is that it shows how

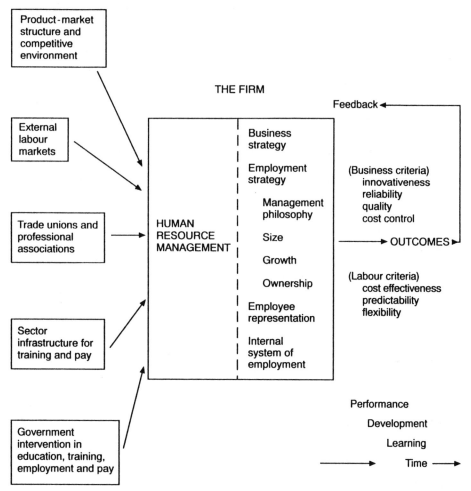

Figure 11.3 *Influences upon company employment strategy and systems*

employment systems within individual firms are a response to a considerable array of factors other than straightforward economic and technical ones. This contrasts with the landmark formulation of labour markets by Doeringer and Piore (1971), which identified their origins simply in technological developments and the extent to which product markets were stable or unstable. Thus, not only do the four kinds of employment system we have characterized – the ILM, ELM, OLM, and TILM – reflect a broader range of influences, but systems in individual companies have idiosyncratic features due to the influence of a wide range of localized factors and history.

The second important point is that often, within the one firm, there will be a number of different employment systems, or ways of managing employees, that are responding to different sets of factors. The way the firm manages these different groups – its 'employment strategy', or 'human resources strategy' – is partly determined by factors it can control and partly an accommodation to those it cannot.

Figure 11.3 attempts to bring together the range of factors which bear upon such strategies and produce the outcomes we see in particular organizations. External to the firm are:

- The competitive environment, industrial structure, and stability of different product-markets, with the resulting requirements for operating successfully in the sector
- The semi-autonomous nature of external labour markets, comprising various sources of labour from local and national sources, influences on levels of labour market participation, and the expectations and work motivations that employees import
- The role of trade unions and professional associations in controlling the supply of labour
- The infrastructure developed by the industry in which the firm operates, to service and regulate the external labour market – that is, sector-specific systems of training, and local and national pay rates
- Government intervention in the labour market, through education and training policies, employment legislation and pay policies, with the influence of public opinion in helping to frame these.

These factors combine most noticeably in the balance of supply and demand for labour, leading to either unemployment or a tight labour market. On the other hand, they can change independently of one another, and even when there is compatibility between pay, training, and the labour market they attempt to regulate at the industry level, there may well be leads and lags in individual firm responses. Thus, these factors are, in turn, mediated by the firm, where:

- Business strategy is decided or evolved
- Technology is adopted and its technical requirements translated into systems of work organization
- Employment (or HRM) strategies are developed, in accordance with management philosophy and capability, and the conditioning effects of factors such as size, the growth stage of the organization, and ownership
- Trade unions, professional associations, or other collectives of employees exercise control over the internal supply of labour through various constitutional or unconstitutional means and, of course,
- There is an existing system of employment.

For example, among the conditioning influences on human resources strategy is size. Small size can put restrictions on recruitment and promotion opportunities. Siebert and Addison (1991) suggest that ILMs, for instance, are less likely to be sustained in firms with under 500 employees.

Mediating these factors on behalf of the firm is HRM. Whether it is a functional specialism or not, HRM can be construed as a boundary-management activity, balancing the factors on the left-hand side with the internal circumstances of the organization. In this box is everything that makes up HRM and the management of employment – recruitment, pay, training, work organization and job design, and so on.

Finally, there are various outcomes from the employment or human resources strategy on the right-hand side, covering the long and short terms. These can be defined in terms of business objectives (such as cost control, quality products, reliable delivery, product innovativeness, and so forth – the kind of criteria identified in Chapter 4). Alternatively, they can be defined in terms of the employment system itself. Osterman (1987), for instance, says that firms have three aims in their employment systems:

- Cost effectiveness (or cost-minimization)
- Maximizing predictability (that is, having available a qualified labour force at foreseeable prices)
- Flexibility (being able to vary the numbers of employees, deploying them freely where they will be most productive, and being able to draw upon broad skills which employees can use readily in new situations).

These objectives are mutually supportive in certain areas (for example, flexible deployment contributes to cost effectiveness), and they parallel outcomes in terms of business objectives. Other writers suggest different lists and definitions – for example, Beer *et al.* (1984) define the goals of HRM as commitment, competence, congruence (between the goals of employees and the organization), and cost effectiveness; and Guest (1987) identifies commitment, quality, flexibility, and strategic integration.

How an organization manages rewards, or pensions, or promotion thus has specific consequences and contributes to a distinctive system of employment. According to the employment systems perspective in this chapter, these differences centre on how four aspects of employment are managed – job classification and job definition, deployment, security, and wage rules (Osterman, 1987). Each system that results fulfils a different balance of objectives. An ELM strategy, for instance, minimizes costs in training, but is vulnerable to higher costs and loss of efficiency through labour turnover (Curtain, 1987). A TILM strategy likewise minimizes training costs, but can add wage costs and lose flexibility. And so on.

However, while such frameworks provide yardsticks, for practical purposes what is most important is to be able to draw out the implicit and explicit objectives that operate in particular organizations.

Employment systems and human resources strategy

This model allows us to move on from the idea of the employment system as something that can be described to the idea of a 'human resources strategy' as something that can be changed. A human resources strategy is the active effort by a firm to manage people and their skills with the immediate and long-term aims of the business in mind. Such a strategy may be explicit to a greater or lesser degree. Often, in fact, it is largely implicit, embedded in a variety of habitual practices.

Because observers focus on the presence of formal manpower planning activities they are led to believe that only a minority of employers do have labour-use strategies (Hakim, 1990). However, as we found in our small–medium firm study, managers can often articulate quite precisely the way their organization recruits and promotes, the reasons for this, and how their approach relates to the commercial and labour markets in which they operate.

As we argued in the previous chapter, the issue is really how actively and systematically an organization monitors and modifies aspects of its total approach to human resources. The 'strategic' firm is one that consciously monitors outcomes (in both business and human resource terms) through the feedback loops described in Figure 11.3, and modifies strategy accordingly. Even so, we should not equate this monitoring with formal, and certainly not with written, planning mechanisms. Management as a judgemental process is going on all the time, in many minds, and being shared through discussions with many people. Adjustments that result, whether radical or incremental, represent a kind of strategic choice.

The bottom-line is that employment systems can be changed: firms can make choices. But equally not just as they choose. Firms make constrained choices:

> No firm is free simply to consider the options . . ., assign weights to goals, and design and implement whichever employment system seems most desirable. In most instances, companies have a system already in place. Management is acclimated to working within specific staff patterns, and the labor force is accustomed to a particular set of arrangements. Any serious change usually will be incremental and in response to external stimuli (Osterman, 1987, p. 59).

and again:

> The notion of choice does not imply that firms continually review and up-date the internal labor market structure for the full range of relevant occupations. Such constant activity is clearly beyond the resources of any company and would almost certainly be counter-productive. . . A given internal employment and training system is not examined or reconsidered until some event – technological change, changing product markets, reduced supply of an appropriate labor force, sharply rising wages, etc. – forces management to attend to the issue (*Ibid.*, p. 53).

Choice, constrained by a variety of external and internal factors and the history that has brought about the present system, results in hybrids that incorporate different elements of the four systems we have described. In a period of change such as we have been experiencing, new forms begin to emerge. In the next two chapters we develop some case examples of how TILM and ELM systems, respectively, are being recast to incorporate elements of what Lawrence calls the 'commitment system' and others call 'HRM'.

Summary

In this chapter we have described four employment systems. We called these the 'internal labour market' (ILM), the 'open external labour market' (ELM), the 'occupational labour market' (OLM), and the 'technical/industrial labour market' (TILM). Table 11.1 summarizes their principal characteristics.

Table 11.1   A typology of employment system characteristics

	Jobs	*Deployment*	*Security*	*Pay*
ILM	Flexible and broad, firm-specific skills, clear rules defined by employer	Seniority/merit, controlled by employer	High	Formalized/individualized, salaried
OLM	Narrow/broad, craft skills, defined by occupation	Controlled by occupation and agreements	High	Well paid, fixed rate/bonuses, job-related, waged/salaried
TILM	Narrow, semi-skilled, tightly defined by employer	Seniority, controlled by employer and agreements, with informal TU control	Low	Job-related, waged
ELM	Narrow, unskilled	Controlled by employer	Low	Low paid/well paid, highly incentivized, job-related, waged

The characterization of employment systems into ILMs, ELMs, OLMs, and TILMs shows:

- How particular employment practices hang together to form a coherent pattern and where the areas of employer–employee tension might be
- Why systems differ between organizations
- Why they are subject to change
- Why they may also be slow to respond to changes which business strategy would like to dictate.

The starting point for a strategic approach to employment is then to ask such questions as:

- 'What kind of employment system do we operate?'
- 'Why?'
- 'What are the consequences of this?'
- 'How might this need to change if we change our technology, business focus, performance objectives and criteria, etc.?'

During the last decade, existing systems, especially the TILM and ILM, have come under increasing strain. The result is that many organizations have been feeling their way towards a new system or systems. Labelling these 'HRM', however, can be confusing, because they often try to reconcile contradictory elements designed to overcome the problems of two systems, not one:

> Employers are therefore in a bind. In the case of blue-collar work, many want to shift to a salaried model. Yet, macro-economic uncertainty and unwillingness to permit labor to become too great a fixed cost generates fears of the high price of employment security. In the case of white-collar employment, firms want to maintain the salaried model but at lower employment levels. These conflicting pressures and firms' efforts to resolve them help explain much confusion and mixed signals about the current direction of work organization. Some employers are attempting to finesse the problem by imposing flexibility via concession bargaining and employer militancy. Other firms are experimenting with a core–periphery model in which they offer job security (or a commitment to make every effort to avoid layoffs) to a core of more or less permanent employees and surround that core with a 'periphery' of temporary, contract, and part-time workers who enjoy less protection (Osterman, 1987, p. 65).

In the following chapters we will look at particular changes in the way firms are managing employment, focusing on white-collar, then blue-collar groups, and then on the core–periphery issue.

Notes

1. The original material for this case was developed by Alan Jones of the Centre for Corporate Strategy and Change.
2. The original material for this case was developed by Michael Arthur of the Centre for Corporate Strategy and Change.

12

Managing the system as a whole: towards HRM (1)

Introduction

In this chapter and the next we look at two extended cases. These are intended to illustrate four things:

- First, they show how employment strategies are adapted to a firm's commercial environment and business strategy.
- Second, they show how the factors which influence firms' employment systems and strategies can produce situations which are a lot more complex than the conventional categorization of employment systems might suggest. In this way, the distinctions between ILMs, OLMs, ELMs, and TILMs set out in Chapter 11 become blurred in practice.
- Third, the two cases show the possibilities for change in existing systems.
- Finally, both cases show different aspects of trends towards HRM, defined in value terms as increasing commitment and flexibility.

The first case is presented against the background of core–periphery trends and the pressure for flexibility over the last decade. The second shows a new firm on a greenfield site taking a deliberate 'strategic' approach to its management of people.

The construction company: an ELM or an ILM?

The first example involves a construction firm. Construction normally is held up as an exemplar of casualized employment. On closer inspection, however, there are strong elements closely associated with internal labour markets, that is, of an ELM overlain with ILM characteristics.

First, there are clear signs of construction firms maintaining an ILM (internal labour market) of core employees. This is entirely compatible, of course, with operating an ELM strategy for other employees – or, in overall terms, following a core–periphery strategy. An interesting question, there-fore, is whether construction firms have been extending the scope and depth of their ILM as a deliberate strategy. At the same time, insofar as construction draws on traditional crafts, the ELM is intercut with occupational labour market (OLM) characteristics.

Second, medium to large construction firms operate through what are in effect extended ILMs, incorporating their sub-contractors. As a result, it is a mistake to look at the construction industry in terms solely of the individual firm. Certainly, there are self-employed workers who come and go as any in a pure ELM. However, if we look at the relationships between the larger firms and their smaller suppliers and sub-contractors, we find they have a strong interest in replicating the operational benefits of an ILM, and will try to provide some stability in this extended network.

To illustrate these themes, we first set out a case featuring a construction firm, with a running commentary on points of note, and then draw on findings from two larger studies to develop some of the implications in further depth.

Construction Co.[1]

Construction Co. provides a good example of the complex interaction between the many factors that bear upon the employment system of a firm. It shows in particular the interaction between commercial strategy and the competitive conditions that give rise to it; the way the labour market impinges on strategy, and how this works in part autonomously of companies; the impact of government policy on employment status and training, which feeds through to company strategy; and, finally, the industry regulative structures which firms, by themselves or with government support, have put together. The result is that construction companies have to manage a complex labour market.

Background, products and markets

'Construction Co.' covers two related businesses in a family-owned construction group. It was founded in 1907 and is based in north-east England. The larger division, Division A, builds to order, with projects covering both new building and reconstruction varying greatly in character and scale. In 1989, turnover in Division A had increased by over a third on the previous year and stood at £19.5 million, but a small profit had turned into a loss of £0.205 million. This pattern of increasing turnover, but fluctuating profits, characterized the 1980s, and serves to highlight the cyclical nature of the industry. As the managing director put it, 'the company has been through every kind of "up and down" imaginable in the past ten years'. Average employment in Division A in 1989 stood at 330 employees, having increased gradually since 1985. However, the actual number varies according to the state of projects.

The smaller division, Division B, grew out of the larger one as a result of partnership deals in the 1970s with the City of

Newcastle to develop low-cost council housing. Around 1981, a dramatic downturn in the construction market and near bankruptcy caused Construction Co. to turn to the building of homes as an alternative source of business and income. Eventually then, in 1987, Division B was established as a separate division to build speculatively. In 1989 sales stood at £8.3 million and profits at a healthy £0.677 million. For the construction industry this represented a very healthy return of 8 per cent on sales. During the 1980s, good profits in one division have thus tended to offset poor results in the other. Division B presently employs between fifty-seven and eighty-one people, again depending on the state of business, while Group handles certain administrative tasks such as wages and personnel.

Competitive environment

The construction industry is highly sensitive to the general state of the economy and tends to exaggerate recessionary and boom conditions. As a result, it has a long tradition of labour sub-contracting and casualization. These provide flexibility to firms in volatile product markets. Following the ending of the 'lump' in the 1960s, a more formalized system of sub-contracting has developed to cope with the volatility of the 1980s. For Construction Co., the flexible control of labour is one of the keys to profitability, and in this respect it can be said to have a highly 'strategic' approach to skill supply.

Company employment structure

The image of casualization is misleading, though. Both divisions of Construction Co. operate with a core of staff (such as estimators, surveyors, and contracts management, including site managers and foremen) and a core of direct employees (principally bricklayers and joiners, plus labourers). In Division A, these represented around 30 per cent (ninety-two) and 50 per cent (176) respectively of total employees in 1989. Turnover is low for a hard core of around 200 of these, but high for the remainder (mainly labourers). In addition, there are highly variable numbers of self-employed tradesmen and labourers (20 per cent of all employees in 1989), among whom turnover is also high. In all, then, around 150 employees will come and go in the course of a year, sometimes these positions turning over three or four times. Finally, there are a wide variety of sub-contracted trades working on sites at different times.

Division B has a similar percentage of staff (twenty-seven out of eighty-one), but the ratio between 'directs' (or 'cards in' employees) and self-employed/sub-contractors is greater because of the short-term, speculative approach to building. Moreover, since the division was formed only two years before, largely by taking on self-employed workers, it has yet to build a strong core of 'loyal' employees. Consequently, in 1989 the ratio between 'cards in' employees and others was around 1:4.

These employment distinctions are recognized through three separate bonus schemes for staff, directs, and the self-employed. The prevalence of bonus systems (even for staff who are salaried) and the high proportion of earnings they account for indicates the importance attached to matching pay to labour productivity. One estimate is that 95 per cent of the site wage bill was through piecework payments.

Business strategy and competitive advantage

However, flexible labour is only one aspect of strategy: 'Building a house is a mixture of timework and teamwork, but 80–90 per cent the latter' (estimator/surveyor, Division B). Teamwork is an integral part of on-site operations, but it is easier to achieve with one's own 'direct' employees than with itinerant site workers. Teamwork is also seen as the key to improved performance more generally, through better procedures and teamwork among staff and between staff and site personnel. The imminence of new European quality standards and certification in 1992 has strengthened this emphasis.

As a result, on taking over in 1988 on the death of his father and after attending action learning and leadership training courses himself, the new group managing director has been pushing the concept of teamwork in both divisions, to change the management style and improve decision making. The highlight of this in 1989 was a weekend teambuilding course attended by eighteen staff from Division A which exceeded the division's whole annual training budget. There has also been increasing attention to the quality of site managers recruited and promoted. This explains what at first might look like a rather unlikely interest, for a construction company, in 'soft' forms of developmental training.

A stable workforce therefore has strategic value from the point of view of internal flexibility and quality control. On a purely financial basis, too, relying heavily on sub-contractors and the self-employed means having to pay premium rates for labour. A core of own employees increases predictability in wage costs. The trick is then to balance these fixed labour costs against the going rate for short-term hirings.

The importance of the wage bill is reflected in the key indicators used in planning. These are slightly different for the two divisions. The broad frame for the Group as a whole is the economic cycle. This is expressed in a ten-year plan, which is updated annually.

More precisely, Division A takes a two- to three-year view of its business, based on a waiting period after tender of three to four months and construction periods of eighteen months. Because work is contracted for, this becomes a fairly firm planning frame. In the short term, however, the key determinant is the annual wage settlement which has to be second-guessed in committing the firm to contract bids.

By contrast, as a speculative builder, Division B works to a five-year plan that covers land acquisition; a six- to nine-month construction cycle; and, in between, a two-year planning frame. The last of these is crucial in managing cash flow. First, it allows for slowing down sitework in the event of adverse economic conditions and reduced house sales; and second, it keeps in view the two-year limit on employment after which redundancy payments become payable.

Smaller construction firms in the sub-contract end of the industry work to much shorter timescales. Normally they find it difficult to plan as much as a year ahead, and during 1990, those engaged in renovations and conversions, for example, were finding it difficult to look beyond a month. At the height of the recession, this obviously got a lot worse.

Employment regulation and the external labour market

Beyond companies' own commercial and labour strategies, however, there have been developments in the labour market independent of the major contractors themselves. Principal among these has been the emergence of the self-employed (the '714s'). The Inland Revenue has always had difficulty getting payment of taxes from casual workers in the construction industry. As a halfway house, therefore, the Revenue agreed to recognize them as a distinct group for taxation purposes, and provide certification (i.e. a '714' tax coding) which, at the same time, absolved them from paying National Insurance. Equally, this absolved companies from making National Insurance contributions on their behalf. Employing '714s' therefore saved companies money and encouraged their use. This has now got to the point where '714s' have become essential to the construction industry.

There are also other underlying reasons for using self-employed workers, quite independent of this, to do with the basic flexibility they provide. For instance, they can divide their time between more than one employer on a day-to-day basis, which can be important in managing the flow of work on a site. The self-employed also value the independence which the '714' status gives them, even though net earnings may not work out much differently from what 'cards in' employees get.

The DSS, however, has never fully accepted the Inland Revenue's certification, and is currently contesting this. If it wins, the economics of employment in the construction industry will change drastically.

The external labour market and sector infrastructure

The other important labour market factor is the interdependency between local-cum-regional and national labour markets. Both divisions of Construction Co. recruit locally, but are dependent on the national labour market for the availability of skills. The national market is made possible, on the one hand, by clearly defined trades, and, on the other by the tradition of itinerant construction workers going where the jobs are. During the mid-1980s, there was a large outflow of workers from the North-east to London and the South-east where construction was booming. With the subsequent downturn hitting construction in the South-east first, 'the trades have been coming home', as the managing director of Construction Co. put it. The result tends to be conditions of feast and famine in local labour markets like the North-east.

The industry as a whole has sought to regulate this situation through national agreements on minimum rates for the different trades, with local markets deciding piecework rates. These are negotiated between the Building Employers Confederation and trade unions, but at company level, at least in Construction Co., trade unions have little impact.

What the industry has not done, however, is maintain the supply of skilled people. In the recession of 1979–1981, it is reckoned that half a million people left the industry. Those aged over 45 left for good, while many younger skilled men left permanently to find more secure employment elsewhere. During the recession and subsequently, companies in the industry stopped training, and despite the efforts of the Construction Industry Training Board (CITB), training did not recover to meet demand.

One reason for this, apart from economic instability, is reckoned to be the spread of bonus systems over the last fifteen to twenty years. The apprenticeship system requires an amount of on-the-job training. But reliance on bonuses acts as a disincentive because it means a skilled person losing time supervising another. The reduction in the period of apprenticeship (from five to three and a half years) is also felt to have caused a drop in standards. Attempts to increase labour supply through short courses for adult retraining have tended to feed only into the more marginal sub-contracting part of the industry. They are then the first to go when a downturn reappears.

The result is that the industry has been struggling against a downward spiral of insufficient basic training and falling standards. The big employers' successful lobbying to get the CITB retained (when the government abolished all the other training boards) is a recognition by employers that a fragmented industry like construction, with lots of small firms, cannot rely on firms themselves to maintain training.

The overall picture, then, is of an occupational labour market (OLM) struggling against skill dilution and external labour market (ELM) casualization pressures.

Company employment strategy

In the face of these external developments, the construction firms use their core employees to manage and control the temporary direct workforce and sub-contract relationships. Within companies, there are firmly established career lines for both staff and trades. Through office experience and part-time studies (notably for membership of the Institute of Builders), staff can achieve management positions in estimating and surveying. At the same time, those in the trades can rise from chargehand, through site manager, to contracts manager, and senior management roles. The industry is thus fairly unique in that such internal labour market (ILM) routes still predominate. On the other hand, there is also an occupational market whereby managers tend to follow one another around between firms.

This ILM structure provides a natural way of retaining experienced employees at a time when they may be becoming less effective physically, and less able and less inclined to work at speed and in all weathers 'on the tools'. Within Construction Co., this is backed up by transferring some older workers into a third division in the Group, called Small Works, which undertakes minor projects. Some of these skilled men are then used to train younger employees and are paid a fixed sum for doing so outside of the bonus system.

While this structure supports the skill requirements of the company, the ILM is sustained by a range of 'side payments' to secure employee loyalty and maintain its character as a family business. For staff (remembering that these are mainly professional employees plus site managers and foremen, and, at 119, number a third of all employees), these include a contributory pension scheme; company cars for 75 per cent of all staff, including all site managers; private medical insurance; and a staff social club. There are also a variety of profit-sharing and bonus schemes for staff, including a general scheme for staff (paying in the range 5-10 per cent), a more highly geared scheme for site management (paying up to 20 per cent on basic salary), and a more highly geared scheme still for directors (paying 30-45 per cent). Divisions A and B, however, differ in their ability to pay out.

Site workers are restricted to standard benefits defined in

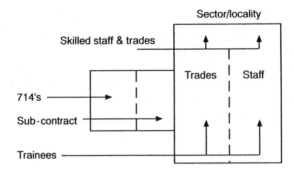

Figure 12.1 *The employment system at Construction Co.*

national agreements, although they have access to the company's social club, and their 'bonuses' are strictly of a piecework nature. The resulting employment system for Construction Co., with its overlay of ELM, ILM, and OLM characteristics, can be summarized in Figure 12.1.

One final point should be made about employment 'strategy' in Construction Co, which is that much of it is implicit and conditioned by industry factors. In 1985 the two-person personnel department disappeared as part of rationalization. Since then, the group managing director's personal secretary has handled personal aspects of personnel, while pay, sickness and injury benefits, layoffs and the like are dealt with by the wages office which reports to the group accountant. Meanwhile, the board does consider certain policy issues such as salaries, benefits, skill shortages, and training. The increasing prominence of training as an issue, however, is creating pressure to re-establish a more professional personnel function.

Business strategy and the extended labour market

With this overview of the way the labour market works in construction in general and in Construction Co. in particular, we can now develop the comments on business strategy and the way in which employment strategy is crucial to performance. This hinges on the idea of networks – a key theme in the analysis of strategy.

Networks are fundamental to the construction industry. Success depends on bringing together and managing a range of resources – above all, people, but also land and finance. Consequently, all types of construction firms, in their different ways, have to build and keep alive networks, in order to get jobs and to carry them through.

First, at the front-end, network relations are important in getting jobs. Larger projects, such as Division A undertakes, may mean getting into consortium relationships in order to tender.

During recession, with bankruptcies disrupting established networks and firms moving across traditional local–regional–national boundaries, this gets increasingly complex and difficult. Construction Co., for instance, as a regional firm, has been recently collaborating with a larger national contractor to subcontract its own labour for work on foundations, brickwork, and joinery. Management time investing in network relationships is therefore important.

Commercial networking works differently in Division B because of its speculative approach. This has consequences for networking in two ways: first, in acquiring land, and second in off-loading risk. As its managing director put it:

> House building is all about outlets, the number and size of them being key features. Shared risk provides better use of finance and allows for putting eggs in multiple baskets.

Consequently, the Division has very strong links with a number of larger competitors for making joint land purchases and in pooling resources in schemes that are too big for it alone.

For both Divisions, local knowledge and contacts are the means by which, as a regionally defined business, it gains a competitive advantage. In the language of strategy, local knowledge and contacts create entry barriers and a defendable niche. As a regional firm, moreover, Construction Co. is attractive to larger national firms because it can contribute its regional experience within a consortium.

Moving towards the operational level, networking is crucial for both divisions in developing long-term relationships with well-run businesses for sub-contracting and materials. Suppliers of materials, such as bricks, timber, and concrete, are an integral part of doing business. Efficient (and therefore profitable) site management relies on knowing suppliers who can perform and will look after you. Concentration in the industry and the increased size of suppliers, however, is making primary relationships more distant and suppliers less responsive to smaller contractors.

One other critical 'supplier' in this respect should not go unnoticed – that is, a firm's bank. Banks are particularly important in construction as a source of working capital because of the unevenness of cash flow in project-based work. It is important therefore to maintain good relations with the firm's bank and to hold regular meetings to discuss both individual projects and the overall requirements of the firm.

Finally, at site level, there is the network relationship with labour sub-contractors. Traditionally, as we have indicated, the main contractor supplies a core of joiners, bricklayers, and general labourers, with typically 50 per cent of the work then subcontracted. The recent trend towards more self-employment among joiners and bricklayers has considerably increased this proportion, and with that the ability to manage employment flexibility. Since profit depends crucially on performing contracted work on time and within budget, juggling the use of their own and sub-contract labour, often between sites, is an important organizational capability.

However, flexibility over wage costs has to be traded off against reliability and the indirect costs of monitoring for and incurring poor quality. Consequently, main contractors like Construction Co. develop strong relationships with two or three sub-contractors in each trade. Typically, these will comprise one or two managers and up to fifty employees. Dependable relationships of this kind allow for more flexible site management and for extracting favours when it may be necessary to get someone on-site at short notice. A number of sub-contractors of this size have thus built themselves off the back of work for Construction Co. While the commercial relationship is based on price always as the first consideration, a main contractor like Construction Co. has a vested interest in spreading its business around its favoured sub-contractors to keep them all in play. In the longer term this ensures price competition among suppliers, as well as maintaining the system of favours. The indirect result of this is to provide greater stability in employment at sub-contract level than otherwise would be the case.

One final aspect of construction industry networks which improve overall stability in the longer term concerns the social networks around which ownership and labour-only sub-contracting revolve. In an industry which is prone to instability, there is a pattern, as the managing director of Construction Co. put it, of 'firms going bust and starting again, while the personalities stay the same'. Thus, personal contacts provide some stability and continuity, and keep contracting relationships intact despite organizations themselves coming and going.

The construction industry: a wider view

The case of Construction Co. shows the competing tendencies between ILM, ELM, and OLM employment structures and practices. Two larger-scale reviews of trends in the contruction industry put these into wider perspective. First, Bryman *et al.* (1987) emphasize construction's ILM characteristics. Evans (1990) on the other hand, describes an industry that has moved towards an increasing freeing up of its labour market.

The Bryman *et al.* study covers the period 1982–1985. The part of their research that deals with construction looked first at forty-three medium-to-large construction projects (i.e. above £2 million) and second, in more detail at site management on three projects. They emphasize the importance of many of the same ILM features which characterize Construction Co.

Central to performance is familiarity among team members, in reducing learning time when starting a new project and in ensuring basic compatibility under pressurized conditions. This applies through the various levels of a team, from the contracts manager to site manager to direct labour. Contracts managers look for site managers who understand their firm's methods, procedures, and working philosophy, and if they are starting from scratch take time to establish this. Similarly, site managers try to take a nucleus of known workers with them from job to job on whom they can rely to delegate. In doing so, 'acceptability' in the form of loyalty, commitment, and reliability are as important in forming the team as 'skills'.

Bryman *et al.* report a similar emphasis on the advantages of long-term familiarity in working relationships in the main contractor's involvement with external organizations such as clients' representatives and sub-contractors. Again, this extends from familiarity with methods to personal knowledge of individuals.

The quality of interpersonal relationships thereby becomes an important factor in translating the formal commercial relationship into a less formal operating structure. This is critical in avoiding contractual 'standoffs' which can slow down projects, especially when there are many different sub-contractors to be coordinated and their participation on projects may vary considerably in duration. This can substantially reduce direct personal contact between the whole team on-site, and therefore familiarity and continuity of experience become the bedrock for the delegation of discretion.

Such considerations produce on a larger scale the same kind of relationships in awarding contracts that are visible in Construction Co. Price comes first, but for each trade a company will work with four or five contractors that are well known to it. As Bryman *et al.* (1987, p. 266) put it, over a period of time this can generate 'a pattern of employment relationships which are "quasi-direct"' – or as one of the people they interviewed said: 'You tend to regard labour-only sub-contractors almost like direct labour, because the same ones are employed by two or three companies only.' As a result,

> a continuing relationship over time with certain sub-contractors may in effect act as a proxy for internal processes of probation and socialisation... The 'authority' of the main contractor as such may extend beyond the specific terms and conditions of work for individual contracts, to a legitimacy more akin to that associated with the existence of longer-term employment relationships. (Bryman *et al.*, 1987, p. 267).

In the absence of such continuity, much more emphasis will be placed upon securing sub-contractors' conformity to the formal terms and conditions of a commercial contract. Indeed, one of the observations Bryman and colleagues make about the leadership skills of site managers is the stylistic distinction between their management of direct labour, which is more inclined towards motivating, educating, and creating team spirit, and that towards sub-contractors, which is more arm's-length and task-oriented.

The study by Evans (1990), by contrast, puts far more emphasis on casualization and fragmenting tendencies in the construction industry and generally gives a much more negative picture. The implication is that creating some stability across sub-contractors is an attempt to minimize the deleterious effects of a looser labour market.

Evans' research was conducted between 1985 and 1987, and involved 150 interviews on fifteen sites and two local labour markets with managers, sub-contractors, employers' organization and trade unions, workers, and public authority clients. It thus covered the sector, firms, and sites. Importantly, it also adopted a perspective which looked back across earlier phases of boom and slump in the industry and at changing trends in casualization.

The context for the study was government policy in the 1980s to free up labour markets in the belief that this would improve productivity in the British economy. A number of measures increased deregulation in construction. These included the repeal of Schedule 11 of the Employment Protection Act 1975 and rescinding the Fair Wages Resolution in 1983, which weakened the application of nationally bargained rates and terms of employment. The Finance Act 1980 reduced the insurance liabilities of self-employed labour-only sub-contractors, creating the '714' situation earlier referred to. Also, a number of measures were designed to weaken the power of contractors to influence the labour practices of sub-contractors.

One focus of this was to undermine direct labour departments in local and central government through compulsory competitive tendering. Another (through the Employment Act 1980, section 18) was to prevent contractors tying sub-contractors into collective agreements, and, through the Local Government Act 1988, to require public authorities to exclude 'non-commercial matters' from consideration when inviting tenders and awarding contracts – such as the contractors' terms and conditions of employment, the composition of its workforce and forms of engagement (i.e. no clauses limiting the use of self-employed labour), and training provision. In other words, public authorities should not use 'contract compliance' methods to influence the labour market, even where, as with training, there could be benefits.

A further significant factor in deregulation was the reduction in construction by local and central government, which fell from a peak of 52 per cent of all construction activity in 1976 to 29 per cent by 1986, part of this being, of course, the enforced slump in public sector house-building. This contributed to the fragmentation of project activity, the reshaping of the industrial structure, and hence of the labour market in the industry. A second influence on this was client demands for faster build times, which implied new contracting arrangements and increased specialization. A third influence was the profit squeeze in construction between 1971 and 1981.

The result in terms of industrial structure has been a polarization, with the number of medium-sized firms reducing and the largest and very small firms increasing in number. Large firms have diversified and extended their activities, while transferring risks and employment costs to chains of dependent sub-contractors and the self-employed. Thus, Evans cites evidence that between 1975 and 1985 firms with seven or fewer employees doubled, the number of single self-employed increased by 150 per cent, while the number of firms with more than 600 employees halved. These trends are confirmed by Abdel-Razek and McCaffer (1987), who note also that smaller firms have increased their share of the value of work done. The result is that the UK has a higher proportion of firms and employees in very small and very large units compared with the EU average (Bannock and Partners, 1990), and the lowest in medium-sized firms having 10–499 employees.

The effect on employment within this pattern of firms has been twofold. First, the proportion of administrative, professional, technical, and clerical staff has increased, while the proportion of manual workers has fallen. Within an overall decline in employment from 1975 to 1985, this is reflected in a sharper decline in the latter (by 31 per cent) compared with a more modest 9 per cent for the former. This in turn has increased the pressure to casualize site labour, since administrative and other such staff constitute an increasing burden of fixed costs. Thus, what started out as a need to employ more 'indirect' staff in areas such as design and more efficient project management begins to drive labour policy elsewhere. The result is the kind of core–periphery pattern we have seen in the case, in which there is a strengthened ILM and a larger ELM.

The resulting casualization has taken the form of increased short-term hiring to supplement regular employees and labour-only sub-contracting. This has also extended into more specialist trades, such as electrical contracting, where it had previously been limited by union agreements. Evans and Lewis (1989) estimate that around 600 000 fall into this latter category – over half the manual workforce – and that the majority of these are on a self-employed basis. Most of these lack a contract of employment and therefore automatically lose statutory rights to notice, redundancy pay, and protection from unfair dismissal.

These are the forces that have been transforming employment in construction. Evans then goes on to assess the longer-term consequences. Some of these have been noted in the case example.

First, there is the question whether the flexible labour market policies which employers in construction have championed actually produce a freer market. While they may loosen the labour market, this may be compensated by increased reliance on ever more complex forms of commercial contract which simply shift the burden of costs elsewhere. Thus, the extreme reliance on precisely drawn contracts within construction reduces flexibility, adds expense, and shifts potential conflicts into a different arena from industrial relations. There is a lesson here for looking at HRM issues in a wider commercial and financial context.

Second, there is the question whether these policies reduce wage costs and increase productivity. Evans echoes others such as Clegg (1979) and Phelps Brown (1968) in arguing that fragmenting national pay scales does not necessarily lead to lower unit costs. The ability of labour-only sub-contractors to shift from site to site in the 1960s and again during the boom years of construction from 1985 to 1988 resulted in earnings being bid up through localized bonus rates. The result was inflated (or one might say, market) rates in the booming South-eastern construction industry (according to people in Construction Co. typically of £800 a week, or five times earnings in the North-east).

Third, there is the question whether productivity is improved by any greater control over employees that might also result. We have seen that the organizational demands of scheduling sub-contractors onto a site and ensuring quality of performance have increased. We have also seen how prime contractors try to manage this by establishing continuous relationships with favoured sub-contractors. This may be more possible in a regional market like the North-east and for a medium-sized firm like Construction Co. Elsewhere and for larger firms, such as in the South-east, it is, as with pay, a question of boom and slump conditions. In a slump, it is easier to exercise discipline through 'market control', but this breaks down in a boom (Winch, 1986).

Fourth, and finally, there is the impact on training and the stock of skills. Even employers in construction have been forced to recognize that the pressure to poach one another's employees discourages firms from training, and that self-employment and labour-only sub-contracting discourage individuals from training. A side-effect of this is the low rate and level of adoption of new technologies and methods in British construction. Employers resorting to casual employment reduces the pressure on them to modernize, and the lack of training limits employees' ability to change their skills.

The effect on skills is made worse by the fact that when skilled workers are forced out of any industry by a recession they tend not to come back in the same numbers as before. (As Lee, 1981, has noted, the biggest source of de-skilling is redundancy and unemployment.) This has been especially true of construction, where less secure employment has been a disincentive to older skilled workers to return. Evans (1990) concludes:

> There is an incongruence between government stimulus to industrial concentration and its labour market policies geared more consistently towards competition and fragmentation which take little account of the necessary inputs for achieving future high productivity rates. Construction demonstrates this particularly vividly (p. 249).

Summary

The construction industry shows how internal labour markets, occupational labour markets, and the pressures towards unregulated external labour markets that produce casualization interact. In this process, financial needs for external flexibility (the ability to manage numbers employed) struggle with operational needs for internal flexibility (the ability to manage through workforce commitment). The result is greater order and stability than might at first appear.

Trends towards greater external flexibility over the last decade in consequence have been accompanied by a continuing and even increased emphasis on the core labour force and in managing the extended labour force through covert ILM strategies. This accounts for the contrasting images of construction in the studies by Bryman *et al.* and by Evans. Put in organizational terms, construction shows the shifting patterns for controlling economic activity and labour through hierarchies, markets, and networks. Evans emphasizes the market processes at work; Bryman *et al.* the network activity. Our case additionally shows both processes in relation to a core organizational hierarchy.

Within this core ILM, construction firms may display surprising elements of HRM, if we define HRM, as many have done, in terms of increasing commitment and flexibility. This includes a continued attachment to an open career structure and an interest in HRD processes of cultural change. However, the hole in its approach to HRM is that this is increasingly confined to a core of employees; basic training is being neglected; and the reliance on time-honoured channels of recruitment implies a passive, 'non-strategic' attitude to skill development.

Note

1. The original material for this case was developed by Michael Arthur of the Centre for Corporate Strategy and Change.

13
Managing the system as a whole: towards HRM (2)

Introduction

Our second case is simpler in terms of its labour markets and the influences on these. It shows, nevertheless, a company trying to break with traditional patterns of employment and restructuring its own system to avoid the latent adversarialism of the technical/industrial labour market (TILM). At the heart of this is an attempt, for sound operational reasons, to overcome the traditional 'status divide' between professional staff and blue-collar manual workers. In taking a much more deliberate approach to the management of its people, its whole approach is also consciously, rather than implicitly, 'strategic'. The result is an example of HRM which embodies core values such as commitment, quality, and flexibility.

From a technical/industrial system to the commitment system and 'HRM'

Fibres

Background, products and markets

Fibres employs 350 people on a modern industrial estate in North Wales. It is a joint venture owned 50:50 by two other companies, one British and one American. These came together to produce optical waveguides (i.e. optical fibre cables) for international telecommunications systems. One provided the technology which it had invented and on which it owned the patents, the other provided market knowledge and connections within telecommunications. The joint venture was established in the late 1970s; a factory was built on a greenfield site; and business commenced in early 1983.

Competitive environment and competitive advantage

Turnover changed little in the years 1985–1989, averaging between £35 million and £40 million. Although results are not published, it is assumed to break-even. In a short space of time, the company has gained 65 per cent of the market in the UK, with four principal customers and BT and Mercury the ultimate users. Having established its domestic base, it began an export drive in 1987 which within three years gave it 45 per cent of the European market. It is now number one in Europe and number three among the world producers. The basis of this success has been reliable quality, close technical cooperation with customers to establish their needs, and dependable technical support. Allied to this and now becoming an increasingly important factor as optical fibres become a mature product is also high production volumes. This has enabled the company to meet rapidly rising demand, take market share, and maintain constantly reducing prices. In contrast, competitors have struggled to achieve volume to reliable specifications.

The key labour factors in this situation are consequently (1) highly qualified technical people who manage and improve the technology and operating systems on which production depends, (2) the technical specialists who maintain customer relationships, and (3) a dependable but not especially skilled workforce who need to adhere to the technical standards laid down.

Company employment structure

Optical fibre production is a process operation, akin to oil refining, flat glass manufacture, and various forms of bulk chemical production. The skill structure of such firms is characterized by complex and varied scientific and technical skills, often in quite considerable numbers, and a less formally skilled direct workforce engaged in production. Because the technology is heavily automated and controlled by computers, even production work is largely concerned with monitoring rather than direct manual work. Ultimately the effectiveness of such operations depends heavily on the attitude of the mass of employees because of the need to maintain continuous production. Interruptions to production not only put the product in jeopardy but can damage plant. Much effort therefore is put into gaining the willing cooperation of the manual workforce and structuring attitudes towards quality.

Firms with major process operations like ICI, Pilkington, and Shell have thus been among the leaders in developing 'progressive' employment policies to encourage company loyalty and eliminate conflict. The smaller proportions of direct employees (to staff) and the lower proportion of operating costs attributable to labour generally have also made it possible for such firms in the past to finance progressive policies.

Fibres conforms very much to this stereotype, in both its

production system and division of skills. It uses a wide range of skills – from machine-minders and 'recorders of information' typical of a process plant, to a high proportion with degrees, including PhDs, in various positions in engineering, technology, marketing, quality, and computing. As the General Manager in charge of the company put it: 'Fibres needs 50 highly qualified people (out of 300–350) of the highest quality, up to world standards.' Direct Production accounts for approximately half only of total employees (168) in four shifts, while plant maintenance includes a further twenty-three. They are supported by another thirty-four employees in various process control and engineering specialisms, and (located under different functional heads) by other groups such as quality engineering and systems (ten) and computing (twenty-four). There is also a group of twenty staff who are responsible for documenting all parts of the production process, for issuing process control documentation to the shopfloor, and for monitoring compliance. This gives an idea of how tightly managed the whole process is. Overall, the proportion of 'indirects' to 'directs' has been increasing since operations began in 1983. The highest concentrations of those with degrees are in marketing (a relatively small section with twelve staff), in computers, and in process control/engineering.

One oddity of the system is the quite large number of employees who are on temporary contracts. Apart from security and catering which are contracted out, twenty-four out of 168 staff in production are on renewable twelve-month contracts. This arose in 1988 after a brief lull in sales when the company remained unsure about the extent of the upturn and wanted to avoid creating a situation where it might have to make subsequent redundancies. The present situation is part and parcel, then, of a policy of ensuring employment stability for the core. However, it is at odds with the philosophy of running a single-status plant and with the strategy of involving employees through the consultative system (see below). Contract employees do not participate in this, and their anomolous position is seen as creating a motivational problem. The opening of a new extension to the plant in 1991, however, was being used to give these employees permanent staff status. Other contract staff are dotted around the company, including five in computing, partly reflecting the peaks and troughs of project activity and partly the market situation for specialist staff.

Technical staff are recruited from a variety of specialist sectoral labour markets at a national level, and for the most specialized jobs can be readily identified within the UK telecoms industry. The operations workforce has been recruited locally, many coming from other process industries such as oil and steel which made large redundancies in the region in the early 1980s. Although, in principle, internal job ladders and promotion prospects exist for technical staff, in practice, opportunities are limited

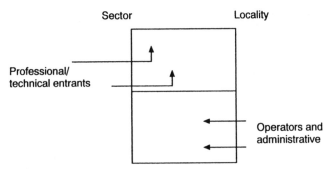

Figure 13.1   *The employment structure at Fibres*

by organizational size. The resulting employment structure can be simply described in terms of two tiers of employees (see Figure 13.1).

Company employment strategy

In outline, then, the company looks like other process businesses. However, it has pursued a distinctive philosophy to avoid a 'them and us' mentality, and in this has gone further than many other such firms in operating 'single-status' policies. Despite the fact that there is a generalized recruitment policy that those in professional and technical grades must have a degree and job titles distinguish engineers, technicians / assistant engineers, administrative, and operators, company philosophy plays down the idea of 'skill' as a differentiating concept:

> 'Skill' is not a word we would use much. We try to play down grade differentials. Job evaluation assesses on the basis of 'what is the contribution to the business'. We compare a PhD and an operator in that sort of way (personnel manager, Fibres).

Although job evaluation is prominent as in a typical TILM system, the chief criterion and method of comparison ('paired comparisons' of each job with every other) are thus less weighted towards predetermined definitions of skills or qualifications. Reflecting this same principle, a 'key job' list has recently been compiled of around a dozen people who are regarded as indispensable to the company and difficult to replace. This includes no managers 'because their skills are not unique to the company' (personnel manager).

The pay structure itself is based on length of service, with ten grades, each with ten increments, so in principle it conforms with the downplaying of individual skill, rather in the Japanese manner. However, since this was inherited from the UK parent company when Fibres was seen as an offshoot, and although it has contributed to the culture, it does not itself reflect a deliberate policy. More obviously on pay is the decision to pay a uniform profit-related bonus (of £1000) to all employees irrespective of grade. Fibres also has a policy to pay in the upper quartile for similar jobs.

Employee representation

The heart of its employment policy, though, is its elaborate and far-ranging consultative system around which it seeks to maintain a distinctive culture. This has three levels: (1) a briefing three times a year by the General Manager covering all aspects of the business; (2) a monthly team-briefing, in which every supervisor receives an authoritative, standard briefing which they then communicate, in cascade fashion, to all who report to them, again on how the business is doing; and (3) 'the hub of the industrial relations wheel', an 'Advisory Board'. In addition to this three-tier structure, comprehensive information is posted on notice boards. The aim of this communications system is that 'no employee should be able to say, "I didn't know" ' (personnel manager).

The Advisory Board system, which was set up at the outset in 1983, represents a deliberate attempt to get away from the traditional union and adversarial culture of its UK parent. On the advice of its American parent, the principle of 'single union, harmonized employment' was adopted (in contrast to the fifteen unions in the UK parent). A number of examples were reviewed, including those at Inmos, DEC, and Toshiba, and a system modelled on Toshiba was chosen. What has come to be called a 'beauty contest' was held with a number of the unions from the UK parent, and EESA, the staff section of the EETPU which had concluded the Toshiba agreement, was selected to represent employees before recruiting began.

This was on the basis, though, of EESA having 'representation' but not 'negotiating', rights. At the same time, the company sought to make the union irrelevant by developing the Advisory Board system and policies such as those on pay. For the first five years, therefore, there were less than a dozen union members, and even after the EETPU pursued a membership drive to justify its single-union agreements within the trade union movement, membership has only reached a quarter of employees.

The focus of employee representation remains the Advisory Board. This is a body of eleven members, elected on a two-year basis, which represents the major groupings ('constituencies') in the firm. It includes representatives of management, one representative from the EETPU/EESA, and various work sections. Since 1990, senior management representation has been reduced to one. The Advisory Board is chaired by the General Manager.

It meets monthly, and receives a review of the business, which it discusses; and it advises on a wide range of personnel issues. The latter includes making recommendations on pay awards.

The way pay awards are decided illustrates the extent to which the company has gone in creating a constitutional system outside the traditional industrial relations structure. The EETPU/EESA is not involved in agreeing pay terms. Instead, pay is agreed 'on a consensus basis' through the Advisory Board, based on information it receives from two sub-committees (composed similarly of employee representatives) – the 14-person job evaluation panel, and a sub-committee which receives data from the personnel manager which it feeds into a computer model. The computer model itself was developed within the sub-committee and members have gone on courses to learn to interpret the output. It takes data from a number of pay surveys, including a local survey of thirty companies.

The result is that the two sub-committees are able to advise on a wide range of pay issues – whether rates are falling behind and which jobs are affected; on general trends in pay settlements; the general award that might be necessary to maintain current differentials with outside jobs; and which jobs would remain anomolous without special awards, with recommendations for these. Only if the Advisory Board, with this information and advice, fails to agree is the union involved in a negotiating capacity. If agreement is still not forthcoming, the issue goes to pendulum arbitration with ACAS.

Apart from pay, the Advisory Board has gained significant additional powers since it was set up. These include the right to scrutinize disciplinary cases, and holding an insurance policy which gives employees access to legal representation over industrial injury and disciplinary appeals. These powers, held by the Advisory Board not the company, take over a further significant part of the traditional role played by trade unions.

To help the functioning of the Board, members have been on a three-day Coverdale training course to improve their skills in negotiation, team-working, managing win–win situations, and handling the report-back to their various constituencies.

Management philosophy

Apart from putting work relationships onto a constitutional setting which marginalizes trade unions, the company has a strong commitment to team-work. This is partly embodied in the Advisory Board, but more generally it emanates from the top team of managers who came together when the company was formed. As they acknowledge, they were people who were seen as rebels in the large company environment. They sought to create a style which was different, less political, more entrepreneurial and more team-oriented. The General Manager has thought seriously about the nature of management in this regard:

> There has been a major change in how we manage a business. Ten years ago, I was managing a £100 million business of 2/3000 people. I could manage it because I could make a reasonable stab at doing any of their jobs. But now it's impossible for anyone to get a total grasp. You can't manage anymore in the old top-down, hands-on sense. Management has become more of a 'secretarial' task, controlling the things people do. For example, computers is now such a specialist area; similarly process technology.
>
> Meredith Belbin in *Management Teams* sums it up well. In the past, management was very much a matter of objective-setting and appraisal of individuals in formal ways. But now it's no longer about individuals, it's about teams and one person not being able to cope with it all. You can't be the 'big white chief' any more. You have to run it as a partnership and formulate joint plans. The role is a coordinating challenge.
>
> The other challenge is deciding what you want to do strategically, and then influencing and persuading others by consensus to want to do it. That's still a problem – not so much at management level, but at supervisory. The old bullying style is no longer appropriate. It's a matter of projecting a vision, a philosophy of the business, to create attitude change.
>
> The Advisory Board has been very significant in the culture formation of the organization – away from the Ford approach, of workers making demands and management being responsible for managing the business, and we've worked hard at developing it.

In order to sustain the team-work philosophy, the intention is to keep employment on-site to around 400 employees. The present expansion can be managed with a limited increase to this number. But setting up a satellite plant elsewhere was a serious possibility if it had involved more.

Commitment and the technical system

In consequence, Fibres combines informality in personal relationships among the top managers, and a high degree of formality (or 'constitutionalism') in employee relationships at large, expressed through the Advisory Board system. To the outsider, the latter can look quite bureaucratic – perhaps an inevitable characteristic of legality and self-imposed rules. Company structure also looks highly functional, reflecting the specialized nature of the many different skills needed. This is why team-work across boundaries acquires a special importance, and why it has had to be worked at.

At root, the culture is highly influenced by the exacting nature of product specifications and the sophistication of the technology. The plant operates on a fully documented process management system, and every stage of the process, from specification by the supplier to delivery, is recorded and has to be signed off. This includes details of the day it was made, barometric pressure on that day, and its progress through the plant for every single length of fibre made.

We come back, then, to the rationale for a social (i.e. employment) system designed to produce team-work and commitment in a highly complex technical system in which people's roles are mutually dependent. As the personnel manager put it:

> We can achieve technical standards others struggle to meet. But it is not a function of technical people. It is a function of systems, and everyone contributes to that.

With half the workforce in operator roles, the security and effectiveness of the operation depends heavily on the operators, even though the system is computer-driven:

> One of the areas we see a need to concentrate on, to eliminate the 0.001 per cent of faults attributable to careless mistakes, is operators. It is important to maintain their morale and they are seen as the weakest link.

Strains in the commitment system

Fibres is relatively unusual in Britain in the effort it has put into creating and sustaining its employee representation structure. There are a few other, high-profile examples. Most of these are influenced by American or Japanese parent companies, including the examples Fibres reviewed when it created its own. They include DEC, Toshiba, Hitachi, and Nissan. Drawing on the prevalent systems in the USA or Japan, all have tried to replace adversarial management–union relationships by creating structures that exclude unions or absorb them into an enterprise union relationship.

A number of other companies, in restructuring existing industrial relations, have imposed single-union agreements by withdrawing recognition and bargaining rights, and, indeed, have introduced harmonized conditions at the same time. These include Tioxide UK and Norsk Hydro (Fox, 1988). They have done so, however, without departing from the basic practices and principles of collective bargaining.

The style of industrial relations at Fibres puts great effort into preventing conflict through consultative structures and resolving it in a constitutional fashion. It replaces the traditional TILM (technical/industrial labour market) system of strong opposed forces, confronting one another in an uneasy truce within procedurally bound collective bargaining, with one which tries to moderate the underlying sources of that antagonism.

Sustaining this system over time, however, is not easy. As one manager at Fibres put it, 'the cracks are beginning to show'. There are three areas in question at Fibres – pay, the management structure and teamwork within it, and training and career development. The emergence of these issues at this point is not altogether surprising. Apart from the fact that no humanly devised system in any sphere is likely to remain serviceable for all time, in organization terms the company has passed through two major 'rites of passage' – a stage of growth which has seen it go from start-up to some maturity in little more than seven years from 1983 to 1990, and from 120 employees at start-up to 350 employees (with 400 in prospect as the second adjacent factory doubles capacity). The broader question, however, is how far the need for change in these areas jeopardizes the core Advisory Board system, and what lessons, if any, this has for constitutional systems of this kind generally.

Pay

The first problem concerns the pay structure. The present structure flattens differentials, with the pay gradient showing a smooth slowly ascending line. The result, as Figure 13.2 shows, is that Fibres overpays in the lower grades, where recruitment and the relevant pay comparisons are local; and underpays for higher grades, where the relevant labour market and pay comparisons are national. The result is some difficulty in recruiting to higher-level posts.

The pay review sub-committees have analysed this problem and prepared a report. The aim is to move to a skill-based system at the lower end. This will pay the 'rate for the job', beginning with a lower 'training rate' on entry and a higher 'proficient' rate at the top of each grade. At present, 60 per cent of process employees could be deemed proficient in three process areas and 20 per cent proficient in two areas. As well as extending scales based on the achievement of skills, rather than increasing pay automatically with service, it makes it possible also to buy out overtime for supervisors and reduce the high proportion of pay attributable to the shift premium. Both of these typically reduce flexibility. Like other companies who have wanted to improve flexibility and curb such costs, Fibres is therefore moving towards a more performance-based system.

While this opens up the structure in the lower grades, it has not yet been decided whether to apply the same principle of rewarding the achievement of skills to the upper grades. People employed for their professional knowledge, for instance, are presumed to be recruited at a high level of proficiency already, and their progress is relatively difficult to grade. The overall effect, nevertheless, will be to give greater emphasis to skill differentials, which in turn may increase status distinctions that undermine the present company culture.

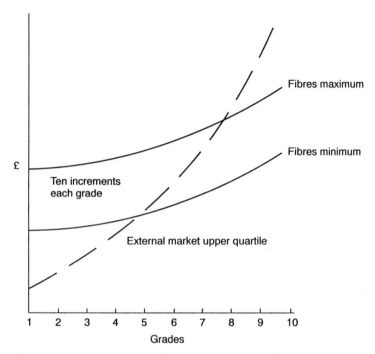

Figure 13.2 *Pay differentials and external relativities at Fibres*

A similar consequence follows from adopting the principle of 'key jobs'. In effect, this means 'key individuals' who have acquired company-specific knowledge. Retaining these individuals by matching higher offers of pay from elsewhere – effectively rewarding the person rather than the job – goes against the grain of job evaluation, and also cannot be anticipated openly since to identify such people would hand over considerable bargaining power.

Overall, then, the problem Fibres is having to address is how to marry internal relativities with external relativities. Pursuing a policy of equity and 'one big happy family' (as Torrington and Chapman (1983, p. 324) put it) through an integrated pay structure can lead to tensions over time with changing market rates for particular skills.

This is a general problem for all companies, but a particular one for such companies adopting this kind of 'commitment system', since pay, in the guise of both external and internal relativities, is one of the major potential sources of grievance a constitutional system seeks to defuse. Removing manual workers' grievances through a policy of harmonization runs the risk of provoking grievances among non-manual ones.

Price (1989, p. 290) notes how Tioxide anticipated this by introducing performance-related merit increases to give 'headroom' for paying more to higher-level employees. Fibres is coming to this late, and then for 'external' reasons to help with recruitment, not because of internal tensions.

The approach to pay by the Fibres company exposes one of the basic contradictions in HRM as a coherent philosophy. On the one hand, HRM is equated with performance-related pay and individualized contracts; on the other, it is associated with harmonization and the reduction of the status divide. The two are essentially incompatible.

Fibres is uncomfortably trying to square elements of performance pay with harmonized conditions. It can probably manage to do so as long as the definition of performance is confined to skill inputs rather than to outputs, and this is conducted within the job-evaluation mechanism. In reality, it is only a little way down this track, and its basic stance on engendering commitment continues to appeal to a collectivist image of the workplace, rather than to a multitude of individual commitments based on rewards through pay, developmental opportunities, and career advancement.

The other point, as the survey by Storey (1992) cited in Chapter 3 showed, is that few companies have as yet much experience of using performance-related pay or practising harmonization. Certainly, few will have explored the limits of compatibility between these. In the meantime, therefore, we are left with an image of HRM as an umbrella term, as firms pick and choose between a range of fashionable schemes which address particular problems of the moment.

The management structure and team-work

A constitutional system runs the risk of bypassing normal lines of management, with all the drawbacks which procedurally bound collective bargaining systems were wont to produce in the 1970s. Line management is emasculated; problems are resolved more slowly than if dealt with face to face; and they are rapidly fanned into major issues by putting them into formal procedure. Fibres has experienced some of this, compounded by the circumstances of a growing organization.

One of the line managers at the sharp end summarized these problems as follows:

> I'm a great supporter of the Advisory Board. But I've consistently struggled with the way it fits in. There's a danger that it bypasses supervisors and formal lines of communication. Managers are frequently accused of not letting on about things, because it is assumed they must know more. But I know no more about the general running of the business than an operator, and I'm not exaggerating. For example, there's a pay briefing next Monday. I will only know what's in it by going to the mass meeting myself. There's a naivety in the way information is spread.
>
> The overall concept and what it has achieved has been outstanding. The weakness is that it has been a little simplistic in some of its structures. It's one of the best places I've been in for the attitude to work and flexibility, etc. But the biggest danger is it detaches management from the day to day, and substitutes that by formal structures. Committees are good, but they are no substitute for eyeball to eyeball.
>
> Because [the personnel manager and general manager] interface with the Advisory Board every month, false impressions creep in that communication is occurring. But the opportunity doesn't occur for supervisors and managers to hear, interact, and even correct what's said. Because people are elected, they feel they've got to raise issues, so it magnifies things into crises which could and should have been handled outside. The recent IR issue was like that. The Advisory Board had to respond to it, but the flames were fanned by that. The issue was raised there without the supervisors getting the chance to speak, and it polarized positions.

This sense among managers and supervisors in the second and third ranks of being excluded and bypassed is aggravated by the natural processes of organization development. The top management team of six has been together, with one exception, since 1982. As a result they have achieved a high degree of cohesion and are seen as an inner, closed group. The effect is like that often found where a single entrepreneur dominates in a small organization. Because everything tends to emanate from the entrepreneur and the organization psychologically is an extension of him or her, entrepreneurs tend to assume that the communications they directly engage in embrace all staff. The enlarged management team is just a second-stage extension of this phenomenon.

By the same token, a strong team culture at one level can reduce team behaviour and cohesion at another. Managers at the second level relate to the top team only through their own boss and have been seen simply as part of the functional line emanating from the members of the top team. The result is a lack of cohesion across functions and of a team culture across functions lower down, contrary to the perceptions top management have had. As the General Manager observes:

> Because we've grown rapidly we have a problem of having recruited experts in their function. That's no longer appropriate, they've got to work in a team, their own job has become more strategic. People like doing what they're good at, so it's hard to stop. We have to build a team below them to take over their work.

As a result, Fibres is now giving active attention to management development at the next level down. We can guess that this will strengthen this group as line managers and as a constituency within the Advisory Board structure. This is likely to require some adjustment in the way the constitutional system works, but need not radically undermine it.

Other companies that have reduced manifest differences between employees through harmonization have offset this by less visible and contestable improvements in opportunity. Johnson and Johnson, for instance, increased the responsibilities of supervisory staff and retrained them to take on this enlarged role (Mullins, 1986). Because harmonization was in place from the beginning, Fibres is in effect doing this belatedly.

Training and career development

Training hitherto has been focused on operators, consequent on making the technology work and absorbing improvements to processes. When the plant was set up, this was done systematically. The transfer of technology from the American parent was effected by two Fibres managers working with an American project leader to learn the principles on which the plant was based. They then recruited and trained the initial batch of operators, using an amended version of the American firm's training package. As production expanded rapidly and the company grew from its initial 140 or so employees, comprehensive training, and certainly comprehensive updating, tended to lapse and become *ad hoc.*

This is not an uncommon phenomenon in fast growth SMEs, as the study by Hendry *et al.* (1991) showed. Like other such companies, Fibres is now addressing this after some five to seven years by reinstating a much more rigorous and systematic approach to training. The stimulus to this is finding that work standards among operators and supervisors have become quite variable as new recruits have been exposed to improvements in operating systems which older employees have missed out on. The prospect of an influx of new operators with the opening of a second factory – in effect, a rerun of the original start-up – gives added momentum to this.

Fibres is tackling this with typical energy and rigour. An outside training consultant has been working with a 'production operator training officer', appointed out of production, in mid-1988. He was sent on a training officer's course first of all to get qualified, and in turn has since trained sixteen operator instructors (four per shift). They remain operators, but get an allowance towards training of 25 per cent of their time. Together, they have analysed the operating procedures in each section, devised checklists for testing all new and existing operators, and devised appropriate training. One aspect of this is the implementation of a 'sixty-day rule', whereby anyone not working on their usual area of operations for sixty days or more will have to take a refresher course on returning. As their training consultant put it, 'They are calibrating the operators in the same way as the machines.' A similar approach is in prospect in developing a systematic programme of training in quality.

As this description indicates, however, the whole style of training has been 'corrective', geared to immediate jobs, and conceived within an 'engineering' frame of reference. The idea of training as development for future jobs has been largely absent. For example, job rotation among operators happens only to a limited extent within sections and between shifts, and not as a matter of policy. The prevalence of this kind of training philosophy represents the persistence of a TILM work system driven by a dominant technology. The alternative is expensive. It does show the Advisory Board system, however, as focused on containing potential industrial relations problems rather than embodying a concept of HRM in which developmental (HRD) concerns are prominent. As the personnel manager acknowledged, 'development is driven by organization requirements, not individual needs.'

Certain departments within Fibres, notably computing, have pursued a philosophy of HRD for some time. The need for a more conscious approach to management development, however, signalled above, means a philosophy of HRD becoming more widely adopted. Thus, staff in the second tier of management are now the deliberate focus of job moves, mentoring, and coaching. The single management policy committee has also been reconstituted as two sub-committees in order to introduce second-tier managers into these and give them more involvement in strategy and policy making:

> It is effectively a management development programme, because it involves thinking about policy, objectives, how to get there, how to manage deviations from plan, finance, and an overview of the ramifications across functions (personnel manager).

As we noted, growth leads to attention being given to HRD through the need to prepare additional layers of management. Likewise, cohort progression means that individual career moves may start to assert themselves some seven to ten years after Fibres began operations, and succession needs to be planned for. How these processes might then impact on company philosophy and culture is unclear, however.

An alternative to the constitutional system: communication, pay, and opportunity at IBM

An alternative route to the constitutional system at Fibres is that followed by IBM (Bassett, 1986). This avoids one of the fundamental problems, that line managers may feel bypassed, by putting the line manager at the very centre of the system. At the same time there are no collectivist institutions such as trade unions, or company-created ones like an Advisory Board, to detract from the centrality of this role.

Communications are managed through the manager–employee relationship. The manager has explicit personnel responsibilities for his or her own staff, and the staff ratio is kept deliberately tight to allow the manager to fulfil these responsibilities (typically 1:9, but varying between departments according to circumstances). All managers also receive a large amount of training a year in people management (thirty-two out of forty days total training in the mid-1980s). Problems are expected to be solved within this relationship, but employees are encouraged to consult with their manager's manager also, to provide a check on this relationship.

There are then two external checks on this system. First, every two years, IBM runs a detailed opinion survey among all employees, which gives information about employee attitudes and how the company is doing by its employees. Second, there are two separate systems of complaint and appeal. Since IBM is a non-union company – that is, it does not recognize unions for collective bargaining purposes in the UK – these substitute for a trade union in giving protection against arbitrary management action.

One system, called 'Speak Up', allows employees to raise business-related problems in confidence around such themes as work organization and procedures, and the working environment. A 'coordinator' then responds in writing. The second system, called 'Open Door', allows an employee to appeal against a manager's decisions. These are adjudged by a higher-level manager or by an appointed investigator. Opinion surveys show, however, that some employees neither understand, nor believe in, the 'Open Door' system, and feel that using it can damage their career prospects.

Like Fibres and other firms operating more collectivist systems, the pay and conditions environment for IBM's system is critical. IBM has a single-status policy in which all employees receive the same basic benefits. Pay awards and external relativities are also determined through a detailed annual survey among comparable lead firms, and a premium is added to place IBM rates above the external average. However, this survey is confidential and rates are centrally determined, and not a matter for collective discussion. Internal relativities are managed through job evaluation, but there is one system for professional and one for non-professional staff.

There is also a very precise individual performance culture. Individuals agree annual performance objectives with their manager, who then makes recommendations for merit increases at the year end. The system gives flexibility to vary individual pay within plus or minus 5 per cent of the pay boundaries for the individual's grade. This produces salaries which range from 15 per cent to 20 per cent above and below the average for the grade.

In these ways, IBM stresses individual relationships and individual achievement, rather than collective contribution. The collective voice is the aggregation of many individuals speaking separately through company channels like the opinion surveys, 'Speak Up', and 'Open Door', rather than through a representative body. The result, nevertheless, is a powerful system of corporate values which is said readily to mark out an IBM employee. IBM provides an alternative model of employment relations, operating without unions or substitute structures, but its efficacy depends on a deep-seated culture that cannot be created overnight.

Summary

Fibres is a company which has a deliberate and distinctive approach to employment. The personnel manager acts consciously as the custodian of company culture embodied in the consultative system and the philosophy of teamwork, and sees his role as being to keep his management colleagues on track with these.

The 'constitutional' system it has created represents one important strand in the concept of HRM. It is strong in engineering commitment by seeking to play down the status-divide between employee groups and by making provision for avoiding and resolving industrial relations disputes. At Fibres, training and development has figured less than in other firms that have developed similar systems, but this is changing.

One difficulty in determining the role of training and development as part of an overall model of HRM alongside a constitutional structure is simply that the firms implementing the latter have tended to be new, greenfield site developments. They are, therefore, subject to the influence, as yet, of life-cycle and growth factors which generate their own structural dynamics and requirements for training and development.

Part Four
Employee Groups

14
Managers and professional employees

Introduction

This is the first of a series of chapters which consider different categories of employee, rather than the system as a whole. This chapter looks at managers, with Chapter 15 discussing the specific issue of managing managers in the international context. Chapter 16 then considers manual and clerical employees, with Chapter 17 providing a case study of technical change. Although this is a crude division, it mirrors the traditional status-divide and allows the exploration of policies and practices typically applied to each.

Chapter 18 then considers a disparate third group, who are linked by a common marginal employment status. This brings out a key theme for employment systems over the last few years – the pursuit of flexibility by firms at the expense of job security for people. Chapter 19 concludes this series of chapters by looking at the system for employment training. If UK plc is to survive in the modern world, it needs to train *all* employees, and, where necessary, retrain people. Only if there is an adequate infrastructure will 'marginal' employees be able to move in and out of employment effectively. Indeed, as long as organizations continue to be as unstable as they have been, we are all, in a sense, 'marginal' employees.

One kind of logic suggests that we should begin with manual employees. An organization should be designed from the bottom-up according to the jobs needed to get the work done. A second logic says that we start with management as the control function. A number of the recent changes affecting management can, in fact, be seen as following on from earlier changes in the role, skills, discretion, and job security of lower-level employees. The fact that we treat managers first is not, then, entirely appropriate.

This chapter begins with a discussion of who we mean by 'management' and what has been happening to management (and professional) employees. This leads on to the issue of management skills (or competences), which necessarily underpins policies and practices for their selection, development, careers, appraisal, and rewards. Simply by concentrating on those themes which dominate current debate, we find ourselves considering the four key levers in Fombrun, Tichy and Devanna's (1984) model of what generates performance in HRM – namely, selection, appraisal, development, and rewards. The concern with skills and the 'psychological contract', however, are more reminiscent of the perspective of Beer (1985) and the Harvard approach to HRM.

The changing shape of management, roles and responsibilities

Estimates of the number of managers and professional employees in the population vary because of different definitional bases. The one certain thing, however, is that their numbers have been rising consistently over the past twenty years and are forecast to go on rising. Separately and together, they represent a substantial slice of employment in most organizations.

In *Management Challenge for the 1990s*, the consultancy firm, Deloitte Haskins & Sells (1989), estimated that almost one in eight employees could be regarded as managers, with an additional number in self-employment and in very small firms. Although this study was not specifically concerned with 'professionals', as Figure 14.1 shows, the latter constituted an even bigger group.

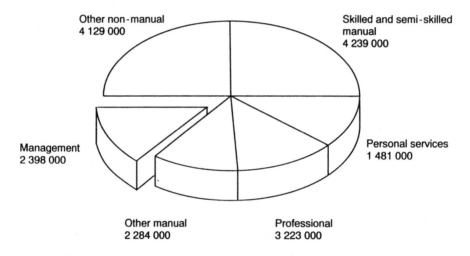

Total population:
17.8 million employees in employment
with organizations of 10 or more employees

Figure 14.1 *How many managers are there in the UK? (Original source: Deloitte Haskins & Sells, 1989)*

The authoritative Institute for Employment Research (Wilson, 1993) shows rather different figures, since they cover all employment and because of the different way of categorizing employees. For instance, Table 14.1 includes approximately 1.3 million 'managers and proprietors in services and agriculture' in the 'managers and administrators' category. 'Professional' and 'associate professional' occupations are also shown separately, while the latter figure includes some groups (such as nurses) who may elsewhere be classified under 'personal services'.

The different sampling apart, both studies agree that managers and professionals (MPEs) constitute a significant group – around 30 per cent of

Table 14.1 Employment status (1991)

	Number of employees (*millions*)	*Percentage*
Managers and administrators (including proprietors at 1.3 million)	3.81	15.0
Professional occupations	2.67	10.5
Associated professional and technical	2.36	9.3
Clerical and secretarial	4.15	16.4
Craft and related manual (including construction)	3.59	14.1
Personal and protective services	1.90	7.5
Sales occupations	1.91	7.5
Plant and machine operatives (including drivers)	2.42	9.6
Other occupations (including farm workers, labourers, and cleaners)	2.56	10.1
Total	25.38	100

Source: Wilson (1993).

all employees. Managerial, professional, associate professional, and skilled personal service occupations are forecast to go on rising in number up to the year 2000 (while job losses will continue, although at a slower rate, in traditional blue collar areas, with clerical and secretarial employment static) (Institute for Employment Research, 1990).

Despite these overall trends, however, MPEs are facing considerable turbulence. In the first place, such growth is not evenly distributed, with middle management being heavily squeezed as organizations 'de-layer'. In many firms, the pyramidal hierarchy had become bell- or pear-shaped. Now firms are cutting down on their middle-aged spread.

In the recession of the early 1980s, manufacturing firms concentrated their efficiency drive on lower levels in the organization. Now, in the recession of the 1990s, these firms have turned their attention to their middle management ranks, helped in some cases by the fact that the raising of skills on the shopfloor and improved shopfloor data-capture make it possible to locate more decision making lower down. Coupled with this, the latest recession has hit the service sector, as it did not previously, forcing efficiencies in white-collar jobs. These latest trends may mean, of course, that earlier predictions of employment growth may not actually materialize.

A second source of turbulence is the way jobs themselves are changing. Part of this results from the redistribution of responsibilities, as the shape of organization changes. But part results from the continuing pace of technical change which causes the skills and knowledge of managers and professionals to become rapidly out of date. These 'disturbances' are reflected differently in the experience of the various groups within the management and professional category.

Middle managers

It has been estimated that just over half of all managers can be regarded as junior managers, and around a third as middle managers (Handy *et al.*, 1987). The remainder (around 14 per cent) are senior managers.

A study of 323 male managers in six large public and private organizations by Goffee and Scase (1986) identified a general dissatisfaction among middle managers and four major influences on their jobs causing this dissatisfaction. These were:

- A decline in organizational growth, leading to shorter, less predictable career paths
- Flatter organization structures which expose middle managers to greater demands for entrepreneurial flair and increased measurement of performance
- Technological change affecting skill requirements
- Socio-economic changes which have undermined the traditional forms of authority managers wield.

A more recent case-based study, however, albeit on a smaller scale, presents a rather different picture (Dopson and Stewart, 1990). This found a general tendency towards:

- Jobs becoming more generalist, with greater responsibilities and a wider range of tasks
- An increasing span of control, with responsibility for a wider mix of staff
- Greater accountability as performance has become more visible through the availability of better, computer-based information (with the opportunity to take better decisions as a result)
- New skills and attitudes to cope with wider responsibilities and more varied staff
- A more strategic role, with a wider understanding of what is happening around them and outside their own department.

The last point sums up much that seems to be changing in the role of the middle manager. A shorter hierarchy means that middle managers are closer to top management and to strategy and policy making. They have a clearer role in creating the means to implement strategies that come down from on-high (Nonaka, 1988). They also have greater control over the resources to get things done and greater freedom to use these resources. Although Dopson and Stewart do not say so, the decentralization we described in Chapter 5 has clearly played a part in this.

These add up to fewer frustrations in the jobs of most middle managers – although Dopson and Stewart note that there seemed to be more resistance to changes from middle managers in the public sector. This is not surprising if we consider that the public sector starts from a different cultural orientation and has arrived at decentralization later. Changes affecting jobs adversely (such as the threat of redundancy) are still working their way through the public sector.

The changing middle management role also means a changing relationship with subordinates and a different way of managing. At a recent seminar organized by the Management Charter Initiative on 'Managing the future', the chairman of Digital Equipment, Geoff Shingles, defined this as follows:

> The role of the manager in the future is going to be to support, serve and coach the experts who are doing the work [and] to empower employees... [This will be] very different to the old 'bridge to engine room' style of management (*Personnel Management*, 1993a).

A critical influence in bringing this about will be the access people increasingly have to information to do and to monitor their jobs for themselves. This in turn requires a more loosely coupled organization in which people are freed from personalized hierarchical controls. This has implications along the whole length of the management hierarchy, and for management style generally.

A visible illustration of the move towards a more supportive, educative role is the initiative by Unipart to set up a 'Unipart University' in which its own managers will provide vocational training for all employees (*Personnel Management plus*, 1993a). In Chapter 20 we will discuss how the 'learning organization' means fundamental change in manager–subordinate relationships and management style.

Supervisors

The picture of a new role being created out of former disorientation is repeated at the supervisor level. Perhaps the most significant development here is a firming up in the role, so that supervisors are now being accepted more readily as part of management. Alternatively, the role is being eliminated entirely because it performs no distinctive function in the particular workplace.

The history of the supervisor over the last hundred years has been one of constant erosion of functions, as specialists have taken over parts of the supervisor's role (Thurley and Wirdenius, 1973). The role has also been eroded from below, first by the scope of shopfloor employees to bypass the supervisor through shop stewards, and more recently by the failure to upgrade supervisors' technical skills as new technology has been introduced in many factories and offices (Chapter 17 provides an instance of this). The supervisor has gone from being the 'man in the middle' (Gardner and Whyte, 1945), to 'marginal man' (Wray, 1949) to 'the man on the way out' (Fletcher, 1973).

Amid all this, however, supervisors seem to have retained some important functions, with more increasingly expected of them (Child and Partridge, 1982) – and more of the blame attaching to them for failures in manufacturing systems' performance. The supervisor retains a key role interfacing between management and the shopfloor and translating plans and policies into action (much as Nonaka, 1988, observed about the middle manager role).

The problem, however, has been the failure to give them the technical abilities to do this job (Partridge, 1989). It has been conceived primarily as a control function, with an emphasis on maintaining employee discipline and ensuring that the production unit and machines did not go 'out of control' in terms of efficiency and quality. During the 1980s, however, a changing perception of manufacturing ('it is important') and a changing emphasis (on 'continuous improvement') have encouraged a reappraisal (Partridge, 1989).

In particular, people have become aware of the role of the supervisor (or *Meister*) in the success of German manufacturing. As we describe in Chapter 19, the *Meister* is the expert; more technically qualified than those under him (or her); respected therefore; with considerable discretion and authority to manage the details of the production unit and in liaising outside it; and with primary responsibility for training the workgroup. The *Meister* role, moreover, is not infringed by the same number of staff specialists as are found in British firms. Partridge (1989) suggests therefore that the supervisory function should:

- Develop into a first-line managerial role (with enhanced status)
- Become more technical
- Be reconstructed with much greater emphasis on the all-round characteristics of the role.

There is evidence that change is taking place, although training to support it is still lacking. For example, in a study of sixteen private and public sector, manufacturing and service organizations, involving interviews with supervisors and those they came into contact with, significant change was found in those areas of work which would normally be regarded as 'management' activity (Kandola, Banerji and Greene, 1989). That is, in 'process' skills such as 'ordering, prioritizing and planning', 'diagnosing, analysing and solving problems', and 'checking, assessing, discriminating'.

The following describes how changes to develop management skills and greater technical competence are being introduced into the supervisory role at British Steel.

Forging a new breed of supervisor at British Steel[1]
British Steel has massively reduced its labour force over the last decade. There has been a substantial decentralisation of management authority, and an emphasis on quality. This has required greater workforce involvement and customer awareness. In turn, this has meant a change in the roles and style of first-line supervisors, to release managers for a more strategic role:

> 'First-line supervisors who possess greater business awareness are key to success... and potentially a prime source of competitive advantage. For this reason British Steel has, as a company, sought a status change for these individuals, lifting them on to our middle management structures for pay and development and involving them more in the business.'

To this end, the company introduced a training programme to create 'multi-functional supervisors' (MFS), involving up to 54 days off-the-job training. This aimed to develop and enhance a wide range of job skills and knowledge, including:
- leading teams,
- relating to internal customers,
- communication skills,

- broader technical understanding, including knowledge of processes and maintenance,
- health and safety, and
- financial understanding of the business.

Among the modules followed were the standard programme which all those new to management at British Steel take, including graduate trainees, and a specially designed business awareness course.

'[This] reinforces the change of status of the people involved by treating them as managers and giving them insights into the problems of their bosses, seeking to integrate them into the management team.'

The result is

'it generates a strong upward pressure for change from an increasingly confident set of supervisors'.

Training is reinforced by a competency-based pay system and by regular appraisal against these – both of which are uncommon for supervisors (Malcolm Ballin, Human Resources Director, British Steel, 1993).

Professional and technical workers

Professional and technical workers cover a wide range of occupations and jobs, including solicitors, doctors, accountants, teachers and lecturers, engineers, IT specialists, and scientists. The range is vast, with the last three groups themselves being enormously diverse. With lower-grade ('associate') professionals in these same areas, they comprise just under 20 per cent of the UK workforce. Meanwhile, the higher-grade 'professional' group (see Table 14.1) showed the most rapid growth of all groups between 1970 and 1990 (Institute for Employment Research, 1992).

'Professionals' are defined as those requiring a first degree or equivalent qualification. They are seen as critical to the dynamic performance of the economy, and represent a heavy investment by individuals and society in their skills. Supply is heavily dependent on flows through the higher education system, and because of the time in training and education, lags in supply are a problem for society, sectors, and firms. Partly for this reason, labour markets are frequently national or international, rather than local. Another relevant characteristic is the greater preponderance of younger people, through the progressive broadening of educational opportunities and recent national policy to increase the output of graduates. Such factors create distinctive issues for HRM around recruitment, retention, and job expectations.

While professional and technical employees are much more likely to be found in large organizations (such as R&D functions), the highest densities of graduates in fact are often in smaller firms, including high-technology firms and in the service sector (Institute for Employment Research, 1992). Faster-growing small firms (which also tend to be younger) are also more likely to employ such specialists (Cambridge SBRC, 1992). The changing structure of the economy and employment opportunities is therefore another potent factor in the management of professional and technical employees –

as well as influencing dominant management styles, as older firms are replaced by new firms with employees having a different outlook.

Apart from a more participative ethos, the motivation profile of employees working in smaller high-technology firms also appears to differ in significant ways from those in larger firms and from other 'knowledge workers' (Slatter, 1992). Employees in small high-tech businesses appear to want money, a comfortable-life style (including a high quality of amenities and physical surroundings at work), recognition and autonomy, but are less motivated by job security, and power and influence over others (Garden, 1987). A similar pattern of priorities, with money featuring prominently, has been observed in studies of Silicon Valley. This combination helps to account for the high job mobility among such employees.

This motivation profile is quite different from that of other types of employee and similar workers and high achievers in large high-technology firms. In the latter, people trade off money and comfort for recognition, power, and autonomy. The smaller high-technology employee wants both. As Slatter (1992, p. 108) puts it, they want to have their cake and eat it.

Certain functions such as finance, computing, R&D, and sales and marketing have also seen a marked move towards higher levels of education. While business expansion and reorganization have been the main driving forces for this, in manufacturing and construction, technological change, upgrading of skills, and deliberate recruitment of graduates as managers have together counted for more. The resulting higher levels of education among management and professional employees have an impact on liberalizing management attitudes and style which are insufficiently appreciated.

The American theorists of HRM saw this changing demography of the workplace as a key element in the emergence of HRM as a phenomenon (Fombrun, Tichy and Devanna, 1984; Beer *et al.*, 1984). In high-technology firms, these tendencies are even more pronounced:

> It is easy to see why many high technology firms tend to exhibit characteristics of the new human resource management system. They are generally younger firms operating in tight labor markets and developing or growing product markets; they employ high proportions of professional and technical employees; and they are often run by their founders and are able to incorporate new technology into plants and offices. The rapidly changing and uncertain character of product markets creates further incentives to build flexibility and high levels of participation into work organization and management systems. . . Moreover, although few of the high technology workers are unionized, the priority placed on union avoidance is quite high.
>
> The confluence of these environmental and organizational forces and the fact that the more innovative organizations were in the growth stages of their business life cycle provided the internal consistency between human resource policy and practices at the different levels of the firms needed to make them durable (Kochan and Chalykoff, 1987, pp. 197/199).

Changing economic conditions and the maturing of the IT sector in particular, however, have put the HRM model under pressure in both new and older high-technology firms. The pressure on IBM to restructure and shed professional and managerial staff, described in Chapter 9, is an instance of a much wider pattern that has been gathering force across the sector since the mid-1980s. Whereas the problem previously was one of retaining IT staff in conditions of skill shortage, targeted retention of key staff has now become a major HR issue. This represents an important shift in human resource priorities.

It is not a challenge that IT and telecommunications firms have shown themselves particularly adept at meeting. When dealing with skill shortages and high voluntary turnover, they understood the use of high pay to attract and hold staff. Some also invented new forms of flexible employment such as home-working to widen the job market they could draw on. In retrenchment, however, retention takes on a new form, focused on skills, and requires the management of a wider range of 'soft' benefits unrelated to pay. This appears to be much harder for them to manage (LeBrasseur, 1994).

Producer IT firms apart, IT has become a major factor in the competitiveness and efficiency of user firms. With responsiveness and value for money becoming a critical issue, IT departments have been experiencing fundamental change in their structure, role and accountability. A survey undertaken by PA Consulting Group in thirty-six large IT users, covering over 13 000 IT employees, found that 86 per cent had been reorganized in the previous two years to achieve closer integration with the business, while almost all envisaged a redefinition of boundaries with other parts of their business (Sparrow, Gratton and McMullan, 1989). The role of the IT specialist has therefore been changing, with certain skills transferred to non-specialists in the organization.

Shifts in job prospects, status, and the efficiency criteria applied to professionals and technical workers point, finally, to a central tension for this group as a whole. How far are they part of a 'middle (service) class' whose lives centre on careers, autonomy and discretion, authority, salaries, fringe benefits, and security? Or how far are they an extension of a technical working class which extends from craft workers upwards, vulnerable to the same insecurities and controls on performance? Much depends on the internal gradations within the group.

In France, for instance, there is a much clearer demarcation of professional engineers, exercising supervisory responsibilities as part of the management function than in Britain (Crawford, 1989; Smith, 1990). National differences like this can be an issue in multinational mergers and acquisitions. More generally, the attack on professional status in the UK, especially in the public sector, is associated with particular policies relating to performance-related pay, appraisal, and reduced job security. Understanding the motivation for, and resistance to, specific human resource practices has to be understood against the backdrop of status issues like these.

Management competences

Since the early decades of the twentieth century, consultants and practitioners like Fayol, Urwick, and Barnard have laid down rules as to what management entails and what skills managers need, while academics such as Mintzberg and Stewart have tried to describe more empirically just what managers do. As management education and training have expanded to keep up with the number of people in management roles, there has been increasing dissatisfaction with these definitions. Latterly, this has resulted in the intense interest in management competences as a more precise measure.

This is now enshrined in the Management Charter Initiative's 'National Standards'. The 'standards' are set out according to three levels of management responsibility. Each starts from (1) four 'key role' activities around the management of resources, but then vary in the detail of (2) 'units of competence', (3) 'elements of competence', and (4) 'performance criteria'. Figure 14.2 provides an overview of roles, unit competences, and elements of competence for first-line managers. In addition, as something of an add-on, the standards also include a second set of 'personal competences' concerned with personal effectiveness. Thus, although the primary focus is on 'tasks', they also embrace a behavioural dimension. The latter, however, is not nearly as developed as in the exclusively behavioural approaches.

The basic idea of all competency models is to create a widely acceptable inventory of competences which make the diagnosis and fulfilment of management development needs easier, as well as underpinning selection, promotion, appraisal and pay. How well do they do this?

A framework of some kind is surely necessary. On the other hand, as we noted in Chapter 10, there are serious shortcomings in the competency approach – although the perception of these is so far based more on instinctive dislike than on proven failure. A paper written in 1978 setting out the requirements for a theory of effective management highlights just why failure beckons (Burgoyne and Stuart, 1978). Any theory must do three things:

1   It must describe the different situations in which managers are required to perform.
2   It must specify all the different possible types of skill or quality that could determine performance in these various situations.
3   It must explain why certain of these qualities and skills determine performance in certain of these situations.

The competency approach faces difficulties in all three areas. The MCI standards, for instance, run into problems over (1) and (2) precisely because they try to specify in such detail; while they appear to avoid the third question entirely.

General versus specific competences

Both the behavioural (Boyatzis, 1982; Schroder, 1989) and job-vocational approaches (Management Charter Initiative) assume that managerial work is similar across different organizations in different sectors in different cultures (Herriot, 1992). The sheer diversity of 'managerial roles' alluded to above indicates the fallacy in this. The first issue, then, is that of general versus specific competences.

While the Management Charter Initiative (MCI) has opted for generalized

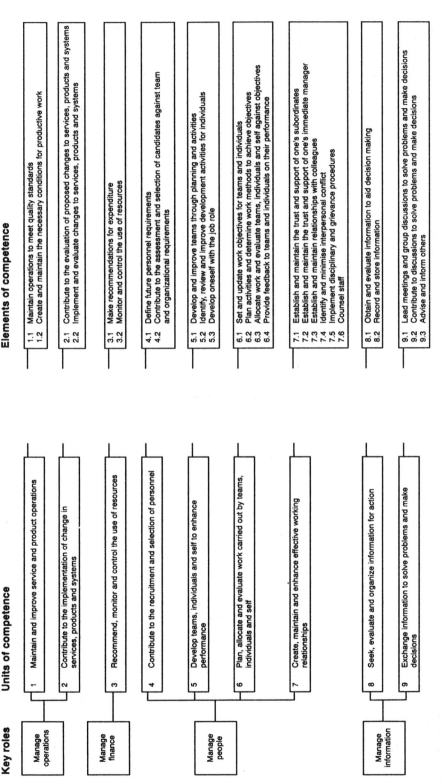

Key roles

Manage operations

Manage finance

Manage people

Manage information

Units of competence

1 Maintain and improve service and product operations

2 Contribute to the implementation of change in services, products and systems

3 Recommend, monitor and control the use of resources

4 Contribute to the recruitment and selection of personnel

5 Develop teams, individuals and self to enhance performance

6 Plan, allocate and evaluate work carried out by teams, individuals and self

7 Create, maintain and enhance effective working relationships

8 Seek, evaluate and organize information for action

9 Exchange information to solve problems and make decisions

Elements of competence

1.1 Maintain operations to meet quality standards
1.2 Create and maintain the necessary conditions for productive work

2.1 Contribute to the evaluation of proposed changes to services, products and systems
2.2 Implement and evaluate changes to services, products and systems

3.1 Make recommendations for expenditure
3.2 Monitor and control the use of resources

4.1 Define future personnel requirements
4.2 Contribute to the assessment and selection of candidates against team and organizational requirements

5.1 Develop and improve teams through planning and activities
5.2 Identify, review and improve development activities for individuals
5.3 Develop oneself with the job role

6.1 Set and update work objectives for teams and individuals
6.2 Plan activities and determine work methods to achieve objectives
6.3 Allocate work and evaluate teams, individuals and self against objectives
6.4 Provide feedback to teams and individuals on their performance

7.1 Establish and maintain the trust and support of one's subordinates
7.2 Establish and maintain the trust and support of one's immediate manager
7.3 Establish and maintain relationships with colleagues
7.4 Identify and minimise interpersonal conflict
7.5 Implement disciplinary and grievance procedures
7.6 Counsel staff

8.1 Obtain and evaluate information to aid decision making
8.2 Record and store information

9.1 Lead meetings and group discussions to solve problems and make decisions
9.2 Contribute to discussions to solve problems and make decisions
9.3 Advise and inform others

Figure 14.2 *The Management Charter Initiative's 'National Standards'.*

(Source: MCI Pocket Directory: First Line Management Standards)

statements of competence, the majority of firms have preferred to develop their own. Thus, a Roffey Park Management Institute survey found that only 10 per cent out of more than 180 organizations using a competency approach followed MCI guidelines. The vast majority had developed competences geared to their own needs (Crofts, 1992). In other words, most organizations recognize that the management competences they need are rooted in their own organizational context.

As Whitley (1989) observes, management competences are relatively 'context-dependent'. Effective managers require detailed knowledge and understanding of their own industry (Kotter, 1982); their skills are specific to situations rather than to problems; and because their activities are primarily concerned with the planning and organizing of resources, the tasks and problems faced by individual managers are highly interconnected. Managerial skills are therefore bound up with the organizations in which they are exercised and are more 'organizational' and less 'individual' than are professional skills.

By attempting to distinguish competences by level in the organization, the MCI approach also runs into the problem that organizations structure roles and responsibilities in different ways – some organizations giving responsibility earlier than others. Indeed, when shopfloor employees can become 'self-managing' in important areas of their work, it raises the question whether 'management' itself is a specific occupational function or merely a set of general capabilities. Many of the elements listed in the MCI standard involve knowledge and skills to be found in many kinds of job. When Peter Wickens, director of personnel and information systems at Nissan, argues that management development is a 'fatally flawed concept', he is making the same point:

> We found that many of the task responsibilities that we had previously regarded as the preserve of people in managerial or supervisory positions were, in fact, an essential part of the job of people at the lowest level (*Personnel Management plus*, 1992, p. 14).

People or competences?

Competency models have certainly gone all-out to satisfy the second require-ment for a general theory of management. They are highly detailed and attempt to cover all possible types of skill and personal qualities. Each competency in most schemes is sub-divided a number of times into units, elements, and performance criteria. The result is they are excessively 'atomistic':

> They break up individuals into parts, with no indication of how these parts are integrated into successful performance. It is people who perform successfully in social situations, not competences that are exercised. We have to consider people in the round, people with emotions, values, and identities; and we have to put them into a social and organizational context (Herriot, 1992, p. 103).

It seems that the more accurate competency schemes attempt to be, the further from reality they get.

The link with performance

Although it has gone through a period of piloting and testing, it is too early to say whether the MCI standards have a bearing on individual performance. The generic behavioural schemes, however, have been subjected to various tests over a number of years. The cognitive elements in Harry Shroder's scheme (information search, concept formation, and conceptual flexibility), for instance, were derived from a fifteen-year research programme into human information processing at Princetown University, and were found to correlate with high performance in uncertain and rapidly changing environments. National Westminster Bank adopted Schroder's scheme (see Table 14.2) and has been testing it further.

The competency–performance link, however, is weak at a number of points. Setting aside issues of measurement and cost, which should not invalidate the basic principle, the central weakness is to do with competences being socially and culturally bound. Since competences have to be practised in organizational situations, they have to be validated in that social context, not in laboratory isolation. Since organizations have cultures which tend to favour the use of particular behavioural styles, there may be considerable variance in how acceptable and effective are behaviours in the interpersonal and achievement-orientation areas.

As an illustration of this, Trent Regional Health Authority carried out a survey on perceptions of management styles and the differences between men and women (*Personnel Management plus*, 1993b). It found that male subordinates viewed their female managers as lacking an 'authoritative' style. Their management technique was perceived to be weak when giving instructions, explaining decisions, motitoring tasks, and delegating.

Competences, then, are embedded in cultural norms, and, as we noted in Chapter 10, are promoted and rewarded by organizational systems. They are socially defined and are not simply the properties of individuals. A competency framework therefore needs to be (1) widely accepted and deeply embedded in an organization and (2) accompanied by necessary changes in the human resource and work systems.

A further issue is that it is neither competences nor individuals but teams which count in many instances. It may not matter that an individual lacks certain competences, if others can compensate. Indeed, providing there is sufficient of a meeting ground among them, some degree of specialization may be beneficial. The classic detective partnerships in fiction are based round this idea of contrasting and complementary qualities (the hard detective–soft detective interrogation technique; the intellectual Inspector Morse and the practical Sergeant Lewis).

These issues around performance are ones which have been well aired in relation to management development over the years. Thus, management development is too narrow an approach; it should be seen as part of a wider process of organization development. Management development is also team development.

Table 14.2 High-performance competences at NatWest

Information search
Gathers many different kinds of information and uses a wide variety of
sources to build a rich informational environment in preparation for
decision making in the organization.

Concept formation
Builds frameworks or models or forms concepts, hypotheses or ideas on the
basis of information; becomes aware of patterns, trends and cause/effect
relations by linking disparate information.

Conceptual flexibility
Identifies feasible alternatives or multiple options in planning and decision
making; holds different options in focus simultaneously and evaluates
their pros and cons.

Interpersonal search
Uses open and probing questions, summaries, paraphrasing, etc. to understand the ideas, concepts and feelings of another; can comprehend
events, issues, problems, opportunities from the viewpoint of another
person.

Managing interaction
Involves others and is able to build cooperative teams in which group
members feel valued and empowered and have shared goals.

Developmental orientation
Creates a positive climate in which individuals increase the accuracy of
their awareness of their own strengths and limitations and provides
coaching, training and developmental resources to improve performance.

Impact
Uses a variety of methods (e.g. persuasive arguments, modelling behaviour,
inventing symbols, forming alliances and appealing to the interest of
others) to gain support for ideas, strategies and values.

Self-confidence
States own 'stand' or position on issues; unhesitatingly takes decisions
when required and commits self and others accordingly; expresses confidence in the future success of the actions to be taken.

Presentation
Presents ideas clearly, with ease and interest so that the other person (or
audience) understands what is being communicated; uses technical, symbolic, non-verbal and visual aids effectively.

Proactive orientation
Structures the task for the team; implements plans and ideas; takes responsibility for all aspects of the situation.

Achievement orientation
Possesses high internal work standards and sets ambitious yet attainable
goals; wants to do things better, to improve, to be more effective and
efficient; measures progress against targets.

Source: Cockerill (1989).

Competences in manager and organizational development

Many of the companies which have developed organization-specific sets of competences, whether from scratch or by customizing a generic model, recognize these issues. They recognize the force of their own culture in the particular slant they give to the behavioural variables. Thus, at BP, Greatrex and Phillips (1989) note that: 'the behaviours listed within the clusters are cultural artefacts of the BP organization and expressed in terms of the language of the organization' (p. 38).

By specifying valued behaviours, it opens them up for discussion and review. For instance, the definition of 'personal drive' – 'self-confident and assertive drive to win, with decisiveness and resilience' – is accompanied by a series of positive and negative indicators. Individual tendencies to score high on one side or the other can then be related to questions and ideas for personal development, involving issues such as the appropriateness of particular behaviours in different situations, impact on others, attitudes to conflict, and so on.

Tony Cockerill at NatWest provides us with a second example, which exemplifies also the issue of individuals versus teams. Here, individuals first identify their 'strengths, adequacies, and limitations' through participation in an assessment centre. They then undertake a three-stage development process:

Using competences to develop managers at NatWest[2]
First, staff devise a plan to make a better contribution to the organization with their strengths. Our experience supports Kotter's notion that managers do not have a clear perception of their strengths; the first benefit of self-insight is that it gives individuals a clear idea of their strengths. Even when staff are aware of their strengths, we find they do not make full use of them; for instance, an individual will gather information very well from a customer in a one-to-one situation but will not be so active at doing this in a group meeting. Staff therefore plan how to use their strengths consistently in different situations and across a fuller range of activities.

Secondly, staff create a plan to compensate for their limitations. Schroder's research in the USA and the UK has found that, on average, managers tend to have three high-performance competences as strengths. These results help to debunk the popular macho belief that managers must be good at everything. We find it comes as quite a relief to staff when they find that they do not have to be supermen or superwomen and that it makes sense to learn how to work co-operatively with others who have different strengths.

This approach also highlights the importance of building managerial teams with individuals who have complementary strengths, so that the team as a whole possesses the full range of competences that are needed for high performance.

Thirdly, staff devise a plan to develop one or two competences which are limitations into strengths. All three plans include ways of measuring whether development is occurring and whether this is raising the level of organizational performance. The plans are implemented in the workplace using the principles of action learning. The relevance and practicality of these plans avoids a problem which is the Achilles heel of many management courses – how to transfer learning back to the workplace (Tony Cockerill, management development adviser with National Westminster Bank, 1989).

In these two examples at BP and NatWest the competency schemes (which turn out to be not markedly different) provide a language for manager development. Another behavioural methodology – Belbin's team role model (outlined in Table 14.3) – provides a similar language to analyse the balance of behaviour in teams. At Cadbury Schweppes, where they use both, the development of such a language is regarded as perhaps the most important factor, helping to create a 'behaviourally literate management population' (Glaze, 1989).

This does raise, however, an interesting parallel with other earlier 'vocabularies' (like Management by Objectives) which in their time provided a common language for management action and development. The language of management 'competences' may raise consciousness for a period of time, and eventually expire as people grow tired of it. Thus, it may be that the behavioural definition of management competences as such has little effect on organizational performance, and that what really matters are the processes of thinking, dialogue, and innovations in learning which it generates.

Table 14.3 Belbin's eight team roles

The coordinator (or chairman): the team's natural chairperson; calm, mature, able to elicit useful contributions from all team members, the social leader. Need not be a brilliant intellect.

The implementer (or company worker): the team's workhorse; practical, logical, reliable, hard-working. May lack imagination.

The plant: the ideas person; imaginative, creative, intelligent, unorthodox. May lack practicality.

The resources investigator: a fixer; extrovert, good at making and using contacts, a salesperson and diplomat. May have a short attention span.

The shaper: may be the self-selected task leader; dynamic, positive, keen to get results. May be impatient or provoke opposition.

The monitor – evaluator: the team's rock; sober, analytical, practical. May lack imagination and motivational skills.

The team-worker: a counselling type; socially oriented, supportive, uncompetitive, perceptive, promotes harmony, a mediator. May be indecisive.

The completer – finisher: a stickler for detail; orderly, spots errors, worries about deadlines. May worry about small things and be reluctant to let go.

Source: Belbin (1981).

Competences for selection and development

The current interest in competences has largely been stimulated by the

Management Charter Initiative's concern with raising the standard of British management education and training. Competences, however, are also used as a basis for selection – for new graduate entrants, in selecting managers for specific appointments, and to identify the potential of employees for promotion. An increasing number of organizations are using competences for these purposes as part of an assessment centre process. (An in-house survey by the consultants, Saville and Holdsworth, in 1989, for example, found that 37 per cent of organizations with over 1000 employees were using assessment centres.)

An assessment centre uses a battery of tests to look at various aspects of performance relating to specific competences which have already been defined. Chapter 10 dealt briefly with these. The core methodology, however, is the use of simulations. A typical assessment centre lasts two days, involves eight candidates, four assessors, and often an external occupational psychologist. Obviously, this does not come cheap. Nevertheless, its supporters argue that getting appointments and selection right is in the long run money well spent. As one of the pillars of a strategic approach to HRM, good selection decisions are obviously vital. Given the prohibitive cost of using this methodology for all employees, it comes down to two questions. How important is the job? How readily available are suitable candidates?

Feedback is supposed to be an essential part of the assessment centre experience, to deal with the anxieties which assessment can induce. If this is properly conducted, it can contribute usefully to development. Both negative and positive consequences reflect the fact that an assessment centre is a social process (Herriot, 1989). Some organizations, such as British Telecom (Beard and Lee, 1990), have recognized both aspects of this and created 'development centres' as a modified form. Among other things, a development centre is longer (and therefore even more expensive); a climate is created in which participants can make mistakes; feedback is on-going during the event; and observers act as facilitators and mentors.

Management learning and development

It is not the intention here to go into detail over the debate about the shortcomings of British management development and how the MCI standards originated. This is very well documented in Silver (1991), *Competent to Manage*. The basic facts are that during the 1980s a series of reports came out which highlighted the deficiencies of British management education and companies' training of managers. These included:

1 *Competence and Competition* (Institute of Manpower Studies, 1984), which compared education and training in three major competitors – West Germany, the USA, and Japan.
2 *A Challenge to Complacency* (Coopers and Lybrands Associates, 1985),

which revealed ignorance and indifference to education and training among top managers in Britain.

3 *The Making of Managers* (Handy *et al.*, 1987), on management education, training and development in the USA, West Germany, France, Japan, and the UK. This was the seminal report in which Charles Handy set out a ten-point plan for raising British standards. It included the suggestion that leading organizations should act as role models for all industry and commerce, which led directly to the formation of the Council for Management Education and Development (CMED) sponsored by the CBI and British Institute of Management and headed by Bob Reid, chairman of Shell UK. The Management Charter Initiative subsequently sprang from this in 1988.

4 *The Making of British Managers* (Constable and McCormick, 1987) – otherwise known as the Constable/McCormick report. This was developed as a companion study to Handy's comparative one and launched on the same day. It provided a comprehensive review of management education and training in Britain.

One point of note is what lay behind this flurry of studies and activity:

> Despite the initial cost-cutting reaction, the 1980-82 recession may come to be seen as a watershed in the history of management training and development in the UK. The recession concentrated attention as never before on weaknesses in British management and on the deficiencies of UK organizations *vis-à-vis* their foreign competitors. (Sadler and Barham, 1988, p. 49).

The principal outcome, meanwhile, has been the development of a set of management vocational standards. Although Silver (1991, pp. 127–130) notes the criticisms levelled at the standards and of the certification based on them, a constant theme running through his review is how the absence of an adequate language to describe management has been a root cause in the lack of attention to management training and development:

> The ill-defined nature of managerial competences, along with the uncertain nature of the link between management education, training and performance, feeds the ambivalent attitude of managers with regard to the need for such training (Silver, 1991, p. 65).

This point was made even more forcibly in an earlier study. Managers were asked to describe skills which were important to their work:

> Many of the respondents provide replies in terms of *functional* skills at a level of abstraction that is of little value, and second, their *vocabulary* of skills is limited.
>
> Many, particularly of those doing little or no training of their managers, were *unable* or *unwilling* to specify the qualities, attributes and skills required of, for example, junior managers. On the other hand, very few were prepared to acknowledge. . .that requirements may very depending upon particular jobs and particular organizational environments.
>
> It would appear from such data generated during the course of interviews that respondents suffer considerable difficulty in finding the *words* which address the area of competency.

> Few replied without prompting and almost all came up with portmanteau terms such as 'good communicator', 'must have leadership skills', and the like. When invited to unpack these terms most proved unable or unwilling so to do (Mangham and Silver, 1986, p. 31).

This is where we came in, then, in the debate over competences, here and in Chapter 10. We have to have some more adequate language than we have had in the past for describing what managers at different levels do, as a basis for suitable training and development. Or do we?

The vocational language that has been developed by MCI is supposed to deal with the 'competences' used on-the-job. It is supposed to be more action-oriented. However, by getting caught up in the desire to professionalize management, like NVQs the management standards have become burdened with assessment and certification. They detract from action. In seeking to draw the further and higher educational system also into the process of certification, the standards also become allied with a particular system of delivering management development and education. Add to this that both management standards and NVQs have created an industry round themselves with exclusive rights to sell their standards, and we have a vast set of vested interests.

If the essence of management is taking action, should we not be more concerned, then, with learning itself than with external assessment and certification and with a particular approach to learning?

Management learning

The IPM has adopted a Code on 'Continuous Development' (IPM, 1990). The essential elements of this are:

- The organization needs to have a strategic plan which spells out in operational terms the knowledge and skills implications for employees
- A readiness to address learning needs as they appear, in terms of the problems and challenges, successes and failures, encountered by employees in their daily work
- The integration of learning and work
- Support from the top management team
- A view that investment in continuous learning is an investment as important as that in research, new products, or capital equipment.

The essence of continuous development is 'self-directed learning' (Wood, 1988, p. 9). It is 'learning from experience', but more than that, it is conscious and reflective learning from experience, consciously promoted or managed in the organization. Wood (1988) and her co-authors go so far as to say that 'CD (continuous development), acknowledged or unrecognized, has all but replaced "systematic training": that is, task analysis carried out by some third party, leading to the setting up of formal training plans' (p. 13).

The basic principle of reflective experiential learning is contained in Kolb's (1984) learning cycle. Formally, it has been given fullest expression in the idea of 'action learning', first enunciated by Revans (1971):

The principles of action learning

First, learning for managers should mean taking effective action. Acquiring information and becoming more capable in diagnosis or analysis has been overvalued in management learning.

Secondly, learning to take effective action necessarily involves actually taking action, not recommending action or undertaking analysis of someone else's problem.

Thirdly, the best form of action for learning is work on a defined project which is significant to the managers themselves. The project should involve implementation as well as analysis and recommendation.

Fourthly, while the managers should have responsibility for their own achievements on their own project, the learning process is a social one; managers learn best with and from each other.

Next, the social process is achieved and managed through regular meetings of managers to discuss their individual projects; the group is usually called a 'set'. The managers are 'comrades in adversity' (Revans).

And finally, the role of people providing help for members of the set is essentially and crucially different from that of the normal management teacher. Their role is not to teach (whether through lecture, case or simulation), but to help managers learn from exposure to problems and to each other. As Revans says, action learning attacks 'the inveterate hankering of the teacher to be the centre of attention' (Mumford, 1991, p. 35).

The 'business development' programme introduced at Pilkington for experienced middle managers in 1987 illustrates what this might look like in practice. The starting point was that it was a 'business development' programme focused on specific business needs, rather than a 'management development' programme based round course attendance. As a result, among the keenest supporters were the front-line works managers who saw it directly meeting some of their business needs, without lengthy periods off the job:

1   Participants first complete a 50-page workbook, designed to get them to think about (a) their business (using tools like SWOT analysis) and (b) their personal development. In doing this, they engage with their superiors, which helps to secure their commitment. This lasts about three weeks.

2   Participants attend a five-day residential course which uses senior executives to review business issues at various levels, from the Pilkington Group down to operating units. This culminates in identification of topics for project work, by sponsoring managers/directors, on the one hand, and by participants, according to their own interests and perception of need, on the other. The criteria for selection of projects are first, that they have a bottom-line benefit to the company, and second, that they develop the individual personally – in that order. Paradoxically, this should produce better learning. Mixed disciplinary teams of three or four people are then assigned to projects outside their usual area of operation.

3   Participants undertake project work on a team basis over a period of

months, first negotiating the time and resources with the sponsoring manager to do it. This identifies further individual developmental and skill needs, which can be met by elective training courses, as well as by compulsory modules in computer appreciation, financial appreciation, and presentation skills. The groups throughout this time are assigned a 'mentor'.

4 Participants reconvene two or three times to share experiences and to review issues for the implementation of proposals.

The whole four-stage process lasts nine to twelve months, and is overseen by a Steering Committee (which includes the personnel director, training manager, and an external consultant). The design ensures that a considerable number of other senior managers are involved at various stages. As a result, one of the early lessons was the need to define more clearly the role of the sponsoring manager and the support he or she needed to give, as well as to confirm the personnel role as that of a facilitator of learning. In this case, participants worked on defined projects; the alternative is to work on on-going problems.

Reviewing Revans's concept of action learning, Mumford (1991) emphasizes four features, which involve some development of his ideas:

> *Interaction* is key – not just within the 'set' of 'fellows in adversity', but including the manager's manager, the project sponsor, and mentors.
> The focus is on addressing real work problems for which the manager is personally accountable, and *implementing* solutions.
> Experiential learning must be *integrated* with appropriate inputs of knowledge and skill. Revans's formula:

$$\begin{array}{ccccc} \text{L} & = & \text{P} & + & \text{Q} \\ \text{(learning)} & & \text{(programmed} & & \text{(questioning} \\ & & \text{knowledge)} & & \text{insight)} \end{array}$$

> was misleading. It needs to be modified as follows to show what he was really describing, and also to show learning as a continuing and iterative process:

$$Q^1 + P + Q^2 = L$$

> This shows that the most effective learning is driven by the need to resolve a managerial problem (Q^1). This leads to the acquisition of relevant knowledge (P) – which then stimulates the identification of further management opportunities (Q^2). The result is learning.
> Finally, such learning needs to be embedded into long-term management processes through *iteration*.

As Mumford then observes:

> The philosophy of action learning is development through significant managerial tasks. It is essentially opportunistic in character, although it provides for careful and considered choices about the opportunities to be pursued. It is a different kind of strategy than that available through the competency approach, which rests on a prefigured, detailed analysis of what managers need.
> Action learning is holistic in its view of the person, the management process

and learning. It is highly situational, flexibly treating elusive problems and combines a social process with individual needs. The competency strategy offers an atomistic, analytical, discrete view of management and learning. It is generalised in its view of what a group of managers need (p. 37).

One might also add that the competency approach is driven from the outside, determining what needs to be learnt. It represents a tradit- ional view of the teacher–learner relationship in which the learner is a passive automaton. This is at odds with the idea of management as taking action.

Action learning versus competences

Action learning should not, however, be confused with haphazard learning from experience. A comparison of management development in four pairs of companies in Japan and Britain (Storey, 1991; Storey *et al.*, 1991) found that British managers were more likely to stress the importance of early challenging experiences in their professional growth, such as being given significant responsibility early on. The Japanese managers, on the other hand, spoke of continuous development, role models, and mentors.

These findings highlight two things. First, the emphasis on learning from experience among the British managers may simply arise by default: they received inadequate preparation and training, and just had to 'sink or swim'. Second, the Japanese training and development system was altogether more coherent, and integrated with manpower planning. Japanese managers came in with a much higher level of basic education; they joined companies with a much more settled framework of training and development; the idea of development was much more broadly based, not confined to 'managers'; and responsibility for developing subordinates was deeply embedded in everyone's expectations. The result is a structure of continuous development (and learning from experience) all the way through a career.

The MCI standards may create a similar settled framework for training and development, reaching from the educational system up through the organization. They also contribute to the development of the mentor role. One of the as-yet unacknowledged benefits of the standards process is the effect which the assessment of competence has on the boss–subordinate relationship. Together, they are obliged to look more explicitly at the work and skills of the subordinate doing the job. This increases mutual under- standing and changes the relationship in helpful and productive ways. It helps to develop the mentoring/coaching role of the boss.

Where weaknesses are identified through this process, moreover, the learning methods adopted to remedy them are not prescribed or limited. Improving competence may mean identifying work opportunities for practis- ing underdeveloped skills; taking time out to look at learning styles; and using the experiential–reflective learning process that underpins action learning.

Managing careers

Almost by definition, managers and professionals are interested in careers. MCI feeds this perspective by creating a structure of certification which documents the level of achievement. Many elements contribute to the career system of an organization, not all of which are in the hands of the HR function (Hirsh, 1984):

- Job design, the grading structure, and the control of posts through current budgets
- The system of rewards
- Entry points into the organization, and the processes of recruitment, selection, and placement
- When and how employees leave organizations, and how organizations discard employees
- The patterns and processes for job movement, promotion and identifying potential
- Who gets training and development, when, and what happens as a result.

All these things communicate messages to employees about what kind of career system operates for them. Often, the HR function will put a lot of effort into the design and management of some aspect of the whole – usually into identifying potential and tracking the careers of an elite few. But meanwhile it fails to address the things which determine the basic 'psychological contract' (Argyris, 1960) the organization has with its employees, and they with it.

The series of positions a person holds in an organization in a sense represents their 'objective' career; but what really matters is their 'subjective' career, their implicit 'psychological contract' with the organization. It is this which holds an organization together over time (Herriot, 1992, p. 7).

Giving primacy to the psychological contract puts a particular slant on strategic HRM. In Chapter 1 we contrasted two versions of HRM. That of Fombrun, Tichy and Devanna (1984) at Michigan talks about formal structure and HR systems driving the strategic objectives of the organization. This leads to a focus on the 'objective' aspects of career management: the systems for managing careers and securing the right people with the right qualities for realizing the business objectives. Implicitly, and often explicitly, it is about fitting people to the organization. In contrast, Beer and his colleagues at Harvard put the emphasis on 'the relationship between the organization and its employees' – in other words on the 'subjective' side which is endorsed and affirmed every working day.

In a sense, this whole book is a running debate about the implications of these two positions. Herriot's emphasis on the psychological contract aligns him clearly with the Harvard group. His comments on the strategic approach in this respect are apposite:

> I have not argued that a human resources strategy should be developed to support strategic business plans. Rather, that business activity by definition requires the active participation and collaboration of all employees. Since this will be achieved by agreement rather than by top-down control, it is the establishment and maintenance of such agreements which come first. . . Organisational missions and strategies follow from these agreements, since employees are the originators as well as the followers of organisational directions (Herriot, 1992, p. 159).

This book takes much the same standpoint, putting the development of people and their skills first. The nature of the psychological contract they have with the organization is then an important linking concept, determining what the organization gains from its people.

Career systems

The psychological contract can be described in terms of career systems. A career system is a particular slant on the broader concept of an 'employment system' which we introduced in Chapter 11. In that chapter, we represented employment systems in terms of (1) the relationship a particular group of employees has with the external labour market and (2) how their movements within the organization are controlled. Narrowing the scope of this slightly for the purpose of describing careers, Sonnenfeld (1989) refers to these two processes as 'supply flow' and 'assignment flow'.

Organizations vary according to (1) how open the career system is to taking people in from the external labour market ('supply flow'); and (2) the pace and pressure for internal career moves generated by such factors as the vacancy rate, organizational growth, and demographic profile ('assignment flow'). These two dimensions give four characteristic types of career system – 'baseball teams', 'academies', 'clubs', and 'fortresses' (Sonnenfeld, Peiperl and Kotter, 1988; Sonnenfeld, 1989). Systems may predominate in particular industries owing to the competitive conditions faced. As we noted in Chapter 11, however, this is by no means the only influence.

'*Baseball teams*' rely upon highly skilled individuals, whose talents are readily transferable. They are open to the external labour market at all levels, to get the best people available and to discard those who no longer fit or are effective. Recruitment is a key activity. Such organizations operate within an elaborate network of agents and intermediaries who facilitate the search for and exchange of 'performers'. The psychological contract is characterized by high cash rewards and the opportunity to star. People tend to identify therefore more with their profession than with the firm. Apart from sports teams, these kind of firms can be found in advertising, law (in the USA but possibly not the UK), consultancy, entertainment, investment banking, and software development.

'*Academies*' aim to develop the knowledge of employees through internal labour markets. They 'make' their talent, rather than buying it. Employees in turn value professional growth. The key human resource activity is development, with firms creating barriers to exit through firm-specific skills and personal qualities. There is low mid-career recruitment and low turn-over – in other words, low openness to the external labour market, beyond the initial entry period. This produces a psychological contract characterized by employment security and loyalty to long-service employees. Reward systems, nevertheless, are based on individual contribution, with promotions often determined by 'tournaments'. There may be dual ladders for management and professional career tracks.

IBM has been held up as the exemplar of the academy, with its extreme reluctance to break its commitment to employment security, even through the turbulent 1980s. Until the recent severance process (described in Chapter 9), it avoided redundancies by restricting hiring, cutting overtime, taking back work from sub-contractors, and redeployment with extensive retraining. To operate like this, such a firm often has to be dominant in its own market. Examples can be found in electronics and computing, pharmaceuticals, and office products. But a number of large firms have had to back away from the commitments involved.

'*Clubs*' are often shielded from the market by regulatory buffers or a monopoly situation. They tend therefore to have less concern for innovation and profitability. They operate an internal labour market, but reward on the basis of seniority, commitment, status, and equal treatment of members. They assign and promote on the basis of group factors rather than individual contribution, with skilful team-work more valued than individualism. In return, employees see the organization as an institution with a mission to serve the public interest. The critical human resource function is retention. This model could be found in public sector utilities, government, banks and insurance, and the military, but has obviously suffered through widespread deregulation and commercialization of public sector activities.

'*Fortresses*' are essentially organizations fighting for survival. As such, they cannot sustain a commitment to careers, but rely on hiring and firing to balance their requirements in unstable market conditions. It may be that the whole industry is in such throes or the particular firm is in a turnaround situation. Examples are textiles, mining, hotels. Employees may have joined in healthier times and became locked in.

With 'clubs' and 'academies' both under threat from changing market conditions, we have seen a general trend with regard to managers and professionals:

- Away from internal labour market systems towards a reliance on, and movements in and out of, the external labour market
- Away from group-based reward systems to an individual emphasis.

At the top, firms search for executive heroes who can turn the organization around, and pay increasingly high salaries to these stars. Meanwhile, the biggest casualties are the loyal ranks of middle managers who have until now given loyalty in exchange for security (Herriot, 1992).

Sonnenfeld relates these four career systems to four patterns of strategic behaviour – prospector, analyser, defender, and reactor (Miles and Snow, 1978). The important point underlying this is that career systems breed attitudes (for example, towards risk); career paths develop structures of knowledge which may be in-bred to the particular company and/or sector; and they influence perspectives and capabilities by the extent to which people pursue generalist or specialist careers. The totality of this management experience has a strong influence on the business strategies firms subsequently pursue (Gunz and Whitley, 1985).

Succession planning

Despite the erosion of careers-for-life, however, management succession remains a primary concern. Although they may not give much thought to other human resource issues, chief executives consider management development for succession a primary responsibility (Coopers & Lybrand Associates, 1985; Bowman, 1986). In a survey of 235 firms, Friedman (1986) also shows that an effective succession system is clearly linked to corporate performance.

Such a system must begin early on, however, with the building of cohorts and cadres to select from, and not rely on pencilling individual names into succession charts. As we saw in the case of IMI in Chapter 5, in an uncertain environment the latter is not viable or realistic. Those in charge of management development need to have a view of career progression in terms of

- The structure of the organization, the breadth of experience required at different levels, and the opportunities for developing experience through these (Derr, Jones and Toomey, 1988)
- The strategic concerns of the CEO and senior management, as to what qualities and experience will be needed in the future (Hall, 1989).

At the same time, it is necessary to modify the idea of a series of 'tournament' stages through which a person progresses and others are eliminated, since this penalizes the late developer and women whose careers get interrupted. Steady career progression of this kind is often simply a reward for seniority and long service: 'Being in the elite stream is not usually a sufficient condition to reaching senior management but it rapidly becomes a self-fulfilling prophecy' (Hirsh, 1984, p. 115).

The disadvantage of such systems is that they are hard to adjust to changes in the environment. They are hard to adjust in terms of numbers of 'high potential' people, because the elite group has been rather rigidly defined. And they are hard to adjust in what 'high potential' means, since the stereotype of a 'successful manager' tends to linger on.

The changing pattern of careers: renegotiating the psychological contract

The worst that could happen is that organizations pay attention just to their elite with top succession in mind, while general career systems continue to erode. Some observers have put a gloss on this increased insecurity by suggesting that the ownership of careers has transferred from the organization to the individual (Golzen and Garner, 1990). In practice, this may simply mean organizations take a *laissez-faire*, 'couldn't care less' attitude, leaving their employees to swim as best they can. Evidence is patchy, but includes:

- A survey showing that two-thirds of middle managers believe their organization pays insufficient attention to their career development (Institute of Management, 1992)
- An in-depth survey in three large UK organizations which showed little sign of a 'psychological contract' operating (reported in Herriot, 1992, pp. 72–80)
- A survey of over 2000 managers which showed job changes being driven primarily by intolerable change and uncertainty, rather than by career plans (Nicholson and West, 1989).

Of course, all this may simply reflect the historic neglect of management development in many organizations. Managerial mobility in British industry has consequently tended to be high, with promotion and higher earnings dependent on moving elsewhere (Crockett and Elias, 1984).

Apart from satisfying the aspirations of managers for more and better training, what can organizations do? At root is the need to give explicit attention to just what kind of 'psychological contract' operates. At present, according to Herriot, organizations are increasingly making multiple, conflicting demands on people, and the demand for commitment is all one-way.

Organizations need to reconcile the expectations of the organization and the individual, and recognize the scope and application of different sets of expectation on the part of each. According to Herriot (1992, pp. 67–68), there are four sets of requirements to keep in balance (see Table 14.4).

Table 14.4 Balancing individual and organizational needs

What the organization wants	*What the individual needs*
Adventure and exploration	Support
Loyalty and commitment	Respect for individuality
Knowledge and its communication	Tolerance and recognition
Environmental intelligence	Trust and autonomy

Source: Herriot (1992).

To some extent, these represent demands and requirements from different employees. This means therefore acknowledging and accepting a diversity of values. Above all, it means making psychological contracting explicit. Part of this contracting must involve making career directions and opportunities (or the lack of them) explicit – that is, clarifying the 'objective' features of a career. Mayo (1991, 1992) suggests that in most organiza[tions] there are four main career directions – (1) manual, clerical, adm[...]

(2) technical/professional; (3) functional management; and (4) general management. There are two things that need to be made visible, then:

- How people progress up a particular ladder
- How people may move from one ladder to another

As Mayo observes, one of the weaknesses of the 'self-development' approach is that the individual usually finds it difficult to engineer such movements. ICL Europe (where Mayo is director of personnel) produces a booklet on career structures for all the main streams which shows how jobs are interconnected; identifies 'career bridges'; and describes 'developmental' positions where a person can begin to make a useful contribution without elaborate preparation beyond a sound basic training. In addition, employees agree a career plan with their boss which identifies a 'career aiming point' five to seven years on, with a profile of the knowledge, skills, attitudes, and experience that will entail. This is reviewed annually. It thus makes appraisal a more meaningful process.

This system presupposes a large organization with the scope and stability to operate what is in effect an internal labour market. The basic principles, however, can be readily adapted to counselling individuals about their career opportunities with the organization, the skills and qualities the organization and sector will need, and what individuals can do to equip themselves with the necessary 'competences'. Thus, one of the attractions of the whole competences approach, especially the MCI standards, is the way it provides a common currency, understood by employees and employers alike, that should facilitate career movements within and between organizations.

If the shift is from 'employment' to 'employability', the obligation on the employer is to equip employees with transferable skills. On the other hand, investing in skills for the benefit of other firms is not something companies have traditionally been enthusiastic about.

Pay and appraisal

This is where the idea of 'aligning human resources with the business strategy' comes down to earth, through pay as supposedly the great motivator. Pay and appraisal thus constitute two of the four levers in Fombrun, Tichy and Devanna's model. Pay is also a principal medium for expressing the 'psychological contract'. Over the last decade this has been increasingly expressed in terms of pay incentives, with the subject of performance-　ᵈ pay (PRP) a constant topic of interest in the pages of professional 　　　ᵉ *Personnel Management* and *Personnel Management plus*.
　　　　　ᶠ this interest lie in the general economic and political
　　　　　　　　with the desire, on the one hand, to instill a more
　　　　　　　　　into managers and, on the other, to make shopfloor
　　　　　　　　　st their pay demands to the state of the business.

Ideas about performance pay, imported with HRM, thus found a ready audience – so much so that, as Torrington and Blandamer (1992) observe, 'The idea of linking pay to performance and to performance management is inextricably linked with the idea of human resource management' (p. 137).

Performance-related pay

Performance-related pay stands in contrast to the philosophy which had animated the design of managerial pay systems for much of the post-war era (Torrington and Blandamer, 1992). This had emphasized 'service', involving the acquisition of experience through steady job tenure, and incremental pay scales. The scope for continuing pay progression through a typical 5-8 point incremental scale was an encouragement to continue in post, while a series of stepped bands promised further progression. Bandwidth and overlap, fitting jobs within the scales, and getting the differentials right were key concerns in the design of such systems. The spread of job evaluation was an attempt to maintain fairness over differentials and increasingly underpinned both managerial and blue-collar pay structures as the use of incentives declined.

Such systems, however, were essentially inward-looking and tied to static conceptions of the organization and its environment. This was reflected in the criticisms increasingly made of job evaluation that it promoted bureaucracy, was costly, rigid, and inflexible, and failed to respond to change (see, for example, the Pilkington case in Chapter 8). One of the main things which has undone job evaluation has consequently been the rapidly changing nature of jobs in many sectors. In the process, the internal labour market model of the firm, implicit here, has increasingly given way to more open systems, with pay geared to individual worth measured by market criteria and performance yardsticks.

Pressures for such change are nicely illustrated in a consultancy report on the banking sector, which for so long typified the 'traditional' model, with its emphasis on equity, hierarchy, control, and permanently defined jobs:

- Traditional salary structures and incremental scales are seen as acting as a brake on change and inhibiting flexibility. They are too strongly related to length of service and inhibit 'sideways' career development moves.
- There is a near-universal view that performance-related pay needs to occupy a greater part of the total remuneration package. The present system is felt to discriminate not at all between the excellent and the adequate performer.
- There is a feeling that the conventionally generous benefits within the financial sector need to be provided on a more selective basis. Regional pay variations, for example, would substantially reduce bank costs. However, this could conflict with the objective of encouraging career moves (Thomas and Tilston, 1987).

What is performance-related pay?

Put simply, performance-related pay is about making a proportion of pay dependent on some objectively defined criterion. This may range from company profits to specific individual output targets, varying according to the nature of the job. As such, PRP is more of a strategy or approach, than a system. It embraces a great variety of schemes and different motivations. In practice, moreover, the efficacy of the relationship between personal contribution and performance outcomes may vary considerably. (Schemes also vary greatly in scope from full-blown 'performance management systems' which embrace all staff, to those which are more exclusively management-oriented.)

While the banks looked on PRP as a way of shaking up attitudes, many local authorities in the mid- to late-1980s, for instance, apparently saw it as a way of overcoming recruitment and retention problems among senior managers (Thatcher, 1993). Like productivity bargaining before it, PRP has thus occasionally been used as a device to reward people more. Tax incentives for profit-related pay schemes (also confusingly referred to by the initials PRP) can easily become a way of enhancing pay at the taxpayer's expense, without any impact on effort or performance.

The problem of a spurious relationship with performance is perhaps nowhere more conspicuous than in the inflation of top executives' salaries, which have run far ahead of pay rises for ordinary managers and workers. As an *Economist* (1990) report put it: 'Amongst Britain's once underpaid bosses, top salaries are beginning to look like libel damages: high and often arbitrary' (p. 30).

At the opposite extreme has been the tendency to set very precise targets as the basis for rewarding performance. Inevitably, targets become focused on the short term and may subvert more significant activities. This is increasingly rife in contracted-out areas of the public sector. The role of the Child Support Agency is a case in point, where targets for reducing the claims of single parents for family income support have led to middle-class fathers, already paying maintenance, being pursued for higher payments, because they are an easier and more lucrative target than poorer fathers making no payment who have disappeared without trace.

The setting of targets for senior executives whose own pay depends heavily on achieving them certainly drives a sense of purpose through an organization. But equally it may create a sense of coercion. Thus, we recall from Chapter 6 that among the fourteen 'quality' principles of Deming were 'eliminate targets', 'eliminate quotas', and 'drive out fear'. Quantitative targets, if adopted, need to be supplemented by qualitative ones.

A satisfactory scheme for performance-related pay has to overcome these and a number of other problems:

- It must in some way be derived from corporate goals and values.
- It must take account of longer-term qualitative performance criteria, as well as what is quantifiably measurable in the short term.
- It must dissociate windfall gains from what is due to staff efforts.
- It must relate rewards to the effective unit of production. In other

words, it must base rewards on the team where team-effort, not individual effort, is what counts. This may go even further and take in interfunctional cooperation.

• Related to this, the member(s) of staff must be able to affect the output goals by their own behaviour. It must cover things for which they can be personally 'accountable'.

In addition, and critical in practice:

• The scheme must involve a way of assessing performance and distributing rewards which is fair and accepted. This includes agreeing individual and team goals in the first place.

• Finally, if it is to be a performance-based system it must actively discriminate between good and bad performance, or between adequate and excellent performance.

The way these 'process' issues are handled can fundamentally affect motivation (which is supposed to be the whole point of the exercise). In practice, systems typically fall down on one of two problems. The first is the problem of subjectivity. Traditional systems of appraisal are wide open to feelings of arbitrariness and unfairness.

The second problem concerns the role of pay as a motivator. This has various ramifications. One way assessors traditionally avoid making invidious judgements between people is by marking the majority 'above average'. Getting one's own staff extra increments is seen as a measure of being a 'good boss': it reflects loyalty on the part of the boss, and inspires loyalty in staff. Some organizations adopting PRP prevent this by setting quotas for performance categories; others (like Citibank) have done so by forcing managers to rank order their staff. Both methods ensure that PRP only pays out to a proportion of staff. Whether this kind of arbitrary determination is motivating or demotivating is debatable. The bigger problem in the end may be getting good performance from those who are demotivated because they failed to get an award, than motivating a few to achieve high performance.

Another fundamental issue is how much performance-related pay is necessary to affect motivation. Some US evidence suggests it would need to be set at 30 per cent of base pay to have an impact. A series of reports from the Institute of Manpower Studies consequently throw doubt on how far existing schemes motivate individuals at all (Bevan and Thompson, 1991; Thompson, 1993).

Competency-based approaches to performance-related pay

Competency-based systems have been proposed as a way of overcoming both problems – the subjectivity and arbitrariness of assessment, and establishing a standard for rewards. Drummond (1993) proposes a task-focused approach which concentrates on a few core functions of management that resemble the MCI standards. Individual objectives may be defined more selectively, however, with a focus on particular projects or areas of activity. The advantage of this is it addresses means, not just ends. In contrast, quantitative target-setting focuses on short-term, ostensible outcomes, without bothering how these are achieved. A task-focused approach asks 'What have you done to ensure this objective is achieved?' not simply 'Have you achieved this objective?' It thus encourages questions to be asked about the details of activity on an on-going basis, thereby embedding performance appraisal in normal processes of management monitoring.

Assessment is then concerned with whether a person has done a broad range of things well, to a minimum expected standard. With extraneous factors outside their control, this is all that can be expected from people in many jobs. Moreover, it does not blindly judge a person without taking account of the circumstances they have had to face.

A skills-based competency approach is obviously a retreat from grander schemes of PRP, with their often-inflated notions of 'excellence'. But for this reason, it may also be more workable and deliver greater organizational benefits in the longer term. Both job-skills and behavioural approaches also have the advantage over systems which rate personal traits (such as 'initiative' and 'attitude to authority') of avoiding the grosser forms of discrimination (Townley, 1990).

Appraisal

One of the abiding lessons in establishing pay systems of any kind is that they work best when 'developed, installed and maintained with the participation of employee representatives' (ACAS, *Introduction to Payment Systems*). Even critical studies of PRP acknowledge that schemes that have involved employees in this way are more likely to be perceived as fair and have a motivating effect (Thompson, 1993). Introduced in any other way, they will be perceived as an unwelcome and arbitrary instrument of control. Thus, PRP requires consent. The conduct of performance appraisal reflects precisely the same issue of willing participation and consent versus feelings of being arbitrarily controlled.

Appraisal has been an area of controversy for many years, a recent study suggesting that over 80 per cent of companies were dissatisfied with the schemes they operated. One of the main problems is the way too many conflicting purposes get loaded on to it. This is partly because organizations do not take it seriously enough and try to use a single session for all purposes. Among these are:

- To assess training and development needs
- To review past performance, and to help improve current performance
- To assess future potential and promotability, and to help career planning decisions
- To set performance objectives
- To determine pay increases and awards

The last of these tended until recently to lag way behind the other uses. IPM surveys, however, suggest that this use almost doubled between 1986 and 1991 (Long, 1986; Bevan and Thompson, 1991). In the process, there has been a continuing shift away from trait-oriented schemes (which rate personality factors) to more quantifiable results-oriented schemes, at least for managers. Interestingly, job behaviour-oriented schemes such as that advocated by Drummond, which avoid the problem of quantifying targets, also feature high.

One final fact about appraisal is that it is much more commonly applied to junior, middle and senior management; increasingly to first-line supervisors and clerical/secretarial staff; to professional workers; and to all these more than to directors (although there are practical problems formally appraising the latter) (Long, 1986).

PRP, and especially fully integrated performance management systems (PMSs) which attempt to develop systematic objectives for all employees, give appraisal a yet more central role. Fletcher (1993) suggests that PMS can help to separate out pay decisions by dealing with these in an objective-setting/performance review tied in to the start of the business year, followed by a developmentally oriented session at a later date. This is helped by the fact that PMS is supposedly driven by line managers, which allows the HR function to guide the developmental process.

The second persistent issue with appraisal is who does it. Organizational changes, such as wider spans of authority and involvement in a multiplicity of teams, make one-to-one appraisal of subordinates by a boss less satisfactory than ever. A combination of self- and superior-appraisal is the most common method, but this can be supplemented further by the involvement of peers, others for whom work is done, and even by one's own subordinates (Fletcher, 1993). The last – the principle of 'upward appraisal' – can take a number of forms:

- Appraisees having space to say what things management could do to help them improve their performance
- Making this more specific by identifying actual occasions when this could have made a difference
- Using an external agency to survey employees on aspects of their bosses' performance, and feeding this back for discussion (more common in the USA).

All these reflect the fact that, increasingly, people do not work in isolation but depend on one another. A sharing of views about individual and group contributions is the basis for improved *organizational* performance. However, such openness equally depends on an initial basis of trust. The power relationship is critical. If employees feel arbitrarily controlled through the way appraisal is conducted it will have limited benefits. If a system operates which has been foisted on people, especially one which uses targets in a coercive way, it will breed precisely the wrong attitudes in the longer term. While the private sector has shown a growing awareness of this, government-inspired schemes in the public sector have tended to do the opposite.

Given that a system needs to engage employees' consent, any organization that is dissatisfied with its system of appraisal could do worse than follow the example of the Nuffield Hospitals group by 'first conducting a staff survey to find out what staff feel about performance appraisals, whether current schemes were succeeding or failing, what managers were actually doing or not doing, and what kind of system people would favour' (Wilson and Cole, 1990).

Career development for organizational performance at Lucas Industries[3]

We end this chapter with an example of what one company, Lucas Industries, has done to implement a strategic HR approach which also embodies a philosophy of 'mutuality'. Figure 14.3 and the paper from which it is taken (Everest, 1993) captures many of the key themes in Chapters 13 and 14:

- It links personal development to business development via the

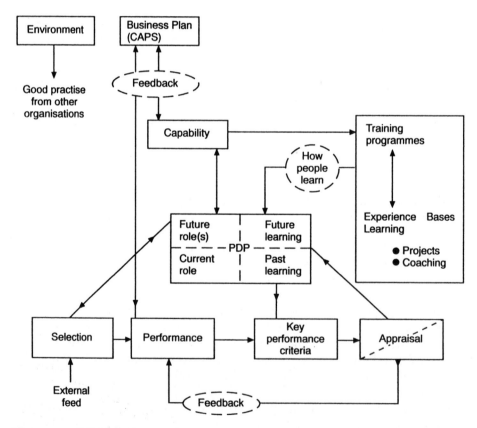

Figure 14.3 *A performance-oriented management-development system. (Source: Everest, 1993)*

business plan (CAP, or Competitiveness Achievement Plan) for each part of the company.

- It does so, however, in relation to broadly defined skills, knowledge, and attributes for the management population as a whole, covering both short-term 'individual performance' and longer-term 'collective capability'. Such skills, etc. are seen as quite specific to Lucas, and therefore there is some scepticism about the generic competency approach.

- Permeating the approach to management development is a belief in continuing learning, and hence the primacy of self-development:

  Seventy per cent of your learning comes from things you have done, twenty per cent from people who have influenced you, and a maximum of ten per cent is derived from off-line training programmes (Everest, 1993, p. 46).

- At the centre is the 'psychological contract' (or 'deal') in the form of a Personal Development Plan (PDP) for all managers (and eventually all employees). This addresses career development in a context of organizational uncertainty, not just for promotion candidates and high flyers. The PDP addresses individual learning requirements in the light of a person's present job and future prospects, and combines individual and organizational interests:

  The individual meets his or her needs for personal development, thus adding value to themselves, within a context prescribed by the needs of the organization. It's this sense of mutuality that must be maintained in an explicit manner (Everest, 1993, p. 44).

- The various components in the whole human resource system (selection, appraisal, pay and benefits, development and training) are managed as a series of inter-connected processes to promote the two key values of personal development and a performance orientation:

  It is important they all pull in the same direction. One important check is to ensure that the factors that drive the pay and benefit system do not conflict with the 'messages' conveyed by the approach to Management Development... Alignment of all the various components which add up to the perception of 'what is valued round here' is an important task for those charged with developing HR strategies in support of business objectives (Everest, 1993, p. 46).

Summary

We began this chapter by describing the size and composition of management with professional employees. We then considered the skills (or competences) managers use. Defining these in some degree is a necessary basis for selection and development. Love it or hate it, at the present time the management competences approach is impossible to ignore. Nevertheless, in keeping with the view developed in Chapter 10, there is a counterargument that action and learning – hence, action learning – are more important. Rather than prescribing competences and hence learning,

learning through action allows fuller play to individual differences and creativity. It also reflects a philosophy where the learner is in control, rather than someone else specifying the competences to learn.

In the context of management careers – something that managers and professionals have uniquely enjoyed – we then discussed the changing nature of the 'psychological contract' which binds managers to organizations. The concept of 'a career for life' has been eroding and internal labour markets have been breaking up. Managers and professionals are having to adjust to being part of an external labour market system, with greater mobility and insecurity. Organizations are also demanding more explicit and varied commitments to performance from managers.

An implicit renegotiation of the 'psychological contract' has been taking place, paralleling tangible changes in the employment contract affecting pay and job security. It is important, then, that negotiating the 'psychological contract' on issues like careers and opportunities is made more explicit, otherwise what organizations demand and expect from people will not be willingly rendered by employees. The 'psychological contract' is thus central to the ability of HRM to deliver on business strategy.

Pay is an important part of this contract. The shift to more performance-oriented systems, away from the idea of 'service' reflected in incremental salary scales, is another manifestation of change, with performance pay tending to be more individualized and attuned to the market. Short-term target-setting and achievement, however, contrasts with the encouragement of a wider set of behaviours which may pay off more in the long run. The use of pay as a sole or prime motivator may, in any case, be fundamentally misconceived. As we noted in Chapter 1, it is important to attend to the whole 'gestalt' of policies, not rely overmuch on pay: 'Pay typically needs to be less tightly tied to specific results or behaviour' (Beer, *et al.*, 1984).

The conduct of appraisal encapsulates these issues. Discussions about performance, development needs, job and career opportunities are the essence of 'psychological negotiating'. If appraisal dwells simply on performance to determine rewards or is used to berate employees, it fails to do its job with the underlying development of the organization in view.

Notes

1   I am grateful to Malcolm Ballin, Human Resources Director of British Steel, for permission to reproduce extracts from this article.
2   I am grateful to Tony Cockerill for permission to reproduce extracts from this article.
3   I am grateful to Nick Everest, Director, Group Management Development & Training for Lucas Industries, for permission to reproduce the diagram used here and for extracts from the article.

15

Managers in an international context

Introduction

The increasing internationalization of business presents many of the issues covered in the previous chapter in a particular form. First, internationalization touches on increasing numbers of managers and professionals. Second, internationalization puts a premium on certain competences (or skills). Third, managerial learning is a critical process in internationalization, with team-work strongly to the fore. Fourth, the management of careers in the context of internationalization gives many firms particular difficulties. In addition to these themes which connect with Chapter 14, organizational culture is a constant issue in most treatments of internationalization.

However, while problems and requirements may be exacerbated, it is important to recognize the continuities with domestic business activity. At a basic level, internationalization is simply about operating in expanded markets, and while geographical and cultural distances may be magnified, it is not helpful to erect mental barriers by thinking of internationalization as a quantum leap (Hendry, 1994).

Staffing in the international firm

International business comes in many forms. It includes domestic firms exporting; firms with subsidiaries abroad; alliances, ranging from joint ventures with shared equity to much looser arrangements to pool resources to purchase, market, research, or produce; and international companies of varying complexity and reach. Each of these calls on specific managerial skills and involves problems of allocating the managerial resource. Even so, there are again common elements and issues across the different forms – notably around processes of networking and team-work.

I have considered these different 'contexts' for internationalization elsewhere at length (Hendry, 1994). Here, we will just concentrate on the international firm as such, since it is where the bulk of 'international managers' are to be found.

International firms themselves vary considerably, depending on how many countries they deal in and how integrated and homogeneous are the markets for their goods in these countries. Successive evolutionary forms include:

- The multinational corporation (MNC)
- The global firm
- The international company
- The transnational organization

The last two have to cope with increasing degrees of complexity, as firms try to combine the advantages of scale and efficiency with responsiveness to local markets (Bartlett and Ghoshal, 1989). The transnational moreover aims to connect resources, innovations, and entrepreneurship which are spread throughout the company, in order to capitalize on the international firm's innovative capacity. This puts a premium on flexibility.

Complexity and flexibility present a challenge to systems of organizational control and to organizational coherence. They imply flexibility and diversity in organization structures and systems, and in management psychology, education, and working practices. Indeed, Bartlett and Ghoshal (1989, p. 17) see the issue as primarily about developing a new management mentality, rather than about a particular organizational form. Flexible thinking and flexible attitudes are the key management qualities in internationalization, whatever form it takes.

A model for staffing

From the beginning, a key issue for the internationalizing firm has been how to exercise and maintain control over its activities abroad. The four types of international organization imply different patterns of control, and consequently different sets of practices for moving staff about the organization. As the focus shifts towards maximizing innovativeness and being responsive to local conditions, the parent company at the centre dominates less. Approaches to staffing consequently vary from the ethnocentric, polycentric, and regiocentric, to the fully geocentric (Perlmutter, 1969), as centralization gives way to more highly devolved practices.

Ethnocentric staffing

With an ethnocentric staffing approach, strategic decisions are made at headquarters, subsidiaries have limited autonomy, and key jobs at home and abroad are filled by employees from headquarters. Nationals from the parent country dominate the organization at home and abroad.

Polycentric staffing

With polycentric staffing, each subsidiary is treated as a distinct national entity with local control of operations. However, headquarters controls key financial targets and investment decisions. Subsidiaries are managed by local nationals, but the key headquarters jobs remain with staff from the parent country.

Regiocentric staffing

Here, control within the group and the movement of staff is managed on a regional basis, reflecting the particular disposition of businesses and operations within the group. Regional managers have greater discretion in decisions. Movement of staff is largely restricted to geographic regions, though, and promotion to the very top jobs continues to be dominated by managers from the parent country.

Geocentric staffing

Finally, with geocentric staffing, business strategy is integrated on a thoroughly global basis. Staff development and promotion is based on ability, not nationality. The board and other parts of the top management structure are thoroughly international in composition. Needless to say, such organizations are uncommon.

Almost everything else in international HRM flows from the way the firm manages its movement of staff in one or other of these ways. Above all, the overall approach to staffing determines the degree of attention given, and the opportunities available, to each of three groups of employee – parent-country nationals (PCNs), host-country nationals (HCNs), and third-country nationals (TCNs) (Dowling and Schuler, 1990).

The typical multinational, for instance, tended to favour PCNs from the home (parent) country where the firm has its corporate headquarters. HCNS – the nationals of the country where subsidiaries are located – might tend to hold secondary positions to those which carry the real power, or gain advancement to placate local political sensitivities. Only in the highly integrated firm might one begin to find TCNs in positions of responsibility – such as where a UK manager takes up a position in a German subsidiary of a US-based firm.

As staffing policy shifts in these ways, so too does the attention given to different kinds of HRM activity. Thus, as a firm becomes progressively more internationalized, attention in HRM can be expected to shift from:

1 The selection of expatriates (PCNs) and the management of their terms and conditions to
2 Training in preparation for assignments and managing staff through a formal career system, with their personal development for international roles in mind – including the gradual extension of this system to an increasingly diverse and dispersed population of HCNs and TCNs to
3 A broader educational effort to internationalize the organization at large, with a focus on cultural change.

Trends in international staffing

In recent years, (2) and (3) have come more to the fore, as international firms provide shorter, more frequent overseas assignments, and as increasing internationalization makes it necessary to influence the attitudes and perspectives of a wider swathe of employees to develop an international outlook. Moreover, while such shifts are driven primarily by the market structures firms are in, socio-cultural and financial environments also have a strong influence. Thus, American multinationals appear to have been cutting back on their use of expatriates, for reasons of cost and politics and the difficulties they have experienced in sending people abroad:

> US MNCs are increasing their use of TCNs and HCNs mainly for cost and political reasons. As they do, the issues of training and retaining TCNs and HCNs will grow in importance and MNCs will have to give more consideration to career opportunities and career paths for TCNs and HCNs (Dowling and Schuler, 1990, p. 70).

This may also represent a necessary readjustment as American firms become less ethnocentric and more responsive to local conditions.

In contrast, Japanese firms rely heavily on expatriates to exercise control and to extend distinctive Japanese management practices. As an illustration:

> [The Japanese firm Kao] has a cadre of sixty expatriate Japanese managers and technicians running overseas operations with only 2,000 employees. This is more than double the number of American expatriates its U.S. based competitor Proctor and Gamble has in an international business with total sales over twenty times larger. More significantly, all of the top management positions in Kao's overseas companies and most of the level below that are Japanese nationals; in P&G only five of the 44 subsidiary general managers are American. A similar contrast can be made between Matsushita and 3M. The former has over 800 expatriates in an international business with 40,000 employees; the American company has less than 100 expatriates to manage its 38,000 employees (Bartlett and Yoshihara, 1988, p. 25).

This kind of direct, close control can be attributed to the Japanese system of *nemawashi* (consensus building) and *ringi* (shared decision making), both of which depend on close physical proximity and shared cultural values (Bartlett and Yoshihara, 1988). However, this is not easily sustained over a long distance except through large numbers of expatriates and frequent trips back and forth from Japan – a practice the Japanese have dubbed 'jet age *nemawashi*'.

Relying on expatriates to this degree is exceedingly expensive. The British company, BP, for instance, has estimated that its use of expatriates costs around $400 million a year (approximately £240 million). A sharp rise in the cost of air travel or an unfavourable shift in the rate of currency exchange (a rapidly rising yen, for example) can make the economics of expatriatism suddenly prohibitive. Equally, as the Japanese move increasingly from an export strategy to direct investment in North America and Europe it puts considerable pressure on their firms to meet the demand for expatriates. Such factors can force a company to change its style of control over overseas subsidiaries.

For the UK, there is a general dearth of information on the numbers of expatriates employed by top companies and the kind of assignments involved, although Scullion (1991) has reported an increasing use of expatriates in a sample of forty-five British and Irish firms, and anecdotal evidence suggests an increasing preference for shorter assignments.

The following sections will now consider the themes of selection (along with the management of terms and conditions), training, careers, and culture as each comes to the fore as the emphasis in internationalization changes.

Selection and management of expatriates

Once a firm begins to send people abroad, the functional tasks for HRM assume a new level of complexity, regardless of how similar the underlying issues are for the managers involved themselves. Expatriate management generates a series of tasks and involvements for the HRM function which are unique to the international setting. These include:

- Additional functions and activities (such as international taxation, relocation and orientation, administrative services for expatriates, host government relations, and language services)
- The need for a broader perspective (an awareness of the complex pay equity issues that arise, for example, when employees of different nationalities work together)
- Greater involvement in employees' lives (such as more direct contact with the employee's family) in smoothing the transition from home to abroad and back again
- Changing the emphasis of activity as the balance of the workforce between PCNs and HCNs varies
- Exposure to greater risk through the financial costs of overseas assignments and the high risk of failure
- More external influences (from governments of different political complexions, differently managed economies, and culturally specific ways of doing business) (Dowling, 1988).

Terms and conditions

For many companies, especially HR departments, it often seems that expatriate management is simply about the terms and conditions under which a person goes abroad. Many seem to view the determination of pay as the only problem they need to address. Admittedly, this is a complex and highly technical area, and consultancies specialize in advising on compensation packages for expatriates. This is especially important for taxation, where the type of package can materially affect the resulting tax burden.

There are two alternative starting points for arriving at a final salary:

- The company's UK salary structure, or
- Local pay scales in the host country.

A third approach combines the two.

The 'home-based system' or 'build-up' method

The first method adjusts the expatriate's equivalent home salary and benefits according to cost-of-living indices and exchange rates in the visiting country.

The 'host country' system

The second approach uses comparable local rates and compensates for additional costs in working overseas. Either of these may form the basis of a company's policy.

The 'balance sheet' approach

The 'balance sheet' approach combines the two and seeks to reconcile overall benefits and costs (Reynolds, 1986). As part of this 'balance sheet', the following factors need to be taken into account:

- Taxation on basic salary, bonuses, and prerequisites (depending on where the salary is paid and in which currency)
- Pension, social security/national insurance, and other company and state contributions and benefits, to provide continuity in such personal schemes to which individuals belong
- Allowances to compensate for additional costs, such as shipping and storage, housing, education, medical cover, and home leave.

Expatriate pay schemes have to try to do three things:

- Maintain relativity with host-based colleagues and protect the purchasing power and standard of living of the assignee
- Protect the terms of domestic contracts (such as pensions)
- Provide motivation for the inconvenience of relocating abroad and compensate for the discomforts of particular locations.

Expatriate compensation has to be perceived as fair and equitable for both the expatriate and those he or she works alongside (taking into account the whole range of national differences in basic levels of pay, taxation, side-benefits, pensions, and so forth). It has to be presented in a clearly understood form. Also, it has to be controlled so that the company does not end up paying inflated rates which encumber it as international activity grows (Barham and Oates, 1991). Similar principles apply to compensation generally.

The failure of expatriate assignments

While pay issues are one dominant concern, a second issue is the failure of expatriate assignments. This is apparently a serious problem for American firms, for whom failure rates have been variously estimated at 25–40 per cent (Mendenhall and Oddou, 1985) to nearer 70 per cent in developing countries (Desatnick and Bennett, 1978). Among European and Japanese multinationals, failure rates are far less (Tung, 1982; Scullion, 1991). However, this should not obscure the fact that all multinationals have a problem. Any level of failure represents a serious problem organizationally and for individual careers since the people concerned are likely to be either senior employees or potential high flyers. Moreover, as Scullion observes, defining failure in terms of premature return or recall before the completion of an assignment may conceal higher levels of effective failure, since companies and the employees concerned may not want to lose face by early recall.

The selection and training of expatriates is a critical issue, therefore. What are the reasons for failure, and what are the rules for success? There is a fair measure of agreement as to the key things to focus on. These cover:

- Selecting for intercultural competence
- Including the family in selection and preparation
- Training.

Selecting for intercultural competence

The criteria for selecting people for assignments abroad in practice are overwhelmingly based on a person's technical competence to do the job. However, a successful domestic track record and knowing a company's systems and procedures are no guarantee of success in an overseas posting. Technical competence is obviously essential – the 'bedrock on which other skills must be founded' (Barham and Oates, 1991, p. 70).

Nevertheless, the lack of attention by comparison to relational abilities is surprising. When asked what they regard as important to success in a foreign assignment, managers themselves tend to cite such skills as 'adaptability to new situations, 'sensitivity to different cultures', 'ability to work in international teams', and 'relationship skills' (Barham and Oates, 1991, p. 102).

However, defining and evaluating such qualities (or 'competences') prospectively is not easy, even though there are psychometric tests around that purport to do so. The majority of studies, in fact, show relatively modest results when it comes to predicting a person's success in a foreign culture (Gertsen, 1990). Certain criteria often assumed to be positive indicators – such as ease in absorbing 'culture shock' – appear on closer investigation to have a negative impact. Thus, if a person is immune to differences in culture, they are not likely to be sensitive in responding to them (Hawes and Kealey, 1981; Ratiu, 1983).

A key factor seems to be the interest a person has in the world around them. At a personal level, this means being interested in other peoples, their history, politics, culture and language. Part of the communication skill involved in this is the way a person interprets behaviour and evaluates individuals. Too great a readiness to categorize and form fixed judgements about people is characteristic of a less adaptive, ethnocentric outlook (Detweiler, 1980; Ratiu, 1983).

Such qualities together are often defined as 'intercultural competence'. They comprise a mix of personality and attitude traits, knowledge and cognitive skills, and communication skills (Gertsen, 1990). The latter must include language ability, but perhaps more important it means the behavioural skills to be able and willing to engage in another language even though linguistically a person is not proficient.

The family

Personal qualities, however, are only part of the problem. The most frequently cited reason for an assignment ending early is the inability of the partner of the person being sent abroad to adjust to a different physical or cultural environment (Tung, 1982). It is usually the partner and children who have to engage most closely with the host culture, including managing the local language, yet they are often neglected in the selection and preparation for an assignment. It is important therefore to include the whole family in discussions about any intended move, and to address basic practical issues such as children's education, housing, and employment for the spouse.

Once abroad, a company can ease the transition by helping the family to develop or connect with a social support network in the host country. The old colonial companies were good at this. Equally, however, they invariably insulated the family from the local population and customs in a colonial ghetto, and risked creating antagonism with the local community. Now this is less the case, at least for UK expatriates, as many more assignments will be in Europe and North America where the standard of living is often higher than in the UK.

Often the family issue intrudes regardless, with employees ruling themselves out from overseas assignments because of family ties. This is increasingly a problem with the growth of dual-career families and an unwillingness to disrupt children's education. Some companies are looking at ways round this by focusing international moves on employees early and late in their careers, allowing for a period of greater stability when staff have school-age children and spouses are building their own careers. This in turn means adjusting the company's career management process. This is a good instance of the changing 'psychological contract' in the international context.

Selection for expatriate management needs to take into account, then, a range of issues to do with the person (centred on the notion of intercultural competence) and a range of situational factors (including family circumstances and job requirements) (Gertsen, 1990).

Preparation and training

In practice, many companies have only a very limited number of people who are suitably qualified technically or who can be spared from the home operation. In such circumstances training and preparation become all the more important. Table 15.1 shows the frequency with which companies use different methods to prepare assignees. As the list in Table 15.1 suggests, training can vary considerably in depth, from 'information-giving approaches', through 'affective (or behavioural) approaches' using devices like role plays, to 'immersion approaches' (Landis and Brislin, 1983; Mendenhall, Dunbar, and Oddou, 1987).

Table 15.1 Preparing managers for international postings

(% of respondents ranking an activity as among the five most important methods in their organization)

Arranging for managers to visit host country	79
Language training for managers	73
Briefing by host country managers	67
In-house general management course	44
Cross-cultural training for managers	42
Cross-cultural training for family	38
General management course at business school	29
Language training for family	23
Training in negotiating within business norms of host country	17

Source: Reproduced with permission from Barham and Oates (1991).

Views differ, however, on the value of pre-training, especially cross-cultural training. While cross-cultural training has strong advocates (for example, Landis and Brislin, 1983), top management tend to see it as unnecessary (Mendenhall and Oddou, 1985), believing that real learning cannot occur until the person is in position abroad. This obviously parallels the wider debate about the value of off-the-job versus on-the-job learning, and the issue of transfer of learning.

A solution is not to look on the skills needed in international assignments as qualitatively unique or different from good management or people skills. Just as the desirable qualities in selection closely resemble good people skills, so training should aim to develop skills of generic application. These can be topped up with knowledge that is then specific to the particular country a person is heading for.

One does not, for instance, have to cross national borders to acquire cross-cultural experiences. Opportunities abound in any country (such as the UK, Holland, or the USA) with diverse religions, racial and ethnic groups, and in the possibilities to mix with groups differentiated by class, age, or sex. As Lobel (1990) argues:

> Skills for global leadership may be quite generic in application to other management contexts... training programmes should attempt to impart generalizable skills by which individuals 'learn how to learn' in any intercultural setting and engage in team building activities with diverse individuals (p. 44).

Organizations can structure normal training activities around such opportunities. What is more, this would make a valuable contribution to equal opportunities generally.

A focused version of this has been used at BP by Neale and Mindel (1992), derived from Indrei Ratiu's (1983) model of 'red and blue loop learning'. This assumes that in order to understand another culture, people have to understand their own culture first – or at least have a working concept of it. They need to understand the processes which helped them to arrive at their own set of values, beliefs, ways of behaving, and perceptions of others. Once they have more awareness of their own cultural frame of reference, they can compare a variety of unfamiliar situations against this, appreciate the differences, and handle communication better.

Having people from other cultures participating obviously helps to focus on differences and promote self-awareness. Cultural training centres (such as Farnham Castle in Kent) work on this principle. Business schools similarly report that the feature students most value on courses is an international student group, so that different ways of looking at problems are highlighted.

The other issue is, when should training for international assignments take place? Too often it is a last-minute activity, consisting therefore of no more than a series of hurried factual briefings. Many advocate that preparation should start up to a year beforehand. Again, this implies a system of company training which encourages qualities and attributes of general application in domestic and international settings.

Managing careers

The attitude firms have towards the training and preparation of employees for overseas assignments marks a significant shift in their perspective on internationalization. The difference is between the firm that neglects training and sees it as a one-off event prior to an assignment and the firm which integrates it into a broader concept of management development and international careers. Training and career development are thus entwined.

Selecting someone for an overseas assignment should be a career management decision, integrated into a system of continuous development. In this way, selecting someone ceases to be a last-minute decision, or if unavoidably an opportunity suddenly arises or things do not go according to plan, the company has people poised to move into place. Part of such a process has to be an open approach to career planning, in which individuals have an understanding of the company's intentions internationally and for themselves, and can therefore initiate relevant self-development, such as learning a language. Again, this implies a mutually negotiated 'psychological contract'.

Organizations typically encounter two problems with expatriates which expose deficiencies in their career systems:

- First is the difficulty they often have in finding suitable people to choose from in making international assignments.
- Second is the problem they have in fitting them back into the organization to the employee's satisfaction and to the advantage of the company.

Expatriate assignments need to be viewed, then, as part of a career process, and managed through a career system which integrates domestic and international requirements.

Expatriation

Many firms face a simple problem of immaturity. The newly internationalizing firm lacks critical mass in the numbers of employees undertaking international assignments and therefore has difficulty managing flows out of and back into domestic operations. For the same reason, effective training in preparation for assignments is less likely to occur without the backing of a career system oriented towards international activity. However, the difficulties firms encounter often reflect on the adequacy in general of their career management.

With an inadequate management cadre to begin with, one of the key decisions is whether to take one's best people from valuable domestic operations to staff international activity. The best, most experienced people are probably already managing important activities. To take such a person(s) may involve significant opportunity costs in resourcing new ventures overseas. One solution is to use not established senior staff but relative newcomers. Newcomers are likely to be more natural 'product champions' for new ventures, since they have a reputation to make, not one to lose.

This approach, however, runs against the grain of selecting people primarily for their technical expertise and company knowledge. Conformity to company practice, however, may not be the quality that is most likely to succeed in strange places.

A second problem that reflects on a management development and career-pathing system more generally is the requirement of internationalization for more rounded general managers. Initial ventures inevitably operate on a smaller scale and therefore involve general management skills. A management development system geared to a larger domestic organization, however, may be more inclined to develop people up functional ladders in their early careers. This virtually compels the firm to staff international ventures with senior staff.

However, as international activity grows, the development of an international cadre, with experience of a variety of functions, businesses, and countries, will tend to acquire its own momentum.

Repatriation

The second career-management problem involves 'repatriates'. This has received far less recognition. For many of the most internationalized British firms, we may surmise that this is in part because becoming an expatriate was for many employees a long-term career decision, which only ended on retirement (and often, not even then).

Where employees return after shorter spells of duty, the problems encountered include:

- Being forgotten once out on assignment
- Becoming disconnected from the power system, decision-making centres, and corporate succession plans
- Returning to less challenging jobs (Torbiorn, 1982; Adler, 1986; Tung, 1989; Derr and Oddou, 1991).

The feeling of being forgotten can be overcome by assigning a personal 'mentor' back home. This relationship should begin before departure in discussing and ironing out likely problems. The mentor should then provide contact while away and help with discussing career changes on return. Bringing the expatriate back at regular intervals for debriefing on business issues, and giving them an opportunity to participate in conferences or workshops at home, are other ways of engaging the expatriate. Repatriation thus becomes part of an overall career management process. Equally important, these mechanisms provide opportunities for the company itself to absorb the knowledge an expatriate has gained on assignment.

The problem of re-entry is compounded by the fact that employees have often become accustomed to a higher level of responsibility and power than they could have expected at home. On return, they have to fit into a longer hierarchy at what feels to be a more junior level. The loss of stimulus and feelings of not being properly valued can therefore make retention a problem. Surveys in the USA have consequently found high levels of turnover among repatriates (Moran, Stahl and Boyer, 1989; Korn/Ferry International, 1986). A mentor can prepare the returning expatriate, deal with the inevitable 'low' during resettlement, and reassure them of their long-term career prospects.

Such problems with repatriates are the obverse of expatriate failure and reveal a failure to sustain long-term career development processes. Expatriate–repatriate problems tend to be linked therefore:

- International assignments are not regarded as developmental, with a

path to top management, and international know-how is not regarded as a source of competitive advantage
- Selection is not backed by a strategic HR planning process that identifies needs and ensures, in turn, that re-entry is to positions identified some while in advance
- Preparation is sporadic
- Support while away is negligible (Derr and Oddou, 1991).

Internationalizing the organization

The discussion above of expatriates and managing careers has been largely ethnocentric, with career movements to and from the parent country. The more thoroughly international a company becomes, however, the more it draws on multiple centres of expertise, and the more the career system is characterized by two-way movements. The career system itself becomes an instrument in maintaining cohesion as the organization becomes more complex.

In addition, integration and cohesion comes to depend increasingly on cultural norms rather than on formal structural controls and reporting relationships. Such norms are promoted through the management development system, as employees move from country to country, as well as through more diffuse educational efforts to internationalize the organization at large. As Evans, Lank and Farquhar (1989) observe:

> Attention in recent years has been focused, with varying degrees of success, on integrating the decentralised firm in more soft and subtle ways – first, through programs to create an overriding corporate culture, and second, through international executive development (p. 117).

Finally, team-work becomes a crucial device for maintaining cohesion.

Internationalizing BP

These elements can be seen coming increasingly to the fore in the evolution of BP. For many years, the focus was on long-term expatriate assignments from the UK to manage overseas oil production sites. Then, in the 1970s and 1980s, as BP acquired non-oil companies, greater use began to be made of short-term secondments to integrate the new acquisitions (while still maintaining an expatriate workforce in oil in the Middle East). Finally, BP has been turning itself into a genuinely international company, with the recognition that the UK can learn from its overseas subsidiaries. As part of this, increasing use has been made of two-way secondments on a two- to three-year basis.

These kind of assignments mean accommodating the interests and development needs of individuals, businesses, and functions.

> This requires negotiation, rather than the old 'postings' culture directed by central personnel, and a sophisticated career management system. In practice, these negotiations are managed through the regional structures of the group and its constituent businesses.
>
> However, while the flow of assignments provides the basis for transferring learning and best practice throughout the organization, the key to making this effective is the management of culture, and specifically the creation of a team culture. Considerable effort has therefore gone into developing a new set of cultural values that emphasize team-work, openness, networking, and less fixation on a person's status. This has included educational programmes to raise awareness of different cultures within the group (as distinct from cultural training simply to prepare people for assignments abroad), along with new reward and appraisal structures to support team-work.

We will now look at the role of corporate culture and team-work in internationalizing management.

Corporate culture

The role of corporate culture as an integrating force in the large international firm is controversial. Many, like Bartlett and Ghoshal (1989) and Barham and Oates (1991), lay particular emphasis on the promotion of core values with which employees (and especially managers) can identify with around the world: 'A clear philosophy and values provide[s] a strong context in which people can plan and act' (Barham and Oates, 1991, p. 46). Others relate this more closely to management development and team-working processes (Evans, Lank and Farquhar, 1989) – in other words, to the essential socializing processes through which values are transmitted.

Shell, one of the world's most internationalized companies (as well as a highly decentralized one), recognizes the formal and informal elements of culture and socialization structures which hold the group together as comprising:

- A strongly communicated set of behavioural values about what is and is not acceptable behaviour
- A written set of ethical business principles, set out in 1984
- A well-understood reward and promotion structure through which senior employees are socialized
- A world-wide expatriate cadre of 5000 managers who act as a corporate resource
- The use of English as the common language among managers in the group (despite the fact that Shell is half Dutch-owned and run).

Despite Shell's success in maintaining cultural coherence the idea of an 'international corporate culture' is a tricky one, since it tends to evoke an ethnocentric worldview, determined centrally in the parent country. The issue is whether corporate culture should be a cultural export, through which the firm, in its parent country, tries to get people to do and think in the same way; or whether national differences are taken seriously and allowed to have expression. Diversity and respect for diversity then become key values in their own right.

Underlying this is the question of which is the more powerful influence on individual behaviour – national or corporate culture? Hofstede's (1980) study of culture in IBM provided a powerful affirmation of national differences at a time when the world was apparently moving towards dominance by large corporations. Thus, his survey of attitudes among IBM employees in fifty countries – in a company renowned for its powerful corporate culture – found systematic differences between nationalities on four dimensions – 'power distance', 'collectivism/individualism', 'feminity/ masculinity', and 'uncertainty avoidance'. He argued therefore that organization culture often operates on behaviour at a relatively superficial level, finding expression principally in symbols, heroes, and rituals.

Similarly, as a result of prolonged studies with managers attending INSEAD programmes, Laurent (1986) has concluded that 'the most powerful determinant of their assumptions was by far their nationality' (p. 93).

While being wary of rigid national stereotypes, such differences between peoples have significant implications for many aspects of managerial and non-managerial work. These include:

- The motivation to work (Adler, 1986)
- The willingness to take risks (Cummings, Harnett and Stevens, 1971)
- Interpersonal skills (Bass and Burger, 1979)
- Speed of decision making and the search for consensus (Harper, 1988; Heller and Yukl, 1969; Axelsson *et al.*, 1991).

Whereas the 'corporate culture' concept slides over these differences, the 'national differences' perspective says that it is necessary to recognize these and work with them. This can be particularly important for HRM where institutional differences and origins are important in the design of systems and practices. National differences within the organization should be explored when seeking to 'export' systems such as appraisal and pay – and equally when applying them to diverse groups at home.

Team-work

Internationalization puts a premium on team-work in a variety of settings and stages of development, although its importance is often not recognized until situations become complex.

Team-work in starting international ventures

The initial step in going international is itself likely to mean bringing together a range of resources and skills. If an organization does not habitually do this, but has groups of specialists working independently, it will have difficulty getting started. Many organizations in the UK and Western countries generally have until recently suffered from compartmentalized organization structures. On this basis, it seems fairly obvious that individualized pay and promotion systems will also not support the necessary cooperation. In such circumstances, international activities may be started by individuals or groups, but as soon as performance suffers a hiccough they are likely to back off from overseas commitments.

Team-work in joint ventures

Western firms have also been castigated for failing to provide the basis for effective learning in joint ventures. This also comes back to lack of team-work. There are other issues involved – such as failing to prepare managers to participate in joint ventures and failure to formulate learning as a prime objective. But organizational fragmentation and a short-term focus in payment and appraisal systems are critical.

In contrast, the superior ability of Japanese firms to learn is attributed to the qualities of team-work at which their firms excel (Pucik, 1988; Hamel, 1991). Team-work helps to translate individual learning into collective knowledge, by making sure it is shared. Thus, the Japanese have 'put in place managerial systems that encourage extensive horizontal and vertical information flow and support the transfer of know-how from the partnership to the rest of the organization' (Pucik, 1988, p. 81). While team-work is a general cultural thing, developed through work practices generally, human resource policies on a wide front can contribute to an effective learning infrastructure.

Managing complexity in the international firm

Finally, team-work is critical in the complex international firm in helping to exploit synergies in products, processes, and research. The role of teams in this process has been described by Weick and Van Orden (1990) in terms of matching the complexity of the environment and of problems with teams which can combine a variety of perspectives and resolve differences in face-to-face communication. Teams and small groups provide the ideal forum for communication on global issues because potentially they can include sufficient internal diversity to match the diversity of the environment with which they are trying to deal.

However, such groups have to be 'effective', with relationships based on trust, honesty, and self-respect among members. Common organizational values (with the reservations previously stated) contribute to the 'strong organizational context' (Barham and Oates, 1991) within which trust can flourish; while common socialization develops a basis of tacit and implicit knowledge which can help teams to function more smoothly.

The following account shows the emphasis placed on face-to-face contacts world-wide in one division of one company.

Team-work at IMI

In 1982, IMI became the world's biggest manufacturer and supplier of drinks-dispensing equipment for soft drinks and beer when it acquired sites in the USA, Canada, and Brazil and a world-wide network of sales and servicing companies to go with five sites it already had in Europe. As an international group fronting up to the likes of Coca-Cola and Pepsi, it was logical to run it as an wholly integrated international group.

Developing this integration meant the transfer of technology and coordination of marketing world-wide. To facilitate this, multidiscipline, multinational teams were set up 'to create the right team spirit, crossing the cultures'. After two to three years, however, this had lost its dynamism as a way of breaking down barriers, and was dissolved in favour of more direct meetings between the three territorial managing directors. Similar direct contacts between other functional heads, such as purchasing, also took place periodically each year. In addition to this, the group managing director fostered a culture of face-to-face relationships 'to get a group cultural rapport':

> Sometimes you think it's a waste of money, to get on a plane, and go across and spend a week in Germany, to understand the mentality. But business is all about people – just to see each other and build up a relationship, and motivate people by letting them know they work for the same company as part of a team. I take them on a few jollies and get them together in a relaxed sort of mentality, whether it's on the beach or some hotel location. They work hard, but then you get a mixed culture and they'll talk to each other. You have to have these informal means of communication.
>
> You have to go under the skin. You have to sniff out, to understand people and what makes them tick. You know some directors are conservative, some over-optimistic. You can set financial targets to them, but figures are one thing, you have to know what's underneath. If you rely on just seeing figures, that's only half the story. That's why I physically go out quarterly to all of them so I can speak to them (Hendry and Pettigrew, 1989, p. 88–92).

International managers

The internationalization of firms means increasing importance for 'international' employees; while the encouragement from the Single European Market to form 'European' firms heralds the emergence of a new breed of

'Euromanager' (Bruce, 1989). It is important, however, to discriminate between the different types of employee who can be expected to be internationally mobile. In one of the few studies on the international managerial labour market, Atkinson (1989) distinguishes four groups:

- Senior managers
- Scientific and technical staff
- Younger managers on development programmes who can expect to experience international assignments
- Graduate recruits.

Senior managers

This group is critical to the success of international businesses, but those with adequate international experience are in short supply (*International Management*, 1986; Scullion, 1992). The numbers involved, however, are very small. Even most multinationals count them in tens rather than hundreds, and even in the largest firms they number only about two hundred. They are 'numerically insignificant' but 'qualitatively vital'.

In the past, firms relied on internal development as much as on external recruitment for this group. Many firms, however, are now looking increasingly to outside recruitment. Among the reasons for this are:

- A shortage of managers with the necessary depth of experience
- The failure of past ways of organizing and developing this cadre to produce the requisite depth and breadth of experience – specifically, the failure of the expatriate system to move people around sufficiently
- Increasing demand as firms move into new geographical markets.

Scientific and technical staff

This group follows the international division of R&D, being attracted by superior resources, job challenge, and the proximity of an academic scientific research milieu. The attraction of a warm climate to work in also ranks high in many sectors. The leading figures tend to be personally known to a company's own R&D staff, although active recruitment is likely to lie with specialist headhunters.

Younger managers

There have been significant changes in internal management development systems in relation to this group. This reflects dissatisfaction with the old expatriate system and new demands affecting senior managers. International firms are seeking to create a larger, more flexible internal labour market of young, internationally experienced managers as a way of overcoming the shortage of suitably qualified senior executives. The result is the emphasis on early, shorter, and more frequent assignments for promising young managers, referred to above.

Graduates

The above groups have a fully international profile. For graduates, however, the European labour market is of more immediate significance, at least as far as British and Continental firms are concerned. As the feedstock to management development programmes and for scientific/technical activity, graduate recruitment is of special interest to companies and policy makers.

Graduates can be expected to be increasingly mobile within Europe because of the imbalances in supply and demand from different educational systems. In this respect, British-based companies seem to be particularly vulnerable to an exodus of young people (Bruce, 1989; Scullion, 1992). All companies, however, face problems in going outside their own country to recruit. The reasons include:

- Lack of knowledge of local labour markets
- Lacking a physical presence in the other country, which makes it harder to attract good local candidates
- Ignorance of the local education system and the status of qualifications
- Variability in the experience and qualifications of graduates, given the different structures of national educational systems
- Trying to transfer native recruitment methods to other countries where different systems may apply
- Language and other cultural problems in conducting interviews
- Pay differences and expectations about pay
- Constraints on and attitudes to mobility (Atkinson, 1989; Barham and Oates 1991; Scullion, 1992).

Summary

This chapter has reviewed the human resource problems international firms face as they become progressively more internationalized. In the process the international firm has to address a range of problems, from managing expatriates through to creating an organizational culture which can act as a 'glue' for people in many different countries. The form such issues take can be traced to a large extent to the model of staffing that permeates the organization.

While we have addressed specific functional issues for HRM, such as how the pay and careers of managers are handled, in describing these processes we have applied a broad perspective to HRM. HRM is not just what HRM managers do. It includes human resource development in its broadest sense – that is, people's skills and how they work together in teams. These can be partly developed through training and planned development; more often they are formed through experience. The line manager, senior executive, and human resource specialist can contribute to this by providing a positive climate for people to develop themselves.

16

Manual and clerical employees

Introduction

In this chapter and the next we look at specific issues for the management of clerical and manual employees. The treatment of these topics is not confined to this chapter, however. Many are addressed elsewhere in the book, as in the extended case examples of Chapters 7, 8, 12, and 13. Hopefully these have provided a variety of insights into managing the employment relationship. In addition, Chapter 3 reviewed the extent to which particular policies associated with HRM have been adopted to promote commitment, flexibility, and quality. To help the reader locate the range of themes, it may be useful, therefore, to take a few moments in the first part of this chapter to recap on those already covered elsewhere.

HRM and the shopfloor: a recap on themes

Chapter 3 concluded by arguing that the 'strategic integration' of employment practices was what most distinguished HRM. The cases developed in the course of this book have therefore emphasized an holistic approach to employment. They show the response to a business situation as a stream of activity searching for a new pattern of coherence. Nevertheless, the cases have also exemplified particular themes.

Commitment and collective bargaining

The Fibres case in Chapter 13 described an attempt to reconstruct employment relationships to foster greater commitment. As an Anglo-American joint venture, Fibres sought to get away from the adversarial industrial relations which prevailed in other of the UK company's sites, with new structures modelled on Japanese firms in the UK. These included harmonized terms of employment, high pay, and an elaborate system of employee communication and involvement focused on a works council (or 'Advisory Board'). The aim was to marginalize, though not to exclude trade unions, since a single-union agreement existed. The system was also 'collectivist', rather than 'individualized', through the range of shared constitutional structures put in place.

In Chapter 8 we saw an established company, Pilkington, pursuing a more indirect approach, with a number of aims directed at involvement, commitment, flexibility, and control over pay. This case illustrated the complex process of decentralization which has been a dominant feature of organizational change and the remodelling of industrial relations over the last fifteen years. Chapter 5 provided a model and further illustration of this.

To summarise, these chapters provide examples of:

- Harmonized terms of employment
- Systems of consultation
- Decentralized collective bargaining.

Flexibility

Flexibility comes in a number of forms. So far, the principal illustration of this has been the 'numerical' flexibility achieved through 'core–periphery' strategies in the Construction Co. case in Chapter 12. Chapter 18 will also address this. Chapter 3 assessed the extent and scope of 'functional (or job) flexibility at some length, noting that it has been at the forefront of efforts to improve productivity in British firms. The fullest treatment of this will come in Chapter 17 with the Hardy Spicer case. 'Financial' flexibility has featured so far only slightly in the chapter on management.

Quality

Chapter 3 defined the pursuit of quality in two ways – developing a quality workforce with suitable skills and promoting consciousness of quality in goods and services produced. We illustrated the latter through programmes for cultural change and TQM with the Barclaycard case in Chapter 7, while noting that quality circles, although their use has increased, have often failed to deliver. Chapter 19 will look at a quality workforce developed through training in terms of the national system, while examples of company practice can be found in most of the case chapters, including Chapter 17 to come.

Strategic coherence

To repeat, however, the key distinguishing feature of HRM is its strategic quality. What personnel and HR professionals should aim at is strategic coherence. It is important to remember, therefore, that the topics in this chapter – 'employee commitment and the skills revolution', 'pay', 'collective bargaining', and 'training' – are not significant in isolation. They take on particular importance under different employment systems. No prescription in any of these areas on its own can be relied on to be effective if it is not supported in other areas. A strategic approach, moreover, is characterized by the way in which problems are tackled as much as by particular solutions. Chapter 17 illustrates this through a case study of technical change.

Employee commitment and the skills revolution

The heading for this section is in fact the title of a recent report in which 3855 people in employment nation-wide were interviewed during May-September 1992 (Gallie and White, 1993). The report begins with the observation that there has been a skills revolution, and that over the last five years this has extended to more and more people. For example, 63 per cent of skilled manual and 70 per cent of lower non-manual workers said that the skills involved in their work had increased. Even among semi- and non-skilled manual workers many more had seen their skills increase than diminish (45 per cent as against 15 per cent).

Computers have been the driving force in this, and have helped to transform the work of women especially. Types of skill have also been changing, with more emphasis on monitoring and social skills. Finally, a majority (62 per cent), across all groups, felt that they were having to work harder.

This trend towards upskilling provides the background to the question of commitment. On this, the survey concludes:

> Employee participation is of fundamental importance for employees' attitudes to the technical and organizational changes that have been transforming British industry. . . (Gallie and White, 1993, p. x).
>
> The most significant type of participation in this respect is the opportunity to take part in decisions that involve changes in the organization of work (Gallie and White, 1993, p. 44).

While employees in general, and most noticeably skilled manual workers, reported an increase in their influence over their immediate work tasks, their influence over technical and organizational change was much less – averaging 32 per cent for all employees, and between 20 and 28 per cent for lower non-manual, skilled manual, and semi- and non-skilled manual workers. In this respect, quality circles (experienced by 20 per cent of the sample) were regarded as highly effective in heightening employee involvement. This figure corresponds fairly closely with the WIRS3 finding that 23 per cent of firms had adopted them (Millward *et al.*, 1992).

The Gallie/White survey is then especially revealing about the influences on specific work performance. The main influences on quality were said to be, in descending order:

- Own discretion

- Clients/customers
- Targets
- One's supervisor/boss.

For quality, the influences altered slightly:

- Own discretion
- Clients/customers
- Supervisor/boss
- Targets.

In comparison, pay incentives featured very low down. The perception and role of supervisors, however, was interesting. The majority of employees did not see their supervisors having a great direct influence over their work, nor was supervision especially tight. However, best practice and actual practice may be at odds, and the report concludes that:

> None the less, we found strong links between supervisory standards and practices on the one hand, and the perceived efficiency of the organization on the other.
>
> Employees evidently recognize that supervisors contribute to organizational effectiveness when they:
>
> - give strong messages about standards
> - monitor performance
> - exercise control over work effort and quality.
>
> Of these three it is the first (providing messages about standards) which emerges as the most universal role of supervision. . .
>
> Even more important than any of these, however, is the supervisor's role in employee development. This proved not only to have a considerable impact upon perceived organizational effectiveness, but also to be critical for the satisfactoriness of the relationship with the supervisor (Gallie and White, 1993, p. 58).

Moroever, supervisory styles that emphasized team-working and down-played status differentials between supervisors and supervised generated the highest levels of satisfaction.

Commitment, supervision, and performance

Attitudinal and perceptual data from employees may be rather one-sided in identifying what matters. It has compelling support, however, from a study which has looked directly at both workplace practices and performance. This concludes that: 'World-class plants have much more active structures for shopfloor problem-solving and improvement; production team leaders play a particularly significant role in these plants' (Oliver, Dellendge, Jones and Lowe, 1994). Evidence on the performance of manufacturing units, in other words, exactly corroborates White and Gallie's comments about employee participation and the role of the supervisor in the work group.

During 1992, Andersen Consulting and Cardiff Business School made a systematic comparison of productivity and work systems in nine UK-based and nine Japanese-based autocomponents plants, in a project known as 'the lean enterprise benchmarking project'. This sought to replicate an earlier study on manufacturing assembly plants worldwide, from which came the concept of 'lean production' (Womack, Jones and Roos, 1990). 'Lean production' has a number of 'systemic' features to do with the number of products, relationships with suppliers, and development times for new products. A key factor, however, is devolving responsibility to the shopfloor.

More generally, world-class plants share a number of features relevant to HRM (Wibberley, 1993):

1 *Empowered team leaders*. Previous studies have suggested that employee involvement is key. The 'lean enterprise benchmarking project' argues that this on its own is not enough:

> At the level of the production team, the differences between the world class plants and the rest are not so great... What is striking, however, is the difference in the input of the production team leader or supervisor in the two groups, which in the world class plants was double that of the rest. For most activities, the world class plants reported *less* input from the production workers than did the other plants (Oliver *et al.*, 1994).

2 *Employee involvement in and contributions to problem solving*. Although the team leader has a pivotal role, this does not diminish the importance of other employees being fully involved. Extensive team-working (through such things as quality circles) is vital for continuous improvement. The quality of solutions improves and commitment to implementation increases.

3 *Company-wide performance appraisal*. World-class organizations create a continuous loop for performance review, feedback, and improvement. They apply this to all employees using common paperwork and processes. (The lessons for properly managed appraisal discussed in Chapter 14 obviously still apply.)

4 *Performance pay top to bottom*. Given the earlier doubts expressed about performance-related pay, this may seem surprising. There seems to be a clear conflict of evidence from the studies sponsored by the IPM and those of world-class organizations, which needs to be cleared up. One explanation may be how performance pay is defined and what it is paid for. For example, Watanebe (1991) comments that quality circles in Japanese firms are closely tied to suggestion schemes which reward employees for their ideas. This system of 'merit pay', moreover, runs 'top to bottom' of the organization insofar as all workers from top management down are effectively obliged to participate in the company's 'total quality' programme. Quality circles rejuvenated the suggestion scheme idea which existed previously.

5 *Single-status terms and conditions*. Despite its undoubted importance for world class plants, Wood (1993) found that single status was among the least popular policies being followed by British manufacturing firms (although adoption was increasing).

6 *Lower absenteeism rates*. Although itself an output, the far lower rates

of absenteeism in the best Japanese firms (2.35 per cent in Japanese UK companies compared with a UK average of 3.97 per cent, according to the Industrial Society) reflect a host of other management practices. (This may, of course, include careful recruitment of younger, inherently healthier people for greenfield sites, backed up by compulsory medical examinations.)

The 'lean production' philosophy implies, then, a wide range of linked practices (which incidentally parallel descriptions of what firms on greenfield sites try to do (Preece, 1993)). At the German firm, Bosch, in Cardiff (a greenfield site), where they have sought to put this into practice, these include:

- Multi-function teams with empowered team leaders
- A flat hierarchy with only five levels
- Minimum staffing levels
- Total personal flexibility with no restricting job descriptions
- A top-to-bottom performance pay system
- Continuous improvement
- Team-work and synergy through extensive use of problem-solving teams
- Single status (as far as possible)
- The idea of internal customers, bringing customer satisfaction close to every employee
- Single-union recognition with the AEEU
- Very low absenteeism
- Daily team briefings at the beginning of each shift
- Training (including training for supplier employees)
- A high level of process automation, with sophisticated planning and control systems
- Extensive performance feedback loops (Wibberley, 1993).

The principal message from 'lean production' firms is therefore that participation and involvement, and schemes that try to create this, are not ends in themselves. Equally, they signal the fact that participation is created and managed by a variety of means (which includes such things as pay). We will look more specifically at performance, via pay, in a moment. Before that, we will review the formal methods that organizations use to create participation.

Creating participation and involvement

Arrangements to promote employee involvement fall roughly into four types (Ramsey, 1992; Marchington, Wilkinson and Ackers, 1993):

1 *Involvement in problem solving through the job.* This includes TQM and customer care programmes; suggestion schemes; and quality circle activities. More generally, it covers all forms of work organization which

increase the discretion of employees over their job and the opportunity to influence change.

2 *Direct communications.* This includes regular team briefings; company newspapers; attitude surveys; and employee reports. In the 1980s, the Industrial Society promoted a model for team briefing which involved:

- Cascading the briefing through successive levels of the organization
- Making it relevant by restricting the amount of corporate information to 30 per cent
- Keeping groups small (five to fifteen people at a time).

This has been widely adopted. Briefings seek to control the giving out of information, while other methods such as attitude surveys are more two--way, designed to elicit what employees think.

3 *Financial participation.* Schemes here include profit sharing; employee share-ownership schemes; and various forms of group bonus across a site. All these attempt to create an identity of interest of the employee with the firm by linking individual rewards to the firm's financial success.

4 *Consultation and representation.* This covers joint consultative committees (JCCs); works councils; health and safety committees; and collective bargaining. A significant difference with these is that trade unions are often more active in them.

The first obvious thing to say is that this list gets longer all the time, with individual firms using more than one of these. Fashions also change. New approaches come and go in waves (Marchington, Wilkinson and Ackers, 1993). In the 1970s, interest centred on joint consultative committees and the prospect of worker directors, with 'industrial democracy' the vogue word. In the mid-1980s, it was team briefing, profit sharing, and quality circles, with 'commitment and communications' the key phrase. Now, it is 'empowerment' through team-working and problem-solving groups.

Interest in earlier forms may not entirely disappear, however. As Marchington and his colleagues found when they looked in-depth at twenty-five firms, schemes that organizations have adopted at one time linger on, sometimes complementing and sometimes conflicting with later initiatives. Figure 16.1 suggests that these can be shown in a series of waves, with the height of each showing how pervasive and important they were and the horizontal how well they have survived.

Applying this to their sample of twenty-five organizations, Marchington and colleagues found that a number of patterns emerged. First, in many manufacturing firms there existed a variety of employee involvement schemes, introduced at different times, as the fashion for these has changed. A second pattern was for private sector service firms also to introduce new techniques, but at a faster rate, so that sometimes they may be implementing more than one at once. The risks of conflict and confusion clearly increase. A final group were even more completely given over to fads and fashions, without any schemes enduring or making significant impact. These tended to be smaller firms or units of decentralized firms with high autonomy.

As a general mapping device – a kind of product-life cycle curve – this kind of analysis can be quite salutary for reflecting on the frequency and longevity of personnel and human resource initiatives generally, and on the

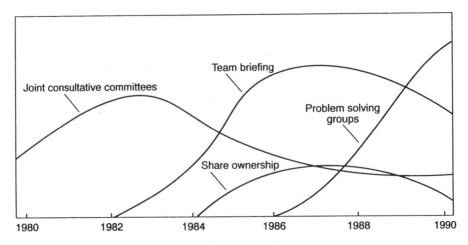

Figure 16.1 *A wave-form approach to viewing the comparative importance and life-cycles of employee-involvement schemes (an example from one organization). (Source: Marchington, Wilkinson and Ackers, 1993)*

consequences and causes. The problems and solutions are likely to be fairly similar to those which Marchington and his colleagues propose for employee involvement:

- Frequent initiatives create a lack of continuity. This happens because of the dynamic career patterns of the managers who champion them, and their not staying long enough to see new schemes fully bedded down. A successor may well lack commitment to an initiative he or she has not introduced.
- Associated with this, middle management and supervisors who bear the brunt of making employee involvement work may not be committed to new schemes. Their own motivation and ability to deliver (team briefings, for example) have not been considered.
- Because of fads and fashions, new packages are bought off the shelf, with consultants asked to help with implementation without establishing relevance or purpose.
- Finally, workforce scepticism, encouraged by all of the above, is the biggest ultimate obstacle.

The solution to these problems is:

- To customize new ideas and develop or amend them in-house (with employee involvement, of course)
- To ensure that they are consistent with other human resource practices
- To allocate sufficient and suitable resources (such as time and training) to implementation, and to ensure that management support is broad-based

- To establish mechanisms for regular monitoring and review.

As we observed in Chapter 3, the test is not how many initiatives a firm can adopt but how far they become part of the fabric of the organization. Simply adopting new techniques for employee involvement whenever they appear is likely to be counter-productive and confusing.

Before leaving this topic, one final thing needs to be said. As the Gallie and White (1993) survey showed, what people value most is the ability to influence what they are doing in their job. Of all the forms of communication, the first – 'Involvement in problem solving through the job' – is the most important.

In a communications audit recently undertaken for Courtaulds Aerospace Advanced Materials Division (Hendry, Jones and Cooper, 1994), this message came through loud and clear:

> The communication people value most is job-related and geared to customer satisfaction. People value job-related meetings with a clear task focus, where they feel they can contribute.

What employees want is a sense of control in their work:

- To be able to influence priorities in their own job
- To know the priorities in their own job and have access to reliable, written information (for example, via computer terminals) so that they can make decisions in the absence of their supervisor or manager
- To know where their work fits in within the company
- To be trained to understand business information
- To have their achievements valued
- To be consulted so that they can make inputs to improve ways of working.

Shopfloor employees can be highly task-focused, especially when jobs are at stake. Corporate communication for its own sake is therefore not especially valued. As one person put it, briefing sessions may simply mean 'we will be the most informed workforce out of work'.

Pay

Pay is a pivotal issue in a strategic approach to employment. First, it is the mechanism through which employers hope to elicit effort and performance geared to organizational objectives. Second, the choice of payment system frequently requires adjustment of a range of devices for developing motivation. Third, the overall pay bill is a key component in a firm's financial strategy, and therefore the area of HRM most liable to engage the active interest of the top management team.

For employees, pay is obviously a prime reason for working, although not the only reason and not the main motivator to good performance in work. Thus, it is often said that while pay is of paramount importance in why people work, pay in itself is a poor motivator for exceptional effort and high-quality work. Thus, when asked in surveys how they rate pay, people's responses vary according to whether this is phrased as:

- What is the most important thing you want from work?
- Is work just a way of earning a living?
- What are the most important characteristics you look for in a job?

The answer to the first question is consistently 'pay'. In fact, the percentage of people rating pay number one has risen considerably over the past twenty years. A survey by MORI (Market and Opinion Research International) for The Sunday Times in 1985 showed 65 per cent of shopfloor workers putting pay first, compared with 44 per cent in an earlier survey in 1976 (*The Sunday Times*, 1986). In 1992, in the Gallie and White (1993, p. 12) survey (admittedly covering all grades of employee), this had gone up to 76 per cent for men, while the figure for women had increased from 37 per cent in 1980, using comparable data, to 53 per cent in 1992.

This does not necessarily mean that people are more financially motivated, however, despite the fact that these responses are against the background of Thatcherism and an increased emphasis in the 1980s on financial incentives. It is just as likely to be bound up with job security, which has markedly declined in the same period. Thus, in the MORI survey, job security ran pay a close second and had moved above an 'interesting enjoyable job' in importance (*The Sunday Times*, 1986).

The importance of job security is underlined by the Gallie and White survey in two ways. First, only 40 per cent of men (again all grades) say they work just to earn a living – in other words, factors other than pay are important. Second, while this figure has stayed constant for men between 1984 and 1992, for women the proportion has risen from 30 per cent to 39 per cent. This implies, as Gallie and White (1993, p. 12) note, 'a sharp rise in women's anxieties about money'. The context here is in part increases in the cost of living, but also the decline in male employment, the increased role of women as the sole breadwinner, and the increase in part-time work. Other data in Gallie and White (1993, p. 14) directly confirm the increased importance of job security – 'by far the biggest change' – up from 40 per cent to 59 per cent for all employees.

When we come to what motivates effort and quality, however, pay as an incentive falls away appreciably to be almost the least important factor (seventh out of eight factors), being rated by less than 20 per cent of all employees as a motivator for effort, and by less than 10 per cent as a motivator for quality (Gallie and White, 1993, p. 47). In each case, 'own discretion' far outranks as a motivator (at 65 per cent and 57 per cent for effort and quality, respectively). However, pay may have a concealed impact to the extent that it is connected to target-setting (which is also highly rated) and to appraisals/reports. On the other hand, targets and appraisals may be more significant for performance in the way they clarify what is expected, than for their link to pay.

All this simply underlines the fact that motivation is complex and that it is important to be clear about the multiple functions different human resource practices and schemes can have. In the case of pay, it is useful therefore to distinguish the different elements that may be involved, and the motivational factors that arise in each case.

The elements of pay

Pay is made up of a number of elements:

- Basic rate
- Overtime
- Incentive pay
- Other premium payments (such as for unsocial hours)
- Fringe benefits (especially occupational pensions)
- Profit sharing
- Merit awards.

This order roughly reflects their importance to manual workers. An example of how these may be combined is given in the next chapter.

Pay schemes can be broadly distinguished according to the balance between these elements, with the extent to which any scheme pays on the basis of time spent at work versus direct incentives for output or performance as the main distinguishing criterion (IDS, 1980). Thus, salary grades, measured day work, and flat rate systems of pay are based on the number of hours spent at work (although measured day work also builds in a bonus for an agreed level of performance). In these cases, there is no clear relationship between effort and variable levels of reward. Piece-work, payment by results (PBR), merit pay, profit- and performance-related pay, in contrast, try to create a relationship between effort and reward in order to induce greater effort.

A second distinction is the extent to which pay in incentive and bonus schemes varies directly with individual effort. Piece-work and PBR establish a close link between individual effort and reward; while profit-related pay and group bonus schemes are only remotely connected to individual effort.

Basic pay

Basic rates of pay are determined by an organization's grading structure, and are varied from time to time by collective bargaining or unilateral employer's action. Getting basic rates right is fundamental to people's perceptions of 'fairness'. This is a cardinal principle in pay, and goes deeper than any attempt to regulate motivation through incentives:

Pay deserves more respect as a source of disincentive than incentive. The most ingenious of bonus schemes and the best of supervision are of little use if the underlying pay structure is felt to be unfair. Consequently, the prudent personnel manager devotes far less time to devising new pay incentives than to tending old notions of fairness (Brown, 1989, pp. 253–254).

Employees have been shown to have a strong sense of what is fair and equitable in pay. This 'felt-fair' (Jaques, 1962) sense describes their feelings about being appropriately rewarded for what they do – people often feel dishonest if they feel they are being overpaid – and their sense of relativities with other workers.

It is a curious fact that the comparisons people tend to make are with those nearest to themselves socially and economically (Behrend, 1973). They react most indignantly when these traditional differentiations are affronted. This is partly why changes in jobs through reorganization and new technology cause such upset. It is not just because of fear of the unknown, or because work may be less satisfying (often it may be more), or because they personally may be worse off, but because the social order is being disrupted. From this point of view, it is unfortunately difficult to see how the readjustments in work organization in the 1980s could have occurred if trade unions had remained strong enough to defend their own members' particular relativities and position.

Regulating the grading structure to prevent grievances and to tidy it up from time to time is therefore a major personnel task. From the late 1960s to the early 1980s job evaluation became increasingly popular as a way of establishing fair differentials within the workplace. It was particularly common in manufacturing and in the nationalized industries, and increased with establishment size. As we saw in the Pilkington case in Chapter 8, however, many large organizations then began to find that job evaluation increased their administrative costs, restricted their flexibility in the labour market, and prevented individual units from adjusting to their competitive environment. Formal job evaluation has therefore gone steadily out of fashion. Moreover, firms may feel they do not need to justify rates of pay to the same extent to their trade unions.

However, in 'skills-based pay' we may be seeing a new form of job evaluation emerging that combines old notions of 'fairness' with new ideas associated with HRM, emphasizing the quality of people skills, flexibility in skills, and work performance. We consider this under 'Pay and HRM' below.

There is one further consideration regarding fairness and pay, and that is the spread of differentials from top to bottom of an organization. A focus on differentials between adjacent groups of workers is a convenient mask for the ultimately more significant gap between the top and bottom of an organization. Earnings differentials between ordinary workers and those at the top of the company hierarchy are vastly greater, for example, in the UK (and the USA) than in Japan. This is bound to have a profound effect on motivation:

> The egalitarian remuneration system is extremely important to workers' morale. Earnings differentials between ordinary workers and those at the top of the company hierarchy are small in Japan: the average annual gross earnings of Japanese company presidents were 5.7 times higher than those of ordinary workers in 1985, whereas board members of US companies earned, on average, 33.5 times more (Watanebe, 1991, p.73).

Furthermore:

> Both groups share the ups and downs in the company business through their
> annual increments and biannual bonuses. In fact, companies reduce their losses
> by cutting the directors' remuneration before the ordinary workers'. . .Conse-
> quently, workers have no reason to suspect that they work hard only to enrich the
> directors and shareholders.

If the underlying reward structure is one-sided, spending time in devising
incentive structures becomes, at best, tinkering, at worst, deception.

Hours, overtime and premium pay

British employees work longer hours than everyone else in the rest of the
European Union – at 44 hours, four more per week than the European
average (*The Guardian*, 1993). While part of this is accounted for by
managerial and professional employees, overtime in many manual industries
is the main reason. Overtime is cheaper for employers than the costs of
taking on extra workers, and boosts workers' take-home pay. It is particularly prevalent in certain sectors like baking, and in railways and the Post
Office in the public sector.

As a result, hours worked have stayed stubbornly high over the last
thirty years despite agreements in various sectors to reduce the official
working week. Latterly, the government has removed some of the constraints on working hours, and in 1993 opposed an EC directive to prevent
forced overtime beyond a working week of 48 hours.

Overtime is the main form of premium payment, far outweighing payments for unsocial hours and adverse working conditions. Above all, it is
more important than incentive pay. In the Gallie and White (1993) survey,
some 70 per cent of skilled manual workers (and 55–60 per cent of clerical
and semi-/non-skilled) had some form of premium pay. This compares with
slightly less than 40 per cent who get incentive pay. Many, moreover, derive
a large proportion of their earnings in this way. Twenty per cent of skilled
manual workers get more than 20 per cent of their earnings from premium
pay, and a further 20 per cent receive 10–24 per cent.

Premium pay (especially overtime) is obviously, then, a major component
of pay, and, not surprisingly, manual workers hold tenaciously onto opportunities to do overtime. How this affects performance, though, is almost
entirely unclear (Brown, 1983). Some have seen 'institutionalized overtime'
as a major contributor to wage inflation, while firms like Pilkington (see
Chapter 8) have tried to eliminate it as source of inefficiency.

Incentives

Of all the topics that have most differentiated the management of blue-
collar and white-collar workers, the stress on matching effort to pay for
manual workers has been among the most striking. Traditionally, the focus
has been on immediate and direct incentives for output, with piece-work

and payment-by-results (PBR) schemes typically believed to pay between 10 and 20 per cent of earnings (although New Earnings Survey figures suggest that it is nearer 30 per cent). More recently there has been a shift towards bonus schemes which reward motivation and performance over the longer term.

Immediate, direct incentives for output (or where a salesperson is paid commission for sales) have persisted for around 40 per cent of the male manual labour force for decades. Precise figures vary depending on the sample base. The latest Workplace Industrial Relations Survey (WIRS3) found that 48 per cent of private manufacturing firms had a form of payment by results (PBR) (Millward *et al.*, 1992); Wood's (1993) survey of 135 manufacturing firms is close to this at 44 per cent; while the New Earnings Survey of individuals themselves comes in at just under 40 per cent for men and 30 per cent for women. As Figure 16.2 shows, however, the numbers are in decline. Few organizations are introducing new schemes, and many firms are withdrawing existing ones.

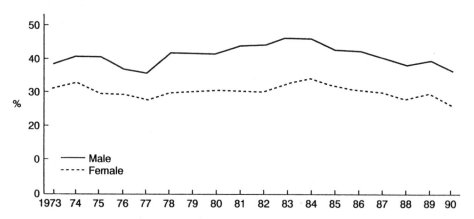

Figure 16.2 *Manual workers on payment-by-results. (Reproduced with permission from Cannell and Long, 1991)*

A joint study, combining interviews and survey, by the IPM and NEDO suggests why this is so (Cannell and Long, 1991). Many of the reasons echo complaints which go back many years:

- The worker cannot always control his or her own pace of work (for example, because the supply of materials or orders are uneven), and therefore earnings may fluctuate.
- Work study values, on which the time allowed to do a job is based, may not be accurate or perceived as fair, and therefore confidence in the whole system is undermined.
- 'Slack' times can be manipulated.
- Piece-rates may penalize skill, through less competent workers being given the easier tasks and being able to maximize their work speed and earnings.
- Individuals may 'satisfice' rather than maximize their work rate and earnings.

- PBR is time consuming and expensive to maintain through work study and clerical personnel, and requires a separate quality control system.

In addition, a number of new factors have come to the fore:

- The emphasis on 'speed' at the expense of 'quality' is less acceptable in today's 'right first time' environment.
- PBR discourages individual initiative and contribution to wider production and commercial goals.
- Shorter production runs and the need for more flexible production systems give less opportunity for workers to gain maximum speed.
- Changes in technology and work organization render individual incentives inappropriate.
- Repetitive work can be both physically and psychologically harmful.

Interestingly, the IPM/NEDO survey showed that private manufacturing was moving away from piece-rate schemes faster than was the public sector.

Profit sharing

While piece-work schemes provide immediate and direct rewards for output, profit sharing rewards motivation and performance of a more general kind over the longer term. Such schemes are almost twice as common among non-manual grades. Nevertheless, the IPM/NEDO survey found 27 per cent of firms at the beginning of the 1990s involved at least some of their manual workers in profit sharing (Cannell and Long, 1991). According to Inland Revenue figures in March 1991, 2.25 million employees were covered by share-option schemes, and 350 000 by registered profit-related pay schemes.

Three developments have encouraged this trend (Brown, 1989):

- More sophisticated accounting systems which enable companies to define profit centres within large companies and to determine the contribution of separate units to profit
- Greater discretion for individual employers to determine rewards, freed from the constraints of industry-wide bargaining
- The series of Finance Acts since 1978 which provide income tax relief on certain types of profit-related payments.

The impact on motivation and performance, however, is disputed. People feel that the amounts of money are too small to be significant and the year-end company performance is remote from what they personally do. However, others argue that the effects on motivation are more diffuse, and that even a small improvement in employee attitudes can be highly significant in the long term (Poole and Jenkins, 1990). It is worth remembering also that the commitment of Japanese employees in major companies derives in large part from features of their system which have a long-term orientation – namely, life-time employment and the seniority promotion system.

Merit Pay

Nowadays, the tendency is to talk about 'performance-related pay' (PRP). To a large extent this is a fancy new term for 'merit pay'. Merit pay/PRP has a double function. It is partly intended to motivate by rewarding exceptional performance, but often for achievements and qualities which lie outside output-based incentive schemes. At the same time, it gives flexibility to reward people outside incremental grade structures. Thus it can be used to retain key people.

Much depends on whether one-off or annual payments of this kind are tied to an explicit structure of objectives and targets. Even then, it may be very difficult to assess the contribution of individual performance to overall organizational performance. Other misgivings echo what has already been said about this topic in relation to professional and managerial employees – principally, that such schemes may do little to motivate the great bulk of employees whose performance falls in the middle range. More may depend on not demotivating this group than on rewarding and penalizing a few.

'Merit pay' has always been frowned on by trade unions, especially manual ones, because of the risks of favouritism (the 'blue-eyed boy' syndrome). As a result, merit pay and performance-related pay have made far less headway among manual and clerical employees. However, there is evidence that this is changing. The IPM/NEDO survey of 390 organizations, for instance, found that 10 per cent of public sector organizations had PRP for some secretarial, clerical, and administrative grades. In the private sector, however, as many as 56 per cent of firms had extended PRP to such grades.

There are alternative ways, moreover, of structuring merit pay, which get round some of the traditional objections. The quality circle system in Japan provides an illustration. Watanebe (1991) observes that within the structure of narrow pay differentials (and in contrast to Western notions) Japanese workers are strongly motivated by financial incentives. Merit pay for suggestions within the quality circle system plays a part in this, although individual payments are usually small, and may be shared by the group. In this case merit pay is tied to a key priority (continuous improvement). Since realizing continuous improvement largely depends on group activity it makes sense to relate merit awards to the group in some way.

A strategic approach to pay

The conclusion from reviewing the elements of pay must be that motivation has both long- and short-term components, and that a sensible approach is to use a range of tactics which encourage both. Having compatible objectives, however, is critical. An individualized incentive system, for example, especially one that is output-based, is likely to preclude other objectives and overshadow other elements of pay.

Second, no payment system continues to operate satisfactorily for ever. Any scheme should be a response to the particular operating situation, defined by factors like technology, work organization, business objectives, social attitudes and beliefs, and labour supply (Lupton and Gowler, 1969). Any number of these may change over time.

All schemes, moreover, tend to lose their edge after a while. This is especially true of incentive and bonus schemes (Brown, 1989). Quite apart from the tendency for original intentions to become distorted and for schemes to 'decay' – through 'grade drift', and incentives and bonuses becoming regarded as an entitlement – the impact of any scheme may simply become blunted through familiarity over time. As Brown (1989) observes: 'Few payment schemes can last a decade without fundamental reform' (p. 259).

Above all, pay is central to a strategic approach to HRM (as the 'human resources cycle' in Chapter 1 argued). It is a pivotal element in directing effort and performance towards organizational objectives: 'Pay is the most direct way of showing workers which types of behaviour management wants to encourage' (Scott, 1993, p. 38), and again: 'Remuneration is a direct, and sometimes blunt, way of expressing the organization's values and beliefs (Murlis and Wright, 1993, p. 33).

It is also next to impossible to detach pay from other systems of the organization. It is hard to change a pay system on its own without tackling a range of other things. Conversely, when major structural changes like decentralization are attempted, changes in the pay system and the way it is managed are central. Examples include the Pilkington case in Chapter 8; decentralization and pay system change at National Power since privatization (Bishop and Lewin, 1993); and developments in the NHS Trusts and other decentralizing public sector organizations (Scott, 1993).

Pay under HRM

Where in all this, however, is HRM? Are there any distinctive developments or trends which add up to an overall new approach? For those who see HRM as a distinctive approach to employment there is both evidence to support their view and confusion. The confusion comes from the contradiction between the individualistic character of performance-related pay and tendencies in other areas to stress team-work and reduce differences.

Three developments expose these contradictions, although none are at all widespread – performance-related pay, harmonization (of terms and conditions), and skills-based pay. Each emphasizes a different aspect of HRM and promotes a different set of objectives:

- Performance-related pay is directed at productivity and efficiency.
- Harmonization aims to promote commitment and flexibility.
- 'Skills-based pay' aims at creating a quality workforce and promoting flexibility.

The last two are closest in spirit, but nevertheless the emphasis is different. Performance-related pay, as presently applied, is the odd one out. This contradiction is of major significance for HRM. However, since PRP has penetrated little as yet down to manual grades, we will reserve discussion of this to Chapter 20, focusing here only on harmonization and skills-based pay.

Harmonization

Harmonization is about reducing or eliminating the differences in treatment of blue- and white-collar workers. Historically, these are real and deep in Britain. Appreciation of this 'status divide' is fundamental to the employment systems approach developed in this book, and is why 'managerial and professional employees' and 'clerical and manual' are treated separately.

The characterization of employment systems in Chapter 11 is largely based around the different styles of treatment afforded to the two groups. Central to this are notions and expectations around commitment and control. Price (1989) usefully summarizes how this originated and why the 'status-divide' is now eroding.

Growth in the scale of early industrial and commercial enterprises led to the development of bureaucratic structures, with management and control vested in a non-manual group. This hierarchy of control was paralleled by the development of tiers of bureaucracy, giving rise to careers as the reward for commitment and compliance. Because of their proximity to the enterprise owner and share in the authority and functions of the employer, non-manual employees

- Exercised more discretion and decision making responsibilities
- Were expected to contribute above and beyond the call of a job description
- Were assumed to be more committed and loyal
- Were assumed to be motivated by more than short-term economic rewards, such as the prospect of careers
- Were better rewarded.

Taylorist work systems institutionalized these differences and their complementary assumptions by:

- Reducing discretion
- Prescribing work tasks, with tight contractual specification of standards of performance
- Tying pay to output through piece-work schemes (thus formalizing short-term economic motivations)
- Enforcing close supervision and disciplinary procedures.

The 'low-trust' relations (Fox, 1974) embodied here contrasted with the high-trust 'responsible autonomy' (Friedman, 1977) strategy extended to white-collar workers.

In public sector bureaucracies, such as the civil service and local government, and in other environments (like banking) which lacked a 'production' ethos and were literally more white-collar, these distinctions were less pronounced and lower-level groups shared in some of the same benefits (such as sick pay). Clerical and administrative employees identified themselves as a distinct group from manual workers, in the main forming separate unions; while employers sponsored staff associations and made concessions to encourage administrative staff to identify with the organization.

This identification of administrative and clerical employees with the enterprise, however, has increasingly eroded as jobs have become more routine and mechanized, as career prospects have declined, and as the number and variety of such jobs have increased. In particular, and fairly on, the reality of this identification was undermined by the 'feminization' of the clerical workforce, with women confined to lower grades, with inferior pay, fewer promotion prospects, and less job security. Latterly, also, microelectronic technology has blurred traditional distinctions by increasing the technical component in a lot of manual work.

In the last twenty years the 'status divide' has come under increasing attack. In the 1970s, this was spearheaded by the turbulence in labour–management relations throughout Europe, and interest in the 'quality of working life' and industrial democracy as ways of re-establishing legitimacy through greater social justice.

In the 1980s, the principal motive force was new technology and the need to utilize its potential through more flexible working. This implies more discretion on the shopfloor and greater reliance on workers' intrinsic commitment. This has been backed by a flood of writings (see, for example, Chapters 3 and 6) which provide ideological justification for treating people better to get more out of them, and examples of Japanese success in managing production systems differently. Tangible examples of Japanese firms abolishing status distinctions and introducing group working in their new plants in the UK have provided an active model for British firms to copy.

The impetus towards harmonization seems, therefore, to be unstoppable. Progress over the last two decades, however, has been steady but slow. It has been slowest in those areas to do with payments for 'non-work periods' (Price, 1989):

- Retirement pensions
- Sick pay
- Lay-off pay
- Short-time working
- Time off for domestic reasons
- Redundancy pay

but considerable progress towards equalization has been achieved on:

- Hours of work
- Holidays

- Payment systems
- Facilities (such as canteens)
- Fringe benefits (for example, insurance and loans).

As Wood (1993) notes, single-status working remains among the least popular initiatives being pursued by British manufacturing firms. One good reason for this is the comprehensive effort required, although a piecemeal approach may work up to a point. A second reason is the costs it may add. However, as firms like Johnson and Johnson have found, additional costs are likely to be offset by increased flexibility and commitment which improve productivity (Mullins, 1986). Although initially a collective bargaining issue, in recent years employers themselves have taken up the case for harmonization. It is therefore likely to continue to spread.

However, another fundamental divide has been opening up, which in a sense may allow firms to buy one kind of harmony at the expense of another. This is the development of 'core–periphery' employment statuses which discriminate against employees in secondary labour markets. Chapter 18 considers this.

Skills-based pay

If the thrust of harmonization is to promote commitment and flexibility, 'skills-based pay' is directed at creating a quality workforce and flexibility. Skills-based pay is an attempt to model a pay/grading structure around the idea of competency or skills. Essentially, employees are progressively rewarded for the achievement of a range of work-based skills within a series of grades. The objectives are:

- To provide a visible and acceptable basis for pay progression
- To emphasize and encourage skill development
- To develop flexibility through employees having a range of skills.

The idea is still in its infancy since national vocational qualifications (NVQs) and behavioural models of competency, which lie behind it, are also relatively new. Nevertheless, some basic issues and guidelines are already emerging.

The initial requirement is a visible hierarchy of processes, activities, and skills. Defining this may actually help organizations to clarify just what they are employing people to do. The scheme developed at Courtaulds Aerospace Advanced Materials at its Performance Fabrics factory (described in Hendry, Jones and Cooper, 1994) illustrates what is involved.

Courtaulds Advanced Materials

The first task was to define discrete areas of skill. This was not too difficult since, in the weaving shed, jobs fell into three natural categories:

- Services operations (at the bottom)
- Preparation (of the yarn) and monitoring
- Process operations (weaving itself, at the top of the skills hierarchy).

Each of these contained a range of existing jobs, with a separation between those whose skills lay in dexterity in managing yarn and those who were more mechanically minded towards the top. At the top, on monthly terms, was a 'super-skilled' group of loom technicians. The problem lay in dealing with a group of jobs based in traditional demarcations, the skills underlying which had become somewhat obscure.

As the company had moved away from traditional weaving skills into industrial weaving (and as the apprenticeship system itself had begun to decay), skills were increasingly acquired by 'sitting next to Nellie'. Standards of skill were becoming uncertain, as were the requirements for moving from one job to another. Also, while there was an implied progression between jobs in terms of skill, there was no clear pay progression or banding, but instead a mix of fixed rates for the job. All of these are familiar ingredients in a 'disordered' pay system.

Working from NVQ principles and with help from the on-going development of standard operating procedures to meet the requirements of BS 5750, the underlying rationale for the three levels of skill was defined. The various jobs and their incumbents could then be slotted in, and the range of specific skills associated with these set out, as Figure 16.3 shows.

Employees in each grade will receive the basic rate and then a series of percentage increments for additional skills. In the first process, an employee has to become competent in all three areas of work to get the full increment; in preparation and monitoring they must achieve a selection of four skills; and in operations (weaving) they must achieve five skills. Similar principles apply in a second area of manufacturing and in administrative jobs.

The scheme was accepted in a workforce ballot in October 1993, and the process of assessment and then training has since been under way. Some lessons can already be drawn, however:

1   As the first objective above suggests – namely, to provide a visible and acceptable basis for pay progression – skills-based pay acts as a form of job evaluation in defining a grading structure, but unlike job evaluation it also assesses a person's skills. This does mean that the desire for pay progression may dominate over the objective of encouraging the development of skills. People will expect to keep raising their skills; they will expect continuing pay progression; and when inevitably the system cannot deliver on these expectations, they will become disillusioned. 'Competency drift' will simply replace 'grade drift' (Murlis and Fitt, 1991).

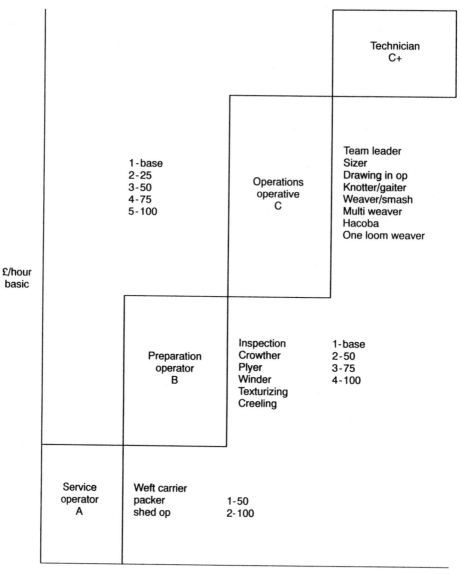

Figure 16.3 *A structure for skills-based pay at Courtaulds Performance Fabrics*

2 It may be necessary to depart from strict adherence to NVQ levels and occupational definitions. Skills-based pay is an opportunity to rethink the organization and its skills hierarchy. Taking a set of skill definitions off-the-peg will not only play into the hands of 'competency drift', and may be inappropriate. It is also an opportunity missed.

3 Skills-based pay involves an organization in a serious commitment to employee learning.

With these points and the overall objectives in mind, the management team at the Performance Fabrics plant set out a series of commitments and principles early on in devising the scheme:

- To pay for competences used
- For these to be agreed between manager and employee
- That management would provide time in working hours for employees to acquire agreed new skills
- That it was management's responsibility to provide the opportunity to acquire and use these
- That employees would be assessed after three months in their use of competences to allow them to gain the increased pay
- That competences would be regularly reassessed, using job rotation if necessary to maintain experience
- That if a skill was no longer needed, payment for it would be phased out
- That the employee would be able to replace that skill over an agreed period to allow them to keep on the same level of pay.

Collective bargaining

There can be little doubt that collective bargaining has ceased to be at the centre of the way employment is managed in the UK. In its two primary functions – to determine pay and to give employees a 'voice' – collective bargaining in many sectors has become a subordinate process.

Market factors are given much greater rein in determining pay levels, while trade union channels and representation are one element in employee involvement policies, not the principal focus. No longer are themes like the forms and machinery of collective bargaining of overwhelming interest. In this sense, industrial relations has become a means, not an end in itself.

Other chapters have dealt with the specific causes of this (Chapter 2), chronicled the extent of the decline in union influence (Chapter 3), and described the restructuring of collective bargaining at company level (Chapters 5, 8, 13). We will, therefore, just briefly say something here about the basic purposes of collective bargaining in relation to the themes of pay and employee 'voice'.

Pay and productivity

The management of pay has a dual focus – designing and maintaining an internal system, and managing the price of labour in relation to the external market. Keeping pay rises in balance with productivity increases inside the firm is critical.

The apparent obduracy of British pay levels to respond to market factors has been a constant complaint of labour market economists for years. The Conservative government's labour market 'reforms' – the weakening of trade union bargaining power through curbs on the right to strike, outlawing the pre-entry closed shop, abolishing wages councils – were intended to make the labour market more responsive and to remove upward pressures on wages.

Greater wage flexibility through the break-up of company-wide and national pay bargaining structures was intended also to contribute. In principle, decentralization should allow firms to be governed more by local labour market rates and by what their international competitors are doing, and less by the domestic sector in the UK.

However, the impact of decentralization on pay levels, some suggest, may be illusory or even negative. Management and unions in large organizations are both likely to have information about claims, strategies, and settlements at different sites, and may well coordinate their overall strategies. Where there are national federated agreements in the background, companies outside may still adhere closely to these agreements as long as union negotiators, especially full-time officials, use them as a yardstick (Jackson and Leopold, 1990).

Others argue that decentralized bargaining is downright inflationary, opening the way for 'leap-frogging' claims (Pickard, 1990). This 'Balkanization' of pay bargaining, as the chairman of ACAS, Douglas Smith, has called it, has therefore encouraged some employers to return to centralized bargaining.

The result is that pay rises have continued to outstrip productivity improvements. As Figure 16.4 shows, UK wage growth exceeded that of Germany throughout the 1980s by a considerable amount. Part of the larger problem has been the expectation among wage bargainers that devaluation at the macro-level would restore the competitive position of firms at the micro-level. The European Exchange Rate Mechanism (ERM) was intended to suppress this inflationary psychology. Thus, since 1983 when the French franc was effectively tied to the German mark inside the ERM, French wage growth rapidly declined and the UK's ran ahead also of France.

A more fundamental problem, however, may be the very obsession with a market approach to labour which gives such priority to price. Britain is, after all, in West European terms, a low-wage economy, on a par with Spain and worsted only by Greece and Portugal in paying low wages. At the same time, capital investment in plant and skills means that units costs are comparatively high (see Hendry, 1994, pp. 143–148). It is this combination which is fatal. As Porter (1990) argues, adverse factor endowments (including high wages) produce a search for more efficient ways of doing things, including investment which puts people's skills to effective use. Put another way, productivity is about the quality as well as the price of people's skills.

The reform of the national training system seeks to do something about the quality of skills available to firms (see Chapter 19). However, company psychology and managerial rewards still act as a barrier. As Campbell

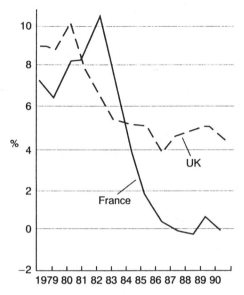

Figure 16.4 *UK and French wage growth differentials with Germany.* (Source: Greenwell Montagu)

(1991) observes, British industry remains too dependent on redundancies as a means of increasing productivity. As we argued in Chapter 2, the productivity increases of the early to mid-1980s were almost entirely the result of cost-cutting through redundancies. The trade union legislation of the last fifteen years has simply encouraged this 'external' labour market approach to industrial change by making redundancies easier as a first resort.

Collective bargaining and employee 'voice'

The existence of collective bargaining and its scope is a key contributor to an environment of 'mutuality'. Using the term favoured by the Harvard writers, it gives employees a 'voice' (Beer *et al.*, 1985). Dealing with a trade union shows an employer willing to take 'mutuality' seriously, or being bound to do so against their worse instincts. Collective bargaining is thus a vital instrument in a pluralist society.

During the 1980s and 1990s, however, collective bargaining has been increasingly constrained, both in extent (through the decline in union representation) and in scope. Chapter 3 cited the latest data from WIRS3 which showed falling union membership and a decline in union recognition (Millward *et al.*, 1992). The second Warwick company-level survey of industrial relations in 1992 confirmed this pattern, with one in five companies employing over 1000 people (in a sample of 176 firms) partially or wholly withdrawing trade union recognition in the previous five years (Marginson *et al.*, 1993). Moreover, of those companies opening up a new site, more than half did not grant recognition to the largest group in the workforce.

The character of collective bargaining, meanwhile, has also become more reduced. Two trends reflect this shift in power (Brewster, 1993):

1   *Varying the subjects covered by agreements* – excluding non-wage issues that had begun to be the subject of joint regulation (such as manning levels), while including clauses on other topics which give management more discretionary power (for example, over flexibility in working hours and tasks).
2   *Reduced formalization* – In the 1960s and 1970s the trend was towards comprehensive written agreements which protect the weaker party. Increasingly, managers prefer to work through informal understandings (for example, in introducing and using new technology).

Certain developments, however, run counter to these trends. Chief among these is harmonization of terms and conditions, which requires detailed negotiations and comprehensive agreements. The shift towards company-level negotiations seems actually to have helped this process which benefits manual employees. Thus, when the Engineering Employers Federation abandoned national bargaining, a number of large firms (like NEI Parsons) welcomed this because it enabled them to finalize negotiations on harmonization (Pickard, 1990).

While some organizations are engaging *more* with their trade unions, rather than less, the diminution of the trade union role, according to the authors of WIRS3, has left a vacuum rather than replaced it with any coherent new form of representation or means of expression. The arguments for employees having a means of collective representation and expression remain, however, the same as they ever were (Kessler and Bayliss, 1992; Kessler, 1993):

1   Most fundamentally, unions are necessary to articulate the interests of employees. What matters to employees is not necessarily what matters most to managers. Unions provide a 'collective voice'.
2   Related to this, unions protect individual rights. Without collective backing, individual rights are precarious:

> Individual rights are enhanced by collective rights and, without collective rights, individual rights, dependent on management largesse, are very fragile. . .the overwhelming case for union membership remains what it always has been, namely the weakness of the individual employee *vis-à-vis* his or her employer (Kessler, 1993, p. 28).

As evidence of this, WIRS3 showed that in 1990 establishments without union recognition dismissed some two and a-half times as many workers per 1000 employed as did those where trade unions were recognized. The rate of compulsory redundancies varied similarly. Private sector workplaces without trade unions were also less than half as likely to have formal health and safety bodies. Unions, in other words, keep managers up to the mark, and may oblige them to look at more difficult and perhaps more fruitful, creative, and productive alternatives.

3   A strong and representative union can present employee views. Other-

wise, managers are bound to assume that they have a monopoly of wisdom, and will tend to attribute failure to 'troublemakers' or 'failure to communicate', rather than addressing the real causes of problems. Unions can thus be a source of ideas.

4 Finally, and critically, union organization can provide an important basis for cooperation in change, since the union can help to deliver employee involvement and consent. There are many instances of technological change being successfully managed through the 1980s and into the 1990s with union support (see, for example, the next chapter).

Unions are thus an essential part of a free, democratic and pluralist society, providing a defence against arbitrary employers and acting as a 'social partner' with management: 'If one doubts this, one needs only to recall how trade unions have invariably been one of the first targets of autocratic and dictatorial regimes throughout the world and throughout modern history' (Kessler, 1993, p. 30). Obviously, unions need to be democratic organizations themselves and responsive to their own membership. During the past fifteen years legislation has contributed towards this. A more fundamental problem, however, is being able to adjust their structures and what they offer so that they are in tune with the increased enterprise-consciousness and individualistic mentality of employees.

It is difficult for an organization wedded to collective ends to square this circle. In the end, a representative organization can only be effective if it is speaking with the same 'voice' as its members. Public attitudes and consciousness on the collectivism–individualism issue, however, are subject to a wide range of influences and liable to change. It will then depend how far companies (and/or government) have created alternative governance structures which reflect the collective interests of people as employees and citizens, as to whether and how far people turn back to trade unions.

Training

Training and the labour market: jobs and careers

If human resource management embraces any one specific value above all others, it is to invest in and develop people's capabilities at work. As Ulrich and Lake (1990) put it: 'The first challenge of any business is to generate the competencies necessary to provide output that will be valued by customers' (p. 79).

As we noted in Chapter 1, one of the central planks of HRM is human capital theory's treatment of people as an asset, rather than a cost, in doing business. Since the mid-1980s, there has been a concerted effort to persuade British-based firms of this. There appears to have been a fair amount of success, with training activity holding up well during the latest recession.

Both Labour Force Survey figures (Stevens and Walsh, 1991) and Gallie and White's (1993) Employment in Britain Survey suggest there has been a 70 per cent increase in the number of people receiving work-related training since the mid-1980s. However, this continues to be concentrated on particular groups – young people, newer employees, those in full-time employment, those already with qualifications, and those in higher-level jobs (*Labour Market and Skill Trends 1994/95*).

Thus, in Gallie and White's (1993) sample of 3458 employees, less than a half (45 per cent) of manual and only one-third (34 per cent) of semi- and non-skilled manual workers had received training in the previous three-year period. The number wanting training in each of these groups exceeds those likely to get it by a far greater proportion than for higher-level employees. There does appear, however, to have been an increase in the amount of training for those in clerical and secretarial jobs (*Labour Market and Skill Trends 1994/95*). Women are also now slightly more likely to receive training than men (reversing the previous pattern).

In sectoral terms, the proportion of employees receiving some training has continued to be greater in those sectors less exposed to international markets – health, education, central government, retail, water and energy supply, and banking and finance (Stevens and Walsh, 1991; *Labour Market and Skill Trends 1994/95*). Trainees in the more internationally open trading sectors like engineering, however, get more training days.

The explanation for this discrepancy, which potentially has severe implications for the international competitiveness of British industry, probably involves several factors. One critical one, however, concerns the different forms of labour market which govern these sectors. The 'service' sectors listed above all tend to operate 'internal labour markets' which give them flexibility in deploying trained staff (Keep, 1989a). In their different ways, with the exception of retail, each has also been able to rely on retaining trained employees and thus benefit from the investment made – many, for instance, being part of a nation-wide public sector now or in the recent past.

In contrast, the manually dominated sectors like engineering, construction, and other manufacturing industries have depended historically on the apprenticeship system which has sustained 'occupational labour markets'. This has limited firms' control over their investment, both in their ability to deploy people flexibly (witness the job demarcations which characterized much of manufacturing until recently) and in guaranteed retention.

The forms the labour market takes have a significant impact, then, on the nature and extent of training which organizations undertake. Training and careers interact. In countries where occupational labour markets predominate (such as Australia), in-firm training (in the absence of State intervention) is thus likely to be relatively scarce (Curtain, 1987). In those like Japan with strong internal labour markets, the pattern is for in-company training.

Bearing this out, there has been a marked trend towards in-house, company-specific training, covering more established employees also, following the collapse of the apprenticeship system in the UK in the early 1980s. The tendency towards shorter, more concentrated periods of training (*Labour Market and Skill Trends 1994/95*) is a further reflection of this.

On the other hand, by giving lower-level employees transferable skills through certification of their competences at work, the system of national vocational qualifications (NVQs and Scottish NVQs) encourages an external labour market. At the same time, however, they define a 'ladder of opportunity' in the larger firm, and thus reinforce an ILM (Hendry, 1991). How these opposed tendencies will work out is unclear.

Firms' training strategies, then, are driven in part by the nature of the labour market (or 'employment systems') and by the way skills and occupations are defined.

Training and business strategy

At the same time, training strategies are driven by business strategy and the competitive environment. In *Training in Britain: Employers' Perspectives on Human Resources*, this stood out as the single most powerful influence driving firms' training activities (Pettigrew, Hendry and Sparrow, 1989).

How the link between strategy and training works out, though, is another matter. In earlier chapters (4 and 10) we have cautioned against the notion of a simple direct link and the fallacy of over-integrated human resource plans. These are likely to remain valid only on paper. Human resource planning needs to be flexibly linked to business 'strategy', and training needs to remain to some extent reactive.

Thus, in our twenty case studies for *Training in Britain*, we found the time horizons for training decisions varied enormously, covering:

- *Ad hoc* requests
- Annual budgeting, on the basis of forecasts of labour turnover, recuitment, and promotion
- Commitments to major projects, which themselves can vary up to five years ahead
- Commitments to groups of employees, such as graduates, which involve a view of skill needs up to five years ahead and beyond
- Long-term manpower plans, such as in the health service where length of training, the numbers involved, career commitments, and resources require careful planning.

All these can be 'strategic', in the sense of being driven by business need – including vital *ad hoc* requests that have suddenly arisen. Meanwhile, on an annual basis, individual training needs arising from the appraisal process have also to be slotted in.

This variety in practice fits with the view in Chapter 4 that 'strategy' can operate according to different timescales. It just so happens that in the mid-1980s firms' training activities were being driven by renewed capital investment, extensive and visible modernization programmes, and systematic training in new skills (associated especially with IT). The timescale for planning 'programmes' like these tended to be in the one- to three-year range (the next chapter is devoted to such an example).

Over the next few years, as the NVQ system takes off and as organizations sign up for Investors in People, however, we can expect 'programmatic' training to be governed increasingly by systematic individual training plans.

A recent interview/questionnaire survey of thirty-five organizations who had won National Training Awards confirms the continuing impact of business-led, high-profile change programmes on training activity and in generating training plans (Sloman, 1993). Business-led programmes which bring direct performance benefits readily engage line managers, and training is likely to be seen as necessary to make new systems work. This overcomes the 'planning gap' whereby line managers have traditionally been the weak link in implementing training plans through their tendency to keep people back from courses or to delay on-the-job training.

At the other end of the planning process, there remains the question of evaluation. There is an enormous literature on this which tends to plough the same ground to little practical effect (given that less than 3 per cent of UK firms systematically evaluate their training (Deloitte Haskins & Sells/ IFF Research Ltd, 1989)). This literature is well summarized in Crittan (1993, Chapter 6).

One of the things which gets in the way is the fallacy, promoted by the Employment Department among others, that the benefits of training can somehow be demonstrated on the bottom-line. As a rhetorical device, it may encourage employers to train by saying 'training pays', but no-one has ever satisfactorily demonstrated this. Firms themselves seem to know better (or at least that the cost of collecting data outweighs the possible benefits). Instead, the more progressive firms use a mix of 'hard' evaluation criteria concerned with near-term measurable performance (such as individual productivity post-training, and quality standards), and 'soft' criteria relating to 'intermediate' human resource goals which benefit the business indirectly (such as reduced employee turnover, ability to recruit, promotability, and providing job cover through flexible skills) (Hendry, 1991).

Training and the human resource system

The lesson is that training cannot be readily separated from other aspects of the human resource system. Evaluation needs to take a holistic view of the inputs and outputs relating to the training event, as Figure 16.5 suggests.

'HRM inputs', for example, include the selection of trainees. Are the right people being targeted? Indeed, is the organization recruiting the right people in the first place? At each stage there is potential for some corrective action. By isolating relevant elements at each stage in relation to particular training cohorts and types of training activity, there may then be scope for more ingenious and creative ways of defining specific business benefits.

The wider human resource system is important conversely in determining whether trainees can put what they have learnt into action. If other people are unsympathetic to new attitudes people learn through training, and if the organization does not reward new behaviours (such as concern for quality), the training activity is likely to be wasted. The question arises as to whether

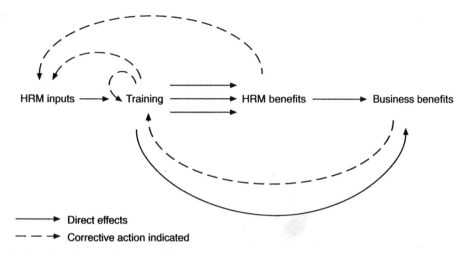

HRM inputs ⟶ Training ⟶ HRM benefits ⟶ Business benefits

⟶ Direct effects
— — ⟶ Corrective action indicated

Figure 16.5 *A general model for evaluating training*

training is really the answer. It rarely is the whole answer: attention often needs to be given also to systems of appraisal, rewards, and supervision. Fairbairns (1991) suggests three questions should therefore be asked before deciding to train:

1 What skills/knowledge/personal attributes are important in a person's job?
2 In what skills/knowledge/personal attributes are they in need of training?
3 What skills/knowledge/personal attributes are likely to encouraged, recognized or rewarded?

Only where the answers to all three coincide is training likely to be effective.

The fact that training can encounter such obstacles draws attention to the fact that training is about more than just developing skills. Even where the direct intention is to increase, improve, remedy, or change skills, a person still has to want to do something a different way. We speak therefore about training addressing skills, knowledge, and attitudes. Training involves personal, as well as conceptual and skill, development.

More than that, however, training can be directly targeted at attitudes, as with culture change and total quality programmes. There are other occasions, also, where a clear byproduct of training, either intended or unexpected, is an improvement in the general climate and working atmosphere in an organization. When Hardy Spicer (see the next chapter) brought shopfloor workers, quality control staff, and production engineers together into groups to learn about SPC (statistical process control), it was the first time there had been joint training like this, and it helped to start breaking down the barriers between these functional groups.

The Ford EDAP (Employee Assistance and Development Programme), launched in 1988, is specifically not about the development of vocational skills. Instead, it can be seen as aimed at fostering a different industrial relations climate and a spirit of 'jointness' which was the object of the earlier Employee Development and Training Programme introduced in America in 1982 (Banas and Sauers, 1989). Like Hardy Spicer with SPC, EDAP brings together individuals from different grades and parts of the workplace to meet in a non-work environment. Training thus has an important role in improving general communications and developing commitment.

Finally, training needs to be seen as part of a broader human resource system in one other essential way. The whole notion of evaluation is based on training as a discrete event – namely, the training course – and justifying the substantial visible costs associated with off-the-job courses and full-time training staff. Take these away, as Hamblin (1974) and Crittan (1993) have observed, and the rationale and pressure for evaluation largely collapses. Evaluation of training events was always a fallacy as long as it ignored the equally important process of practice back on the job which ensures that training transfers.

The proper role of evaluation is then as part of a corrective cycle (formative evaluation) and helping to make judgements about means (for example, the balance between on- and off-the-job training to develop particular skills).

To summarize, training relates to the broader human resource system in four ways:

- Other human resource processes, such as recruitment and selection, have an important input into training.
- Other parts of the whole system, like pay and rewards, have a powerful influence on behaviour and affect training transfer.
- Training can fulfil many purposes, not just to do with skills.
- Formal training needs to be complemented by practice on-the-job.

Learning and training

Finally, how do people on the shopfloor learn? Increasingly, we are getting away from the divisive notion that managers are 'developed' while the shopfloor are merely 'trained'. The principles of adult learning apply to each. Much of what was said in the previous chapter about learning therefore applies equally here.

Often, for manual and clerical employees, 'training' as a concept is inadequate because they have got out of the habit of learning. The statistics on who gets trained above makes it obvious why this is so. The challenge is therefore 'to regenerate the learning process in people who [have] got out of the habit of learning' (Halsen, 1990, p. 38). Since the mid-1980s, with help from Brunel University's Centre for the Study of Human Learning, the Post Office has tackled this problem through a major programme of learning and change, which embodies the following principles:

- Learning is a skill that can be learnt or relearnt – acquiring or re-acquiring learning skills is therefore a prime task.

- The learner must see a need for learning in personal terms.
- Because each individual's experience is unique, learning needs to be individualized in a practical and financially viable way.
- Responsibility for learning rests largely with the learner (while the organization has a duty to provide the necessary resources and opportunities to learn).
- Most people learn better when given the support of a group or partner between whom there is trust.
- Much more is learnt through learning on-the-job than through prescribed training.

Other principles could be added to this. For example, adults especially work within a highly developed complex of knowledge, values, and principles for action. If learning is to be meaningful in personal terms, they must be able to connect it to this totality of experience. This underpins, therefore, the argument for experiential learning (Jones and Hendry, 1994).

The secret of adult learning, and the difference between training and development, is that the learner is in control. This has been a key principle, along with other adult learning ideas, in work recently carried out at Courtauld's Aerospace Advanced Materials by Neville Cooper (Hendry, Jones and Cooper, 1994).

Adult learning at Courtaulds Advanced Materials

This began with a small but influential group of twelve senior and middle managers taking part in a programme to develop their teaching skills, with a view to the eventual adoption of training for NVQs. This 'tutor skills programme' was designed in a learner-centred way. Health and safety training happened then to become a priority issue and provided an opportunity for the group to practice and apply their skills. Health and safety training was consequently also managed in a learner-centred way. The result has been widespread diffusion of adult learning principles across the site:

- All employees have been exposed to the learner-centred culture in the classroom through health and safety training.
- New forms of relationship have been forged – between manager and shopfloor, between people from different functions, and between people from different parts of the site. People have begun to see one another as engaged in shared learning.
- Shopfloor employees have become active partners in problem solving through the conduct of health and safety audits around the site.

In this way (and supported by other initiatives), a learning community is being built.

The notion of workplace-based 'communities of practice', described in Chapter 10 as the secret of continuous improvement, embodies similar ideas. People at work learn from one another. Given a suitable focus, sufficient opportunities, and access to knowledgeable resources, they can continually learn.

This is more than 'sitting next to Nellie', which has constantly been disparaged as a way of learning. Nevertheless, people learn from those in closest proximity. The problem has been sitting only next to Nellie; being exposed to Nellie's limited experience; and picking up her bad habits:

> By creating a working environment where people have opportunities to watch, work with, talk ideas over, and share problems with others, organizations create the conditions for lively 'communities of practice'. When people then have a need to learn, they know which combination of people can help, and can assemble their own 'learning community' to solve their problem (Hendry, Jones and Cooper, 1994, p. 1).

Quality circles are a way of formalizing this, with groups of people who can bring diverse relevant experience and have a direct interest in, and ability to implement, improved ways of working.

Finally, the kinds of learning described here have profound implications for the training function. Instead of being a provider or organizer of training, the professional trainer becomes a facilitator. Moreover, to help the mass of employees learn, trainer skills need to be widely diffused as coaching skills to line managers at all levels.

Summary

In this chapter we have reviewed some of the key issues and developments in HRM affecting manual and clerical employees. The overriding principle, however, remains the pursuit of strategic coherence. The HR manager needs to be aware of how changes fit with the type of employment system currently operating in the organization. Four themes were considered:

- Employee commitment
- Pay
- Collective bargaining
- Training.

Commitment is created and managed by a variety of means, including pay. Communication alone cannot produce commitment. Involvement in problem solving through the job is of greatest importance.

Pay is a pivotal issue in a strategic approach to employment, in three ways:

- It is the mechanism through which employers hope to elicit effort and performance (or, as it is usually crudely put, the means of motivating people).

- The choice of payment system frequently also means adjusting other devices for developing motivation.
- The overall pay bill is critical to a firm's financial strategy, and therefore attracts top management interest.

We then reviewed the elements of pay, and the different ways they affect motivation in the long and short term, noting new developments in pay. Among these, although each is still a minority interest (as new ideas inevitably are), are performance-based pay, harmonization of terms and conditions, and skills-based pay. Each of these is governed by different objectives.

The decline of trade union power makes it possible to see the functions of collective bargaining from an enterprise perspective more clearly, without the distraction of rethinking trade union structures. In its two primary functions – to determine pay, and to give employees a 'voice' – collective bargaining in many sectors has become a subordinate process to open market forces. The weakening of trade unions, however, may actually damage competitiveness in one sense, by encouraging firms to adopt an 'external' labour market approach to industrial change through redundancies to cut costs, rather than to pursue improved productivity through more sustainable means.

Finally, training exemplifies the need for a strategic view of HRM. The employment system (or labour market) in which an organization operates or is involved has a significant impact on the training it undertakes. At the same time, training strategies are driven by business strategy and the competitive environment. In responding to the latter, however, human resource planning (and its training component) needs to retain flexibility. Above all, training should not be seen as a simple solution to solve people problems (as it often is). Training depends heavily on other aspects of the human resource system for its effect. For this reason, evaluation also needs to take a holistic view.

The last theme – how people on the shopfloor learn – brings us on to common ground with professionals and managers. The principles of adult learning are being increasingly recognized as being of general application to each. If anything, they matter more to the 'training' of manual and clerical grades because of the way continuous improvement is rooted in workplace-based 'communities of practice'.

In the next chapter we will illustrate some of these themes in concrete terms through a case study of how one company has introduced technical change and begun to build a learning organization on top of this.

17
Managing technical and organizational change at GKN Hardy Spicer

Introduction

This chapter is primarily concerned with the introduction of technical change on the shopfloor of an engineering firm. As such, it links with the previous chapter on manual employees, looking at changes in shopfloor practices and the process of implementing them.

This process has continued for ten years, and during the latter part it has begun to take on a more organizational character, transforming the relations between managerial and technical staff with the shopfloor to a much greater extent. In this respect, this chapter also has something to say about the changing managerial and professional role. The specific innovation in organizational structure around the philosophy of 'concept-to-customer' is closely akin to 'business process re-engineering', an idea which is attracting widespread interest at present. Such a philosophy changes the whole shape of an organization.

A third feature is what this case has to say about the way we look at strategy and change. It takes the 'long view', revealing processes over a period of time. It shows how effective change is not just about what happens at the moment of implementing technical change. On the contrary, technical change may begin in anticipatory changes to recruitment and training which precede the need for higher levels of skill. It will also benefit from the previous development of sound traditions in employee relations.

These can have a significant influence on the kind of technical change that is attempted. Anticipatory change will also speed up the process of change, since favourable conditions cannot be created overnight. Finally, building new traditions consistently (for example, in skills) creates subsequent opportunities for further technical enhancement. In other words, technical change should not be seen as a once-and-for-all event involving the adoption of a particular piece of hardware (Winner, 1977).

In this way, the chapter supports the 'emergent', incremental view of strategy advanced in Chapter 4, and the idea of a 'strategic' human resource management which is about building organizational capability and competences. Nevertheless, the case is also a classic example of a 'planned' approach to implementing a specific programme of technical change.

In tracing these changes, the case exemplifies two other particular themes. The first concerns the role of trade unions in helping with change. The second relates to employee flexibility (specifically task, or 'functional', flexibility) through the development of flexible skills.

The need for change at GKN Hardy Spicer[1]

The company in question, GKN Hardy Spicer, is a subsidiary of GKN, acquired in 1966 along with a number of other companies as part of GKN's diversification into automotive components. At that time, its main product was in conventional propeller ('prop') shafts for rear-wheel-drive vehicles. However, it had also developed a special joint – the constant velocity (cv) joint – for use in front-wheel-drive cars. During the 1960s and 1970s, its cv joint production grew as car manufacturers increasingly switched to front-wheel-drive, and cv joints became one of GKN's most profitable businesses.

While Hardy Spicer is the only manufacturer of cv joints in the UK, it is just one of a number of such companies within GKN, other subsidiaries having been acquired (in Germany, France, and Spain), established on greenfield sites (in the USA), or been the subject of joint venture deals (various non-European countries). The result is that Hardy Spicer's performance is constantly measured against facilities in other countries by both GKN and its customers. This has been a continuing feature from the early 1980s, when Hardy Spicer's cost structure began to deteriorate relative to the newer plants, right up to the present time. Together, these plants give GKN a very strong global presence in automotive component manufacture.

The process of technical change at Hardy Spicer in the 1980s was stimulated by three factors:

- The pressure for lower prices and higher quality around 1980 from customers themselves under increasing threat from Japanese car manufacturers
- The looming expiry of its patents in 1988, with the loss of both significant royalty income and the threat of open competition from Japanese cv joint manufacturers
- The collapse during the recession of 1979–1982 of the UK truck and agricultural vehicle markets which cut profits and sales from its other major product line, propeller shafts.

The financial problems from the last of these led to the closure of three peripheral plants, the transfer of 'propeller' shafts to another company within the Group, and a concentration on cv joints at the main Birmingham site. During this rationalization employee numbers were reduced from nearly 3700 to just over 2000. This produced a significant recovery in profitability.

The company was still at serious risk, however, of losing one or more of its three principal customers, and only avoided this by agreeing a series of five-year sales contracts at lower prices. This forced the issue of plant modernization to reduce operating costs and secure more reliable quality.

In late 1983 Hardy Spicer employed consultants to come up with a plan to improve productivity. Cutting manufacturing costs pointed to a reduction in the overall labour force of around 40 per cent – 50 per cent in direct and line-related indirect labour (setters, inspectors, labourers) and 25 per cent for other indirect employees (tooling, maintenance supervision, and quality control).

Improving productivity also meant reinvestment. The existing plant comprised nearly 1400 machines. Half were more than fifteen years old and a third more than twenty years old, dating back to the first production of cv joints. These varied from 'stand-alone', manually loaded and operated machines to modern CNC (computer numerically controlled) machine tools with some automation of materials transfer. The age and diversity of this machine stock contributed to the inefficiency, quality problems, and material waste.

Modernization meant a substantial reduction in the machine population and improved layout, making use of the latest in CNC technology and robotics. As the consultants argued: 'The basis for achieving the substantial cost reduction required is a significant investment in flexible automation, including "state of the art" machine tool and materials handling technology.' However, they also noted this would require a 'step-change in people policies'.

New system design

The need to cut manning and reduce work-in-progress, coupled with relatively high product volumes (thirty-three types of cv joint, three major customers, and a projected annual output of around 6 million joints) led Hardy Spicer to adopt a form of 'just-in-time' manufacture which they termed an 'integrated flexible flow-line'. This approach was applied to the five components of the cv joint – bells, bar shafts, tulips, cages, and inners. For each of the components except 'tulips' (where new lines had already been laid down in 1980) this meant a substantial investment in new lines.

The centrepiece was the 'bell' line. This comprised seven CNC cells carrying out various machining operations, plus induction hardening, and a 'crack-detection' facility for final inspection before assembly. Each cell was linked by a conveyor system, with robot arms transferring components to and from machine operations along the 100-metre line. Three shorter lines produced the bar shafts, cages, and inner races.

The original plan was for three sets of such lines, entirely replacing old technology for all but rework and short runs, with a total investment of £28 million, spread over three phases. This included radical improvements in manufacturing support services such as quality control, plant maintenance, tooling, and materials handling, and improved design and development through the purchase of CAD/CAM (computer-aided design/computer-aided manufacture). This meant that most of the support functions had to raise their levels of expertise and standards, and develop a new sense of their role involving tighter disciplines and management control. The consultants' report, for example, pointed to the urgent need to strengthen production engineering as the critical function in managing the technical side of implementation. In this connection, a new engineering director was recruited and during 1984–1986 fifteen new graduate and professional engineers were recruited, with less qualified staff being redeployed into production supervision and maintenance.

The biggest rethinking of roles and skills, however, concerned direct production employees. Two factors were critical – reducing the numbers of production employees (as shown in Table 17.1) and the need to maintain continuous running of the integrated flow-lines. Taken together, these factors implied that operators would have to take all 'first-level' decisions at the point of production to keep the line running. This included basic fault-finding and maintenance, and validating and editing of programmes to set up machines for production. To provide flexibility with reduced manning it also meant they should operate as a team (with backing from a small 'central resource' of specialist maintenance engineers).

Table 17.1 Changes in occupational categories within manufacturing in GKN Hardy Spicer 1984–1992

| | 1984 | 1989/1990 | 1992 | |
	Actual	*Projected*	*Actual*	
Supervisors	2	24	18	
Production Foremen	30	0	0	
Chargehands	2	218	142	Technical Operatives
Setter-Operators/Toolsetters	220	21	79	
Direct Operators	837	182	390	
Labourers	91	24	16	
Others	6	49	58	
Apprentices/Research Inspectors	101	37	43	
Mechanical maintenance	71	56		
			55	
Electrical maintenance	28	28		
Maintenance labourers	28	0	1	
			20	New Tech.
Maintenance Toolroom	63	51	32	
			63	Stores and Drivers
	1529	730	917	

These technological imperatives signalled a need to develop multi-skilled 'technical operatives' (as the company called them), with a knowledge of machining, programming, hydraulics, electrics, and electronics. Electrical and mechanical maintenance staff would also have to become multi-skilled, with the elimination of formal demarcations. It was also intended to replace foremen with 'team leaders'. In practice, however, this did not materialize until 1990.

The plans approved in July 1984 envisaged installation of the new lines in three phases over five years. Total cost was one consideration; a second was the need to maintain production on the same site through the implementation; a third, however, was the fundamental issue of not over-stretching existing human resources (such as the production engineering expertise) and people's capacity to cope with change. As the Chairman said in 1982: 'A company can only take so much change.' The first lines were installed from autumn 1985 and came into production in March 1986. The second entered production in November 1987. Meanwhile, the CAD/CAM system was introduced in July 1986.

In the event, however, plans for a third set of flow-lines were abandoned in favour of a series of manufacturing cells. There were a number of reasons for this. The introduction of a night shift in August 1986 (subsequently replaced in November 1987 by a Continental-style, 12-hour double-day shift system) gave round-the-clock production and went a long way towards creating the capacity which a third line would have provided. A third flow-line, with new machining centres, robots, and conveyor systems, was also extremely expensive. Finally, cells gave greater flexibility in the commercial climate of the late-1980s with the more diversified order book which Hardys had by then built up.

The technology introduced since 1990 has therefore been radically different in concept and design. Six machining cells, plus assembly cells and a third bar shaft line, were installed during 1991–1993 (modelled on a prototype cell set up in 1989). Cells therefore now account for all assembly work and a third of bell production. Each cell contains the full range of operations (like a flow-line), but produces the component for a particular customer (or in some cases two). It is thus more customer-focused. Cell 1 serves Rover and Ford; Cell 2 serves Volvo and Chrysler; Cell 3 serves Nissan; and Cell 4 serves Land Rover.

Implementing technical change

The first phase of technical change provides an excellent example of a 'planned' approach to change. It followed a logical order involving the following activities:

1 Communication   (November 1983 to early 1984)

2 Negotiation   (January to June 1984)

3   Training Needs Analysis (August to October 1984)

4   Selection   (November 1984 to February 1985)

5   Training   (March to November 1985)

Moreover, as writers on planned organizational change often recommend, this was preceded by a diagnosis of the state of the organization, using the consultants as a sounding-board. Thus, a substantial part of the feasibility study was devoted to the implications for people; identifying the necessary action steps; and doing some preliminary thinking about jobs, skills, and training needs.

Introducing change in a unionized environment

The way Hardy Spicer went about introducing technical change in 1984 stood out against two well-publicized trends of the time – the move to locate major new investment on greenfield sites and the belief that management should limit the role of trade unions. When the investment proposals were put to the main board in 1984, everyone in the company was aware of the recent precedent of another West Midlands car components firm, Lucas, going to a greenfield site at Telford. The argument for greenfield sites emphasizes the opportunity to introduce new values and employment practices (Preece, 1993). However, relocation in this way can underestimate the difficulties of finding an appropriate skill base elsewhere, and the value of building on an existing skill base.

Although the new flow-lines at Hardy Spicer would not use machining skills directly, such skills and know-how have been shown to be indispensable to CNC operation (Jones, 1982; Scott, 1985). There are obviously, then, economies in developing the skills of an existing workforce.

One factor in investing on the existing ('brownfield') site was, therefore, the faith in the skills of the existing workforce. Hardy Spicer's managing director, David Mackin, for instance, was strongly committed to training, especially apprentice training, and believed in the ability of the workforce to raise their level of skills. The company had been one of the few West Midlands firms to maintain its apprentice training during the 1980–1982 recession, and its training school was equipped with the latest robotics and CNC equipment. Second, they had raised their recruitment and training standards. Traditionally, half the annual intake of twelve to sixteen apprentices had gone into production as quality engineers, setters, and occasionally tooling, with the others entering engineering and design. In anticipation of 'new tech', the standards of intake had been raised in 1981–1982, and the company had begun to sponsor apprentices on to engineering degree courses at university. Six out of sixteen apprentices a year were being sponsored in this way by 1984 when the planning of the new lines began.

The high pay culture was also felt to give the company a highly motivated workforce. In retrospect, therefore, David Mackin believed that it had actually been easier to manage the process as a 'brownfield' development. The major factor in favour of development on the 'brownfield' site, however – certainly in the eyes of the GKN board – was the history of cooperation between management and workforce in adopting new technology and in already achieving big reductions in employment.

In effect, the company was already a 'single-union' site. One union, the Metal Mechanics (then part of TASS), represented 70 per cent of the workforce and dominated the company, with the then AEU having 20 per cent and the EEPTU and TGWU a handful each. While the bulk of the Metal Mechanics' membership were machine operators, union representation, moreover, did not split strictly along job and skill lines. The result was that the ten shop stewards on the joint industrial council (JIC) formed a highly cohesive group under the leadership of a well-respected convenor. Joint consultation was well developed and the relationship between management and the unions was open, cooperative, and pragmatic. As one union member put it:

> Everything gets sorted out here. The industrial relations are brilliant – basically because we don't have inter-union problems, and because of the JIC. We don't stop work while we're sorting a problem out.

Or as the personnel director, Brian Clamp, said:

> We discuss everything and anything. The style is to make a lot of noise, and settle. The biggest rows are not about pay issues, but where the convenor feels a lack of consultation has put him on the spot and he hasn't a ready answer for his members.

In their audit of human resource issues, the consultants noted this positive industrial relations climate and the pragmatism of the unions as a major plus which would help with the implementation of change over the next five years.

Communication

With this tradition of consultation, the unions were brought into the picture as soon as the consultants appeared on the scene to do the technical study. As the outlines of the new lines then began to firm up during early 1984, a scale model was built and presentations were made to the JIC, and then jointly by managers and shop stewards in a series of meetings with all employees. As Brian Clamp stated:

> We talked and talked about the concept of the new line. We showed them the model. And we said, the alternative is that we don't do it here. In our conversations, the union really said, 'you've got a free hand, we don't want you saying that the union blocked you. So you tell us what you want, and we will see if we can help you deliver it'. It became increasingly clear to them that we were in a survival situation. We had to invest, and if we invested, it would have a dramatic effect on all their existing agreements.

For the union's part, the likely scale of job losses was quickly evident. However, regretfully, they saw it (as Daniel and Millward, 1983, observed about unions and new technology generally) as a commitment to the future of the company and a way of preserving jobs in the long run:

> With 'new tech' we lose five jobs and gain one. If we hadn't got an agreement to put 'new tech' in here, it would probably have been done elsewhere, and we would have lost all five jobs. At least there is some security, and the workforce is better equipped with skills for the future if we do fail (Graham Gould, convenor).

The fact that 'new tech' would be phased in helped considerably, given the age profile of the workforce (see Table 17.2).

Table 17.2   The age profile at GKN Hardy Spicer (1984)

	Total	Staff		Works	
		M	F	M	F
16–20	68	7	4	55	2
21–25	119	30	6	81	2
26–30	198	37	6	155	—
31–35	147	25	5	115	2
36–40	191	35	6	145	5
41–45	247	42	4	195	6
46–50	254	29	4	211	10
51–55	299	38	6	248	7
56–60	211	19	6	185	1
61–65	55	10	—	45	—
	1789	272	47	1435	35

One of the distinctive aspects of technical change at Hardy Spicer at the outset was therefore the active involvement of the trade unions in the process, and the role of the personnel director and industrial relations manager in maintaining consultation. This is not the unitaristic model of HRM in which management attempt to squeeze out trade unionists. Indeed, the company tacitly rejected the consultants' suggestion that there should be less reliance on the union and convenor as a channel for communication with the workforce, and preferred to continue working closely with its unions. This remained a continuing feature in the industrial relations style throughout the period, and a consistent theme into the 1990s. As Brian Clamp put it:

> We've got a very participative style of operating. The convenor plays a very influential part in the way this company operates, and we're happy to work that way because it's successful.

Negotiating new terms and conditions

During the first half of 1984 new terms and conditions were agreed relating to 'new tech'. The key points covered:

- Selection for the new jobs
- Gradings and pay
- A training rate
- Shifts
- Flexibility between maintenance crafts
- Arrangements and terms for voluntary redundancy.

Traditionally, access to the most highly paid jobs under piece-work was governed by length of service, with the Metal Mechanics exercising considerable leverage over the allocation of jobs. However, with the investment it was making and the demands of new technology, the company insisted that it had to break those links. Equally, the union side were concerned that selection should not be open to management favouritism. The result was an agreement to select through tests open to all employees – despite the absence of a testing tradition (other than for apprentices) and the Metal Mechanics' traditional opposition to tests.

The second major departure was over pay. Machine operators enjoyed high status and piece-work enabled them to earn relatively high wages (in 1984, around £220) rather more than machine-setters, electricians, fitters, foremen, and the toolroom, who were all on the 'skilled' rate, and more than some even on the bottom of the production engineers' scale. In Hardy Spicer, 'the piece-worker was king'. Piece-work, however, was not appropriate to machine-paced lines, and the overall structure of shopfloor pay in any case had become rather obscure. A proposal to combine a variable section bonus with personal proficiency rates on top of a basic rate was considered (see Figure 17.1). However, a simpler, single basic rate 'technical operative' grade was introduced instead. Views continued to differ, however, as to the importance of having some form of incentive bonus payment in production, in an environment traditionally so oriented to piece-work.

The union was also concerned about parity between the rate for working

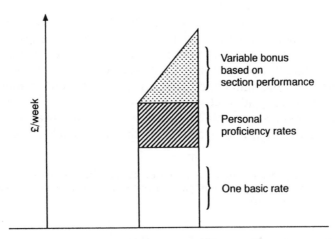

Figure 17.1 *The proposed pay structure for technical operatives at GKN Hardy Spicer*

on 'new tech' and what its other members could earn. When the first lines came onstream in 1985, therefore, technical operatives' pay, on the new 'skilled' rate, remained below what top piece-workers could earn, and only later achieved parity. For the same reason, to avoid technical operatives becoming a privileged group, the union sought a training rate £40 (around 20 per cent) less than the top piece-worker could earn, and supported a 'trainee clawback' of training costs from any trainee leaving within an unreasonable period. With these agreements applying to new technology, the old and new were then symbolically separated by putting a fence round the area of the factory cleared for the new lines.

Skills, selection and training

The definition of tasks, jobs, skills, the type of people needed, and the design of training is a good example of systematic training needs analysis. When the lines were first conceived during 1983 and early 1984 an outline picture was first formed, and the details were then firmed up. As described above, it was apparent that the new system would require multi-skilled 'technical operatives' and that they would need to function as a team.

As agreed with the trade unions, selection used a combination of numerical and manual aptitude tests, along with the 16PF personality test to identify qualities of team-worker orientation and self-reliance. Supervisors' reports were additionally used to identify any significant problems of bad timekeeping or discipline. Half the workforce (some 800 employees) opted to take the tests. Since only a small number could be initially chosen, however, care had to be taken not to demotivate those not selected for the first phase by 'failing' them. Instead, employees were told if there were particular weaknesses in education or attitude, which they could remedy.

It was difficult in 1984–1985, when the detailed design of the new lines was still being done, to predict required manning levels accurately, and therefore how many people needed training. Brian Clamp and his training manager, Paul Trenberth, decided to go for a first training cohort of 40. The training programme which began in March 1985 was central to the whole project. This consisted of six months' off-the-job training, covering team-building, drawing and measurement, basic machining, cutting tools, CNC programming and operation, and hydraulics, electrics, and electronics for fault-finding and maintenance.

This was carried out using a combination of the company's own training school, practice on existing CNC equipment in the factory, short courses with private training providers, and modules (especially on electronics and electrics) developed with the local college. Trainees followed the various modules in groups of eight. Smaller numbers of maintenance staff from both the electrical and mechanical side (nine in the first phase) also followed individual programmes to fill gaps in their background and experience.

In addition to the formal programme of training, technical operatives also visited the machine suppliers (mostly abroad) to receive some direct training. They then participated in the 'signing off' procedures for the equipment in conjunction with quality and production engineers, and carried out the installation. The effect of this was to develop 'ownership' of the new lines.

Similar training continued as successive phases were commissioned in 1985–1987, 1989 and 1992 (with some modification to the amount of electronics taught, and the addition of on-the-job training on lines already installed). Up to 1990, some 160 technical operatives were trained, with another forty undergoing training during 1992 and a further twenty central service maintenance staff retrained.

Beyond implementation

Developing jobs and skills

Multi-skilling of technical operatives had implications for a number of other skill groups:

1 It eliminated setters and first-line inspection.
2 It threatened the roles of production management and supervision as traditionally conceived – first, because the system itself was machine-paced; and second, by introducing the concept of teams and team leaders.
3 Technical operatives interfaced with maintenance and production engineering, and potentially intruded on their roles.

How far the technical operative role developed depended, therefore, on how these other roles also evolved under the impact of the same technology. In technical change, because a wide variety of jobs and roles are often affected, there is thus fertile ground for processes of 'contest' and 'negotiation' (Wilkinson, 1983).

The interface with maintenance staff turned out in practice to be the least problematic. The skills of works maintenance had been considerably enhanced to cope with more sophisticated plant and with multi-skilling of their own. Many of these service engineers came from the mechanical side and had a lot to do to 'upskill' themselves. They were therefore very glad to encourage technical operatives on the line to take on as much of the basic fault-finding and repairs as possible to relieve them of workload.

The relationship with production engineering was potentially more fraught. The original programmes for CNC were produced by a combination of means – some written by the machine-tool companies, others by production engineers (for robotics), and others by technical operatives (for all grinding machines). Technical operatives continued to do simple editing of programmes for set-up and modification purposes.

The extent to which they extended their programming tasks in the long run, however, depended on two opposing factors – the withdrawal by production engineering from hands-on 'tool-proving' activity and the implementation of DNC (direct numerical control). This in turn depended on recognition of what the technical operatives were capable of doing and the willingness of production engineers to relinquish such tasks. As with maintenance staff, the new technology was itself a key factor, by raising the demands on production engineers and calling for new levels of skill from them.

It was evident from the beginning that the relationship between technical operatives and production management would need to be different from that on old technology. Technical operatives were selected and trained to be resourceful and self-reliant. However, the style and structure of supervision remain unresolved. On the one hand, the training of production management, other than in some of the technical aspects, was limited, largely because the habits and outlook of production management at the time were unsympathetic to change. On the other, pressures to reach designed levels of efficiency helped to shift emphasis back to a more directive style. As further phases of new technology come onstream, however, the balance of manufacturing between old and new began to change, and production supervision needed to become more technical. This sharpened the challenge to their role, capability, and style.

Accommodating and managing these complex adjustments in role, motivation, and careers over time is one of the more subtle tasks for HRM facing both the professional HRM/personnel manager and the line manager. Internally, at GKN Hardy Spicer it focused on the abolition of foremen and adoption of team leaders (see below). Externally, it focused on the need to stem the loss of engineers with increasing experience on leading-edge technology to higher salaries elsewhere. Consequently, in 1987 a new pay and grading structure was introduced, geared more to external market rates and emphasizing professional qualifications and responsibilities, to attract and retain professional engineers.

Upskilling?

In all these areas evolution of the technical operative role depended, in part, on how far they themselves wanted to extend their skills and responsibilities. The job engaged their new skills most when a machine broke down. On a smoothly running line, multi-skilling therefore risked overeducating them. Training had broadened skills, encouraged autonomy, and raised expectations. With the novelty worn off, and the line running with fewer teething problems, the work theoretically should become no more than sophisticated machine-minding for much of the time, and this could lead to a loss of morale. In practice, however, this was not a real problem, insofar as new phases created continuing challenges and the demands of becoming fully efficient were considerable (see below).

In the longer run, nevertheless, technical change of this kind demands a rethinking of factory work. It may mean establishing career routes into middle management and specialist areas like maintenance and production engineering. Traditionally these have been open only to apprentices, not to the shopfloor in general. It may also mean more precise selection standards, so that those with most promise prepare for jobs in maintenance and production engineering from the outset, where diagnostic and problem-solving skills can find constant expression.

On the other hand, we should be careful how we interpret multi-skilling. First, there is the question 'what do technical operatives actually do?' Second, the discipline or job background 'multi-skilled' people come from can colour their views significantly. 'Multi-skilling' is not necessarily the same as upskilling (Lee, 1981; Kern and Schumann, 1984; Hendry, 1990b).

In the selection for the first phase, 'skilled' grades initially predominated (including many who had come through the apprenticeship system), with only about a third having been machine operators. In the second and later phases, as the apprentice source was exhausted, the ratio of formerly skilled/unskilled grades was more even. The result was therefore sometimes a considerable difference in job satisfaction between former machinists and former apprentices. For example: 'At the end of the day, I didn't expect to be a glorified piece-worker.' Allowing skills to evolve and opening up career paths from the technical operative role into factory management and production engineering is therefore important as it provides a safety valve for frustrated expectations, knowledge, and energy.

Developing flexibility

'New tech' training aimed to develop an understanding of basic principles so that trainees could continue to build specific knowledge and skills subsequently on-the-job. For this reason, the company knowingly over-trained. The hope was that eventually technical operatives would be flexible between all machines on the line, and even between lines. In fact, this was modified for reasons others have noted elsewhere (Clark, 1993):

- Individuals are suited to different kinds of work.
- Encouraging specialist knowledge is good for motivation as well as efficiency.
- Allowing ownership of particular work areas encourages commitment and higher quality.
- Specialization supports on-the-job training of newcomers.
- Learning and skill retention is limited when people move around too much.
- Tight staffing levels in direct production jobs limit movement which requires additional training.

Task flexibility was a central objective at Hardy Spicer. It is important, however, to understand the reasons for this. Flexibility is often talked and written about as if managers seek only one goal with it. At Hardy Spicer it was not pursued because it gave management a freer rein to exercise control; nor to intensify work (the piece-work system already sustained a high level of effort); nor was it pursued independently of other objectives such as the maintenance of equity. Indicative of this was the fact that the company rejected the consultants' view that there should be 'clear rules, discipline and strong line management/supervision over the control of work'. (The role of consultants, rather than managers, in promoting Tayloristic systems of control is not fully appreciated.)

Instead, Brian Clamp and his team put the emphasis on personal responsibility and self-regulating groups, with team leaders performing many of the traditional functions of the foreman. Jobs and work organization were modelled on ideas of 'responsible autonomy', with minimal specification of tasks and a minimum of supervision. As the managing director put it: 'We wrote all the nice words in the plan about the Japanese style of management and operator involvement, while trying to get away from the idea of "operators".'

While flexibility was a goal, however, it was not pursued as an end in itself or as a humanistic ideal, but to make the technology work. Brian Clamp saw the actual design as a logical and pragmatic result of the type of technology they had opted for:

> The start point was 'we're going to have few people on the slab... What are we going to do?... They've got to be multi-skilled... They've got to be flexible.'

Flexibility, moreover, was bound up with the idea of employee commitment – maintaining commitment in the way new technology was introduced; developing commitment through new skills and participative forms of working; and fostering commitment through opportunities for additional learning and personal development. Consequently, flexibility was not pursued primarily through a bargaining process, as some kind of 'negotiated flexibility', as, for example, at Pirelli (Clark, 1993). There were never, for instance, any written job descriptions, and the terms and conditions agreed with the unions in 1984 said very little about the jobs themselves. As one technical operative stated:

> There is no limit to the job we've got. There's nothing laid down in writing about what the job is. The job is whatever needs to be done.

The process of evolving skills through training was thus more important. Obviously, such flexibility is more productive from a company's point of view.

Throughout the 1980s, however, flexibility as an objective was largely confined to the shopfloor. While the first era of technical change did impact on wider organizational relationships, changes in these relationships were slow to come about until the second era of technical change tackled them more directly. Progess towards flexibility can therefore be described in terms of three periods:

- The negotiation of formal agreements, the definition of skills, selection, and training in the immediate period 1984–1986
- The struggle towards efficiency and the gradual acceptance of fundamental changes in the concept of supervision between 1986 and 1990
- The wider cultural and organizational change post-1990, associated

with changes in senior management and cell manufacture but made possible also by the progressive investment in skills over a number of years.

Before turning to the third of these which has involved a further step change, we will briefly fill in the gap covering the period 1986–1990.

Achieving efficiency (1986–1990)

Nine months on from start-up, by late 1986, the new lines in Phase 1 had reached only 30 per cent efficiency (although this was on the unrealistic basis of maximum output achievable in 24 hours' continuous operation). The production manager attributed the number and length of shutdowns to the high proportion (75 per cent) of ex-'indirect' employees selected for the first phase, while the managing director blamed it on their training:

> I wouldn't take shopfloor people off for 6–9 months training again. They've lost the work ethic. We've trained them in everything else except achievement and there is no impatience to get things done. They switch the line off for hours, and have lost sight of what it is all about. You can almost hear them saying 'break down, break down, I want to use the skills I've got'. I've actually got the convenor saying to me, 'we've got to watch this multi-skill thing, because it's too interesting for them'.

To correct this, a more directive style of supervision was introduced, retreating further from the team leader concept which the 'new-tech' teams had themselves so far been unwilling to adopt. A traditional foreman was put in charge of 'new tech', with more technically oriented, non-production supervisors working closely with the line to overcome technical problems.

To technical operatives and maintenance staff, however, the problem was managers not appreciating the difficulties of making the new plant work. As one technical operative said:

> Where they went completely wrong was they educated us, then they said 'we'll get you a couple of managers'. If I'm going to change my attitudes, then they've got to change theirs, and they should be part of a team.

Figures for training days in 1986 reveal this very starkly – 'management and supervisory training' accounting for only 251 days out of a total of 31 159.

While the question of supervision, along with that of incentive pay, rumbled on through the late 1980s, the company decided it needed to run the existing lines round the clock. Since this proposal for a night shift in August 1986 went back on the original 'new-tech' agreements, it was resented – especially since most technical operatives and maintenance staff, not having been machine operators before, had not had to work night shifts on 'old tech'. For a period of twelve months the union agreed to provide a voluntary rota while a more permanent solution was worked out. In November 1987 a proposal for a Continental-style, 12-hour double-day shift was approved by ballot, and Phase 2 came into operation in 1987 on this basis. The increased capacity from this eliminated the need for a third set of lines.

Problems persisted, however, in achieving expected levels of efficiency. In Phase 1 there were problems with particular pieces of equipment on cages, bells, and shafts, while the switch to UK machines (with the lack of standardization) for Phase 2 produced a host of new problems. Gradually these were overcome. Modifications were made to the bell line to reduce bottlenecks, including additional turning capacity off-line, and automatic inspection was replaced by visual checking and manual loading off the line. People became more familiar with the equipment. Scheduling improved to reduce downtime. Product design was changed slightly to improve machinability. Eventually, after much argument, a group bonus scheme was introduced in July 1990 which paid up to a quarter of total pay. The cumulative impact was to double output over a couple of months to between 70 and 80 per cent of the design maximum of 240 parts an hour.

The second wave of technical and organizational change

Despite these improvements, however, Hardy Spicer was failing to meet corporate targets and in 1990 faced renewed financial losses (aggravated by additional divisional charges and exceptional redundancy costs). This was due in part to continuing pressures for improved productivity from lower prices and reliable quality. Also in part it was caused by a loss of control in other areas – in planning and in top-level customer liaison. The result was the departure of David Mackin as managing director in 1990.

From 1990, under new leadership a broader programme of organizational change began to take place through the influence of three factors:

- The accumulated benefits from the way the company had approached technical change in the first place – specifically the emergence of a learning culture as former 'new-tech' trainees developed an interest in continuing further education
- A more participative style at the top, a rethinking of organizational structures across the company (including the introduction of team-based working on the factory floor), and an explicit commitment to culture change from greater employee involvement
- The introduction of cell manufacture which began to spread team-based working and addressed the systematic training needs of 'old-tech' employees for the first time.

Commitment to change and the creation of a learning culture

Two factors contributed more than anything else to the continuing commitment of employees to technical change – the phasing of redundancy which allowed employees to manage the onset of retirement and the extent of training. As we noted above, because they lacked the engineering expertise in 1984 and because of the human costs involved, Hardy Spicer's management recognized that they could not manage all the investment in one go. The skewness of the workforce's age profile meant they were then able to phase the loss of jobs over a five-year period through natural wastage and early retirement. Coupled with this, the intensive investment in training demonstrated a continuing commitment to the workforce and secured their goodwill for further change.

'New tech' gave many established employees a taste of training and education for the first time since they had left school and joined the company (although the introduction of 'statistical process control' (SPC) in 1984 also had a notable impact). 'New tech' also introduced principles of adult training into the company. The participative style adopted proved important both for motivation and in setting the tone for self-reliance and team-work later on the job. Finally, 'new-tech' training laid the basis for a flexibly skilled workforce in the longer term. The six-month programme was conceived not simply as 'training' but as an education in some of the basic principles. This allowed people to deepen their knowledge and take on increasing responsibility over time.

In these ways, 'new tech' created a new climate for training, and represented a shift towards continuing education and personal development. Many 'new-tech' trainees went on after their initial training to take further courses under BTEC and City and Guilds, and progressed into jobs in engineering and production. The company also provided literacy and numeracy courses at the request of employees. Finally, since 1990, with the training function taking over the budget for management development, supervisors and managers have increasingly been drawn into a 'learning culture'.

Organizational change and team-working

The original flow-line manufacture of the 'bell' line was modelled on principles of team-work. In a sense, however, the custodians of this ideal were in personnel. Departmental barriers largely persisted despite attempts to break them down. In 1990, however, a new managing director, Tom Wood, and a new manufacturing director, Geoff Pearce (combining responsibilities for production and production engineering), introduced a new philosophy of management and gave greater impetus to team-work throughout the company.

Production teams and team leaders

From 1986 to 1990, the idea of team leaders on 'new tech' had made only halting progress. Traditional factory management were suspicious of a shift in role from foremen as 'gofers' to the factory manager, to team leaders acting more independently. Technical operatives meanwhile were reluctant to take on additional responsibilities for no extra pay, and thought that the idea of a group leader conflicted with that of personal responsibility and independence that they had been taught. Everyone meanwhile was preoccupied with getting the new plant up and running efficiently.

The boost to the idea of team leaders came with Tom Wood. In 1988–1989 BRD (a local sister company of Hardy Spicer) had implemented the team leader concept under Tom Wood, who was then its managing director. Unlike his more autocratic predecessor at Hardy Spicer, he had a strong belief in delegation and that if you gave people ownership, it would release potential. At BRD, the foremen were seen as blocking that energy, so BRD had got rid of foremen. In October 1990, Hardy Spicer followed suit, appointing team leaders and abolishing foremen across the whole factory.

Since then, the team leader principle, originally conceived in 1983–1984 in relation to 'new tech', has been adopted wholesale. However, to make this happen two other things have been necessary first:

1 Teams had to be formed. The flow-lines had defined teams from the beginning. On 'old tech', however, some reorganization had to take place to define work areas more clearly. Some twenty-five to thirty teams per shift were therefore provisionally defined (in addition to the eight teams per shift on 'new tech'), with numbers per team ranging from five to twenty workers.
2 Individual piece-work had to be abolished and replaced by a system of team bonuses. Thus, in 1990 when team bonuses were adopted in 'new tech', it was part of a wider process.

The team leader concept at Hardy Spicer has certain characteristics which may differ from those at other firms:

- Team leaders are elected or nominated by the team, and not appointed by management (although management have the power of veto). They receive a small allowance of £10 a week, although initially at the convenor's request they were not paid.
- The team leader is an active working member of the team, responsible for improving team efficiency and liaising with other departments and sections. He or she has no disciplinary or supervisory role, however, and no administrative functions (as traditional foremen might have).
- The role operates at a lower hierarchical level than, for example, at BRD, where they are called 'facilitators'. The higher the level, the more potential there is for conflict between a trade union role and a 'supervisory' role (since some team leaders are also shop stewards). Role conflict is not easy to avoid completely, however.

Engineering and factory management teams

Alongside these changes at shopfloor level there have been two other re-organizations that touch the higher echelons of the company and strike at functional boundaries which had more or less remained intact through the 1980s – a reorganization of product engineering around the philosophy of 'concept-to-customer' and the adoption of the 'small-factory concept'.

Towards the end of 1990, Hardy Spicer adopted the philosophy of 'concept-to-customer' to provide better coordination of functions in product design and development. Five product engineering teams (PETs) of four to seven people were formed, dedicated to particular customers. These comprise staff from applications engineering, production engineering, quality engineering, sales, and purchasing, and work closely with customers and manufacturing. A lot of work has been done on team-building with these groups, linked to accreditation under the Management Charter Initiative. Against the background of a general dearth in management training, this represents an important broadening of the whole training effort in the company.

While some production engineers were assigned to commercial engineering in this way, the remainder were assigned to a reorganized factory system and located in new offices on the factory floor. Since autumn 1990, manufacturing has been reorganized into five separate factories (for the five components of the cv joint), each with its own group of decentralized production engineers and maintenance engineers under a factory manager and two shift deputies. The resulting 'small-factory concept' is intended to give people a greater sense of ownership. However, this also means a change in management style, and it remains a weakness.

In addition to these specific reorganizations, other team-oriented initiatives include:

- The formation of cross-functional project teams to work on specific problems of performance in different parts of the company
- A TQM-type project with a major customer, Nissan, in conjunction with NEDO's 'Strategies for Success' scheme
- Development of a vision statement to provide a framework for business-focused mission objectives for each function (following the example of Rover's 'Rover 2000' vision and mission statement).

In this way, the need for 'new ways of managing' is being framed within a cultural statement focused on customer need.

Cell (or 'cellular') manufacture

Since 1991 the adoption of cell manufacture, with its associated principles of team-working, has sharpened up the whole system of team-working and acted as a stimulant to systematic training to underpin it. Cells consist of a group of activities, arranged in a 'U'-shape, which produce or assemble a whole component for a particular customer. They contain the same sequence of processes and range of machines as, for instance, on the 'bell' line. The difference is there is no automation of material flow (that is, no robots and no moving conveyors), although the just-in-time principle still applies. In some respects, therefore, it involves a lower level of technology. Implementation has involved investment in some new machines and refurbishment of existing ones, and restructuring to improve process flow. For assembly, cellular manufacture has been modelled on the system in Hardy Spicer's sister company in Spain.

Employees have greater control of the process and a sense of ownership, however, in that they produce a complete component. They are closer to the quality problems and can intervene more quickly. They also have the motivation to do so because the six or so people in each cell (one of whom is also the team leader) are physically closer together and get a common bonus. This is a major change from 'old tech', especially for assembly workers, whom 'new tech' entirely passed by.

To support the introduction of cells (and teams generally) there has been an unparalleled effort to assess individual training needs. This includes:

- Testing and training in basic numeracy, literacy, and the ability to read technical drawings
- Writing detailed training manuals
- Appointment of some ninety-plus trainers-cum-team leaders to cover all sections in every shift
- A six-week full-time training programme for all employees prior to the setting up of each cell
- Novel use of video by trainees to analyse their work processes.

These represent a systematic effort to raise work standards all round.

Because there is no moving line, however, there are not the same technological imperatives for multi-skilled, technical operatives which automation of the 'transfer' process (Bell, 1972) under 'just-in-time' demanded. Although cellular manufacture means operators managing a number of machines and for some learning to operate CNC for the first time, such changes belong to an earlier period of automation. It remains an open question therefore whether the traditional 'old-tech' system of setters and operators should be retained or whether the company should go, nevertheless, for multi-skilled setter-operators. The desire to flatten the organizational structure certainly points to the latter.

All this raises the possibility that management are being guided by a belief in people's potential as much as by engineering considerations. Thus, there is a retreat from automation, partly influenced by capital considerations and increased product complexity, but based also on a belief that people are more flexible than machines and that we have tended to overengineer jobs. This has radical implications, involving the rejection of Taylorism.

Summary

This chapter has described the introduction of technical change and its evolution into a more thorough programme of organizational change. As such, it is about change in a manufacturing environment, although in fact technical change has been more common for non-manual workers (Millward *et al.*, 1992). We have also represented this as a long-term, continuing process of change. Technical change should not be seen as a once-and-for-all event.

One of the characteristics of HRM is, of course, its attempt to address organizational change in a comprehensive way. Similarly, technical change has often neglected the need for accompanying organizational change, leading to sub-optimization of systems and failed implementations (Bessant, 1991). While the first era of technical change at Hardy Spicer certainly included organizational change, the second era has begun to do so in an even more comprehensive way.

The first phase of technical change at Hardy Spicer encouraged the 'humanistic' design of work organization, with teams of multi-skilled technical operatives. The automation of the transfer process, combined with 'just-in-time' principles, was crucial in this respect. Automation of the materials 'transfer' process, when combined with reduced manning, is likely to have a radical impact on jobs, skills, and roles – more so than automation of the material 'transformation' process alone, which may simply de-skill (Hendry, 1990b).

Nevertheless, this first phase involved a relatively determinist view of technology (Clark *et al.*, 1988; McLoughlin and Clark, 1993). The second era since 1990, however, has seen a greater degree of organizational change and a lower level of technical change. Technical change now appears to be framed within organizational change, rather than the other way round. In the second period, management philosophy has begun to assume a more independent and decisive role.

This raises the interesting prospect that certain models of technology currently being adopted in advanced factories allow greater scope for management choice in their social and organizational arrangements, and encourage a greater role to be given to the human element in the operation of these systems (Bessant, 1993). This suggests a happy conjunction between new systems of technology and HRM, where HRM is defined as a philosophy of employee involvement and the use of human potential. This implies that the opportunities provided by a paradigm shift in the design and use of technology may be fundamental to the realization of HRM itself as a paradigm shift in the management of people. A number of factors altogether may be involved:

- Managers' perceptions of what can be expected of employees may simply rise. Technical change and training can set a virtuous spiral in motion (as critics who compare the impact of the German system of training on company strategies argue (Steedman and Wagner, 1987)).

- A new generation of managers have been exposed to ideas about human potential drawn from the socio-democratic tradition and to the specific influence of HRM. Managerial values are conditioned by societal values.
- The philosophy of manufacturing itself allows the human factor a more significant role while organizing employees into business-related units. The critical factor is the transition from a manufacturing-led form of organization to one that is customer-led, as in the restructuring of design and manufacturing at Hardy Spicer (Bessant, 1993). People, and people issues, consequently become of more direct strategic importance.
- Customer influence is significant. Hardy Spicer's new Japanese customers, Nissan and Toyota, and older customers like Ford and Rover who have been influenced by Japanese practices, were becoming more and more visible on the shopfloor during this period. They create pressure for team-working and for employees to take responsibility for quality, delivery and continuous improvement. In turn, these performance criteria demand a different order of commitment that goes beyond a simple conception of skill.

Such influences, which are visible at Hardy Spicer, are highly relevant in the wider context of manufacturing where:

- Training standards are rising
- Managers are becoming more educated
- Nearly three-quarters of UK engineering firms (according to the management engineering consultants, Ingersoll) have adopted cell manufacture (or 'mini-business cells')
- The influence of Japanese customers and Japanese manufacturing practice continues to spread.

Note

1 A more detailed version of this case can be found in Hendry, C. (1993), 'Personnel leadership in technical and human resource change', in J. Clark (ed.), *Personnel Management and Technical Change*, London/Newbury Park/New Delhi:Sage.

18
Flexible employees: flexible firms

Introduction

In this book we have tried to capture developments in employment at three levels – at the level of the economy, the firm, and in relation to employees and employee groups. The issue of flexibility engages with all three levels.

At the macro-economic level, it is associated with the supposed decline of mass markets and mass production techniques. Piore and Sabel (1984) characterized this as 'flexible specialization'; others refer to it as 'post-Fordism' (Murray, 1985). The result has been a reordering of the economic structure, including a shift from manufacturing to services and a revitalization of the small-medium firm sector.

Firms have responded with a range of flexible employment practices (Atkinson and Meager, 1986), including:

- Flexible deployment within the firm (task or functional flexibility) and
- Matching overall levels of business activity to staffing needs through numerical flexibility (temporary and casual employment, part-time work, job-share, self-employment and sub-contracting).

We reviewed these tactics in Chapter 3, along with the other lesser forms of temporal and pay flexibility.

For people themselves, 'functional flexibility' may mean increased skills and therefore enhanced job prospects. So-called 'numerical flexibility', however, is likely to mean for many people less job security and pressure to accept lower pay (although for some, especially women, part-time work may mean a way back into the job market). 'Flexibility' therefore has important economic and social implications for individuals. It can result in people's job prospects and position in the labour market becoming institutionalized and reinforced. Those already disadvantaged become condemned to a twilight of inferior work, pay, terms, and conditions.

Insofar as firms' needs for flexibility are fed by particular groups and consequently discriminate against them, flexibility thus perpetuates social disadvantage. Governments can intervene to protect and advance such groups, or they can (as Conservative governments have done since 1979) reduce the protection afforded by legislation, trade unions, and other institutions (like wage councils), in the interests of a more flexible labour market at the macro-economic level.

In the longer term, however, this may backfire by encouraging firms to pursue low-pay employment strategies which undermine the development of skills. Such firms are then condemned to compete in low added-value markets where cost minimization is at a premium. If large parts of the economy are in this trap, there are repercussions for overall GDP, international competitiveness, consumer spending, taxation, and the public services that can be afforded.

The flexibility question exposes linkages like this between different levels of analysis. On the one hand, it brings out the interdependency between labour market phenomena and business strategy. It encourages us to look at the dynamics in the economy, not just to describe surface changes and trends. On the other, it connects firms' behaviour to individuals' life chances. Flexible employment is thus a social question as well as something firms do in pursuit of their own perceived interests.

This chapter will look at what flexible employment strategies mean for the firm and what flexible employment means for employees.

Flexible workers, flexible firms

In the 1980s, the flexibility debate was crystallized by the model of the 'flexible firm' (see Figure 18.1) proposed by John Atkinson (1985). The distinctive feature of this was the suggestion that firms have begun to divide their workforces into 'core' and 'periphery' workers. *Core workers* are the full-time, permanent employees who enjoy job security and high earnings. In return, they perform a range of tasks and work flexibly across traditional skill boundaries. They are 'functionally' flexible. The firm invests training in them, and they develop new skills which separate them increasingly from the external labour market. Typical members of this group are managerial and professional staff and multi-skilled workers. Core workers, in other words, are managed within an internal labour market, or its derivative the 'commitment system', described in Chapter 11.

Outside this core group are a great variety of peripheral workers. They exist in a series of layers. The *first peripheral group* are also full-time, but enjoy less job security and inferior career prospects. They are hired to do specific jobs, usually of a semi-skilled nature, and are therefore prone to higher labour turnover. Because they are easily recruited and easily fired, firms can vary their numbers according to levels of activity. They are 'numerically flexible'. The 'technical/industrial labour market' of Chapter 11 broadly describes their situation.

The *second peripheral group* includes part-timers and people on job-share, and a variety of temporary workers (agency staff, people on short-term contracts, and those on government schemes). They perform the same kind of jobs as the first peripheral group (for example, part-timers in retail). Like the first group, they give the firm numerical flexibility in the face of fluctuating business activity and allow it to cope with uncertain growth.

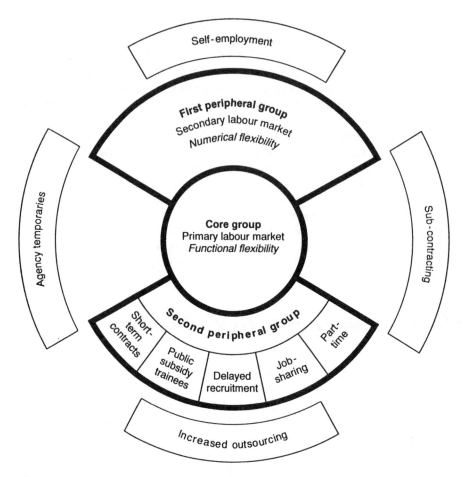

Figure 18.1   *The flexible firm. (Source: Atkinson 1985)*

Outside the firm, there are then a variety of *external workers* who perform either very routine tasks (such as cleaning and security) or very specialized ones. Among the latter would be sub-contract, agency staff, and home-workers in various areas of computing. Both groups enable the firm to cope with predictable 'blips' in activity. It would probably be more accurate to say that they provide financial, rather than numerical, flexibility, since they enable the firm to limit its financial commitment. In the case of the less skilled, sub-contracting of routine services in recent years has frequently been accompanied by reduced pay and costs. With the more specialized group, a firm may be forced down this route because such workers are in short supply. Low-skill 'external workers' and the 'second peripheral group' would tend to fall within the 'open external labour market' model of Chapter 11; while those with higher skills belong to the 'occupational labour market'.

The core–periphery, flexible firm is an 'ideal-type' model of the firm. Although in some ways it is a useful synthesis (Hakim, 1990), it has been challenged on two grounds:

- What is the evidence for increased flexibility?
- Are firms behaving any differently from in the past (Atkinson suggested they were)?

The evidence for flexibility

Atkinson based his model on evidence from case studies and surveys. The latter included the NEDC (1985) survey of seventy-two firms in the food and drink, engineering, retail, and financial services industries. This identified widespread increases in numerical flexibility in the early 1980s. Other studies around the same time, however, failed to find significant evidence of change in employment practices. This includes the more representatively based 1984 Workplace Industrial Relations Survey (Millward and Stevens, 1986).

Subsequent surveys, including ACAS (1988), point to a modest increase in different forms of numerical flexibility. For example, sub-contracting is most common and has increased in manufacturing, in larger organizations, and in parts of the public sector (such as health and the civil service). Job-sharing has made some advance in, for example, banking where there are particular problems of balancing staffing and workload. Most commentators are sceptical, however, about how far such practices have spread and how generalized they are (Pollert, 1988; Marginson *et al.*, 1988; Wood and Smith, 1989; Hakim, 1990; Casey, 1991).

These negative views might seem at odds with the evidence of increasing numbers of 'flexible employees'. Two particular groups – part-time employees and the self-employed – have steadily increased in number.

In 1981, there were just over 4 million people in Britain working part-time; in September 1993, there were just under 6 million. This growth has occurred at the expense of full-time jobs. In the single year to September 1993, part-time workers increased by 227 820 to 5 998 112, while full-time jobs declined by 275 464 to 14 889 977. Over the whole period, 1981–1992, the number of part-time jobs rose by 1.25 million, while full-time jobs declined by 0.5 million. In the process, the share of part-time jobs in the British economy has increased from 19 per cent to 24 per cent. This trend is set to continue to the year 2000, when there are forecast to be 6.5 million part-time jobs, or 25 per cent of all jobs (Employment Department, 1994).

As Figure 18.2 shows, the proportion of the self-employed in the UK workforce also increased substantially throughout the 1980s, at a slightly faster rate (68 per cent up compared with 50 per cent) than the increase in part-time employees. In 1990 there were nearly 3.4 million self-employed – around one in eight of the total workforce.

Both trends, however, can be largely explained by wider economic effects rather than indicating the deliberate adoption of novel core–periphery strategies. First, there is the restructuring of the economy. Full-time jobs have been disappearing in manufacturing while the more part-time-oriented service sector has been adding jobs. What has happened is not a large-scale swap of full-time jobs for part-time ones, implying a change of strategy by firms, but more of the same in those sectors where part-time working is

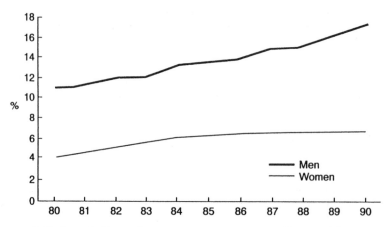

Figure 18.2 *Self-employment as a proportion of the workforce in employment (June 1980 to June 1990). (Source: Employment Department, 1992)*

traditional. (Having said that, there are also specific cases of firms like Forte, the hotel group, changing staff contracts from 40 hours to 20 hours to adjust to trading conditions.) Similarly, self-employment is concentrated in three sectors where it has always been traditional – distribution, hotels and catering, and construction.

Second, it is possible to argue that the growth in part-timers and the self-employed also reflects recessionary influences. One common explanation for self-employment, for instance, is that it is a temporary response to what would otherwise be unemployment. However, the growth in the self-employed has been fairly consistent over the whole period since 1980, through the peak as well as the troughs of the economic cycle.

However we intepret such data, it is a mistake nevertheless to equate increased 'casualization' in the labour market, measured by these two groups, with flexible employment policies inside firms (Allen, 1988). What matters are employers' labour-use strategies in the workplace rather than aggregate trends in the labour market.

Employers' labour-use strategies

The Employers' Labour Use Strategies (ELUS) survey carried out in 1987 indicated that only about 5 per cent of employers with twenty-five or more employees had adopted a core–periphery strategy (or, at most 15 per cent if allowance is made for possible undercounting). Such firms covered no more than 1.27 million employees, of whom 0.27 million could be regarded as peripheral out of a total of 8 million 'casualized' workers in the economy at large:

> It follows that the vast majority of peripheral workers are working in or for establishments where management is *not* making sharp distinctions between core and periphery, but simply pursuing traditional reasons for employing part-time

and temporary employees, contract and freelance staff, supplemented by a large measure of *ad hoc* response to opportunities and problems as they arise (Hakim, 1990, p. 178).

Researchers who have done 'micro' studies of firms' behaviour which get at individual managers' rationales for adopting particular practices echo these sentiments. (As we noted in Chapter 3, the problem with large data sets is that they are wide open to attributing erroneous motives to employers and managers.)

The follow-up study on the ELUS survey by Hunter and MacInnes (1991) is particularly useful because it is the result of progressively focusing on those workplaces having the most marked tendency to employ peripheral workers. ELUS was based on the 1984 Workplace Industrial Relations Survey and focused on those workplaces which indicated that they made use of peripheral workers of various kinds. It visited 877 of these – roughly half of the WIRS sample (Hakim, 1990). Hunter and MacInnes then took a sub-sample of thirty-nine establishments from the ELUS survey which had identified themselves as having a clear labour-use strategy, or whose questionnaire returns indicated that they were heavy users of non-standard labour contracts. They then conducted interviews, during late 1988 and early 1989, to establish whether the employer was following a deliberate strategy and how far it involved a core–periphery strategy.

They begin by clarifying the kinds of occupational group which predominated in these firms – that is, who these 'peripheral' workers were. Three groups were identified (Hunter and MacInnes, 1991, p. 40):

1   First, there were a set of skilled professional and technical occupations comprising large numbers of freelance, agency and self-employed workers who preferred self-employed status. They were able to maintain this in the face of employers' preferences that they should be full-time direct employees, because demand exceeded the supply of people with such skills. The main occupations were draughtspersons, design engineers, and computing specialists. Overwhelmingly, these workers were fairly high-paid men. Around one in ten of those on non-standard contracts fell into this category.

2   Second, there was a much more diverse group of manual and non-manual workers who were seen by their employers as having a low level of skill or as easily transferable. The jobs they did were thought not to require much learning or training. As we note below, these assumptions may be inaccurate. Overwhelmingly, these workers were women (around 90 per cent of this group). Again, as we note below, the work done by women is often systematically undervalued. The range of contracts among this group was more varied – usually it involved direct employment (Atkinson's 'first peripheral group') on a temporary or part-time basis, but occasionally such workers were agency temps or self-employed. Mostly it was employers who had decided on the non-standard form of contract as part of a deliberate strategy corresponding to patterns of work. This was especially true of packing, cleaning, catering and shop work. In some cases however (with secretarial, clerical, nursing

and paramedical staff), there were elements of both employer and employee preference. With these workers, part-time hours were attractive to both parties and could increase the supply of female labour.

3   Finally, there was a smaller third group between the other two which covered a range of skilled and unskilled jobs that were dependent in some way on limited contracts and a tendering process. These included workers in civil engineering and construction. At the time of interviewing, these sectors were relatively buoyant and many workers were able to benefit from or preferred self-employed status (as we saw in the construction case in Chapter 12). The others in this group were predominantly public sector workers in local authorities, hospitals, and universities where funding was for a limited duration (for example, contract researchers who now comprise a high proportion of academic staff in many universities).

Hunter and MacInnes conclude that while employers have been extending their use of non-standard contracts with these groups, there is little evidence of core-periphery-type strategies:

> We have been unable to detect any significant trend towards a new employment strategy, in the sense of a forward-looking plan which systematicaly relates labour use patterns to the coprorate or business strategy of the employing organization. The evidence suggests a much more *ad hoc* approach to labour use, but predominantly exploiting existing types of flexible contract and, for the most part, applying them in quite conventional ways (Hunter and MacInnes, 1991, Summary).

Other studies that find employers pursuing clear strategies have flatly contradicted the core–periphery model. The most apposite one here concerns retailing – a sector which is well known for its flexible labour-utilization strategy. Thus, Doogan (1992) argues that modern retailers in Britain have been moving up-market. The top twenty retailers, covering all kinds of product area, have attempted to improve the calibre of staff and change the perception of shop work:

> Personnel strategy seeks to reduce staff turnover, shift attitudes and motivation, and to inculcate a strong sense of company culture in the workforce. This has resulted in significant improvement in wage and non-wage benefits and the virtual erosion of differentials between full and part-time staff in the large companies.
> Shop workers, therefore, simply do not conform to the profile laid down by the core and periphery model (Doogan, 1992, p. 38).

Other case studies provide supporting evidence for this view (Sparrow, 1988).

However, erosion of pay differentials may count for little in a context where there has been a massive shift from full- to part-time work since the 1960s, and where rates of pay remain low compared with other industries. On the other hand, work patterns in retail need to be seen against the background of the equally massive decline in the small, self-employed retailer. In macro terms, jobs have effectively transferred from full-time, independent self-employment, to part-time employment in large retailers.

An assessment of the core–periphery model

The flexible firm model synthesizes ideas from a number of disciplines. It incorporates older concepts of primary and secondary labour markets, and puts these within the context of the firm as the main agent in structuring employment. In doing so, it reflects a shift in labour market segmentation theory away from the characteristics of workers towards the characteristics of jobs and the role of firms in defining these (Rubery, 1988; Peck, 1989).

By incorporating different groups of workers within one model it provides a framework for thinking about the whole set of labour markets which may be combined within any one firm. It thus brings together the four or five labour markets described in Chapter 11 and suggests how firms manage the boundaries between them.

The question, however, is whether Atkinson's dichotomy into core and periphery groups illuminates or obscures the issues involved. Does the attachment to a core–periphery thesis put a straitjacket on thinking about how different employee groups and labour markets within any one organization are being managed, and can be managed, in the real world?

There are two principal objections. The first is that it encourages a polarized view of employment strategies (and employable workers) in terms of a core of 'polyvalent' task-flexible workers and a numerically flexible periphery of unskilled labour (Child, 1985). The second is that through the excessive attention it has received, sometimes of an ideological kind, the core–periphery model has been a distraction. The real issue is 'flexibility' itself, with its various costs and benefits.

Numerical flexibility is a response to many factors

As we argued in Chapter 11, employment strategies are a response to a wide range of factors – not only economic and technical ones but also to the state of the labour market itself. Figure 11.3 highlighted five sets of external factors interacting with factors internal to the firm, while others have grouped these together in terms of labour demand factors, labour supply factors, and the role of the State.

Flexible employment strategies in recent years have been a response to three principal factors – the first to do with demand, the other two reflecting labour supply:

1 *Competitive pressures*: As Hunter and MacInnes (1991) observed, the guiding force behind organizations' behaviour, in both the private and public sector, has been to obtain a better resourcing fit with short-term competitive or budgetary constraints. Part-time and temporary employees are cheaper from an employer's point of view because they avoid paying certain benefits and can hire and fire more freely. Part-time workers also tend to be more productive on an hourly basis and are less often absent. For example, full-time workers may 'pace' themselves, while part-timers are both fresher and may feel more vulnerable to dismissal for sub-standard (slower) performance.

2 *Labour market shortages*: Recession since 1990 has tended to obscure this factor. In the period 1987–1990, however, the British economy had scarcely begun to tackle accumulated high unemployment than skilled labour shortages started to reappear. The reduction in the number of school-leavers and an ageing population will exacerbate this in the medium-term once recession passes. Faced with this 'demographic down-turn', the National Economic Development Office (NEDO) and Employment Department were urging firms in the late 1980s to open up employment to under-represented groups through more flexible forms of employment (see Chapter 2). Part-time work is to some extent, therefore, a response to skill shortages.

3 *Changing life-style preferences and career patterns*: As the Hunter and MacInnes (1991) observations on employee groups above indicate, there will always be those who, by virtue of having special skills in short supply, can dictate their own terms of employment. Moreover, in recent years the notion of 'free agent careers' (Kanter, 1989) has gained ground, with entrepreneurial individuals preferring to be less tied to one employer.

The balance between such factors is liable to change over time. In the 1980s organizations were responding to a particularly stringent set of economic conditions – uncertainty, unsettled product markets, competitive pressures on costs and profits in the private sector; increased financial disciplines and budget controls in the public sector. In just a few years, the economy has gone from boom through inflation into recession, and is now emerging to face the predicted demographic downturn once again. Meanwhile, larger structural changes (such as those affecting the distribution of jobs in retailing between large and small firms) further obscure trends in employment practice. It is therefore difficult to predict what form labour-utilization strategies will take in the longer term, and whether flexibility strategies are a short- or a long-term phenomenon.

The costs of flexibility

As we saw in the case of retail, however, the real issue is not whether firms are pursuing core–periphery strategies but the fact of flexible (i.e. 'casual-ized') employment combined with low pay. While numerically flexible employment provides benefits to employers, it also brings disadvantages, including drawbacks for firms themselves. For example, a flexible workforce is harder to manage and imposes higher administrative costs in areas like recruitment. Commitment may also be a problem.

The greater cost, however, is borne by the individual and the State (Brewster *et al.*, 1992). The State has to pick up the unemployment costs of people between temporary jobs and, for part-time workers in low-paid jobs, the cost of income subsidies. Employers using workers on government-assisted training schemes as a source of cheap labour also benefit from effective State subsidies. For the individual, anything other than permanent, full-time employment tends to mean lower pay and fewer non-wage benefits.

Part-time and temporary work also makes training and promotion less likely; reduces involvement in decisions affecting jobs; and decreases access to trade union protection.

These are immediate, direct effects. There are also more fundamental, long-term effects which arise from the stereotyping of and discrimination against part-time and temporary workers in less specialized jobs. In this respect, the very idea of 'core' and 'periphery' tends to downgrade the importance of those in part-time jobs. As Walsh (1990) observes, talking about part-timers as 'peripheral' in sectors like retailing, where they comprise up to two-thirds of all employees and firms rely on them during the hours of peak demand, is misleading and derogatory. Nevertheless, such workers have low status and temporary and part-time work tends to encourage this. It allows the employer to treat them as less skilled and to pay less. This is reinforced socially as people then perceive the work and the worker to be less unskilled and of low status. This affects the self-image and expectations of the employees themselves. A self-fulfilling dynamic is thereby set up of 'low-skilled' workers for low-status, 'low-skilled' jobs, regardless of their actual technical content (Rubery, 1988). Such patterns are evident in many jobs employing women.

On the one hand, then, firms shape the labour market through their recruitment, training, and reward strategies, and create and reinforce inequalities. On the other, they get workers with low expectations which they themselves have helped to create. While this increases the employer's freedom as regards employment strategies, it potentially also limits the commercial strategies they are able to pursue.

This is the real consequence of employment practices. What matters is effects, not intentions. It matters less that employers appear to have been largely adopting *ad hoc* approaches to employment (Hunter and MacInnes, 1991), as against explicit core–periphery strategies, but that this *ad hoc* behaviour can readily become habitual, permanent, and irreversible (especially when encouraged by government (Hakim, 1990)). A labour-utilization strategy may be no less effective and embedded if it is tacit and implicit than if it is articulated and made explicit.

Secondary employment groups and equal opportunities

The above discussion touches on the issue of discrimination and equal opportunities. As a result of actual practices in respect of recruitment, training, promotion, and rewards, the labour market becomes segmented in a variety of ways. The most prominent and controversial of these concern gender and race. Here we will consider specifically the issue of gender and discrimination against women, since this is related directly to the flexibility question.

Discrimination on the basis of race or ethnic origins is both more complex (because of the diversity of non-white, non-English races) and less subtle (being rooted in colonial relationships). For a discussion of the origins, extent, and forms of racial discrimination in employment, the reader is referred to the analysis of the Labour Force Survey in *Britain's Ethnic Minorities* (Jones, 1993) and to Jenkins (1988).

Equal opportunities and women

In Chapter 16 we considered the 'status divide' between manual and non-manual groups as a primary form of segmentation in the workplace. Arguably, however, the real 'status divide' has long shifted to that between men and women. This has two aspects (1) the segregation of women into women's jobs, and (2) direct discrimination when doing similar jobs.

As Price (1989) observes, the latter arose very early in the employment of women. When women began to be employed in large numbers in clerical and related jobs men fiercely opposed this, fearing that their own pay and prospects would be reduced. Women tended, therefore, to be segregated into special grades, at lower wages, with fewer promotion opportunities, less job security, and lower status (Walby, 1986). The employment structure in banking, for example, is a legacy of this.

Direct discrimination of this kind has been made harder by legislation on equal pay (Equal Pay Act 1970, amended in 1983) and the promotion of equal opportunities through statute and the Equal Opportunities Commission (Sex Discrimination Acts 1975 and 1986). However, the explosion in part-time work and the fact that women fill such jobs disproportionately tends to institutionalize more indirect forms of discrimination. Increased rates of female participation in the labour force are therefore deceptive.

As we saw in Chapter 2, the participation rate for women has increased consistently since the 1970s, while that of men has fallen (see Figure 2.3). These trends are forecast to continue, with the gap between the participation rates of men and women of working age closing to 84 per cent and 76 per cent, respectively, by 2006 (Employment Department, 1994, p. 35). This will be most marked among women in the 25-44 age group.

However, as Figure 18.3 shows, much of this has been and will continue to be in part-time jobs. In 1992, in the UK 46 per cent of women were part-timers (compared with 11 per cent of men). With the exception of the Netherlands (at nearly 60 per cent), this is the highest in the European Union – double that, for instance, of France. Put another way, 90 per cent of part-timers are women.

Increased participation rates and part-time work have therefore gone hand in hand in Britain. The suggestion is that inferior rights attaching to part-time work mean that women's inferior position in the labour market has paradoxically also to some extent been reinforced. This means that equal opportunities legislation on its own is not enough if, at the same time, the labour market is governed by market forces which push women into jobs with inferior pay and conditions.

In an interesting study, Whitehouse (1992) tested this proposition by comparing data on women's pay in thirteen OECD countries, including Britain. This showed a strong association between high relative earnings for

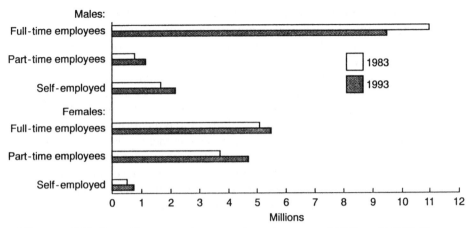

Figure 18.3 *Change in the type of employment, 1983 and 1993. (Source: Employment Department, 1994)*

women, on the one hand, and centralized wage-fixing arrangements (through unionized bargaining structures) and government employment, on the other. Both of these act as a constraint on localized (company- or establishment-based) market factors being used as a criterion for judging the worth of a job. It is these more localized processes which allow biased evaluations of women's work to creep in and escape the terms of equal pay legislation (Ghobadian and White, 1987).

At the same time, Whitehouse found that centralized wage-fixing arrangements were negatively correlated with female participation rates (indicating that regulation tended to restrict the participation-through-casualization that characterizes the UK). These findings do not mean that legislation is unimportant (although relatively high pay was achieved in leading countries such as Denmark, Finland, Norway, and Sweden in advance of equal pay and equal opportunities legislation). The Equal Pay Act 1975, for instance, is widely regarded as having significantly closed the pay gap (Zabalza and Tzannatos, 1985). Of immense contemporary importance also is the ruling by the House of Lords in March 1994 that the provisions of the Employment Protection Act 1978, giving weaker employment rights on redundancy and unfair dismissal to those working fewer than 16 hours a week, contravene European Union law on on equal pay and treatment for men and women and are invalid (*The Guardian*, 1994). This opens the way for similar challenges on pensions and maternity rights.

Nevertheless, it does mean that the prospects for women depend on much more than the enactment of legislation. They rely on supporting institutions and policies. Indeed, the willingness of judges in the British House of Lords to intepret the impact of 1978 Act in the way they have done is indicative of a change of attitude and perspective as much as anything else. Among the critical 'institutional' factors is the provision of public childcare facilities, which are relatively poor in the UK. This deficiency enforces a work pattern whereby women interrupt employment and careers to bring up a young family. They often then return to work on a part-time basis and lose position in the career market. This puts a different gloss on the argument which says many women 'prefer' part-time work.

In addition, participation rates are misleading as an indicator of labour force equality – even for full-time jobs (see Figure 18.3) – when they do not indicate the kind of jobs into which women are being drawn. Women's employment is still concentrated in personal services (such as catering, cleaning, and hairdressing); in retail; in clerical jobs; in textiles and clothing within manufacturing; and in health, welfare, and education for professional and quasi-professional jobs (Employment Department, 1994, p. 12). Many of these jobs are liable to be undervalued either because women's skills and attributes are undervalued or because the jobs are in sectors where the ability of firms to pay is low because of low productivity through lack of investment (Craig *et al.*, 1982) Two problems persist, then:

- The inherent undervaluing of part-time jobs, disproportionately filled by women and
- The undervaluing of women's attributes and skills in full-time jobs where they happen to be concentrated (Horrell, Rubery and Burchell, 1990).

Women in management

One area where this bias is especially insidious is in the qualities demanded in management jobs. Even when the grosser barriers have been removed – such as unreasonable requirements to be geographically mobile – women in management experience particular obstacles and stresses in having to conform to a male culture (Ashburner, 1991). In the first place, promotion is made more difficult because of the masculine bias in valuing attributes and skills. Then having progressed into management, women are liable to encounter a range of special difficulties rooted in cultural values. These cover attitudes favouring long working hours to the detriment of home commitments – to beliefs about 'proper' managerial behaviours involving such things as delegation, participation, and the inclination to play organizational politics (Davidson and Cooper, 1983). Even working with other women gives problems, since women in lower-hierarchy jobs have often been socialized into submissive roles and are (said to be) either uncomfortable taking orders from another woman or expect clearer hierarchical boundaries than the woman manager may be inclined to give.

A recent survey by Scase and Goffee (1990) shows that women continue to feel that they are under greater pressure than their male counterparts. The major sources of pressure reported were:

- Conflicting demands of home and work
- Expectations of colleagues
- Working relationships with men
- Visibility as (token) women managers.

Summary

This chapter has considered a central phenomenon in the way employment has developed in recent years, namely the growth in 'numerical' flexibility. It has considered this from the point of view both of the firm and what it means for employees. In doing this we have stressed the 'circular' effect whereby firms construct the labour market and the labour market acts back on the firm, determining the kind of employees available to it.

The flexibility debate has been considerably influenced since the mid-1980s by the model of the 'flexible firm' proposed by John Atkinson. The evidence suggests, however, that firms have been less intent on pursuing 'core–periphery' strategies than in simply responding to supply and demand factors, especially competitive pressures. The result is a large increase in the numbers of 'flexible employees', but largely confined to sectors which have traditionally relied on casualized employment.

The real issue is that such *ad hoc* employment approaches become permanent and institutionalize the disadvantages which accompany part-time and temporary employment. The impact of this falls especially on women.

The trend towards flexible working patterns has been occurring all over Europe, with part-time employment particularly on the increase in the Netherlands, Germany, and the UK (Brewster *et al.*, 1993). The driving forces for this vary – from economic pressure to permissive legislation (in Germany and Scandinavia) which gives women legal rights to work part-time. At the same time, work patterns and their impact are influenced by institutional factors like the provision of childcare.

The nature and extent of 'flexibility' and its impact on people thus depends on the particular labour market context and the economic and social systems which underpin the operation of the labour market (Rubery, 1989). A special aspect of this wider context is the national educational and training system. This has a profound influence on mobility and the terms on which people enter employment, as well as, of course, in underpinning the capacity of firms to pursue commercial strategies.

The next chapter picks up this issue and compares the working of the UK training system with that of Germany, the USA, and Japan, with the implications for companies of the kind of labour market created.

19

Skills and training in the European Union and beyond

Introduction

The Single European Market, which came into existence on 1 January 1993, looks forward to the creation of a high skill, high added value economy. Some Member States, especially Germany, have already gone a long way towards achieving this, as have others outside Europe such as Japan. Across Europe as a whole, this implies that there will have to be an education and training drive to create a workforce with up-to-date knowledge and flexible skills. British politicians of all parties also seem agreed on this. How far, however, is Europe in general and Britain in particular placed to create such a workforce? What kind of employment opportunities are likely to result from the national system of training in Britain?

Beginning with a brief overview of EU policy and comparative performance among EU countries, this chapter looks at the system of vocational education and training (VET) in the UK and how it has changed in recent years. We then compare this with the systems in three of our major competitors – the USA, Japan, and Germany – the latter two of which especially have been held up as exemplars to be copied.

The impact of the Single European Market on jobs and skills

In the run-up to 1993, the Institute for Employment Research at Warwick University did some forecasts on the consequences of the Single European Market (SEM). It considered three possible scenarios for the economy of the European Community, as it was then called, as a result of removing barriers to trade:

- An 'efficiency' scenario, resulting from vigorous product-market competition and increased labour market flexibility, would produce an increase of 1.1 million jobs by the turn of the century. These would be largely in service industries, however, and in part-time, low-paid jobs.

- A 'cost-cutting' scenario, involving fierce price competition between European competitors, would effectively negate these benefits. This would be detrimental to services in general and to certain areas of manufacturing.
- A 'quality' scenario, however, in which Europe moves towards a high-added value/high-skill economy, would double the benefits and increase employment. These effects were likely to be especially marked in chemicals, construction and banking. The benefits for individual countries would differ, however, according to how well they were placed in sectors that were strong or weak internationally (Institute for Employment Research, 1991). Regrettably, the UK has more weak or averagely performing sectors than most other EU countries, except Greece and Spain (Directorate-General, Employment, Industrial Relations and Social Affairs, 1990; Hendry, 1994, pp. 135–138).

Since the SEM was conceived, the European Commission has been committed to the third scenario. Its expectations and objectives for the SEM rest on the enhancing of technological progressiveness and a belief in upgrading skills through increased training and development:

> The importance attached to an education-training drive is not equally shared throughout the Community. Yet such a drive is essential as it must make it possible to renew existing qualifications, increase comparative advantages in terms of the ratio of real salary/level of qualification and therefore stimulate other types of investment (that is, not concentrated solely on industries with a high labour content) (Directorate-General for Economic and Financial Affairs, 1990, p. 99).

Other commentators also assume the need to follow a high-skill strategy in order to combat the dominance of the USA and Japan in high-technology sectors and to match the development of the Pacific Rim countries (Rajan, 1990; Lane, 1991). Such an 'education-training drive' will ensure that workers have good basic, up-to-date knowledge and broad, flexible skills.

An education and training strategy for Europe?

European initiatives to improve knowledge and raise skills have been at two levels: (1) EU-wide training programmes and (2) the setting of common objectives for national training systems. There are a large number of EU programmes covering initial training and education, with exotic names like Erasmus, Comett, Lingua, Eurydice, Arion, Petra, Eurotecnet, and Iris. A number of these are targeted at graduate students to develop their mobility as employees with the EU. There are also schemes operating at national level for youth exchanges. Four of the twelve 'fundamental social rights' enshrined in the Social Chapter of the Mastricht Treaty also directly or indirectly concern vocational training.

The second approach – setting common objectives for training – is made difficult, however, by the enormous diversity between national systems: 'Not only are the training systems of Member States institutionally diverse but they are also embedded in broader systems of social relations with which they interact' (Rainbird, 1992, p. 3). As Warner (1987) and others have observed, this diversity is based in historical developments which make fundamental changes in national systems difficult to carry through and slow to produce results:

> Whilst in some countries vocational training is provided by the state within the education system, in others it is provided primarily within the company. This is often reflected in ministerial responsibility for VET falling with either the Ministry of Education or the Ministry of Labour, or both. In some instances VET will be regulated by law, in others by collective agreements or arrangements made between individuals and their employers. Young people undergoing training may have the status of employees, trainees or students and will be paid a wage, an allowance or receive nothing, accordingly. The division of financial responsibility between the state, employers and employees varies from one country to another, as does the relative emphasis given to initial and continuing training (Rainbird, 1992, p. 3–4).

The performance of European training systems

The diversity in institutional systems makes it very difficult to establish meaningful cross-country comparisons of Member States' performance on training, and the extent to which they are responding to the call for an education-training drive. Thus, company expenditure on training reflects differences in who trains (companies or the State); whether or not there is legislative compulsion (as in France); and simply how efficient companies are at accounting for training. As studies of VET in Britain have shown, there is enormous variability in activities counted as training and the elements of cost taken into account (Pettigrew, Hendry and Sparrow, 1989). This problem is widespread in Europe (Holden, 1991), with company practices in recording expenditure extremely variable even in Germany.

The annual review begun by Price Waterhouse/Cranfield on human resource trends in Europe will improve the availability of systematic data on training, and the understanding of the institutional background.

Educational standards

The structure for initial training combines with the educational system. Again there are marked differences in the school-leaving age, participation rates, and leaving qualifications. For example, in Portugal the school-leaving age is thirteen years of age, whereas in most other EU states it is sixteen.

Figure 19.1 shows the proportion of young people in post-14 education. Only Portugal has a lower figure than the UK in the 14-18 age group, while the UK has the lowest figure for both the 19-22 and 23-24 age group. The UK is also near the bottom among the wider group of OECD countries (Rajan, 1990). However, these figures are influenced by factors such as shorter degrees in the UK. In the UK, most first degrees (except some such as medicine and engineering) take three years: in Germany five to six years is more normal.

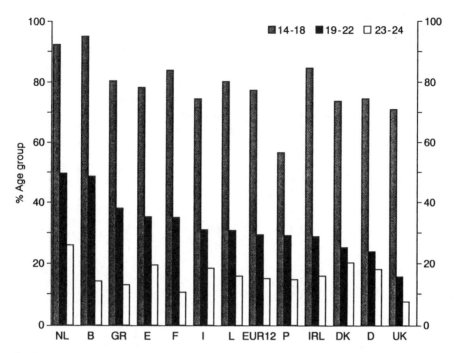

Figure 19.1 *Share of young people in education in the Member States [1988]. (Source Directorate-General, Employment, Industrial Relations and Social Affairs, 1990)*

Table 19.1, which features seven of the twelve Member States in 1989, consequently shows that the UK has the highest percentage of people with university degrees, despite its low participation rate. This low participation rate in the UK has, in any case, dramatically changed in the 1990s, increasing from around 14 per cent in 1990 to nearer 25 per cent.

On the other hand, in contrast with the then West Germany, Table 19.1 also shows a relatively small proportion of young people receiving an extended non-academic, vocational education. Arguably, this is more important in forming the backbone of a progressive economy than is academic training of a graduate elite. The other countries listed, however, lack even the UK's level of further training.

Such figures on their own are not conclusive of national disadvantage given the way different elements in each country's system support one another. Nor do they say anything about standards. However, low numbers in advanced secondary and higher education cannot but be a stumbling block in sustaining high-technology, knowledge-based sectors and shifting more traditional sectors onto a higher technological footing.

We now look at this more deeply in terms of the institutional structure for VET in the UK, Germany, the USA, and Japan. Underlying education and training in each case is a prevailing model of the labour market. We will mention specific features of this as appropriate.

Table 19.1 Level of education of the population aged twenty and over (%) (1989)

	Completed upper secondary education only	Additional vocational non-academic education and training	Post-secondary education	University degree
Belgium				
Male	21.4			14.6
Female	17.3			12.0
West Germany				
Male	10.3	60.5	3.9	6.0
Female	7.3	45.3	1.2	3.2
Italy				
Male	22.6			5.5
Female	20.7			3.7
Netherlands				
Male	31.5		14.1	6.1
Female	27.7		10.2	1.9
Portugal				
Male	8.4		0.8	3.4
Female	6.3		2.5	2.0
Spain				
Male	24.3		4.3	4.1
Female	19.5		4.5	2.1
United Kingdom				
Male	6.5	28.8		16.1
Female	6.3	6.8		14.8

Source: Directorate-General for Economic and Financial Affairs (1990) (reproduced from OECD *Employment Outlook*, July 1989).

The training system in the UK

While the majority of EU States have some form of regulation in their training systems and also incorporate trade union interests into the policy-making process for training, the UK is an exception. In the UK, vocational training is treated as the responsibility of the individual employer – thus mirroring the *laissez-faire* approach in the related area of collective bargaining.

The national structure

For a time, in the 1960s and 1970s, a more interventionist philosophy prevailed. The Training Act 1964 created a system of tripartite Industrial Training Boards (ITBs) and gave them powers to impose a levy to fund training. They then returned this money to firms in the form of grants. Apart from the impact the ITBs had on training standards and pioneering new training methods, the levy system stimulated many companies to establish training departments for the first time in order to provide a mechanism for recouping the levy.

The levy/grant was subsequently transformed into a levy/grant/exemption system in 1973 (by the Employment and Training Act), to make it less bureaucratic and less punitive for those firms which carried out training as a matter of course. The 1973 Act also created the Manpower Services Commission (MSC) to oversee the ITBs and to compensate for particular defects in the ITB system. Among these were the failure of ITBs to address youth unemployment and adult retraining, as they were largely geared to sustaining the apprenticeship system.

In 1981 the Conservative government abolished the majority (seventeen) of the twenty-four ITBs as part of its 'rolling back of the State', and reverted to a more 'voluntarist' system. Paradoxically, at the same time, however, the MSC expanded its centralist role by taking on the management of national programmes for youth training (YTS) and subsequently training for the adult unemployed (ET). In 1988 this tripartite/corporatist approach to training finally ended, with the decision to turn the MSC first into the Training Commission and then into the Training Agency, before becoming a full part once again of the Department of Employment. The remaining ITBs were abolished (with exception of the Construction Industry Board, on the insistence of the employers), and a system of local training bodies was set up from April 1991, run by employers through boards modelled on private sector lines. Trade unions were formally excluded, although a few TECs and LECs have chosen to involve trade unionists and educationalists.

In England and Wales there are seventy such bodies known as Training and Enterprise Councils (TECs), and twelve in Scotland, known as Local Enterprise Companies (LECs). They are funded from central sources, and initially had to produce development plans to obtain approval to operate. Apart from being constituted in a way intended to maximize employer involvement and commitment to training, the TECs/LECs also represent a shift from a sectoral approach to training to one which exercises influence in local labour markets. This reflects the criticism of the ITBs that, being sectorally based, they were unable to address skill shortages which often had a local character.

Responsibility for the management of YTS (and the upgraded two-year version Youth Training (YT) which replaced it), plus ET, have passed to the TECs/LECs. The TECSs/LECs also manage new schemes such as 'Business Growth Training' (for small–medium enterprises), and accreditation for 'Investors in People' which since 1991 has been spearheading the national effort to raise in-company training standards.

Alongside the TECs/LECs there remain some ninety-four voluntary industrial training organizations (ITOs) at sectoral level, supported by companies in their industry and by the earnings they generate. These 'non-statutory training organizations' are relatively underfunded, however, and, despite the valuable contribution they can yet make, they have become something like Cinderellas in the training system, confining themselves in many cases to disbursing grants and information. What was formerly the largest ITB, the Engineering Industry Training Board, meanwhile has been reconstituted as a company limited by guarantee (i.e. the Engineering Training Authority).

Although the new locally based, employer-led system is modelled on the regional 'Chambers of Craft Industries' in Germany, and to a lesser extent on the 'Private Industry Councils' (PICs) in the USA, it fundamentally differs in the discouragement to trade unions and educationalists to participate in the management of the system. In Germany, trade unions play an active role and help to determine the structure and content of training, through nationally agreed syllabuses with employers and the government. Similarly, educationalists are an integral part of the German system on account of the dual character of vocational training. That is, it combines two days in school with three days working in a company, during the period of apprenticeship from the age of 16 to 19. Moreover, initial and further training in the German company is organized within the broader framework of worker–management cooperation which characterizes company-level industrial relations.

While the UK has thus retreated from state involvement in training, there are still voices which urge the need for a compulsory element to promote training in companies, not just in the Labour Party but also within the Department of Employment itself. Given the control they now exercise over the system of training, the TECs/LECs are perhaps the last chance for employers to justify the voluntary approach.

The tasks of the training system

Chapter 2 outlined some of the basic changes in the UK system in the 1980s, while Chapter 16 described the training provided by the British system in terms of the internal labour market and occupational labour market structures predominating in services and manufacturing. Thus, the manually dominated sectors of engineering and construction, among others, have depended historically on the apprenticeship system which sustained occupational labour markets.

The big change since the early 1980s has been the collapse of the apprenticeship system. Whereas in 1964 there were some 240 000 apprentices in British manufacturing industry, by 1979 this had dropped to 155 000, and by 1986 it had reduced to just 63 700 (MSC, 1986). It took the recession of 1980–1982 to force employers and unions finally to face up to the faults of the existing system in which one had had a vested interest in preserving and the other had tolerated (Keep, 1989a). That is:

- Under the traditional apprenticeship, school-leavers (predominantly male) were attached to individual employers
- They qualified by serving a set period of time (hence, apprenticeships were 'time-served')
- Training was largely on-the-job (although in more recent years there was more time spent off-the-job at a college of further education or a government training centre)
- The skills learnt were specific to an occupation, or 'exclusive', rather than providing a broad range of transferable skills.

The drawbacks of this were considerable:

- Entry to apprenticeships was closely controlled by trade unions with a view to regulating access to jobs, and hence the numbers trained nationally were meagre.
- In turn, job demarcations were rigidly preserved through the narrow definition of trades. This acted as a disincentive to employers to train semi- and unskilled workers, since it was next to impossible to put them into the jobs of 'skilled' men. It also discouraged the adoption of new technology or prevented employers getting the best from such investment, because inefficient job demarcations persisted.
- Finally, standards of on-the-job training and supervision were themselves variable, and the level of competence actually achieved was doubtful in the absence generally of external standards and testing.

When the apprenticeship system finally withered in the face of recession, the MSC started to put in place an alternative national system of training for school-leavers with the launch of its 'New Training Initiative' in 1981. The centrepiece of this was the one-year Youth Training Scheme (YTS), introduced in 1983 and subsequently upgraded into the two-year Youth Training (YT) in 1986.

YTS/YT combined in-company training with a period in further education. It also emphasized broader qualities (such as the development of appropriate work attitudes) and introduced the principle of testing achieved competences. YTS achieved considerable scale in a short time, with some 230 000 (or 27 per cent) of all 16-year-olds on YTS in 1986. In the better-designed schemes it also acted as a catalyst for other areas of company training by setting new standards – including acting as a stimulus to the renewal of surviving apprenticeship schemes in building, chemicals, and engineering.

On the debit side, both YTS and YT have been bedevilled by the confusion of motives which brought YTS into being – namely, their image as a palliative for youth unemployment. The rush to do something about this also on occasion compromised standards. Above all, like the TOPS scheme before it, many employers have tended to see YTS/YT as a source of temporary cheap labour, and have not integrated it into their manpower planning and training structures. Unemployment and low, subsidized training rates in fact partly explain the numbers of training places created in such a short space of time. Consequently, YT still has a long way to go before it seriously matches what is available in countries such as Germany and Japan (Keep, 1989a).

Alongside YTS/YT, however, the NVQ initiative since then has arguably taken a major step forward towards a national system. As the name implies, the purpose of NVQs (National Vocational Qualifications) is to rationalize and simplify the patchwork of vocational courses and qualifications which has hitherto existed. This process has been carried out through 'lead industry bodies' defining standards of skill across a wide range of occupations, and getting these adopted by qualifying institutions in further and higher education. NVQs, and Scottish NVQs, aim to do three things:

- To provide background criteria to guide programmes such as YT
- To provide a framework to integrate a variety of existing qualifications into a coherent, understandable national system, and to integrate elements of education and training
- Through a series of four levels to create a progressive system which knits together initial training and adult training into a single system of continuing training.

Following on from this, the CBI, with the endorsement of the government, in 1991 set out eight specific targets for foundation learning and a lifetime of learning, with the objective of creating a learning culture throughout British society (see Table 19.2).

Table 19.2 The national training targets for education and training

---

Foundation Learning Targets

1 By 1997, 80% of all young people to attain NVQ/SNVQ level 2 or its academic equivalent (i.e. four GCSE grades A-C or Standard Grades in Scotland).

2 Education and training to NVQ/SNVQ level 3 or its academic equivalent (two A-levels, or three Scottish Highers) for all young people who can benefit.

3 By the year 2000, 50 per cent of young people to attain NVQ/SNVQ level 3 or its academic equivalent, as a basis for further progression.

4 All education and training provision to be structured and designed to develop self-reliance, flexibility and broad competence as well as specific skills.

Lifetime Learning Targets

5 By 1996, all employees to take part in training or development activities as a norm.

6 By 1996, at least half of the employed workforce to be aiming for qualifications or units within the NVQ/SNVQ framework, preferably in the context of individual action plans and with support from employers.

7 By the year 2000, 50 per cent of the employed workforce to be qualified to NVQ/SNVQ level 3 or its academic equivalent as a minimum.

8 By 1996, at least half of all medium-sized and larger organizations to qualify as 'Investors in People'.

It is too early to say yet whether NVQs, which are at the core of these targets, are working. Critics say that the whole approach is too bureaucratic, unrealistic, and unworkable. The biggest problem is likely to be in assessing employees' achievement of specific on-the-job skills in the workplace. In smaller firms and small establishments – the vast majority – it is hard to visualize an employer devoting sufficient time to this. There is a risk also that NVQ standards simply reflect the way jobs are done now, especially since few 'lead industry bodies' have researched international comparisons (Stevens and Walsh, 1991).

The evidence on progress towards achieving the targets themselves is also not promising. The National Training Taskforce's successor, the employer-led National Advisory Council on Education and Training Targets (Nacett), in its first annual report, for example, admitted that some of the targets are not strictly measurable, others pose a 'major challenge', and only three look to be achievable. Moreover, among these, progess towards Foundation Targets 1 and 3 has been largely the result of improved performance at school, rather than higher standards of vocational training (Pickard, 1994).

Despite these criticisms, however, NVQs begin to give vocational training in the UK the coherence and reach it has long had in Germany, and provide a basis for continuing upgrading of standards. For example, having got away from the shortcomings of the apprenticeship system, there are moves now to reinvent its positive features (of quality and breadth), with the decision of the government to fund up to 150 000 'modern apprentice' training places at NVQ level 3 (*Personnel Management plus*, 1993c).

Perhaps the most intriguing feature of the new system, however, is the blend being created between internal and external labour markets. The replacement of the apprenticeship system by YTS/YT represented a shift from an occupational system to a more open labour market one. Indeed, the reduction in employment protection for young people, as for employees generally, could be seen as an encouragement to casualization.

The NVQ system also encourages flexibility to the extent that it provides portable qualifications. However, these are far more occupationally defined (although for some critics, insufficiently so), and the vocational version depends on acquiring skills in-company. This may be an encouragement to organizations to create internal ladders of opportunity to reward and retain people. Typically, however, they have managed internal labour markets like this in the past by building on organization-specific skills and personal qualities.

The training system in the USA

It is worth reflecting briefly on the US system, since a number of the initiatives described above (such as TECs and LECs) have been copied from there, along with others not mentioned in the educational sphere, such as school-employer 'Compacts' and City Technology Colleges. The problem is that VET in the US mirrors many of the faults of the UK system:

> The American training 'system', whether we are talking about the training of new labour market entrants or experienced workers, is not a system, but a patchwork of programmes targeted at different clients, financed in different ways, provided by different sources, and designed for different purposes.
>
> Increasingly, this patchwork is being seen less as 'flexible' and more as chaotic and costly for individuals and those who finance it.
>
> Our cultural preferences for a decentralized public sector (especially in education) and an unregulated, free market private sector encourage us to idealise the value of local action... and work against the development of the national performance standards and certification process which are key to any national training system (Berryman, 1991, pp. 111–112).

The result is a reliance on employer-sponsored training and a bias in training with which we are also familiar:

> Employer-sponsored training in the United States is a substantial, but largely invisible, human-capital-producing and wealth-producing system that disproportionately benefits white-collar workers, the initially better-educated, and the not-so-new labour market entrant. Thus, it does not compensate in any systematic way for the haphazard and often mediocre training otherwise available to non-college bound youth and young adults (Berryman, 1991, p. 116–117).

Women and non-white employees receive less training. Like Britain, also, small firms spend less. On the positive side, larger American employers do spend large sums on training, and one can understand, therefore, why it has been seen in the UK as a model for an employer-led training system. Some well-known companies (such as IBM, Xerox, and Motorola) are thus committed to continuous training. However, Berryman suggests that they are exceptions.

This paradox should be familiar from the American literature on HRM which emphasizes 'people development' and frequently quotes examples of model companies. The general rule is – when an ideology or new philosophy like HRM argues for the virtues of particular practices or ways of managing people, and especially when they then hold up particular companies as exemplars, it is a sure sign that such companies are an exception and the propagandists are really talking about a widespread malaise. The more aggressive the propaganda, the more serious the underlying problem only indirectly alluded to.

In fact, America is experiencing the same trends in its economy as Britain and Europe, with implications strikingly similar to those that follow from the high-skill, 'quality' scenario painted for the Single European Market:

- Supervisory and problem-solving responsibilities are devolving downwards in organizations, so that employers will have to reconsider who gets training within the firm
- The US workforce is growing more slowly and the growth rate will continue to fall, so that employers will have to increase their retraining of older workers
- Meanwhile, the ties between employers and workers are weakening,

as a result of sub-contracting, use of part-timers with high turnover rates, and generally greater reliance on external recruitment for qualified people

- This means greater dependence on skills and credentials acquired externally, less investment by employers themselves, and stronger divisions between higher-level employees who enter in this way and less educated workers who become stranded therefore either in low-level jobs in the company or in unemployment outside
- In the process, responsibility for receiving training shifts from the employer to employee, which disadvantages those with least initial education and limited financial resources
- Finally, firms are becoming smaller, and smaller firms are less apt to train.

These trends are incompatible for the creation of a high-skill workforce. The central problem is the focus of training on an advantaged (employed) elite to the neglect of the (casualized or unemployed) majority. The American system is an extreme combination of internal and external labour market practices. An ILM 'seniority system' survives in (male) blue-collar work (Piore, 1986), while 'flexibility' prevails in (female) clerical and retail jobs (Osterman, 1984) and latterly in white-collar jobs.

The final quotation provides another striking reflection on the options that face the UK:

> Many American companies have held on to a mass production mentality, where front-line workers need to be not educated so much as reliable and steady. Instead of moving to high skill and high performance work, these employers retain old organizations of work. They have tried to stay competitive by cutting labour costs; by exporting work to countries with cheap labour; by automating; and, as we have seen, by moving to market-mediated and part-time work arrangements. These companies are functioning with a low skills equilibrium (Berryman, 1991, p. 126).

The problem for the USA is not what is spent on training but its focus, spread, and efficiency. Tax codes subsidize employer-provided training by allowing them to write off investments in training (including trainees' wages). At the same time, the fees that employers pay for the third of training that takes place in the outside education and training system are well below full cost. The 'patchwork' system means that this is inefficient and is increasingly narrowly targeted, when the modern economy requires a broad base of broadly skilled people. As Berryman notes, US companies will have radically to rethink who gets trained, how often, and how.

What the US system lacks is what NVQ in Britain purports to offer – a framework for skills, embodying ladders of opportunity. Such a system can provide a focus and incentive for both individual and company efforts. However, for the USA this is extremely counter-cultural and also impractical because of its size and federal structure. In this respect, America's problem mirrors the long-term ambitions for the EU. First, how culturally acceptable and viable is a European-wide systematic approach? Second, is the effort to develop European-wide skills and qualifications standards feasible, given population numbers, geographical spread, and national differences?

Vocational education and training in Japan

Whereas the American training system is primarily orientated towards an open labour market, the Japanese system tends to be seen in terms of strong, company-based internal labour markets. This is inaccurate, however (Whittaker, 1990). It is more properly a 'dual' system, comprising around a third of all employees (mostly male) in large (often multinational) companies, enjoying the privileges of 'lifetime employment'. The rest form a large 'non-core' or 'secondary' labour force, in predominatly small–medium firms, serving the industrial conglomerates and bearing the brunt of economic downturns.

While the UK has something to learn from the sheer size and resilience of the medium–firm sector (in both Japan and Germany), it is the primary sector which has been most admired. This is essentially a closed system in which the ties between employee and employer are exceedingly strong. Inohara (1990) has sketched the elements of this, enough to see that Britain both lacks similar basic cultural values and that our VET system has been going in a diametrically opposite direction in recent years in the promotion of vocationalism during secondary education.

The starting point is to appreciate that the Japanese are a highly educated people. They place great value on education, and receive a secondary education which is general, cultural, and scientific (including mathematics to a much higher standard than in the UK), rather than being narrowly technical and vocational. Thus, there are only about 200 public vocational training schools in Japan (around 5 per cent of all public and private schools). (Incidentally, this is very different from the German system, where technical schools are prominent – although, within this, the German system also aims at breadth.) These vocational schools serve people who change jobs in mid-career and move between small enterprises (Inohara, 1990). The whole education system, otherwise, is geared to a broad general education:

> The overwhelming majority of blue-collar workers have twelve years of formal schooling. They are able to read and understand technical and administrative instructions, participate in meaningful discussions with supervisors and managers, and propose useful suggestions for the improvement of work processes. Any company training and development program takes this condition as a given: it considers that the employees, with practically no exception, have enough potential to continuously learn new things and improve human and technical qualitities (Inohara, 1990, p. 68).

From school or college, new employees all go through a pre-employment programme which is more extended and thorough than that found in most

UK companies. These orientation programmes are held in the company's own centre and involve several nights together. (Smaller firms will use training institutes, the parent company, or the local trade association to which they are affiliated.) The aim is to create the team-work and family spirit, and the beginnings of group discipline, which is fundamental to the work style of the Japanese firm. Basic technical training then follows through a series of job assignments managed by the personnel department. This will vary from three to six months, according to educational background and the kind of business.

These features may not appear particularly distinctive, but they lay the basis for the whole appoach to VET thereafter. First, the company takes responsibility for training and development. It is therefore almost entirely in-house. The company is *expected* to take care of the development of its members – indeed, Inohara speaks of 'members' rather than 'employees'. The employee is a member of the company family. The company is an extension of the natural family. Conversely, and second, the results of training are a corporate asset and not that of the individual trainee. The trainee is expected to share fully with his or her co-workers what they have learned from the training provided by the company. This rests on a particular attitude to skill in Japanese society. Skill is not the exclusive or particular possession of individuals. As a result, occupations themselves are blurred and not a distinctive source of status (Asanuma, 1982).

This outlook underpins the third feature of Japanese VET – its reliance on face-to-face teaching and communication between co-workers on-the-job: 'Technology is believed to be best transferred and taught face to face, person to person, and skill is best learned by performing the job with co-workers' (Inohara, 1990, p. 69). The resulting emphasis on on-the-job 'training' among co-workers accounts for the fact that employee training costs in Japan are unexpectedly low, amounting during the 1980s to a constant 3 per cent of total labour costs (compared with 8.1 per cent for the UK on the basis of Deloittes/IFF's (1989) estimates for 1986/1987). Co-worker training also means that development is continuous and long term, although often informal.

The effect of sharing knowledge and co-training, and the non-proprietorial attitude to skill, is to dilute occupational or professional pride on the part of the individual and to make job demarcation almost unheard of. Not only are Japanese employees therefore ready to accept temporary or permanent job transfers as necessary, but Japanese employers resort to transfers before ever they will consider making employees redundant. This makes for an employment system with internal flexibilty, rather than one which tries to gain flexibility through the external market (like the American and, increasingly, the British).

This leads to the fourth related feature – the stress on developing generalists oriented to company performance rather than specialists orientated to their own careers and job interest. A system that produces specialists tends to emphasize individual performance and encourages individuals to regard themselves as superior to colleagues. Developing generalists means, then, development on a broad front:

> The purpose of training and development is multiple; it is to meet at any time all the basic and changing needs of the company: product quality and productivity, good human relations at work, and technological innovation (Inohara, 1990, p. 70).

Since the ability and willingness to communicate expertise and ideas is vital to co-worker improvement, development aims at personal maturity and sociability as a goal equal in importance to technical skills. Training thus aims to upgrade the technical level *and* morale of the *whole* workforce.

These attitudes to skill and its transmission can be traced back to the specific relationship between the skilled worker and master craftsman in pre-industrial Japanese society. On the face of it, this is little different from the relationship which has persisted in the British and German apprenticeship systems. However, it remains pervasive and its deep roots are reflected in the word *nenko*, which occurs in a variety of word combinations (Thurley, 1991). Meaning 'merit of years of service', it reflects the importance of seniority, the respect for the person who can communicate skill, and the necessary deference between individuals.

Nenko blurs the distinction between skill and age-based seniority. Status resides not so much in the skill as in the inferred superiority which seniority and longer experience confers. Skill is a collective rather than an individual attribute. When one person acquires knowledge and skill, for instance, they are receiving the collected wisdom of past generations. Many workers in traditional British industries have instinctively had a similar perception, but in Japan these beliefs are more institutionalized at the highest level in companies and society.

The example of Japan suggests, therefore, that it is necessary to understand attitudes to skill in the particular society when assessing systems of VET and especially in planning reforms (Thurley, 1991). We need to look critically at how people see the acquisition of competence in its broadest sense, through the whole of a person's life, and not narrowly within a formal framework for VET.

Along with this, an historical view of national systems is also essential. Lifetime employment and the seniority wage system, for instance, did not arise by chance but were deliberately adopted to stop the mobility of skilled workers in the early decades of this century. At that time, hiring was managed through sub-contract labour bosses whom groups of workers followed from company to company (not so very different from the old foreman sub-contract labour system in Britain (Gospel, 1983) or modern hiring practices in construction). The attachment of the skilled worker to the master craftsman (*nenko*) thus had a specific character. The modern Japanese system has incorporated this older value into the firm. In this way, national systems of VET and employment practice represent a conjunction of ingrained historical patterns and values, and contemporary policy adjustments.

By the same token, the Japanese employment system is currently vulnerable to erosion from changing economic circumstances (Takahashi, 1990), with companies wanting to give job performance greater weight against seniority. This would seem to reflect imminent problems from the ageing of the Japanese workforce.

Vocational education and training in Germany

Within Europe, Britain tends to look towards the German system. German VET is based in a twin-track State system of academic and vocationally oriented schools – the *Gymnasium* for the academically inclined and the *Realschule* and *Hauptschule* for the vocationally oriented. While the *Gymnasium* have highest status, the *Realschule* (or technical schools) are sustained by the prestige which skills and skill training have in Germany. This itself derives from the impetus which Bismarck gave to technical education in the nineteenth century, and further back from medieval craft traditions. The result is that many parents opt to send their children to *Realschule*, rather than to *Gymnasium* which are the passport to university.

The apprenticeship system

The heart of vocational training proper is the apprenticeship system. Every occupation, of which there are around 400 recognized in Germany, has its own scheme, with national standards, syllabuses and practical examinations. On leaving school, some 550 000–600 000 pupils sign apprenticeship contracts with companies each year. Over a period of two to three-and-a-half years, these apprentices spend three days a week working for the company, and two days in the vocational school, divided roughly 50:50 between continuing basic education (in maths, German, and general studies) and the technical aspects of their chosen trade.

Local chambers of commerce accredit instructors and organize the examinations, but the whole system is tightly regulated by statute. To make major changes in syllabuses, the mutual consent of employers, unions, and government is needed. Even so, the system is flexible. Apart from the fact that national syllabuses are general, to allow companies and schools to take account of changing technology and work organization, more than half the syllabuses, accounting for 96 per cent of apprentices, have been updated over the last twenty years. The number of recognized occupations has also been reduced (from 465 in 1980 to 332 in 1988) (Policy Studies Institute, 1991).

This process of modernization has been slow but thorough. The programme for metalworkers, for instance, was updated during the 1980s in a process lasting eight years in the large-firm sector (1979–1987) and six years among small firms (1983–1989), with employers and unions undertaking detailed functional analysis of jobs before they agreed comprehensive changes. Such updating is carried out under the guidance of the Federal Vocational Training Institute, which also finances and asseses new training models and methods and makes training materials available to all concerned.

Over the years, companies have shown a continuing commitment to this system (although it was originally imposed on them by Bismarck). Indeed,

421

in the early 1980s it was experiencing something of a crisis, as the number of young people unable to find training places soared and those qualifying were having difficulty finding permanent jobs. Companies responded, however, by increasing places and unemployment diminished. However, the fall in the numbers of school-leavers played an important part, with the numbers declining by twice the UK rate of fall, as 35 per cent fewer young people entered the labour market. In the recent recession the situation has been rather different, with the added tension of a large pool of well-educated East Germans, used to lower rates of pay, also seeking employment.

Currently, employers spend around DM50 billion a year (approximately £17 billion) on apprenticeships. This represents about 80 per cent of the total cost of the dual system. British employers, in contrast, were reckoned to spend £18 billion on all forms of training in 1986/1987 (Deloittes/IFF, 1989), with about 40 per cent, or £7.2 billion, going on young entrants. Another way of looking at this is that employers contribute around 55 per cent of the total training expenditure in Britain. On the other hand, most of the costs of further training (such as *Meister* training described below) are borne by individuals, both in course fees and in wage premia (such as overtime) foregone.

Apprenticeships in Germany are attractive also to school-leavers. In 1989, for instance, 73.5 per cent of young people started an apprenticeship on leaving full-time schooling (Policy Studies Institute, 1991). The result has been that German output of qualified personnel far exceeds that of Britain, and also France. In mechanical engineering, output has been about five times that of Britain and of electricians about four times. In other areas where qualifying training is even less formalized in Britain, such as office work, the difference is tenfold (Wagner, 1991).

Such differences in output are, moreover, cumulative to the stock of skills nationally. The national training target for the UK quoted above is for 50 per cent of young people to attain NVQ level 3 equivalent (two A-levels) by the year 2000. Germany, however, already had 60 per cent of its young people qualifying at that level in 1978. In 1994, the actual figure for the UK was still only 37 per cent. Similarly, in 1988, Britain had 64 per cent with no vocational qualifications whatsoever, compared with France's 53 per cent and Germany with just 28 per cent (Steedman, 1990).

The German system is dependent, however, on its reputation and the attractiveness of apprenticeships *vis-à-vis* alternative routes in industry and commerce. Unemployment, for instance, can shake this confidence. In 1991 the numbers of those enrolling to go to university for the first time exceeded those going into apprenticeships, and this has caused some heart-searching in Germany at the thought that apprenticeships are losing status. Those areas attracting young people, moreover, are in white-collar occupations, where skills are seen to be more transferable. Although hardly on a scale with the problem in the UK, it mirrors the loss of status of manufacturing employment which successive recessions in 1974/1975 and 1980/1982 have caused in Britain. The crisis of the early 1980s, where there was a shortfall of places, has, within the former West Germany, now become a problem of too few applicants, as a result of demographic change.

The *Meister* system

Initial qualifications are only part of the German story, though. The crucial difference between Germany and the UK lies in the advanced technical training which produces a class of industrial worker which is almost lacking in the UK – what Campbell (1991) calls the 'excluded middle'. The backbone of German training and industrial performance is the *Meister* system.

The *Meister* examinations can be taken for a variety of occupations, following two years' work experience after completing an apprenticeship. Courses and examinations are regulated nationally, although delivered locally usually by chambers of commerce. Syllabuses are flexible to allow for developments in technology to be covered, and include some general business subjects and trainer skills. The focus, however, is on advanced technical skills.

In contrast, the British equivalent – NEBSS (the National Examinations Board for Supervisory Studies) – is not concerned with improved technical proficiency, and is based on only a quarter of the hours of instruction (240 hours compared with an average of 950 hours in the *Meister*). In 1988 46 000 people passed the *Meister* examinations in the main industrial trades, plus another 5000 in agriculture and public and private domestic services (Wagner, 1991). By comparison, 6000 passed the NEBSS certificate and diploma courses, and 1100 the Certificate in Supervisory Management – a differential of over 7:1.

The *Meister* has higher status, authority, and pay than a skilled worker, with a pay differential of more than 40 per cent, compared with a British foreman who earns only about 20 per cent more than other workers. Indeed, Wagner (1991), and elsewhere in the same volume, Walter Eltis, then Director General of NEDO, regard the pay differentials between the apprentice, qualified worker, and *Meister* as a critical factor in the motivation of employees and employers in supporting the German training system. Thus, the German apprentice receives only 30-40 per cent of the pay of the qualified skilled worker (strictly, what they receive is an allowance), compared with a figure that was traditionally nearer 75 per cent in Britain. (Consequently, one of the aims of YTS/YT was to lower trainees' expectations on pay.)

The importance of the *Meister* to the German industrial system is the technical leadership they give. This includes their role as trainers, for which they receive explicit training themselves. Thus, when apprentices spend their three days in the workplace, they encounter someone who takes training seriously.

There are direct benefits from this and also indirect economies, in that more responsibility can be devolved to them as first-line supervisors. The result is that Germany tends to make do with one layer of supervision on the shopfloor, whereas in Britain and France two layers are typical (Maurice, Sorge and Warner, 1980). The trend through the technical changes of the 1980s, as we have described in various chapters of this book, has been to reduce layers of supervision in British firms. To do this successfully, however, requires either higher levels of skill in foremen or operators, or both. The combination of high skill levels in both in Germany is a major contributory factor to the superior productivity of German firms (Daly, Hitchens and Wagner, 1985; Steedman and Wagner, 1989).

A second area where the *Meister* system is important is in the legal requirement that a person setting up in business of any kind must hold a *Handwerksmeister* certificate (one of the two forms *Meister* training takes). Thus, small firms, from sole traders upwards, are qualified persons. Whether this is unnecessarily restrictive on 'enterprise' is another matter.

Technicians

A second important layer of 'super-skilled' craft workers are technicians. In most cases, they have completed an apprenticeship, but undertake a higher level of formal technical education over a longer period. Thus, technician training involves two years full-time study or four years part-time, for a total of 2400 hours of instruction. Again, the curriculum is a national one, and leads to a State certificate (the *Staatlich geprufter Techniker*). The British equivalent is the HNC and HND, and, like those, the subjects studied prepare a person for jobs in support functions, such as production control, rather than for shopfloor supervision. Again, however, Germany has more of these (some 790 000 according to Wagner), qualified to higher levels – 36 per cent with technician qualifications in Germany, compared with 14 per cent in Britain and 21 per cent in France.

One interesting facet of this, however, is that Britain has a much higher proportion of graduates in technician roles. This is not necessarily the source of advantage it might appear. It suggests, for instance, that graduates are being employed below their capabilities to fill gaps created by an intermediate skills shortage. Sorge and Warner (1986) have referred to this in terms of an 'early extraction of elites' and a 'flight of skills from the factory floor'. As Campbell (1991, p. 159) observes:

> There has been a tendency in Britain to make savings at the shopfloor level and then to pay higher overheads in terms of white-collar and graduate staff... it suggests that in Germany [technical graduates] have been deployed more effectively than in Britain, in a way that complements craft and technical skills, rather than as a substitute for them (p. 159).

This is in keeping with a German industry that makes intensive use of craft skills on the shopfloor, compared with the tendency in Britain to automate and remove skills from the factory floor. These represent two very different directions for industrial development. The question is whether both are equally viable. The EU's 'quality' scenario (echoing Piore and Sabel's 1984, vision of smaller production runs of customized products in flexible manufacturing units) suggests that the German approach is more viable in the long run.

Continuing development and business strategies

The final element in the German system is, as in Britain, the continued updating of skills. Much of this is uncertificated and in response to needs as they arise. As in Britain and the USA, it also tends to be concentrated on those already qualified: however, many more employees in Germany start out qualified. The numbers receiving training in this way each year are substantial (800 000 in 1988), while a total of 1.3 million in 1988 received various forms of out-company training. Employers financed around half the cost of this, with the chambers of commerce providing around half the courses. As in Japan, however, updating on a day-to-day basis in the workplace is emphasized even more.

The hidden factor in on-the-job development, however, stems from the basic direction of the firm:

> The amount of additional skills which can be learnt depends very much on opportunities, e.g. how many innovative products and production processes the companies introduce. . .British companies tended more to standardized products than their German counterparts which means that British employees on all hierarchical levels have many fewer opportunities to update their skills on the job and therefore the above identified gap between their skill levels widens further (Wagner, 1991, p. 144).

The study of company training by Pettigrew, Hendry and Sparrow (1989) showed the importance of company strategy as a driving force. Equally important, however, is the direction of strategy in ensuring that training is not a once-and-for-all event (Hendry, 1991). Employers' expectations of employee skills and the product-market strategies they build on these are thus critical in creating a virtuous cycle of development. Will, then, a stronger supply of skills in the UK alter employers' expectations and cause them to pursue product and process strategies which utilize employee skills effectively, while providing a better environment for continuous learning?

Summary

EU policy has been directed towards achieving both 'efficiency' and 'quality' in the human resources of the Union – 'efficiency', by encouraging labour mobility to spread scarce skills more efficiently across the Union, and 'quality', through improved education and training. The second of these has so far been much more important. In this chapter we have looked at the strengths and weaknesses of different VET systems and how the UK compares. The VET system in the UK has undergone major reforms in the last few years, modelled above all on the German system.

Traditionally, Germany has had an institutional system of VET which is much superior to Britain's. It is a system rooted in formal, externally monitored standards. It offers a broader off-the-job education to support on-the-job specific skills. It therefore produces a more flexible set of skills and it achieves much wider coverage of occupations. Through the *Meister* system it also provides the basis for continuous development of skills which was almost completely lacking from the British apprenticeship system. The new system of YT in Britain and especially NVQs adopt many of the following principles:

- Externally-monitored standards
- The combination of on-the-job skill development and off-the-job education
- Comprehensive coverage of a wide range of occupations through 'lead industry bodies' responsible for drawing up NVQ standards
- A progressive system of skill development and continuous learning through NVQ levels.

Where the new British system differs from the old apprenticeship system and from the present German one is in the commitment to output-based measures in the form of NVQs. In contrast, Germany (and Italy) still prefer input-based measures (that is, the achievement of formal qualifications).

The German system is based on a hybrid conjunction of occupational and in-company internal labour markets. It depends heavily on company commitment to provide structured training opportunities, sustained by high barriers to employee mobility. Strictly, this is a matter of reducing the power of the employer to make forced redundancies and temporary lay-offs through the involvement of trade unions in works councils (Wächter and Stengelhofen, 1992). The obverse of this, however, is to reduce employee motivation to move jobs and lose job security. Likewise, large pay differentials between grades encourage people to stick.

The downside of this has been a growing perception of uncompetitiveness on pay and loss of employment flexibility – certainly compared with the USA which has had considerable success in creating new jobs. (Critics argue, however, that the US success is illusory since it has been accompanied by falling real blue-collar wages and growth in part-time employment.)

Continuing growth in part-time and temporary employment which circumvents legal restrictions has been one response in Germany (Piore, 1986; Brewster *et al.*, 1993). Opening up factories and transferring jobs to Eastern Europe, where pay levels are vastly lower, has been another since 1989 when the Communist regimes fell. In the long run these developments may put the German system of training under considerable strain.

Allied to this is the need to ensure flexibility in skills training. The German system, for instance, has been criticized for creating 'occupational and status ghettoes' (Grosser, 1989, p. 30). This matters particularly to smaller firms where flexibility, in tasks and skills, is at a premium (Hendry, Jones and Arthur, 1991), and is all the more important when SMEs are becoming a more prevalent organizational form.

Within the EU, much will depend on the success of the Social Chapter of the Maastricht treaty in providing a suitable framework for employment – in particular, its ability to prevent a free-for-all in which Member countries try to undercut one another's wage rates (otherwise known as 'social dumping'). The British government's opposition to the Social Chapter is clearly designed to retain 'social dumping' as a policy option – or, as it would prefer to say, to maintain international wage competitiveness.

The idea that the only route to international competitiveness is through low wages, however, is, at best, short-sighted and, at worst, may be fundamentally wrong. There is a view – most recently expressed by Porter (1990) – that factor disadvantages such as high wages are an important incentive to innovation in technology and work practices. For example:

> German [print machinery] firms had to cope with high factor costs. Wages and social benefit costs were higher and working hours were shorter than those in competitor nations. These selective factor disadvantages led German firms continually to rationalize production as well as to develop the highest-technology machines (Porter, 1990, p. 188).

Low wages are simply an excuse for putting off investment in new methods and equipment because margins can be maintained in the short run via depressed wages. Competitive strategies based on low wages simply undermine the demand for higher skills (Finegold and Soskice, 1988). In contrast, higher wages, accompanied by high levels of skill through investment in training, increase the readiness of employees to accept improvements and smooth economic and technological transitions. As Porter (1990) notes in connection with the above example, as far back as the 1920s:

> The thorough training in Germany was in stark contrast to the situation in the United States, where printers received only on-the-job training. The sophistication of German printers led to a receptivity to new innovations as well as a continual dialog (sic) with manufacturers on technical matters (p. 189).

Put crudely: 'If labour costs alone determined international competitiveness there would be no industry in high wage countries' (Mosley, 1990, p. 161). Policies directed at securing wage cost advantages are likely therefore to be successful only in the short term – as the recurrent skill shortages in Britain indicate.

Part Five
Conclusion

20

Future scenarios: issues for the 1990s and beyond

Introduction

In this final chapter we draw together some of the key themes of this book, and identify what are likely to be important issues for the future of HRM. These are:

A   Emerging Models of HRM – including whether we are likely to see a convergence towards a European model (or models) which transcend national differences

B   From Conflict and Control to Growth and Development – including the future of industrial relations, the rise of the learning organization, and issues of organizational governance

C   New Organizational Forms – in the private, public, and quasi-public sectors

D   The Future of the Personnel and Human Resources Function – and what this means for the IPM as a professional institution and for teaching HRM.

In conclusion, we recap on the virtues of a strategic perspective. Central to the argument of this book is that employment systems and skill supply two essential concepts for a strategic perspective in personnel management and HRM.

Emerging models of HRM

As we saw in Chapter 1, the theory of HRM coming out of America in the mid-1980s had two distinct elements:

- A 'philosophy' which saw people as a valuable resource, and focused on ways of developing and harnessing their contribution and skills to the organization (Beer *et al.*, 1984; Walton and Lawrence, 1985)
- A 'strategic' perspective which argued that the systems for managing people should be 'aligned' with the business strategy and with one another, so that they pulled in the same direction (Fombrun, Tichy and Devanna, 1984).

Much of the debate since then has been about whether HRM is a particular human resources strategy to encourage commitment and reduce the influence of trade unions or whether, as a strategic approach which attempts to 'match' (Boxall, 1993) employment practices to a variety of internal and external circumstances and goals, it is not confined to one substantive model. Chapter 3 concluded that a convincing empirical case could not be made for HRM being equated with policies to promote commitment, flexibility, and quality, and the undermining of trade unions.

The employment systems perspective described in Chapter 11, nevertheless, is an encouragement to look for emerging patterns of some kind. The mistake has been to try to lump together all recent innovations in employment into one. This has been rather premature and unrealistic, in any case. A coherent set of new employment practices is hardly likely to become embedded in a wide number of firms in such a short space of time. Moreover, the last ten to fifteen years have been a time of unprecedented economic uncertainty and structural change, not to mention political and social turbulence (see Chapter 2). In such circumstances, it is reasonable to see management as being engaged in a phase of 'practical experimentation' (Streeck, 1987), feeling their way gradually and incrementally towards viable new ways of managing people. This is indeed how 'strategic learning' occurs (Boxall, 1993).

As a result of work carried out by Stephen Wood and colleagues at the London School of Economics, I believe we can now begin to see more clearly that there is not one model of HRM, but two, or even three:

1 First, there is the *'commitment system'* described by Walton and Lawrence (1985), in which training and trainability, team-working, and career progression are key elements (Wood, 1993). This places an emphasis on certain kinds of flexibility, such as job flexibility and flexible working hours; on commitment; and on raising the quality of people through training and development. In employment systems terms, this equates fairly closely with the traditional 'internal labour market' model, but is weaker on job security.

2 Second, there is a *'performance management approach'* (Wood, 1993) in which pay is the main lever. Wood and others like Lockyer (1992) equate this with Peters and Waterman's (1982) 'excellence' philosophy, with individual pay being tied to qualitative objectives through profit-sharing and merit pay, and a stress on high performance throughout the organization. It is a 'bought' commitment, with a strong strategic orientation, providing the organization with financial flexibility. In some ways, this departs furthest from traditional models by combining employer control, medium-to-low job security, and incentive pay with the potential for high earnings, while (unlike incentivized systems in the past) encouraging broad job responsibilities.

3 Third, there is a *'core–periphery'* strategy in which job security for some is achieved at the expense of insecurity for others. Its novelty lies not so much in any single organization increasing the casualization of its own labour force (although there are examples of this) but in firms pushing

non-core jobs into contracting firms where terms and conditions are of a lower standard and employees are more vulnerable. This is all about numerical flexibility and lower costs. It combines a traditional 'internal labour market' or modern 'commitment system' with an equally traditional 'external labour market' approach based on casualization. The result is a reinforcement of the 'dual labour market'.

Wood's study has usefully begun to discriminate between these different sets of employment practices, although its primary finding is to separate out (1) from (2). Most other commentators treat the 'performance management approach' as integral to the 'commitment system', with Lockyer (1992, p. 250), for instance, suggesting that 'undoubtedly, the symbolic system of HRM is performance-related pay'.

The brief discussion here suggests that the type of flexibility a firm pursues is a significant discriminator of its overall approach to employment. Further clarification may come from distinguishing which of these it is that organizations emphasize. Above all, Wood's analysis pinpoints the contradictions within HRM and reinforces the idea of 'strategic coherence' between different practices as the key discriminating factor.

Towards a European model of HRM?

The basic ideas of human resource management have come from the USA and attracted widespread attention outside that country. As with other widely disseminated management ideas (such as Taylorism, quality circles, strategic planning, and divisionalized organization structures) does this mean that organizations are becoming more alike and are developing common models of employment?

One problem is distinguishing between normative models and actual practice (Legge, 1989). This applies as much to the USA where, as various authors have noted, HRM values (both of the 'commitment' and 'strategic' variety) are in stark contrast to critiques of American business practice in the 1980s (Guest, 1990; Hendry and Pettigrew, 1990; Brewster, 1993b). Separating 'what some say' from 'what others do' in respect of just one country, as we have seen in the case of Britain, is a considerable task. For countries where there is a less developed tradition of empirical research into personnel management – for example, Germany (Wächter and Stengelhofen, 1992) – it may be even more difficult. (The compensating factor in countries like Germany, however, may be that a powerful institutional structure imposes more conformity and makes it easier to generalize. Of course, this may also mean that such a system is more impervious to adopt foreign management ideas.)

Despite these difficulties, HRM has entered the international language very quickly – indeed, it has done a lot to create a common language for comparing people management. This is no doubt due in part to the mobility of academics and the speed with which ideas are nowadays transmitted. In part, it is also due to the internationalization of business itself, and the scope that creates for transferring and reflecting on 'best practice'. The result is that 'convergence in employment systems is back on the political and intellectual agenda' (Cressey and Jones, 1991, p. 493). This is especially relevant for Europe where there are powerful institutional forces towards convergence through the European Union.

Since HRM is an American import, a contrast with American cultural values makes a useful starting point (Brewster, 1993b). Individualism and autonomy, and a belief in being able to shape one's environment, are a powerful underlying set of assumptions (Adler and Jelinek, 1986; Springer and Springer, 1990). The whole notion of corporate strategy, an American idea which dates only from the 1960s, is about how organizations can get better control of their business environments. Changing organizational cultures embodies a similar objective and set of assumptions about the internal environment. As Brewster (1993b) observes, European organizations are far less autonomous: 'Their autonomy is constrained at a national level, by culture and legislation; at the organizational level, by patterns of ownership; and, at the HRM level, by trade union involvement and consultative arrangements' (p. 766).

The system of education and training (with the exception of the UK), for example, is more highly regulated by the State (Rainbird, 1992). As we saw in the previous chapter, Germany has an elaborate structure for certificating training and education and for managing it nationally through a partnership of firms, trade unions, and educational institutions. In France, too, formal qualifications are highly valued. The way skills are developed and certificated is a form of labour market regulation and therefore has a profound impact on firms' employment strategies (Eyraud, Marsden and Silvestre, 1990).

Legal structures also play a much greater role in regulating industrial relations in Europe. The prime instance of this is the legal underpinning for employee involvement in works councils in many countries of Europe, with Denmark, the Netherlands, and Germany additionally giving a role for employee representatives on the boards of companies. Again, Britain is the exception, being closer to the American presumption of an unfettered right of management to manage. The corporatism of the German system of 'co-determination' is therefore neither uniquely German, nor is it new: '"Organised capitalism" in Germany has always included a social dimension' (Wächter and Stengelhofen, 1992, p. 22).

Germany developed systems of social security and consensus-management to alleviate the strains of industrial life in the late nineteenth century. The formal system of works councils and board representation themselves date from the First World War (much as consultative systems did in the UK during the Second) to ensure industrial harmony to support the war effort. A second aspect of corporatism – the close ties between banks and industry and cooperative interfirm relationships – stem from the same sense of needing to pull together:

> Cartels, close ties between banks and industry, and exchange of know-how between firms have always been a dominant feature of German capitalism. Even today, the awareness of being largely dependent on conquering and defending world market shares, and thus the notion of 'sitting in one boat' is – although frequently derided – a lingering fact of German economic and social life. Being

prepared for fierce world market competition can hardly be ignored, in view of Germany's dependence on exports (Wächter and Stengelhofen, 1992, p. 22).

Interlocked structures like these (which also characterize Japan) mean less pressure for short-term profits, less incentive to drive competitors out of the marketplace (Randlesome *et al.*, 1990), and, conversely, less need for firms to assert their autonomy.

Corporatist structures are thus common in many areas of German life. The reunification of East and West Germany provides further illustration, with all the social factors – State authorities, employers' associations, and trade unions – being committed to full employment, and various schemes for temporary employment and retraining being adopted:

> The impact of a 'social dimension' on economic decisions, a concern for building up human capital in the firm, and worker participation, are generally accepted by all parties involved – in spite of major differences in putting them to work. This shapes the daily practice of personnel management (Wächter and Stengelhofen, 1992, p. 34).

At company level, such influences are especially marked in the procedural and legal constraints on enforced redundancies and relocating employees within the workplace.

Such arrangements mark out Germany from the UK and the USA. In the UK and USA it is possible to speak of 'human resource strategy' because firms have relative freedom to vary the way they manage employment. 'Strategy' only exists where there are choices. Within a tighter institutional structure, German firms have less scope for varying their employment strategy. Germany's centralized, industry-level bargaining structures similarly limit freedom of action, in contrast to the UK, where bargaining has been increasingly decentralized to company and plant level. This is partly why there is less interest in innovations associated with HRM, and why the term HRM is not well liked in Germany. Initiatives such as quality circles, for example, are perceived as a direct threat to established collective procedures (Wächter, 1992).

While this means that Germany will be less likely to adopt American forms of HRM, employment legislation increasingly governing all countries of the European Union will tend in the long run to produce a convergence of institutional systems. In the process, it is hardly likely that Germany and its neighbours who share 'social market economies' will opt for the less regulated Anglo-American system.

Within each type of system, the preference for collectivism versus individualism is, indeed, a major discriminator (notwithstanding the discussion in Chapter 3). On the one hand, this is a function of the degree of unionization. Although there are marked differences among the European countries themselves, Europe is in general much more heavily unionized than the USA, with membership ranging from 85 per cent of the working population in Sweden to around 10 per cent in France, compared with only 6 per cent in the USA. Similar disparities exist in company recognition of unions.

The absence of trade union protection in the USA, on the other hand, is compensated for by a greater tendency for individuals and interest groups to use the law to gain redress (Springer and Springer, 1990). This has a powerful influence on companies introducing progressive and equitable policies for equal opportunities. The absence of collective protection also accounts for preoccupations within HRM which Europeans may not appreciate. Interest in novel pay structures is an example. With a private insurance-based health system, medical cover is a major benefit provided by employers. This exerts strong upward pressure on pay costs (especially given the relative inefficiency of insurance-based systems). Consequently, there has been far more interest in America in 'cafeteria' pay schemes as a way of reducing the burden.

In conclusion, then, American-style HRM is different and likely to remain so from any European model. In any case, there is no one European model at present (Pieper, 1990; Sparrow and Hiltrop, 1993). However, as Britain gains increasing exposure to Continental European systems and EU regulations take effect a distinctly European model may evolve. This is more likely to build on the social democratic traditions of Germany than the *laissez-faire* approach of the UK. It will also, however, need to be more flexible than the often bureaucratic German firm. Such a model (already forming in European multinationals like Shell, Olivetti, and Siemens) is likely to:

- Provide for dialogue between the 'social partners' at all levels
- Promote a democratic form of enterprise
- Allow for multi-culturalism in organizations to preserve different ways of thinking and behaving and the expression of different cultural identities in Europe
- Provide for continuous learning and a scientific attitude to adopting best practice (Thurley, 1990).

Ultimately, models of HRM, like those of personnel management over the years, express what sort of society we want to be and reflect our institutional structures:

> The fundamental issue posed by European integration in the end comes down to the question of what type of society is being proposed. In this sense, personnel management must become one of a number of critical political issues (Thurley, 1990, p. 57).

Personnel management and HRM are therefore part of a wider institutional debate, and need actively to take part in that.

From conflict and control to growth and development

One of the major shifts in recent years has been a change in firms' preoccupations, from dealing with conflict and seeing the employment relationship in terms of control to looking for ways to promote employee development and growth. In this sense, there has been a real shift towards embracing a core value within HRM, which is that employees are an asset. This shift raises questions about the long-term future of industrial relations and is reflected in current interest in the learning organization. Both of these also touch on a third issue, that of organizational governance. Together, these three themes are central to the institutional debate referred to above.

Reassessing trade unions and collective bargaining

During the 1980s and into the 1990s trade unions have been engaged not so much in a long march as in a long retreat. The decline in their influence can be measured in five trends (Rose, 1993):

- *Exclusion*, through the dismantling of tripartite ('corporatist') arrangements in many spheres, including decisions and discussions on the economy
- *Pacification*, with a sharp decline in industrial action of all kinds, including fewer strikes and overtime bans, shorter stoppages, and fewer working days lost (Edwards, 1991)
- *Juridification*, that is, restriction on union powers through laws against the closed shop and secondary picketing (1980, 1990), requirements for secret ballots before strikes, election of leaders, and membership approval for political funds (1984), stronger individual rights *vis-à-vis* the union (1988), and loss of legal immunities in respect of strikes and strikers, both official and unofficial (1982, 1990)
- *Contraction*, with total membership falling from over 13 million in 1979 to below 10 million
- *Demoralization*, as employers either directly confronted and reduced trade union power and influence (in major setpiece strikes) or circumvented it through new ways of managing (including, suggests Rose, HRM and Japanese models).

The question for the 1990s and beyond is whether this decline is permanent and irreversible. Put in a negative light, are we likely to see a resurgence of militancy? More positively, are we likely to see a revival of influence, in either a new or old guise?

Strikes have tended to occur in waves (Edwards, 1991). Throughout the industrialized world, there have been periodic peaks in strike activity – notably around 1920 and 1970. The beginning of the 1990s has been a low point (see Table 2.2). As old issues and traditional groups of workers disappear, however, new issues arise and new groups of workers discover the use of industrial action (inventing new forms of action in the process). Thus, new forms of discontent may develop, around, for instance, work intensification, appraisal systems, promotion practices, and health and safety (Edwards, 1991). Such issues have been a source of discontent and confrontation in, for example, schools during the early 1990s.

In this view, strikes and other forms of 'militancy' are not in any case random but are the result of grievances. These may be 'genuine' grievances in the sense that they are provoked by bad management and 'militant' employers or they may arise in protecting privileged and feather-bedded situations. Recent confrontations in the public sector have elements of both. Both nevertheless provide a continuing *raison d'être* for trade unions in exercising a representative function in the workplace (Kessler, 1993; Kessler and Bayliss, 1992). Rose (1993, p. 296) terms this the 'arrestable decline' position on British trade unionism (see also Chapter 16). This will depend, however, on two factors:

- The ability of trade unions to surmount structural economic and social change
- The ability of trade unions to accommodate changes in social attitudes without fatally compromising their collectivist character.

Trade unions were undermined during the 1980s by the erosion in their traditional constituency of male manual workers located in large enterprises. Job losses, especially among the semi-skilled, the demoralizing effects of unemployment, and the fragmentation of large units have all tended to undermine the solidary relationships derived from relatively standardized patterns of residence and consumption which nourished traditional unionism (Hyman, 1991). In its place there has been a growth in white-collar, professional and skilled workers; an increase in female employment; an increase in part-time work and self-employment; a shift from large urban workplaces to smaller, more dispersed sites; and a move from public to private sector employment. All these make it harder for trade unions to recruit and organize. They do not, however, make it impossible (Hyman, 1991).

As we suggested in Chapter 16, a more fundamental problem may be for trade unions to adjust their structures and what they offer to be more in tune with the increased enterprise-consciousness and individualistic mentality of employees. Although it has always been dangerous to infer radical attitudinal change from changing work experiences and life-styles (often involving, as this does, an idealized picture of working-class consciousness), this does need to be taken seriously (Hyman, 1991).

It is difficult for an organization wedded to collective ends to square the circle with individualism. A representative organization has to speak with the same 'voice' as its members – which means satisfying individualized interests. The obvious route to take is towards an American-style 'business unionism' where trade unions vie to deliver benefits to their members and stand or fall by that. The fate of American trade unions in this respect is not promising, however.

Hyman (1991) suggests, instead, 'business unionism with a social conscience' (p. 637). This is a watered-down version of the role which British trade unions have traditionally taken, in which they have sought to combine (1) sectional economic defence and reform in the workplace, (2) the furtherance of broad class interests through political lobbying, and (3) radical political opposition. In other European countries these roles have tended to be divided between competing union movements. Since 1979, the broader political role has been greatly eroded with the dismantling of 'corporatism'.

The linchpin of corporatism and the measure of trade union success in its political role, in Britain and across Europe, was the achievement of the 'social wage' – that is, benefits in health, education, and welfare in addition to direct earnings (Martinez Lucio and Simpson, 1992). The economic crisis of the 1970s, which began with the first oil price rise of 1973, raised questions about the State's ability to maintain this – encapsulated in the theory of the 'overburdened State' (Offe, 1984). The Conservative government's solution to this was to reduce the power of the trade union movement to make demands on national resources politically, and over time to reduce the amount and cover of the 'social wage', while at the same time reducing the power to bargain on pay itself and ensuring that pay claims were aligned to what the country (through companies) could pay. The devolution of pay bargaining to company and plant-level has therefore been double-edged. On this reading, the crisis of trade unionism in Britain (and, to a lesser extent, Europe, where corporatism has stronger roots), is a crisis about both its industrial and social role.

Just as an historical perspective suggests that the present lull in trade union militancy may be a passing phenomenon, however, so an historical perspective suggests that the involvement of trade unions in social-wage politics has itself been a twenty-year temporary phase in post-war Europe (Baglioni and Crouch, 1990). In more precise terms: 'unions may have a long-term future, but do union *movements*?' (Crouch, 1990, p. 359).

Some would conclude that the larger aspiration is misguided:

> Unions practically everywhere are handicapped by an enduring view that they are (in countries like France, must be) social movements as well as economic pressure-groups. Such self-images seriously limit the ability to offer new types of service to members, or to devise new ways of rolling with the management punch by developing their own 'productivist' alternatives for work organization, training, and even 'career development' (Rose, 1993, p. 305).

In contrast, the more 'engaged' attitude of German trade unions, through participation in works councils, and the stronger grounding of German workers and trade unionists in a technical education, have meant German unions have been more successful in developing coherent alternatives on work organization (Turner, 1991). In contrast, British and American trade unions, which have maintained more adversarial relationships, have not accepted or equipped themselves for such a role.

While this indicates the direction the 'new unionism' should take, two factors are likely to perpetuate a socio-political profile. One is the pressure of multinationals to develop common operational requirements across Europe and hence to encourage supra-national trade union strategies (Mueller and Purcell, 1992). The other is the potential through European legislation and directives to achieve workplace benefits 'through the back door'.

If 'social Europe' becomes a reality through legislation, we may see a revival of trade union ambitions. This will mean reshaping, not discarding, trade union-based industrial relations. The challenge for HRM will then come from its accommodation and incorporation within collective structures, rather than the other way round, as the UK comes into closer contact with Continental European systems of industrial relations and employment (notwithstanding Conservative opposition to the Social Chapter of the Maastricht treaty).

The learning organization

Within HRM, one of the 'big themes' at the present moment is the idea of the 'learning organization'. Chapter 16 discussed how this affects ordinary workers, with Chapter 14 elaborating on the learning principles that lie behind it. The learning organization represents a real shift towards adopting the human asset philosophy. It thus embraces a core value in the Harvard perspective on HRM. Accompanying notions like 'empowerment' are a realization of the 'from control to commitment' philosophy (Walton, 1985a, b).

Various writers have associated the learning organization with organizational transformation (Pedler, Boydell and Burgoyne, 1988). More precisely, it is about how encouragement to learning can facilitate continuous improvement (Hendry, Jones and Cooper, 1994). The particular methodologies adopted in this respect are critical. It helps at one level to stimulate people's interest and confidence in learning and to communicate the fact that the company cares about this. Schemes like Ford's EDAP, Peugeot–Talbot's imitation of this, and Rover's learning company work like this.

More important, however, is the way learning becomes integrated into work. In Chapters 10 and 16 we described 'communities of practice' as a basic vehicle for organizational learning. 'Communities of practice' have an immediate pragmatic focus – 'How do I do this job better?' 'How do I solve this problem?' – and they involve experiential learning – people learning from one another. Learning methodologies like action learning attempt to formalize these principles. Programmes such as TQM (total quality management) likewise provide a framework by focusing attention on relationships through work processes. For instance:

> Grasping the concept of continuous learning has been made easier by TSB's introduction of TQM ... This has emphasised continuous improvement, through reviewing and enhancing workplace processes: in other words, learning from reality (Taylor, 1992, p. 55).

What TQM and action learning do is to close the loop between individual learning and organizational concerns for efficiency and innovation. (The problem for TQM is the way it is often introduced and promoted.) Closing this loop depends, however, on individuals being able to experiment with new ways of working, based on their direct experience of the conditions involved in work processes and within a framework of system objectives, and then getting feedback on the consequences. This process is well known through Kolb's learning cycle (Kolb, Rubin and McIntyre, 1974), while there are also strong echoes of Senge's (1990) five 'disciplines' in creating a learning organization (systems thinking, personal mastery, mental models, shared vision, and team learning).

Layers of management and supervision, along with formalism in organization, tend to act as barriers, however, to both experimentation and feedback processes. The learning organization therefore if it has any chance of being realized is a challenge to management jobs and roles. Certainly it requires flatter management structures. In its favour at present is the trend towards cutting middle-management jobs to reduce overheads. This has enabled some companies like Kimberley-Clark in North Wales to rebuild their organization round 'self-managing teams'. More generally, it requires managers to develop a different style, as coach, tutor, and mentor. It also means a fundamental change in the trainer's role, towards facilitating the overall learning environment in which work-based learning takes place (Crittan, 1993).

A serious problem with this, however, is in determining which are the significant 'communities of practice'. It is too easy to dismiss the role of supervisors and middle management. (As we noted in Chapter 16, the supervisor is being increasingly recognized as a critical element in team functioning.) Middle managers often possess essential knowledge about how systems work, and play a vital role in translating strategies and plans into operational terms. By stripping out middle management, organizations may be denuding themselves of vital experience. They, too, are a 'community of practice'. 'Employee empowerment' has to embrace all levels.

Organizational governance

One of the ironies with 'employee empowerment' is the renewed emphasis on the employee as a central figure. This follows years of being told that the 'customer comes first' and of downright denigration of producer interests by Conservative governments. Empowerment, according to PA Consultant, Lance Lindon,

> Involves the introduction of training policies and a culture which places the employee, rather than the customer, first. It is supposed to produce a far more motivated and committed workforce with the power to respond more directly to customers' needs (Bernoth, 1994, p. 3.7).

The logic of this is sensible: if you have demoralized staff, you do not get dynamic, resourceful people.

What the rediscovery of the worker is about is a rethinking of stakeholder rights and obligations. That means reconciling customer and employee interests. It also includes the community and shareholders. The role of profit in guiding organizations and the returns to shareholders are consequently also being rethought. Hampden-Turner (1990), for instance, is critical of the overfocus on profit because in various ways it subverts the means to better performance, and therefore is in effect anti-industrial and anti-wealth creation. For instance, it does not give advance warning of problems, it is motivationally too narrow a desire to learn from, it conflicts with values which have higher priority (such as market share), and produces sub-optimal behaviour in people. Other writers, like Handy (1994), are similarly critical of the variant of capitalism we have in the UK which elevates profit and shareholder interests above all others.

Balancing competing values like these – employee, customer, community, shareholder, plus family – is an institutional and a personal issue. At the personal level a manager constantly has to reconcile value dilemmas. Confronting and reconciling such dilemmas is a source of creativity

(Hampden-Turner, 1990) and of moral development (Kohlberg, 1973; Ma-cLagan, 1990; Jones and Hendry, 1994). Managers themselves frequently recognize this moral dimension:

> Throughout the accounts given to me by managers when I ask them about 'what management is' or about any 'theories which they have come across or have developed about managing' is a strong suggestion that, central to managerial work, are *moral* rather than technical matters and that these moral matters are closely related to the manager's personal integrity (Watson, 1992, p. 12).

At the institutional level, a rethinking of stakeholder rights and obligations is currently taking place through the theme of 'corporate governance'. The Cadbury Committee provided an initial stimulus with its report advocating stronger checks to prevent corporate wrongdoing. The RSA (Royal Society for the encouragement of Arts, Manufactures & Commerce) subsequently initiated a wide-ranging review of company performance, behaviour, and governance directed at industry's short-termism. The resulting *Tomorrow's Company* report argues for an 'inclusive approach' (*RSA Journal*, 1994) which takes account of a wider range of stakeholder interests in the way companies are run. This consciously embraces the 'learning organization' and the social responsibilities of management. The RSA argues that a broader stakeholder perspective leads to better companies and better business decisions.

Such ideas link back directly to the Harvard perespective on HRM, in which employee practices ('HRM choices') aim to satisfy a variety of stakeholder interests. Inevitably, this brings us back to the role of trade unions. If companies (and/or government) fail to create governance structures which reflect the collective interests of people as employees and citizens, people are likely to turn back to trade unions to secure themselves a 'voice'. As the Harvard theorists (and others before them) have recognized, management legitimacy and 'employee influence' processes are at the heart of any model of the firm. Although trade unions have backed off from pursuing political and social objectives through the workplace, they could find themselves drawn back into this role.

New organizational forms

The practice of personnel and human resource management is shaped by the organizational forms in which people are employed. Over the last fifteen years the UK economy has been undergoing fundamental change and the structure of organizations and the relationships between them have been transformed. Big organizations have grown bigger in the sense that both the world economy and that of the UK are dominated by transnational corporations. Between a quarter and one fifth of total GNP in the world is thus accounted for by 600 firms (UNCTC, 1988).

On the other hand, large firms have become less significant as employers of people. Large production units have become increasingly a thing of the past, and large companies now tend to consist of business units managed relatively independently. 'Business process re-engineering', with its philosophy of hiving off ancillary and expensive tasks to suppliers and automating remaining functions, is the latest contributor to this trend (Hammer and Champey, 1993).

The same phenomenon of decentralization is evident in the public sector, where the National Health Service, schools, and further education colleges, for example, have all been subject to devolved budgets and fragmentation. Public sector industries like British Coal and the railways, and the electricity industry before them, have likewise been broken up into smaller business units prior to privatization.

One result has been a higher profile for small–medium firms. A majority of the population are employed in firms with fewer than 200 employees. Even discounting the self-employed and those firms with fewer than five employees, small–medium firms account for 53 per cent of the employed population (Bannock and Daly, 1990). From a low point between 1968 and 1973, when the future of small firms was in some doubt (leading to the setting up of the Bolton Commission of Enquiry), the percentage in manufacturing employed in small–medium firms has returned to levels not seen since the 1930s (Stanworth and Gray, 1991).

These trends affect personnel and HRM in various ways:

- Smaller firms and establishments mean a more personalized style – not necessarily more progressive, but more face to face
- Smaller units may require less complex and sophisticated systems of personnel management, but may also be less able to sustain them in areas like management development
- Smaller units are less able to sustain a specialist personnel management function. As the IPM President said:

> Are there going to be large corporations in the future in which large traditional personnel administration departments can flourish? I don't think so, or at least not many (Bett, 1993, p. 41).

- On the other hand, the business and human challenges of operating in this kind of environment are becoming greater. The contribution of HRM will then be in facilitating the processes which support the development of the enterprise, rather than, as traditional personnel management has done, in administering systems for controlling people. Internationalization is a case in point (Hendry, 1994).

The basic challenge to HRM and enterprise management comes from the changing character of competition. The issue is not large firms or small firms but large firms, medium firms, *and* small firms. Competition in many sectors is no longer between individual firms, large or small, but between constellations of firms (Best, 1990). In the international sphere, for instance, major companies operate through a complex web of strategic alliances of varying degrees of permanence (Dicken, 1992).

The same pattern is seen domestically in the increasingly close relationships which large (often transnational) firms forge with their local suppliers. In the motor vehicle and electronics sectors, for example, buyer–supplier relationships have been transformed by the need for cooperation in the pursuit of reliability, continuous quality, product improvements, and shorter developmental lead times. Such relationships depend on regular exchanges of people and information-exchange through IT.

Often (for example, in the motor industry) a single large firm is surrounded by suppliers in close geographical proximity. While this is obviously efficient from a delivery and communication point of view, and firms consider such factors in choosing a location, it also indicates that competition, especially international competition, is between clusters of firms in 'industrial districts' (Porter, 1990). As a result, the development of the single firm depends increasingly on the development of the locality and the sector as a whole (Best, 1990). This includes the development of specialized skilled labour (technical and managerial) managed flexibly within the local labour market (Storper and Scott, 1989; Hendry, Arthur and Jones, 1995), and the public sector in providing an appopriate regulatory environment and a supportive structure of services and facilities (Goodman, Bamford and Saynor, 1989).

These changes in economic structure and patterns of competition mean that managers generally, including human resource professionals, will have to cope with the implications of networked relations more and more, in place of the more comfortable hierarchical relationships which dominated most people's experience of organizations until recently. In the public sector, meanwhile, the fragmentation and commercialization of unitary bodies like the NHS, local government, and central government departments give more scope to human resource strategies, in the sense that staff resources are more actively geared to customer-focused, unit objectives and financial resources. Indeed, as George Thomason (1990) observes, personnel management itself only really developed in the NHS after the reorganization of 1974 (and then half-heartedly) when the demand for a stronger performance-orientation led to a more managerial approach. Reorganization in local government in 1974 had a similar impact (Kessler, 1990).

The issue for both sectors now is how far a 'strategic' approach (with its implications of choice) is feasible within an ethic of service to all members of the community. Either the public service abandons this mission, or in retaining it limits the scope to manage employee resources flexibly in accordance with localized unit objectives.

The future of the personnel and human resources function

Since its formation in 1947 the IPM has enjoyed enormous growth as the professional institution representing those working in personnel. From 8000 members in 1967 numbers increased to 35 000 in 1989, and in 1994 had gone up to over 53 000.

This growth is closely related to the reform of its examination system in the early 1970s. This established a programme of study and qualification route which has become increasingly accepted. The concurrent development of management education in the former polytechnics and elsewhere meanwhile provided the local infrastructure for teaching the IPM course. Further changes to the curriculum in the early 1980s and again in 1991 have maintained its relevance and appeal. The importance of the professional examination to the IPM's success can be gauged by the number of members who are students at any one time – 30 000 out of 53 000 in 1994.

The result is that personnel professionals are relatively highly educated compared with British management generally, and the IPM is more entrenched in higher education than most other management specialisms in the UK (Berridge, 1992). For example, the percentage of personnel specialists who are not graduates or IPM-qualified rapidly declines as one goes up the hierarchy from junior personnel officer (67 per cent without a degree or IPM) to personnel director (15 per cent without either). These links into the higher education system also make the personnel profession in the UK unique within Europe (Kenny, 1989; Torrington, 1993). Personnel practitioners and the IPM have been highly successful in adopting'an expert-professional stance'(Berridge, 1992), reinforced through publications, research, and a network of local branches.

However, personnel professionals and the IPM currently face two threats to their exclusive claim to professional competence. First, there is the fact that in many firms, especially smaller ones, responsibility for personnel matters is either combined with other specialisms or is a line or general management responsibility. The decline of large organizations and reorganization ('decentralization') into smaller units means than many large centralized personnel departments have been greatly reduced. Line managers have taken on more of the operational responsibilities for things like selection and training, while non-professionals have been brought in as personnel directors and combined this with other portfolios.

These changes in the structure of firms in the UK both reduce the scope for specialized experience in more junior posts and reduce opportunities for promotion to the highest ranks (Torrington, Mackay and Hall, 1985). However, firms are also making greater use of specialist consultancy services and this creates possibilities for various combinations of generalist and specialist roles (Fowler, 1992a; see Chapter 5). According to the President of the IPM, this outsourcing of personnel activities and the growth of personnel consultancies is likely to be the pattern for the future (Bett, 1993).

The second threat is related to this dilution of responsibility. As part of the general effort to establish a structure of vocational qualifications in the UK for all crafts and occupations, the National Council for Vocational Qualifications has set up a Personnel Standards Lead Body, independent of the IPM (although the IPM is well represented), to develop a set of standards of job-related competences in personnel management. Among the data it collected from employers was a specific desire for qualifications that 'reflect broad business competence and include financial skills, an understanding of commercial pressures and of the link between HR and organizational objectives' (McKiddie, 1994, p. 33). As a result, the 'functional map' of competences which the Lead Body has developed gives more

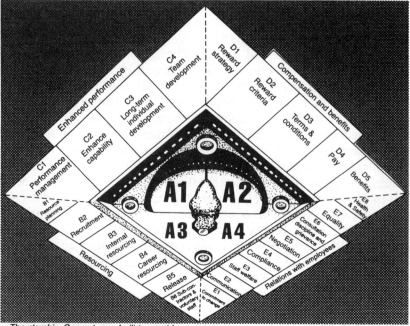

The starship *Competence*, built to provide
strategic support to the better-known *Enterprise*, is
based on the Lead Body's 'functional map' –
essentially a job description of personnel.

The core module Ⓐ Strategy and the organization,
is at the centre of the model, and subdivides into
the following key elements:
A1 Contributions to organizational strategy
A2 Personnel strategy
A3 Organizational structure and process
A4 Culture and values

Figure 20.1 *The Personnel Standards Lead Body's map of competences.*
(Reproduced with permission from McKiddie, 1994)

weight to organizational and personnel strategy than the IPM syllabus (see
Figure 20.1).

The division of functional skills and knowledge into resourcing, enhanced
performance (embracing training and development), compensation and
benefits, and relations with employees also has a different emphasis than
the IPM syllabus's core themes of employee resourcing, employee development, and employee relations. These proposals for an NVQ structure are
clearly designed to accommodate the high proportion of generalists with
personnel responsibilities and to bring personnel management into closer
relationship with business preoccupations.

The IPM has responded to these challenges by initiating a wide-ranging
review of its mission and the role of personnel practitioners in the light of
the changing shape of business and society (*Managing People – The Changing Frontiers*). Above all, it has agreed a merger with the more specialized
Institute of Training and Development (ITD) which has 20 000 members

(after an earlier attempt some fifteen years earlier). Among the benefits this is seen as bringing are:

- A single body of 73 000 members able to speak with one voice for the profession, and more able to command the attention of government and policy makers on employment and training (with the added bonus that it will make chartered status more likely)
- A higher profile for training and development in the work of personnel/HR professionals (in the words of the IPM director general, the merger will create 'a new unified professional body promoting the values of continuous learning and improvement of people'
- An acknowledgement that personnel work demands holistic, integrated solutions to business problems, not a narrow functional expertise (*Personnel Management*, 1993b; *Personnel Management plus*, 1994a–c).

The merger into a new Institute of Personnel and Development symbolizes the shift in the personnel management role away from industrial relations and control towards a concern with employee growth and development, skills and training.

The changes to the boundaries of personnel management, meanwhile, make the general argument of HRM for a strategic, integrative perspective increasingly relevant, as well as encouraging the development of specific frameworks for thinking and planning strategically. Personnel work is likely to include more direct involvement in the day-to-day realization of strategy through job design, work organization design, the development of skills, and the adoption of methods for improving productivity – areas which have traditionally been more the concern of line managers and technical support functions. With a team approach to these issues, the personnel professional will get closer to the core issues of operations and strategy. 'Skill' could also then become more obviously a core concept in HRM.

Closer involvement with business problems and the fact that HR specialists may increasingly find themselves working through consultancies means also adopting a more entrepreneurial style. According to the IPM President, Mike Bett:

> Personnel professionals with an entrepreneurial spirit will increasingly set themselves up in business to meet the personnel needs of smaller businesses. . .
> We must show we have moved on from being industrial relations gun-fighters, and are now about developing people and organizations for competitive success (*Personnel Management plus*, 1994d, p. 8).

While there will remain a place for basic personnel skills and knowledge (for instance, over employee contracts), these kind of changes suggest that at higher levels of the profession an education in HRM will have more of the qualities and syllabus associated with a general MBA and be less technique-oriented. That is, it will be strategic, international, and problem focused, while developing personal qualities such as creativity. At higher levels of the profession it also means gearing HR training and education to non-specialists. If personnel professionals want to be part of general management, the profession must also admit general management into its area of expertise.

Summary

In this final chapter we have reviewed four interconnected themes – emerging models within HRM, the shift in focus from conflict and control to employee growth and development, new organizational forms, and the future of the personnel and human resources function. Many of the issues arising point to the importance of the institutional and political context in framing the agenda with which HRM has to contend. It may well be that we are at a watershed in the dominance of a market-oriented, right-wing ideology, and that the next few years will see a return to more communitarian attitudes and institutions. Clearly, this will directly affect the public sector, but it will also affect the environment for the private sector. The role of the State in the training system is one obvious area which is ripe for a more interventionist approach.

While addressing contemporary themes, we have aimed in this book to develop a perspective which will survive political change. We will therefore conclude with a restatement of the core theme of the book. While HRM challenges basic values in the way people are managed, it is above all about taking a strategic approach. In this, internal 'strategic coherence' is more important than external 'strategic fit'.

Personnel management has been generally defective in its strategic frameworks. Although HRM purports to offer a strategic perspective, it too is weak, with very few tools for thinking and planning strategically. Two concepts can fill this gap.

First, the notion of an employment system makes it possible to analyse company practices in terms of the different patterns for treating people which they sustain. Thus, all organizations manage different groups of employees according to some combination of an internal labour market, occupational labour market, open external (or casualized) labour market, and technical/ industrial labour market, with the 'commitment system' and 'performance management approach' as emerging new types (Chapter 11). Because the employment systems perspective defines patterns, it provides a measure for assessing internal coherence or 'strategic integration' between aspects of personnel management. However, the framework of selection, appraisal, development, and rewards used by Fombrun, Tichy and Devanna (1984) does not provide any normative yardstick for measuring 'alignment'. The types of employment system, however, do.

Moreover, they provide a connection to business strategy (external 'strategic fit') through the concept of skill. Thus, an employment system is fundamentally a way of securing skills and effort for an organization. The internal labour market system, for example, tends to exist where firm-specific knowledge and skills are at a premium or where it is desirable to secure predictable effort for some other reason. The implications of being in a particular product-market in terms of getting, retaining, developing, and discarding skills will indicate the type of employment system which a firm may need to operate, alongside the labour market constraints within which they have to work.

Within a framework of employment systems, personnel management therefore also needs to have a concept of skill at its centre. In the past this has not been the case. The obvious reason for this is that it has been more concerned with managing conflict and effecting control over employees than with promoting employee growth and development.

Skill is thus a way of defining the human implications of business strategy and the technology required to implement it. Increasingly, theorists are recognizing that successful business strategies begin 'from the inside out'. That is, they are developed around the 'core competences' or skills of the organization, rather than being driven primarily by an assessment of market opportunity. Personnel management and human resource strategy should therefore be driven by an assessment of skill requirements, changing skills, and skill deficits, since these frame the possibilities for a business.

Finally, if HRM adopts an employment systems perspective it provides a common basis for comparing national systems of personnel management through the types of pattern that predominate. Factors which contribute to these patterns by underpinning or restricting labour mobility – such as national training systems – can then be isolated, understood, and even reformed. Understanding these will help to define the limits for convergence towards one or more models of HRM in different European countries and world-wide.

References

Abdel-Razek, R. and McCaffer, R. (1987). 'A change in the UK construction industry structure: implications for estimating', *Construction Management and Economics*, **5**, 227–242.

Abernathy, W., Clark, K.B. and Kantrow, A.M. (1981). 'The new industrial competition', *Harvard Business Review*, October, 69–77.

ACAS (1988). *Labour Flexibility in Britain: the 1987 ACAS survey*, Occasional paper 41. London: ACAS.

Adler, N.J. (1986). *International Dimensions of Organisational Behaviour*, Boston, MA: Kent Publishers.

Adler, N.J. and Jelinek, M. (1986). 'Is "organisation culture" culture bound?' *Human Resource Management*, **25**, 1, 73–90.

Ahlstrand, B. and Purcell, J. (1988). 'Employee relations strategy in the multi-divisional company', *Personnel Review*, **17**, 3, 3–11.

Allen, J. (1988). 'Fragmented firms, disorganized labour', in J. Allen and D. Massey (eds), *The Economy in Question*, London/Newbury Park/New Delhi: Sage, 184–228.

Althauser, R.P. and Kalleberg, A.L (1981). 'Firms, occupations and the structure of labor markets: a conceptual analysis', in I. Berg (ed) *Sociological Perspectives on Labor Markets*, New York: Academic Press, 119–149.

Angle, H.L., Manz, C.C. and Van de Ven, A.H. (1985). 'Integrating human resource management and corporate strategy: a preview of the 3M story', *Human Resource Management*, **24**, 51–68.

Ansoff, H.I. (1965). *Corporate Strategy: An Analytic Approach to Business Policy for Growth and Expansion*, New York: McGraw-Hill.

Argyris, C. (1960). *Understanding Organisational Behaviour*, Homewood, IL: Dorsey Press.

Argyris. C. (1964). *Integrating the Individual and the Organisation*, Wiley: New York.

Argyris, C. and Schon, D.A. (1974). *Theory in Practice: Increasing Professional Effectiveness*, London: Jossey-Bass.

Arkin, A. (1993). 'An education in training', *Personnel Management*, December, 42–45.

Armstrong, M. (1979). *Case Studies in Personnel Management*, London: Kogan Page.

Armstrong, M. (1987). *A Handbook of Human Resource Management*, London: Kogan Page.

Asanuma, K. (1982). 'The social context of industrial skill and its training implications', Unpublished paper, University of Sussex, Brighton.

Ashburner, L. (1991). 'Men managers and women workers: women as an under-used resource', *British Journal of Management*, **2**, 1, 3–15.

Atkinson, J. (1984). 'Manpower strategies for flexible organisations', *Personnel Management*, August, 28–31.

Atkinson, J. (1985). *Flexibility, Uncertainty and Manpower Management*,

Institute of Manpower Studies, Report No. 89, Falmer, University of Sussex.

Atkinson, J. (1989). *Corporate Employment Policies for the Single European Market. IMS Report No. 179*, Institute of Manpower Studies, University of Sussex.

Atkinson, J. and Meager, N. (1986). *Changing Patterns of Work: How Companies Introduce Flexibility to Meet Changing Needs*, Falmer, Sussex: Institute for Manpower Studies.

Axelsson, R., Cray, D., Mallory, G.R. and Wilson, D.C. (1991). 'Decision style in British and Swedish organisations: a comparative examination of strategic decision making', *British Journal of Management*, **2**, 67–79.

Bacon, R.W. and Eltis, W.A. (1976). *Britain's Economic Problem: Too Few Producers*, London: Macmillan.

Badaracco, J.L. (1991). *The Knowledge Link – How Firms Compete through Strategic Alliances*, Boston, MA: Harvard Business School Press.

Baglioni, G. and Crouch,C. (eds) (1990). *European Industrial Relations: The Challenge of Flexibility*, London/Newbury Park/New Delhi: Sage.

Bain, G.S. and Price, R. (1983). 'Union growth: dimensions, determinants and destiny', in G.S. Bain (ed.), *Industrial Relations in Britain*, Oxford: Blackwell.

Baird, L. and Meshoulam, I. (1988). 'Managing two fits of strategic human resource management', *Acadamy of Management Review*, **13**, 1, 116–128.

Baird, L., Meshoulam, I. and Degive, G. (1983). 'Meshing human resources planning with strategic business planning: a model approach', *Personnel*, September-October, 14–25.

Ballin, M. (1993). 'Forging a new breed of supervisor', *Personnel Management*, April, 34–37.

Banas, P. and Sauers, R. (1989). *The Relationship between Participative Management and Employee Involvement*, Dearborn, MI: Ford Motor Company.

Bannock, G. and Daly, M. (1990). 'Size distribution of UK firms', *Employment Gazette*, May.

Bannock and Partners (1990). *Enterprises in the European Community*, Brussels/Luxembourg: Commission of the European Communities.

Barham, K. and Oates, D. (1991). *The International Manager*, London: Economist Books.

Barney, J.B. (1986). 'Organizational culture: Can it be a source of sustained competitive advantage?' *Academy of Management Review*, **11**, 656–665.

Bartholomew, D.J. (1969). *Stochastic Models of Social Processes*, Chichester: Wiley.

Bartlett, C.A. and Ghoshal, S. (1989). *Managing Across Borders: The Transnational Solution*, Boston, MA: Harvard Business School Press.

Bartlett, C.A. and Yosihara, H. (1988). 'New challenges for Japanese multinationals: is organisation adaptation their Achilles heel?', *Human Resource Management*, **27**, 1, 19–43.

Bass, B.M. and Burger, P.C. (1979). *Assessment of Managers: An International Comparison*, New York: Free Press.

Bassett, P. (1986). *Strike Free*, London: Macmillan.

Bassett, P. (1988). 'Non-unionism's growing ranks', *Personnel Management*, March, 44–47.

Beard, D. and Lee, G. (1990). 'Improved connections at BT's development centres', *Personnel Management*, April, 61–63.

Beaumont, P. and Townley, B. (1985). 'Greenfield sites, new plants and work practices', in V. Hammond (ed.), *Current Research in Management*, London: Frances Pinter.

Beckhard, R. and Harris, R.T. (1987). *Organisational Transitions*, 2nd edition, Reading, MA: Addison-Wesley.

Beer, M. (1976). 'The technology of organisation development', in M. D. Dunnette (ed.), *Handbook of Industrial and Organisational Psychology*, Chicago, IL: Rand McNally.

Beer, M., Eisenstet, R. and Spector, B. (1990). *The Critical Path to Organizational Renewal*, Boston, MA: Harvard Business School Press.

Beer, M., Spector, B., Lawrence, P.R., Mills, Q.N., and Walton, R.E. (1984). *Managing Human Assets*, New York: Free Press.

Behrend, H. (1973). *Incomes Policy, Equity and Pay Increase Differentials*, Edinburgh: Scottish University Press.

Belbin, M. (1981). *Management Teams: why they succeed or fail*, London: Heinemann.

Bell, R.M. (1972). *Changing Technology and Manpower Requirements in the Engineering Industry*, Sussex University Press.

Bennison, M. and Casson, J. (1984). *The Manpower Planning Handbook*, Maidenhead: McGraw-Hill.

Bernoth, A. (1994). 'Mindbenders explore the future at Mercury', *The Sunday Times*, 24 April, 3.7.

Berridge, J. (1992). 'Human resource management in Britain', *Employee Relations*, **14**, 5, 62–92.

Berryman, S.E. (1991). 'Training in the United States: the state of play and future directions', in J. Stevens and R. Mackay (eds), *Training and Competitiveness*, London: NEDO/Kogan Page, 111–131.

Bessant, J. (1991). *Managing Advanced Manufacturing Technology: The Challenge of the Fifth Wave*, Oxford: NCC/Blackwell.

Bessant, J. (1993). 'Towards Factory 2000: designing organizations for computer-integrated technologies', in J. Clark (ed.), *Human Resource Management and Technical Change*, London/Newbury Park/New Delhi: Sage, 192–211.

Best, M.H. (1990). *The New Competition*, Cambridge, MA: Harvard University Press.

Bett, M. (1993). 'Pioneering a new role for personnel', *Personnel Management*, November, 40–43.

Bevan, S. and Hutt, R. (1985). 'Company perspectives on the Youth Training Scheme', Report No.104, University of Sussex, Institute of Manpower Studies.

Bevan, S. and Thompson, M. (1991). 'Performance management at the crossroads', *Personnel Management*, November.

Birley, S. and Westhead, P. (1990). 'Growth and performance contrasts between 'types' of small firms', *Strategic Management Journal*, **11**, 535–557.

Bishop, G. and Lewin, R. (1993). 'Short-circuiting old bargaining machinery', *Personnel Management*, February, 28–32.

Blyton, P. (1993). 'The search for workforce flexibility', in B. Towers (ed.), *The Handbook of Human Resource Management*, Oxford: Blackwell.

Bowen, D.E. and Schneider, B. (1988). 'Services marketing and management: implications for organizational behaviour', *Research in Organizational Behaviour: Vol 10*, Greenwich, CT: JAI Press, 43–80.

Bowey, A.M. (1974). *A Guide to Manpower Planning*, London: Macmillan.

Bowman, E.H. (1986). 'Concerns of the CEO', *Human Resource Management*, **25**, 267–285.

Boxall, P.F. (1993). 'The significance of human resource management: a reconsideration of the evidence', *International Journal of Human Resource Management*, **4**, 3, 645–664.

Boyatzis, R. (1982). *The Competent Manager*, New York: Wiley.

Bramham, J. (1975). *Practical Manpower Planning*, London: IPM.

Braverman, H. (1974). *Labor and Monopoly Capitalism: The Degradation of Work in the Twentieth Century*, New York and London: Monthly Review Press.

Brewster, C. (1993a). 'Collective agreements: old and new styles', in B. Towers (ed.), *A Handbook of Industrial Relations Practice*, 2nd edition, London: Kogan Page, 152–166.

Brewster, C. (1993b). 'Developing a 'European' model of human resource management', *International Journal of Human Resource Management*, **4**, 4, 765–784.

Brewster, C. and Smith, C. (1990). 'Corporate strategy: a no-go area for personnel?' *Personnel Management*, July, 36–40.

Brewster, C., Hegewisch, A., Lockhart, T. and Mayne, L. (1993). *Flexible Working Patterns in Europe*, Wimbledon: IPM.

Brown, C.V. (1983). *Taxation and the Incentive to Work*, Oxford: Oxford University Press.

Brown, J.S. and Duguid, P. (1991). 'Organizational learning and communities of practice: toward a unified view of working, learning, and innovation', *Organization Science*, **2**, 1, 40–57.

Brown, W. (1989). 'Managing remuneration', in K. Sisson (ed.), *Personnel Management in Britain*, Oxford: Blackwell, 249–270.

Bruce, L. (1989). 'Wanted: more mongrels in the corporate kennel', *International Management*, January, 35–37.

Bryant, D.T. (1965). 'A survey of the development of manpower planning', *British Journal of Industrial Relations*, **3**, November, 279–290.

Bryman, A., Bresnen, M., Beardsworth, A.D., Ford, J., and Keil, E.T. (1987). 'The concept of the temporary system: the case of the construction project', in S.B. Bacharach and N. DiTomaso (eds), *Research in the Sociology of Organizations, Volume 5*, Greenwich, CT: JAI Press, 253–283.

Buchanan, D. (1989). 'Principles and practice in job design', in K. Sisson (ed.), *Personnel Management in Britain*, Oxford: Blackwell.

Buller, P.F. and Napier, N.K. (1993). 'Strategy and human resource management integration in fast growth versus other mid-sized firms', *British Journal of Management*, **4**, 77–90.

Burgoyne, J. and Stuart, R. (1978). 'Managerial skills', in J. Burgoyne and R. Stuart (eds), *Management Development: Context and Strategies, A Personnel Review*, Monograph, Aldershot: Gower, pp. 51–73.

Burns, T. and Stalker, G.M. (1966). *The Management of Innovation*, London: Tavistock.

Burnes, B. and Weekes, B. (1988). 'Planning profit from advanced manufacturing technology, *Personnel Management*, December, 50–53.

Business Week (1984). 'Who's excellent now: some of the best-seller's picks haven't been doing so well lately', *Business Week*, 5 November, 76–94.

Cahill, J. and Ingram, P. (1988). *Changes in Working Practices in British Manufacturing Industry in the 1980s: a study of employee concessions made during wage negotiations*, London: Confederation of British Industry.

Calori, R. and Sarnin, P. (1991). 'Corporate culture and economic performance: a French study', *Organisation Studies*, **12**, 1, 49–74.

Cambridge Small Business Research Centre (1992). *The State of British Enterprise: Growth, innovation and competitive advantage in small and medium-sized firms*, University of Cambridge: Small Business Research Centre.

Campbell, A. (1991). 'Issues of training strategy in British manufacturing', in J. Stevens and R. Mackay (eds), *Training and Competitiveness*, London: Kogan Page/NEDO, pp. 111–131.

Cannell, M. and Long, P. (1991). 'What's changed about incentive pay?' *Personnel Management*, October, 58–63.

Cartwright, S. and Cooper, C.L. (1990). 'The Impact of Mergers and Acquisitions on People at Work: Existing Research Issues', *British Journal of Management*, 1, 2, pp. 65–76.

Cartwright, S. and Cooper, C.L. (1993). 'The role of culture compatibility in successful organizational marriage', *Academy of Management Executive*, **7**, 2, 57–70.

Casey, B. (1991). 'Survey evidence on trends in "non-standard" employment', in Pollert, A. (ed.), *Farewell to Flexibility?* Oxford: Blackwell.

Caulkin, S. (1983). 'Manufacturing's last stand', *Management Today*, March, 51–61.

Chakravarthy, B.S., (1984). 'Strategic self-renewal: a planning framework for today', *Academy of Management Review*, **9**, 3, 536–547.

Chandler, A.D. (1962). *Strategy and Structure*, Cambridge, MA: MIT Press.

Channon, D.F. (1972). 'Corporate strategy and organization structure in British industry', *Journal of Business Policy*, **3**, 1, 60–72.

Channon, D.F. (1982). 'Industrial structure', *Long Range Planning*, **15**, 5, 78–93.

Channon, D.F. (1991). 'Le Défi Americain ou le Défi Japonais: Quelle est la difference?' paper to the 11th Annual Strategic Management Society International Conference, Toronto, 23–26 October.

Child, J. (1977, 1984). *Organization: A Guide to Problems and Practice*, London: Harper and Row.

Child, J. (1985). 'Managerial strategies, new technology and the labour process', in D. Knights, H. Willmott and D. Collinson (eds), *Job Design*, Aldershot: Gower, 107–141.

Child, J. and Partridge, B.E. (1982). *Lost Managers*, Cambridge: Cambridge University Press.

Churchill, N.C. and Lewis, V.L. (1983). 'The five stages of small business growth', *Harvard Business Review*, **61**, May-June, 30–50.

Clark, J. (1993). 'Full flexibility and self-supervision in an automated factory', in J. Clark (ed.), *Human Resource Management and Technical Change*, London: Sage, 116–136.

Clark, J. McLoughlin, I., Rose, H. and King, R. (1988). *The Process of Technological Change: New Technology and Social Choice in the Workplace*, Cambridge: Cambridge University Press.

Claydon, T. (1989). 'Union derecognition in Britain in the 1980s', *British Journal of Industrial Relations*, **27**, 214–223.

Clegg, H.A. (1979). *The Changing System of Industrial Relations in Great Britain*, Oxford: Blackwell.

Cockerill, T. (1989). 'The kind of competence for rapid change', *Personnel Management*, September, 52–56.

Constable, J. (1986). 'Diversification as a factor in UK industrial strategy', *Long Range Planning*, **19**, 1, 52–60.

Constable, J. and McCormick, R. (1987). *The Making of British Managers*, London: British Institute of Management.

Cook, D.S. and Ferris, G.F. (1986). 'Strategic human resource management and firm effectiveness in industries experiencing decline', *Human Resource Management*, Fall, 441–557.

Cooke, R. and Armstrong, M. (1990). 'The search for strategic HRM', *Personnel Management*, December, 30–33.

Coopers and Lybrands Associates (1985). *A Challenge to Complacency*, London: National Economic Development Office and Manpower Services Commission.

Coopey, J. and Hartley, J. (1990). 'Tensions in organizational commitment', British Psychology Conference, Windermere, January.

Cowe, R. (1990). 'Could nineties engineer an exciting new age?', *The Guardian*, 11 January.

Cowling, K., Stoneman, P., Cubbin, J., Cable, T., Hall, G., Domberger, S. and Dutton, P. (1980). *Mergers and Economic Performance*, Cambridge: Cambridge University Press.

Craig, C., Rubery, J., Tarling, R. and Wilkinson, F. (1982). *Labour Market Structure, Worker Organisation and Low Pay*, Cambridge: Cambridge University Press.

Crawford, S. (1989). *Technical Workers in an Advanced Society: The Work, Careers and Politics of French Engineers*, Cambridge: Cambridge University Press.

Cressey, P. and Jones, B. (1991). 'A new convergence? Introduction to a Special Issue of work employment and European society', *Work, Employment and Society*, **5**, 4, 493–495.

Crittan, P. (1993). *Investing in People: Towards Corporate Capability*, Oxford: Butterworth-Heinemann.

Crockett, G. and Elias, P. (1984). 'British managers: A study of their education, training, mobility and earnings', *British Journal of Industrial Relations*, **XXII**, 1, 34–46.

Crofts, P. (1992). 'Employers find MCI approach "too mechanistic"', *Personnel Management plus*, **3**, 11, 1.

Crouch, C. (1990). 'Afterword', in G. Baglioni and C. Crouch (eds), *European Industrial Relations: The Challenge of Flexibility*, London/Newbury Park/New Delhi: Sage, 356–362.

Crowther, S. and Garrahan, P. (1988). 'Invitation to Sunderland: corporate power and the local economy', *Industrial Relations Journal*, **19**, 1, 51–59.

Cuming, M.W. (1985). *The Theory and Practice of Personnel Management*, 5th edition, London: Heinemann.

Cummings, L.L., Harnett, D.L. and Stevens, O.J. (1971). 'Risk, fate, conciliation, and trust: an international study of attitudinal differences among executives', *Academy of Management Journal*, 285–304.

Curtain, R. (1987). 'Skill formation and the enterprise', *Labour & Industry*, **1**, 1, 8–38.

Cutler, T., Haslam, C., Williams, J. and Williams, K. (1989). *1992 – The Struggle for Europe: A Critical Evaluation of the European Community*, New York: Berg.

Daly, A., Hitchens, D.M. and Wagner, K. (1985). 'Productivity, machinery and skills in a sample of British and German manufacturing plants', *National Institute Economic Review*, February.

Daniel, W.W. (1987). *Workplace Industrial Relations and Technical Change*, London: Frances Pinter/Policy Studies Institute.

Daniel, W.W. and Millward, N. (1983). *Workplace Industrial Relations in Britain: The DE/PSI/ESRC Survey*, London: Heinemann.

Davidson, M. and Cooper, C. (1983). *Stress and the Woman Manager*, Oxford: Martin Robertson.

Deal, T. and Kennedy, A. (1982). *Corporate Cultures: The Rites and Rituals of Corporate Life*, Reading, MA: Addison-Wesley.

Deloitte Haskins & Sells (1989). *Management Challenge for the 1990s*, Sheffield: Training Agency.

Deloitte Haskins & Sells/IFF Research Ltd (1989). *Training in Britain: Employers' Activities*, London: HMSO.

Denison, D.R. (1984). 'Bringing corporate culture to the bottom line', *Organisational Dynamics*, Autumn, 4–22.

Denison, D.R. (1990). *Corporate Culture and Organizational Effectiveness*, New York: Wiley.

Department of Education and Science (1990). *Statistical Bulletin 1/90*, London: DES.

Department of Employment (1981). *A New Training Initiative: A Programme for Action*, Cmnd 8455, London: HMSO.

Derr, C.B. and Oddou, G.R. (1991). 'Are US multinational adequately preparing future American leaders for global competition?' *International Journal of Human Resource Management*, **2**, 2, 227–244.

Derr, C.B., Jones, C., and Toomey, E.L. (1988). 'Managing high-potential employees: current practices in thirty-three U.S. corporations', *Human Resource Management*, **27**, 3, 273–290.

DeSanto, J.F. (1983). 'Workforce planning and corporate strategy', *Personnel Administrator*, **28**, 33–36.

Desatnick, R.L. and Bennett, M.L. (1978). *Human Resource Management in the Multinational Company*, New York: Nichols.

Detweiler, R. (1980). 'Intercultural interaction and the categorisation process: a conceptual analysis and behavioural outcome', *International Journal of Intercultural Relations*, **4**, 275–293.

Deutscher, I. (1973). *What We Say/What We Do: sentiments and acts*, Glenview, IL: Scott Foresman.

Devanna, M.A., Fombrun, C.J. and Tichy, T.M. (1984). 'A framework for strategic human resource management', in C.J. Fombrun, N.M. Tichy, and M.A. Devanna, *Strategic Human Resource Management*, New York: Wiley.

Dicken, P. (1992). *Global Shift*, 2nd edition, London: Paul Chapman.

Directorate-General for Economic and Financial Affairs (1990). *European Economy: Social Europe. The impact of the internal market by industrial sector: the challenge for the Member States*, Brussels: Commission of the European Communities.

Directorate-General, Employment, Industrial Relations and Social Affairs (1990). *Employment in Europe*, Luxembourg: Commission of the European Communities.

Doeringer, P.B. and Piore, M.J. (1971). *Internal Labour Markets and Manpower Analysis*, Lexington, MA: Heath.

Doogan, K. (1992). 'Flexible labour? Employment and training in new service industries: The case of retailing', Working Paper 105, School for Advanced Urban Studies, University of Bristol.

Dopson, S. and Stewart, R. (1990). 'What *is* happening to middle management?' *British Journal of Management*, **1**, 1, 3–16.

Dosi, G. (1988). 'Sources, procedures, and microeconomic effects of innovation', *Journal of Economic Literature*, **26**, 1120–1171.

Dowling, P.J. (1988). 'International and domestic personnel/human resource management: similarities and differences', in R.S. Schuler, S.A. Youngblood and V.L. Huber (eds), *Readings in Personnel and Human Resource Hanagement*, 3rd edition, St Paul, MN: West Publishing Co.

Dowling, P.J. and Schuler, R.S (1990). *International Dimensions of Human Resource Management*, Boston, MA: PWS-Kent.

Drucker, P.F. (1954). *The Practice of Management*, New York: Harper.

Drummond, H. (1993). 'Measuring management effectiveness', *Personnel Management*, March, 38–41.

du Gay, P. (1991). 'Enterprise culture and the ideology of excellence', *New Formations*, **13**, 45–61.

Dyer, L. (1983). 'Bringing human resources into the strategy formulation process', *Human Resource Management*, **22**, 257–271.

Economist, The (1990). 'Doing nicely, old man', 27 October, 30.

Edwards, P.K. (1991). 'Industrial conflict: will the giant awake?' *Personnel Management*, September, 26–29.

Employment Department (1992). *Labour Market & Skill Trends 1991/92: Planning for a Changing Labour Market*, Sheffield: Employment Department Group.

Employment Department (1994). *Labour Market & Skill Trends 1994/95*, Sheffield: Skills and Enterprise Network.

Evans, P., Lank, E. and Farquhar, A. (1989). 'Managing human resources in the international firm: lessons from practice', in P. Evans, Y. Doz and A. Laurent (eds), *Human Resource Management in International Firms*, London: Macmillan.

Evans, S. (1990). 'Free labour and economic performance: evidence from the construction industry', *Work, Employment and Society*, **4**, 2, 239–252.

Evans, S. and Lewis, R. (1989). 'Restructuring and deregulation in the construction industry'. in S. Tailby and C. Whitston (eds), *Manufacturing Change: Industrial Relations and Restructuring*, Oxford: Blackwell.

Everest, N. (1993). 'Striking the balance in management development', Crystal Lecture, University of Wolverhampton, *Journal of Industrial Affairs*, **2**, 43–49.

Eyraud, F., Marsden, D. and Silvestre, J.-J. (1990). 'Occupational and internal labour markets in Britain and France', *International Labour Review*, **129**, 4, 501–517.

Fairbairns, J. (1991). 'Plugging the gap in training needs analysis', *Personnel Management*, February, 43–45.

Fazey, I.H. (1987). *The Pathfinder*, London: Financial Training Publications.

Ferner, A. (1989). 'Ten years of Thatcherism: changing industrial relations in British public enterprises', Warwick University, Warwick Papers in Industrial Relations.

Fiedler, F.E. (1967). *A Theory of Leadership Effectiveness*, New York: McGraw-Hill.

Financial Times (1993). 'A very British clash', 30/31 October, 6.

Finegold, D. and Soskice, D. (1988). 'The future of training in Britain: analysis and prescription', *Oxford Review of Economic Policy*, **4**, 3.

Finniston, M. (1990). 'Building on steel's strong foundations', letter to the *Sunday Times*, 28 October, 38.

Flanders, A. (1970). *Management and Unions: The Theory and Reform of Industrial Relations*, London: Faber.

Fletcher, C. (1973). 'The end of management', in J. Child (ed.), *Man and Organization*, London: Allen & Unwin.

Fletcher, C. (1993). 'Appraisal: an idea whose time has gone', *Personnel Management*, September, 34–37.

Folger, R. and Konovsky, M.A. (1989). 'Effects of procedural and distributive justice on reactions to pay raise decisions', *Academy of Management Journal*, **32**, 1, 115–130.

Fombrun, C. (1982). 'Conversation with Reginald H. Jones and Frank Doyle', *Organizational Dynamics*, **10**, 3, 42–63.

Fombrun, C.J. (1983). 'Strategic management: integrating the human resource systems into strategic planning', in *Advances in Strategic Management, Vol. 2*. Greenwich, CT: JAI Press.

Fombrun, C.J. and Tichy, N.M. (1983). 'Strategic planning and human resources management: at rainbow's end', in R. Lamb (ed.), *Recent Advances in Strategic Planning*, New York: McGraw-Hill.

Fombrun, C.J., Tichy, N.M. and Devanna, M.A. (1984). *Strategic Human Resource Management*, New York: Wiley.

Fowler, A. (1987). 'When chief executives discover HRM', *Personnel Management*, January, 3.

Fowler, A. (1992a). 'Structure a personnel department', *Personnel Management plus*, **3**, 1, 22–23.

Fowler, A. (1992b). 'Two routes to quality', *Personnel Management*, November, 30–34.

Fox, A. (1974). *Beyond Contract: Work, Power, and Trust Relations*, London: Faber.

Fox, J. (1988). 'Norsk Hydro's new approach takes root', *Personnel Management*, January, 37–40.

Fox, S. and McLeay, S. (1992). 'An approach to researching managerial labour markets: HRM, corporate strategy and financial performance in UK manufacturing', *International Journal of Human Resource Management*, 3, 3, pp. 523–554.

Fox, S., McLeay, S. and Tanton, M. (1990). 'Smoothies, trendies and sharpbenders: human resource management in financially distinctive firms', Annual Congress of the European Accounting Association, Maastricht, The Netherlands, April.

Freedman, A. (1985). *The New Look in Wage Policy and Employee Relations*, Report No. 865. New York: Conference Board Inc.

Friedman, A. (1977). *Industry and Labour*, London: Macmillan.

Friedman, S.D. (1986). 'Succession systems in large corporations: characteristics and correlates of performance', *Human Resource Management*, **25**, 191–214.

Galbraith, J.R. and Nathanson, D.A. (1978). *Strategy Implementation: The Role of Structure and Process*, St Paul, MN: West Publishing.

Gallie, D. and White, M. (1993). *Employee Commitment and the Skills Revolution*, London: Policy Studies Institute.

Garden, A. (1987). 'The Motivation and job excitement of software professionals', unpublished paper, London Business School.

Gardner, B.B. and Whyte, W.H. (1945). 'The man in the middle: position and problems of the foreman', *Applied Anthropology*, **4**, 1–28.

Gershuny, J. and Miles, I. (1985). *The New Service Economy*, London: Frances Pinter.

Gertsen, M.C. (1990). 'Intercultural competence and expatriates', *International Journal of Human Resource Management*, **1**, 3, 341–362.

Ghobadian, A. and White, M. (1987). 'Job evaluation and equal pay', Research Paper No. 58, London: Department of Employment.

Glaze, T. (1989). 'Cadbury's dictionary of competence', *Personnel Management*, July, 44–48.

Gluck, F.W., Kaufman, S.P. and Walleck, A.S. (1980). 'Strategic management for competitive advantage', *Harvard Business Review*, July-August, 154–161.

Goffee, R. and Scase, R. (1986). 'Are the rewards worth the effort? Changing managerial values in the 1980s,' *Personnel Review*, **15**, 3–6

Golden, K.A. and Ramanujam, V. (1985). 'Between a dream and a nightmare: on the integration of the human resource management and strategic business planning processes', *Human Resource Management*, Winter, 429–452.

Golzen, G. and Garner, A. (1990). *Smart Moves*, Oxford: Basil Blackwell.

Goodman, E., Bamford, J. with Saynor, P. (eds) (1989). *Small Firms and Industrial Districts in Italy*, London: Routledge.

Goodmeasure Inc. (1985). *The Changing American Workplace: Work Alternatives in the 1980s*, New York: American Management Association.

Goold, M. and Campbell, A. (1987). *Strategies and Styles: The Role of the Centre in Managing Diversified Corporations*, Oxford: Blackwell.

Goold, M. and Quinn, J, (1990). *Strategic Milestones for Long-Term Performance*, London: Hutchinson.

Gospel, H. (1983). 'The development of management organisation in industrial relations: a historical perspective', in K. Thurley and S. Wood (eds), *Industrial Relations and Management Strategy*, Cambridge: Cambridge University Press.

Gospel, H.F. (1992). *Markets, Firms, and the Management of Labour in Modern Britain*, Cambridge: Cambridge University Press.

Gospel, H. and Littler, C.R. (1983). *Managerial Strategies and Industrial Relations: An Historical and Comparative Study*, London: Heinemann.

Gowler, D. (1969). 'Determinants of the supply of labour to the firm', *Journal of Management Studies*, **6**, 1, 73–93.

Greatrex, J. and Phillips, P. (1989). 'Oiling the wheels of competence', *Personnel Management* , August, 36–39.

Greer, C.R., Jackson, D.L. and Fiorito, J. (1989). 'Adapting human resource planning in a changing business environment', *Human Resource Management*, 28, 1, 105–123.

Greiner, L. (1972). 'Evolution and revolution as organizations grow', *Harvard Business Review*, July-August, 37–46.

Grinyer, P.H. and Spender, J.-C. (1979). 'Recipes, crises and adaptation in mature businesses', *International Studies of Management and Organisation*, **IX**, 113–123.

Grinyer, P.H., Mayes, D. and McKiernan, P. (1988). *Sharp Benders: The Secrets of Unleashing Corporate Potential*, Oxford: Blackwell.

Grosser, A. (1989). 'The future of education in Europe', *Vocational Training*, **1**, 28–30.

Guardian, The (1987). 'Manufacturers shift spending to overseas jobs', 5 May.

Guardian, The (1993). 'British workers likely to stay at top of long-hours league', 2 June.

Guardian, The (1994). 'Part-timers win rights', 4 March, 1.

Guest, D.E. (1987). 'Human resource management and industrial relations', *Journal of Management Studies*, **24**, 5, 503–521.

Guest, D.E. (1989). 'HRM: implications for industrial relations', in J. Storey (ed.), *New Perspectives on Human Resource Management*, London and New York: Routledge.

Guest, D.E. (1990). 'Human resource management and the American dream', *Journal of Management Studies*, **27**, 4, 377–397.

Guest, D.E. (1992). 'Human resource management in the United Kingdom', in B. Towers (ed.), *The Handbook of Human Resource Management*, Oxford: Blackwell.

Gunz, H. and Whitley, R. (1985). 'Managerial cultures and industrial strategies in British firms', *Organisation Studies*, **6**, 3, 247–273.

Gupta, A.K., (1986). 'Matching managers to strategies: point and counterpoint', *Human Resource Management*, **25**, 2, 215–234.

Gupta, A.K. and Govindarajan, V. (1984). 'Business unit strategy, managerial characteristics, and business unit effectiveness at strategy implementation', *Academy of Management Journal*, **27**, 25–41.

Hakim, C. (1990). 'Core and periphery in employers' workforce strategies: evidence from the 1987 ELUS survey', *Work, Employment and Society*, **4**, 2, 157–188.

Hall, D.T. (1989). 'How top management and the organization itself can block effective executive succession', *Human Resource Management*, **28**, 1, 5–24.

Halsen, B. (1990). 'Teaching supervisors to coach', *Personnel Management*, 36–39/53.

Hamblin, A.C. (1974). *Evaluation and Control of Training*, Maidenhead: McGraw-Hill.

Hambrick, D.C. and Finkelstein, S. (1987). 'Managerial discretion: a bridge between polar views of organizational outcomes', in L.L. Cummings and B. Staw (eds), *Research in Organizational Behaviour*, Vol. 9, Greenwich, CT: JAI Press.

Hamel, G. (1991). 'Competition for competence and inter-partner learning within international strategic alliances', *Strategic Management Journal*, **12**, 83–103.

Hampden-Turner, C. (1990). *Charting the Corporate Mind: From Dilemma to Strategy*, Oxford: Blackwell.

Hammer, M. and Champey, J. (1993). *Re-engineering the Corporation, a manifesto for business revolution*, London: Brealey publishing.

Handy, C. (1976). *Understanding Organizations*, Harmondsworth: Penguin.

Handy, C. (1989). *The Age of Unreason*, London: Hutchinson.

Handy, C. (1994). *The Empty Raincoat*, London: Hutchinson.

Handy, C., Gow, I., Gordon, C., Randelsome, C. and Moloney, M. (1987). *The Making of Managers: a Report on Management Education, Training and Development in the United States, West Germany, France, Japan, and the UK*, London and Sheffield: MSC/NEDO/BIM.

Harper, S.C. (1988). 'Now that the dust has settled: learning from Japanese management', *Business Horizons*, July-August.

Harrigan, K.R. (1981). *Strategies for Declining Industries*, Lexington, MA: Lexington Books.

Harrison, R. (1972). 'How to describe your organization', *Harvard Business Review*, September/October.

Hawes, F. and Kealey, D.J. (1981). 'Canadians in development: an empirical study of Canadian technical assistance', *International Journal of Intercultural Relations*, **5**, 239–258.

Hayek, F.A. (1945). 'The use of knowledge in society', *The American Economic Review*, **35**, 4, 519–530.

Hayes, R.H. and Abernathy, W.J. (1980). 'Managing our way to economic decline', *Harvard Business Review*, July-August, 67–77.

Hayes, C., Anderson, A. and Fonda, N. (1984). *Competence and Competi-*

tion: Training and Education in the Federal Republic of Germany, the United States, and Japan, London: NEDO/MSC.

Hax, A.C. and Majluf, N.S. (1984). *Strategic Management: An Integrative Perspective*, Englewood Cliffs, NJ: Prentice Hall.

Hedley, B. (1977). 'Strategy and the business portfolio', *Long Range Planning*, **11**, 1, 12–24.

Heller, F.A. and Yukl, G. (1969). 'Participation, managerial decision-making and situational variables', *Organisational Behaviour and Human Performance*, **4**, 227–241.

Hendry, C. (1987). *Strategic Change and Human Resource Management in Retail Banking and Financial Services: An Overview*, Centre for Corporate Strategy and Change, University of Warwick.

Hendry, C. (1990a). 'The corporate management of human resources under conditions of decentralisation', *British Journal of Management*, **1**, 2, 91–103.

Hendry, C. (1990b). 'New technology, new careers: the impact of company employment policy', *New Technology, Work and Employment*, **5**, 1, 31–43.

Hendry, C. (1991). 'International comparisons of human resource management: putting the firm in the frame', *International Journal of Human Resource Management*, **2**, 3, 415–440.

Hendry, C. (1994). *Human Resource Strategies for International Growth*, London and New York: Routledge.

Hendry, C. and Pettigrew, A. (1986). 'The practice of strategic human resource management', *Personnel Review*, **15**, 5, 3–8.

Hendry, C. and Pettigrew, A.M. (1987). 'Banking on HRM to respond to change', *Personnel Management*, November, 29–32.

Hendry, C. and Pettigrew, A.M. (1988). 'Multiskilling in the round', *Personnel Management*, April, 36–43.

Hendry, C. and Pettigrew, A. (1989a). *Strategic Change and Human Resource Management in Pilkington PLC*, Centre for Corporate Strategy and Change, University of Warwick.

Hendry, C. and Pettigrew, A. (1989b). *Strategic Change and Human Resource Management in Central Retail Services Division, Barclays Bank ('Barclaycard')*, Centre for Corporate Strategy and Change, University of Warwick.

Hendry, C. and Pettigrew, A. (1989c). *Strategic Change and Human Resource Management in IMI*, Centre for Corporate Strategy and Change, University of Warwick.

Hendry, C. and Pettigrew, A. (1990). 'Human resource management: an agenda for the 1990s', *International Journal of Human Resource Management*, **1**, 1, 17–43.

Hendry, C. and Pettigrew, A. (1992). 'Patterns of strategic change in the development of human resource management', *British Journal of Management*, **3**, 3, 137–156.

Hendry, C., Arthur, M.B. and Jones, A.M. (in press). *Strategy through People*, London and New York: Routledge.

Hendry, C., Jones, A.M. and Arthur, M.B. (1991). 'Skill supply, training, and development in the small–medium enterprise', *International Small Business Journal*, **10**, 1, 68–72.

Hendry, C., Jones, A.M. and Cooper, N. (1994). *Creating A Learning Organization: Strategies for Change*, Birmingham: Man-made Fibres Industry Training Organization.

Hendry, C., Pettigrew, A. and Sparrow, P. (1988). 'Changing patterns of human resource management', *Personnel Management*, November, 37–41.

Hendry, C., Jones, A.M., Arthur, M.B. and Pettigrew, A. (1991). 'Human resource development in small to medium sized enterprises', Research Paper No. 88, Sheffield: Department of Employment.

Henry, M. (1984). 'Company finances and investment in the United Kingdom', *Barclays Review*, November, 90–93.

Herriot, P. (1989). 'Selection as a social process' in J.M. Smith and I.T. Robertson (eds), *Advances in Selection and Assessment*, Chichester: Wiley.

Herriot, P. (1992). *The Career Management Challenge: Balancing Organizational and Individual Needs*, London/Newbury Park/New Delhi: Sage.

Hill, S. (1991). 'Why quality circles failed but total quality management might succeed', *British Journal of Industrial Relations*, **29**, 4, 541–568.

Hirsh, W. (1984). *Career Management in the Organization: a guide for developing policy and practice*, IMS Report No. 96, Institute of Manpower Studies, University of Sussex.

Hitt, M. and Ireland, D. (1987). 'Peters and Waterman revisited: the undending quest for excellence', *Academy of Management Executive*, **1**, 2, 91–98.

Hofer, C.W. (1977). 'Conceptual constructs for formulating corporate and business strategies', Intercollegiate Case Clearing House, Boston, No. 9–378–754, 34 in Hofer and Schendel (1978).

Hofer, C.W. and Schendel, D. (1978). *Strategy Formulation: Analytical Concepts*, St Paul, MN: West Publishing.

Hofstede, G. (1980). *Culture's Consequences*, Beverly Hills, CA: Sage.

Hofstede, G. (1991). *Cultures and Organisations: Software of the Mind. Intercultural Cooperation and its Importance for Survival*, Maidenhead: McGraw-Hill.

Holden, L. (1991). 'European trends in training and development', *International Journal of Human Resource Management*, **2**, 2, 113–131.

Horrell, S., Rubery, J. and Burchell, B. (1990). 'Gender and skills', *Work, Employment and Society*, **4**, 2, 189–216.

Huczynski, A.A. (1993). 'Explaining the succession of management fads', *International Journal of Human Resource Management*, **4**, 2, 443–463.

Huff, A.S. (1982). 'Industry influences on strategy reformulation', *Strategic Management Journal*, **3**, 119–131.

Hunter, L.C. and MacInnes, J. (1991). 'Employers' labour use strategies – case studies', Research Paper No. 87, London: Department of Employment.

Hyman, R. (1989). *The Political Economy of Industrial Relations*, London: Macmillan.

Hyman, R. (1991). 'European unions: towards 2000', *Work, Employment and Society*, **5**, 4, 621–639.

IDS (1980). *Guide to Incentive Payment Schemes*, London: Income Data Services.

IFF Research Ltd (1985). *Adult Training in Britain*, Sheffield: MSC.

Iles, P., Mabey, C., and Robertson, I. (1990). 'HRM practices and employee commitment: possibilities, pitfalls and paradoxes', *British Journal of Management*, **1**, 147–157.

Iles, P.A., Robertson, I.T., and Rout, U. (1989). 'An investigation of assessment-based development centres', *Journal of Managerial Psychology*, **4**, 3, 11–16.

Inohara, H. (1990). *Human Resource Development in Japanese Companies*, Tokyo: Asian Productivity Organization.

Institute for Employment Research (1990). *The Economy and Employment in the 1990s*, Bulletin No. 8, University of Warwick.

Institute for Employment Research (1991). *Employment in the Single European Market*, Bulletin No. 10. University of Warwick.

Institute for Employment Research (1992). *Skills and Dynamic Performance*, Bulletin No. 14, University of Warwick.

Institute of Management (1992). *Who's Managing the Managers?* London: Institute of Management.

Institute of Manpower Studies (1984). *Competence and Competition: Training and Education in the Federal Republic of Germany, the United States, and Japan*, London: National Economic Development Office and Manpower Services Commission.

Institute of Manpower Studies (1989). *How Many Graduates in the Twenty-First Century?* IMS, University of Sussex.

Institute of Personnel Management (1963). 'Statement on personnel management and personnel policies', *Personnel Management*, March, 11–15.

Institute of Personnel Management (1988). *Follow up to the IPM Statement on Human Resource Planning: Initial Analysis of Survey Results*, London: Institute of Personnel Management.

Institute of Personnel Management (1990). *Continuous Development: People and Work*, 3rd edition, Wimbledon: IPD.

International Management (1986). 'Expansion abroad: the new direction for European firms', November.

Jackson, M. and Leopold, J. (1990). 'Casting off from national negotiations', *Personnel Management*, April, 64–66.

Jackson, S.E., Schuler, R.S., and Rivero, J.-C. (1989). 'Organizational context characteristics as predictors of personnel practices', *Personnel Psychology*.

Janger, A. (1977). *The Personal Function: Changing Objectives and Organisation*, Report No. 712, New York: Conference Board.

Jaques, E. (1962). 'Objective measures for pay differentials', *Harvard Business Review*, January-February, 133–137.

Jenkins, R. (1988). 'Discrimination and equal opportunity in employment: ethnicity and "race" in the United Kingdom', in D. Gallie (ed.), *Employment in Britain*, Oxford: Blackwell, pp. 310–343.

Johnson, G. (1990). 'Managing strategic change: the role of symbolic action', *British Journal of Management*, **1**, 183–200.

Johnson, G. and Scholes, K. (1988). *Exploring Corporate Strategy*, 2nd edition, Hemel Hempstead: Prentice Hall International.

Jones, A.M. and Hendry, C. (1994). 'The learning organization: adult learning and organizational transformation', *British Journal of Management*, **5**, 153–162.

Jones, B. (1982) 'Destruction or redistribution of engineering skills', in S. Wood (ed.), *The Degradation of Work?* London: Hutchinson, 179–200.

Jones, T. (1993). *Britain's Ethnic Minorities*, London: Policy Studies Institute.

Kandola, R. and Pearn, M. (1992). 'Identifying competences', in P.R. Sparrow and R. Boam (eds), *Designing and Achieving Competency*, Maidenhead: McGraw-Hill, 31–49.

Kandola, R.S., Banerji, N.A. and Greene, M.A. (1989). *The Role of Supervisors in Human Resource Development*, Sheffield: Training Agency.

Kanter, R.M (1984). *The Change Masters: Corporate Entrepreneurs at Work*, London: Allen & Unwin.

Kanter, R.B. (1989). *When Giants Learn to Dance: mastering the challenge of strategy, management and careers in the 1990s*, New York: Simon & Schuster.

Kanter, R.M. and Buck, J.D. (1985). 'Reorganizing part of Honeywell: from Strategy to structure', *Organization Dynamics*, Winter, 4–25.

Katz, H. and Sabel, C. (1985). 'Industrial relations and adjustment in the car industry', *Industrial Relations*, **24**, 3, 295–315.

Keat, R. and Abercrombie, N. (eds), (1991). *Enterprise Culture*, London and New York: Routledge.

Keenoy, T. (1990). 'Human resource management: rhetoric, reality and contradiction', *International Journal of Human Resource Management*, **1**, 3, 363–384.

Keep, E. (1986). 'Designing the stable door: a study of how the Youth Training Scheme was planned', Warwick Papers in Industrial Relations No.8, University of Warwick, Industrial Relations Research Unit.

Keep, E. (1989a). 'A training scandal?' in K. Sisson (ed.), *Personnel Management in Britain*, Oxford: Basil Blackwell, 177–202.

Keep, E. (1989b). 'Corporate training strategies: the vital component?' in J.Storey (ed.), *New Perspectives on Human Resource Management*, London and New York: Routledge.

Kelly, J. (1988). *Trade Unions and Socialist Politics*, London: Verso.

Kelly, J. (1990). 'British trade unionism 1979–89: change, continuity and contradictions', *Work, Employment and Society*, May, 29–65.

Kenny, T.P. (1975). 'Stating the case for welfare', *Personnel Management*, September, 18–21/35.

Kenny, T. (1989). 'Personnel management 20 Years On', *Personnel Management*, May, 30–41.

Kern, H. and Schumann, M. (1984). *Das Ende der Arbeitsteilung? Rationalisierung in der industriellen Produktion*, Munich: Beck.

Kerr, C. (1954). 'The Balkanisation of labor markets', in E. W. Bakke *et al.* (eds), *Labor Mobility and Economic Opportunity*, Cambridge, MA: MIT Press, pp. 92–110.

Kerr, J., (1982). 'Assigning managers on the basis of the life cycle', *Journal of Business Strategy*, **2**, 4, 58–65.

Kessler, I. (1990). 'Personnel management in local government: the new agenda', *Personnel Management*, November, 40–44.

Kessler, S. (1993). 'Is there still a future for the unions?' *Personnel Management*, July, 24–30.

Kessler, S. and Bayliss, F. (1992). *Contemporary British Industrial Relations*, London: Macmillan.

Kinnie, N. (1987). 'Bargaining within the enterprise: centralised or decentralised?' *Journal of Management Studies*, **24**, 5, 463–477.

Kirkland, R.I. (1985). 'Are service jobs good jobs?' *Fortune*.

Kitching, J. (1967). 'Why do mergers miscarry?' *Harvard Business Review*, November-December, 84–101.

Kitching, J. (1973). *Acquisitions in Europe: Causes of Corporate Successes and Failures*, Geneva: Business International.

Knights, D. and Morgan, G. (1991). 'Corporate strategy, organizations, and subjectivity: a critique', *Organization Studies*, **12**, 2, 251–273.

Kochan, T. and Capelli, P. (1984). 'The transformation of the industrial relations and personnel function', in P. Osterman (ed.), *Internal Labor Markets*, Cambridge, MA: MIT Press.

Kochan, T.A. and Chalykoff, J.B. (1987). 'HRM and business life cycles: some preliminary propositions', in A. Kleingartner and C.S. Anderson (eds), *HRM in High Tech Firms*, Lexington, MA: Lexington Books.

Kochan, T., Katz, H. and McKersie, R. (1986). *The Transformation of American Industrial Relations*, New York: Basic Books.

Kohlberg, L. (1973). 'Continuities in childhood and adult moral development revisited', in P.B. Baltes and K.W. Schaie (eds), *Life-Span Developmental Psychology: Personality and Socialisation*, New York: Academic Press.

Koike, K. (1984). 'Skill formation systems in the US and Japan: a comparative study', in M. Aoki (ed.), *The Economic Analysis of the Japanese Firm*, Amsterdam: Elsevier Science Publishers.

Kolb, D.A. (1984). *Experiential Learning: experience as the source of learning and development*, Englewood Cliffs, NJ: Prentice Hall.

Kolb, D.A., Rubin, I.M. and McIntyre, J.M. (1974). *Organizational Psychology*, Engelwood Cliffs, NJ: Prentice Hall.

Korn/Ferry International (1986). *A Survey of Corporation Leaders in the '80s*, Korn/Ferry International, 237 Park Avenue, PO Box 2459, Grand Central Station, New York 10017, USA.

Kotter, J.P. (1982). *The General Managers*, New York: Free Press.

Kumon, H. (1992). 'Multinationalization at Toyota Motor Company', *Journal of International Economic Studies*, **6**, 80–99.

Labour Market and Skill Trends 1994/95, Sheffield: Skills and Enterprise Network.

Landis, D. and Brislin, R. (1983). *Handbook on Intercultural Training*, Vol. 1, New York: Pergamon Press.

Lane, C. (1991). 'Industrial reorganization in Europe: patterns of convergence and divergence in Germany, France and Britain', *Work, Employment and Society*, **5**, 4, 515–539.

Laurent, A. (1986). 'The cross-cultural puzzle of international human resource management', *Human Resource Management*, **25**, 1, 91–102.

Lave, J. and Wenger, E. (1990). *Situated Learning: Legitimate Peripheral Participation*, IRI report 90–0013, Palo Alto, CA: Institute for Research on Learning.

Lawrence, J. (1973). 'Manpower and personnel models in Britain', *Personnel Review*, **2**, 4–26.

Lawrence, P. (1985). 'The history of human resource management in American industry', in R.E. Walton and P.R. Lawrence (eds), *HRM Trends and Challenges*, Boston: Harvard Business School Press, 15–34.

Lawrence, P.R. and Lorsch, J.W. (1967). *Organization and Environment*, Boston, MA: Harvard Business School Press.

Lawrence, P.R. and Lorsch, J.W. (1969). *Developing Organisations: Diagnosis and Action*, Reading, MA: Addison-Wesley.

LeBrasseur, R. (1994). *Skill Supply Strategies in High Technology Organizations*, unpublished doctoral thesis, University of Warwick.

Lee, D.J. (1981). 'Skill, craft and class: a theoretical critique and a critical case', *Sociology*, **15**, 1, 56–78.

Legge, K. (1978). *Power, Innovation, and Problem-solving*, Maidenhead: McGraw-Hill.

Legge, K. (1988). 'Personnel management in recession and recovery: a comparative analysis of what the surveys say', *Personnel Review*, **17**, 2, 2–72.

Legge, K. (1989). 'Human resource management: a critical analysis', in J.Storey (ed.), *New Perspectives on Human Resource Management*, London and New York: Routledge, 19–40.

Lester, T. (1991). 'A structure for Europe', *Management Today*, January, 76–78.

Levitt, T. (1965). 'Exploit the product life cycle', *Harvard Business Review*, November/December, 81–94.

Lewin, K. (1952). *Field Theory in Social Science*, London: Tavistock Publications.

Lieberson, S. and O'Connor, J.F. (1972). 'Leadership and organizational performance: a study of large corporations', *American Sociological Review*, **37**, 2, 117–130.

Lobel, S.A. (1990). 'Global leadership competencies: managing to a different drumbeat', *Human Resource Management*, **29**, 1, 39–47.

Lockyer, C. (1992). 'Pay, performance and reward' in B. Towers (ed.), *The Handbook of Human Resource Management*, Oxford: Blackwell, 238–256.

Lodge, G.C. (1985). 'Ideological implications of changes in human resource management', in R.E. Walton and P.R. Lawrence (eds), *HRM Trends and Challenges*, Boston, MA: Harvard Business School Press

Long, P. (1986). *Performance Appraisal Revisited*, London: IPD.

Lorange, P. and Murphy, D. (1984). 'Bringing human resources into strategic planning: Systems design and considerations', in C. Fombrun, N.M. Tichy and M.A Devanna (eds) *Strategic Human Resource Management*, New York: Wiley.

Lorenz, A. (1990). 'Out of the Race', *The Sunday Times*, 22 July.

Lupton, T. and Gowler, D. (1969). *Selecting a Wage Payment System*, London: Kogan Page.

MacInnes, J. (1987). *Thatcherism at Work*, Milton Keynes: Open University Press.

Mackay, L. (1986). 'The macho manager: it's no myth', *Personnel Management*, **18**, 1, 25–27.

MacLagan, P. (1990). 'Moral behaviour in organizations: the contribution of management education and development', *British Journal of Management*, **1**, 17–26.

McGregor, D. (1960). *The Human Side of Enterprise*, New York: McGraw-Hill.

McKiddie, T. (1994). 'Personnel NVQs: preparing for take-off', *Personnel Management*, February, 30–33.

McLoughlin, I.P. and Clark, J. (1993). *Technological Change at Work*, 2nd edition, Milton Keynes: Open University Press.

Mangham, I.L. and Silver, M.S. (1986). *Management Training: Context and Practice*, London and Bath: ESRC, DTI and University of Bath.

Marchington, M., Wilkinson, A. and Ackers, P. (1993). 'Waving or drowning in participation?', *Personnel Management*, March, 46–50.

Marginson, P., Armstrong, P., Edwards, P.K. and Purcell, J. with Hubbard, N. (1993). *The Control of Industrial Relations in Large Companies*, Warwick Papers in Industrial Relations, No.45, IRRU, University of Warwick.

Marginson, P., Edwards, P.K., Martin, R., Purcell, J. and Sisson, K. (1988). *Beyond the Workplace: managing industrial relations in the multi-establishment enterprise*, Oxford: Blackwell.

Marsh, C., McAuley, R. and Penlington, S. (1990). 'The road to recovery? Some evidence from vacancies in one labour market', *Work, Employment and Society*, **4**, 1, 31–58.

Martinez Lucio, M. and Simpson, D. (1992). 'Discontinuity and change in industrial relations: the struggles over its social dimensions and the rise of human resource management', *International Journal of Human Resource Management*, **3**, 2, 173–190.

Maslow, A.H. (1943). 'A theory of human motivation', *Psychological Review*, **50**, 370–396.

Marsden, D. and Thompson, M. (1990). 'Flexibility agreements and their significance in the increase in productivity in British manufacturing since 1980', *Work, Employment and Society*, **4**, 1, 83–104.

Martin, J., Anterasian, C. and Siehl, C. (1988). 'Externally espoused values and the legitimation of financial performance', Working Paper, Graduate School of Business, Stanford University, Palo Alto, CA.

Maurice, M., Sorge, A. and Warner, M. (1980). 'Societal differences in organizing manufacturing units: a comparison of France, West Germany, and Great Britain', *Organization Studies*, **1**, 1, 59–86.

Maynard, G. (1988). *The Economy Under Mrs Thatcher*, Oxford: Basil Blackwell.

Mayo, A. (1991). *Managing Careers – strategies for organisations*, London: IPD.

Mayo, A. (1992). 'A framework for career management', *Personnel Management*, February, 36–39.

Mendenhall, M. and Oddou, G. (1985). 'The dimensions of expatriate acculturation: a review', *Academy of Management Review*, **10**, 39–47.

Mendenhall, M., Dunbar, E. and Oddou, G. (1987). 'Expatriate selection, training, and career pathing: a review and critique', *Human Resource Management*, **26**, 331–345.

Meyer, J.P., and Allen, N.J. (1988). 'Links between work experiences and organizational commitment during the first year of employment: a longitudinal analysis' *Journal of Applied Psychology*, **61**, 195–209.

Miles, R.E. and Snow, C.C. (1978). *Organizational Strategy, Structure, and Process*, New York: McGraw-Hill.

Miller, P. (1989). 'Managing corporate identity in the diversified business', *Personnel Management*, March, 36–39.

Mills, D.Q. (1985). 'Planning with people in mind', *Harvard Business Review*, **63**, July/August, 97–105.

Millward, N. and Stevens, M. (1986). *British Workplace Industrial Relations 1980–84*, Aldershot: Gower.

Millward, N., Stevens, M., Smart, D. and Hawes, W.R. (1992). *Workplace Industrial Relations in Transition: The ED/ESRC/PSI/ACAS Surveys*, Aldershot: Gower.

Mintzberg, H., (1978). 'Patterns in strategy formation', *Management Science*, **24**, 9, 934–948.

Mintzberg, H. (1979). *The Structuring of Organizations*, Englewood Cliffs, NJ: Prentice Hall.

Mintzberg, H. (1987a). 'The strategy concept 1: Five Ps for strategy', *California Management Review*, **30**, 1, 11–24.

Mintzberg, H. (1987b). 'Crafting strategy', *Harvard Business Review*, July-August, 66–75.

Mintzberg, H. and Waters, J.A. (1985). 'Of strategies, deliberate and emergent', *Strategic Management Journal*, 257–272.

Moran, Stahl and Boyer (1989). 'A report on expatriation and repatriation of *Fortune 500* client firms', paper given to the Academy of Management Annual Conference, New Orleans, August.

Morgan, G. (1989). *Riding the Waves of Change: Developing Managerial Competences for Turbulent World*, Oxford: Jossey-Bass.

Morris, J. (1974). 'Developing resourceful managers', in B. Taylor and G.L. Lippitt (eds), *Management Development and Training Handbook*, New York: McGraw-Hill.

Morris, P. (1991). 'Freeing the spirit of enterprise', in R. Keat and N. Abercrombie (eds). *Enterprise Culture*, London and New York: Routledge.

Morris, T. and Lydka, H. (1992). 'Managing the terms of exchange: employee commitment and human resource policies', British Academy of Management Conference, Bradford, September.

Mosley, H.G. (1990). 'The social dimension of European integration', *International Labour Review*, **129**, 2, 147–164.

Mueller, F. and Purcell, J. (1992). 'The Europeanization of manufacturing and the decentralization of bargaining: multinational management strategies in the European automobile industry', *International Journal of Human Resource Management*, **3**, 1, 15–34.

Mullins, T. (1986). 'Harmonisation: the benefits and the lessons', *Personnel Management*, March, 38–41.

Mumford, A. (1987). 'Myths and realities in developing directors', *Personnel Management*, February, 29–33.

Mumford, A. (1991). 'Learning in action', *Personnel Management*, July, 34–37.

Murlis, H. and Fitt, D. (1991). 'Job evaluation in a changing world', *Personnel Management*, May, 39–43.

Murlis, H. and Wright, V. (1993). 'Decentralising pay decisions: empowerment or abdication?' *Personnel Management*, March, 28–33.

Myers, C. and Davids, K. (1992). 'Knowing and doing: tacit skill at work', *Personnel Management*, February, 45–47.

Neale, R. and Mindel, R. (1992). 'Rigging up multicultural teamworking', *Personnel Management*, January, 36–39.

National Economic and Development Council (1985). *Changing Working Patterns and Practices*, London: NEDC.

NEDO/Training Agency (1988). *Young People and the Labour Market*, London: NEDO.

Nelson, R.R. (1991). 'Why do firms differ, and how does it matter?' *Strategic Management Journal*, **12**, 61–74.

Nelson, R.R. and Winter, S.G. (1982). *An Evolutionary Theory of Economic Change*, Cambridge, MA: Belknap.

Nicholson, N. and West, M. (1989). *Managerial Job Change: Men and Women in Transition*, Cambridge: Cambridge University Press.

Nicholson, N., Rees, A. and Brooks-Rooney, A. (1990). 'Strategy, innovation and performance', *Journal of Management Studies*, **27**, 5, 511–534.

Nightingale, M. (1980). 'UK productivity dealing in the 1960s' in T. Nichols (ed.), *Capital and Labour: A Marxist Primer*, London: Fontana.

Niven, M.M. (1967). *Personnel Management, 1913–1963*, London: IPD.

Nkomo, S.M. (1987). 'Human resource planning and organization performance: an exploratory analysis', *Strategic Management Journal*, **8**, 387–392.

Nonaka, I. (1988). 'Towards middle up/down management: accelerating information creation', *Sloan Management Review*, Spring, **29**, 9–18.

Offe, C. (1984). *The Contradictions of the Welfare State*, London: Hutchinson.

Ogilvie, J.R. (1986). 'The role of human resource management practices in predicting organizational commitment', *Group and Organization Studies*, **11**, 4, 335–359.

Ohmae, K., (1982). *The Mind of the Strategist*, New York: McGraw-Hill.

Oliver, N. Delbridge, R., Jones, D. and Lowe, J. (1994, in press). 'World class manufacturing: Further evidence in the lean production debate', *British Journal of Management*.

Orr, J. (1990). *Talking about Machines: An Ethnography of a Modern Job*, unpublished doctoral thesis, Cornell University.

Osterman, P. (1982). 'Employment structures within firms', *British Journal of Industrial Relations*, **XX**, 3, 349–361.

Osterman, P. (1984). 'White-collar internal labor markets', in P. Osterman (ed.), *Internal Labor Markets*, Cambridge, MA: MIT Press, 163–190.

Osterman, P. (1987). 'Choice of employment systems in internal labour markets', *Industrial Relations*, **26**, 1, 46–67.

Ouchi, W. (1981). *Theory Z: How American Business Can Meet the Japanese Challenge*, Reading, MA: Addison-Wesley.

Partridge, B. (1989). 'The problem of supervision', in K. Sisson (ed.), *Personnel Management in Britain*, Oxford: Blackwell, 203–221.

Pascale, R.T. and Athos, A.G. (1981). *The Art of Japanese Management*, New York: Simon & Schuster.

Payne, R. (1991). 'Taking stock of corporate culture', *Personnel Management*, **July**, 26–29.

Peach, L. (1992). 'Parting by mutual agreement: IBM's transition to manpower cuts', *Personnel Management*, March, 40–43.

Pearn, M.A. and Kandola, R.S. (1988). *Job Analysis: A Practical Guide for Managers*, London: IPD.

Peck, J.A. (1989). 'Labour market segmentation theory', *Labour & Industry*, **2**, 1, 119–144.

Pedler, M., Boydell, T. and Burgoyne, J. (1988). *Learning Company Project*, Sheffield: Training Agency.

Penley, L.E. and Gould, S. (1988). 'Etzioni's model of organizational involvement: a perspective for understanding commitment to organizations', *Journal of Organizational Behaviour*, **9**, 43–59.

Perlmutter, H.V. (1969). 'The tortuous evolution of the multinational corporation', *Columbia Journal of World Business*, January-February, 9–18.

Perry, L.T. (1985). 'Cutbacks, layoffs, and other obscenities: making human resource decisions', *Business Horizons*, July-August, 68–75.

Personnel Management (1993a). 'Management education', November, 64.

Personnel Management (1993b). 'IPM/ITD: The case for combination', December, 26–33.

Personnel Management plus (1992). 'A fatally flawed concept', May, 14.

Personnel Management plus (1993a). 'Unipart invests in an in-house 'university', September, 11.

Personnel Management plus (1993b). 'Health authority staff criticise women managers' techniques', August, 2.

Personnel Management plus (1993c). 'Plan for 'modern apprentices', December, 1.

Personnel Management plus (1994a). 'Council shows overwhelming support for a combined IPM/ITD institute', February, 3.

Personnel Management plus (1994b). 'Adding value in a new institute', February, 4.

Personnel Management plus (1994c). 'A new institute for people in the change business?' February, 16–18.

Personnel Management plus (1994d). 'HR entrepreneurs will aim to service small businesses', April, 8.

Peters, T.J. (1988). *Thriving on Chaos: A Handbook for a Management Revolution*, London: Macmillan.

Peters, T.J. and Waterman, R.H. (1982). *In Search of Excellence: Lessons from America's Best-Run Companies*, New York: Harper and Row.

Pettigrew, A.M. (1979). 'On studying organizational cultures', *Administrative Science Quarterly*, **24**, 570–581.

Pettigrew, A.M. (1985). *The Awakening Giant: Continuity and Change in Imperial Chemical Industries*, Oxford: Blackwell.

Pettigrew, A.M. (1987). 'Context and action in the transformation of the firm', *Journal of Management Studies*, **24**, 6, 649–668.

Pettigrew, A.M. (1989). 'How organizations effect strategic change', presentation to CCSC conference on 'Managing Strategic Change: New Research Findings', University of Warwick, March.

Pettigrew, A., Hendry, C. and Sparrow P. (1989). *Training in Britain: Employers' Perspectives on Human Resources*, London: HMSO.

Pettigrew, A.M. and Whipp, R. (1991). *Managing Change for Competitive Success*, Oxford: Basil Blackwell.

Pfeffer, J. (1985). 'Organizational demography: implications for management', *California Management Review*, **28**, 1, 67–81.

Phelps Brown, E.H. (1968). *Report of the Committee of Inquiry under Professor E.H. Phelps Brown into Certain Matters Concerning Labour in Building and Civil Engineering*, Cmnd 3714, London: HMSO.

Pickard, J. (1990). 'Engineering tools up for local bargaining', *Personnel Management*, March, 40–43/55.

Pickard, J. (1992). 'Shell UK pulls responsibility back to centre', *Personnel Management plus*, **3**, 4, 1.

Pickard, J. (1994). 'Why targets are in danger of missing the mark', *Personnel Management plus*, March, 12.

Pieper, R. (ed.) (1990). *Human Resource Management: An International Comparison*, Berlin: Walter de Gruyter.

Piore, M.J. (1986). 'Perspectives on labor market flexibility', *Industrial Relations*, **25**, 2, 146–183.

Piore, M.J. and Sabel, C.F. (1984). *The Second Industrial Divide*, New York: Basic Books.

Policy Studies Institute (1991). 'Recent developments in West Germany's apprenticeship system'.

Pollert, A. (1988). 'The flexible firm: fixation or fact?' *Work, Employment and Society*, **2**, 281–316.

Pollert, A. (1991). 'The orthodoxy of flexibility', in A. Pollert (ed.), *Farewell to Flexibility*, Oxford: Blackwell.

Polanyi, M. (1966). *The Tacit Dimension*, London: Routledge and Kegan Paul.

Poole, M. (1988). 'Factors affecting the development of employee financial participation in contemporary Britain', *British Journal of Industrial Relations*, **26**, 1.

Poole, M. and Jenkins, G. (1990). 'Human resource management and profit sharing: employee attitudes and a national survey', *International Journal of Human Resource Management*, **1**, 3, 289–328.

Poole, M. and Mansfield, R. (1992). 'The movement towards human resource management: evidence from a national sample', British Academy of Management Conference, September, Bradford.

Porter, M.E. (1980). *Competitive Strategy*, New York: Free Press.

Porter, M.E. (1985). *Competitive Advantage*, New York: Free Press.

Porter, M.E. (1987). 'From competitive advantage to corporate strategy', *Harvard Business Review*, May-June.

Porter, M. J. (1990). *The Competitive Advantage of Nations*, New York: Free Press.

Porter, M.E. (1991). 'Towards a dynamic theory of strategy', *Strategic Management Journal*, **12**, 95–117.

Preece, D. (1993). 'Human resource specialists and technical change at greenfield sites', in J. Clark (ed.), *Human Resource Management and Technical Change*, London: Sage.

Price, R. (1989). 'The decline and fall of the status divide?' in K. Sisson (ed.), *Personnel Management in Britain*, Oxford/New York: Basil Blackwell, pp. 271–295.

Price Waterhouse/Cranfield (1990). *The Price Waterhouse/Cranfield Project on International Strategic Human Resource Management: Report 1990*, London: Price Waterhouse.

Pucik, V. (1988). 'Strategic alliances, organisational learning and competitive advantage', *Human Resource Management*, **27**, 1, 77–93.

Purcell, J. (1982). 'Macho managers and the new industrial relations', *Employee Relations*, **4**, 1, 3–5.

Purcell, J. (1989). 'How to manage decentralised bargaining', *Personnel Management*, May, 53–55.

Quinn, J.B. (1977). Strategic goals: process and politics', *Sloan Management Review*, Fall, 21–37.

Quinn, J.B. (1991). 'Strategies for change', in H. Mintzberg and J.B. Quinn (eds), *The Strategy Process: Concepts, Contexts, Cases*, Englewood Cliffs, NJ: Prentice Hall International.

Quinn, J.B. and Mintzberg, H. (1991). *The Strategy Process: Concepts, Contexts, Cases*, Englewood Cliffs, NJ: Prentice Hall International.

Rainbird, H. (1990). *Training Matters. Union perspectives on industrial restructuring and training*, Oxford: Blackwell.

Rainbird, H. (1992). 'The European dimension on training', in M. Gold (ed.), *Europe: The Social Dimension*, London: Macmillan.

Rajan, A. (1990). *1992: A Zero-Sum Game*, London: Industrial Society Press.

Ramsey, H. (1992). 'Commitment and involvement', in B. Towers (ed.), *The Handbook of Human Resource Management*, Oxford: Blackwell, pp. 208–237.

Randlesome, C., Brierley, W., Bruton, K., Gordon, C. and King, P. (1990). *Business Cultures in Europe*, Oxford: Heinemann.

Ratiu, I. (1983). 'Thinking internationally: A comparison of how international executives learn', *International Studies of Management and Organisation*, **13**, 1–2, 139–150.

Revans, R.W. (1971). *Developing Effective Managers*, London: Longman.

Revans, R.W. (1982). *The Origins and Growth of Action Learning*, Bromley: Chartwell-Brett.

Reynolds, C. (1986). 'Compensation of overseas personnel', in J.J. Famularo (ed.) *Handbook of Human Resources Administration*, 2nd edition, New York: McGraw-Hill.

Rice, A.K., Hill, J.M. and Trist, E.L. (1950). 'The representation of labour turnover as a social process', *Human Relations*, **3**, 349–372.

Risto, H. (1990). 'Sociology as a discursive space – the coming age of a new orthodoxy?' *Acta Sociologica*, **33**, 4, 305–320.

Rodger, D. and Mabey, C. (1987). 'BT's leap forward from assessment centres' *Personnel Management* , July, 32–35.

Rose, M. (1975). *Industrial Behaviour*, London: Allen Lane.

Rose, M. (1993). 'Trade unions – ruin, retreat, or rally?' *Work, Employment and Society*, **7**, 2, 291–311.

Rothwell, S.G. (1984). 'Company employment policies and new technology in manufacturing and service sectors', in M. Warner (ed.), *Microprocessors, Manpower and Society*, London: Gower.

Rowland, K. and Summers, S. (1981). 'Human resource planning: A second look', *Personnel Administrator*, December, 73–80.

RSA Journal. (1994). 'Tomorrow's company', April, 8–10.

Rubery, J. (1988). 'Employers and the labour market', in D. Gallie (ed.), *Employment in Britain*, Oxford: Blackwell, 251–280.

Rubery, J. (1989). 'Labour market flexibility in Britain', in F. Green (ed.), *The Restructuring of the UK Economy*, Hemel Hempstead: Harvester Wheatsheaf, 155–176.

Rumelt, R.P., Schendel, D. and Teece, D.J. (1991). 'Strategic management and economics', *Strategic Management Journal*, **12** (S), 5–30.

Sadler, P. and Barham, K. (1988). 'From Franks to the future: 25 years of management training presciptions', *Personnel Management*, May, 48–51.

Sako, M. and Dore, R. (1986). 'How the Youth Training Scheme helps employers', *Employment Gazette*, June, 195–204.

Salter, M.S. (1973). 'Stages of corporate development', in B. Taylor and K. MacMillan (eds), *Business Policy*, Bradford: Crosby Lockwood.

Scase, R. and Goffee, R. (1990). 'Women in management: towards a research agenda', *International Journal of Human Resource Management*, **1**, 1, 107–125.

Schein, E.H. (1983). 'The role of the founder in creating organizational culture', *Organisational Dynamics*, Summer, 13–28.

Schon, D.A. (1987). *Educating the Reflective Practitioner*, San Francisco, CA: Jossey-Bass.

Schroder, H.M. (1989). *Managerial Competence: The Key to Excellence*, Iowa: Kendall Hunt.

Schuler, R.S. (1989). 'Strategic human resource management and industrial relations', *Human Relations*, **42**, 2, 157–184.

Schumpeter, J. (1939). *Business Cycles: A Theoretical, Historical and Statistical Analysis of the Capitalist Process*, New York: McGraw-Hill.

Schwartz, H. and Davies, S.M. (1983). 'Matching corporate culture and business strategy', MAP Concept Paper, Cambridge, MA.

Scott, B.R. (1971). *Strategies of corporate development*, Harvard Business School.

Scott, P. (1985) 'Automated machining systems and the role of engineering craft skills', in H. J. Bullinger (ed.), *Proceedings of the Second International Conference on Human Factors in Manufacturing*, Bedford, IFS Publications, 121–130.

Scott, R. (1993). 'Getting ready for a move to local bargaining', *Personnel Management*, September, 38–41.

Scullion, H. (1991). 'Why companies prefer to use expatriates', *Personnel Management*, November, 32–35.

Scullion, H. (1992). 'Attracting management globetrotters', *Personnel Management*, January, 28–32.

Senge, P.M. (1990). *The Fifth Discipline: The Art and Practice of the Learning Organization*, New York: Doubleday/Currency.

Sewell, G. and Wilkinson, B. (1993). 'Human resource management in 'surveillance' companies', in J. Clark (ed.), *Human Resource Management and Technical Change*, London: Sage.

Shrivastava, P. (1985). 'Integrating strategy formulation with organizational culture', *Journal of Business Strategy*, **5**, 3, 103–111.

Siebert, W.S. and Addison, J. (1991). 'Internal labour markets: causes and consequences', *Oxford Review of Economic Policy*, **7**, 1, 1–17.

Siehl, C. and Martin, J. (1990). 'Organisational culture: a key to financial performance?' in B. Schneider (ed.), *Organizational Culture and Climate*, San Francisco, CA: Jossey-Bass.

Silver, M. (1991). *Competent to Manage*, London and New York: Routledge.

Silverman, D. (1970). *The Theory of Organizations*, London: Heinemann.

Simons, R. (1991). 'How new top managers use formal systems as levers of strategic control', paper presented at the 11th Annual International Strategic Management Society Conference, Toronto, October.

Singh, A. (1977). 'UK industry and the world economy: a case of de-industrialisation', *Cambridge Journal of Economics*, **1**, 2, 113–136.

Sisson, K. (ed.) (1989). *Personnel Management in Britain*, Oxford: Blackwell.

Sisson, K. and Scullion, H. (1985). 'Putting the corporate personnel department in its place', *Personnel Management*, December, 36–39.

Slatter, S. (1992). *Gambling on Growth: How to Manage the Small High-Tech Firm*, Chichester: Wiley.

Sloman, M. (1993). 'Training to play a lead role', *Personnel Management*, July, 40–45.

Smircich, L. (1983). 'Concepts of culture and organizational analysis', *Administrative Science Quarterly*, **28**, 339–358.

Smith, C. (1990). 'How are engineers formed? Professionals, nation and class politics', *Work, Employment and Society*, **3**, 4, 451–470.

Smith, C., Child, J. and Rowlinson, M. (1991). *Reshaping Work: The Cadbury Experience*, Cambridge: Cambridge University Press.

Smith, J.E., Carson, K.P., and Alexander, R.A. (1984). 'Leadership: it can make a difference', *Academy of Management Journal*, **27**, 765–776.

Smith, M. and Robertson, I. (1992). 'Assessing competences', in P.R. Sparrow and R. Boam (eds), *Designing and Achieving Competency*, Maidenhead: McGraw-Hill, 50–75.

Smith, P. and Morton, G. (1990). A change of heart: union exclusion in the provincial newspaper sector', *Work, Employment and Society*, **4**, 1, 105–124.

Smith-Gavine, S. and Bennett, A. (1990). *Index of Percentage Utilisation of Labour*, De Montfort University and Aston University.

Sonnenfeld, J.A. (1989). 'Career system profiles and strategic staffing', in M.B. Arthur, D.T. Hall and B.S. Lawrence (eds), *Handbook of Career Theory*, Cambridge: Cambridge University Press.

Sonnenfeld, J.A., Peiperl, M.A. and Kotter, J.P. (1988). 'Strategic determinants of managerial labour markets: a career systems view', *Human Resource Management*, **27**, 4, 369–388.

Sparrow, P.R. (1988). 'Strategic human resource management issues in retailing', Centre for Corporate Strategy and Change, University of Warwick.

Sparrow, P.R. (1992). 'Building human resource strategies around competences: a life cycle model', Working Paper No. 235, Manchester Business School.

Sparrow, P.R. and Boam, R. (1992). 'Where do we go from here?' in P.R. Sparrow and R. Boam (eds), *Designing and Achieving Competency*, Maidenhead: McGraw-Hill, 175–197.

Sparrow, P. and Hiltrop, J.M. (1993). *European Human Resource Management in Transition*, Englewood Cliffs, NJ: Prentice Hall.

Sparrow, P.R. and Pettigrew, A.M. (1988a). 'Strategic human resource management in the UK computer supply industry' *Journal of Occupational Psychology*, **61**, 1, 25–42.

Sparrow, P.R. and Pettigrew, A.M. (1988b). 'How Halfords put its HRM into top gear', *Personnel Management*, June, 30–34.

Sparrow, P.R., Gratton, L. and McMullan, J. (1989). *Human Resource Issues In Information Technology*, London: PA Consulting Group.

Springer, B. and Springer, S. (1990). 'Human resource management in the U.S. – celebration of its centenary', in R. Pieper (ed.), *Human Resource Management: An International Comparison*, Berlin: Walter de Gruyter, 41–60.

Stanworth, J. and Gray, C. (eds) (1991). *Bolton 20 Years On: The Small Firm in the 1990s*, London: Small Business Research Trust.

Steedman, H. (1990). 'Improvements in workforce qualifications: Britain and France 1979–88', *National Institute Economic Review*, No. 133.

Steedman, H. and Wagner, K. (1987). 'A second look at productivity, machinery and skills in Britain and Germany', *National Institute Economic Review*, November.

Steedman, H. and Wagner, K. (1989). 'Productivity, machinery and skills: clothing manufacture in Britain and Germany', *National Institute Economic Review*, No. 128.

Stevens, J. and Walsh, T. (1991). 'Training and competitiveness', in J. Stevens and R. Mackay (eds), *Training and Competitiveness*, London: Kogan Page/NEDO, 25–58.

Stogdill, R.M. (1974). *A Handbook of Leadership: A Survey of theory and research*, New York: Free Press.

Storey, J. (ed.) (1989). *New Perspectives on Human Resource Management*, London and New York: Routledge.

Storey, J. (1991). 'Do the Japanese make better managers?' *Personnel Management*, August, 24–28.

Storey, J. (1992a). 'HRM in action: the truth is out at last', *Personnel Management*, April, 28–31.

Storey, J. (1992b). *Developments in the Management of Human Resources: an Analytical Review*, Oxford: Basil Blackwell.

Storey, J., Okazaki-Ward, L., Gow, I., Edwards, P.K. and Sisson, K.

(1991). 'Managerial careers and management development: a comparative analysis of Britain and Japan', *Human Resource Management Journal*, **1**, 3, 33–57.

Storper, M. and Scott, A.J. (1989). 'The geographical foundations and social regulation of flexible production complexes', in J. Wolch and M. Dear (eds), *The Power of Geography: How Territory Shapes Social Life*, Boston, MA: Unwin Hyman, 25–43.

Streeck, W. (1987). 'The uncertainties of management in the management of uncertainty: employers, labor relations and industrial adjustment in the 1980s', *Work, Employment and Society*, **1**, 3, 281–308.

Sunday Times, The (1986). 'Shopfloor stalemate', 5 January, 17.

Szilagyi, A.D. and Schweger, D.M. (1985). 'Matching managers to strategies: a review and a suggested framework', *Academy of Management Review*, **9**, 4, 626–637.

Takahashi, Y. (1990). 'Human resource management in Japan', in R. Pieper (ed.), *Human Resource Management: An International Comparison*, Berlin: Walter de Gruyter, 211–232.

Taylor, S. (1992). 'Managing a learning environment', *Personnel Management*, October, 54–57.

Thatcher, M. (1993). 'Rewarding managers for competence', *Personnel Management plus*, March, 20–21.

Thomas, M. (1985). 'In search of culture: holy grail or gravy train?' *Personnel Management*, September, 24–27.

Thomas, M. and Tilston, D. (1987). *Human Resources Strategy in the Retail Financial Services Sector*, London: PA Management Consultants.

Thomason, G.F. (1976, 1978). *A Textbook of Personnel Management*, 2nd and 3rd editions, London: IPM.

Thomason, G.F. (1990). 'Human resource strategies in the health sector', *International Journal of Human Resource Management*, **1**, 2, 173–194.

Thompson, J.D. (1967). *Organizations in Action*, New York: McGraw-Hill.

Thompson, M. (1993). *Pay and Performance II: the employees' experience*, Institute of Manpower Studies, University of Sussex.

Thurley, K. (1990). 'Towards a European approach to personnel management', *Personnel Management*, September, 54–57.

Thurley, K. (1991). 'The utilisation of human resources', in C. Brewster and S. Tyson (eds), *International Comparisons in Human Resource Management*, London: Pitman, 15–32.

Thurley, K.E. and Wirdenius, H. (1973). *Supervision: A Reappraisal*, London: Heinemann.

Thurley, K. and Wood, S. (eds) (1983). *Industrial Relations and Management Strategy*, Cambridge: Cambridge University Press.

Tichy, N.M. (1983). *Managing Strategic Change: Technical, political, and cultural dynamics*, New York: Wiley.

Timperley, S. and Sisson, K. (1989). 'From manpower planning to human resource planning?' in K. Sisson (ed.), *Personnel Management in Britain*, Oxford: Blackwell, 103–124.

Torbiorn, I. (1982). *Living Abroad: Personal Adjustment and Personnel Policy in the Overseas Setting*, New York: Wiley.

Torrington, D. (1989). 'Human resource management and the personnel function', in J.Storey (ed.), *New Perspectives on Human Resource Management*, London and New York: Routledge.

Torrington, D. (1993). 'How dangerous is human resource management? A reply to Tim Hart', *Employee Relations*, **15**, 5, 40–53.

Torrington, D. and Blandamer, W. (1992). 'Competency, pay, and performance management', in R. Boam and P. Sparrow (eds), *Designing and Achieving Competency*, Maidenhead: McGraw-Hill.

Torrington, D. and Chapman, J. (1983). *Personnel Management*, 2nd edition, London: Prentice Hall.

Torrington, D., Mackay, I. and Hall, L. (1985). 'The changing nature of personnel management', *Employee Relations*, **7**, 5, 10–16.

Towers, B. (ed.) (1992). *The Handbook of Human Resource Management*, Oxford: Blackwell.

Townley, B. (1990). 'A discriminating approach to appraisal', *Personnel Management*, December, 34–37.

Trevor, M. (1988). *Toshiba's New British Company*, London: Policy Studies Institute.

Tung, R.L. (1982). 'Selection and training procedures of U.S., European and Japanese multinationals', *California Management Review*, **25**, 1, 57–71.

Tung, R.L. (1989). 'International assignments: strategic challenges in the 21st century', paper presented to Academy of Management International Management Symposium on 'Career Issues', Washington, DC, August.

Turner, L. (1991). *Democracy at Work: Changing World Markets and the Future of Labor Unions*, London and Ithaca, NY: Cornell University Press.

Tushman, M.L., Newman, W.H. and Romanelli, E. (1986). 'Convergence and upheaval: managing the unsteady pace of organizational evolution', *California Management Review*, **29**, 1, 29–44.

Tyson, S. (1983). 'Personnel management in its organisational context', in K. Thurley and S. Wood (eds), *Industrial Relations and Management Strategy*, Cambridge: Cambridge University Press.

Tyson, S. and Fell, A. (1986). *Evaluating the Personnel Function*, London: Hutchinson.

Ulrich, D. and Lake, D. (1990). *Organizational Capability: Competing from the Inside Out*, New York: Wiley.

UNCTC (United Nations Centre on Transnational Corporations) (1988). *Transnational Corporations in World Development: Trends and Prospects*, New York: UN.

Wächter, H. (1992). 'German co-determination: an outdated model?' in J.J.J. van Dijck and A.A.L.G. Wentick (eds.), *Transnational Business in Europe, Economic and Social Perspectives*, Tilburg: Faculty of Social Sciences, 258–264.

Wächter, H. and Stengelhofen, T. (1992). 'Human resource management in a unified Germany', *Employee Relations*, **14**, 2, 21–37.

Wagner, K. (1991). 'Training efforts and industrial efficiency in West Germany', in J. Stevens and R. Mackay (eds), *Training and Competitiveness*, London: NEDO/Kogan Page, 132–149.

Walby, S. (1986). *Patriarchy at Work*, Cambridge: Polity Press.

Walsh, T.J. (1990). 'Flexible labour utilisation in the private service sector', *Work, Employment and Society*, **4**, 4, 517–530.

Walton, R.E. (1985a). 'Toward a strategy of eliciting employee commitment based on policies of mutuality', in R.E. Walton and P.R. Lawrence (eds). *HRM Trends and Challenges*, Boston, MA: Harvard Business School Press.

Walton, R.E. (1985b). 'From control to commitment in the workplace', *Harvard Business Review*, March-April, 77–94.

Walton, R.E. and Lawrence, P.R. (eds) (1985). *HRM Trends and Challenges*, Boston, MA: Harvard Business School Press.

Warner, M. (1987). Industrialization, Management Education and Training Systems: A Comparative Analysis, *Journal of Management Studies*, **24**, 1, 91–112

Watanebe, S. (1991). 'The Japanese quality circle: Why it works' *International Labour Review*, **130**, 1, 57–80.

Watson, T.J. (1992). 'Managing management', paper presented at to the British Academy of Management Annual Conference, University of Bradford, September.

Weick, K.E. and Van Orden, P.W. (1990). 'Organising on a global scale: a research and teaching agenda', *Human Resource Management*, **29**, 1, 49–61.

Weiner, N. and Mahoney, T.A. (1981). 'A model of corporate performance as a function of environmental, organizational, and leadership influences', *Academy of Management Journal*, **24**, 453–470.

Wensley, R. (1982). 'PIMS and BCG: new horizons or a false dawn?' *Strategic Management Journal*, **3**, 2, 147–158.

Whitehouse, G. (1992). 'Legislation and labour market gender inequality: an analysis of OECD countries', *Work, Employment and Society*, **6**, 1, 65–86.

Whitley, R.D. (1989), 'On the nature of managerial tasks and skills', *Journal of Management Studies*, **26**, 3, 209–224.

Whittaker, D.H. (1990). *Managing Innovation: A Study of British and Japanese Factories*, Cambridge: Cambridge University Press.

Wibberley, M. (1993). 'Does "lean" necessarily equal "mean"?' *Personnel Management*, July, 32–35.

Wickens, P. (1987). *The Road to Nissan*, London: Macmillan.

Wilensky, H. (1967). *Organizational Intelligence*, New York: Basic Books.

Wilkinson, A. (1993). 'Managing human resources for quality', in B.G. Dale (ed.), *Managing Quality*, 2nd edition, Englewood Cliffs, NJ: Prentice Hall.

Wilkinson, B. (1983). *The Shopfloor Politics of New Technology*, London: Heinemann.

Wilkinson, B. and Oliver, N. (1992). Human resource management in Japanese manufacturing companies in the UK and USA', in B. Towers (ed.), *The Handbook of Human Resource Management*, Oxford: Blackwell.

Williamson, O.E. (1975). *Markets and Hierarchies*, New York: Free Press.

Willmott, H. (1993). 'Strength is ignorance; slavery is freedom: managing culture in modern organizatons', *Journal of Management Studies*, **30**, 4, 515–552.

Wilson, D.C. (1992). *A Strategy of Change*, London and New York: Routledge.

Wilson, R.A. (1993). *Review of the Economy and Employment 1992/3: Occupational Assessment*, Institute for Employment Research, University of Warwick.

Wilson, J. and Cole, G. (1990). 'A healthy approach to performance appraisal', *Personnel Management*, June, 46–49.

Winch, G.M. (1986). 'The labour process and the labour market in construction', *International Journal of Sociology and Social Policy*, **6**, 2, 103–116.

Winner, L. (1977). *Autonomous Technology*, Cambridge, MA: MIT Press.

Winter, S.G. (1987). 'Knowledge and competence as strategic assets', in D. Teece (ed.), *The Competitive Challenge – Strategies for Industrial Innovation and Renewal*, Cambridge, MA: Ballinger.

Wissema, J.G., Brand, A.F. and Van der Pol, H.W. (1981). 'The incorporation of management development in strategic management', *Strategic Management Journal*, **2**, 4, 361–377.

Witcher, B. and Wilkinson, A. (1992). 'Holistic TQM must take account of political processes', *Journal of Total Quality Management*, **4**, 1, 49–57.

Womack, J., Jones, D. and Roos, D. (1990). *The Machine that Changed the World*, New York: Rawson Associates.

Wood, D. and Smith, P. (1989). *Employers' Labour Use Strategies: First Report on the 1987 Survey*, Research Paper No.63. London: Department of Employment.

Wood, S. (ed.) (1988). *Continuous Development: The Path to Improved Performance*, Wimbledon: IPD.

Wood, S. (1993). 'Human resource management or paying for productivity: the British case', unpublished paper, London School of Economics.

Woodruffe, C. (1992). 'What is meant by a competency?' in P.R. Sparrow and R. Boam (eds), *Designing and Achieving Competency*, Maidenhead: McGraw-Hill, 16–30.

Wray, D.E. (1949). 'Marginal men of industry: the foremen', *American Journal of Sociology*, **54**, 5, 298–301.

Wrigley, L. (1970). *Divisional Autonomy and Diversification*, unpublished doctoral thesis, Harvard Graduate School of Business.

Zabalza, A. and Tzannatos, Z. (1985). *Women and Equal Pay: the Effects of Legislation on Female Employment and Wages in Britain*, Cambridge: Cambridge University Press.

Index